Third Canadian Edition

Strategic Management

Competitiveness and Globalization CONCEPTS

Michael A. **Hitt**
Texas A&M University

R. Duane **Ireland**
Texas A&M University

Robert E. **Hoskisson**
Arizona State University

W. Glenn **Rowe**
The University of Western Ontario

Jerry P. **Sheppard**
Simon Fraser University

NELSON / EDUCATION

NELSON / EDUCATION

Strategic Management: Competitiveness and Globalization—Concepts
by Michael A. Hitt, R. Duane Ireland, Robert E. Hoskisson, W. Glenn Rowe, and Jerry P. Sheppard

**Associate Vice President,
Editorial Director:**
Evelyn Veitch

**Editor-in-Chief,
Higher Education:**
Anne Williams

Acquisitions Editor:
Amie Plourde

Marketing Manager:
Kathaleen McCormick

Developmental Editor:
Tracy Yan

Permissions Coordinator:
Sandra Mark

Senior Content Production Manager:
Imoinda Romain

Production Service:
ICC Macmillan Inc.

Copy Editor:
Kelli Howey

Proofreader:
Dianne Fowlie

Indexer:
Dave Luljak

Senior Manufacturing Coordinator:
Joanne McNeil

Design Director:
Ken Phipps

Managing Designer:
Franca Amore

Cover Design:
Sasha Moroz

Cover Images:
Brem Stocker/Shutterstock (globe),
jstan/Shutterstock (sphere)

Compositor:
ICC Macmillan Inc.

Printer:
Edwards Brothers

**Library and Archives Canada
Cataloguing in Publication**

Strategic management :
competitiveness and globalization :
concepts / Michael A. Hitt ...
[et al.].—3rd Canadian ed.

Includes bibliographical references
and index.
ISBN 978-0-17-650006-1

1. Strategic planning—
Textbooks. I. Hitt, Michael A.

HD30.28.S728 2008   658.4'012
C2008-903875-4

ISBN-10: 0-17-650006-5
ISBN-13: 978-0-17-650006-1

To my family for all of your love and support over the years

—Michael A. Hitt

To all of my family: You mean the world to me. Thank you for your never-ending love, support and nurturing over many years and many projects.

—R. Duane Ireland

To my wonderful wife and companion, Kathy, for all of your love and support. With you the future is always bright.

—Robert E. Hoskisson

To Fay, Gillian, and Ryan! You are so important to me and I love you all so very much. Your achievements continue to amaze me.

—W. Glenn Rowe

To the wisest of counsellors, Marnie, I love you and I'm so proud of all you've accomplished. To my other bright lights in this cloudy place: Ben, Bailey, and Jesse; to my parents, Rose and Rocky; and to Barb, Harvey, Helen, Alan, and Carol.

—Jerry P. Sheppard

Brief Contents

Contents

Chapter 6   Competitive Rivalry and Competitive Dynamics   166

Chapter 7	Corporate-Level Strategy 198

Chapter 10   Cooperative Strategy   296

Part 3 *Strategic Actions: Strategy Implementation* 329

Chapter 13   Strategic Leadership   396

About This Book

As with the earlier Canadian edition, to develop this third Canadian edition of *Strategic Management: Competitiveness and Globalization—Concepts* we have carefully integrated cutting-edge research with practical applications that examine companies competing in global markets. We continue to use this approach because we strongly believe that melding research findings with managerial practices provides you, our readers, with a comprehensive, timely, and accurate explanation of how companies use the strategic management process to successfully compete in the 21st century's dynamic and challenging competitive landscape. Our goals in preparing this edition remain as they were for the first edition: (1) to introduce the strategic management process in a way that illustrates both traditional approaches and the dynamics of strategic change; (2) to describe the full set of strategic management tools, techniques, and concepts available, as well as how firms use them to develop competitive advantages; and (3) to present contemporary strategic thinking and issues affecting 21st-century firms and the strategic decisions made in those companies. Thus, our major goal in preparing this edition has been to present you, our readers, with a concise, complete, accurate, up-to-date, and interesting explanation of the strategic management process as it is used by firms competing in the global economy.

Using an engaging, action-oriented writing style, we have taken great care to sharpen our presentation of strategic management tools and concepts. We have carefully rewritten the chapters to make them clear and concise. Although we fully describe all relevant parts of the strategic—and interesting—management process, the chapters in this edition are more succinct. However, the noticeable reduction in chapter length has not come at the expense of informative, practical examples. In fact, while reading the chapters you'll find descriptions of many different types of firms as we explore the strategic management process. These examples are current and show how firms are competing in today's constantly changing global environment.

New Features and Updates

Many new features and updates to this edition enhance the book's value.

- All-new chapter *opening cases* (14 in total).
- All-new *Strategic Focus* boxes (one to two per chapter for a total of 27).
- New *company-specific examples* illustrating each chapter's central themes.
- Full coverage of *strategic issues* that are prominent in the 21st-century competitive landscape. Chapter 14, for example, focuses on strategic entrepreneurship. Important in established firms as well as in start-up ventures, strategic entrepreneurship is concerned with combining opportunity-seeking behaviour with advantage-seeking behaviour. As we describe in Chapter 14, firms that learn how to use a strategic perspective to identify and exploit entrepreneurial opportunities increase their ability to outperform their rivals. In Chapter 6, we've sharpened the discussion of patterns of competition that occur between firms as they try to outperform each other.

- *Discussion of new topics.* In this edition, we discuss the use of the Balanced Scorecard as a means of measurement and control and the concept of corporate social responsibility as a performance measure including material on the triple bottom line in Chapter 2. These new tools are gaining importance as parts of an effective strategic management process.
- A continued emphasis on *global coverage*, with more emphasis on the international context and issues.
- Updated *review questions* at the end of each chapter.
- *Experiential exercises* at the end of each chapter. New to this edition, these exercises present real-life strategic management issues and are followed by questions. The exercises can be individual or group-based, and are sophisticated yet simple to use.
- Enhanced readability and pedagogical treatment.

These new features and updates provide a unique competitive advantage for this book. With 14 new opening cases and 27 new Strategic Focus boxes, we offer 41 major case examples in the chapters. In addition, virtually all of the shorter examples used throughout each chapter are completely new.

This new edition also emphasizes a global advantage with comprehensive coverage of international concepts and issues. In addition to comprehensive coverage of international strategies in Chapter 9, references to and discussions of the international context and issues are included in every chapter. The opening cases, Strategic Focus boxes, and individual examples in each chapter cover numerous global issues.

Importantly, this new edition solidifies a research advantage for our book. For example, each chapter averages more than 100 references. On average, 60 percent of these references are new to this third Canadian edition. Drawn from business literature and academic research, the materials in these references are vital to our explanations of how firms use the strategic management process.

The Book's Focus

The strategic management process is our book's focus. Organizations use the strategic management process to understand competitive forces and to develop competitive advantages. The magnitude of this challenge is greater today than it has been in the past. A new competitive landscape exists in the 21st century as a result of the technological revolution (especially in e-commerce) and increasing globalization. The technological revolution has placed greater importance on innovation and the ability to rapidly introduce new goods and services to the marketplace. The global economy, one in which goods and services flow relatively freely among nations, continuously pressures firms to become more competitive. By offering either valued goods or services to customers, competitive firms increase the probability of earning above-average returns. Thus, the strategic management process helps organizations identify what they want to achieve as well as how they will do it.

The Strategic Management Process

Our discussion of the strategic management process is both traditional and contemporary. In maintaining tradition, we examine important materials that have historically been a part of understanding strategic management. For example, we thoroughly examine the concept of performance (see Chapter 2), how to analyze a firm's external environment (see Chapter 3), and how to analyze a firm's internal environment (see Chapter 4). To help students be aware of where they are as they progress through the strategic management process, we have included Figure 1.1 on the opening page of each chapter with the current chapter highlighted.

Contemporary Treatment

To explain the aforementioned important activities, we keep our treatments contemporary. In Chapter 4, for example, we emphasize the importance of identifying and determining the value-creating potential of a firm's resources, capabilities, and core competencies. The strategic actions taken as a result have a direct link with the company's ability to establish a competitive advantage, achieve strategic competitiveness, and earn above-average returns.

Our contemporary treatment is also shown in the chapters on the dynamics of strategic change in the complex global economy. In Chapter 6, for example, we discuss the competitive rivalry between firms and the outcomes of their competitive actions and responses. Chapter 6's discussion suggests a firm's strategic actions are influenced by its competitors' actions and reactions. Thus, competition in the global economy is fluid, dynamic, and fast-paced. Similarly, in Chapter 8 we explain the dynamics of strategic change at the corporate level, specifically addressing the motivation and consequences of mergers, acquisitions, and restructuring (e.g., divestitures) in the global economy.

We also emphasize that the set of strategic actions known as strategy formulation and strategy implementation (see Figure 1.1) must be carefully integrated for the firm to be successful.

Contemporary Concepts

Contemporary topics and concepts are the foundation for our in-depth analysis of the strategic actions that firms take to implement strategies. In Chapter 11, for example, we describe how different corporate governance mechanisms (e.g., boards of directors, institutional owners, and executive compensation) affect strategy implementation. Chapter 12 explains how firms gain a competitive advantage by effectively using organizational structures that are properly matched to different strategies. The vital contributions of strategic leaders and the concept of strategic leadership are examined in Chapter 13. In Chapter 14, we describe the important relationship between the ability to find and exploit entrepreneurial opportunities through competitive advantages.

Key Features

Several features are included in this book to increase its value for you.

Knowledge Objectives

Each chapter begins with clearly stated knowledge objectives. Their purpose is to emphasize key strategic management issues you will learn while studying each chapter. To both facilitate and verify learning, you can revisit the knowledge objectives while preparing answers to the review questions presented at the end of each chapter.

Opening Cases

An opening case follows the knowledge objectives in each chapter. The opening cases describe current strategic issues in modern companies such as Sony, Hewlett-Packard, and Walmart among many others. The purpose of the opening cases is to demonstrate how specific firms apply an individual chapter's strategic management concepts. Thus, the opening cases serve as a direct and often distinctive link between the theory and application of strategic management in different organizations and industries.

Key Terms

Key terms that are critical to understanding the strategic management process are bold-faced throughout the chapters. Definitions of the key terms appear in chapter margins as well as in the text. Other terms and concepts throughout the text are italicized, signifying their importance.

Strategic Focus Segments

Each chapter presents one or two all-new Strategic Focus boxes. As with the opening cases, the Strategic Focus boxes highlight a variety of high-profile organizations, situations, and concepts and describe issues that can be addressed by applying a chapter's strategy-related concepts.

End-of-Chapter Summaries

Closing each chapter is a summary that revisits the concepts outlined in the knowledge objectives. The summaries are presented in a bulleted format to highlight each chapter's concepts, tools, and techniques.

Review Questions

Review questions are directly tied to each chapter's knowledge objectives, prompting readers to reexamine the most important concepts in each chapter.

Social Responsibility Review

The Social Responsibility Review exercises bring relevant social issues into the context of each chapter.

Experiential Exercises

Each experiential exercise provides an action-oriented opportunity for readers to enhance their understanding of strategic management. Materials come to life as readers use a chapter's materials to answer questions concerned with strategic management issues. We appreciate the work of Luis Flores, Northern Illinois University, who developed several of these experiential exercises.

Examples

In addition to the opening cases and Strategic Focus boxes, each chapter is filled with real-world examples of companies in action. These examples illustrate key strategic management concepts and provide realistic applications of strategic management.

Indexes

Besides the traditional end-of-book subject and name indexes, we offer a company index as well. The company index includes the names of the hundreds of organizations discussed in the text. The three indexes help to locate where subjects are discussed, a person's name is used, or a company's actions are described.

Support Material for the Instructor

Instructor's Resource CD-ROM

Key ancillaries (Instructor's Resource Manual, Test Bank, ExamView® Testing Software, and PowerPoint® Slides) are provided on CD-ROM (ISBN 978-0-17-647495-9), giving instructors the ultimate tool for customizing lectures and presentations. See the descriptions on the following page.

Instructor's Resource Manual

The manual provides instructors with a wealth of additional material and presentations that effectively complement the text. Using each chapter's knowledge objectives as an organizing principle, the manual has been completely revised to integrate the best knowledge on teaching strategic management to maximize student learning. The manual includes ideas about how to approach each chapter and how to emphasize essential principles with additional examples that can be used to explain points and to stimulate active discussions in your classrooms. Lecture outlines, detailed answers to the review questions at the end of each chapter, additional assignments, and transparency masters are also included, along with instructions for using each chapter's experiential exercise. Flexible in nature, these exercises can be used in class or in other ways, such as homework or as an out-of-classroom assignment.

Test Bank

The test bank has been thoroughly revised and enhanced for this edition and includes new questions for each opening case and Strategic Focus box, as well as a set of scenario-based questions for each chapter to add an innovative problem-solving dimension to exams. All objective questions are linked to chapter knowledge objectives and are ranked by difficulty level, among other measures.

ExamView® Testing Software

All of the test questions are available in ExamView®, a computerized format available in Windows and Macintosh versions. ExamView® is easy-to-use test-creation software that makes it possible for instructors to easily and efficiently create, edit, store, and print exams.

PowerPoint® Slides

An all-new set of PowerPoint® slides designed to be used with this text can be downloaded from the Web site at www.concepts3e.nelson.com. The easily followed presentations include clear figures based on the text and innovative adaptations to illustrate the text concepts.

For the Student

Infotrac® College Edition

Infotrac® College Edition gives students access—anytime, anywhere—to an online database of full-text articles from hundreds of scholarly and popular periodicals, including *Newsweek* and *Fortune*. Fast and easy search tools help you find just what you're looking for from among tens of thousands of articles, updated daily, all at a single site. For more information or to log on, please visit http://www.infotrac-college.com. Just enter your passcode as provided on the subscription card packaged free with new copies of *Strategic Management*.

For the Student and Instructor

Web site—www.concepts3e.nelson.com
This edition's Web site offers students and instructors access to several useful resources, including quizzes for self-testing, Web links, and a wealth of other material.

Acknowledgments

We want to thank those who helped us prepare the third Canadian edition. The professionalism, guidance, and support provided by the editorial and production teams of Evelyn Veitch, Amie Plourde, Tracy Yan, Imoinda Romain, and Kelli Howey are gratefully acknowledged. We appreciate the excellent work of our research assistants: Ashley Orser and Marnie Young. In addition, we owe a debt of gratitude to our colleagues at Texas A&M University, Arizona State University, the University of Western Ontario, and Simon Fraser University. Finally, we are sincerely grateful to those who took time to read and provide feedback on drafts of either this third Canadian edition or the previous edition of our book. Their insights and evaluations have enhanced this text, and we list them below with our thanks.

Ann Dulhanty, Acadia University

Tom Cooper, Memorial University

Ian Lee, Carleton University

Roumen Solov, Concordia University

Gary Bissonette, Queen's University

Final Comments

Organizations face exciting and dynamic competitive challenges in the 21st century. These challenges, and effective responses to them, are explored in this third Canadian edition of *Strategic Management: Competitiveness and Globalization—Concepts*. The strategic management process conceptualized and described in this text offers valuable insights and knowledge to those committed to successfully meeting the challenge of dynamic competition. Thinking strategically, as this book challenges you to do, will increase the likelihood that you will help your company achieve strategic success. In addition, continuous practice with strategic thinking and the use of the strategic management process gives you skills and knowledge that will contribute to career advancement and success. Finally, we want to wish you all the best and nothing other than complete success in all of your endeavours.

Michael A. Hitt

R. Duane Ireland

Robert E. Hoskisson

W. Glenn Rowe

Jerry P. Sheppard

Third Canadian Edition

Strategic Management

Competitiveness and Globalization | **CONCEPTS**

Strategic Management Inputs

1

Strategic Management and Strategic Competitiveness

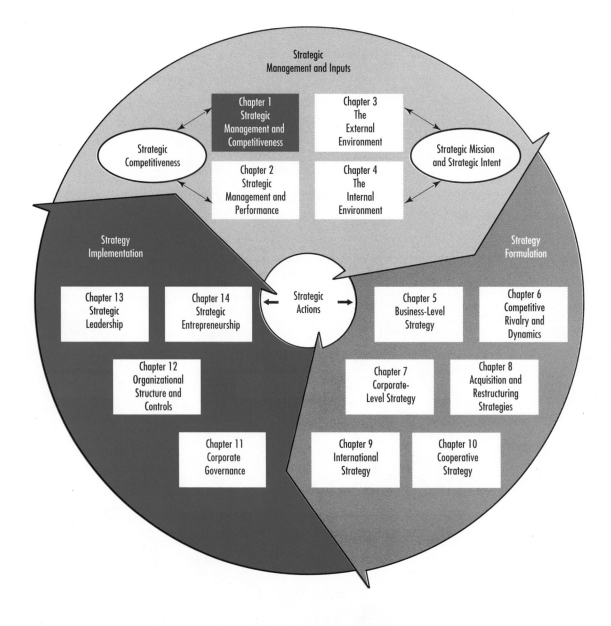

Knowledge Objectives

Studying this chapter should provide you with the strategic management knowledge needed to:

1. Define strategic competitiveness, strategy, competitive advantage, above-average returns, and the strategic management process.

2. Describe the 21st-century competitive landscape and explain how globalization and technological changes shape it.

3. Use the industrial organization (I/O) model to explain how firms can earn above-average returns.

4. Use the resource-based model to explain how firms can earn above-average returns.

5. Describe vision and mission and discuss their value.

6. Define stakeholders and describe their ability to influence organizations.

7. Describe the work of strategic leaders.

8. Explain the strategic management process.

How Cool Is Canada?

In late 2003, Britain's *The Economist* pronounced, "Canada is now rather cool." The magazine noted Canada not only had overcome serious problems in its public finances but also had made bold social moves, like allowing gay marriage and considering marijuana legalization. However, one might not consider Canadian business all that cool. So when one thinks of world-class competitors, Canada may not immediately come to mind. Yet Canada is the world's third largest diamond producer, has the world's second largest oil reserves, and is the world's largest uranium supplier.

www.bombardier.com	www.magna.com
www.cameco.com	www.mccain.com
www.cirquedusoleil.com	www.masonite.com

Only Russia and Botswana produce a greater value of diamonds than Canada. Part of that value stems from the fact that most Canadian diamonds come from some very cool places: the Northwest Territories and Nunavut. Because Canadian diamond mining is so remote, the industry is able to maintain tight controls on the gems. This allows the government to register, certify, and laser-inscribe an identification number on each diamond. Because of this, buyers know that these are not blood diamonds, and the gems can command at least a 20-percent premium. ("Blood diamonds" are stones acquired by rebel armies and smuggled into legitimate markets so their profits can fund a war—as has happened in Angola, the Congo, Liberia, and Sierra Leone.)

After Saudi Arabia, Canada possesses the world's largest proven oil reserves. By developing the Alberta oil-sands, the Syncrude consortium and others created a process for producing crude oil that is reliable enough to allow industry experts to include the oil-sands as part of Canada's oil reserves. "Reserves" are the oil that is commercially recoverable with current technology. By including oil-sands in the calculations, Canada increased its oil reserves from 5 billion to about 180 billion barrels and made Canada the number-two world oil-reserve holder, just behind Saudi Arabia.

One-third of all the world's uranium is produced by Canada. Saskatoon's Cameco is the world's largest uranium producer and, by itself, accounts for 20 percent of world production. By law, none of Canada's uranium is to be used in weapons production, so this resource has a huge potential for power generation—though it is just as likely the country may not need it, as Canada is also the largest producer of hydro-electric power in the world.

And, for sheer market power and control over a critical resource, no one tops McCain Foods Limited. McCain, as the world leader, makes almost one-third of the world's french fries.

When you walk out the door, chances are it is a Canadian-made door. The world's largest door maker is Toronto's Masonite International. The company has a well-thought-out strategy—it focuses only on doors, and on intelligent production location decisions: the company has 70 locations in 12 countries. Doors are heavy to transport, and locating close enough to customers turns out to be a critical consideration.

If you board a train or a take a short hop on a plane, you may well be using a product made by Montreal's Bombardier. Bombardier provides not only trains but also whole computerized transit systems; it is also the world's largest producer of regional aircraft. If you decide to drive, some part of that car may have been made by Aurora, Ontario's Magna International, the world's largest producer of auto parts. Magna makes a wide array of parts and even assembles cars.

Say you reach a vacation destination and see a show. If you are in Las Vegas, chances are Montreal's Cirque du Soleil had something to do with its production. While no one imagined a group of street performers would create an organization that does a half-billion dollars' worth of business and dominates the world of live entertainment, particularly in Las Vegas, this is exactly what Cirque has done. In 20 years, Cirque's nearly 4,000 employees have produced shows that have been performed in more than 100 cities and played to tens of millions of people. There have been times when Cirque simultaneously performed seven different shows on four continents. The company has IMAX movies, CDs, boutiques, and permanent facilities in Las Vegas and Walt Disney World.

One might say you can go anywhere on Earth and find Canadian connections. Some you can find if you leave Earth. The big extendable robotic arm on the space shuttle—with "Canada" and the Canadian flag stamped on the side—is called the Canadarm. And, you guessed it: It is Canadian too.

SOURCES: 2000, The entertainers: Cirque du Soleil, *Maclean's* (Toronto ed.), September 4; G. Marr, 2003, Doormaker to the world, *National Post*, November 4, FP7; S. Burgess, 2003, They really like us, eh? *Maclean's* (Toronto ed.), October 13, 53–55; 2003, Canada's new spirit, *The Economist*, September 27, 15; 2003, McCain Web page, http://www.mccain.com/McCainWorldWide/Leadership; 2007, Diavik Mines Web page, http://www.diavik.ca, October 1; 2007, UN Conflict Diamonds web page, http://www.un.org/peace/africa/Diamond.html, March 7; Amnesty International Diamonds Web page, http://www.amnestyusa.org/diamonds, March 6; 2003, Syncrude Web page, http://www.syncrude.ca/who_we_are/index.html, April 30; K. MacNamara, 2003, Oilsands: Coming to America, *National Post*, December 24, FP6; 2007, Cirque du Soleil Web page, http://www.cirquedusoleil.com/CirqueDuSoleil/en/Pressroom/cirquedusoleil/factsheets/cds_glance.htm, October 1.

The actions undertaken by companies like Cameco, Masonite, Bombardier, and Cirque du Soleil are designed to help the firms achieve the levels of success desired by people who have a stake in the firm's performance. As we will discuss in Chapter 2, if an organization has above-average performance it is likely that shareholders, employees, suppliers, customers, local communities, and others affected by the company are satisfied with the firm's current accomplishments. In the final analysis, though, we can be confident in believing that those leading the above organizations want their firms to be highly competitive (something we call a condition of *strategic competitiveness*). This is an important outcome firms seek to accomplish when using the strategic management process (see Figure 1.1). The strategic management process is fully explained in this book and we will introduce you to this process in the next few paragraphs.

Figure 1.1	The Strategic Management Process

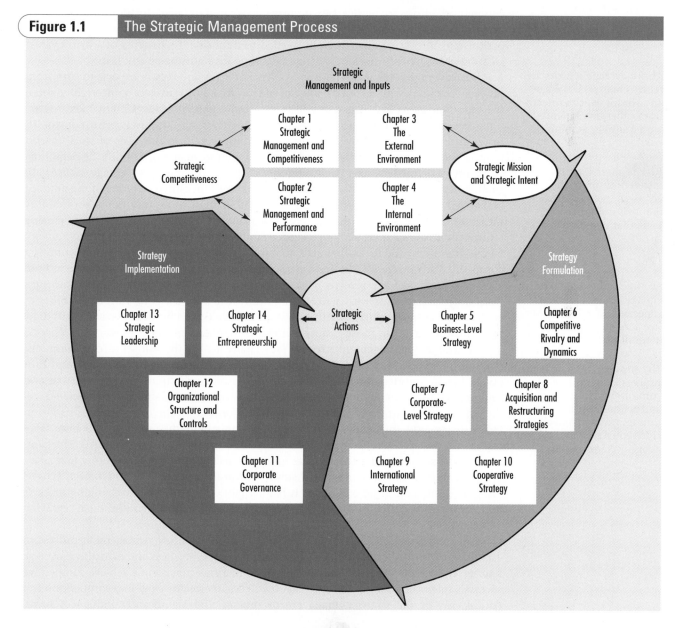

Chapter 1 / Strategic Management and Strategic Competitiveness

Strategic competitiveness is achieved when a firm successfully formulates and implements a value-creating strategy.

A strategy is an integrated and coordinated set of commitments and actions designed to exploit core competencies and gain a competitive advantage.

A firm has a **competitive advantage** when it implements a value-creating strategy that competitors are unable to duplicate or find too costly to try to imitate.

Above-average returns are returns in excess of what an investor expects to earn from other investments with a similar amount of risk.

Risk is an investor's uncertainty about the economic gains or losses that will result from a particular investment.

Average returns are returns equal to those an investor expects to earn from other investments with a similar amount of risk.

The **strategic management process** is the full set of commitments, decisions, and actions required for a firm to achieve strategic competitiveness and earn above-average returns.

Strategic competitiveness is achieved when a firm successfully formulates and implements a value-creating strategy. A **strategy** is an integrated and coordinated set of commitments and actions designed to exploit core competencies and gain a competitive advantage. When choosing a strategy, firms make choices among competing alternatives. In this sense, the chosen strategy indicates what the firm intends to do as well as what it does not intend to do. Sony Corp., for example, unveiled a new strategy in September 2005 that was intended to restore the firm's ability to earn above-average returns. Changes in the manufacture and distribution of televisions and in its portable music players are examples of issues Sony addressed when altering its strategy. Comments by Howard Stringer, Sony's new CEO, demonstrate that choices were being made: "We cannot fight battles on every front. We have to make choices . . . and decide what the company's priorities ought to be."[1]

A firm has a **competitive advantage** when it implements a strategy competitors are unable to duplicate or find too costly to try to imitate.[2] An organization can be confident that its strategy has resulted in one or more useful competitive advantages only after competitors' efforts to duplicate its strategy have ceased or failed. In addition, firms must understand that no competitive advantage is permanent.[3] The speed with which competitors are able to acquire the skills needed to duplicate the benefits of a firm's value-creating strategy determines how long the competitive advantage will last.[4]

Above-average returns are returns in excess of what an investor expects to earn from other investments with a similar amount of risk. **Risk** is an investor's uncertainty about the economic gains or losses that will result from a particular investment.[5] Returns are often measured in terms of accounting figures, such as return on assets, return on equity, or return on sales. Alternatively, returns can be measured on the basis of stock market returns, such as monthly returns (the end-of-the-period stock price minus the beginning stock price, divided by the beginning stock price, yielding a percentage return). In smaller new venture firms, performance is sometimes measured in terms of the amount and speed of growth (e.g., in annual sales) rather than more traditional profitability measures[6] (the reason for this is that new ventures require time to earn acceptable returns on investors' investments).[7] Understanding how to exploit a competitive advantage is important for firms that seek to earn above-average returns.[8] Firms without a competitive advantage or that are not competing in an attractive industry earn, at best, average returns. **Average returns** are returns equal to those an investor expects to earn from other investments with a similar amount of risk. In the long run, an inability to earn at least average returns results in failure. Failure occurs because investors withdraw their investments from those firms earning less-than-average returns.

The **strategic management process** (see Figure 1.1) is the full set of commitments, decisions, and actions required for a firm to achieve strategic competitiveness and earn above-average returns. The firm's first step in the process is to analyze its external and internal environments to determine its resources, capabilities, and core competencies—the sources of its "strategic inputs." With this information, the firm develops its vision and mission and formulates its strategy. To implement this strategy, the firm takes actions toward achieving strategic competitiveness and above-average returns. The summary of the sequence of activities is as follows: effective strategic actions that take place in the context of carefully integrated strategy formulation and implementation actions result in desired strategic outcomes. It is a dynamic process, as ever-changing markets and competitive structures must be coordinated with a firm's continuously evolving strategic inputs.[9]

In the remaining chapters of this book, we use the strategic management process to explain what firms should do to achieve strategic competitiveness and earn above-average returns. These explanations demonstrate why some firms consistently achieve competitive success while others fail to do so.[10] As you will see, the reality of global competition is a critical part of the strategic management process and significantly influences firms' performances.[11] Indeed, learning how to successfully compete in the globalized world is one of the most significant challenges for firms competing in the 21st century.[12]

Several topics are discussed in this chapter. First, we describe the 21st-century competitive landscape. This challenging landscape is being created primarily by the emergence of a global economy, globalization resulting from that economy, and rapid technological changes. Next, we examine two models that firms use to gather the information and knowledge required to choose their strategies and decide how to implement them. The insights gained from these models also serve as the foundation for forming the firm's vision and mission. The first model (industrial organization or I/O) suggests that the external environment is the primary determinant of a firm's strategic actions. The key to this model is identifying and competing successfully in an attractive (i.e., profitable) industry.[13] The second model (resource-based) suggests that a firm's unique resources and capabilities are the critical link to strategic competitiveness.[14] Thus, the first model is concerned with the firm's external environment, while the second model focuses on the firm's internal environment. After discussing vision and mission, direction-setting statements influencing the choice and use of organizational strategies, we describe the stakeholders that organizations serve. The degree to which stakeholders' needs can be met directly increases when firms achieve strategic competitiveness and earn above-average returns. Closing the chapter are introductions to strategic leaders, the elements of the strategic management process, and the critically important topic of organizational ethics.

What Is Strategy?

For simplicity, we have defined **strategy** as an integrated and coordinated set of commitments and actions designed to exploit core competencies and gain a competitive advantage. Yet defining strategy is a bit more complicated. There may be no single agreed-to definition of strategy. Some of the diversity in the definitions of strategy is presented below.[15]

A **strategy** is an integrated and coordinated set of commitments and actions designed to exploit core competencies and gain a competitive advantage.

"The formulation of basic organizational missions, purposes, and objectives; policies and program strategies to achieve them; and the methods needed to assure that strategies are implemented to achieve organizational ends." (Steiner & Miner, 1977:7)

"A unified, comprehensive, and integrated plan designed to ensure that the basic objectives of the enterprise are achieved." (Glueck, 1980:9)

"The pattern or plan that integrates an organization's major goals, policies, and action sequences into a cohesive whole. A well formulated strategy helps to marshal and allocate an organization's resources into a unique and viable posture based on its relative internal competencies and shortcomings, anticipated changes in the environment, and contingent moves by intelligent opponents." (Quinn, 1980)

"Strategy is a pattern of resource allocation that enables firms to maintain or improve their performance. A good strategy is a strategy that neutralizes threats and exploits opportunities while capitalizing on strengths and avoiding or fixing weaknesses." (Barney, 1997:17)

McGill University's Henry Mintzberg gives five definitions of strategy: a plan, a ploy, a pattern, a position, and a perspective. More than one of these may apply at any one time.[16]

By *plan*, Mintzberg means that an organization is undertaking a conscious and intended course of action to deal with a situation. For example, when Montreal's Domtar suffered a loss of $271 million in the fourth quarter of 2005, the company created a plan to cut costs through mill closures that refocused the company's product line on higher-valued paper items.[17]

Strategy as a *ploy* means that the firm is attempting some kind of specific "manoeuvre" intended to outwit an opponent or competitor. In 2004, Telus made an unfriendly takeover bid to buy Microcell—the people who own Fido. Fido was the fourth-ranked competitor after Bell, Telus, and Rogers. The $1.1-billion bid was far short of what the Microcell board thought the company was worth, and the technology employed by Telus's cell phones was incompatible with Microcell's. For competitive reasons, it was unlikely that regulators would let Bell acquire Microcell, thus, Rogers Communications—whose technology *was* compatible with Microcell's—purchased Microcell for nearly $1.5 billion. Telus, without spending any of its own money, had started a process by which it had eliminated a weak competitor. [18]

The third view of strategy is that it is a *pattern* of fairly consistent actions rather than a set of intended courses of actions. For example, Tim Hortons started out serving just coffee and doughnuts but has added a fuller line of baked goods (danishes, doughnut holes, cookies, cakes, pies, muffins, croissants, and bagels) and expanded its beverages (flavoured cappuccino, mochas, and blended iced cappuccino). Further extensions have included Tim's soups, chilli, sandwiches, wraps, hot breakfast sandwiches, and yogurt with berries. What holds all this together, however, is that through the years Tim Hortons has worked to establish a down-home reputation. Though a national chain, their locations are essentially the community gathering place in many of the communities in which they do business. Franchisees strive to be an integral part of their communities by actively supporting community sports and recreation programs and assisting the parent company in sponsoring summer camps for economically disadvantaged children.[19]

Strategy as a *position* reflects placing the organization in a particular environment (i.e., a market niche) that puts the organization at a competitive advantage and allows it to produce a greater than normal rate of return. Richard Branson's Virgin Group does this over a wide range of products. The Virgin name has been used to add a trendy label to planes, trains, phones, music, health clubs, and so on. Often, the name is used under agreements that involve little investment on the part of the corporate parent but still allow further exposure and expansion of the Virgin name.[20]

Lastly, strategy may reflect a *perspective*—or the organization's "ingrained way of perceiving the world" (i.e., there's the right way, the wrong way, and the way we do it here). For example, Vancity is Canada's largest credit union, with 50 branches, more than 300,000 members, and over $10 billion in assets. Vancity's perspective is to integrate social responsibility into all that it does. Innovations include the Shared Success program, which returns 30 percent of bank profits back to members and the community; EnviroVISA, where 5 percent of card profits go to an environmental fund; and Circadian mutual funds, which invest in progressive companies.[21]

Mintzberg makes another important contribution to our understanding of strategy when he differentiates among intended, emergent, and realized strategies (see Figure 1.2).[22] Intended strategies are those plans or conscious courses of action required to deal with a specific situation that lead to deliberate strategies. Intended strategies are usually top-down from senior management and reflect a hierarchical view of strategy. This hierarchical perspective suggests that corporate senior managers are responsible for the corporate mission and objectives, business unit senior managers are responsible for business unit strategies flowing from corporate missions and objectives, and functional area managers within the division are responsible for tactics/policies that flow from the business unit strategies.

Emergent strategies are patterns of actions that come about over time in an unintended manner. They are actions and decisions that a firm's senior managers may not have intended to pursue but nevertheless have ended up perusing. They may be a by-product of other intended strategies, or may be strategies that emerge from bottom-up as opposed to top-down initiatives. Emergent strategies are thus those strategies that result from the pattern of everyday actions and behaviours engaged in by managers and employees almost without conscious thought or planning.

When U.S. electronics retailing giant Best Buy entered the Canadian market, it did so by purchasing one of the companies that was likely to be its main competitor: Future Shop. The intended strategy was to run both chains as low-cost, low-pressure electronics retailers. This meant that Best Buy would have to eliminate Future Shop's well-developed sales commissions system. After the purchase, however, Best Buy discovered that Future Shop's "Customers for Life" relationship with consumers yielded better sales performance, and the commission-free system became an unrealized strategy at Future Shop. The emergent strategy was for each retail chain to pursue its traditional strategies: commissions at Future Shop and no commissions at Best Buy. The deliberate strategy of running both chains, however, did become part of the realized strategy.[23]

What is important about this view of strategy is the awareness that realized strategies are the result of what everyone (senior managers, middle managers, and employees) in an organization does as they go about their daily activities. This means that senior managers must appreciate the need for all members of their organizations to be aware of, understand, embrace, and, on a day-to-day basis, act in accordance with the proposed strategy of the firm and its subordinate business units. In an organization where senior managers do not have a clear mission or clear objectives—and, therefore, no clear strategy—the actions that emerge may destroy shareholder wealth. Thus, the need to develop a clear strategy is critical to the success of the organization. To this end, we now turn to two models used in strategic analysis to generate the strategic inputs needed to successfully formulate and implement strategies.

The 21st-Century Competitive Landscape

The fundamental nature of competition in many of the world's industries is changing.[24] The pace of this change is relentless and is increasing. Even determining the boundaries of an industry has become challenging. Consider, for example, how advances in interactive computer networks and telecommunications have blurred the boundaries of the entertainment industry. Today firms like ABC, CBC, CBS, NBC, CTV, and HBO compete not only among themselves but also with AT&T, Microsoft, Rogers, Sony, Bell, Telus, and others.

Partnerships among firms in different segments of the entertainment industry further blur industry boundaries. For example, MSNBC is co-owned by NBC (which itself is owned by General Electric) and Microsoft.[25] With full-motion video and sound rapidly making their way to mobile devices, cell phones are also competitors for customers' entertainment expenditures. Wireless companies, for example, are partnering with the music industry to introduce music-playing capabilities into mobile phones.[26] To provide digital music to its phone and Internet users, Bell Canada purchased a minority interest in digital music provider Puretracks[27] and also owns ExpressVu satellite broadcasting. Entertainment giant Walt Disney Company is selling wireless-phone plans to children.[28] That Disney videos can be streamed through phones is yet another example of the difficulty of determining industry boundaries.

Other characteristics of the 21st-century competitive landscape are noteworthy as well. Conventional sources of competitive advantage such as economies of scale and huge advertising budgets are not as effective as they once were. Moreover, the traditional managerial mind-set is unlikely to lead a firm to strategic competitiveness. Managers must adopt a new mind-set that values flexibility, speed, innovation, integration, and the challenges that evolve from constantly changing conditions. The conditions of the competitive landscape result in a perilous business world, one where the investments required to compete on a global scale are enormous and the consequences of failure are severe.[29] Developing and implementing strategy remains an important element of success in this environment. It allows for strategic actions to be planned and to emerge when the environmental conditions are appropriate. It also helps to coordinate the strategies developed by business units in which the responsibility to compete in specific markets is decentralized.[30]

Hypercompetition is a term often used to capture the realities of the 21st-century competitive landscape. Under conditions of hypercompetition, "assumptions of market stability are replaced by notions of inherent instability and change."[31] Hypercompetition results from the dynamics of strategic manoeuvring among global and innovative combatants. It is a condition of rapidly escalating competition based on price–quality positioning, competition to create new know-how and establish first-mover advantage, and competition to protect or invade established product or geographic markets.[32] In a hypercompetitive market, firms often aggressively challenge their competitors in the hopes of improving their competitive position and ultimately their performance.[33]

Several factors create hypercompetitive environments and influence the nature of the 21st-century competitive landscape. The two primary drivers are the emergence of a global economy and technology, specifically rapid technological change.

The Global Economy and Globalization

A **global economy** is one in which goods, services, people, skills, and ideas move freely across geographic borders.

A **global economy** is one in which goods, services, people, skills, and ideas move freely across geographic borders. Relatively unfettered by artificial constraints, such as tariffs, the global economy significantly expands and complicates a firm's competitive environment.[34]

Numerous opportunities and challenges are associated with the emergence of the global economy.[35] Europe, not the United States, is now the world's largest single market. The European Union and the other Western European countries in combination now have a gross domestic product that is the world's largest.[36] Because of the size of Canada's economy relative to these markets, Canadian business has more frequently than not needed to seek out foreign markets. Obviously, companies like Bombardier need to go global—there are only so many Canadian cities that are likely to buy billion-dollar computerized transit systems. Companies like Toronto's Apotex, with a billion dollars in sales, need to sell their generic pharmaceuticals worldwide in order to recoup development costs.

Even small Canadian companies need to address the global market. Richmond Hill, Ontario–based Aecometric—a designer and manufacturer of custom burners and controls for heavy industry—has done business in the U.S. from its start in 1978. By the new millennium, 80 percent of the company's business was in the U.S. When U.S. manufacturers became skittish about new investments after Sept. 11, Aecometric's revenues dropped in half. Since the company's staff reflected Canada's cultural mosaic, it was able to develop contacts in India and China. The company was able to triple its business, and while 50 percent of the business is still in the U.S., other foreign accounts now make up 40 percent of Aecometric's sales.[37]

China's economy is now larger than Canada's, causing an analyst to suggest, "It's hard to talk meaningfully about the world economy any more without China being included."[38] One indicator of the rapid rise in the capabilities of China's economy is the fact that from roughly 1986 to 2005, China lifted "some 400 million of its 1.3 billion people out of grinding $1-a-day poverty."[39] India, the world's largest democracy, has an economy that also is growing rapidly and now ranks as the world's fourth largest.[40] By 2050, the United States, China, India, Japan, Britain, France, Germany, and South Korea are expected to be the world's largest economies. Russia and Italy are two economies projected to decline in size and influence between 2005 and 2050.[41]

Statistics detailing the nature of the global economy reflect the realities of a hyper-competitive business environment. This environment challenges individual firms to think seriously about the markets in which they will compete. U.S. industrial giant General Electric (GE) expects that as much as 60 percent of its revenue growth between 2005 and 2015 will come from rapidly developing economies (e.g., China and India). According to one analyst, GE is doing what it must to sustain its business: "Developing countries are where the fastest growth is occurring and more sustainable growth."[42] Based on its analyses of world markets, GE estimates that by 2024, China will be the world's largest consumer of electricity and will be the world's largest consumer and consumer-finance market (all GE businesses). GE is making strategic decisions today to make significant investments in China and India in order to improve its competitive position in what the firm believes are becoming vital sources of revenue and profitability. Similarly, FedEx estimates that in less than 10 years the firm will generate the bulk of its revenue growth from business activities outside North America. Brazil and India are two markets in which the firm is now making significant investments in anticipation of revenue growth possibilities.[43]

Globalization is the increasing economic interdependence among countries and their organizations as reflected in the flow of goods and services, financial capital, and knowledge across country borders.[44] Globalization is a product of a larger number of firms competing against one another in an increasing number of global economies.

In globalized markets and industries, financial capital might be obtained in one national market and used to buy raw materials in another one. Manufacturing equipment bought from a third national market can then be used to produce products that are sold in yet a fourth market. Thus, globalization increases the range of opportunities for companies competing in the 21st-century competitive landscape.[45]

Wal-Mart, for instance, is trying to achieve boundaryless retailing with global pricing, sourcing, and logistics. Through boundaryless retailing, the firm seeks to make the movement of goods and the use of pricing strategies as seamless among its international operations as it has historically among its U.S. stores. The firm developed this type of retailing on an evolutionary basis; most of Wal-Mart's original international investments were in Canada and Mexico, because it was easier for the firm to rehearse its global practices in countries geographically close to its U.S. home. Based on what it learned, the firm expanded into Europe, South America, and Asia. Today, Wal-Mart is the world's largest retailer (with more than 3,600 total units). Internationally, Wal-Mart now employs over 330,000 people in its more than 1,500 international units.[46]

Globalization is the increasing economic interdependence among countries and their organizations as reflected in the flow of goods and services, financial capital, and knowledge across country borders.

The challenge to companies experiencing globalization is to understand the need for culturally sensitive decisions when using the strategic management process and to anticipate ever-increasing complexity in their operations as goods, services, people, and so forth move freely across geographic borders and throughout different economic markets. For example, though headquartered in Montreal, SNC-Lavalin has done construction projects in 120 countries, and at any one time has ongoing projects on five continents. Some projects may be done across continents. Projects may have cost estimates produced in North America, engineering done in India, and construction performed in Africa with equipment from Europe. SNC-Lavalin not only makes all these disparate elements work together, but also wins awards in design, engineering, and safety in doing so. Though Canada still accounts for a majority of its multi-billion-dollar revenues, Europe and Africa consistently provide about half of its off-shore sales (about 20 percent of total revenues, the majority of this from Africa).[47]

Thus, globalization makes it increasingly difficult to think of firms headquartered in various economies throughout the world as domestic-only companies—as we have seen with SNC-Lavalin. In the global environment, ownership attributes get blurred as well. Consider a quintessentially Canadian company: Tim Hortons. A Canadian company from its founding, it was bought by Wendy's International in 1995. As part of Wendy's it was, then, an American company. In 2006, Wendy's spun off Tim Hortons into a separate company. The company is incorporated in the U.S. state of Delaware. The company's stock, mostly owned by Americans, is traded on the New York Stock Exchange. Some might consider it a U.S. company. However, the company is also listed on the Toronto Stock Exchange, its financial statements are now remunerated in Canadian dollars, more than 80 percent of its outlets are in Canada, and it is headquartered in Oakville, Ontario. So maybe it is quintessentially Canadian after all.[48]

Globalization also affects the design, production, distribution, and servicing of goods and services. In many instances, globalization results in higher-quality goods and services. Global competitor Toyota Motor Company provides an example of how this happens. Because Toyota initially emphasized product reliability and superior customer service, the company's products are in high demand across the globe. Because of the demand for its products, Toyota's competitive actions have forced its global competitors to make reliability and service improvements in their operations.[49] Indeed, almost any car or truck purchased today from virtually any manufacturer is of higher quality and is supported by better service than was the case before Toyota began successfully competing throughout the global economy.

Overall, it is important for firms to understand that globalization has led to higher levels of performance standards in many competitive dimensions, including those of quality, cost, productivity, product introduction time, and operational efficiency. In addition to firms competing in the global economy, these standards affect firms competing on a domestic-only basis. The reason for this is that customers will purchase from a global competitor rather than a domestic firm when the global company's good or service is superior. Because workers now flow rather freely among global economies, and because employees are a key source of competitive advantage, firms must understand that, increasingly, "the best people will come from . . . anywhere."[50] Overall, firms must learn how to deal with the reality that in the 21st-century competitive landscape only companies capable of meeting, if not exceeding, global standards typically have the capability to earn above-average returns.[51]

As we have explained, globalization creates opportunities (such as those being pursued by Aecometric, GE, Wal-Mart, SNC-Lavalin, and Toyota, among many other firms). However, globalization is not risk free. Collectively, the risks of participating outside of a firm's domestic country in the global economy are labelled a "liability of foreignness."[52]

One risk of entering the global market is that typically a fair amount of time is required for firms to learn how to compete in markets that are new to them. A firm's performance can suffer until this knowledge is either developed locally or transferred from the home market to the newly established global location.[53] As well, a firm's performance may suffer with substantial amounts of globalization. In this instance, firms may over-diversify internationally beyond their ability to manage such operations.[54] The result of over-diversification can have strong negative effects on a firm's overall performance.[55]

Thus, entry into international markets, even for firms with substantial experience in the global economy such as GE, SNC-Lavalin, and Toyota, requires proper use of the strategic management process. In this regard, firms should choose to enter more markets that are international only when there is a viable opportunity for them to do so and when they have the competitive advantages required to be successful in those markets.

It is also important to note that while global markets are attractive strategic options for some companies, they are not the only source of strategic competitiveness. In fact, for most companies, even for those capable of competing successfully in global markets, it is critical to remain committed to and strategically competitive in their historical markets.[56] A firm's historical base can create and provide unique opportunities. For example, Scotiabank's roots in the Maritimes created a situation early in its history where it was important for the bank to become involved in the Caribbean. In the 1800s the bank began to assist seafarers involved in the trade that was occurring between the Maritimes and the Caribbean regarding fish, sugar, and rum. In 1889, the bank first expanded internationally into Kingston, Jamaica. To further serve customers in the shipping business, the bank opened offices in Puerto Rico in 1910 and the Dominican Republic in 1920. Scotiabank's early start in these islands allowed it to develop a large presence in the Caribbean, Central America, and South America. Today, the bank has almost 60 branches in the Dominican Republic and has expanded to over 20 countries in the Caribbean, nine countries in Central America and South America, and is the third largest bank in Peru.[57]

Technology and Technological Changes

There are three categories of trends and conditions—technology diffusion and disruptive technologies, the information age, and increasing knowledge intensity—through which technology is significantly altering the nature of competition and contributing to unstable competitive environments as a result of doing so.

Increasing Rate of Technological Change and Diffusion

Both the rate of change of technology and the speed at which new technologies become available and are used have increased substantially over the last 15 to 20 years. Consider the following rates of technology diffusion: It took the telephone 35 years to get into about 25 percent of all homes in North America. It took television 26 years. It took radio 22 years. It took personal computers 16 years. It took the Internet 7 years.[58]

Perpetual innovation is a term used to describe how rapidly and consistently new, information-intensive technologies replace older ones. The shorter product life cycles resulting from these rapid diffusions of new technologies place a competitive premium on being able to quickly introduce new, innovative goods and services into the marketplace.[59] In fact, when products become somewhat indistinguishable because of the widespread and rapid diffusion of technologies, speed to market with innovative products may be the primary source of competitive advantage (see Chapter 6).[60] Indeed, some argue that the global economy is increasingly driven by or revolves around constant innovations. Not surprisingly, such innovations must be derived from an understanding of global standards and global expectations in terms of product functionality.[61]

Another indicator of rapid technology diffusion is that it now may take only 12 to 18 months for firms to gather information about their competitors' research and

Perpetual innovation is a term used to describe how rapidly and consistently new, information-intensive technologies replace older ones.

development and product decisions.[62] In the global economy, competitors can sometimes imitate a firm's successful competitive actions within a few days. Once a source of competitive advantage, the protection firms previously possessed through their patents has been stifled by the current rate of technological diffusion. Today, patents may be an effective way of protecting proprietary technology in a small number of industries like pharmaceuticals. Indeed, many firms competing in the electronics industry often do not apply for patents to prevent competitors from gaining access to the technological knowledge included in the patent application.

Disruptive technologies—technologies that destroy the value of an existing technology and create new markets[63]—surface frequently in today's competitive markets. Think of the new markets created by the technologies underlying the development of products such as iPods, PDAs, WiFi, and the browser.[64] Products such as these are thought by some to represent radical or breakthrough innovations[65] (we talk more about radical innovations in Chapter 14). A disruptive or radical technology can create what is essentially a new industry or can harm industry incumbents. Some incumbents, though, are able to adapt based on their superior resources, experience, and ability to gain access to the new technology through multiple sources (e.g., alliances, acquisitions, and ongoing internal basic research).[66] When a disruptive technology creates a new industry, competitors follow. As explained in the Strategic Focus, the Research In Motion (RIM) BlackBerry created a new industry, if not an entirely new culture, by making use of a disruptive technology we know as the Internet.

In addition to providing innovative access to the Internet, the company has developed a device with a unique degree of connectedness. Certainly, it connects to the Internet—but with a phone to make calls with, a user-friendly keyboard, and Bluetooth-enabled connectivity, the BlackBerry allows users to connect in a variety of different ways to a variety of different devices. RIM makes the devices compliant with Java and gives away free, fully integrated development environment tools and device simulators for every handheld model. This means that RIM gives developers access to a simulated environment for every aspect of the BlackBerry platform and allows a multitude of vendors to develop an array of programs for the device. Clearly, RIM understands the importance of information sharing and knowledge (topics we discuss next) as competitive tools for the 21st-century competitive landscape.[67]

The Information Age

Dramatic changes in information technology have occurred in recent years. Personal computers, cellular phones, artificial intelligence, virtual reality, and massive databases (e.g., LexisNexis) are a few examples of how information is used differently as a result of technological developments. An important outcome of these changes is that the ability to effectively and efficiently access and use information has become an important source of competitive advantage in virtually all industries.[68]

Both the pace of change in information technology and its diffusion will continue to increase. For instance, the number of personal computers in use around the world is estimated at 1.3 billion.[69] The declining costs of information technologies and the increased accessibility to them are also evident in the 21st-century competitive landscape. The global proliferation of relatively inexpensive computing power and its linkage on a global scale via computer networks combine to increase the speed and diffusion of information technologies. Thus, the competitive potential of information technologies is now available to companies of all sizes throughout the world, not only to large firms in Europe, Japan, and North America.

As noted in the Strategic Focus on Research In Motion, the Internet and associated computer and telecommunications applications are other technological innovations contributing to hypercompetition. Available to an increasing number of people throughout the world, the cell phone and the Internet provide an infrastructure that

Constant Change at Research In Motion

In 1984, while attending the University of Waterloo, Mike Lazaridis and Doug Fregin founded Research In Motion (RIM). They picked a name that reflected their notion the company would strive for constant innovation. By 1988, the company was active in the transmission of wireless data.

Lazaridis, now co-CEO of RIM, recalls that in 1988, "We were doing wireless point-of-sale integration with another company's radios. I remember thinking, 'Hey, we can build a better radio than this.' And we did. That got us into paging, and we turned ourselves into experts in terms of the specifications of the paging network. We soon realized that, even though it was designed for one-way communication, you could incorporate a back channel so messages could go both ways."

When RIM began its foray into the wireless data industry, the main challenge was to get the devices' batteries to work for extended periods of time. The desire was to move battery life from hours to days. Current models of RIM's product have a battery life of weeks, not days.

What is RIM's product? It is a wireless handheld communication device called a BlackBerry. Lazaridis calls the BlackBerry a "synch engine," because "it synchronizes data across a mobile work force." This means that a BlackBerry can send and receive e-mail via a wireless/cell phone carrier. New messages can be pushed to the device as they are received. The BlackBerry has a browser capable of viewing a variety of Web-friendly formats (e.g., HTML files) and common image types, and supports JavaScript. Corporate clients can access secure intranet sites, which allows the BlackBerry to wirelessly synchronize Outlook contacts, calendar, tasks, and mail messages between your desktop computer and your handheld. The BlackBerry does all this on a device that includes a trackwheel, a full standard QWERTY keyboard, and an array of programmable shortcut keys.

RIM is not one to ever stop developing the product. The innovations and features just keep coming. Adding Bluetooth to new models allowed for the addition of a foldout wireless keyboard and a product that allows you to print to any Bluetooth-enabled printer. If your BlackBerry has the Global Positioning Satellite (GPS) feature, available products will speak directions to you as you drive—including a "Caffeine Finder" service that locates the nearest coffee shop relative to your GPS coordinates. That GPS might come in handy in finding your way around the world, because in 2002 RIM entered European and Asian markets in a big way. They added General Packet Radio Service wireless handhelds to their product list. This technology lets handhelds operate on the protocol for cell phones in about 140 countries, including throughout Europe. The technology opened international markets for RIM in the United Kingdom, the Netherlands, Germany, Ireland, and Italy.

If you wanted to buy a BlackBerry-like handheld—say, a Palm Pilot or a Handspring—you would still be getting some Research In Motion technology. In 2002, RIM began licensing its famous thumb-controlled keyboard to those two main rivals. The company preferred to do this rather than spend a huge sum of money fighting contestable patent protection in the courts. Besides, with so much more to offer than just a keyboard, the BlackBerry's cult-like loyalty is not likely to diminish.

Indeed, the BlackBerry cult just keeps growing. In 2007, RIM hit the 10-million-subscriber mark and shipped its 20 millionth handset. Most importantly, more than half the new cult members—that is, half of RIM's new subscribers in North America—were "non-enterprise." This means new users are not large corporations or big government departments, but the mass market. With the number of personal computers in use in the world estimated at about 1.3 billion a lot of people want to stay connected to the Internet, and RIM are the folks who can help them do so.

Yet RIM's influence goes beyond the BlackBerry device. Three examples give some idea of the device's range of influence: (1) "BlackBerry thumb" has been added to a list of modern-day ailments that includes "tech neck," "mouse wrist," and "iPod finger." According to the

(continued)

Canadian Physiotherapy Association, the global pervasiveness of technology-induced afflictions was among the hottest topics at a recent World Confederation of Physical Therapy Congress in Vancouver. (2) the BlackBerry's security features are so good that an internal RCMP "threat assessment" on organized crime devoted an entire section to the device. It seems that busy drug lords, like busy corporate executives, are enamoured with the device. In this case, gangsters like the device because it is much harder for police to tap into. Last but not least, (3) RIM is such a large influence on the stock market it is recognized as a major influence on the S&P/TSX composite index. Though RIM comprises less than 3.5 percent of the weight of the index, RIM's stock alone accounted for about 20 percent of the index's total gains in 2007.

SOURCES: Government of Canada, 2005, Case 7: Research In Motion Limited, innovation in Canada, http://www.innovation strategy.gc.ca/gol/innovation/site.nsf/en/in04212.html, October 15, 2007; W. Dabrowski, 2007, RIM passes key development milestones: BlackBerry hits 10 million subscribers as it ships its 20 millionth handset, *The Gazette,* October 6, C8; D. Berman, 2007, Our fortunes tied to RIM: Blackberry maker a giant influence, *National Post,* October 9, FP8; 2007, The BlackBerry gains popularity among tech-savvy B.C. crime lords, *National Post,* October 9, A6; M. Harris, 2007, Technology has become a pain in the neck: Tech neck, mouse wrist, iPod finger: Devices like computers and BlackBerries are having an effect on our health, *The Gazette,* October 9, A4; D. Mabe, 2007, What is a BlackBerry? O'Reilly Wireless DevCenter, http://www.oreillynet.com/ub/a/wireless/2005/09/15/what-is-blackberry.html?, October 14.

allows the delivery of information to a range of devices in any location. Access to significant quantities of relatively inexpensive information yields strategic opportunities for a number of companies in global markets. Being continually connected to the Net thus becomes critically important, and devices like the BlackBerry allow people to do so. Keeping such high-tech equipment current in such a fast-changing environment is also critical, and firms like Research In Motion must be constantly working to keep pace.

Increasing Knowledge Intensity

Knowledge (information, intelligence, and expertise) is the basis of technology and its application. In the 21st-century competitive landscape, knowledge is a critical organizational resource and is increasingly a valuable source of competitive advantage.[70] Indeed, starting in the 1980s, the basis of competition began shifting from hard assets to intangible resources. For example, "Wal-Mart transformed retailing through its proprietary approach to supply chain management and its information-rich relationships with customers and suppliers."[71] Relationships are an example of an intangible resource.

Knowledge is gained through experience, observation, and inference and is an intangible resource (tangible and intangible resources are described in Chapter 4). The value of intangible resources, including knowledge, is growing as a proportion of total shareholder value.[72] The probability of achieving strategic competitiveness in the 21st-century competitive landscape is enhanced for the firm that realizes its survival depends on the ability to capture intelligence, transform it into usable knowledge, and diffuse it rapidly throughout the company.[73] Therefore, firms must develop (e.g., through training programs) and acquire (e.g., by hiring educated and experienced employees) knowledge, integrate it into the organization to create capabilities, and then apply it to gain a competitive advantage.[74] In addition, firms must build routines that facilitate the diffusion of local knowledge throughout the organization for use everywhere it has value.[75] Firms are better able to do these things when they have strategic flexibility.

Strategic flexibility is a set of capabilities used to respond to various demands and opportunities existing in a dynamic and uncertain competitive environment. Thus, strategic flexibility involves coping with uncertainty and its accompanying risks.[76] Firms should try to develop strategic flexibility in all areas of their operations. However, those working within firms to develop strategic flexibility should understand that this is not an easy task, largely because of inertia that can build up over time.[77]

Strategic flexibility is a set of capabilities used to respond to various demands and opportunities existing in a dynamic and uncertain competitive environment.

Be Ready to Change, It Can't Be Avoided!

In the 21st-century competitive landscape, some argue that competition is about change—being able to change effectively, quickly, and in ways competitors find difficult to imitate. Through change, organizations have opportunities to grow and to learn. In a continuous cycle, new learning resulting from one change is the foundation for a new cycle of growth and future change. Without change and the resulting learning that pushes this continuous, reinforcing cycle, the likelihood of organizational decline and eventual death greatly increases. Being able to rapidly and successfully change is increasingly an irreplaceable dimension of being able to earn above-average returns in the global economy.

In spite of its importance, change is difficult for individuals and organizations. If we think of individuals, it may surprise us to learn that roughly 90 percent of heart-bypass patients do not change their lifestyles, even at the risk of dying. The difficulty individuals experience trying to change their behaviour suggests the challenge of achieving change in an organization—which, after all, is a collection of what often are change-resistant people! Nonetheless, there are interesting cases about organizational change, two of which we discuss next.

In the 1990s, Montreal's Gildan Activewear did what was fairly typical for an apparel maker: it used cheaper offshore labour to keep costs down. Gildan also handled non-Canadian sales out of lower-tax countries to keep its tax burden down, and invested heavily in cost-saving vertical integration. The company moved into all aspects of production—yarn spinning, knitting, dyeing, finishing, cutting, and sewing—located in cost-efficient environments. Since Gildan sold its product as T-shirt blanks to others who added their own designs and logos, the company was able to build sales and production volumes for less cost. Gildan used the wholesale channel to grow rapidly as a manufacturer and marketer of high-quality T-shirts in the North American and European Union (EU) imprinted sportswear markets.

As the new millennium dawned, however, there were clouds on the horizon. Under the 1995 World Trade Organization Agreement on Textiles and Clothing, quotas maintained by Western countries on imports of textiles and clothing were scheduled for a phased-out removal beginning in 2005. This meant Chinese manufacturers—with their extremely low labour costs—would gain greater access to Western markets. Gildan, with no operations in China, would need to change to survive in this labour-intensive industry.

Gildan sent a team of employees around the world to study the global price of clothing and determine the benchmark prices Gildan would need to reach to stay in business. According to Glenn Chamandy, CEO of Gildan, "The first thing we did from day one was to make sure that we benchmarked ourselves against the global market." Chamandy notes that, "We said, 'This is where we need to set our selling price,' and every year from then on we started declining our selling prices in anticipation of getting ready for more of a global market."

How did Gildan manage to lower its costs? Starting in 1998, Gildan relocated its sewing facilities to Honduras, Mexico, Haiti, and Nicaragua. In 2001, Gildan built huge, state-of-the-art textile processing facilities in Honduras and the Dominican Republic. The company's Honduras plant is the largest such operation in the world. From these facilities Gildan makes enough T-shirts to give one to everybody in St. John's, every day—that's 400 million every year.

While wages in Gildan's factories are about four times higher than those in Chinese plants, Gildan's wages are still relatively low by world standards and advanced technology has taken much of the labour out of textile processing. Chamandy points out, "Today, if you look at our basic wholesale product, a white 100 percent cotton heavyweight tee-shirt, we're selling it for just over a dollar." He adds, "The costs for a similar landed product from China today would be 10% to 15% higher."

Another critical component to the changes at Gildan has been closely studying bilateral and regional trade agreements around the world. Gildan strategically located facilities to ensure it can ship duty-free anywhere into North America, the EU countries, and Australia.

(continued)

Chamandy notes, "We've set our manufacturing up for every one of our markets, so that we can ship without quota and duty."

In 2006, the company began selling socks, sweatshirts, packaged T-shirts, and golf shirts directly to retailers like Wal-Mart. This action took the company head-to-head with a larger number of Chinese manufacturers. To compete in the retail market, Gildan built a copy of its Honduran plant in the Dominican Republic (where wages are more than one-third lower than in Honduras).

Importantly, the company has studied the market enough to recognize other factors that may add to its chance of success. An often-deciding factor in the retail market is a supplier's "response time." Since inventory is expensive, retailers do not like to hold stock. Thus, retailers have pushed inventory management responsibility onto suppliers. Now the producer who sells at the right price and can deliver the product closest to the date it is needed will get the sale. Proximity to the North American market is thus an important advantage. Gildan's proximity to North America not only saves a significant amount in shipping costs, but also allows the company to quickly refill its warehouses. Chamandy notes, "Our cycle time from offshore is three weeks, from China it's three months." Gildan has built a distribution network in each of its markets to meet the needs of customers for faster response. "One of the biggest opportunities is our service and fast response," notes Chamandy. "We have vendor management inventory systems that can ship to our customers in 24 hours from the time they place their order."

What can organizations do to improve their ability to change? One thing to recognize is that there are no shortcuts. Helping a firm learn how to change is hard work—work requiring dedicated efforts on the parts of many. To help firms learn how to effectively and consistently engage in change, research suggests that strategic leaders (whom we talk about more later in this chapter and in full detail in Chapter 13) should engage in a number of actions including the following: (1) phrasing the need for change in ways that appeal to employees' emotions as well as their cognitions, (2) casting the need for change as providing positive outcomes, (3) developing a story to describe the needed change that is simple, straightforward, and appealing, and (4) continuously developing and describing stories about the firm's success with different change efforts. While these actions won't lead to organizational change without disruption and some trepidation on the part of some employees, they do facilitate efforts to improve the chance of success when engaging in organizational change efforts.

SOURCES: J. Sanford, 2005, Beat China on cost, *Canadian Business,* 78(22): 51–56; A. Deutschman, 2005, Making change, *Fast Company,* May, 52–62; M. Arndt, A. Carter, & C. Arnst, 2005, Needed: More bite to fight fat, *BusinessWeek,* January 31, 36; J. A. Bryne, 2005, The case for change, *Fast Company,* April, 12; J. A. Bryne, 2005, Great work if you can get it, *Fast Company,* April, 14.

To be strategically flexible on a continuing basis and to gain the competitive benefits of such flexibility, a firm has to develop the capacity to learn. In the words of John Browne, CEO of British Petroleum: "In order to generate extraordinary value for shareholders, a company has to learn better than its competitors and apply that knowledge throughout its businesses faster and more widely than they do."[78] Continuous learning provides the firm with new and up-to-date sets of skills, which allow it to adapt to its environment as it encounters changes.[79] Firms capable of rapidly and broadly applying what they have learned have strategic flexibility and the resulting capacity to change in ways that will increase the probability of being able to successfully deal with uncertain, hypercompetitive environments. As we discuss in the Strategic Focus, some firms must change dramatically to remain competitive or to again become competitive.

Will the changes at Gildan noted in the Strategic Focus allow the company to address the demands of the changing global market in the face of strong competition? Time will provide the answer to this question. What we do know is that being prepared to consistently engage in change improves the likelihood of a firm achieving above-average returns across time.

Next, we describe two models firms use to generate the information they need to form their vision and mission and then to select and decide how to implement one or more strategies.

The I/O and Resource-Based Models of Above-Average Returns

The industrial organization or I/O model (examined in Chapter 3) specifies that the industry a firm chooses to compete in has a stronger influence on the firm's performance than choices managers make inside the firm.[80] A firm's performance is viewed to be determined mainly by a range of industry properties, including economies of scale, barriers to market entry, diversification, product differentiation, and the degree of concentration of firms in the industry.[81]

The I/O model has four underlying assumptions. One, the external environment imposes constraints that determine the strategies that result in above-average returns. Two, firms competing in an industry control similar resources and pursue similar strategies. Three, resources to implement strategies are mobile across firms and resource differences between firms will be short lived. Four, organizational decision makers are rational and committed to acting to maximize the firm's profits.[82] The I/O model challenges firms to locate the most attractive industry and learn how to use their resources to implement the strategy required by the industry's characteristics.

The five forces model of competition is an analytical tool used to help firms with this task. The model suggests that an industry's profitability is a function of interactions among suppliers, buyers, competitive rivalry, product substitutes, and potential entrants to the industry.[83] Firms can earn above-average returns by producing standardized products at lower cost (a cost-leadership strategy) or by making differentiated products that can command a premium price (a differentiation strategy).

As shown in Figure 1.3 on page 22, the I/O model suggests that above-average returns are earned when firms implement the strategy dictated by the characteristics of the general, industry, and competitor environments. Companies that develop or acquire skills needed to implement these strategies are likely to succeed; those that do not are likely to fail. This model suggests that external characteristics rather than the firm's unique internal resources and capabilities primarily determine returns.

Alternatively, the resource-based model assumes each organization's unique collection of resources and capabilities are the primary basis for the firm's strategy and returns rather than industry characteristics. **Resources** are inputs into a firm's production process, such as capital equipment, the skills of individual employees, patents, finances, and talented managers. A **capability** is the capacity for a set of resources to perform a task or an activity in an integrative manner. This model suggests that capabilities evolve and must be managed dynamically.[84] Furthermore, firms acquire different resources and develop unique capabilities, and since resources may not be highly mobile across firms the differences in resources may be the real basis for competitive advantage.

The strategy chosen should allow a firm to best exploit its core competencies relative to opportunities in the external environment. Not all firm resources and capabilities have the potential to be the basis for a core competency. This potential is realized when resources and capabilities are (1) *valuable*—allowing a firm to take advantage of opportunities or neutralize external threats, (2) *rare*—possessed by few current or potential competitors, (3) *costly to imitate*—other firms either cannot obtain them or are at a cost disadvantage in obtaining them, and (4) *organized to be exploited*—firms have the correct structure, control, and reward systems to support each advantage.[85] When these four criteria are met, resources and capabilities become core competencies. **Core competencies** are resources and capabilities that serve as a source of competitive advantage for a firm. Often related to functional skills, core competencies, when developed and applied throughout a firm, may result in strategic competitiveness.

Resources are inputs into a firm's production process, such as capital equipment, the skills of individual employees, patents, finances, and talented managers.

A **capability** is the capacity for a set of resources to perform a task or an activity in an integrative manner.

Core competencies are resources and capabilities that serve as a source of competitive advantage for a firm over its rivals.

Figure 1.3 The I/O and Resource-Based Models

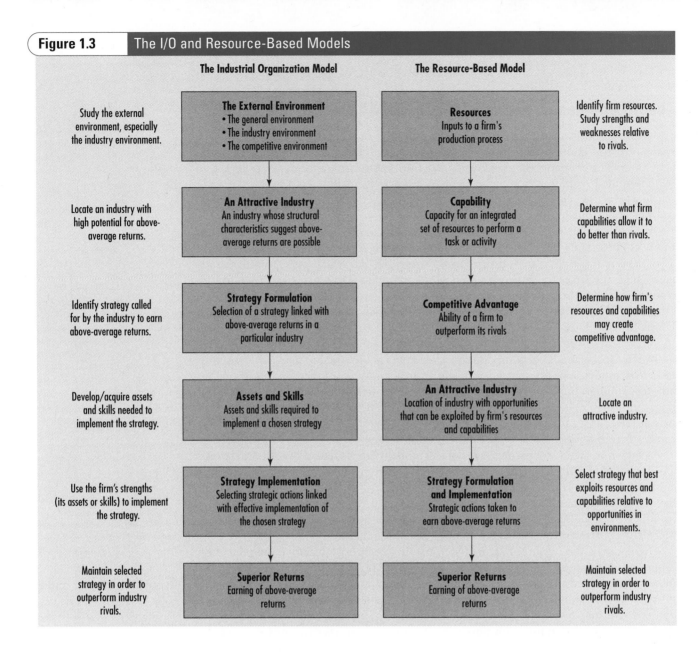

The Industrial Organization Model

The Resource-Based Model

Study the external environment, especially the industry environment.

The External Environment
- The general environment
- The industry environment
- The competitive environment

Resources
Inputs to a firm's production process

Identify firm resources. Study strengths and weaknesses relative to rivals.

Locate an industry with high potential for above-average returns.

An Attractive Industry
An industry whose structural characteristics suggest above-average returns are possible

Capability
Capacity for an integrated set of resources to perform a task or activity

Determine what firm capabilities allow it to do better than rivals.

Identify strategy called for by the industry to earn above-average returns.

Strategy Formulation
Selection of a strategy linked with above-average returns in a particular industry

Competitive Advantage
Ability of a firm to outperform its rivals

Determine how firm's resources and capabilities may create competitive advantage.

Develop/acquire assets and skills needed to implement the strategy.

Assets and Skills
Assets and skills required to implement a chosen strategy

An Attractive Industry
Location of industry with opportunities that can be exploited by firm's resources and capabilities

Locate an attractive industry.

Use the firm's strengths (its assets or skills) to implement the strategy.

Strategy Implementation
Selecting strategic actions linked with effective implementation of the chosen strategy

Strategy Formulation and Implementation
Strategic actions taken to earn above-average returns

Select strategy that best exploits resources and capabilities relative to opportunities in environments.

Maintain selected strategy in order to outperform industry rivals.

Superior Returns
Earning of above-average returns

Superior Returns
Earning of above-average returns

Maintain selected strategy in order to outperform industry rivals.

Research findings suggest both environment and firm characteristics play a role in determining a firm's profitability. These findings show that about 20 percent of the variance in a firm's profitability is determined by the industries in which the firm operates, and 36 percent of the variance in profitability could be attributed to the firm's characteristics and actions.[86] Thus, there is likely a reciprocal relationship between the environment and the firm's strategy, thereby affecting the firm's performance.[87] As a result, executives must integrate the two models to develop the most effective strategy.

As noted previously, research shows that both the industry environment and a firm's internal assets affect that firm's performance over time.[88] Thus, to form a vision and mission, and subsequently to select one or more strategies and to determine how to implement them, firms use both the I/O and the resource-based models.[89] In fact, these models complement each other in that one (I/O) focuses outside the firm while the other (resource-based) focuses inside the firm. In Chapter 3 we describe how firms use the I/O model, and in Chapter 4 we discuss how firms use the resource-based model.

Successful strategy formulation and implementation actions result only when the firm properly uses both models. Next, we discuss the forming of the firm's vision and mission—actions taken after the firm understands the realities of its external (Chapter 3) and internal (Chapter 4) environments.

Vision and Mission

After studying the external environment and the internal environment, the firm has the information it needs to form a vision and a mission (see Figure 1.1). Stakeholders (those who affect or are affected by a firm's performance, as discussed later in the chapter) learn a great deal about a firm by studying its vision and mission. Indeed, a key purpose of vision and mission statements is to inform stakeholders of what the firm is, what it seeks to accomplish, and whom it seeks to serve.

Vision

Vision is a picture of what the firm wants to be and, in broad terms, what it wants to ultimately achieve.[90] Thus, a vision statement articulates the ideal description of an organization and gives shape to its intended future. In other words, a vision statement points the firm in the direction of where it would eventually like to be in the years to come. Vision is "big picture" thinking with passion that helps people *feel* what they are supposed to be doing.[91] People feel what they are to do when their firm's vision is simple, positive, and emotional.[92] A vision stretches and challenges people and evokes emotions and dreams. Imagine the dreams evoked and the emotions felt when employees learn that as part of the firm's vision, the new CEO of LG Electronics says, "We must be a great company with great people."[93]

It is also important to note that vision statements reflect a firm's values and aspirations and are intended to capture the heart and mind of each employee and, it is hoped, many of its other stakeholders. A firm's vision tends to be enduring, while its mission can change in light of changing environmental conditions. A vision statement tends to be relatively short and concise, making it easily remembered. Examples of vision statements include the following: [94]

Vision is a picture of what the firm wants to be and, in broad terms, what it wants to ultimately achieve.

Our vision is to be the quality **leader in everything we do. (Tim Hortons)**

To be an international leader in protection and wealth management. (Sun Life Financial)

SOURCES: Courtesy of Sun Life Financial, URL: http://www.sunlife.com/worldwide/v/index.jsp?vgnextoid=597e5a366ccb0110Vgn VCM1000006c90d09fRCRD&vgnextchannel=597e5a366ccb0110VgnVCM1000006c90d09fRCRD&; Courtesy of The TDL Group Corp.

As a firm's most important and prominent strategic leader, the CEO is responsible for working with others to form the firm's vision. It is important for the CEO to do this because, in the words of Dan Rosensweig, chief operating officer (COO) for Yahoo!, "With a clear vision and strong leadership, you can make almost anything happen."[95]

Experience shows that the most effective vision statement results when the CEO involves a host of people (e.g., other top-level managers, employees working in different parts of the organization, suppliers, and customers) to develop it. In addition, to help the firm reach its desired future state, a vision statement should be clearly tied to the conditions in the firm's external and internal environments and it must be achievable. Moreover, the decisions and actions of those involved with developing the vision, especially the CEO and the other top-level managers, must be consistent with that vision. In fact, there is nothing worse than for the firm's top-level strategic leaders' actions to be inconsistent with the vision. At Tim Hortons, for example, a failure to openly provide employees with what they need to quickly and effectively serve customers would be a recipe for disaster.

Mission

A **mission** specifies the business or businesses in which the firm intends to compete and the customers it intends to serve.

The vision is the foundation for the firm's mission. A **mission** specifies the business or businesses in which the firm intends to compete and the customers it intends to serve.[96] As we will learn in Chapter 5, today's customers tend to be quite demanding when it comes to their expectations for product variety and quality.[97]

The firm's mission is more concrete than its vision. Yet, like the vision, a mission should establish a firm's individuality and should be inspiring and relevant to all stakeholders.[98] Together, vision and mission provide the foundation the firm needs to choose and implement one or more strategies. The probability of forming an effective mission increases when employees have a strong sense of the ethical standards that will guide their behaviours as they work to help the firm reach its vision.[99] Thus, business ethics are a vital part of the firm's discussions to decide what it wants to become (its vision) as well as whom it intends to serve and how it desires to serve those individuals and groups (its mission).[100]

As with the vision, the final responsibility for forming the firm's mission rests with the CEO, though the CEO and other top-level managers tend to involve a larger number of people in forming the mission. The main reason for this is that mission deals more directly with product markets and customers. Compared with the CEO and other top-level managers, middle- and first-level managers and other employees have more direct contact with customers and the markets in which they are served. Examples of mission statements include the following:[101]

> Our guiding mission is to deliver superior quality products and services for our customers and communities through leadership, innovation and partnerships. Our vision is to be the quality leader in everything we do. (Tim Hortons)

> To provide enabling technologies used to capture, process, store, and transmit information to drive the Digital Age. We will achieve this by anticipating our customers' requirements and by integrating our high-speed microprocessor, mixed signal and communications system technologies to deliver semiconductor solutions with superior quality service and technical support. (PMC Sierra)

> SOURCES: Courtesy of PMC-Sierra; Courtesy of The TDL Group Corp.

Notice how the Tim Hortons mission statement flows from its vision of delivering quality. PMC Sierra's mission statement describes the business areas (high-speed microprocessor, mixed signal and communications system technologies) in which the firm intends to compete and integrate.

While reading the vision and mission statements presented above, you likely recognized that the earning of above-average returns (also called profit maximization) was not mentioned in any of them. The reasons for this are that all firms want to earn above-average returns (meaning that this intention does not differentiate the firm from its rivals) and that desired financial outcomes result from properly serving certain customers while trying to achieve the firm's intended future. In other words, above-average returns are the fruits of the firm's efforts to achieve its vision and mission. In fact, research has shown that having an effectively formed vision and mission has a positive effect on performance as measured by growth in sales, profits, employment, and net worth.[102] In turn, positive firm performance increases the firm's ability to satisfy the interests of its stakeholders (whom we discuss next). The flip side of the coin also seems to be true—namely, the firm without an appropriately formed vision and mission is more likely to fail than the firm that has properly formed vision and mission statements.[103]

Stakeholders

Every organization involves a system of primary stakeholder groups with whom it establishes and manages relationships.[104] **Stakeholders** are the individuals and groups who can affect, and are affected by, the strategic outcomes achieved and who have enforceable claims on a firm's performance.[105] Claims on a firm's performance are enforced through the stakeholders' ability to withhold participation essential to the organization's survival, competitiveness, and profitability.[106] Stakeholders continue to support an organization when its performance meets or exceeds their expectations.[107] Also, recent research suggests that firms effectively managing stakeholder relationships outperform those that do not. Stakeholder relationships can therefore be managed to be a source of competitive advantage.[108]

Although organizations have dependency relationships with their stakeholders, they are not equally dependent on all stakeholders at all times;[109] as a consequence, not every stakeholder has the same level of influence. The more critical and valued a stakeholder's participation, the greater a firm's dependency on it. Greater dependence, in turn, gives the stakeholder more potential influence over a firm's commitments, decisions, and actions. Managers must find ways to either accommodate or insulate the organization from the demands of stakeholders controlling critical resources.[110]

> **Stakeholders** are the individuals and groups who can affect, and are affected by, the strategic outcomes achieved and who have enforceable claims on a firm's performance.

Classifications of Stakeholders

The parties involved with a firm's operations can be separated into at least three groups.[111] As shown in Figure 1.4, these groups are the capital market stakeholders (shareholders and the major suppliers of a firm's capital), the product market stakeholders (the firm's primary customers, suppliers, host communities, and unions representing the workforce), and the organizational stakeholders (all of a firm's employees, including both non-managerial and managerial personnel).

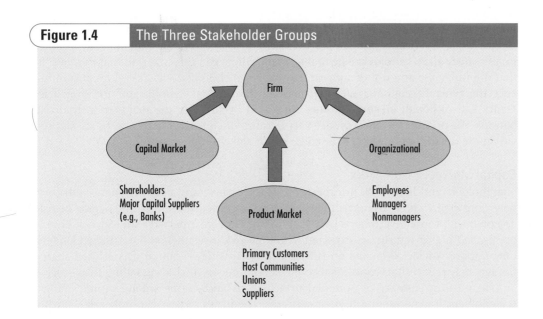

| Figure 1.4 | The Three Stakeholder Groups |

Each stakeholder group expects those making strategic decisions in a firm to provide the leadership through which its valued objectives will be reached.[112] The objectives of the various stakeholder groups often differ from one another, sometimes placing those involved with the strategic management process in situations where trade-offs have to be made. The most obvious stakeholders, at least in U.S. organizations, are *shareholders*—individuals and groups who have invested capital in a firm in the expectation of earning a positive return on their investments. These stakeholders' rights are grounded in laws governing private property and private enterprise.

Shareholders want the return on their investment (and, hence, the value of their investment) to be maximized. Maximization of returns sometimes is accomplished at the expense of investing in a firm's future. Gains achieved by reducing investment in research and development, for example, could be returned to shareholders, thereby increasing the short-term return on their investments. However, this short-term enhancement of shareholders' wealth can negatively affect the firm's future competitive ability, and sophisticated shareholders with diversified portfolios may sell their interests if a firm fails to invest in its future. Those making strategic decisions are responsible for a firm's survival in both the short and the long term. Accordingly, it is not in the interests of any stakeholders for investments in the company to be unduly minimized.

In contrast to shareholders, another group of stakeholders—the firm's customers—prefers that investors receive a minimum return on their investments. Customers could have their interests maximized when the quality and reliability of a firm's products are improved, but without a price increase. High returns to customers might come at the expense of lower returns negotiated with capital market shareholders.

Because of potential conflicts, each firm is challenged to manage its stakeholders. First, a firm must carefully identify all important stakeholders. Second, it must prioritize them, in case it cannot satisfy all of them. Power is the most critical criterion in prioritizing stakeholders. Other criteria might include the urgency of satisfying each particular stakeholder group and the degree of importance of each to the firm.[113]

When the firm earns above-average returns, the challenge of effectively managing stakeholder relationships is lessened substantially. With the capability and flexibility provided by above-average returns, a firm can more easily satisfy multiple stakeholders simultaneously. When the firm is earning only average returns, it is unable to maximize the interests of all stakeholders. The objective then becomes one of at least minimally satisfying each stakeholder. Trade-off decisions are made in light of how important the support of each stakeholder group is to the firm. For example, environmental groups may be very important to firms in the energy industry but less important to professional service firms.[114] A firm earning below-average returns does not have the capacity to minimally satisfy all stakeholders. The managerial challenge in this case is to make trade-offs that minimize the amount of support lost from stakeholders. Societal values also influence the general weightings allocated among the three stakeholder groups shown in Figure 1.4. Although all three groups are served by firms in the major industrialized nations, the priorities in their service vary because of cultural differences. Next, we provide more details about each of the three major stakeholder groups.

Capital Market Stakeholders

Shareholders and lenders both expect a firm to preserve and enhance the wealth they have entrusted to it. The returns they expect are commensurate with the degree of risk accepted with those investments (that is, lower returns are expected with low-risk investments, and higher returns are expected with high-risk investments). Dissatisfied lenders may impose stricter covenants on subsequent borrowing of capital. Dissatisfied shareholders may reflect their concerns through several means, including selling their stock.

When a firm is aware of potential or actual dissatisfactions among capital market stakeholders, it may respond to their concerns. The firm's response to stakeholders who are dissatisfied is affected by the nature of its dependency relationship with them (which, as noted earlier, is also influenced by a society's values). The greater and more significant the dependency relationship is, the more direct and significant the firm's response becomes. Given the situation the major North American auto producers find themselves in, it is reasonable to expect that the CEO and top-level managers at GM and Ford are thinking seriously about what should be done to improve their firms' financial performance in order to satisfy its capital market stakeholders.

Product Market Stakeholders

Some might think that product market stakeholders (customers, suppliers, host communities, and unions) share few common interests. However, all four groups can benefit as firms engage in competitive battles. For example, depending on product and industry characteristics, marketplace competition may result in lower product prices being charged to a firm's customers and higher prices being paid to its suppliers (the firm might be willing to pay higher supplier prices to ensure delivery of the types of goods and services that are linked with its competitive success).

As is noted in Chapter 3, customers, as stakeholders, demand reliable products at the lowest possible prices. Suppliers seek loyal customers who are willing to pay the highest sustainable prices for the goods and services they receive. Host communities want companies willing to be long-term employers and providers of tax revenues without placing excessive demands on public support services. Union officials are interested in secure jobs, under highly desirable working conditions, for employees they represent. Thus, product market stakeholders are generally satisfied when a firm's profit margin reflects at least a balance between the returns to capital market stakeholders (i.e., the returns lenders and shareholders will accept and still retain their interests in the firm) and the returns in which they share.

Organizational Stakeholders

Employees—the firm's organizational stakeholders—expect the firm to provide a dynamic, stimulating, and rewarding work environment. As employees, we are usually satisfied working for a company that is growing and actively developing our skills, especially those skills required to be effective team members and to meet or exceed global work standards. Workers who learn how to use new knowledge productively are critical to organizational success. In a collective sense, the education and skills of a firm's workforce are competitive weapons affecting strategy implementation and firm performance.[115] As suggested by the following statement, strategic leaders are ultimately responsible for serving the needs of organizational stakeholders on a day-to-day basis: "[T]he job of [strategic] leadership is to fully utilize human potential, to create organizations in which people can grow and learn while still achieving a common objective, to nurture the human spirit."[116]

Strategic Leaders

Strategic leaders are people located in different parts of the firm using the strategic management process to help the firm reach its vision and mission. Regardless of their location in the firm, successful strategic leaders are decisive and committed to nurturing those around them[117] and are committed to helping the firm create value for customers and returns for shareholders and other stakeholders.[118]

When identifying strategic leaders, most of us tend to think of chief executive officers (CEOs) and other top-level managers. Clearly, these people are strategic leaders. And, in the final analysis, CEOs are responsible for making certain their firm effectively uses the strategic management process. Indeed, the pressure on CEOs to do this is stronger than ever.[119] However, there are many other people in today's organizations who help choose a

Strategic leaders are people located in different parts of the firm using the strategic management process to help the firm reach its vision and mission.

firm's strategy and then determine actions to be taken to successfully implement it.[120] The main reason for this is that the realities of 21st-century competition that we discussed earlier in this chapter (e.g., the global economy, globalization, rapid technological change, and the increasing importance of knowledge and people as sources of competitive advantage) are creating a need for those "closest to the action" to be the ones making decisions and determining the actions to be taken.[121] In fact, the most effective CEOs and top-level managers understand how to delegate strategic responsibilities to people throughout the firm who influence the use of organizational resources.[122]

Organizational culture refers to the complex set of ideologies, symbols, and core values that are shared throughout the firm and that influence how the firm conducts business.

Organizational culture also affects strategic leaders and their work. In turn, strategic leaders' decisions and actions shape a firm's culture. **Organizational culture** refers to the complex set of ideologies, symbols, and core values that are shared throughout the firm and that influence how the firm conducts business. It is the social energy that drives—or fails to drive—the organization. For example, highly successful Southwest Airlines is known for having a unique and valuable culture. Its culture encourages employees to work hard but also to have fun while doing so. Moreover, its culture entails respect for others—employees and customers alike. The firm also places a premium on service, as suggested by its commitment to provide POS (Positively Outrageous Service) to each customer. Wal-Mart claims that its continuing success is largely attributable to its culture.[123]

Some organizational cultures are a source of disadvantage. Look back over Nortel Networks' recent history. One can see the battle it has gone through due to a dysfunctional corporate culture. In early 2004, Nortel fired its chief executive officer, chief financial officer, and comptroller.[124] The firings were prompted by the investigations then underway by the Brampton, Ontario–based company's Audit Committee. An independent review covered the years 2000 to 2003 and focused on management's practices regarding accruals and provisions that could materially impact their stated earnings.[125] Simply, these executives tried to paint an overly rosy picture of the company's performance. The dysfunctional culture at the company's top levels ran so deep that eventually another half-dozen senior executives were dismissed from Nortel due to the accounting scandal. In 2007, The U.S. Securities and Exchange Commission charged the three former Nortel executives mentioned above with seven counts of accounting fraud aimed "to bridge gaps between Nortel's true performance, its internal targets and Wall Street expectations."[126] New Nortel CEO Mike Zafirovski, formerly a senior executive at Motorola, has taken actions to correct the dysfunctional aspects of Nortel's culture and recover the company's reputation, but he is likely to have a long road ahead of him given the depth of the damage that has been done.

Not all corporate cultures are as dysfunctional as the one at Nortel. However, Linda Duxbury of Ottawa's Carleton University has stated that, "More than half of corporate cultures right now in Canada are completely dysfunctional." A survey of hundreds of corporations shows most companies fail in developing a positive corporate culture. This could mean anything from bosses demanding that workers work through the night without giving so much as a thank-you, to screaming at their workers. Professor Duxbury notes that having a mission statement and corporate values policy is not enough: firms need to include values and performance and reward employees who effectively demonstrate both.[127]

It is important for strategic leaders to understand, however, that whether the firm's culture is functional or dysfunctional, their work takes place within the context of that culture. There is a continuing reciprocal relationship between organizational culture and strategic leaders' work, in that the culture shapes how they work while their work helps shape what is an ever-evolving organizational culture.

The Work of Effective Strategic Leaders

Perhaps not surprisingly, hard work, thorough analysis, a willingness to be brutally honest, a penchant for wanting the firm and its people to accomplish more, and common sense are prerequisites to an individual's success as a strategic leader.[128] As well, strategic leaders must be able to "think seriously and deeply . . . about the purposes of the organizations they head or functions they perform, about the strategies, tactics, technologies, systems, and people necessary to attain these purposes and about the important questions that always need to be asked."[129]

Additionally, effective strategic leaders work to set an ethical tone in their firms. One of the world's richest people, Warren Buffett, has said, "It takes 20 years to build a reputation and five minutes to ruin it."[130] And as Peter Robinson, CEO of Mountain Equipment Co-op, noted, "Ethics is the new competitive environment."[131] The importance of ethics to this CEO has helped Mountain Equipment earn a rank in the top 15 in *Corporate Knights'* "Best Fifty Corporate Citizens" list.[132]

Strategic leaders, regardless of their location in the organization, often work long hours, and the work is filled with ambiguous decision situations for which effective solutions are not easily determined.[133] However, the opportunities afforded by this work are appealing and offer exciting chances to dream and to act.[134] The following words, given as advice to the late Time Warner chairman and co-CEO Steven J. Ross by his father, describe the opportunities in a strategic leader's work: There are three categories of people—the person who goes into the office, puts his feet up on his desk, and dreams for 12 hours; the person who arrives at 5 a.m. and works for 16 hours, never once stopping to dream; and the person who puts his feet up, dreams for one hour, then does something about those dreams.[135]

The organizational term used for a dream that challenges and energizes a company is vision (discussed earlier in this chapter). Strategic leaders have opportunities to dream and to act, and the most effective ones provide a vision as the foundation for the firm's mission and subsequent choice and use of one or more strategies.

The Importance of Social Responsibility and Ethics in Leadership

It is important to emphasize that, primarily because they are related to how a firm interacts with its stakeholders, almost all strategic management process decisions have an impact on society and thus have ethical dimensions.[136] A firm's decisions are a product of the core values that are shared by most or all of a company's managers and employees. In the turbulent and often ambiguous 21st-century competitive landscape, those making decisions that are part of the strategic management process are challenged to recognize that their decisions affect capital market, product market, and organizational stakeholders differently and to evaluate their social responsibility to such stakeholders and the ethical implications of their decisions on virtually a daily basis.[137] Decision makers failing to recognize these realities accept the risk of putting their firm at a competitive disadvantage when it comes to consistently engaging in social responsibility through ethical business practices.[138]

Effective leaders commonly have a strong set of core values or guiding principles that include ethics and integrity.[139] According to Robert D. Haas, Chair and CEO of Levi Strauss, high ethical standards must be modelled by management and woven into the fabric of the company.[140] It seems that more organizations are attempting to implement a code of ethics or code of conduct. While a vision may be a firm's desired end-state, and its mission a delineation of the company's businesses and the customers it intends to serve, an organization's ethical codes defines the framework within which all employees must work. Such codes are essentially the company's moral compass.

How the organization's top leader behaves sets the standard that lower levels of management and employees will follow. A classic case is that of Hollinger International. The company's Code of Business Conduct and Ethics was an excellent one. It called for the company and management to have honest and ethical conduct, no conflicts of interest, accurate and timely disclosures, legal compliance, and fair internal reporting that allowed for whistle-blowing.[141] There were claims that virtually none of these standards were actually applied in the company by its owner, Montreal native Conrad Black. Beginning in 2005, Lord Black began a losing battle against charges that he was involved in numerous acts of fraud and, in a related act, attempted to obstruct justice.[142]

However, if there is sincere intent on the part of top management to address ethical issues, and the organization's decision-making processes regarding such issues are transparent and honest, people will sense it and be open to discussing ethics.[143] For example, BMO Financial Group (Bank of Montreal) highlights the organization's core values in its Corporate Responsibility Report and Public Accountability Statement: [144]

We care about our customers, shareholders, communities and each other.

We draw our strength from the diversity of our people and our businesses.

We insist upon respect for everyone and encourage all to have a voice.

We keep our promises and stand accountable for our every action.

We share information, learn and innovate to create consistently superior customer experiences.

SOURCE: Courtesy of BMO Financial Group.

Notice that BMO organizational values note major stakeholder groups and address the needs the organization will try to fulfill. The report also includes a signed statement by BMO's President and CEO William A. Downe endorsing the report. Others in the organization have taken up the call. Rose M. Patten, BMO's Senior Executive Vice-President, Head of Human Resources, and Senior Leadership Advisor, has stated, "I do take the position that ethical conduct and corporate values must become front and centre in our priorities on the personal level and on the institutional level."[145] BMO also backs up its public statements with a reporting of its social activities and charitable giving. BMO is also ranked in the top 10 in *Corporate Knights'* "Best Fifty Corporate Citizens" list.

Another financial institution on the *Corporate Knights* "Best Fifty Corporate Citizens" list is Vancouver City Savings—Vancity for short. Ranked number three on that list, Vancity, the largest credit union in Canada, uses its ethical stance as part of its strategy. The credit union has numerous ethical investment funds that are an integral part of its product mix, has plans to become carbon neutral by 2010, and it pays all of its profits back to its most important stakeholders, its members.[146]

In some cases, an organization's ethical stance can be a vital part of its strategy. Just down the street from a Vancity branch in Abbotsford, B.C. is one of the two locations of the Ethical Addictions Coffee House. Ethical Addictions pays a living wage to its coffee growers, supports numerous charities, and you can even get a fine cup of coffee there.

Predicting Outcomes of Strategic Decisions: Profit Pools

Strategic leaders attempt to predict the outcomes of their decisions before taking efforts to implement them. This is difficult to do, in that many decisions that are a part of the strategic management process are concerned with an uncertain future and the firm's place in that future.[147]

Mapping an industry's profit pool is something strategic leaders can do to anticipate the possible outcomes of different decisions and to focus on growth in profits rather than strictly growth in revenues. A **profit pool** entails the total profits earned in an

A **profit pool** entails the total profits earned in an industry at all points along the value chain.

industry at all points along the value chain (value chain is explained in Chapter 4 and further discussed in Chapter 5).[148] Analyzing the profit pool in the industry may help a firm see something others are unable to see by helping it understand the primary sources of profits in an industry. There are four steps to identifying profit pools: (1) define the pool's boundaries, (2) estimate the pool's overall size, (3) estimate the size of the value-chain activity in the pool, and (4) reconcile the calculations.[149]

Let's think about how Gildan Activewear might map the apparel industry's profit pools. First, Gildan would need to define the industry's boundaries and, second, estimate their size. These boundaries would include markets across the globe. Gildan would then be prepared to estimate the amount of profit potential in each part of the value chain (step 3). Are product design and product quality more important sources of potential profits than distribution channels? These are the types of issues to be considered with the third step of actions used to map an industry's profit pool. Gildan would then have the information and insight needed to identify the strategies to use to be successful where the largest profit pools are located in the value chain.[150] As this brief discussion shows, profit pools are a tool to use to help the firm's strategic leaders recognize the actions to take to increase the likelihood of increasing profits.

The Strategic Management Process

As suggested by Figure 1.1, the strategic management process is a rational approach firms use to achieve strategic competitiveness and earn above-average returns. Any discussion should begin with what "above-average returns" really means. For that reason, we devote Chapter 2 to a discussion of performance measures. Figure 1.1 also outlines the topics we examine in this book to present the strategic management process to you.

There are three parts to this book. In Part 1, we provide a general overview of the topic of strategic management (Chapter 1), we review a variety of performance measures (Chapter 2), and we describe what firms do to analyze their external environment (Chapter 3) and internal environment (Chapter 4). These analyses are completed to identify marketplace opportunities and threats in the external environment (Chapter 3) and to decide how to use the resources, capabilities, and core competencies in the firm's internal environment to pursue opportunities and overcome threats (Chapter 4). With knowledge about its external and internal environments, the firm forms its vision and mission.

The firm's strategic inputs (see Figure 1.1) provide the foundation for choosing one or more strategies and deciding how to implement them. As suggested in Figure 1.1 by the horizontal arrow linking the two types of strategic actions, formulation and implementation must be simultaneously integrated if the firm is to successfully use the strategic management process. Integration happens as decision makers think about implementation issues when choosing strategies and as they think about possible changes to the firm's strategies while implementing a currently chosen strategy.

In Part 2 of this book, we discuss the different strategies firms may choose to use. First, we examine business-level strategies (Chapter 5). A business-level strategy describes a firm's actions designed to exploit its competitive advantage over rivals. A company competing in a single product market (e.g., a locally owned grocery store operating in only one location) has but one business-level strategy. As you will learn, a diversified firm competing in multiple product markets forms a business-level strategy for each of its businesses. In Chapter 6, we describe the actions and reactions that occur among firms while using their strategies in marketplace competitions. As we will see, competitors respond to and try to anticipate each other's actions. The dynamics of competition affect the strategies firms choose to use as well as how they try to implement the chosen strategies.[151]

For the diversified firm, corporate-level strategy (Chapter 7) is concerned with determining the businesses in which the company intends to compete as well as how resources, capabilities, and core competencies are to be allocated among the different businesses. Other topics vital to strategy formulation, particularly in the diversified corporation, include acquiring other companies and, as appropriate, restructuring the firm's portfolio of businesses (Chapter 8) and selecting an international strategy (Chapter 9). With cooperative strategies (Chapter 10), firms form a partnership to share their resources and capabilities in order to develop a competitive advantage. Cooperative strategies are becoming increasingly important as firms try to find ways to compete in the global economy's array of different markets.[152] For example, Microsoft, the world's largest software company, and Toshiba, the world's third-largest maker of notebook PCs, have formed a joint venture to combine some of their resources and capabilities in order to develop software for notebook computers and other mobile devices.[153]

To examine actions taken to implement strategies, we consider several topics in Part 3 of the book. First, we examine the different mechanisms used to govern firms (Chapter 11). With demands for improved corporate governance being voiced today by many stakeholders,[154] organizations are challenged to learn how to simultaneously satisfy their stakeholders' different interests. Finally, we address the organizational structure and actions needed to control a firm's operations (Chapter 12), the patterns of strategic leadership appropriate for today's firms and competitive environments (Chapter 13), and strategic entrepreneurship (Chapter 14) as a path to continuous innovation.

As you will discover, the strategic management process examined in this book calls for disciplined approaches to the development of competitive advantage. These approaches provide the pathway through which firms will be able to achieve strategic competitiveness and earn above-average returns in the 21st century. Mastery of this strategic management process will effectively serve you, our readers and the organizations for which you will choose to work.

Summary

- Firms use the strategic management process to achieve strategic competitiveness and earn above-average returns. Strategic competitiveness is achieved when a firm has developed and learned how to implement a value-creating strategy. Above-average returns (in excess of what investors expect to earn from other investments with similar levels of risk) provide the foundation a firm needs to simultaneously satisfy all of its stakeholders.

- The fundamental nature of the competition landscape in the 21st century is different. As a result, those making strategic decisions must adopt a different mind-set, one that allows them to learn how to compete in highly turbulent and chaotic environments that produce disorder and uncertainty. The two primary factors contributing to the turbulence of the 21st-century competitive landscape are the globalization of industries and their markets, and rapid and significant technological changes.

- Firms use two major models to help them form their vision and mission and then choose one or more strategies to use in the pursuit of strategic competitiveness and above-average returns. The core assumption of the I/O model is that the firm's external environment has more of an influence on the choice of strategies than do the firm's internal resources, capabilities, and core competencies. Thus, the I/O model is used to understand the effects an industry's characteristics can have on a firm when deciding what strategy or strategies to use to compete against rivals. The logic supporting the I/O model suggests that above-average returns are earned when the firm locates an attractive industry and successfully implements the strategy dictated by that industry's characteristics. The core assumption of the resource-based model is that the firm's unique resources, capabilities, and core competencies have more of an influence on selecting and using strategies than does the firm's external environment. Above-average returns are earned when the firm uses its valuable, rare, costly-to-imitate, and organized-to-exploit resources and capabilities to compete against its rivals in one or more industries. Evidence indicates that both models yield insights that are linked to successfully selecting and using strategies. Thus, firms want to use their unique resources, capabilities, and core competencies as the foundation for one or more strategies that will allow them to compete in industries they understand.

- Vision and mission are formed in light of the information and insights gained from studying a firm's internal and external environments. Vision is a picture of what the firm wants to be and, in broad terms, what it wants to ultimately achieve. Flowing from the vision, the mission specifies the business or businesses in which the firm intends to compete and the customers it intends to serve. Vision and mission provide direction to the firm and signals important descriptive information to stakeholders.

- Stakeholders are those who can affect, and are affected by, a firm's strategic outcomes. Because a firm is dependent on the continuing support of stakeholders (shareholders, customers, suppliers, employees, host communities, etc.), stakeholders have enforceable claims on the company's performance. When earning above-average returns, a firm has the resources it needs to at least minimally simultaneously satisfy the interests of all stakeholders. However, when earning only average returns, different stakeholder groups must be carefully managed in order to retain their support. A firm earning below-average returns must minimize the amount of support it loses from dissatisfied stakeholders.

- Strategic leaders are people located in different parts of the firm using the strategic management process to help the firm reach its vision and mission. In the final analysis, though, CEOs are responsible for making certain that their firms properly use the strategic management process. Today, the effectiveness of the strategic management process increases when it is grounded in ethical intentions and behaviours. The strategic leader's work demands decision trade-offs, often among attractive alternatives. It is important for all strategic leaders, and especially the CEO and other members of the top-management team, to work hard, conduct thorough analyses of situations, be brutally and consistently honest, and ask the right questions of the right people at the right time.

- Strategic leaders must predict the potential outcomes of their strategic decisions. To do so, they must first calculate profit pools in their industry that are linked to value chain activities. In so doing, they are less likely to formulate and implement ineffective strategies.

Review Questions

1. What are strategic competitiveness, strategy, competitive advantage, above-average returns, and the strategic management process?

2. What are the characteristics of the 21st-century landscape? What two factors are the primary drivers of this landscape?

3. According to the I/O model, what should a firm do to earn above-average returns?

4. What does the resource-based model suggest a firm should do to earn above-average returns?

5. What are vision and mission? What is their value for the strategic management process?

6. What are stakeholders? How do the three primary stakeholder groups influence organizations?

7. How would you describe the work of strategic leaders?

8. What are the elements of the strategic management process? How are they interrelated?

Social Responsibility Review

1. Check out *Corporate Knights* magazine (www. corporateknights.ca) and go to their annual 50 Best issue. Select one of the companies listed and, from your own personal perspective, describe why you think the company is a socially responsible organization.

2. Go to *Corporate Knights* magazine's (www. corporateknights.ca) annual 50 Best issue. Select the company on the list you think is the most and least ethical. Why do you think *Corporate Knights* includes both companies? What does this tell you about the differing perspectives of different stakeholders? Do you think business or society wants an organization to develop strategies that will satisfy *all* stakeholders?

3. Do you know to whom you're giving your money? Pick from any of the largest banks in Canada and search their Web site for the words "social responsibility" or "ethics." What does this list tell *you* about how the organization treats the topic—for example, to whom is it important within the organization? Does the company have a code of conduct and what stakeholders does it address?

Creating Value

Strategy is about creating value. In this chapter, we learned about the two lenses through which managers seek to create above-average returns—the I/O model and the resource-based model. In each model, the way in which returns are measured is important. For example, in the text, risk adjustment is discussed as one criterion that has to be taken into account when accounting profits are compared, particularly with firms in different industries. However, the way in which returns are calculated may also affect firm rankings relative to an industry average, even among firms in the same industry. Three widely used measures of return are as follows:

1. *Percentage of sales.* This is the most commonly used measure of performance. It is simply the firm's net income expressed as a percentage of sales revenues.

2. *Return on capital employed.* This measure considers what was earned for each dollar that shareholders and bondholders invested. It is a good measure of how well those leading and managing firms have used the capital society has entrusted to them. The numerator for this measure is the firm's profit prior to tax and interest (EBIT). The denominator is the firm's total assets minus its current liabilities.

3. *Total return to shareholders.* This measure captures the total gain to a shareholder over a year as a percentage of the price of a share on the first day of the year. The numerator here is the change in price of a share of stock from the first day to the last day of the year plus all dividends paid on that share. The denominator is the price of the share at the beginning of the year.

When firms within the same industry are ranked in terms of these three performance measures, who is "above average" and who is "below average" often changes significantly. In other words, a firm may perform well with respect to one of these performance measures but may perform poorly (compared to competitors) on another measure.

In Groups

Select an industry with at least six publicly traded firms that are dominated by a single business. Banking, airlines, brewing, and fast food are examples of industries from which you may choose. Look at the annual report data for the last calendar year for six firms within the industry you chose and calculate the return measures listed above as well as the industry average for each. Present your results to the class and discuss which measure your group thinks yields the best indication of managerial performance from the perspective of the firm's stakeholders. Be prepared to explain your reasoning.

The March of Globalization

Foreign direct investments (FDI) and international trade patterns demonstrate globalization's rapid spread across many of the world's economies. For example, both FDI and international trade have been growing at a faster rate than the Canadian economy as a whole for some time. And there are other patterns of importance. As the text points out, significant investment in developing countries such as India and China has shifted investment from well-established economies to emerging economies over the last 10 to 15 years. Looking at these patterns can be very informative with respect to understanding how global business patterns are changing. Managers in the 21st century must be aware of these patterns if they are to successfully lead their firms. In particular, strategic managers who have responsibility for establishing the firm's vision and making certain that the firm pursues its mission must have a broad awareness of the shifting trends in global business practices and the different nature of different nations' economics.

Go to the main Web page for the Organisation for Economic Co-operation and Development (OECD) at www.oecd.org. After reading the background information about the OECD, locate its statistical portal. In the "Data by Topic" area, you will find a significant and valuable amount of information that is relevant to understanding the march of globalization. Under "International Trade," look for the latest report on global trade; it is published quarterly. Open that document and you should find import and export numbers for the world in the last five years. Then look for the report on trade among OECD members. This report is usually published on the same date each quarter, as is the world report. Use the data you have found to answer the following questions.

1. What are the trends in global trade over the last five years that most stand out? How does the change in trade volumes match with the growth of the global economy over the same period? What is influencing the patterns you have observed?

2. What are the trends in OECD trade over the last four years that most stand out? How do the changes in trade volumes among the OECD members compare to those numbers you saw for the world as a whole? What do you think is causing the patterns you have observed?

Mission Statements and Stakeholders

Effective mission statements, which are derived from the firm's vision, are externally focused in order to speak to the needs of a range of stakeholders. They focus the firm in a certain direction with respect to products, customers, and performance. A mission statement has a different meaning for different stakeholders. For each stakeholder group, though, the mission statement should provide a mental frame in which a group's members can evaluate a firm's actions to verify that they are consistent with the mission.

The mission statements of five pharmaceutical firms are presented in the following table. Each of these mission statements is posted on the firm's Web site for all stakeholders to see. In each case, the statement has remained unchanged for at least three years.

Using materials in the chapter and discussions of those materials during class, evaluate each of the five mission statements and assign a grade of A, B, C, D, or F based on the perspective of each one of the stakeholder groups. If you give a high grade, be prepared to defend it. If you give a low grade, be ready to tell what you think is wrong with the statement and how it should be improved.

| Firm and Mission Statement | Stakeholder Group | | |
	Capital Market Stakeholders	Product Market Stakeholders	Organizational Stakeholders
GlaxoSmithKline GSK's mission is to improve the quality of human life by enabling people to do more, feel better, and live longer.			
Bristol-Myers Squibb Our company's mission is to extend and enhance human life by providing the highest quality of pharmaceuticals and health care products.			
Merck The mission of Merck is to provide society with superior products and services by developing innovations and solutions that improve the quality of life and satisfy customer needs, and to provide employees with meaningful work and advancement opportunities, and investors with a superior rate of return.			
Novartis We want to discover, develop, and successfully market innovative products to cure diseases, to ease suffering, and to enhance the quality of life. We also want to provide a shareholder return that reflects outstanding performance and to adequately reward those who invest ideas and work in our company.			
Pfizer We will become the world's most valued company to patients, customers, colleagues, investors, business partners, and the communities where we work and live.			
Pharmascience Pharmascience is a Canadian company dedicated to profitable growth through research and development, manufacturing and distribution of affordable healthcare products and related services. Flexibility, innovation, speed, trust and tenacity define us; customer service drives us and our employees make it happen.			

Notes

1. N. Layne, 2005, Sony to unveil new strategy in September, Reuters, www.reuters.com, retrieved June 22.
2. J. B. Barney & T. B. Mackey, 2005, Testing resource-based theory, In D. J. Ketchen Jr. & D. D. Bergh (eds.), *Research Methodology in Strategy and Management* (2nd ed.), London: Elsevier, 1–13; D. G. Sirmon, M. A. Hitt, & R. D. Ireland, 2007, Managing firm resources in dynamic environments to create value: Looking inside the black box, *Academy of Management Review*, 32: 273–292.
3. D. Lei & J. W. Slocum, 2005, Strategic and organizational requirements for competitive advantage, *Academy of Management Executive*, 19(1): 31–45; T. J. Douglas & J. A. Ryman, 2003, Understanding competitive advantage in the general hospital industry: Evaluating strategic competencies, *Strategic Management Journal*, 24: 333–347.
4. K. Shimizu & M. A. Hitt, 2004, Strategic flexibility: Organizational preparedness to reverse ineffective strategic decisions, *Academy of Management Executive*, 18(4): 44–59; D. J. Teece, G. Pisano, & A. Shuen, 1997, Dynamic capabilities and strategic management, *Strategic Management Journal*, 18: 509–533.
5. P. Shrivastava, 1995, Ecocentric management for a risk society, *Academy of Management Review*, 20: 119.
6. F. Delmar, P. Davidsson, & W. B. Gartner, 2003, Arriving at a high-growth firm, *Journal of Business Venturing*, 18: 189–216.
7. T. Bates, 2005, Analysis of young, small firms that have closed: Delineating successful from unsuccessful closures, *Journal of Business Venturing*, 20: 343–358.
8. A. M. McGahan & M. E. Porter, 2003, The emergence and sustainability of abnormal profits, *Strategic Organization*, 1: 79–108; T. C. Powell, 2001, Competitive advantage: Logical and philosophical considerations, *Strategic Management Journal*, 22: 875–888.
9. R. D. Ireland & C. C. Miller, 2004, Decision-making and firm success, *Academy of Management Executive*, 18(4): 8–12.
10. P. Nutt, 2004, Expanding the search for alternatives during strategic decision-making, *Academy of Management Executive*, 18(4): 13–28; S. Dutta, M. J. Zbaracki, & M. Bergen, 2003, Pricing process as a capability: A resource-based perspective, *Strategic Management Journal*, 24: 615–630.
11. S. Tallman & K. Fladmoe-Lindquist, 2002, Internationalization, globalization, and capability-based strategy, *California Management Review*, 45(1): 116–135; M. A. Hitt, R. D. Ireland, S. M. Camp, & D. L. Sexton, 2001, Strategic entrepreneurship: Entrepreneurial strategies for wealth creation, *Strategic Management Journal*, 22 (Special Issue): 479–491; S. A. Zahra, R. D. Ireland, & M. A. Hitt, 2000, International expansion by new venture firms: International diversity, mode of market entry, technological learning and performance, *Academy of Management Journal*, 43: 925–950.
12. R. Kirkland, 2005, Will the U.S. be flattened by a flatter world? *Fortune*, June 27, 47–48.
13. A. Nair & S. Kotha, 2001, Does group membership matter? Evidence from the Japanese steel industry, *Strategic Management Journal*, 22: 221–235; A. M. McGahan & M. E. Porter, 1997, How much does industry matter, really? *Strategic Management Journal*, 18 (Special Issue): 15–30.
14. D. G. Sirmon & M. A. Hitt, 2003, Managing resources: Linking unique resources, management and wealth creation in family firms, *Entrepreneurship Theory and Practice*, 27(4): 339–358; J. B. Barney, 2001, Is the resource-based "view" a useful perspective for strategic management research? Yes, *Academy of Management Review*, 26: 41–56.
15. G. A. Steiner & J. B. Miner, 1977, *Management Policy and Strategy: Text, Readings and Cases*, New York: MacMillan, 7; W. F. Glueck, 1980, *Business Policy and Strategic Management*, New York: McGraw-Hill, 9; J. B. Quinn, 1980, *Strategies for Change: Logical Incrementalism*, Homewood, IL: Irwin; K. J. Hatten & M. L. Hatten, 1988, *Effective Strategic Management*, Englewood Cliffs, NJ: Prentice-Hall, 1; J. B. Barney, 1997, *Gaining and Sustaining Competitive Advantage*, Don Mills, ON: Addison Wesley Publishing, 17.
16. H. Mintzberg, 1987, Five Ps for strategy, *California Management Review*, Fall, reprinted in H. Mintzberg & J. B. Quinn, 1996, *The Strategy Process: Concepts, Contexts and Cases*, Upper Saddle River, NJ: Prentice-Hall, 10–17.
17. Z. Patakfalvi, 2007, Domtar: High quality paper at Windsor, *Pulp and Paper Canada*, 108(4): 24–25.
18. S. Schick, 2004, Rogers Wireless hatches GSM plan with $1.4B Fido bid, *Computing Canada*, 30(14): 12.
19. R. Thompson, 2006, Tim Hortons is one of Canada's great growth stories . . ., *Financial Post Business*, March, 24–25; 2007, Tim Hortons Web page, http://www.timhortons.com/en/pdfs/en_media_kit.pdf and /goodwill/childrens_about.html, October 6.
20. P. McCosker, 2007, Stretching the brand: A review of the Virgin Group, in *Strategic Management, Competitiveness and Globalization*, 2nd ed., M. A. Hitt, R. D. Ireland, R. E. Hoskisson, J. P. Sheppard, & W. G. Rowe, eds., Toronto: Thomson Nelson: 305–311; 2007, Virgin Group Web page, http://www.virgin.com/home.aspx, October 6.
21. M. Dickie, 2007, Vancity: CSR as brand identity: CSR takes hold, *Strategy*, August, 47.
22. H. Mintzberg & J. B. Quinn, 1996, *The Strategy Process*, Upper Saddle River, NJ: Prentice-Hall, 12.
23. J. Schmidt, 2007, personal communication, October 14.
24. M. A. Hitt, B. W. Keats, & S. M. DeMarie, 1998, Navigating in the new competitive landscape: Building competitive advantage and strategic flexibility in the 21st century, *Academy of Management Executive*, 12(4): 22–42; R. A. Bettis & M. A. Hitt, 1995, The new competitive landscape, *Strategic Management Journal*, 16 (Special Issue): 7–19.
25. 2005, NBC could combine network and cable news—*NY Post*, www .reuters.com, retrieved June 30.
26. B. Alptert, 2005, Apple's iPod faces threat, *Bryan-College Station Eagle*, July 3, E5.
27. 2007, Bell Canada acquires majority interest in Puretracks, nation's premiere online digital music service, BCE Web page, http://www.bce.ca/en/news/releases/bcinternet/2006/03/01/73399.html, October 8.
28. C. Harrison, 2005, Is it Goofy to give your child a phone? *Dallas Morning News*, July 7, D1, D3.
29. G. Probst & S. Raisch, 2005, Organizational crisis: The logic of failure, *Academy of Management Executive*, 19(1): 90–105; M. A. Hitt & V. Pisano, 2003, The cross-border merger and acquisition strategy, *Management Research*, 1: 133–144.
30. R. M. Grant, 2003, Strategic planning in a turbulent environment: Evidence from the oil majors, *Strategic Management Journal*, 24: 491–517.
31. G. McNamara, P. M. Vaaler, & C. Devers, 2003, Same as it ever was: The search for evidence of increasing hypercompetition, *Strategic Management Journal*, 24: 261–278.
32. R. A. D'Aveni, 1995, Coping with hypercompetition: Utilizing the new 7S's framework, *Academy of Management Executive*, 9(3): 46.
33. R. A. D'Aveni, 2004, Corporate spheres of influence, *MIT Sloan Management Review*, 45(4): 38–46; W. J. Ferrier, 2001, Navigating the competitive landscape: The drivers and consequences of competitive aggressiveness, *Academy of Management Journal*, 44: 858–877.
34. S.-J. Chang & S. Park, 2005, Types of firms generating network externalities and MNCs' co-location decisions, *Strategic Management Journal*, 26: 595–615; S. C. Voelpel, M. Dous, & T. H. Davenport, 2005, Five steps to creating a global knowledge-sharing systems: Siemens/ShareNet, *Academy of Management Executive*, 19(2): 9–23.
35. R. Belderbos & L. Sleuwaegen, 2005, Competitive drivers and international plant configuration strategies: A product-level test, *Strategic Management Journal*, 26: 577–593.
36. 2005, Organisation for Economic Co-operation and Development, *OCED Statistical Profile of the United States—2005*, www.oced.org; S. Koudsi & L. A. Costa, 1998, America vs. the new Europe: By the numbers, *Fortune*, December 21, 149–156.
37. S. Ruderi, 2005, Asia or Bust, *Profit*, 24(5): 51–52.
38. T. Raum, 2005, Awakening economic powerhouses eye G8, Washington Post Online, www.washingtonpost.com, retrieved July 3.
39. Kirkland, Will the U.S. be flattened by a flatter world? 47.
40. A. Virmani, 2005, India a giant economy? Yes, by 2035! Rediff.com, www.rediff.com, retrieved January 21.

41. Raum, Awakening economic powerhouses.

42. K. Kranhold, 2005, GE pins hopes on emerging markets, Wall Street Journal Online, www.wsj.com, retrieved March 2.

43. 2005, Delivering the goods at FedEx, *BusinessWeek*, June 13, 60–62.

44. P. Williamson & M. Zeng, 2004, Strategies for competing in a changed China, *MIT Sloan Management Review*, 45(4): 85–91; V. Govindarajan & A. K. Gupta, 2001, *The Quest for Global Dominance*, San Francisco: Jossey-Bass.

45. T. Khanna, K. G. Palepu, & J. Sinha, 2005, Strategies that fit emerging markets, *Harvard Business Review*, 83(6): 63–76.

46. 2005, Wal-Mart at a glance, www.walmart.com, retrieved July 3.

47. 2007, SNC-Lavalin Web page, www.snclavalin.com/en/, October 13. Regional data from 2005/2006 financial statements.

48. 2007, Tim Hortons Web page, http://www.timhortons.com/en/pdfs/ en_media_kit.pdf, October 12.

49. P. Barwise & S. Meehan, 2004, Don't be unique, be better, *MIT Sloan Management Review*, 45(4): 23–26.

50. M. A. Prospero, 2005, The march of war, *Fast Company*, May, 14.

51. G. Fink & N. Holden, 2005, The global transfer of management knowledge, *Academy of Management Executive*, 19(2): 5–8; M. Subramaniam & N. Venkataraman, 2001, Determinants of transnational new product development capability: Testing the influence of transferring and deploying tacit overseas knowledge, *Strategic Management Journal*, 22: 359–378.

52. S. Zaheer & E. Mosakowski, 1997, The dynamics of the liability of foreignness: A global study of survival in financial services, *Strategic Management Journal*, 18: 439–464.

53. R. C. May, S. M. Puffer, & D. J. McCarthy, 2005, Transferring management knowledge to Russia: A culturally based approach, *Academy of Management Executive*, 19(2): 24–35.

54. M. A. Hitt, R. E. Hoskisson, & H. Kim, 1997, International diversification: Effects on innovation and firm performance in product-diversified firms, *Academy of Management Journal*, 40: 767–798.

55. D'Aveni, Coping with hypercompetition, 46.

56. G. Hamel, 2001, Revolution vs. evolution: You need both, *Harvard Business Review*, 79(5): 150–156.

57. 2007, Scotiabank at 175 Web page, http://www.scotiabank.com/cda/index/0, LIDen_SID15,00.html.

58. K. H. Hammonds, 2001, What is the state of the new economy? *Fast Company*, September, 101–104.

59. L. Yu, 2005, Does knowledge sharing pay off? *MIT Sloan Management Review*, 46(3): 5.

60. L. Valikangas & M. Gibbert, 2005, Boundary-setting strategies for escaping innovation traps, *MIT Sloan Management Review*, 46(3): 58–65; K. M. Eisenhardt, 1999, Strategy as strategic decision making, *Sloan Management Review*, 40(3): 65–72.

61. J. Santos, Y. Doz, & P. Williamson, 2004, Is your innovation process global? *MIT Sloan Management Review*, 45(4): 31–37.

62. C. W. L. Hill, 1997, Establishing a standard: Competitive strategy and technological standards in winner-take-all industries, *Academy of Management Executive*, 11(2): 7–25.

63. C. Gilbert, 2003, The disruptive opportunity, *MIT Sloan Management Review*, 44(4): 27–32; C. M. Christiansen, 1997, *The Innovator's Dilemma*, Boston: Harvard Business School Press.

64. P. Magnusson, 2005, Globalization is great—sort of, *BusinessWeek*, April 25, 25.

65. R. Adner, 2002, When are technologies disruptive? A demand-based view of the emergence of competition, *Strategic Management Journal*, 23: 667–688; G. Ahuja & C. M. Lampert, 2001, Entrepreneurship in the large corporation: A longitudinal study of how established firms create breakthrough inventions, *Strategic Management Journal*, 22 (Special Issue): 521–543.

66. C. L. Nichols-Nixon & C. Y. Woo, 2003, Technology sourcing and output of established firms in a regime of encompassing technological change, *Strategic Management Journal*, 24: 651–666; C. W. L. Hill & F. T. Rothaermel, 2003, The performance of incumbent firms in the face of radical technological innovation, *Academy of Management Review*, 28: 257–274.

67. D. Mabe, 2007, What is a BlackBerry? O'Reilly Wireless DevCenter, http:// www.oreillynet.com/ub/a/wireless/2005/09/15/what-is-blackberry.html?, October 14.

68. G. Ferguson, S. Mathur, & B. Shah, 2005, Evolving from information to insight, *MIT Sloan Management Review*, 46(2): 51–58.

69. Estimate is for 2010; J. LeClaire, 2004, Worldwide PC market to double by 2010, Forrester says, *TechNewsWorld*, http://www.technewsworld.com/story/ 39010.html, October 14, 2007.

70. A. C. Inkpen & E. W. K. Tsang, 2005, Social capital, networks, and knowledge transfer, *Academy of Management Review*, 30: 146–165; A. S. DeNisi, M. A. Hitt, & S. E. Jackson, 2003, The knowledge-based approach to sustainable competitive advantage, in S. E. Jackson, M. A. Hitt, & A. S. DeNisi (eds.), *Managing Knowledge for Sustained Competitive Advantage*, San Francisco: Jossey-Bass, 3–33.

71. M. Gottfredson, R. Puryear, & S. Phillips, 2005, Strategic sourcing: From periphery to the core, *Harvard Business Review*, 83(2): 132–139.

72. K. G. Smith, C. J. Collins, & K. D. Clark, 2005, Existing knowledge, knowledge creation capability, and the rate of new product introduction in high-technology firms, *Academy of Management Journal*, 48: 346–357; S. K. McEvily & B. Chakravarthy, 2002, The persistence of knowledge-based advantage: An empirical test for product performance and technological knowledge, *Strategic Management Journal*, 23: 285–305.

73. S. K. Ethirau, P. Kale, M. S. Krishnan, & J. V. Singh, 2005, Where do capabilities come from and how do they matter? *Strategic Management Journal*, 26: 25–45; L. Rosenkopf & A. Nerkar, 2001, Beyond local search: Boundary-spanning, exploration, and impact on the optical disk industry, *Strategic Management Journal*, 22: 287–306.

74. Sirmon, Hitt, & Ireland, Managing firm's resources.

75. K. Asakawa & M. Lehrer, 2003, Managing local knowledge assets globally: The role of regional innovation relays, *Journal of World Business*, 38: 31–42.

76. R. E. Hoskisson, M. A. Hitt, & R. D. Ireland, 2004, *Competing for Advantage*, Cincinnati: Thomson South-Western; K. R. Harrigan, 2001, Strategic flexibility in old and new economies, in M. A. Hitt, R. E. Freeman, & J. S. Harrison (eds.), *Handbook of Strategic Management*, Oxford, UK: Blackwell Publishers, 97–123.

77. Shimizu & Hitt, Strategic flexibility, 45.

78. L. Gratton & S. Ghoshal, 2005, Beyond best practice, *MIT Sloan Management Review*, 46(3): 49–55.

79. K. Uhlenbruck, K. E. Meyer, & M. A. Hitt, 2003, Organizational transformation in transition economies: Resource-based and organizational learning perspectives, *Journal of Management Studies*, 40: 257–282.

80. E. H. Bowman & C. E. Helfat, 2001, Does corporate strategy matter? *Strategic Management Journal*, 22: 1–23.

81. A. Seth & H. Thomas, 1994, Theories of the firm: Implications for strategy research, *Journal of Management Studies*, 31: 165–191.

82. Ibid., 169–173.

83. M. E. Porter, 1985, *Competitive Advantage*, New York: Free Press; M. E. Porter, 1980, *Competitive Strategy*, New York: Free Press.

84. C. Lee, K. Lee, & J. M. Pennings, 2001, Internal capabilities, external networks, and performance: A study on technology-based ventures, *Strategic Management Journal* 22 (special issue): 615–640; C. C. Markides, 1999, A dynamic view of strategy, *Sloan Management Review*, 40(3): 55–72; Abell, Competing today while preparing for tomorrow.

85. J. B. Barney, 1991, Firm resources and sustained competitive advantage, *Journal of Management*, 17: 99–120; Barney, 1995, Looking inside for competitive advantage, *Academy of Management Executive*, 9 (4): 56; Barney, 1997, *Gaining and Sustaining Competitive Advantage*; J. B. Barney, 2001, Is the resource based "view" a useful perspective for strategic management research? Yes, *Academy of Management Review*, 26: 41–56.

86. A. M. McGahan, 1999, Competition, strategy and business performance, *California Management Review*, 41(3): 74–101; A. M. McGahan & M. E. Porter, 1997, How much does industry matter, really? *Strategic Management Journal*, 18 (special summer issue): 15–30.

87. R. Henderson & W. Mitchell, 1997, The interactions of organizational and competitive influences on strategy and performance, *Strategic Management Journal* 18 (special summer issue): 5–14; C. Oliver, 1997, Sustainable competitive advantage: Combining institutional and resource-based views, *Strategic Management Journal,* 18: 697–713; J. L. Stimpert & I. M. Duhaime, 1997, Seeing the big picture: The influence of industry, diversification, and business strategy on performance, *Academy of Management Journal,* 40: 560–583.

88. G. Hawawini, V. Subramanian, & P. Verdin, 2003, Is performance driven by industry- or firm-specific factors? A new look at the evidence, *Strategic Management Journal,* 24: 1–16.

89. M. Makhija, 2003, Comparing the resource-based and market-based views of the firm: Empirical evidence from Czech privatization, *Strategic Management Journal,* 24: 433–451; T. J. Douglas & J. A. Ryman, 2003, Understanding competitive advantage in the general hospital industry: Evaluating strategic competencies, *Strategic Management Journal,* 24: 333–347.

90. R. D. Ireland, R. E. Hoskisson, & M. A. Hitt. 2006, *Understanding Business Strategy,* Cincinnati: Thomson South-Western, 32–34.

91. 2005, The CEO's secret handbook, *Business 2.0,* July, 69–76.

92. A. Deutschman, 2005, Making change, *Fast Company,* May, 53–62.

93. M. Ihlwan, C. Edwards, & R. Crockett, 2005, Korea's LG may be the next Samsung, *BusinessWeek,* January 24, 54–55.

94. 2007, Tim Hortons Web page, http://www.timhortons.com/en/pdfs/en_media_kit.pdf, October 21; 2007, Sun Life Financial Web page, http://www.sunlife.com/worldwide/v/index.jsp?vgnextoid=597e5a366ccb0110VgnVCM1000006c90d09fRCRD&vgnLocale=en_CA&chnpath=%2FAbout+SLF6, October 20.

95. P. B. Brown, 2005, What I know now, *Fast Company,* February, 96.

96. R. D. Ireland & M. A. Hitt, 1992, Mission statements: Importance, challenge, and recommendations for development, *Business Horizons,* 35(3): 34–42.

97. V. Postrel, 2005, So many choices, *Dallas Morning News,* June 26, P1, P5.

98. W. J. Duncan, 1999, *Management: Ideas and Actions,* New York: Oxford University Press, 122–125.

99. P. Martin, 1999, Lessons in humility, *Financial Times,* June 22, 18.

100. J. A. Pearce & J. P. Doh, 2005, The high impact of collaborative social initiatives, *MIT Sloan Management Review,* 46(3): 30–39.

101. 2007, Tim Hortons Web page, http://www.timhortons.com/en/pdfs/en_media_kit.pdf, October 21; 2007, PMC Sierra mission statement Web page, http://www.pmc-sierra.com/company/mission_statement. html, October 21.

102. I. R. Baum, E. A. Locke, & S. A. Kirkpatrick, 1998, A longitudinal study of the relation of vision and vision communication to venture growth in entrepreneurial firms, *Journal of Applied Psychology,* 83: 43–54.

103. J. Humphreys, 2004, The vision thing, *MIT Sloan Management Review,* 45(4): 96.

104. P. A. Argenti, R. A. Howell, & K. A. Beck, 2005, The strategic communication imperative, *MIT Sloan Management Review,* 46(3): 83–89; J. Frooman, 1999, Stakeholder influence strategies, *Academy of Management Review,* 24: 191–205.

105. T. M. Jones & A. C. Wicks, 1999, Convergent stakeholder theory, *Academy of Management Review,* 24: 206–221; R. E. Freeman, 1984, *Strategic Management: A Stakeholder Approach,* Boston: Pitman, 53–54.

106. G. Donaldson & J. W. Lorsch, 1983, *Decision Making at the Top: The Shaping of Strategic Direction,* New York: Basic Books, 37–40.

107. S. Sharma & I. Henriques, 2005, Stakeholder influences on sustainability practices in the Canadian Forest products industry, *Strategic Management Journal,* 26: 159–180.

108. A. J. Hillman & G. D. Keim, 2001, Shareholder value, stakeholder management, and social issues: What's the bottom line? *Strategic Management Journal,* 22: 125–139.

109. J. M. Stevens, H. K. Steensma, D. A. Harrison, & P. L. Cochran, 2005, Symbolic or substantive document? The influence of ethics codes on financial executives' decisions, *Strategic Management Journal,* 26: 181–195.

110. R. E. Freeman & J. McVea, 2001, A stakeholder approach to strategic management, in M. A. Hitt, R. E. Freeman, & J. S. Harrison (eds.), *Handbook of Strategic Management,* Oxford, UK: Blackwell Publishers, 189–207.

111. Ibid.

112. C. Caldwell & R. Karri, 2005, Organizational governance and ethical systems: A covenantal approach to building trust, *Journal of Business Ethics,* 58: 249–267; A. McWilliams & D. Siegel, 2001, Corporate social responsibility: A theory of the firm perspective, *Academy of Management Review,* 26: 117–127.

113. C. Hardy, T. B. Lawrence, & D. Grant, 2005, Discourse and collaboration: The role of conversations and collective identity, *Academy of Management Review,* 30: 58–77; R. K. Mitchell, B. R. Agle, & D. J. Wood, 1997, Toward a theory of stakeholder identification and salience: Defining the principle of who and what really count, *Academy of Management Review,* 22: 853–886.

114. S. Maitlis, 2005, The social process of organizational sensemaking, *Academy of Management Journal,* 48: 21–49.

115. T. M. Gardner, 2005, Interfirm competition for human resources: Evidence from the software industry, *Academy of Management Journal,* 48: 237–256.

116. J. A. Byrne, 2005, Working for the boss from hell, *Fast Company,* July, 14.

117. D. Brady & D. Kiley, 2005, Short on sizzle, and losing steam, *BusinessWeek,* April 25, 44.

118. E. T. Prince, 2005, The fiscal behavior of CEOs, *MIT Sloan Management Review,* 46(3): 23–26.

119. D. Brady & J. Weber, 2005, *BusinessWeek,* April 25, 88–96.

120. A. Priestland & T. R. Hanig, 2005, Developing first-level managers, *Harvard Business Review,* 83(6): 113–120.

121. R. T. Pascale & J. Sternin, 2005, Your company's secret change agent, *Harvard Business Review,* 83(5): 72–81.

122. 2005, Jim Collins on tough calls, *Fortune,* June 27, 89–94.

123. 2005, About Wal-Mart, www.walmart.com, retrieved July 3.

124. B. Lindsay, 2004, Nortel executives, postpones results, Network World Canada, 14 (9): 5.

125. J. Bagnall, 2007, Fixing the RCMP: Lessons from Nortel: Can the new man at the top fix the dysfunctional force?, *The Ottawa Citizen,* July 7, A1 [final edition].

126. 2007, SEC files first charges in Nortel accounting scandal, TelecomWeb News Break, March 13, 1.

127. D. Sankey, 2005, Is your boss a jerk? Then take a walk, *Montreal Gazette,* October 15, B7 [final edition].

128. D. Rooke & W. R. Tolbert, 2005, Seven transformations of leadership, *Harvard Business Review,* 83(4): 66–76.

129. T. Leavitt, 1991, *Thinking about Management,* New York: Free Press, 9.

130. 2007, Quotations from business and thought leaders on ethics . . . , http://www.interpraxis.com/quotes.htm, October 23.

131. Ibid.

132. 2007, Best Fifty Corporate Citizens, *Corporate Knights,* 6(1): 24–26.

133. D. C. Hambrick, S. Finkelstein, & A. C. Mooney, 2005, Executive job demands: New insights for explaining strategic decisions and leader behaviors, *Academy of Management Review,* 30: 472–491; J. Brett & L. K. Stroh, 2003, Working 61 plus hours a week: Why do managers do it? *Journal of Applied Psychology,* 88: 67–78.

134. J. A. Byrne, 2005, Great work if you can get it, *Fast Company,* April, 14.

135. M. Loeb, 1993, Steven J. Ross, 1927–1992, *Fortune,* January 25, 4.

136. J. R. Ehrenfeld, 2005, The roots of sustainability, *MIT Sloan Management Review,* 46(2): 23–25; L. K. Trevino & G. R. Weaver, 2003, *Managing Ethics in Business Organizations,* Stanford, CA: Stanford University Press.

137. J. R. Ehrenfeld, 2005, The roots of sustainability.

138. 2005, Corporate citizenship on the rise, *BusinessWeek,* May 9, S1–S7.

139. G. Miller, 2004, Leadership & integrity: How to ensure it exists in your organization, *The Canadian Manager,* 29(4):15–17.

140. J. Sherren, 2005, Ethics in the workplace, *Summit,* 8(4): 4–5. The pun about "ethical standards ... woven into the fabric of the company" at Levi's is in the original article.

141. M. McClearn, 2004, Did anybody even read this?, *Canadian Business,* 77(11): 14.

142. 2007, Biography of Conrad Black, *Financial Post,* http://www.canada.com/nationalpost/financialpost/conradblack/story.html?id=ff18a624-c20b-481c-ab6b-822b4111258c, October 27.

143. 2002, Leadership ethics: Finale, *Management Matters,* 84: 1–3.
144. 2007, Corporate Responsibility Report and 2007 Public Accountability Statement: Taking the Initiative, BMO Financial Group, http://www2.bmo.com/bmo/files/images/7/1/BMO_CRPAS2007en.pdf, retrieved April 2, 2008.
145. 2003, Remarks made to the Canadian Centre for Ethics & Corporate Policy in Toronto on April 24, 2003, http://www.ethicscentre.ca/EN/resources/april%202003_luncheon.pdf, October 27, 2007.
146. 2007, Shared success, Vancity Web page, https://www.vancity.com/MyCommunity/CommunityFunding/CarbonOffsetProgram/?id=communityMain, October 28; 2007, Vancity carbon offset program, Vancity Web page, https://www.vancity.com/MyCommunity/Membership/MemberBenefits/SharedSuccess/, October 27.
147. Collins, Jim Collins on tough calls.
148. O. Gadiesh & J. L. Gilbert, 1998, Profit pools: A fresh look at strategy, *Harvard Business Review,* 76(3): 139–147.
149. O. Gadiesh & J. L. Gilbert, 1998, How to map your industry's profit pool, *Harvard Business Review,* 76(3): 149–162.
150. M. J. Epstein & R. A. Westbrook, 2001, Linking actions to profits in strategic decision making, *Sloan Management Review,* 42(3): 39–49.
151. D. J. Ketchen, C. C. Snow, & V. L. Street, 2004, Improving firm performance by matching strategic decision-making processes to competitive dynamics, *Academy of Management Executive,* 18(4): 29–43.
152. P. Evans & B. Wolf, 2005, Collaboration rules, *Harvard Business Review,* 83(7): 96–104.
153. 2005, Microsoft, Toshiba to develop electronics, Reuters, www.reuters.com, retrieved June 27.
154. Pearce & Doh, The high impact of collaborative social initiatives, 30–39.

Chapter Two

Strategic Management and Firm Performance

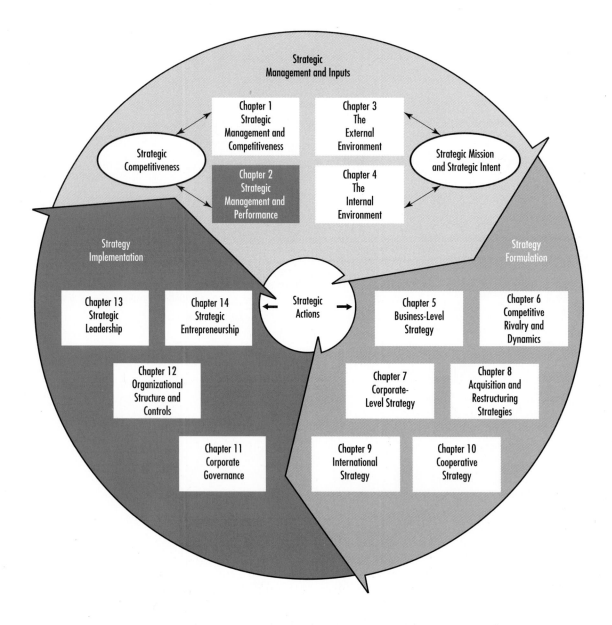

Knowledge Objectives

Studying this chapter should provide you with the strategic management knowledge needed to:

1. Understand the ultimate goal of strategic management—to impact organizational performance.

2. Define performance, particularly the differences among above-average returns, average returns, and below-average returns.

3. Discuss the different ways in which organizational performance is measured.

4. Know the strengths and weaknesses of different measures of organizational performance.

5. Define corporate social responsibility, sustainability, and the triple bottom line.

The Triple Bottom Line: A New Measure of Firm Performance

In recent years, a very different measure of firm performance has emerged and is continuing to gain prominence. This measure is called corporate social responsibility, also referred to as the "triple bottom line." Corporations today are looking past the bottom line and are demonstrating to their customers, investors, and the general public that they are acting in society's best interests and are investing in sustainable development initiatives. This includes employment diversity, environmental consciousness, and more. Firms are becoming more transparent and are required to disclose more information about their practices around social, environmental, and governance issues.

To this end, studies have shown that investors are becoming increasingly aware of the "link between environmental and financial performance." This explains the rationale behind some firms in specific industries assigning departments to be accountable for things like environmental management.

The term "triple bottom line" was originally coined by John Elkington, co-founder of the business consultancy SustainAbility and author of *Cannibals with Forks: The Triple Bottom Line of 21st Century Business*. The basic theory behind SustainAbility is that there are numerous measures of firm performance beyond the financial statements. For example, the triple bottom line, which represents "people, planet, and profit," takes into account the fact that firms are no longer responsible only to shareholders, but instead are held accountable to *all* stakeholders, representing "anyone who is influenced, either directly or indirectly, by the actions of the firm."

According to *CMA Management*, "companies that incorporate triple bottom line (social, environmental, and financial) objectives into their strategies have superior share returns." Today, many consulting firms specialize in sustainability and corporate social responsibility. For example, EthicScan Canada Limited, a Toronto-based business ethics consultancy, corporate responsibility research house, and educational resource centre, "help(s) organizations and individuals behave more ethically." EthicScan provides clients with the research, tools, and training necessary to integrate socially responsible behaviour into firms' business models.

www.ethicscan.ca

www.jantziresearch.com

In offering its clients a social responsibility benchmark, Jantzi Research, a firm focused on evaluating and monitoring the "social and environmental performance of securities," launched the Jantzi Social Index© (JSI) in conjunction with the Dow Jones indexes and Montreal-based investment management firm State Street Global Advisors. This index uses the market capitalization of 60 Canadian firms as a benchmark to measure against other securities' social and environmental performance. In addition to the JSI, Jantzi Research uses its Best-of-Sector™ investment screening to help its clients "work toward their social goals while maintaining their obligations and fiduciary responsibilities."

SOURCES: 2007, Message from Deloitte about the Best 50 ranking, *Corporate Knights*, http://www.corporateknights.ca/content/page.asp?name=2007deloitte, June 24; V. Magness, 2007, Lean or green, *CMA Management*, March 1; 2008, Triple bottom line, Wikipedia, http://en.wikipedia.org/wiki/Triple_bottom_line, accessed January 10; 2008, EthicScan Canada Ltd., http://www.ethicscan.ca/, accessed January 10; 2008, Jantzi Research, Home, http://www.jantziresearch.com/, accessed January 10; 2008, Jantzi Social Index, About the JSI, http://www.jantzisocialindex.com/, accessed January 10.

In Chapter 1, we stressed the importance of understanding how to exploit competitive advantages to ensure that a firm earns above-average returns. This is consistent with most definitions of strategy that have at least one attribute in common: they focus on the effect of a firm's strategy on performance in the short and/or long term. The definition of strategy as the allocation of resources to enable the maintenance or enhancement of performance illustrates this point very well.[1] In addition, this emphasis on performance is explicit in the description of the strategic management process in Chapter 1: *The strategic management process is the full set of commitments, decisions, and actions required for a firm to achieve strategic competitiveness and earn above-average returns.*[2]

An important question in the study of organizations is: What is performance? In some settings, the notion of performance is very clear. In athletics, the person who throws the javelin the farthest, the person who runs 100 metres the fastest, the person who jumps the highest in a pole vaulting competition—all these people have outperformed their competition. In sports, the team that wins the Stanley Cup in the National Hockey League playoffs, the team that wins the World Series in baseball, the team that wins the National Basketball Association's league championship—these teams are considered to have outperformed the rest of the teams in their respective sports. However, in many organizations, the definition of performance is more complicated. In this chapter, we present one reasonable approach to defining performance. Then we examine several measures of organizational performance. Finally, we suggest that there is no single measure of performance that is flawless and that using multiple approaches is an appropriate perspective for conducting strategic analyses.[3]

Defining Performance Conceptually

To understand performance conceptually, it is necessary to define what is meant by an organization. An organization is an association of productive assets (including people) who have voluntarily come together to accomplish a set of goals—in the case of the business organization, the goal is to gain an economic advantage.[4] For the coming together to occur there must be a point of equilibrium between contributions to the organization and inducements from the organization, such that people and other productive assets are willing to stay with the organization. In simple terms, it must be worth it for people and other productive assets to be involved with the organization.[5] In addition, owners of productive assets must be satisfied with the use of these assets by an organization and, therefore, be willing to permit the organization to retain the assets and continue to exist.[6] Further, the owners of assets will voluntarily make these assets available to an organization if, and only if, they are satisfied with the income they are receiving. They will be satisfied only if the income they are receiving—as adjusted for risk—is at least as high as the next best alternative.[7]

Building on the above insights, strategy researcher Jay Barney developed a conceptual definition of performance that compares the actual value created by an organization using its productive assets with the expected value that the assets' owners anticipated the organization would create.[8] The comparison of the actual value created with the value that owners expected leads to three levels of performance: below-normal, normal, and above-normal. *Below-normal performance* occurs when an organization's actual value created is less than the value owners expected. *Normal performance* occurs when the actual value created is equal to the expected value. Finally, *above-normal performance* occurs when the actual value created is greater than the expected value. The positive difference between actual value created and expected value is also known as *economic rent*. Barney argues that resources and capabilities that are sources of competitive disadvantage will lead to below-normal performance, while those that are sources of competitive parity will lead to normal performance, and those that are sources of either temporary or sustained competitive advantage will lead to above-normal performance. We will discuss these concepts in depth in Chapter 4.

Before proceeding further, we will define and briefly discuss the concept of value. One marketing researcher has defined value as what is received for what is given. In the context of creating customer value, he argues that customers give their money, time, energy, or effort, and incur psychological and sensory costs (negative aspects of the setting where the interaction takes place, such as noise, drafts, or uncomfortable seats). After a transaction, the customer will ask, "Did I receive more than I gave?"[9] If the answer is yes, value was created—but if the answer is no, value was destroyed. For shareholders, value creation means receiving more from an investment than could have been received from another investment with similar risk. As a student, ask yourself whether you are receiving value for the money, time, and effort invested in buying and reading this textbook. Have Hollinger International's shareholders received more than they have given? Considering the testimony of a long-time partner of Conrad Black, who "accuses current management of . . . presiding over the destruction of 95 percent of Hollinger's shareholder value,"[10] some would argue, no.

The terms below-normal, normal, and above-normal performance were derived from microeconomic theory and refer to levels of firm performance achieved under conditions of perfect competition. If a firm uses its resources to create just enough value to fully compensate the owners of all resources (including a rate of return that is risk-adjusted for the suppliers of capital), it is achieving normal performance, and the owners of resources will keep those resources in that firm. These firms are surviving.[11] When firms are achieving below-normal performance, the owners of resources will move their resources to another firm where it is expected they will be used to achieve at least normal performance. When this happens to all of a firm's resources the firm no longer exists economically, and eventually may cease to exist legally. Certainly, firms such as Eaton's, Woodward's, and Canadian Airlines no longer exist economically because they created less value than the owners of their resources expected them to create. Firms achieving above-normal performance will retain their current productive resources and will attract even more productive resources. These firms can be said to be prospering.

Building on the above insights and using terminology from Chapter 1, we state that when a firm achieves strategic competitiveness and successfully exploits its competitive advantages, it is able to accomplish its primary objective—achieving above-average returns. **Above-average returns** are returns in excess of what an investor expects to earn from other investments with a similar amount of risk. Firms that are competing without any competitive advantages will earn, at best, average returns.

Average returns are returns equal to what an investor expects to earn given a similar amount of risk. If a firm does not achieve at least average returns, the result is failure. Failure occurs because the owners of productive assets will choose to withdraw their investments from these firms and invest in firms that are earning at least average returns. This last group of firms is said to be earning below-average returns. **Below-average returns** are returns that are less than an investor expects given a similar level of risk. Table 2.1 presents the relationships among the expected value of a firm's resources, their actual value, and firm performance.

This conceptual approach to defining performance has several advantages.[12] It is consistent with the perspective from microeconomics, it is consistent with most definitions of performance developed in organization behaviour and organization theory, and it can be used to analyze the impact of a firm's resources, capabilities, and environment on its performance. Unfortunately, this definition of performance is hard to measure, and we present several measures of performance in the next section. We suggest that those assessing performance use more than one measure of performance.

Above-average returns are returns in excess of what an investor expects to earn from other investments with a similar amount of risk.

Average returns are returns equal to what an investor expects to earn given a similar amount of risk.

Below-average returns are returns that are less than an investor expects given a similar level of risk.

Table 2.1	The Relationships among Expected Value, Actual Value, and Firm Performance
Average Returns	A firm creates with its resources' value **equal to** what owners of those resources expected the firm to create given similar levels of risk.
Below-Average Returns	A firm creates with its resources' value **less than** what owners of these resources expected the firm to create given similar levels of risk.
Above-Average Returns	A firm creates with its resources' value **greater than** what owners of these resources expected the firm to create given similar levels of risk.

SOURCE: Barney, Jay B., *Gaining and Sustaining Competitive Advantage*, 2/E, © 2002, p. 27. Adapted by permission of Pearson Education, Inc., Upper Saddle River, NJ.

The Measure of Firm Performance

Firm performance can be measured through the use of a variety of techniques. All of these techniques have limitations, and they all have their critics and supporters. Because of the limitations associated with each technique, it is advisable that multiple measures of performance be used when conducting a strategic analysis of a firm. Eight approaches to measuring firm performance will be described in the following sections. We will review the strengths and weakness of several of these approaches when applicable.

Firm Survival and Performance

One measure of performance is the ability of a firm to survive over an extended period of time. Obviously, if a firm survives for an extended period of time, it is creating at least average returns as defined in Table 2.1. The logic behind this statement is that firms generating less than average returns will not survive in the long term unless they receive some kind of subsidy, either from government or some private benefactor.[13]

Strengths of Using Firm Survival

This measure of firm performance is relatively easy to use. It does not require detailed information about a firm's economic condition. The only information required is whether a firm is still continuing operations. If this is the case, then the firm must be generating average returns as, if it were not, the owners of the assets would have transferred them elsewhere.[14]

Weaknesses of Using Firm Survival

Unfortunately, the firm survival measure of performance has several important limitations. First, it is sometimes difficult to know when a firm no longer exists. Although determining when some firms no longer exist may be easy—as in the case of smaller firms, such as individually owned gas stations, restaurants, and small newspapers—for larger firms it may not be so easy to assess whether a firm has ceased to exist. For example, when two companies merge together, arguably neither of the individual firms exists anymore, but the assets of both can still remain relatively intact. For example, the two firms may serve many of the same customers they did before the merger, which makes it difficult to say that the two firms cease to exist.

In addition, does a firm cease to exist when it declares bankruptcy? Air Canada filed for bankruptcy protection under the Companies' Creditors Arrangement Act on April 1, 2003, to facilitate its operational, commercial, financial, and corporate restructuring. Today, the reorganized Air Canada operates under a new parent company, ACE Aviation Holdings, and is considered to be "Canada's largest airline and flag carrier."[15]

Similar to a legal acquisition, many bankrupt firms continue to use the same productive assets, service the same customers, and compete against the same firms. In fact, some firms appear to do better after declaring bankruptcy, as is the case with Air Canada. Some evidence suggests the possibility that strategic bankruptcies—bankruptcies filed in order to deal with some specific problem[16]—may be a way to maintain or even improve performance. Some firms are declaring bankruptcies to enable restructuring with the intention of being a stronger, better performing firm in the future. Yet, other research shows that any circumstance in which a strategic bankruptcy may be profitably employed is so limited as to be useless as a strategy.[17]

A second limitation is that the death of a firm can occur over an extended period of time. This is particularly true when a firm has generated above-average returns and therefore acquired many assets that are of value and whose liquidation can extend a firm's survival. During such times, it is not clear whether the firm is going out of business or facing temporary setbacks. This means that using survival as the only definition of performance may lead to results being ambiguous.[18]

A final limitation regarding the use of survival as a performance measure is that it does not provide any information concerning above-average returns. Survival differentiates only between below-average returns and average returns/above-average returns as a group. Some of the firms generating at least average returns may be generating slightly above-average returns, or well-above-average returns. In strategic management, we are interested in conditions that enable firms to earn above-average returns. With a focus concentrated only on survival, these insights are not available.[19]

This is not to say that financial ratios and other indicators (such as the quality of the board of directors) that are related to survival are not important. Slack financial resources (i.e., high liquidity or low debt-to-equity ratio) and quality board members (i.e., boards that may have many personal connections with other corporate boards) will aid a firm's condition and chances for survival. In fact, in one piece of classic research, Edward Altman combined several financial measures that were indicative of a firm's likelihood of survival. His measure, known as Altman's Z (shown below), uses measures of profitability, liquidity, and solvency to evaluate a company's likelihood of bankruptcy or default on bondholders (major stakeholders).[20] Altman's Z scores of less than 1.8 represent very high potential for failure, scores between 1.8 and 3.2 represent a grey zone, and scores greater than 3.2 indicate the likelihood of survival. However, we must note that the simple act of surviving (without looking at any indicators related to the likelihood of survival, such as the accounting measures discussed below or Altman's Z) is insufficient to allow a complete picture of the performance of the organization.

$$\text{Altman's Z} = .012(\text{WC/TA}) + .014(\text{RE/TA}) + .033(\text{EBIT/TA}) + .006(\text{MVE/BVE}) + .100(\text{SALE/TA})$$

where, WC = Working capital

TA = Total assets

RE = Retained earnings

EBIT = Earnings before interest & taxes

MVE = Market value of equity (shares outstanding × average market value)

BVD = Book value of debt

SALE = Net sales

Therefore, while survival is an important technique in assessing firm performance, it is only one measure. Other authors have suggested several reasons for the limited ability of survival as a performance measure. First, it is hard to apply to new organizations. Second, it gives no guidance to short-term decision making. Third, it is possible that a firm will survive because of the intervention of others, such as government support, therefore making the measure artificial. Finally, it is possible that focusing solely on survival may cause senior managers to ignore other important goals and objectives that are essential for the firm's long-term well-being.[21] We now turn our attention to accounting measures of performance.

Accounting Measures and Performance

Accounting measures of firm performance are the most frequently used measures in strategic management.[22] Some would suggest that the reason for the popularity of accounting measures is that the data are easily available for publicly traded firms. Others contend that accounting numbers are important because managers use them when making strategic decisions, and because accounting numbers actually provide insights into economic rates of return.[23] However, others have criticized accounting measures of performance because accounting numbers have a built-in short-term bias, are subject to manipulation by managers, and undervalue intangible assets.[24]

In defence of accounting data, it is necessary to understand that such criticisms were developed to defend large U.S. firms in anticompetition or antitrust suits against charges that these firms were earning monopoly rents. Thus, it was important to argue that accounting rates of return did not reflect economic rates of return. In addition, some finance scholars note that stock exchanges like the Toronto Stock Exchange put great emphasis on the quality of accounting data so that investors may better estimate a firm's future returns.[25] Finally, some researchers have defended the use of accounting measures of performance by arguing that if one assumes that stock market data are indicative of economic profits, then accounting information must also provide insights into economic performance to some degree, particularly if investors consider accounting numbers useful.[26] Thus, while accounting-based measures of performance may present certain problems, there is broad support for their use as a measure of financial performance.

The more common approach to using accounting data to assess firm financial performance is to use ratio analysis. Some of the more important ratios and what they mean with respect to firm performance are listed in Table 2.2 on page 48. The categories most used are (1) profitability ratios (a measure of profitability is used as the numerator, and a measure of size is used as the denominator), (2) liquidity ratios (the ability of a firm to pay its short-term debts), (3) leverage ratios (the amount of a firm's indebtedness), (4) activity ratios (the level of activity in a firm), and (5) miscellaneous ratios (ratios that do not fall into one of the previously mentioned categories).

The following sources are available to access Canadian and U.S. industry averages in order to judge a particular firm's ratios relative to its closest competitors in a particular industry:

- Statistics Canada, *Market Research Handbook*, available at www.statcan.ca/english/ads/ 63-224-XPB.
- Dun & Bradstreet, *Industry Norms & Key Business Ratios*, available at http://kbr.dnb. com/login/KBRHome.asp
- L. Troy, 2006, *Almanac of Business and Industrial Financial Ratios*, CCH Incorporated, IL: Wolters Kluwer.

Limitations Associated with Using Accounting Measures

There are three important limitations to using accounting measures to assess firm performance. These are managerial discretion, short-term bias, and valuing intangible resources and capabilities.[27]

Table 2.2 Key Financial Accounting Ratios, Their Calculation, and What They Mean

Ratio	Calculation	What the Ratio Means
Profitability Ratios		
• Gross Profit Margin	$\dfrac{\text{(Sales – cost of goods sold)}}{\text{Sales}}$	Measures the revenue left to cover operating expenses after taking out the cost of procurement
• Operating Profit Margin	$\dfrac{\text{(Profit before interest \& taxes)}}{\text{Sales}}$	Assesses firm profitability without regard to interest charges as a result of the capital structure
• Net Profit Margin (Return on Sales)	$\dfrac{\text{Profit after taxes}}{\text{Sales}}$	After-tax profits per dollar of sales
• Return on Total Assets	$\dfrac{\text{Profit after taxes}}{\text{Total assets}}$	Measures the return on the total investment in the firm
	$\dfrac{\text{(Profit after taxes + interest)}}{\text{Total assets}}$	It is appropriate to add interest to the numerator to obtain a measure of returns to both debt and equity of investors
• Return on shareholders' equity	$\dfrac{\text{Profit after taxes (PAT)}}{\text{Total shareholders' equity}}$	Rate of return to shareholders given their investment in the firm
• Return on common equity	$\dfrac{\text{(PAT – preferred stock dividends)}}{\text{Total shareholders' equity}}$	Return on investment which common shareholders have made in the firm
• Earnings per share	$\dfrac{\text{(PAT – preferred stock dividends)}}{\text{\# of common shares outstanding}}$	Earnings available to common shareholders
Liquidity Ratios		
• Current ratio	$\dfrac{\text{Current assets}}{\text{Current liabilities}}$	Measure of ability to cover short-term debt by assets convertible to cash in approximately same period as short-term debt matures
• Quick ratio (Acid-Test Ratio)	$\dfrac{\text{(Current assets – inventory)}}{\text{Current liabilities}}$	Measure of ability to pay off short-term debt without relying on inventory (most difficult current asset to convert to cash)
• Inventory to net working capital	$\dfrac{\text{Inventory}}{\text{Current assets – Current liabilities}}$	Measure of the extent to which a firm's working capital is tied up in inventory
Leverage Ratios		
• Debt-to-assets ratio	$\dfrac{\text{Total debt}}{\text{Total assets}}$	Measures use of debt to finance operations
• Debt-to-equity ratio	$\dfrac{\text{Total debt}}{\text{Total shareholders' equity}}$	Measures use of debt relative to shareholders' investment in firm
• Long-term debt-to-equity ratio	$\dfrac{\text{Long-term debt}}{\text{Total shareholders' equity}}$	Measures balance between debt and equity in the long-term capital structure of firm
• Times interest earned	$\dfrac{\text{(Profits before interest and taxes)}}{\text{Total interest charges}}$	Measures how much profits can decline before firm unable to meet interest obligations
• Fixed-charge coverage	$\dfrac{\text{(Profits before taxes and interest + lease obligations)}}{\text{(Interest charges + lease obligations)}}$	A more inclusive measure of ability of firm to handle all of its fixed-charge obligations.

(continued)

Ratio	Calculation	What the Ratio Means
Activity Ratios		
• Accounts receivable turnover	Annual credit sales / Accounts receivable	Measures average time to collect on credit sales
• Average collection period	Accounts receivable / Total sales/365	Average time it takes to receive payment for a sale
• Inventory turnover	Cost of goods sold / Average inventory	Measure speed with which firm is turning over its inventory
• Fixed-assets turnover	Sales / Fixed assets	Measures sales productivity and plant & equipment utilization
• Total assets turnover	Sales / Total assets	Measures utilization of a firm's assets. If below industry average, a firm is not generating the volume expected given its investment in assets
Shareholders' Return and Other Ratios		
• Dividend yield on common stock	Annual dividends per share / Current market price per share	Measures return to common shareholders
• Price–earning ratio	Current market price per share / After-tax earnings per share	Indicates market perception of the firm. Usually, faster growing or less risky firms tend to have higher P/E ratios than more risky or slower growing firms
• Dividend payout ratio	Annual dividends per share / After-tax earnings per share	Indicates dividends paid out as a percentage of profits
• Cash flow per share	After-tax profits + depreciation / # of common shares outstanding	Measures total cash per share available to firm
• Break-even analysis	Fixed costs / Contribution margin Where Contribution Margin = (Selling price/unit) − (variable price/unit)	Measures the number of units of product or service that need to be sold to begin to make a profit on that product or service

Managerial Discretion

Managers have some discretion when they choose methods of accounting.[28] Managers decide when to account for revenues and/or costs, how to value inventory, and how to depreciate assets. Consequently, accounting measures of performance may reflect managerial preferences and interests.

Short-Term Bias

A second limitation is the built-in short-term bias in accounting measures.[29] This short-term bias occurs because longer term, multi-year investments are generally treated as costs in a year when they do not generate identifiable revenues. This means that investments in research and development, human resource management training and development, and market research may be expensed in the short term rather than viewed as an investment in the long term. If managers' bonuses are based on short-term financial results, they may reduce these types of strategic investments.

Valuing Intangible Resources and Capabilities

A third limitation is the valuation of intangible resources.[30] Intangible resources and capabilities are productive assets that have a significant effect on performance but are difficult to observe, describe, and value through the use of accounting measures. Resources such as brand awareness, a sense of affiliation and identity with the firm, trust and friendship among managers and employees, close relationships with suppliers and customers, and close relations with shareholders are hard to assess and measure but are critical components of firm success.[31]

These limitations do not mean that accounting measures are bad or should be ignored. They do suggest that judgment and care should be used when assessing firm performance using accounting measures. Next, we examine the multiple stakeholder view of performance.

The Multiple Stakeholder Approach and Performance

The conceptual approach described earlier suggests a stakeholder approach to measuring performance.[32] This approach views a firm's performance relative to the preferences of those stakeholders who are important to the firm and can impact firm performance. Stakeholders who may impact firm performance include customers, employees, suppliers, managers, top executives, equity holders, debt holders, communities where plants and offices are located, and governments (local, provincial, and federal). The problem is that different stakeholders may have differential interests in how the firm should be managed. These differential interests may be a result of how much of each resource is being supplied by each stakeholder and the effect that firm decisions will have on each stakeholder.

Different stakeholders use different criteria to judge firm performance. Consequently, it is difficult to formulate and implement strategies that will satisfy each stakeholder with an interest in the firm. It could be that firms which sell their products at a lower than optimal price may satisfy their customers but may not have the financial resources to satisfy employees with better pay, managers with better furnishings, and governments with higher taxes.

While the multiple stakeholder approach to performance is intuitively appealing, it is very difficult to apply in performing strategic analyses that lead to formulating and implementing appropriate strategies. As one strategy researcher wrote, "Each [stakeholder] group, and perhaps each individual stakeholder, may define performance in an idiosyncratic way."[33] As a result, there may be several and varied dimensions firms may have to assess. This multiple approach could become very cumbersome and cause performance for the few very important stakeholders to deteriorate. Consequently, it may be necessary to adopt those measures that emphasize a few stakeholders over others. These stakeholders need not always be the owners, and in cases where others are more critical to the firm's interest in the short run, their interests may take precedence. For example, the CEO of Starbucks, Howard Schultz, decided early in the history of Starbucks to emphasize employee satisfaction as well as customer satisfaction. He considered that this would mean better service for customers and higher shareholder returns in the long term. In the field of higher education, universities are becoming more student-oriented. This focus is a major shift from the 1980s when they were faculty-oriented. We would argue that universities must be faculty-, staff-, student-, and alumni-oriented if they are to satisfy some of their more important stakeholders. But this is difficult given the differing needs and perceptions of what value means even among this small group of stakeholders.

Present Value and Performance

One measure of performance, grounded in finance theory, is the present value of cash flows.[34] This approach seeks to avoid some of the limitations of other performance measures. It avoids short-term bias by measuring cash flows over time, and it values all resources made available to a firm by using the discount-rate concept. Firms that use the present-value approach estimate both their net cash flows and their expected discount rates for several years into the future. This approach allows them to assess firm performance and individual project performance on a forward-looking basis. Table 2.3 shows the relationship between net present value and firm performance.

Strengths and Weaknesses of Present-Value Measures

This method of measuring performance has several strengths. First, there is the close link between present value and the conceptual definition of performance proposed by Jay Barney.[35] In addition, research suggests that firms who apply present-value principles and invest in positive net present-value strategies are able to maximize value creation and through value creation the wealth of shareholders. These firms will probably also generate enough cash to satisfy other stakeholders, such as employees, managers, customers, suppliers, and governments.

However, several weaknesses also have been highlighted in the literature. The first is the problem of accurately predicting cash flow patterns several years into the future. Misjudging these cash flows on projects worth several billion dollars and lasting several decades may be problematic. Second, measuring the discount rate is problematic. Estimating the discount rate means that one needs to assess the firm's systematic risk (beta). Unfortunately, the measurement of beta may be problematic and may change over time. Finally, many researchers question the adequacy of the economic model (the Capital Asset Pricing Model [CAPM]) on which the estimation of beta is based.[36]

Does this mean we should not use net present-value measures? Of course not! Just as we suggested with other measures, the use of net present value must be done with its limitations in mind. In fact, using this measure may allow for a deeper understanding of firm performance.

Market-Based Measures and Performance

In recent years, strategy researchers have increasingly relied on market-based measures of firm performance, either alone or in conjunction with accounting-based measures, when assessing a firm's financial performance.[37] This increased use of market-based measures of firm performance may partially be a response to the criticisms of accounting-based measures outlined earlier. The theoretical basis for using market-based performance measures is that they are a more accurate reflection of a firm's economic performance

Table 2.3	The Relationships between Net Present Value and Firm Performance
Net Present Value < 0	Below-average returns
Net Present Value $= 0$	Average returns
Net Present Value > 0	Above-average returns

SOURCE: Barney, Jay B., *Gaining and Sustaining Competitive Advantage*, 1/E, © 1997. Adapted by permission of Pearson Education, Inc., Upper Saddle River, NJ.

Chapter 2 / Strategic Management and Firm Performance

than accounting-based measures. This argument is based on the semi-strong form of the efficient market hypothesis[38] that suggests that all publicly available information is immediately reflected in a firm's stock price. This assumption has led to the use of the Capital Asset Pricing Model (CAPM) to determine systematic (beta) and unsystematic risks, and risk-free firm returns as measured by Jensen's Alpha, which we define below.

Some researchers have argued that, while accounting data may be used to measure the effects of a firm's strategies *post hoc*, they are not useful for assessing the economic value of a given strategy or for choosing between strategies that are being evaluated for possible implementation.[39] Another viewpoint suggests that market-based measures are intrinsically different from accounting-based measures because the former focus on the present value of future streams of income (i.e., on the expected value of future cash flows), whereas accounting-based measures focus on past performance.[40] Thus, we will examine several measures of firm performance based on stock market data. However, before we do, we will discuss the manner in which these measures are developed.

Stock Market Measures

Stock market measures are based on the assumption that capital markets are semi-strong form efficient. This means that all publicly available information is reflected in the price of a firm's equity and debt. Accepting this assumption allows us to develop measures of risk and performance for a publicly traded firm. To develop these measures we need prices for the firm's stock over a period of time and values for the market index on which the stock is traded. For example, let's take a hypothetical firm that is traded on the Toronto Stock Exchange. In our example, we will examine the change in our firm's closing stock price for a period of 250 trading days. We take these closing stock price changes and regress them (in a statistical procedure called linear regression) on the daily change in the closing values of the TSX 300. This is reflected below:

$$S - RFR = a + b(M - RFR) + e$$

where, S = the percentage change in daily closing stock prices over 250 trading days

RFR = a measure of the risk-free rate of return for each of the 250 trading days

a = Jensen's Alpha, the risk-free rate of return for the firm's stock

b = beta, the systematic risk or risk associated with movements in the stock market

M = the percentage change in daily closing value of the stock market index (e.g., TSX 300) for each of the 250 trading days

e = the residual obtained when estimating alpha and beta

Once this regression is conducted, it is possible to obtain measures of risk. The standard deviation of "S" is used as the measure of total risk. Beta is used as the measure of systematic risk, and the standard deviation of "e" is used as the measure of unsystematic risk. Market performance can now be assessed using four different measures: (1) the Sharpe measure, (2) the Treynor measure, (3) Jensen's Alpha, and (4) the Appraisal Ratio.[41]

The Sharpe measure is used to assess return per unit of total risk. The formula is:

The Sharpe measure = $(S - RFR)$ / Standard Deviation of "S"

The Treynor measure is used to assess return per unit of systematic risk. The formula is:

The Treynor measure $= (S - RFR)/Beta$

Jensen's Alpha is used to assess a risk-free return and is measured by "a"

Jensen's Alpha $= a$

The Appraisal Ratio is used to measure the risk-free return per unit of unsystematic risk. The formula is:

Appraisal Ratio $=$ Jensen's Alpha/Standard deviation of "e"

In summary, the Sharpe measure compares a firm's stock market performance to the firm's total risk. The higher the value of the Sharpe measure, the better the firm is performing. The Treynor measure compares a firm's stock market performance to the firm's systematic risk. As with the Sharpe measure, a higher Treynor measure indicates better firm performance. Jensen's Alpha compares a firm's stock market performance to the firm's risk-adjusted expected performance. A Jensen's Alpha greater than zero (two standard deviations or more above the mean) suggests that the firm is outperforming the market and achieving above-average returns. A Jensen's Alpha equal to zero (between $+2$ and -2 standard deviations from the mean) suggests that the firm is performing as well as the market and achieving average returns. A Jensen's Alpha less than zero (two standard deviations or more below the mean) suggests that the firm is underperforming the market and achieving below-average returns. Table 2.4 summarizes the relationship between Jensen's Alpha and firm performance. The Appraisal Ratio is a measure of the abnormal return per unit of risk that the firm could diversify away by becoming more diversified in the scope of its product markets. The higher the Appraisal Ratio the better a firm is performing.

Limitations of Market Measures

The first limitation of these measures is that they were not originally designed for the measurement of firm performance, but for the assessment of investment portfolio performance. Recently, however, strategy researchers have used them as a measure of firm performance.[42] A related problem is that both the Sharpe and Treynor measures implicitly use the risk-free rate as the cost of capital. This application may not be as much of a problem as it once was for large, publicly traded firms in the United States. The cost of capital and the rate of return on capital are available for the largest 1,000 U.S. firms from the Stern Stewart 1000 performance lists. Unfortunately, Stern Stewart no longer publishes a Canadian 300 performance list. The loss of this Canadian performance list has recently become a problem for Canadian firms. In addition, it is a problem when assessing smaller firms in both countries.

A second, related problem is that the Treynor measure uses the firm's systematic risk (beta), which assumes that any unsystematic risk is fully diversified away. This approach

Table 2.4	Relationship between Jensen's Alpha and Firm Performance
Jensen's Alpha < -1	Below-average returns
Jensen's Alpha $= 0$	Average returns
Jensen's Alpha $> +1$	Above-average returns

may be appropriate for investment portfolios but may not be appropriate for firms. Finally, some have questioned the use of market indexes. It is possible for some firms to have an inordinate effect on a market index. For example, in its "glory days" Nortel had a significant influence on the country's stock indices. At its peak, "Nortel alone accounted for more than a third of the value of the entire TSE 300 Composite Index (now known as the S&P/TSX Composite Index)."[43] This was largely due to the fact that it had an inordinate number of shares outstanding, which meant its stock was given a much higher weighting. As a result, changes in Nortel's stock performance moved the index on its own in some cases.[44]

Although the four market measures presented have limitations, they do provide insight into the ability of a firm to achieve above-average returns, average returns, or below-average returns. Empirically, the Sharpe measure, the Treynor measure, Jensen's Alpha, and the Appraisal Ratio are highly correlated. One study found that the correlations of the Sharpe measure, the Treynor measure, and Jensen's Alpha were in the 0.84 to 0.90 range.[45] Another study found that the Sharpe measure, the Treynor measure, and the Appraisal Ratio had correlations in the same range.[46] However, both studies found that the correlations between the accounting measures described earlier and the market measures were only in the 0.15 to 0.30 range. Although statistically significant, the results suggest that market measures tell us more about performance than the accounting measures do. We next discuss Market Value Added and Economic Value Added.

Market Value Added and Economic Value Added and Performance

Market Value Added (MVA) and Economic Value Added (EVA) are measures of performance that some firms may use to judge their performance. In this section, we describe these two concepts and discuss their limitations. These two concepts, developed by Stern Stewart, allow for the appraisal of performance and evaluation. They further suggest that using MVA and EVA will enhance benchmarking, assessing business and financial risk, setting goals, spotting investments, and screening acquisition targets, among others.[47]

Market Value Added

Market Value Added (MVA) is the difference between the cash that investors expect to receive (given the current market value of the firm) and the amount of cash that debt and equity holders have invested in the firm since its inception.

Market Value Added is believed to be a definitive measure of firm performance, with performance being defined as shareholder wealth maximization through the most efficient management and allocation of firm resources. **Market Value Added** (MVA) is the difference between the cash that investors expect to receive (given the current market value of the firm) and the amount of cash that debt and equity holders have invested in the firm since its inception. For example, for a firm that has received $20 billion from its debt holders and $15 billion from its equity holders, has retained $30 billion through its operations, and currently has a total market value of $75 million, the MVA equals $10 billion. This $10 billion represents the cumulative amount that the firm has increased its shareholder wealth. Of course, a negative MVA would represent the cumulative amount that the firm has destroyed shareholder wealth.[48]

A leader in international management consulting, Stern Stewart & Company argued that MVA not only is a good measure of shareholder wealth creation or destruction but also captures the ability of a firm to manage scarce capital resources. The reasoning behind this argument is that MVA is considered an estimate of the net present value of all the firm's capital projects, both those currently being pursued and those that are being anticipated by investors. Just as a net present value analysis takes the up-front investment and subtracts it from the present value of the expected cash flows of a future project, MVA takes the capital investment in the firm to date and subtracts it from the firm's current gross market value (the expected present value of the firm's future cash flows). The difference is the firm's net present value. Positive MVAs suggest that firms are maximizing shareholder wealth and that these firms are efficiently allocating the resources flowing to them.[49]

Consequently, MVA shows how much shareholder wealth has been increased and how well the firm's senior leaders are managing the firm's capital. This measurement of firm performance is a better measure of success than rankings that focus on measures of size, such as sales, revenue, or market capitalization.

Changes in MVA over a period of time are significant and should be examined closely by a firm's stakeholders, as these changes may be a more effective measure than absolute MVA at a particular point in time. A positive increase in MVA means that the firm's market value grew more than the amount of any additional funds obtained through debt, equity, or retained earnings. This increase indicates that the firm's net present value increased and so did the wealth of its shareholders. A decrease in MVA means that the firm's net present value was reduced and that shareholder wealth was destroyed. Stern Stewart argues that a change in MVA could be the result of many factors, including a change in stock market values, changes in expectations for a specific industry, and/or the effectiveness of a firm's senior leaders and the strategic choices they have made.

Economic Value Added

Economic Value Added (EVA) is an internal measure of a firm's ability to generate MVA in the future. It is measured by taking the amount of operating capital at the beginning of each year and multiplying it by the difference between the rate of return on capital and the weighted average cost of the debt and equity capital employed. Measurements are made at the beginning of the year because new capital investments take at least a full year to reach maturity. As mentioned earlier, EVA is linked to MVA in that MVA is the present value of all projected EVAs.

Obviously, there are several ways to create shareholder value, but they all relate to doing one of the following three,[50] all of which will improve EVA:

- Improve return on capital already employed (i.e., generate more profits without employing more capital);
- Invest more capital in strategies that have a greater rate of return than the cost of the capital employed; and
- Withdraw capital from strategies or projects that have a cost of capital greater than their rate of return.

Economic Value Added (EVA) is an internal measure of a firm's ability to generate MVA in the future. It is measured by taking the amount of operating capital at the beginning of each year and multiplying it by the difference between the rate of return on capital and the weighted average cost of the debt and equity capital employed.

Limitations of MVA and EVA

Several writers do not agree with the many benefits of MVA/EVA touted by Stern Stewart. The authors of an article in *CMA Management* listed seven weaknesses that they considered were associated with the use of MVA/EVA.[51] First, EVA does not assess economic value or profit. The authors argued that economic value is a firm's expected cash flows discounted at the firm's cost of capital. Economic profit is the difference in economic value at two different points in time. The authors suggested that EVA does not measure cash flow but measures accounting net income that has been accrued. In addition, they suggested that EVA does not measure future cash flows but past accounting income. Second, the authors argued that there is a lack of consistent definitions for EVA, capital, and net operating profit after taxes. Third, EVA is too complex in that it requires 160 accounting adjustments to the generally accepted accounting principles (GAAP). Fourth,

EVA is an inadequate single measure for any decision in that it measures only short-term profitability, which is not appropriate. Fifth, given that EVA is a short-term measure, it may be inappropriate to reward managers based only on EVA. Sixth, EVA is not appropriate for capital budgeting.

Finally, EVA is easy for managers to manipulate. The authors suggest five ways that managers can manipulate EVA and reduce firm performance:

- EVA requires the capitalization of R&D. This could allow the capitalization of R&D expenditures as assets rather than as expenses when the expenditures have no future value.
- Managers could develop a short-term bias.
- Managers could decide to spend little or no time on quality improvement.
- EVA permits the capitalization of restructuring charges, which could lead to unnecessary restructuring.
- EVA permits the holding back of expenditures in asset accounts. Expenditures with no future value could be recorded as assets.

The EVA and MVA methodologies are still fairly new concepts, with many people for, and some against, their use. Although both have been used successfully by large firms such as General Electric (GE) and Coca-Cola, a common limitation is the proprietary nature of the methodology; to have EVA/MVA applied to your firm in accordance with the Stern Stewart philosophy means hiring consultants from Stern Stewart. Of course, as the methodology has become better known, others have applied their own version of the Stern Stewart MVA/EVA techniques and the proprietary nature of the techniques become much less of a barrier.

For example, the sdEffect™, an initiative developed by the Corporate Knights Inc., the Sustainable Investment Group (SIG), and Yachnin & Associates, uses EVA as a tool for measuring the financial impact of corporate sustainable development for companies.[52] Combined with other measures like discounted cash flow and ratio analyses, the sdEffect™ has set out to "... demonstrate that [sustainable development], a business aspect traditionally viewed as 'soft' by the financial community, can have a 'hard', material and calculable impact on share price and company value."[53]

The Balanced Scorecard and Performance

The *Balanced Scorecard* is a relatively new way of measuring performance. The creators of this system, Robert S. Kaplan and David P. Norton, argue that the Balanced Scorecard is a synthesis of a firm's long-range competitive capabilities and its historical-cost financial accounting model. The goal is to integrate long-term and short-term perspectives into one performance management system. Financial measures tell about past events; however, they are inadequate for the evaluating and directing required for the creation of future value through investing in suppliers, employees, customers, processes, technology, and innovation. The Balanced Scorecard brings financial measures of previous performance together with measures of the drivers of future performance. Its measures and objectives are determined from an organization's vision and strategy.

The framework used translates a firm's vision and strategy into operational terms by asking four interrelated questions, illustrated in Table 2.5. For each question, it is critical to identify the objectives, determine how each objective will be measured, and set appropriate targets and initiatives to achieve the targets. It is important to remember that each of these questions is interrelated with all of the others, and that all the questions are driven by the organization's vision and strategy. Robert Kaplan and David Norton have written several articles and a book on the Balanced Scorecard, which the reader is encouraged to obtain and read for further information.[54] We return to the Balanced Scorecard in Chapter 12, where we discuss the need to pursue appropriate controls such as strategic controls and financial controls.

	Area	Question	Objectives	Measures	Targets	Initiatives
Vision Strategy	Customer	To achieve our vision, how should we appear to our customers?				
	Financial	To succeed financially, how should we appear to our shareholders?				
	Internal Business Processes	To satisfy our shareholders and customers, what business processes must we excel at?				
	Learning & Growth	To achieve our vision, how will we sustain our ability to change and improve?				

Table 2.5 The Balanced Scorecard

SOURCE: Reprinted by permission of *Harvard Business Review*. Adapted from "Using the Balanced Scorecard as a Strategic Management System" by R.S. Kaplan and D.S. Norton (January-February), p. 76. Copyright © 1996 by the Harvard Business School Publishing Corporation, all rights reserved.

Corporate Social Responsibility

To be socially responsible, a corporation is said to "voluntarily tak[e] further steps to improve the quality of life for employees and families as well as for the local community and society at large."[55] The business case for corporate social responsibility (CSR) generally lies within four broad areas: brand differentiation, human resources, risk management, and licence to operate.[56] In saturated markets, firms constantly look for points of differentiation to set them apart in "the minds of consumers."[57]

In terms of human resources, a company that is seen as being socially responsible will generally have better results in recruitment and employee retention. Companies that make sure they invest in sustainable projects and make socially responsible decisions generally protect themselves from the risk of "corruption scandals or environmental accidents."[58] Lastly, "good corporate citizens" generally avoid conflict with regulators and tax law: "By taking substantive voluntary steps [corporations] can persuade governments and the wider public that they are taking current issues like health and safety, diversity or the environment seriously and so avoid intervention."[59]

Corporate social responsibility has many aspects, and there is an increasing importance for senior leaders of companies to have an awareness that they are being watched by shareholders, customers, employees, and other stakeholders who are interested in how the companies they invest in, work for, buy from, and interface with are interacting with society and the environment. In addition, many organizations are assessing the ability of Canadian firms to interact in a responsible manner.

In addition to the GLOBE Awards (see the Strategic Focus), since 2002 *Corporate Knights* magazine has published yearly listings of "Canada's Best 50 Corporate Citizens." These lists score companies on several key indicators, which in 2007 fell into three distinct categories: environment, social, and governance.[60] Table 2.6 lists the top 20 firms in the 2007 study.[61]

Table 2.6	The 2007 Best 50 Corporate Citizens

2007 Rank	Company Name
1	Royal Bank Of Canada
2	Alcan Inc.
3	Vancouver City Savings C.U.
4	Dofasco Inc.
5	Hydro-Quebec
6	Hewlett-Packard Canada
7	Canadian Tire Corporation Ltd.
8	Bank Of Montreal
9	General Electric Canada
10	Petro-Canada
11	IBM Canada
12	McKesson Canada
13	Mountain Equipment Co-op
14	Potash Corporation Of Sask. Inc.
15	Enbridge Inc.
16	Cascades Inc.
17	Transcontinental Inc.
18	Sun Life Financial Inc.
19	Canadian Pacific Railway Ltd.
20	Sherritt International

SOURCE: Reprinted by permission of Corporate Knights.

Sustainability and the Triple Bottom Line

Many researchers are becoming concerned with the sustainability of the current growth-based market system that seems to be an outcome of a philosophy that gives little thought to the needs of society or the environment. As mentioned in the Opening Case, there is a growing movement to include the triple bottom line when assessing performance. Sustainability is the recognition that the Earth is a closed system with limits that we are approaching, not an open, boundless system. Sustainability is defined as the capability of present generations to meet their needs without compromising the capability of future generations to meet *their* needs. Among the many Canadian firms that are starting to report on the triple bottom line, BC Hydro has shown a strong commitment in this regard. BC Hydro stated in its annual report that, "reporting on the three bottom lines also allows [it] to benchmark [its] performance with other organizations to ensure [it] continue[s] to remain in the forefront as a sustainability leader."[62]

While assessing performance is difficult, it is expected that, as stakeholders require firms to be environmentally and socially responsible as well as financially responsible, measuring performance will become even more difficult. There is a growing sense that the firms that hope to achieve better financial performance are those that are also socially and environmentally responsible, as measured by their triple bottom line.

Reputation and Recognition as Key Performance Measures

As we mentioned in the Opening Case, investors—and, more broadly, stakeholders—are holding Canadian firms accountable for their corporate citizenry. A firm's reputation is becoming an important measure of performance that should also be discussed. Every year, Canadian firms are recognized for their outstanding corporate citizenship. One particular award, the GLOBE Award for Environmental Excellence, is based on a study conducted by the GLOBE Foundation (a Vancouver-based, not-for-profit private business foundation established to " . . . promote the business case for sustainable development") and *The Globe and Mail.*

The annual GLOBE Awards for Environmental Excellence " . . . recognize the creativity, initiative and leadership of Canadian enterprises towards environmental excellence." In 2007, awards were given in four distinct categories, with a winner and up to three finalists announced in each category. The categories for the 2007 GLOBE Awards covered areas such as technology innovation and application, sustainable investment and banking, and excellence in urban sustainability. Each category focused largely on environmental sustainability. Every May, the winners are presented at the EECO Environment and Energy Conference in Toronto. The results of the 2007 GLOBE Awards are outlined below.

The GLOBE Awards

Category	Winner	Finalists
The Corporate Competitiveness Award	Teknion Corporation	AMEC (AMEC Americas Ltd.) Home Depot Canada Inc. Vancity Group
The Award for Technology Innovation and Application	Earthcycle Packaging Ltd.	EnviroTower Inc. Remsoft Inc.
The Capital Markets Award for Sustainable Investment & Banking	Mercer Investment Consulting	Innovest Strategic Value Advisors Yachnin & Associates and Sustainable Investment Group Ltd.
The Award for Excellence in Urban Sustainability	Greater Vancouver Transportation Authority (Vancouver Transit Centre)	Diamond and Schmitt Architects Incorporated (University of Ontario Institute of Technology) HOK (Toronto Studio and Office)

They say on the GLOBE Awards Web site that it takes dedication, a competitive nature, and an ability to endure many challenges to work toward becoming a sustainable enterprise. It would seem, then, that having average or above-average returns is no longer enough. These returns must be generated through ethical and environmentally and socially responsible actions.

SOURCES: 2004–2008, The GLOBE Awards 2007 Award Winners, http://www.theglobeawards.ca/winners.cfm, accessed January 11, 2008; 2007, The GLOBE Foundation: Advancing Opportunities for Enterprise and the Environment, http://www.globe.ca/about_us.cfm, accessed January 10, 2008; 2007, The GLOBE Foundation, Globe Communications: Immediate Information and Environmental Kudos, http://www.globe.ca/communications.cfm, accessed January 10, 2008; 2008, The 2008 GLOBE Awards: Categories, http://www.theglobeawards.ca/categories.cfm, accessed January 10.

Summary

- Performance is the comparison of the actual value created by an organization using its productive assets with the value that the assets' owners expected the organization to create. The comparison of actual value created with the value the owners of assets expected the organization to create leads to three levels of performance. These three levels are below-normal, normal, and above-normal performance. When an organization's actual value created is less than the value owners of assets expected, it is below-normal performance; when the actual value created is equal to the expected value, it is normal performance; and when the actual value created is greater than the expected value, it is above-normal performance.

- Firm survival is one measurement of firm performance that is easily applied. If a firm survives over an extended period of time, it is creating at least average returns.

- One common approach to measuring firm performance is the use of accounting data. The types of data used are (1) profitability ratios (a measure of profitability is used as the numerator, and a measure of size is used as the denominator), (2) liquidity ratios (the ability of a firm to pay its short-term debts), (3) leverage ratios (the amount of a firm's indebtedness), (4) activity ratios (the level of activity in a firm), and (5) miscellaneous ratios (ratios that do not fall into one of the previously mentioned categories).

- Another method of measuring firm performance is the stakeholder approach. This method views a firm's performance relative to the preferences of those stakeholders who are important to the firm and can impact firm performance. Some stakeholders who may impact firm performance are customers, employees, suppliers, managers, top executives, equity holders, debt holders, communities where plants and offices are located, and governments (local, provincial, and federal).

- Net present value begins with the measurement of future cash flows, discounts them using an appropriate discount rate, and then subtracts the up-front investment. This approach seeks to avoid some of the limitations of other performance measures. The net present value method avoids short-term bias by measuring cash flows over time, and it values all resources made available to a firm by using the discount rate concept. Firms that use the present-value approach estimate their net cash flows and expected discount rates for several years into the future. This approach allows them to assess firm performance and individual project performance on a forward-looking basis.

- Market-based measures have been used to measure firm performance in recent years. The measures used have been the Sharpe measure, the Treynor measure, Jensen's Alpha, and the Appraisal Ratio. These measures rely on the assumptions underlying the Capital Asset Pricing Model, especially the semi-strong market efficiency argument, and have been criticized for this reason.

- Market Value Added is the difference between the cash that investors expect to receive (given the current market value of the firm) and the amount of cash that debt and equity holders have invested in the firm since its inception.

- Economic Value Added is an internal measure of a firm's ability to generate MVA in the future. It is measured by taking the amount of operating capital at the beginning of each year and multiplying it by the difference between the rate of return on capital and the weighted average cost of the debt and equity capital employed.

- Corporate social responsibility, sustainability, and triple bottom line are terms coming more and more into the language of business in recent years. Sustainability is defined as the capability of present generations to meet their needs without compromising the capability of future generations to meet their needs. The triple bottom line is closely related to this definition of sustainability. It can be defined as a framework for measuring and reporting firm performance against economic, environmental, and social parameters. Both of these definitions embrace the concept of corporate social responsibility.

Review Questions

1. Discuss the conceptual meaning of performance. Is this a theoretically sound way to think about firm performance? Does this conceptual definition help us focus on the challenge of strategic management? Explain.

2. Briefly describe survival as a performance measure. What are its strengths and weaknesses?

3. Why are accounting measures of performance so popular? Is their continued use to measure performance justified? Why?

4. Is the stakeholder approach a useful performance measure? Describe how you would use this measure.

5. Net present value is a well-grounded financial performance measure. Discuss this measure conceptually, based on your

finance textbooks. Do the authors of these textbooks agree or disagree with the limitations discussed in this chapter?

6. Stock market–based measures have been used recently to measure performance. Borrow an investment textbook from one of your finance friends, and use material from the textbook to conceptually discuss whether market-based measures are appropriate for assessing firm performance.

7. Describe in detail what the measures Market Value Added and Economic Value Added mean. Are they valid measures of firm performance?

8. Briefly discuss the underlying principles of the Balanced Scorecard. Feel free to read the material in Chapter 12 as well as the material in Chapter 2.

9. Discuss the concepts of corporate social responsibility, sustainability, and triple bottom line. Are these valid ways of describing an organization's performance?

Social Responsibility Review

1. What we can quantify tends to drive what we can qualify. In other words, numbers tend to drive our view of how we measure performance. Without using quantifiable indicators, what measures of performance do you think better describe the quality of companies as product producers, employers, and environmentally sustainable enterprises?

2. Under what conditions do you think accounting-based measures might give some degree of performance measurement with regard to the environment? Is it possible to develop such measures for environmental stakeholders?

Experiential Exercise

Go to the Web site of a Canadian company you would like to work for after graduation. Assess this company using accounting-based measures and market-based measures. In

addition, assess this company's level of corporate social responsibility. After conducting this assessment, determine whether you would still want to work there.

Notes

1. J. B. Barney, 1997, *Gaining and Sustaining Competitive Advantage,* Don Mills, ON: Addison-Wesley Publishing Company, 30–64.
2. R. P. Rumelt, D. E. Schendel, & D. J. Teece (eds.), 1994, *Fundamental Issues in Strategy,* Boston: Harvard Business School Press, 527–30; A. D. Meyer, 1991, What is strategy's distinctive competence? *Journal of Management,* 17: 821–33.
3. W. G. Rowe & J. L. Morrow Jr., 1999, A note on the dimensionality of the firm financial performance construct using accounting, market and subjective measures, *Canadian Journal of Administrative Sciences,* 16(1): 58–70.
4. A. Alchian & H. Demsetz, 1972, Production, information costs, and economic organization, *American Economic Review,* 62: 777–95; R. H. Coase, 1937, The nature of the firm, *Economica,* 4: 386–405; R. H. Hall, 1987, *Organizations: Structures, Processes, and Outcomes,* 4th ed., Englewood Cliffs, NJ: Prentice-Hall Inc.; M. C. Jensen & W. H. Meckling, 1976, Theory of the firm: Managerial behavior, agency costs, and ownership structure, *Journal of Financial Economics,* 3: 305–60; J. P. Sheppard, 1994, Strategy and bankruptcy: An exploration into organizational death, *Journal of Management,* 20: 795–833; H. A. Simon, 1976, *Administrative Behavior,* 3rd ed., New York: MacMillan.
5. Barney, *Gaining and Sustaining Competitive Advantage;* Simon, *Administrative Behavior.*
6. Barney, *Gaining and Sustaining Competitive Advantage;* Coase, The nature of the firm; Jensen and Meckling, Theory of the firm: Managerial behavior, agency costs, and ownership structure.
7. Alchian & Demsetz, Production, information costs, and economic organization; Barney, *Gaining and Sustaining Competitive Advantage.*
8. Barney, *Gaining and Sustaining Competitive Advantage.*
9. J. G. Barnes, 2001, *Secrets of Customer Relationship Marketing: It's All about How You Make Them Feel,* Montreal, QC: McGraw-Hill.
10. 2007, The Conrad Black trial, Macleans.ca, http://www.macleans.ca/article.jsp?content=20070425_091159_9668 &source=srch, April 25.
11. Sheppard, Strategy and bankruptcy: An exploration into organizational death.
12. Barney, *Gaining and Sustaining Competitive Advantage.*
13. Barney, *Gaining and Sustaining Competitive Advantage;* H. Demsetz, 1973, Industry structure, market rivalry, and public policy, *Journal of Law and Economics,* 16: 1–9.
14. Barney, *Gaining and Sustaining Competitive Advantage.*
15. 2008, Air Canada, Wikipedia, http://en.wikipedia.org/wiki/Air_Canada#21st_century, January 9.

16. K. J. Delaney, 1992, *Strategic Bankruptcy: How Corporations and Creditors Use Chapter 11 to Their Advantage*, Berkeley, CA: University of California Press; W. N. Moulton & H. Thomas, 1993, Bankruptcy as a deliberate strategy: Theoretical considerations and empirical evidence, *Strategic Management Journal*, 14(2): 125–35; J. P. Sheppard, 1992, When the going gets tough, the tough go bankrupt: The questionable use of Chapter 11 as a strategy, *Journal of Management Inquiry*, 1(3): 183–92.

17. J. P. Sheppard, 1993, Corporate diversification and survival, *Journal of Financial and Strategic Decisions*, 6(1): 113–32.

18. Barney, *Gaining and Sustaining Competitive Advantage*.

19. Ibid.

20. Altman, E. I., 1968, Financial ratios, discriminant analysis and the prediction of corporate bankruptcy, *The Journal of Finance*, 23(4): 589–609; Altman, E. I., 1982, *Corporate Financial Distress: A Complete Guide to Predicting, Avoiding, and Dealing with Bankruptcy*, New York: John Wiley and Sons.

21. Barney, *Gaining and Sustaining Competitive Advantage*; R. M. Kanter & D. Brinkerhoff, 1981, Organizational performance: Recent developments in measurement, *Annual Review of Sociology*, 7: 321–49.

22. Rowe & Morrow Jr., A note on the dimensionality of the firm financial performance construct using accounting, market and subjective measures; Barney, *Gaining and Sustaining Competitive Advantage*.

23. I. Horowitz, 1984, The misuse of accounting rates of return: Comment, *American Economic Review*, 74: 492–93; R. Jacobson, 1987, The validity of ROI as a measure of business performance, *American Economic Review*, 77: 470–78; W. F. Long & D. J. Ravenscraft, 1984, The misuse of accounting rates of return: Comment, *American Economic Review*, 74: 494–500.

24. G. Bentson, 1982, Accounting numbers and economic values, *Antitrust Bulletin*, Spring, 161–215; F. M. Fisher & J. J. McGowan, 1983, On the misuse of accounting rates of return to infer monopoly profits, *American Economic Review*, 73: 82–97; R. L. Watts & J. L. Zimmerman, 1978, Towards a positive theory of the determination of accounting standards, *Accounting Review*, 53: 112–33; R. L. Watts & J. L. Zimmerman, 1990, Positive accounting theory: A ten-year perspective, *Accounting Review*, 65: 131–56.

25. T. E. Copeland & J. F. Weston, 1983, *Financial Theory and Corporate Policy*, Reading, MA: Addison-Wesley.

26. Long & Ravenscraft, The misuse of accounting rates of return.

27. Rowe & Morrow Jr., A note on the dimensionality of the firm financial performance construct using accounting, market and subjective measures; Barney, *Gaining and Sustaining Competitive Advantage*.

28. Watts & Zimmerman, Towards a positive theory of the determination of accounting standards; Watts & Zimmerman, Positive accounting theory: A ten-year perspective.

29. Barney, *Gaining and Sustaining Competitive Advantage*.

30. H. Itami, 1987, *Mobilizing Invisible Assets*, Cambridge, MA: Harvard University Press; Barney, *Gaining and Sustaining Competitive Advantage*.

31. Barney, *Gaining and Sustaining Competitive Advantage*.

32. R. W. Sexty, 1995, *Canadian Business and Society*, Scarborough, ON: Prentice Hall Canada Inc.

33. Barney, *Gaining and Sustaining Competitive Advantage*, 46.

34. S. A. Ross, 1996, *Fundamentals of Corporate Finance*, 2nd Canadian ed., Toronto: Irwin; Barney, *Gaining and Sustaining Competitive Advantage*.

35. Barney, *Gaining and Sustaining Competitive Advantage*.

36. W. F. Sharpe, G. J. Alexander, J. V. Bailey, and D. J. Fowler, 1997, *Investments*, 2nd Canadian ed., Scarborough, ON: Prentice Hall Canada, Inc.; Z. Bodie, A. Kane, A. J. Marcus, S. Perrakis, and P. J. Ryan, 1997, *Investments*, 2nd Canadian ed., Toronto: McGraw-Hill Ryerson, Ltd.

37. Rowe & Morrow Jr., A note on the dimensionality of the firm financial performance construct using accounting, market and subjective measures; R. E. Hoskisson, M. A. Hitt, R. A. Johnson, & D. D. Moesel, 1993, Construct validity of an objective (entropy) categorical measure of diversification strategy, *Strategic Management Journal*, 14: 215–35; R. E. Hoskisson, R. A. Johnson, &

D. D. Moesel, 1994, Corporate divestiture intensity in restructuring firms: Effects of governance, strategy, and performance, *Academy of Management Journal*, 37(5): 1207–51.

38. Z. Bodie, A. Kane, & A. J. Marcus, 1993, *Investments*, 2nd ed., Boston, MA: Irwin.

39. M. Hergert & D. Morris, 1989, Accounting data for value chain analysis, *Strategic Management Journal*, 10: 175–88.

40. A. Seth, 1990, Value creation in acquisitions: A re-examination of performance issues, *Strategic Management Journal*, 11: 99–115.

41. Sharpe, Alexander, Bailey, & Fowler, *Investments*; Bodie, Kane, Marcus, Perrakis, & Ryan, *Investments*.

42. Rowe & Morrow Jr., A note on the dimensionality of the firm financial performance construct using accounting, market and subjective measures; R. E. Hoskisson, M. A. Hitt, R. A. Johnson, & D. D. Moesel, Construct validity of an objective (entropy) categorical measure of diversification strategy; Hoskisson, Johnson, & Moesel, Corporate divestiture intensity in restructuring firms: Effects of governance, strategy, and performance.

43. 2006, In-depth: Nortel: The wild ride of Canada's most-watched stock, CBC News Online, December 1.

44. Ibid

45. Hoskisson, Hitt, Johnson, & Moesel, Construct validity of an objective (entropy) categorical measure of diversification strategy.

46. W. G. Rowe, 1996, Persistence and Change in CEO Succession Processes, College Station, TX: Texas A&M University, unpublished doctoral dissertation.

47. I. Ross, 1998, The 1997 Stern Stewart Performance 1000, *Journal of Applied Corporate Finance*, 10(4): 116–20; I. Ross, 1997, The 1996 Stern Stewart Performance 1000, *Journal of Applied Corporate Finance*, 8(4): 115–28; L. Walbert, 1995, The 1994 Stern Stewart Performance 1000, *Journal of Applied Corporate Finance*, 7(4): 104–18.

48. Stern Stewart Management Services, 1997, *The Stern Stewart Performance 1000*, New York: Stern Stewart Management Services.

49. Ibid.

50. Ibid.

51. D. Keys, M. Azamhuzjaev, & J. MacKey, 1999, EVA: To boldly go?, *CMA Management*, September, 30–33; B. Schofield, 2000, EVA, *CMA Management*, December/January, 8–9.

52. 2006, Yachnin & Associates, Sustainable Investment Group Ltd., sdEffect™: Translating sustainable development into financial valuation measures, http://www.sdeffect.com/sdEffectFeb2006.pdf, accessed January 10, 2008.

53. Ibid

54. R. S. Kaplan & D. P. Norton, 1992, The balanced scorecard: Measures that drive performance, *Harvard Business Review*, January–February, 71–79; R. S. Kaplan & D. P. Norton, 1996, Using the balanced scorecard as a strategic management system, *Harvard Business Review*, January–February, 71–79; R. S. Kaplan & David P. Norton, 1996, *The Balanced Scorecard: Translating Strategy into Action*, Boston: Harvard Business School Press.

55. 2008, Corporate Social Responsibility, Wikipedia, http://en.wikipedia.org/wiki/Corporate_social_responsibility, retrieved January 11.

56. Ibid

57. Ibid

58. Ibid

59. Ibid

60. 2007, Methodology for 2007 Best 50 Corporate Citizens, Corporate Knights, May 22, http://www.corporateknights. ca/content/page.asp?name=2007methodology, retrieved January 10, 2008.

61. 2007, The 2007 Best 50 Corporate Citizens, Corporate Knights, http://www.corporateknights.ca/content/page.asp?name=best50_2007_list, retrieved January 11, 2008.

62. 2007, BC Hydro, 2007 Annual Report: Reporting on triple bottom line performance, July 11, http://www.bchydro.com/info/reports/reports853.html, retrieved January 11, 2008.

Chapter Three

The External Environment: Opportunities, Threats, Industry Competition, and Competitor Analysis

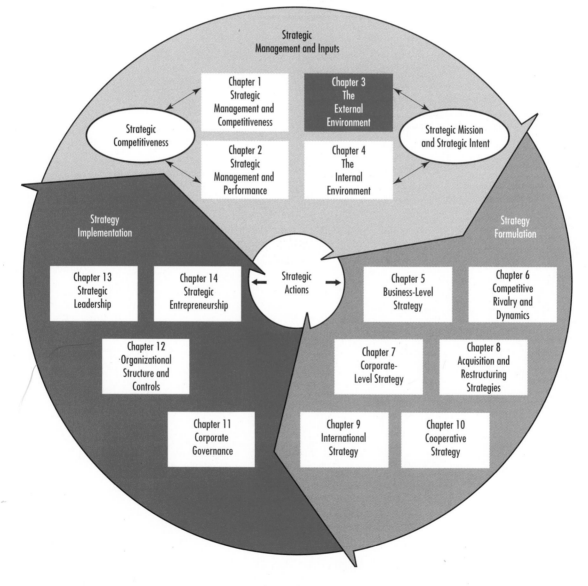

Knowledge Objectives

Studying this chapter should provide you with the strategic management knowledge needed to:

1. Explain the importance of analyzing and understanding the firm's external environment.

2. Define and describe the general environment and the industry environment.

3. Discuss the four activities of the external environmental analysis process.

4. Name and describe the general environment's six segments.

5. Identify the five competitive forces and explain how they determine an industry's profit potential.

6. Define strategic groups and describe their influence on the firm.

7. Describe what firms need to know about their competitors and different methods (including ethical standards) used to collect intelligence about them.

The Five Forces of Competition, the Retail Industry, and Wal-Mart

When considering the five forces of competition and how they dictate the profit potential for a given industry, it is useful to consider Wal-Mart and its role in the discount retail industry. Wal-Mart demonstrates how a firm can obtain high profits despite unattractive industry characteristics. On average, the discount retail industry is not an attractive industry to compete in. In fact, some players like K-Mart are struggling to stay afloat, while still others have declared bankruptcy. It is important to note that this is not due to factors like a high threat of entrants, because there are high barriers to entry (i.e., the ability to gain favourable leases, locations, and supply contracts, and to successfully compete with well established, vertically integrated retail chains like Wal-Mart that have standardized buying procedures), which translates to a low threat of entry. Nor is this due to a high threat of substitutes; rather, it comes from extreme competition from Wal-Mart combined with medium supplier power. These factors, competitive rivalry and supplier power, have had a substantial impact on the industry and have squeezed some retailers' profit margins to the point of no return.

www.wal-mart.ca

The Wal-Mart phenomenon has transformed the discount retail industry. According to a Global Insight independent research study, "the existence of Wal-Mart between 1985 and 2004 resulted in a 3.1% cumulative reduction in consumer prices by 2004."

Wal-Mart's strategy of selling a range of products at the lowest price possible has given it substantial control over the discount retail industry. And, as a result, it has gained extreme bargaining power over its suppliers, from which Wal-Mart can demand extremely low prices; as one reporter put it, "a contract with a large retailer such as Wal-Mart can make-or-break a small supplier."

A PBS article entitled "Wal-Mart: Impact of a Retail Giant" demonstrates just how powerful Wal-Mart is in this industry: "Wal-Mart's revenues are greater than the combined sales of its top competitors Target, Sears Roebuck, Costco Wholesale, Home Depot and The Kroger Co."

The discount retail industry "faces stiff competition and has slow market growth." The implication is that industry players must battle for market share by slashing prices and offering loyalty cards and membership plans to increase customer retention.

Wal-Mart has had amazing success in the discount retail industry, boasting $351.14 billion in revenue and $11.3 billion in profits for the fiscal year ending January 2007. It has reshaped the industry as a whole and forced retailers to change the way they do business if they want to survive. However, as Jay Barney explains it, when companies like Wal-Mart have success in an industry characterized by extreme competition and generally unattractive factors, it shows that "a firm's competitive environment is not the only determinant of a firm's profit potential." That is, a firm's internal capabilities and general strategy have the ability to surpass an industry's profit potential. These factors will be discussed in further detail in subsequent chapters.

SOURCES: 2008, The price impact of Wal-Mart: An update through 2006, Global Insight, http://www.globalinsight.com/MultiClientStudy/MultiClientStudyDetail2438.htm, retrieved February 27; 2008, Wal-Mart: Impact of a retail giant, PBS, http://www.pbs.org/newshour/bb/business/wal-mart/unique.html, retrieved February 27; 2008, The Industry Handbook—The Retailing Industry, Investopedia, http://www.investopedia.com/features/industry handbook/retail.asp, retrieved February 27; J. Barney, 2007, *Gaining and Sustaining Competitive Advantage* (3rd edition), Upper Saddle River, NJ: Pearson Prentice-Hall.

As the Opening Case on Wal-Mart and the retail industry attests and as research suggests, the external environment affects firm growth and profitability.[1] Major events like the U.S.–Canada softwood lumber dispute, which led to the Softwood Lumber Agreement in September 2006, have affected the forest sector in a positive light (i.e., created a stable and predictable legal environment for Canadian lumber companies exporting to the United States). Major political events such as the war in Iraq, the strength of separate nations' economies at different times, and the emergence of new technologies are a few examples of conditions in the external environment that affect firms in Canada and throughout the world. External environmental conditions such as these create threats to, and opportunities for, firms that in turn have major effects on their strategic actions.[2]

Regardless of the industry, the external environment is critical to a firm's survival and success. This chapter focuses on what firms do to analyze and understand the external environment. As the discussion of the retail industry shows, the external environment influences the firm's strategic options as well as the decisions made in light of them. The firm's understanding of the external environment is matched with knowledge about its internal environment (discussed in the next chapter) to form its vision, to develop its mission, and to take actions that result in strategic competitiveness and above-average returns (refer to Figure 1.1 on page 68).

As noted in Chapter 1, the environmental conditions in the current global economy differ from those previously faced by firms. Technological changes and the continuing growth of information gathering and processing capabilities demand more timely and effective competitive actions and responses.[3] The rapid sociological changes occurring in many countries affect labour practices and the nature of products demanded by increasingly diverse consumers. Governmental policies and laws also affect where and how firms may choose to compete.[4] To achieve strategic competitiveness and thrive, firms must be aware of and understand the different dimensions of the external environment.

Firms understand the external environment by acquiring information about competitors, customers, and other stakeholders to build their own base of knowledge and capabilities.[5] On the basis of the new information, firms may take actions to build new capabilities and buffer themselves against environmental effects, or to build relationships with stakeholders in their environment.[6] In order to take successful action, they must effectively analyze the external environment.

The General, Industry, and Competitor Environments

An integrated understanding of the external and internal environments is essential for firms to understand the present and predict the future.[7] As shown in Figure 3.1, a firm's external environment is divided into three major areas: the general, industry, and competitor environments.

The **general environment** is composed of dimensions in the broader society that influence an industry and the firms within it.[8] We group these dimensions into six environmental *segments:* demographic, economic, political/legal, sociocultural, technological, and global. Some, but not all, of the *elements* analyzed in each of these segments are shown in Table 3.1 on page 68.

The **general environment** is composed of dimensions in the broader society that influence an industry and the firms within it.

Firms cannot directly control the general environment's segments and elements. Accordingly, successful companies gather the information required to understand each segment and its implications for the selection and implementation of the appropriate strategies. For example, most firms have little individual effect on the strength of the Canadian dollar, although the move to parity with the U.S. dollar on September 20, 2007, for first time since November 1976, had a major effect on each firm's ability to operate if their operations include exporting to other geographic regions, especially the United States. Canadian companies in manufacturing industries were finding parity with

Figure 3.1 The External Environment

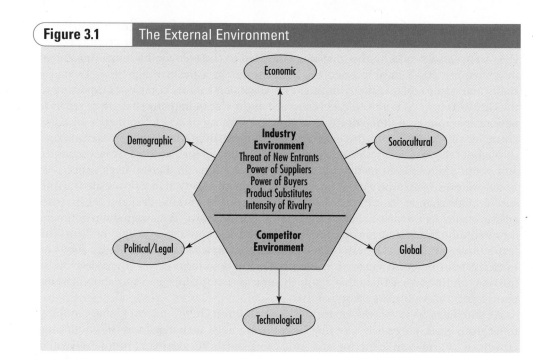

Table 3.1 The General Environment: Segments and Elements

Demographic Segment	• Population size • Age structure • Geographic distribution	• Ethnic mix • Income distribution
Economic Segment	• Inflation rates • Interest rates • Trade deficits or surpluses • Budget deficits or surpluses	• Personal savings rate • Business savings rates • Gross domestic product
Political/Legal Segment	• Antitrust laws • Taxation laws • Deregulation philosophies	• Labour training laws • Educational philosophies and policies
Sociocultural Segment	• Women in the workforce • Workforce diversity • Attitudes about the quality of work life	• Concerns about the environment • Shifts in work and career preferences • Shifts in preferences regarding product and service characteristics
Technological Segment	• Product innovations • Applications of knowledge	• Focus of private and government-supported R&D expenditures • New communication technologies
Global Segment	• Important political events • Critical global markets	• Newly industrialized countries • Different cultural and institutional attributes

the U.S. dollar particularly difficult in the early part of 2008, as parity had happened too quickly for them to get their house in order. On the other hand, companies in the service industry were finding it easier to deal with parity between the Canadian and U.S. dollars.

The **industry environment** is the set of factors that directly influences a firm and its competitive actions and competitive responses: the threat of new entrants, the power of suppliers, the power of buyers, the threat of product substitutes, and the intensity of rivalry among competitors. In total, the interactions among these five factors determine an industry's profit potential. The challenge is to locate a position within an industry where a firm can favourably influence those factors or where it can successfully defend against their influence. Canada's beer market is dominated by large players—in Ontario, the two biggest brewers control the distribution and sale of competitors' products. Labatt and Molson Coors own and operate Ontario's 441 Beer Stores under a provincial monopoly. Therefore, two multinational corporations (Molson Coors, headquartered in Colorado, and InBev, the Belgian parent of Labatt) run the stores in that they control everything from policy to space, displays, promotions, and listing fees. In essence, the greater a firm's capacity to favourably influence its industry's environment the greater the likelihood the firm will earn above-average returns.

How companies gather and interpret information about their competitors is called *competitor analysis.* Understanding the firm's competitor environment complements the insights provided by studying the general and industry environments. For example, understanding its competitor environment was critical for Air Canada in its competitive battle with WestJet.

Analysis of the general environment is focused on the future; analysis of the industry environment is focused on the factors and conditions influencing a firm's profitability within its industry; and analysis of competitors is focused on predicting the dynamics of competitors' actions, responses, and intentions. In combination, the results of the three analyses the firm uses to understand its external environment influence its vision, mission, and strategic actions. Although we discuss each analysis separately, performance improves when the firm integrates the insights provided by analyses of the general environment, the industry environment, and the competitor environment.

The **industry environment** is the set of factors that directly influences a firm and its competitive actions and competitive responses: the threat of new entrants, the power of suppliers, the power of buyers, the threat of product substitutes, and the intensity of rivalry among competitors.

The I/O Model of Above-Average Returns

From the 1960s through the 1980s, the external environment was thought to be the primary determinant of strategies that firms selected to be successful.[9] The industrial organization (I/O) model of above-average returns explains the external environment's dominant influence on a firm's strategic actions. The model specifies that the industry in which a company chooses to compete has a stronger influence on performance than do the choices managers make inside their organizations.[10] The firm's performance is believed to be determined primarily by a range of industry properties, including economies of scale, barriers to market entry, diversification, product differentiation, and the degree of concentration of firms in the industry.[11]

Grounded in economics, the I/O model has four underlying assumptions. First, the external environment is assumed to impose pressures and constraints that determine the strategies that would result in above-average returns. Second, most firms competing within an industry or within a certain segment of that industry are assumed to control similar strategically relevant resources and to pursue similar strategies in light of those resources. Third, resources used to implement strategies are assumed to be highly mobile across firms, so any resource differences that might develop between firms will be short-lived. Fourth, organizational decision makers are assumed to be rational and committed to acting in the firm's best interests, as shown by their profit-maximizing behaviours.[12] The I/O model challenges firms to locate the most attractive industry in which to compete. Because most firms are assumed to have similar valuable resources that are mobile across companies, their performance generally can be increased only when they operate in the industry with the highest profit potential and learn how to use their resources to implement the strategy required by the industry's structural characteristics.[13]

The five forces model of competition is an analytical tool used to help firms with this task. The model (see Figure 3.3 later in this chapter) encompasses several variables and tries to capture the complexity of competition. The five forces model suggests that an industry's profitability (i.e., its rate of return on invested capital relative to its cost of capital) is a function of interactions among five forces: suppliers, buyers, competitive rivalry among firms currently in the industry, product substitutes, and potential entrants to the industry.[14] Firms can use this tool to understand an industry's profit potential and the strategy necessary to establish a defensible competitive position, given the industry's structural characteristics. Typically, the model suggests that firms can earn above-average returns by manufacturing standardized products or producing standardized services at costs below those of competitors (a cost leadership strategy), or by manufacturing differentiated products for which customers are willing to pay a price premium (a differentiation strategy). The cost leadership and product differentiation strategies are fully described in Chapter 4.

As shown in Figure 3.2, the I/O model suggests that above-average returns are earned when firms implement the strategy dictated by the characteristics of the general,

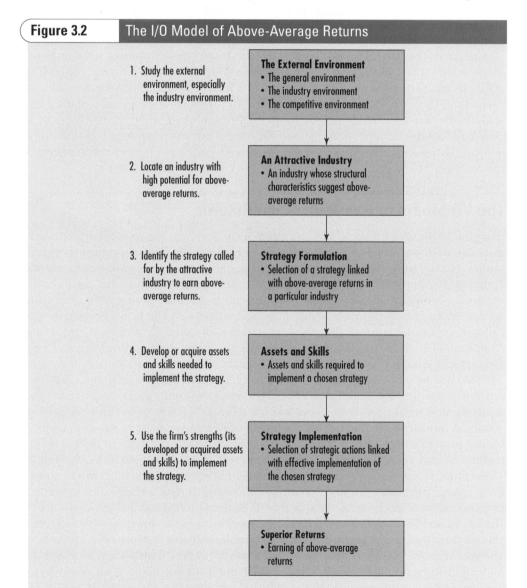

Figure 3.2   The I/O Model of Above-Average Returns

1. Study the external environment, especially the industry environment.

   The External Environment
   • The general environment
   • The industry environment
   • The competitive environment

2. Locate an industry with high potential for above-average returns.

   An Attractive Industry
   • An industry whose structural characteristics suggest above-average returns

3. Identify the strategy called for by the attractive industry to earn above-average returns.

   Strategy Formulation
   • Selection of a strategy linked with above-average returns in a particular industry

4. Develop or acquire assets and skills needed to implement the strategy.

   Assets and Skills
   • Assets and skills required to implement a chosen strategy

5. Use the firm's strengths (its developed or acquired assets and skills) to implement the strategy.

   Strategy Implementation
   • Selection of strategic actions linked with effective implementation of the chosen strategy

   Superior Returns
   • Earning of above-average returns

industry, and competitor environments. Companies that develop or acquire the internal skills needed to implement strategies required by the external environment are likely to succeed, while those that do not are likely to fail. Hence, this model suggests that returns are determined primarily by external characteristics rather than by the firm's unique internal resources and capabilities.

Research findings support the I/O model, in that approximately 20 percent of a firm's profitability can be explained by the industry in which it chooses to compete. This research also shows, however, that 36 percent of the variance in profitability could be attributed to the firm's characteristics and actions.[15] This suggests that both the environment and the firm's characteristics play a role in determining the firm's specific level of profitability. Thus, there is likely a reciprocal relationship between the environment and the firm's strategy, thereby affecting the firm's performance.[16]

As you can see, the I/O model considers a firm's strategy to be a set of commitments, actions, and decisions that are formed in response to the characteristics of the industry in which the firm has decided to compete. The resource-based model, discussed in Chapter 4, takes a different view of the major influences on strategy formulation and implementation.

External Environmental Analysis

Most firms face external environments that are highly turbulent, complex, and global—conditions that make interpreting them increasingly difficult.[17] To cope with what are often ambiguous and incomplete environmental data and to increase their understanding of the general environment, firms engage in a process called external environmental analysis. The continuous process includes four activities: scanning, monitoring, forecasting, and assessing (see Table 3.2). Those analyzing the external environment should understand that completing this analysis is a difficult, yet significant, activity.[18]

An important objective of studying the general environment is identifying opportunities and threats. An **opportunity** is a condition in the general environment that, if exploited, helps a company to achieve strategic competitiveness. Canadian banks have expressed their interest in taking advantage of an opportunity that may seem disconnected from normal banking services. Canada's greying population suggests interesting opportunities in wealth management; the Bank of Montreal and the Royal Bank of Canada announced in 2007 that they are training staff in bereavement services. As one newspaper suggested, if a customer's parent dies, it is possible for that customer to request the bank's bereavement services staff plan the funeral, ask Canada Post to redirect the parent's mail, and even settle any outstanding debts.[19]

A **threat** is a condition in the general environment that may hinder an organization's efforts to achieve strategic competitiveness.[20] Above, we used Canada's greying population as an example of an opportunity for banks. However, Canada's aging population

An **opportunity** is a condition in the general environment that, if exploited, helps a company to achieve strategic competitiveness.

A **threat** is a condition in the general environment that may hinder a company's efforts to achieve strategic competitiveness.

Table 3.2	Components of the External Environmental Analysis
Scanning	Identifying early signals of environmental changes and trends
Monitoring	Detecting meaning through ongoing observations of environmental changes and trends
Forecasting	Developing projections of anticipated outcomes based on monitored changes and trends
Assessing	Determining the timing and importance of environmental changes and trends for firms' strategies and their management

Chapter 3 / The External Environment

also poses a threat. A 2007 report from Statistics Canada suggested that Canada's population was aging so fast that by 2017 more people could be leaving the workforce than would be entering it. This poses a major threat to organizations striving to achieve strategic competitiveness through an experienced workforce.[21]

Several sources can be used to analyze the general environment, including a wide variety of printed materials (such as trade publications, newspapers, business publications, and the results of academic research and public polls), trade shows and suppliers, customers, and employees of public-sector organizations. People in "boundary-spanning" positions can obtain much information. Salespersons, purchasing managers, public relations directors, and customer service representatives, each of whom interacts with external constituents, are examples of individuals in boundary-spanning positions. Expatriates in multinational corporations can act as significant boundary spanners as they act in and return from their foreign assignments.[22]

Scanning

Scanning entails the study of all segments in the general environment. Through scanning, firms identify early signals of potential changes in the general environment and detect changes that are already underway.[23] When scanning, the firm often deals with ambiguous, incomplete, or unconnected data and information. Environmental scanning is critically important for firms competing in highly volatile environments.[24] In addition, scanning activities must be aligned with the organizational context; a scanning system designed for a volatile environment is inappropriate for a firm in a stable environment.[25]

Many firms use special software to help them identify events that are taking place in the environment and announced in public sources. For example, news event detection procedures use information-based systems to categorize text and reduce the trade-off between an important missed event and false alarm rates.[26] The Internet provides multiple opportunities for scanning. For example, similar to many Internet companies, Amazon.ca records significant information about individuals visiting its Web site, particularly if a purchase is made. Amazon then welcomes these customers by name when they visit the Web site again. The firm even sends messages to them about specials and new products similar to those purchased in previous visits.

Monitoring

When *monitoring,* analysts observe environmental changes to see if an important trend is emerging from among those spotted by scanning.[27] Critical to successful monitoring is the firm's ability to detect meaning in different environmental events and trends. For example, Staples Business Depot recognized that small business is one of the fastest-growing segments of the Canadian economy. In response, it partnered with BizLaunch and Women Entrepreneurs of Canada (40 percent of solo self-employed people in Canada are women) to offer seminars to small business owners across Canada. The Canadian Federation of Independent Business reported that 7 out of 10 Canadians work for an employer with 10 or fewer employees.[28]

Effective monitoring requires the firm to identify important stakeholders. Because the importance of different stakeholders can vary over a firm's life cycle, careful attention must be given to the firm's needs and its stakeholder groups across time.[29] Scanning and monitoring are particularly important when a firm competes in an industry with high technological uncertainty.[30] Scanning and monitoring not only can provide the firm with information but also serve as a means of importing new knowledge about markets and about how to successfully commercialize new technologies that the firm has developed.[31]

Forecasting

Scanning and monitoring are concerned with events and trends in the general environment at a point in time. When *forecasting,* analysts develop feasible projections of what might happen, and how quickly, as a result of the changes and trends detected through scanning and monitoring.[32] For example, analysts might forecast the time that will be required for a new technology to reach the marketplace, the length of time before different corporate training procedures are required to deal with anticipated changes in the composition of the workforce, or how much time will elapse before changes in governmental taxation policies affect consumers' purchasing patterns.

Forecasting events and outcomes accurately is challenging. Canada's manufacturing sector, concentrated in Ontario and Quebec, suffered major blows as the loonie appreciated in 2007. Nearly 250,000 jobs were cut from 2004 to 2007 in an attempt to reduce costs. Despite the widespread troubles, some Canadian-based manufacturers who imported materials showed particular resilience and reaped the rewards of parity between the Canadian and U.S. dollars.

Assessing

The objective of *assessing* is to determine the timing and significance of the effects of environmental changes and trends on the strategic management of the firm.[33] Through scanning, monitoring, and forecasting, analysts are able to understand the general environment. Going a step further, the intent of assessment is to specify the implications of that understanding for the organization. Without assessment, the firm is left with data that may be interesting but are of unknown competitive relevance. Despite the importance of studying the environment, evidence suggests that only a relatively small percentage of firms use formal processes to collect and disseminate such information. Even if formal assessment is inadequate, the appropriate interpretation of that information is important. "Research found that how accurate senior executives are about their competitive environments is indeed less important for strategy and corresponding organizational changes than the way in which they interpret information about their environments."[34] Thus, although gathering and organizing information is important, investing money in the appropriate interpretation of that intelligence may be equally important. Accordingly, after information has been gathered, assessing whether a trend in the environment represents an opportunity or a threat is extremely important.

Segments of the General Environment

The general environment is composed of segments that are external to the firm (refer to Table 3.1). Although the degree of impact varies, these environmental segments affect each industry and its firms. The challenge to the firm is to scan, monitor, forecast, and assess those elements in each segment that are of the greatest importance. These efforts should result in recognition of environmental changes, trends, opportunities, and threats. Opportunities are then matched with a firm's core competencies (the matching process is discussed further in Chapter 4).

The Demographic Segment

The **demographic segment** is concerned with a population's size, age structure, geographic distribution, ethnic mix, and income distribution.[35] Often, demographic segments are analyzed on a global basis because of their potential effects across countries' borders and because many firms compete in global markets.

The **demographic segment** is concerned with a population's size, age structure, geographic distribution, ethnic mix, and income distribution.

Population Size

By mid 2007, the world's population was over 6.6 billion, up from 6.1 billion in 2000. Combined, China and India accounted for one-third of the world's population. Experts speculate that the population might stabilize at 10 billion after 2200 if the deceleration in the rate of increase in the world's head count continues. By 2050, India (with over 1.5 billion people projected) and China (with just under 1.5 billion people projected) are expected to be the most populous countries.[36] Interestingly, only slightly over one billion people live in developed countries, whereas over five billion live in developing countries. Canada's population grew from just over 32,000,000 in 2004 to an estimated 33,091,200 in late 2007. Net international migration accounted for a major proportion of Canada's population increase in late 2007 as over 70,000 people immigrated to Canada in the third quarter of 2007.[37]

Observing demographic changes in populations highlights the importance of this environmental segment. For example, it is projected that, by 2006, 20 percent of Japan's citizens will be at least 65, while the United States and China will not reach this level until 2036. In Japan this is up 10 percent from just 20 years ago. Government officials hope that by encouraging the employees to work longer through incentives for improved retirement—71 percent of Japanese aged 60 to 64 continue to work—will counteract lower birthrates enough to prevent a significant decline in the overall workforce. Without older citizens' increasing willingness to work longer, Japan would likely experience cost overruns in its pension system. Like Japan, Italy will reach 20 percent over 65 in 2006, and Germany will reach it in 2009. However, workers in these two countries tend to retire at an earlier age than the Japanese. Their policymakers have encouraged this in order to reduce the unemployment rate. But with workers retiring earlier than the Japanese, these countries are looking at higher expenses in their pension systems and a significant loss of skilled labour that may affect productivity rates.[38] Interestingly, the United States has a higher birthrate and significant immigration, placing it in a better position than Japan and other European nations.

Age Structure

As noted above, in Japan and other countries, the world's population is rapidly aging. In North America and Europe, millions of baby boomers are approaching retirement. However, even in developing countries with large numbers of people under the age of 35, birth rates have been declining sharply. In China, for example, by 2040 there will be 400 million people over the age of 60. The 90 million baby boomers in North America are fuelling the current economy because they seem to continue to spend as they age. They are also thus expected to fuel growth in the financial planning sector as they inherit $1 trillion over the next 15 years and rush to save more before retirement. However, the future surrounding baby boomers is clouded in at least two areas. One problem is the significant increase in health care costs. For instance, Canadian health care, which has strong government subsidies, is predicted to consume 40 percent of all government tax revenues by 2040. The other problem is that as the number of retired baby boomers swells, the number of workers paying Canada/Quebec Pension Plan and other taxes will decrease significantly. This will leave governments in North America and Europe facing significant choices: it seems that governments will have to raise the retirement age (as have the Japanese through incentives to stay in the workforce), cut benefits, raise taxes, and/or run significant budget deficits.[39]

Although emerging-economy populations are aging as well, they still have a significantly younger labour force. The consumer products being produced so cheaply in China are helping North American consumers to contain inflation. However, the basic prices of commodities such as copper, oil, and gas have been rising in North America as China increases its productivity and seeks to maintain employment levels for its large population. As the workforce in the West ages and education levels rise in emerging economies, the United States and Canada will be accepting larger numbers of immigrant workers. At the same time, Western firms are outsourcing work to such countries as India, which has a growing high-tech sector.[40] As can be seen, changes in the age structure have significant impacts on firms in an economy.

Geographic Distribution

In Canada, 28 metropolitan areas have accounted for nearly three-quarters of the growth in employment in the country during the past seven years. Between 2000 and 2006, employment in Canada rose by just over 1.7 million. Of this total, census metropolitan areas accounted for an estimated 1.3 million, or about 73 percent. During this seven-year period, employment in these large metropolitan areas increased 12.6 percent, compared with growth of only 9.6 percent in the smaller urban and rural areas in the rest of the nation.[41] In contrast, the U.S. population has been shifting from the north and east to the west and south. Similarly, the trend of relocating from metropolitan to non-metropolitan areas continues. These trends are changing local and state governments' tax bases. In turn, business firms' decisions regarding location are influenced by the degree of support that different taxing agencies offer as well as the rates at which these agencies tax businesses.

The geographic distribution of populations throughout the world is also affected by the capabilities resulting from advances in communications technology. Through computer technologies, for example, people can remain in their homes, communicating with others in remote locations to complete their work.

Ethnic Mix

The ethnic mix of countries' populations continues to change. For firms, the challenge is to be sensitive to these changes. Within Canada, the ethnicity of provinces and their cities varies significantly because of changes that have occurred through immigration. Through careful study, firms can develop and market products that satisfy the unique needs of different ethnic groups. Changes in the ethnic mix also affect a workforce's composition and cooperation.[42] In Canada, the population and labour force will continue to diversify as immigration accounts for a sizable part of growth. The resulting workforce diversity, if effectively managed, can be a source of competitive advantage. For example, a firm considering internationalizing a product could use an ethnic group in Canada similar to the ethnicity of the country in which they intend to market and sell their products and/or services to assess the likelihood of success. This test could be conducted by employees who are members of the same ethnic background.

Income Distribution

Understanding how income is distributed within and across populations informs firms of different groups' purchasing power and discretionary income. Studies of income distributions suggest that although living standards have improved over time, variations exist within and between nations.[43] Of interest to firms are the average incomes of households and individuals. For instance, the increase in dual-career couples has had a notable effect on average incomes of households. Although real income has been declining in general, the household income of dual-career couples has increased. This type of information is strategically relevant for firms as research indicates that whether an employee is part of a dual-career couple can strongly influence the willingness of the employee to accept an international assignment.[44]

The Economic Segment

The health of a nation's economy affects individual firms and industries. Because of this, organizations study the economic environment to identify changes, trends, and their strategic implications. The **economic environment** refers to the nature and direction of

The **economic environment** refers to the nature and direction of the economy in which a firm competes or may compete.

the economy in which a firm competes or may compete.[45] Because nations are interconnected as a result of the global economy, firms must scan, monitor, forecast, and assess the health of economies outside their host nation. Many nations throughout the world are affected by the U.S. economy, and this impact is especially relevant to Canadians. In 2006, exports to the U.S. accounted for roughly 80 percent of Canada's $456 billion of exports. Imports from the U.S. accounted for approximately 65 percent of Canada's $404 billion of imports. Although these percentages were down from the 2001 percentages of 83.5 and 72.5, respectively, it is clear that the U.S. economy is important to Canada's economic health—as is noted in the Strategic Focus. In 2007, there were indications that China's economic health would impact nations, such as Canada, that are resource-rich.

The Political/Legal Segment

The **political/legal segment** is the arena in which organizations and interest groups compete for attention, resources, and a voice in overseeing the body of laws and regulations guiding the interactions among nations.[46] Essentially, this segment represents how organizations try to influence government and how governments influence them. As the politics of regulations change, for example, this segment influences the nature of competition through changing the rules (for other examples of political/legal elements, refer to Table 3.1).

Firms must carefully analyze a new political administration's business-related policies and philosophies. Competition laws, taxation laws, industries chosen for deregulation, labour training laws, and the degree of commitment to educational institutions are areas in which an administration's policies can affect the operations and profitability of industries and individual firms. Stephen Harper's Conservative minority government has pursued policies that are different from those of Paul Martin's Liberal government. For example, on January 1, 2008, the GST was reduced from 6 percent to 5 percent by the Harper government. This followed a previous reduction from 7 percent to 6 percent. Often, firms develop a political strategy to influence governmental policies and actions that might affect them. The effects of global governmental policies on a firm's competitive position increase the importance of forming an effective political strategy.[47]

Business firms across the globe confront an interesting array of political/legal questions and issues. For example, the debate continues over trade policies. Some believe that a nation should erect trade barriers to protect its companies' products. However, as countries continue to join the World Trade Organization (WTO), more countries seem to believe that free trade across nations serves the best interests of individual countries and their citizens. A Geneva-based organization, the WTO establishes rules for global trade. For instance, after joining the World Trade Organization, China ended a 40-year-old global textile-quota system regulating its exports. Earlier, to ease the problems created for other countries, China had voluntarily enacted transition tariffs. When the quota system expired in early 2005, Chinese textiles flooded global markets, threatening domestic textile industries. Several countries responded by imposing even higher tariffs to level the playing field.[48]

The Sociocultural Segment

The **sociocultural segment** is concerned with a society's attitudes and cultural values. Because attitudes and values form the cornerstone of a society, they often drive demographic, economic, political/legal, and technological conditions and changes. Sociocultural segments differ across countries. A significant trend in Canada is increased workforce diversity due to immigration from socioculturally diverse countries. As noted

The **political/legal segment** is the arena in which organizations and interest groups compete for attention, resources, and a voice in overseeing the body of laws and regulations guiding the interactions among nations.

The **sociocultural segment** is concerned with a society's attitudes and cultural values.

How the High-Flying Loonie Crashed Retailers

In late 2007, when the loonie climbed to its highest point against the U.S. dollar in more than 30 years, it was not its namesake majestic waterfowl that could be heard uttering a lamenting wail. It was Canadian retailers. Over the years, as the Canadian dollar had sunk against the U.S. greenback, prices on everything coming from the U.S. grew higher and higher. On every book, magazine, calendar, greeting card, or other object that displayed the price of the product in both currencies, it was patently obvious that one paid more for it in Canadian dollars. But when the Canadian dollar reached parity with the U.S. dollar in late September 2007, it looked like Christmas would be coming early for Canadian shoppers hunting bargains south of the border.

Canadian retailers, however, struggled with the impact of the high dollar. Not only were many Canadian shoppers taking their business south of the border, but consumer pressure was mounting at home to have Canada's retailers reduce prices and offer more discounts. The situation became dire for independent merchants. Pat Caven, manager of Perfect Books, an independent bookstore in Ottawa, complained, ". . . after surviving Chapters, Costco, Pharma Plus getting into the book business, now we're being pitted against one another and I just think that's incredibly unfair." It was, in fact, the book industry that faced one of the toughest battles because most of its products have both the American and Canadian price listed on the cover. "It's reduced our revenues," said Joseph Stewart, manager of Blackberry Books Ltd., an independent bookstore in Vancouver. "We're selling about the same amount of books . . . but it's bringing in less money per book." The store began putting reduced-price stickers on many of its books, in large part because Random House of Canada had begun discounting its merchandise to help retailers offset the impact of the high dollar. Now, some books are priced only a few dollars higher than in the U.S., Stewart said. "No other publisher has done anything quite as dramatic."

Major Canadian stores, including Zellers and Canadian Tire, began dropping their prices due to the rising dollar. Yet retailers "have a lot of goods on the shelf that they may have purchased several months ago on the basis of a considerably lower dollar," said Perrin Beatty, president and chief executive officer of the Canadian Chamber of Commerce. "It was much more expensive for them to buy and suddenly they're confronted with a situation of having to compete with retailers across the border."

To make matters worse, Finance Minister Jim Flaherty said consumers should pressure retailers to drop prices, without taking into account the fact that the merchants were still being charged high rates by suppliers. "We are encouraging the retailers to reflect as quickly as possible the increased purchasing value of the Canadian dollar for the sake of Canadian consumers and quite frankly, for the sake of Canadian retailers as well so that they will have the business volumes they would like to have," Flaherty said during question period in the House of Commons. Retailers quickly protested that argument, saying they were stuck in a no-win situation because suppliers were still charging high rates—maybe because they saw an opportunity to gain extra profit, or maybe because they were unsure about the stability of the Canadian dollar. After all, like its namesake the loon, the loonie might be just as capable of diving quickly as it was of flying high.

SOURCES: C. Weeks, 2007, Retailers cut prices, but bleed profits, because of high dollar, CanWest News, October 23; 2007, In depth economy, parity and beyond, how high will the loonie go?, CBC News, October 31, http://www.cbc.ca/news/back ground/economy/loonie.html, retrieved February 29, 2008.

earlier, effective management of a culturally diverse workforce can produce a competitive advantage. For example, heterogeneous work teams have been shown to produce more effective strategic analyses, more creativity and innovation, and higher-quality decisions than homogeneous work teams.[49] However, evidence also suggests that diverse work teams are difficult to manage and achieve integration. As such, not all diverse work teams are able to achieve these positive outcomes.[50]

Labour force diversity has increased significantly as more women and minorities from a variety of cultures have entered the labour force. The number of new businesses started by women continues to increase, and thus women own a larger percentage of the total number of businesses.

The growing gender, ethnic, and cultural diversity in the workforce creates challenges and opportunities,[51] including combining the best of both men's and women's traditional leadership styles. Although diversity in the workforce has the potential to add improved performance, research indicates there are important conditions requiring management of diversity initiatives in order to reap these organizational benefits. Human resource practitioners are being trained to successfully manage diversity issues to enhance positive outcomes.[52]

Another major sociocultural trend is the continued growth of suburban communities in Canada and abroad. The increasing number of people living in the suburbs has a number of effects. For example, because of the resulting often-longer commute times to urban businesses, there is pressure for better transportation systems and superhighway systems (e.g., outer beltways to serve the suburban communities such as the new Express Toll Route [ETR 407] from Hamilton, Ontario, to Ajax, Ontario, which also spans a 108-km section north of downtown Toronto). On the other hand, some businesses are locating in the suburbs closer to their employees. Suburban growth also has an effect on the number of electronic telecommuters, which is expected to increase rapidly in the 21st century. This work-style option is feasible because of changes in the technological segment, including the Internet's rapid growth and evolution.

The Technological Segment

The **technological segment** includes the institutions and activities involved with creating new knowledge and translating that knowledge into new outputs, products, processes, and materials.

Pervasive and diversified in scope, technological changes affect many parts of societies. These effects occur primarily through new products, processes, and materials. The **technological segment** includes the institutions and activities involved with creating new knowledge and translating that knowledge into new outputs, products, processes, and materials.

Given the rapid pace of technological change, firms must thoroughly study the technological segment.[53] These efforts are important as early adopters of new technology often achieve higher market shares and earn higher returns. Thus, executives must verify that their firm is continuously scanning the external environment to identify potential substitutes for technologies that are in current use, as well as to spot newly emerging technologies from which their firm could derive a competitive advantage.[54]

Internet technology is playing an increasingly important role in global commerce. Internet pharmacies in Canada have benefited from the access that U.S. senior citizens enjoy, via the Internet, to cheaper drugs in Canada. Legislation was passed in the United States in 2003 to ensure that U.S. citizens could continue to access drugs from Canada.[55] While the Internet was a significant technological advance providing substantial power to companies utilizing its potential, the use of handheld computers with wireless network connectivity, Web-enabled mobile phone handsets, and other emerging platforms (e.g., consumer Internet-access devices) is expected to increase substantially, soon becoming the dominant form of communication and commerce.[56]

The Internet and wireless communication forms are important technological developments. One reason for their importance is that they facilitate the diffusion of other technology and knowledge critical for achieving and maintaining a competitive advantage.[57]

Companies not only must stay current with technologies as they evolve, but also must be prepared to act quickly to embrace important new disruptive technologies shortly after they are introduced.[58] Globally, the technological opportunities and threats in the general environment have an effect on whether firms obtain new technology from external sources (such as by licensing and acquisition) or develop it internally.

The Global Segment

The **global segment** includes relevant new global markets, existing markets that are changing, important international political events, and critical cultural and institutional characteristics of global markets.[59] Globalization of business markets creates both opportunities and challenges for firms.[60] For example, firms can identify and enter valuable new global markets.[61] In addition to these valuable opportunities, firms should recognize potential competitive threats. China presents many opportunities and some threats for international firms.[62] Creating some opportunities is China's 2001 admission to the World Trade Organization. However, the low cost of Chinese products threatens many firms in the textile industry. China's average labour costs are much lower than those in North America and Europe (90 percent lower than in the U.S. and Italy). Furthermore, their manufacturers are more efficient than garment manufacturers in other low-cost countries such as India or Vietnam could not can in both places and were disrupted not are disrupted.[63]

Exemplifying the globalization trend is the increasing amount of global outsourcing. For example, many firms are outsourcing jobs to different countries. Telus outsourced the jobs of thousands of call centre and back office employees to the Philippines.[64] However, recent research suggests that there is a trade-off between flexibility and efficiency if all work in a particular function or product is outsourced. Custom work to fill special orders, for example, is more efficiently done through domestic manufacturing; outsourcing standard products to an offshore facility needs to save at least 15 percent to be justified. Even in the textile industry, where much outsourcing is done for efficiency reasons, many order adjustments or special orders require flexibility and cannot be readily handled by low-cost offshore producers.[65]

Moving into international markets extends a firm's reach and potential. Toyota receives almost 50 percent of its total sales revenue from outside Japan, its home country. Over 60 percent of McDonald's sales revenues and almost 98 percent of Nokia's sales revenues are from outside their home countries.[66] Firms can also increase the opportunity to sell innovations by entering international markets. The larger total market increases the probability that the firm will earn a return on its innovations. Certainly, firms entering new markets can diffuse new knowledge they have created and learn from the new markets as well.[67]

Firms should recognize the different sociocultural and institutional attributes of global markets. Companies competing in South Korea, for example, must understand the value placed on hierarchical order, formality, and self-control, as well as on duty rather than rights. Furthermore, Korean ideology emphasizes communitarianism, a characteristic of many Asian countries. Korea's approach differs from those of Japan and China, however, in that it focuses on *inhwa*, or harmony. Inhwa is based on a respect of hierarchical relationships and obedience to authority. Alternatively, the approach in China stresses *guanxi*—personal relationships or good connections—while in Japan, the focus is on *wa*, or group harmony and social cohesion.[68] The institutional context of China suggests a major emphasis on centralized planning by the government. The Chinese government provides incentives to firms to develop alliances with foreign firms having sophisticated technology in hopes of building knowledge and introducing new technologies to the Chinese markets over time.[69]

Firms based in other countries that compete in these markets can learn from them. For example, the cultural characteristics above suggest the value of relationships. In

The **global segment** includes relevant new global markets, existing markets that are changing, important international political events, and critical cultural and institutional characteristics of global markets.

particular, guanxi emphasizes the importance of social capital when one is doing business in China.[70] Although social capital is important for success in most markets around the world,[71] problems can arise from its strict ethic of reciprocity and obligation. It can divide, for example, loyalties of sales and procurement people who are in networks outside the company. Sales and procurement people need to have their loyalties focused on the company with which they are employed.[72] Global markets offer firms more opportunities to obtain the resources needed for success.

A key objective of analyzing the general environment is identifying anticipated changes and trends among external elements. With a focus on the future, the analysis of the general environment allows firms to identify opportunities and threats. As a result, it is necessary to have a top management team with the experience, knowledge, and sensitivity required to effectively analyze this segment of the environment.[73] Also critical to a firm's future operations is an understanding of its industry environment and its competitors; these issues are considered next.

Industry Environment Analysis

An **industry** is a group of firms producing products that are close substitutes.

An **industry** is a group of firms producing products that are close substitutes or strategically equivalent. In the course of competition, these firms influence one another. Typically, industries include a rich mix of competitive strategies that companies use in pursuing strategic competitiveness and above-average returns. In part, these strategies are chosen because of the influence of an industry's characteristics.[74]

When compared with the general environment, the industry environment often has a more direct effect on the firm's strategic competitiveness and above-average returns.[75] The intensity of industry competition and an industry's profit potential are a function of five forces of competition: the threats posed by new entrants, the power of suppliers, the power of buyers, product substitutes, and the intensity of rivalry among competitors (see Figure 3.3). These are illustrated in the Strategic Focus on the global automobile industry.

The five forces model of competition expands the arena for competitive analysis. Historically, when studying the competitive environment, firms concentrated on companies with which they competed directly. However, firms must search more broadly to identify current and potential competitors by identifying potential customers as well as

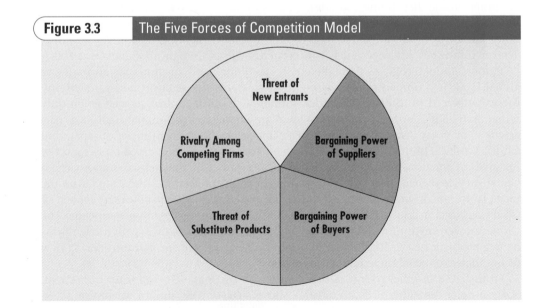

Figure 3.3 The Five Forces of Competition Model

Threat of New Entrants

Rivalry Among Competing Firms

Bargaining Power of Suppliers

Threat of Substitute Products

Bargaining Power of Buyers

Competitive Forces in the Global Automobile Industry

Because of the globalizing nature of the automobile industry, competition is increasing among domestic operations in Canada and the United States. General Motors' market share in North America dropped to 25.2 percent during the first quarter of 2005, from 26.3 percent one year earlier. U.S. automakers dropped below 50 percent market share for the first time in history in July 2007. GM sales dropped 22.3 percent when compared to a strong July 2006, while Ford declined 19.1 percent and Chrysler fell 8.4 percent. Even Toyota Motor Corp., which had been posting strong gains, reported a decline of 7.4 percent after a record-setting July 2007. The drop was attributed to rising rates on home equity loans and adjustable mortgages and higher gas prices, leaving consumers with less money to buy cars.

The market share captured by the Big Three in the first three months of 2008 had slipped to 52.9 percent—four percentage points lower than the previous year's share at the same point. Most of the import nameplates, on the other hand, had a good quarter. Toyota, Honda, Nissan, Mazda, and Hyundai all sold more vehicles.

Toyota Motor Corp. became the world's top auto seller in the first three months of 2007, passing rival General Motors Corp. for the first time. Toyota has gained steadily on GM in recent years and analysts have been saying it is only a matter of time before it eclipses its Detroit-based rival, which has seen its market share shrink in the United States even as it leads sales in China. While GM has struggled to shore up earnings with job cuts and plant closures, Toyota has expanded rapidly, thanks in part to the popularity of its fuel-efficient cars, including the Camry, Corolla, and the Prius gas–electric hybrid.

In regard to potential new entrants, Shanghai Automotive Industry Corp. (SAIC) produced over 600,000 vehicles in joint ventures with Volkswagen and General Motors in China. Originally SAIC did not produce any vehicles under its own brand name, but because China has a large growing market for automobiles, and the government requires joint ventures, SAIC will have a significant role to play in the global automobile industry.

Because General Motors and Ford are experiencing financial difficulties due to their market share loss, they have pushed these difficulties upstream to their suppliers by requiring them to reduce their costs. Both Delphi and Visteon, formerly part of General Motors and Ford, respectively, have experienced difficulties in recent years because General Motors and Ford have demanded lower prices in light of their own competitive difficulties. Consequently, these auto parts companies have increased their losses beyond the requests by their dominant buyers because of pricing difficulties in the face of rising costs for steel and other commodities.

Similarly, much of General Motors' and Ford's inventory difficulties have been pushed forward onto rental car companies. Ford, for example, has a substantial ownership position in Hertz rental cars. Both firms also own substantial dealership networks through which they have offered incentives to lower their substantial inventory in the face of overcapacity in the global auto industry. Accordingly, General Motors and Ford have significant market power through these ownership arrangements in regard to significant customer groups.

While there are not many substitutes for autos, with increasing gas prices many individuals might turn to mass transit or other forms of transportation where available. Bicycles are not much of a substitute given the fast-moving pace of transportation these days.

Finally, competition in the global automobile industry, as noted in the opening paragraph, is intense. The primary reason for *global* competition is that the economies of scale necessary to produce automobiles—and especially high-value-added parts such as engines and transmissions—often require companies to expand beyond their national borders. Also, when a downturn occurs in one country, the immediate reaction is to seek to sell in another country. Although China, for instance, has had the hottest market as far as growth and future expectations for growth, even as sales have dampened in the short term in China firms have considered manufacturing vehicles there for export to other markets such as Europe and

(continued)

North America because manufacturing costs are low in China relative to the rest of the world.

Although firms such as Toyota have continued to make money in a difficult environment, even they are experiencing a downturn of profits due to the highly competitive environment. However, Toyota continues to make inroads, as do Honda and Nissan, in the North American market. This has caused severe problems for both Ford and General Motors. These trends are illustrative of the nature of Porter's five forces, discussed in this chapter.

SOURCES: 2007, U.S. automakers drop below 50 per cent market share for 1st time, AutosDaily.com, http://autos-daily.com/us-automakers-drop-below-50-per-cent-market-share-for-1st-time/,retrieved February 27, 2008; 2007, GM and Ford's Canadian sales fall as "import" sales rise, CBC News, April 3, http://www.cbc.ca/story/money/national/2007/04/03/ autosales.html, retrieved February 27, 2008; 2007, Toyota tops GM as world's top auto seller, CBC News, April 24, http://www.cbc.ca/money/story/2007/04/24/toyota-gm.html, retrieved February 27, 2008; 2005, China hopes to be next nation to make major inroads in U.S. car market, *USA Today,* April 25, B4; N. E. Boudette, Power play: Chrysler's storied hemi motor helps it escape Detroit's gloom, *Wall Street Journal,* June 17, A1, A10; J. Fox, 2005, A CEO puts his job on the line, *Fortune,* May 2, 17–21; L. Hawkins, 2005, GM shifts to a loss of $1.1 billion, *Wall Street Journal,* April 20, A3, A6; J. Sapsford, 2005, Nissan to sell China vans made in the U.S., *Wall Street Journal,* March 17, A14; D. Welch, D. Beucke, K. Kerwin, M. Arndt, B. Hindo, E. Thornton, D. Kiley, & I. Rowley, 2005, Why GM's plan won't work . . . and the ugly road ahead, *BusinessWeek,* May 9, 84–92; J. B. White & J. S. Lublin, 2005, Visteon, Delphi seek to revamp, as woes mount, *Wall Street Journal,* A3, A4; A. Taylor, III, 2004, Shanghai Auto wants to be the world's next great car company, *Fortune,* October 4, 103–109.

the firms serving them. Competing for the same customers and thus being influenced by how customers value location and firm capabilities in their decisions is referred to as the *market microstructure.*[76] Understanding this area is particularly important, because in recent years industry boundaries have become blurred. For example, Canadian banks are now providing bereavement services to customers who have lost loved ones, telecommunications companies now compete with cable broadcasters, software manufacturers provide personal financial services, airlines sell mutual funds, and automakers sell insurance and provide financing.[77] In addition to the focus on customers rather than on specific industry boundaries to define markets, geographic boundaries are also relevant. Research suggests that different geographic markets for the same product can have considerably different competitive conditions.[78]

The five forces model recognizes that suppliers can become a firm's competitors (by integrating forward), as can buyers (by integrating backward). Several firms have integrated forward in the pharmaceutical industry by acquiring distributors or wholesalers. In addition, firms choosing to enter a new market and those producing products that are adequate substitutes for existing products can become a company's competitors. We now examine each of these five forces in detail.

Threat of New Entrants

It is often difficult to identify new competitors. Doing so is important because they can threaten the market share of existing competitors.[79] One reason new entrants pose such a threat is that they bring additional production capacity. Unless the demand for a good or service is increasing, additional capacity holds consumers' costs down, resulting in less revenue and lower returns for competing firms. Often, new entrants have a keen interest in gaining a large market share. As a result, new competitors may force existing firms to be more effective and efficient and to learn how to compete on new dimensions (for example, using an Internet-based distribution channel).

The likelihood that firms will enter an industry is a function of two factors: barriers to entry and the retaliation expected from current industry participants. Entry barriers make it difficult for new firms to enter an industry and often place them at a competitive disadvantage even when they are able to enter. As such, high entry barriers increase the returns for existing firms in the industry and may allow some firms to dominate the industry.[80]

Barriers to Entry

Existing competitors try to develop barriers to entry. In contrast, potential entrants seek markets in which the entry barriers are relatively insignificant. An absence of entry barriers increases the probability that a new entrant can operate profitably. There are several kinds of potentially significant entry barriers.

Economies of Scale. *Economies of scale* are derived from incremental efficiency improvements through experience as a firm gets larger. Therefore, as the quantity of a product produced during a given period increases, the cost of manufacturing each unit declines. Economies of scale can be developed in most business functions, such as marketing, manufacturing, research and development, and purchasing.[81] Increasing economies of scale enhances a firm's flexibility. For example, a firm may choose to reduce its price and capture a greater share of the market. Alternatively, it may keep its price constant to increase profits. In so doing, it likely will increase its free cash flow, which is helpful in times of recession.

New entrants face a dilemma when confronting current competitors' scale economies. Small-scale entry places them at a cost disadvantage. Alternatively, large-scale entry, in which the new entrant manufactures large volumes of a product to gain economies of scale, risks strong competitive retaliation. This is the situation faced by potential new entrants from China. Although Chinese firms have significant capacity to produce cars and parts they do not have the brand recognition necessary to challenge larger global auto firms.

Some competitive conditions reduce the ability of economies of scale to create an entry barrier. Many companies now customize their products for large numbers of small customer groups. Customized products are not manufactured in the volumes necessary to achieve economies of scale. Customization is made possible by new flexible manufacturing systems. In fact, the new manufacturing technology facilitated by advanced information systems has allowed the development of mass customization in an increasing number of industries. While customization is not appropriate for all products, mass customization is becoming increasingly common in manufacturing products.[82] In fact, online ordering has enhanced the ability of customers to obtain customized products. They are often referred to as "markets of one."[83] Companies manufacturing customized products learn how to respond quickly to customers' desires rather than develop scale economies.

Product Differentiation. Over time, customers may come to believe that a firm's product is unique. This belief can result from the firm's service to the customer, effective advertising campaigns, or being the first to market a good or service. Companies such as Coca-Cola, PepsiCo, and the world's automobile manufacturers spend a great deal of money on advertising to convince potential customers of their products' distinctiveness. Customers valuing a product's uniqueness tend to become loyal to both the product and the company producing it. Typically, new entrants must allocate many resources over time to overcome existing customer loyalties. To combat the perception of uniqueness, new entrants frequently offer products at lower prices. This decision, however, may result in lower profits or even losses.

Capital Requirements. Competing in a new industry requires a firm to have resources to invest. In addition to physical facilities, capital is needed for inventories, marketing activities, and other critical business functions. Even when competing in a new industry is attractive, the capital required for successful market entry may not be available to pursue an apparent market opportunity. For example, defence industries would be very difficult to enter because of the substantial resource investments required to be competitive. In addition, because of the high knowledge requirements of the defence industry, a firm might enter the defence industry through the acquisition of an existing firm. For example, through a series of acquisitions and joint ventures with local players, the French defence contractor Thales SA entered the markets of Britain, the Netherlands, Australia, South Africa, South Korea, and Singapore.[84] But it had access to the capital necessary to do it.

Switching Costs. *Switching costs* are the one-time costs customers incur when they buy from a different supplier. The costs of buying new ancillary equipment and of retraining employees, and even the psychic costs of ending a relationship, may be incurred in switching to a new supplier. In some cases, switching costs are low, such as when the consumer switches to a different soft drink. Switching costs can vary as a function of time. For example, in terms of credit hours toward graduation, the cost to a student to transfer from one university to another as a freshman is much lower than it is when the student is entering the senior year. Occasionally, a decision made by manufacturers to produce a new, innovative product creates high switching costs for the final consumer. Customer loyalty programs, such as airlines' frequent flier miles, are intended to increase the customer's switching costs. If switching costs are high, a new entrant must offer either a substantially lower price or a much better product to attract buyers. Usually, the more established the relationship between parties, the greater is the cost incurred to switch to an alternative offering.

Access to Distribution Channels. Over time, industry participants typically develop effective means of distributing products. Once a relationship with its distributors has been developed, a firm will nurture it to create switching costs for the distributors.

Access to distribution channels can be a strong entry barrier for new entrants, particularly in consumer nondurable goods industries (for example, in grocery stores where shelf space is limited) and in international markets. New entrants have to persuade distributors to carry their products, either in addition to or in place of those currently distributed. Price breaks and cooperative advertising allowances may be used for this purpose; however, those practices reduce the new entrant's profit potential.

Cost Disadvantages Independent of Scale. Sometimes, established competitors have cost advantages that new entrants cannot duplicate. Proprietary product technology, favourable access to raw materials, desirable locations, and government subsidies are examples. Successful competition requires new entrants to reduce the strategic relevance of these factors. Delivering purchases directly to the buyer can counter the advantage of a desirable location; new food establishments in an undesirable location often follow this practice. Similarly, automobile dealerships located in unattractive areas (perhaps in a city's downtown area) can provide superior service (such as picking up the car to be serviced and then delivering it to the customer) to overcome a competitor's location advantage.

Government Policy. Through licensing and permit requirements, governments can also control entry into an industry. Liquor retailing, radio and TV broadcasting, banking, fishing, and trucking are examples of industries in which provincial and federal government decisions and actions affect entry possibilities. Also, governments often restrict entry into some industries because of the need to provide quality service or the need to protect jobs. Some of the most publicized government actions are those involving competition issues.

Expected Retaliation. Firms seeking to enter an industry also anticipate the reactions of firms in the industry. An expectation of swift and vigorous competitive responses reduces the likelihood of entry. Vigorous retaliation can be expected when the existing firm has a major stake in the industry (for example, it has fixed assets with few, if any, alternative uses), when it has substantial resources, and when industry growth is slow or constrained. For example, any firm attempting to enter the automobile industry at the current time can expect significant retaliation from existing competitors due to the overcapacity inherent in the industry.

Locating market niches not being served by incumbents allows the new entrant to avoid entry barriers. Small entrepreneurial firms are generally best suited for identifying and serving neglected market segments. When Honda first entered the North American market, it was forced by market conditions to concentrate on small-engine motorcycles. Fortunately for Honda this was a market niche that firms such as Harley-Davidson had ignored. By targeting this neglected niche, Honda avoided competition. After consolidating its position, Honda used its strength to attack rivals by introducing larger motorcycles and competing in the broader market. Competitive actions and competitive responses between firms are discussed more fully in Chapter 6.

Bargaining Power of Suppliers

Increasing prices and reducing the quality of their products are potential means used by suppliers to exert power over firms competing within an industry. If a firm is unable to recover cost increases by its suppliers through its own pricing structure, its profitability is reduced by its suppliers' actions. A supplier group is powerful when

- It is dominated by a few large companies and is more concentrated than the industry to which it sells.
- Satisfactory substitute products are not available to industry firms.
- Industry firms are not a significant customer for the supplier group.
- Suppliers' goods are critical to buyers' marketplace success.
- The effectiveness of suppliers' products has created high switching costs for industry firms.
- It poses a credible threat to integrate forward into the buyers' industry. Credibility is enhanced when suppliers have substantial resources and provide a highly differentiated product.

The airline industry is an example of an industry in which suppliers' bargaining power is changing. Though the number of suppliers is low, the demand for the major aircraft is also relatively low. Boeing and Airbus strongly compete for most orders of major aircraft.[85] However, the shift in airline strategy to short-haul flights and low costs has enhanced the fortunes of other aircraft manufacturers who make smaller and more efficient aircraft.

Bargaining Power of Buyers

Firms seek to maximize the return on their invested capital. Alternatively, buyers (customers of an industry or a firm) want to buy products at the lowest possible price—the point at which the industry earns the lowest acceptable rate of return on its invested capital. To reduce their costs, buyers bargain for higher quality, greater levels of service, and lower prices. These outcomes are achieved by encouraging competitive battles among the industry's firms. Customers (buyer groups) are powerful when

- They purchase a large portion of an industry's total output.
- The sales of the purchased product account for a significant portion of the seller's annual revenues.
- They could switch to another product at little, if any, cost.
- The industry's products are undifferentiated or standardized.
- The buyers pose a credible threat if they were to integrate backward into the sellers' industry.

Armed with greater amounts of information about the manufacturer's costs and the power of the Internet as a shopping and distribution alternative, consumers appear to be increasing their bargaining power in many industries. One reason for this shift is that individual buyers incur virtually zero switching costs when they decide to purchase from one manufacturer rather than another or from one dealer as opposed to a second or third one. These realities are also forcing airlines to change their strategies. There is very little differentiation in air travel, and the switching costs are very low.

Threat of Substitute Products

Substitute products are goods or services from outside a given industry that perform the same or similar functions as a product that the industry produces. As a sugar substitute,

NutraSweet places an upper limit on sugar manufacturers' prices—NutraSweet and sugar perform the same function, though with different characteristics. Other product substitutes include e-mail and fax machines instead of overnight delivery, plastic containers rather than glass jars, and tea instead of coffee. Newspaper firms have experienced a circulation decline gradually over a number of years. The declines are due to substitute outlets for news including Internet sources, cable television news channels, and e-mail and cell phone alerts.[86] These products are increasingly popular, especially among younger people, and as product substitutes they have significant potential to continue to reduce overall newspaper circulation sales.

In general, product substitutes present a strong threat to a firm when customers face few, if any, switching costs and when the substitute product's price is lower or its quality and performance are equal to or greater than those of the competing product. Differentiating a product along dimensions valued by customers (i.e., quality, service after the sale, and location) reduces a substitute's attractiveness. Or, pursuing a cost leadership strategy that allows firms to offer their products at a lower price will reduce the threat of substitutes.

Intensity of Rivalry among Competitors

Because an industry's firms are mutually dependent, actions taken by one company usually invite competitive responses. In many industries, firms actively compete against one another. Competitive rivalry intensifies when a firm is challenged by a competitor's actions or when a company recognizes an opportunity to improve its market position.

Firms within industries are rarely homogeneous; they differ in resources and capabilities and seek to differentiate themselves from competitors.[87] Typically, firms seek to differentiate their products from competitors' offerings in ways that customers value and in which the firms have a competitive advantage. Visible dimensions on which rivalry is based include price, quality, and innovation.

The competitive rivalry is intense in the automobile industry, as described in the Strategic Focus. In fact, the rivalry is so intense that both General Motors and Ford have experienced significantly lower earnings due to price cuts, which in turn have led to their debt ratings being lowered below investment grade or to "junk" levels.[88] Various factors influence the intensity of rivalry between or among competitors. Next, we discuss the most prominent factors that experience shows to affect the intensity of firms' rivalries.

Numerous or Equally Balanced Competitors

Intense rivalries are common in industries with many companies. With multiple competitors, it is common for a few firms to believe that they can act without eliciting a response. However, evidence suggests that other firms generally are aware of competitors' actions, often choosing to respond to them. At the other extreme, industries with only a few firms of equivalent size and power also tend to have strong rivalries. The large and often similar-sized resource bases of these firms permit vigorous actions and responses. The competitive battles between Airbus and Boeing exemplify intense rivalry between relatively equivalent competitors.[89]

Slow Industry Growth

When a market is growing, firms try to effectively use resources to serve an expanding customer base. Growing markets reduce the pressure to take customers from competitors. However, rivalry in no-growth or slow-growth markets becomes more intense as firms battle to increase their market shares by attracting competitors' customers.

High Fixed Costs or High Storage Costs

When fixed costs account for a large part of total costs, companies try to maximize the use of their productive capacity. Doing so allows the firm to spread costs across a larger volume of output. However, when many firms attempt to maximize their productive capacity, excess capacity is created on an industry-wide basis. To reduce inventories, individual companies typically cut the price of their product and offer rebates and other special discounts to customers. However, these practices often intensify competition. A pattern of excess capacity at the industry level followed by intense rivalry at the firm level is observed frequently in industries with high storage costs. Perishable products, for example, lose their value rapidly with the passage of time. As their inventories grow, producers of perishable goods often use pricing strategies to sell products quickly.

Lack of Differentiation or Low Switching Costs

When buyers find a differentiated product that satisfies their needs, they frequently remain loyal purchasers over time. Industries with many companies that have successfully differentiated their products have less rivalry, resulting in lower competition for individual firms. Firms that develop and sustain a differentiated product that cannot be easily imitated by competitors often earn higher returns.[90] However, when buyers view products as commodities (that is, as products with few differentiated features or capabilities), rivalry intensifies as firms compete on price. Typically, buyers' purchasing decisions are based on price and, to a lesser degree, service. Personal computers are becoming a commodity. Thus, the competition among Dell, HP, and other computer manufacturers is intense and is expected to become more intense.

The effect of switching costs is identical to the effect of differentiated products. The lower the buyers' switching costs the easier it is for competitors to attract buyers through pricing and service offerings. High switching costs at least partially insulate the firm from rivals' efforts to attract customers.

High Strategic Stakes

Competitive rivalry is likely to be high when it is important for several of the competitors to perform well in the market. For example, although it is diversified and is a market leader in other businesses, Samsung has targeted market leadership in the consumer electronics market and is doing quite well. This market is quite important to Sony and other major competitors, such as Hitachi, Matsushita, NEC, and Mitsubishi. There is substantial rivalry in this market, and it is likely to continue over the next few years.

High Exit Barriers

Sometimes companies continue competing in an industry even though the returns on their invested capital are low or negative. Firms making this choice likely face high exit barriers, which include economic, strategic, and emotional factors causing companies to remain in an industry when the profitability of doing so is questionable. Common exit barriers are:

- Specialized assets (assets with values linked to a particular business or location).
- Fixed costs of exit (such as labour agreements).
- Strategic interrelationships (relationships of mutual dependence, such as those between one business and other parts of a company's operations, including shared facilities and access to financial markets).
- Emotional barriers (aversion to economically justified business decisions because of fear for one's own career, loyalty to employees, and so forth).
- Government and social restrictions.

Interpreting Industry Analyses

Effective industry analyses are products of careful study and interpretation of data and information from multiple sources. A wealth of industry-specific data is available to be analyzed. Because of globalization, international markets and rivalries must be included in the firm's analyses. In fact, research shows that in some industries, international variables are more important than domestic ones as determinants of strategic competitiveness. Furthermore, because of the development of global markets, a country's borders no longer restrict industry structures. In fact, movement into international markets enhances the chances of success for new ventures as well as more established firms.[91]

Following a study of the five forces of competition, the firm can develop the insights required to determine an industry's attractiveness in terms of the firm's potential to earn adequate or superior returns on its invested capital. In general, the stronger competitive forces are, the lower is the profit potential for an industry's firms. An unattractive industry has low entry barriers, suppliers and buyers with strong bargaining positions, strong competitive threats from product substitutes, and intense rivalry among competitors. These industry characteristics make it very difficult for firms to achieve strategic competitiveness and earn above-average returns. Alternatively, an attractive industry has high entry barriers, suppliers and buyers with little bargaining power, few competitive threats from product substitutes, and relatively moderate rivalry.[92] Next, we turn to strategic groups operating within industries.

Strategic Groups

A **strategic group** is a set of firms emphasizing similar strategic dimensions to use a similar strategy.

A set of firms within an industry emphasizing similar strategic dimensions and using similar strategies is called a **strategic group**.[93] The competition between firms within a strategic group is greater than the competition between a member of a strategic group and companies outside that strategic group. Another way of saying this is that intra–strategic group competition is more intense than is inter–strategic group competition. In fact, there is more heterogeneity in the performance of firms within strategic groups than across groups. The performance leaders within groups are able to follow strategies similar to those of other firms in the group and yet maintain strategic distinctiveness to gain and sustain a competitive advantage.[94]

The extent of technological leadership, product quality, pricing policies, distribution channels, and customer service are examples of strategic dimensions that firms in a strategic group may treat similarly. Patterns of competition within strategic groups may be described this way: "Organizations in a strategic group occupy similar positions in the market, offer similar goods to similar customers, and may also make similar choices about production technology and other organizational features."[95] Thus, membership in a particular strategic group defines the essential characteristics of the firm's strategy.[96]

The notion of strategic groups can be useful for analyzing an industry's competitive structure. Such analyses can be helpful in diagnosing competition, positioning, and the profitability of firms within an industry.[97] High mobility barriers, high rivalry, and low resources among the firms within an industry will limit the formation of strategic groups.[98] However, research suggests that after strategic groups are formed, their membership remains relatively stable over time, making analysis easier and more useful.[99] Using strategic groups to understand an industry's competitive structure requires the firm to plot companies' competitive actions and competitive responses along strategic dimensions such as pricing decisions, product quality, distribution channels, and so forth. Doing this shows the firm how certain companies are competing similarly in terms of how they use similar strategic dimensions.

Strategic groups have several implications. First, because firms within a group offer similar products to the same customers, the competitive rivalry among them can be intense. The more intense the rivalry, the greater the threat to each firm's profitability. Second, the strengths of the five industry forces (the threats posed by new entrants, the power of suppliers, the power of buyers, product substitutes, and the intensity of rivalry among competitors) differ across strategic groups. Third, the closer the strategic groups are in terms of their strategies, the greater is the likelihood of rivalry between the groups.

Competitor Analysis

The competitor environment is the final part of the external environment requiring study. Competitor analysis focuses on each company against which a firm directly competes. For example, Air Canada and WestJet, Home Depot and Rona, the Richard Ivey School of Business and the Rotman School of Management, and CTV and Global National are Canadian organizations that should be keenly interested in understanding each other's objectives, strategies, assumptions, and capabilities. Furthermore, intense rivalry creates a strong need to understand competitors.[100] In a competitor analysis, the firm seeks to understand

- What drives the competitor, as shown by its *future objectives.*
- What the competitor is doing and can do, as revealed by its *current strategy.*
- What the competitor believes about the industry, as shown by its *assumptions.*
- What the competitor's capabilities are, as shown by its capabilities (its *strengths* and *weaknesses*).[101]

Information about these four dimensions helps the firm prepare an anticipated response profile for each competitor (see Figure 3.4). The results of an effective competitor analysis help a firm understand, interpret, and predict its competitors' actions and responses. Understanding the actions of competitors clearly contributes to the firm's ability to compete successfully within the industry.[102] Interestingly, research suggests that analyzing possible reactions to competitive moves is not often carried out by executives.[103] This suggests that those firms that do work at such analyses can obtain a competitive advantage over firms that do not.

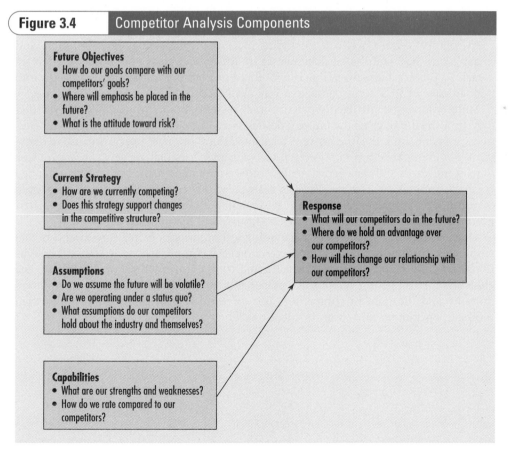

Figure 3.4   Competitor Analysis Components

Future Objectives
- How do our goals compare with our competitors' goals?
- Where will emphasis be placed in the future?
- What is the attitude toward risk?

Current Strategy
- How are we currently competing?
- Does this strategy support changes in the competitive structure?

Assumptions
- Do we assume the future will be volatile?
- Are we operating under a status quo?
- What assumptions do our competitors hold about the industry and themselves?

Capabilities
- What are our strengths and weaknesses?
- How do we rate compared to our competitors?

Response
- What will our competitors do in the future?
- Where do we hold an advantage over our competitors?
- How will this change our relationship with our competitors?

Competitor intelligence
is the set of data and
information the firm
gathers to better
understand and better
anticipate competitors'
objectives, strategies,
assumptions, and
capabilities.

Complementors are the
network of companies that
sell complementary goods
or services or are
compatible with the focal
firm's own product or
service.

Critical to an effective competitor analysis is gathering data and information that can help the firm understand its competitors' intentions and the strategic implications resulting from them.[104] Useful data and information combine to form **competitor intelligence**: the set of data and information the firm gathers to better understand and better anticipate competitors' objectives, strategies, assumptions, and capabilities. In competitor analysis, the firm should gather intelligence not only about its competitors, but also regarding public policies in countries around the world. Such intelligence facilitates an understanding of the strategic posture of foreign competitors.

Through effective competitive and public policy intelligence, the firm gains the insights needed to create a competitive advantage and to increase the quality of the strategic decisions it makes when deciding how to compete against its rivals.

One must also pay attention to the complementors of a firm's products and strategy.[105] **Complementors** are the network of companies that sell complementary goods or services or are compatible with the focal firm's own product or service. This could also include suppliers and buyers who have a strong "network" relationship with the focal firm. A strong network of complementors can solidify a competitive advantage. If a complementor's good or service adds value to the sale of the focal firm's good or service it is likely to create value for the focal firm.

Ethical Considerations

Firms should follow generally accepted ethical practices in gathering competitor intelligence. Industry associations often develop lists of these practices that firms can adopt. Practices considered both legal and ethical include (1) obtaining publicly available information (such as court records, competitors' help-wanted advertisements, annual reports, financial reports of publicly held corporations, and legal filings), and (2) attending trade fairs and shows to obtain competitors' brochures, view their exhibits, and listen to discussions about their products.

In contrast, certain practices (including blackmail, trespassing, eavesdropping, and stealing drawings, samples, or documents) are widely viewed as unethical and often are illegal. To protect themselves from digital fraud or theft by competitors that break into their employees' PCs, some companies buy insurance to protect against PC hacking.[106]

Some competitor intelligence practices may be legal, but a firm must decide whether they are also ethical, given the image it desires as a corporate citizen. Especially with electronic transmissions, the line between legal and ethical practices can be difficult to determine. For example, a firm may develop Web site addresses that are very similar to those of its competitors and thus occasionally receive e-mail transmissions that were intended for those competitors. The practice is an example of the challenges companies face when deciding how to gather intelligence about competitors while simultaneously determining what to do to prevent competitors from learning too much about them.

Open discussions of intelligence-gathering techniques can help a firm to ensure that employees, customers, suppliers, and even potential competitors understand its convictions to follow ethical practices for gathering competitor intelligence. An appropriate guideline for competitor intelligence practices is to respect the principles of common morality and the right of competitors not to reveal certain information about their products, operations, and strategic intentions.[107]

Summary

- The firm's external environment is challenging and complex. Because of the external environment's effect on performance, the firm must develop the skills required to identify opportunities and threats existing in that environment.

- The external environment has three major parts: (1) the general environment (elements in the broader society that affect industries and their firms), (2) the industry environment (factors that influence a firm, its competitive actions and responses, and the industry's profit potential), and (3) the competitor environment (in which the firm analyzes each major competitor's future objectives, current strategies, assumptions, and capabilities).

- The external environmental analysis process has four steps: scanning, monitoring, forecasting, and assessing. Through environmental analyses, the firm identifies opportunities and threats.

- The general environment has six segments: demographic, economic, political/legal, sociocultural, technological, and global. For each segment, the firm wants to determine the strategic relevance of environmental changes and trends.

- Compared with the general environment, the industry environment has a more direct effect on the firm's strategic actions. The five forces model of competition includes the threat of entry, the power of suppliers, the power of buyers, product substitutes, and the intensity of rivalry among competitors. By studying these forces, the firm finds a position in an industry where it can influence the forces in its favour or where it can buffer itself from the power of the forces in order to increase its ability to earn above-average returns.

- Industries are populated with different strategic groups. A strategic group is a collection of firms that follow similar strategies along similar dimensions. Competitive rivalry is greater within a strategic group than it is between strategic groups.

- Competitor analysis informs the firm about the future objectives, current strategies, assumptions, and capabilities of the companies with whom it competes directly. Firms should also examine complementors that sustain a competitor's strategy.

- Different techniques are used to create competitor intelligence: the set of data, information, and knowledge that allows the firm to better understand its competitors and thereby predict their likely strategic and tactical actions. Firms should use only legal and ethical practices to gather intelligence. The Internet enhances firms' capabilities to gather insights about competitors and their strategic intentions.

Review Questions

1. Why is it important for a firm to study and understand the external environment?

2. What are the differences between the general environment and the industry environment? Why are these differences important?

3. What is the external environmental analysis process? What does the firm want to learn when using this process?

4. What are the six segments of the general environment? Explain the differences among them.

5. How do the five forces of competition in an industry affect its profit potential? Explain.

6. What is a strategic group? Of what value is knowledge of the firm's strategic group in formulating that firm's strategy?

7. What is the importance of collecting and interpreting data and information about competitors? What practices should a firm use to gather competitor intelligence and why?

8. Discuss the ethical issues inherent in conducting general environment, industry environment, and competitor analyses. Go beyond what is discussed in the chapter.

Social Responsibility Review

1. In a perfectly competitive market, all businesses are price takers. Yet it seems that by our study on market forces in this chapter we are trying to ensure that our business does not become a price taker in a commodity market. Is this just business or an illegitimate attempt to thwart market forces? What does this mean for you as a customer, as a manager in the organization, or as a supplier to the organization?

2. Barriers to entry allow the formation of oligopolies. Such an industry structure tends to raise prices above what a perfectly

competitive market would create. Is it legitimate that businesses pursue barriers to entry to raise prices? Is it proper that duly elected governments fight such moves by business? Should suppliers and customers negotiate in such a way that organizations cease to be economically viable? Is this being socially responsible on the part of suppliers and customers?

3. Gathering information about the competition is critical for any organization, yet there are some methods that are immoral, if not illegal. In the chapter we mentioned the idea that a firm may develop Web site addresses that are very similar to those of its competitors and thus occasionally receive e-mail transmissions that were intended for those competitors. How legitimate a practice is this? Should it be illegal? Is it being socially responsible to engage in such practices?

Experiential Exercises

Industry Boundaries

Think about the nature of the following industries:

- Telecommunications
- Computers and peripheral equipment
- Computer software
- Consumer electronics

Work in groups to do the following exercises.

Part One

Establish the boundaries that your group thinks define each of the four industries. As you do so, identify the challenges you are experiencing in completing this task. Where there seems to be overlap and ambiguity, set out a decision rule for your classifications. One thing that may help your group decide on the boundaries is how the five forces apply to firms competing against each other. For example, you could ask if their products or services are "rivals," or "substitutes," for each other. Then identify 12 well-known Canadian and/or international firms that are currently important participants in one of these four industries. Please include Research In Motion, Telus, Bell Canada Enterprises, and Rogers Communications, for a total of 16 firms. Your selections must have at least four firms in each category.

Part Two

Go online to a business Web site such as finance.yahoo.ca and find its industry classification scheme for the firms you are examining. Next, obtain the annual reports to investors from a large Canadian mutual fund that invests broadly in the stock market and from a retirement equity fund, such as the one run by OMERS or another similar organization. These documents should be available on each organization's Web site. Study how each equity fund classifies the firms you are considering to complete this task. Compare your classification of industry boundaries with those developed by the investment funds. Are there differences between the industry boundaries you developed and those prepared by the investment fund companies? If so, what are the differences? As you study the differences, if any, do they make sense to you? Why or why not? What underlying assumptions might cause differences in the industry boundaries you are examining?

Part Three

Based on the information collected and the responses you prepared for Part Two above, answer the following questions:

- Do the different classifications of industry boundaries you observed create problems when firms try to analyze an industry? If so, describe those problems.
- What is the effect of different industry classifications on a firm's use of the five forces model to analyze an industry?
- What additional information, perspectives, and analysis would you suggest be a part of industry analysis in the light of your findings?

Strategic Groups and Restaurants

In Groups. Develop a strategic group map of the restaurant industry in your town. Establish strategic groups and offer a rationale for the groupings you have created. Explicitly identify the criteria for defining each group and for distinguishing it from the other groups. Include three to five competing restaurants in each strategic group and be prepared to discuss the competitive similarities of the restaurants within each strategic group and the competitive differences between and among the strategic groups.

Whole Class. Compare the different strategic group maps developed by the different groups in class. Each group should give the logic of its classification independent of what other groups say. Discuss the differences that may exist both in terms of the strategic group structure of the industry and where particular restaurants are placed within the group structure.

Five Forces and the Airline Industry

It is often noted that if all of the profits and losses ever reported by all publicly traded passenger airline companies in the United States were summed up, the total would be negative. With that one fact it might be easy to conclude that the airline industry is a tough one to be in. However, several firms operate profitably in the airline industry in the United States and in Canada. Some, such as WestJet (WJA), Southwest (LUV), JetBlue (JBLU), and AirTran (AAI), have done so quite regularly in recent years in spite of the industry's troubled times. Clearly, these firms' management teams have a sophisticated understanding of the forces that are at work in the airline industry. Using this understanding, these managers have found positions within a difficult industry in which their firms are protected against the profit-destroying potential of the five forces.

The five forces model can help you see how all of these firms shape their strategy to fit industry conditions when a careful and thoughtful application is made. In this exercise, you will both analyze the five forces that affect an industry and identify the ways adverse forces are being managed. Clearly, in the commercial passenger airline business there are many negative forces, and the solutions go beyond simplistic answers such as "cut costs" or "raise revenue." But note too that there are some positive aspects of the airline industry—aspects firms should exploit to their advantage.

In Groups. Using one of the pairs of airlines appearing below, your group will conduct an analysis that looks at the nature of each of the five forces affecting the industry and how the two firms in your pair are managing each force. For the "discount carrier" in your analysis, the management is likely part of an ongoing successful strategy. For the older "legacy carrier," the actions may be those managers have taken to restructure their firm after coming out of bankruptcy. Importantly, note that all management teams have to cope with industry forces. Moreover, regardless of their past performance, management must be working to position the firm so that negative forces are neutralized and positive ones are exploited.

- WestJet and Air Canada/Air Canada Jazz

- Southwest and US Airways/America West

- AirTran and United

- JetBlue and Delta

For the analysis of each force, note all of the key sources of profit impact your group identifies, both those that make it difficult to earn above-average returns and those that make it easier to earn above-average returns. Remember that every force is rich with multiple components that require thoughtful analysis and the application of economic principles. Use industry information sources from the business press, the Internet, stockbroker analysts, and other sources to gain a good understanding of the pressures managers face in this industry. Only after working through your analysis of each of the forces should your group turn to an analysis of the firm pair you have been assigned.

For each of the carriers you have been assigned, use the same multiple sources to gain an understanding of how each firm is coping with the specific force facing it. Note that answers such as "cutting costs" or "raising revenue" are incomplete in and of themselves without explaining how and why the actions will be effective in managing or exploiting an industry force.

After a classwide discussion of the group's conclusions on the nature of the five forces, each group will present its analysis of the pair it was assigned and the likely effectiveness of the managers' current actions.

	Rivalry Among Firms	Bargaining Power of Suppliers	Bargaining Power of Customers	Threat of New Entry	Threat of Substitutes
Analysis of the Force					
Discount Carrier's Current Response					
Legacy Carrier's Current Response					

Chapter 3 / The External Environment

1. C. Williams & W. Mitchell, 2004, Focusing firm evolution: The impact of information infrastructure on market entry by U.S. telecommunications companies, 1984–1998, *Management Science,* 5: 1561–1575; D. J. Ketchen Jr. & T. B. Palmer, 1999, Strategic responses to poor organizational performance: A test of competing perspectives, *Journal of Management,* 25: 683–706.

2. J. Tan, 2005, Venturing in turbulent water: A historical perspective of economic reform and entrepreneurial transformation, *Journal of Business Venturing,* 20: 689–704; J. T. Eckhardt & S. A. Shane, 2003, Opportunities and entrepreneurship, *Journal of Management,* 29: 333–349; P. Chattopadhyay, W. H. Glick, & G. P. Huber, 2001, Organizational actions in response to threats and opportunities, *Academy of Management Journal,* 44: 937–955.

3. J. Gimeno, R. E. Hoskisson, B. D. Beal, & W. P. Wan, 2005, Explaining the clustering of international expansion moves: A critical test in the U.S. telecommunications industry, *Academy of Management Journal,* 48: 297–319; C. M. Grimm, H. Lee, & K. G. Smith, 2005, *Strategy as Action: Competitive Dynamics and Competitive Advantages,* New York: Oxford University Press.

4. S. Rangan & A. Drummond, 2004, Explaining outcomes in competition among foreign multinationals in a focal host market, *Strategic Management Journal,* 25: 285–293; J. M. Mezias, 2002, Identifying liabilities of foreignness and strategies to minimize their effects: The case of labor lawsuit judgments in the United States, *Strategic Management Journal,* 23: 229–244.

5. K. G. Smith, C. J. Collins, & K. D. Clark, 2005, Existing knowledge, knowledge creation capability, and the rate of new product introduction in high-technology firms, *Academy of Management Journal,* 48: 346–357.

6. R. M. Grant, 2003, Strategic planning in a turbulent environment: Evidence from the oil majors, *Strategic Management Journal,* 24: 491–517.

7. M. Song, C. Droge, S. Hanvanich, & R. Calantone, 2005, Marketing and technology resource complementarity: An analysis of their interaction effect in two environmental contexts, *Strategic Management Journal,* 26: 259–276; D. M. De Carolis, 2003, Competencies and imitability in the pharmaceutical industry: An analysis of their relationship with firm performance, *Journal of Management,* 29: 27–50.

8. L. Fahey, 1999, *Competitors,* New York: John Wiley & Sons; B. A. Walters & R. L. Priem, 1999, Business strategy and CEO intelligence acquisition, *Competitive Intelligence Review,* 10(2): 15–22.

9. R. E. Hoskisson, M. A. Hitt, W. P. Wan, & D. Yiu, 1999, Swings of a pendulum: Theory and research in strategic management, *Journal of Management,* 25: 417–456.

10. E. H. Bowman & C. E. Helfat, 2001, Does corporate strategy matter? *Strategic Management Journal,* 22: 1–23.

11. J. Shamsie, 2003, The context of dominance: An industry-driven framework for exploiting reputation, *Strategic Management Journal,* 24: 199–215; A. Seth & H. Thomas, 1994, Theories of the firm: Implications for strategy research, *Journal of Management Studies,* 31: 165–191.

12. Seth & Thomas, 169–173.

13. L. F. Feldman, C. G. Brush, & T. Manolova, 2005, Co-alignment in the resource-performance relationship: Strategy as mediator, *Journal of Business Venturing,* 20: 359–383.

14. M. E. Porter, 1985, *Competitive Advantage,* New York: Free Press; M. E. Porter, 1980, *Competitive Strategy,* New York: Free Press.

15. A. M. McGahan, 1999, Competition, strategy and business performance, *California Management Review,* 41(3): 74–101; McGahan & Porter, How much does industry matter, really?

16. R. Henderson & W. Mitchell, 1997, The interactions of organizational and competitive influences on strategy and performance, *Strategic Management Journal,* 18 (Special Issue): 5–14; C. Oliver, 1997, Sustainable competitive advantage: Combining institutional and resource-based views, *Strategic Management Journal,* 18: 697–713; J. L. Stimpert & I. M. Duhaime, 1997, Seeing the big picture: The influence of industry, diversification, and business strategy on performance, *Academy of Management Journal,* 40: 560–583.

17. R. D. Ireland & M. A. Hitt, 1999, Achieving and maintaining strategic competitiveness in the 21st century: The role of strategic leadership, *Academy of Management Executive,* 13(1): 43–57; M. A. Hitt, B. W. Keats, & S. M. DeMarie, 1998, Navigating in the new competitive landscape: Building strategic flexibility and competitive advantage in the 21st century, *Academy of Management Executive,* 12(4): 22–42.

18. L. Välikangas & M. Gibbert, 2005, Boundary-setting strategies for escaping innovation traps, *MIT Sloan Management Review,* 46(3): 58–65; Q. Nguyen & H. Mintzberg, 2003, The rhythm of change, *MIT Sloan Management Review,* 44(4): 79–84.

19. T. Perkins, 2007, They'll even plan your funeral, *Globe and Mail Report on Business,* September 29.

20. G. Panagiotou, 2003, Bring SWOT into focus, *Business Strategy Review,* 14(2): 8–10.

21. D. Ljunggren, 2007, Aging population poses problems for Canada: Report, Reuters, July 17.

22. K. Y. Au & J. Fukuda, 2002, Boundary spanning behaviors of expatriates, *Journal of World Business,* 37(4): 285–296; L. Rosenkopf & A. Nerkar, 2001, Beyond local search: Boundary-spanning exploration, and impact in the optical disk industry, *Strategic Management Journal,* 22: 287–306.

23. K. M. Patton & T. M. McKenna, 2005, Scanning for competitive intelligence, *Competitive Intelligence Magazine,* 8(2): 24–26; D. F. Kuratko, R. D. Ireland, & J. S. Hornsby, 2001, Improving firm performance through entrepreneurial actions: Acordia's corporate entrepreneurship strategy, *Academy of Management Executive,* 15(4): 60–71.

24. K. M. Eisenhardt, 2002, Has strategy changed? *MIT Sloan Management Review,* 43(2): 88–91; I. Goll & A. M. A. Rasheed, 1997, Rational decision-making and firm performance: The moderating role of environment, *Strategic Management Journal,* 18: 583–591.

25. J. R. Hough & M. A. White, 2004, Scanning actions and environmental dynamism: Gathering information for strategic decision making, *Management Decision,* 42: 781–793; V. K. Garg, B. A. Walters, & R. L. Priem, 2003, Chief executive scanning emphases, environmental dynamism, and manufacturing firm performance, *Strategic Management Journal,* 24: 725–744.

26. C.-P. Wei & Y.-H. Lee, 2004, Event detection from online news documents for supporting environmental scanning, *Decision Support Systems,* 36: 385–401.

27. Fahey, *Competitors,* 71–73.

28. 2007, Launch pad for entrepreneurs, *National Post,* October 4, JV1–JV2.

29. K. Buysse & A. Verbke, 2003, Proactive strategies: A stakeholder management perspective, *Strategic Management Journal,* 24: 453–470; I. M. Jawahar & G. L. McLaughlin, 2001, Toward a prescriptive stakeholder theory: An organizational life cycle approach, *Academy of Management Review,* 26: 397–414.

30. M. L. Perry, S. Sengupta, & R. Krapfel, 2004, Effectiveness of horizontal strategic alliances in technologically uncertain environments: Are trust and commitment enough, *Journal of Business Research,* 9: 951–956; M. Song & M. M. Montoya-Weiss, 2001, The effect of perceived technological uncertainty on Japanese new product development, *Academy of Management Journal,* 44: 61–80.

31. M. H. Zack, 2003, Rethinking the knowledge-based organization, *MIT Sloan Management Review,* 44(4): 67–71; H. Yli-Renko, E. Autio, & H. J. Sapienza, 2001, Social capital, knowledge acquisition, and knowledge exploitation in young technologically based firms, *Strategic Management Journal,* 22 (Special Issue): 587–613.

32. Fahey, *Competitors.*

33. Fahey, *Competitors,* 75–77.

34. K. M. Sutcliffe & K. Weber, 2003, The high cost of accurate knowledge, *Harvard Business Review,* 81(5): 74–82.

35. L. Fahey & V. K. Narayanan, 1986, *Macroenvironmental Analysis for Strategic Management,* St. Paul, MN: West Publishing Company, 58.

36. 2004, World population prospects: 2004 revision, www.un.org/esa/population/unpop.htm; 1999, Six billion . . . and counting, *Time,* October 4, 16; 2008, World Census Data, U.S. Census Bureau, http://www.census.gov/cgi-bin/ipc/idbagg, retrieved February 27.

37. 2007, Canada's population estimates, http://www.statcan.ca/Daily/English/071219/d071219b.htm, December 19, accessed January 3, 2008.

38. S. Moffett, 2005, Fast-aging Japan keeps its elders on the job longer, *Wall Street Journal,* June 15, A1, A8.

39. T. Fennell, 2005, The next 50 years, www.camagazine.com, April.

40. Ibid.

41. 2007, Study: Unemployment in Canada's metropolitan areas, http://www .statcan.ca/Daily/English/070125/d070125b.htm, January 25, accessed January 3, 2008.

42. J. A. Chatman & S. E. Spataro, 2005, Using self-categorization theory to understand relational demography-based variations in people's responsiveness to organizational culture, *Academy of Management Journal,* 48: 321–331.

43. E. S. Rubenstein, 1999, Inequality, *Forbes,* November 1, 158–160.

44. R. Konopaske, C. Robie, & J. M. Ivancevich, 2005, A preliminary model of spouse influence on managerial global assignment willingness, *International Journal of Human Resource Management,* 16: 405–426.

45. Fahey & Narayanan, *Macroenvironmental Analysis,* 105.

46. [1]J.-P. Bonardi, A. J. Hillman, & G. D. Keim, 2005, The attractiveness of political markets: Implications for firm strategy, *Academy of Management Review,* 30: 397-413; G. Keim, 2001, Business and public policy: Competing in the political marketplace, in M. A. Hitt, R. E. Freeman, and J. S. Harrison (eds.), *Handbook of Strategic Management,* Oxford, UK: Blackwell Publishers, 583–601.

47. M. D. Lord, 2003, Constituency building as the foundation for corporate political strategy, *Academy of Management Executive,* 17(1): 112–124; D. A. Schuler, K. Rehbein, & R. D. Cramer, 2003, Pursuing strategic advantage through political means: A multivariate approach, *Academy of Management Journal,* 45: 659–672; A. J. Hillman & M. A. Hitt, 1999, Corporate political strategy formulation: A model of approach, participation, and strategy decisions, *Academy of Management Review,* 24: 825–842.

48. C. Hutzler, 2005, Beijing rescinds textile duties, slams U.S., EU on import limits, *Wall Street Journal,* May 31, A3.

49. D. M. Schweiger, T. Atamer, & R. Calori, 2003, Transnational project teams and networks: Making the multinational organization more effective, *Journal of World Business,* 38: 127–140; G. Dessler, 1999, How to earn your employees' commitment, *Academy of Management Executive,* 13(2): 58–67.

50. L. H. Pelled, K. M. Eisenhardt, & K. R. Xin, 1999, Exploring the black box: An analysis of work group diversity, conflict, and performance, *Administrative Science Quarterly,* 44: 1–28.

51. C. A. Bartlett & S. Ghoshal, 2002, Building competitive advantage through people, *MIT Sloan Management Review,* 43(2): 33–41.

52. M. E. A. Jayne & R. L. Dipboye, 2004, Leveraging diversity to improve business performance: Research findings and recommendations for organizations, *Human Resource Management,* 43: 409–425.

53. A. L. Porter & S. W. Cunningham, 2004, *Tech mining: Exploiting new technologies for competitive advantage,* Hoboken, NJ: Wiley.

54. C. W. L. Hill & F. T. Rothaermel, 2003, The performance of incumbent firms in the face of radical technological innovation, *Academy of Management Review,* 28: 257–274; A. Afuah, 2002, Mapping technological capabilities into product markets and competitive advantage: The case of cholesterol drugs, *Strategic Management Journal,* 23: 171–179.

55. J. Baglole, 2003, Canada's southern drug drain, Wall Street Journal Online, www.wsj.com, March 31.

56. N. Wingfield, 2003, Anytime, anywhere: The number of Wi-Fi spots is set to explode, bringing the wireless technology to the rest of us, *Wall Street Journal,* March 31, R6, R12.

57. A. Andal-Ancion, P. A. Cartwright, & G. S. Yip, 2003, The digital transformation of traditional businesses, *MIT Sloan Management Review,* 44(4): 34–41; M. A. Hitt, R. D. Ireland, & H. Lee, 2000, Technological learning, knowledge management, firm growth and performance, *Journal of Technology and Engineering Management,* 17: 231–246.

58. Y. Y. Kor & J. T. Mahoney, 2005, How dynamics, management, and governance of resource deployments influence firm-level performance, *Strategic Management Journal,* 26: 489–497; C. Nichols-Nixon & C. Y. Woo, 2003, Technology sourcing and output of established firms in a regime of encompassing technological change, *Strategic Management Journal,* 24: 651–666.

59. W. P. Wan, 2005, Country resource environments, firm capabilities, and corporate diversification strategies, *Journal of Management Studies,* 42: 161–182; M. Wright, I. Filatotchev, R. E. Hoskisson, & M. W. Peng, 2005, Strategy research in emerging economies: Challenging the conventional wisdom, *Journal of Management Studies,* 42: 1–30; W. P. Wan & R. E. Hoskisson, 2003, Home country environments, corporate diversification strategies and firm performance, *Academy of Management Journal,* 46: 27–45.

60. F. Vermeulen & H. Barkema, 2002, Pace, rhythm, and scope: Process dependence in building a multinational corporation, *Strategic Management Journal,* 23: 637–653.

61. J. Lu & P. Beamish, 2004, International diversification and firm performance: The S-curve hypothesis, *Academy of Management Journal,* 47: 598–609; L. Tihanyi, R. A. Johnson, R. E. Hoskisson, & M. A. Hitt, 2003, Institutional ownership differences, and international diversification: The effects of boards of directors and technological opportunity, *Academy of Management Journal,* 46: 195–211.

62. G. D. Bruton & D. Ahlstrom, 2002, An institutional view of China's venture capital industry: Explaining the differences between China and the West, *Journal of Business Venturing,* 18: 233–259.

63. M. Fong, 2005, Unphased by barriers, retailers flock to China for clothes, *Wall Street Journal,* May 27, B1, B2.

64. 2005, Telus International Inc. and Singapore Computer Systems Ltd. form strategic partnership to invest in Ambergris Solution, Outsource 2 Philippines, http://www.outsource2philippines.com/news/020505.asp, retrieved February 29, 2008.

65. K. Cattani, E. Dahan, & G. Schmidt, 2005, Offshoring versus "Spackling," *MIT Sloan Management Review,* 46(3): 6–7.

66. R. D. Ireland, M. A. Hitt, S. M. Camp, & D. L. Sexton, 2001, Integrating entrepreneurship and strategic management actions to create firm wealth, *Academy of Management Executive,* 15(1): 49–63.

67. Z. Emden, A. Yaprak, & S. T. Cavusgil, 2005, Learning from experience in international alliances: Antecedents and firm performance implications, *Journal of Business Research,* 58: 883–892; M. Subramaniam & N. Venkataraman, 2001, Determinants of transnational new product development capability: Testing the influence of transferring and deploying tacit overseas knowledge, *Strategic Management Journal,* 22: 359–378.

68. G. D. Bruton, D. Ahlstrom, & J. C. Wan, 2003, Turnaround in East Asian firms: Evidence from ethnic overseas Chinese communities, *Strategic Management Journal,* 24: 519–540; S. H. Park & Y. Luo, 2001, Guanxi and organizational dynamics: Organizational networking in Chinese firms, *Strategic Management Journal,* 22: 455–477; M. A. Hitt, M. T. Dacin, B. B. Tyler, & D. Park, 1997, Understanding the differences in Korean and U.S. executives' strategic orientations, *Strategic Management Journal,* 18: 159–167.

69. M. A. Hitt, D. Ahlstrom, M. T. Dacin, E. Levitas, & L. Svobodina, 2004, The institutional effects on strategic alliance partner selection: China versus Russia, *Organization Science,* 15: 173–185.

70. Park & Luo, Guanxi and organizational dynamics.

71. M. A. Hitt, H. Lee, & E. Yucel, 2002, The importance of social capital to the management of multinational enterprises: Relational capital among Asian and Western firms, *Asia Pacific Journal of Management,* 19: 353–372.

72. W. R. Banhonacker, 2004, When good guanxi turns bad, *Harvard Business Review,* 82(4): 18–21.

73. C. A. Bartlett & S. Ghoshal, 2003, What is a global manager? *Harvard Business Review,* 81(8): 101–108; M. A. Carpenter & J. W. Fredrickson, 2001, Top management teams, global strategic posture and the moderating role of uncertainty, *Academy of Management Journal,* 44: 533–545.

74. V. K. Narayanan & L. Fahey, 2005, The relevance of the institutional underpinnings of Porter's five forces framework to emerging economies: An epistemological analysis, *Journal of Management Studies,* 42: 207–223; N. Argyres & A. M. McGahan, 2002, An interview with Michael Porter, *Academy of Management Executive,* 16(2): 43–52; Y. E. Spanos & S. Lioukas, 2001, An examination into the causal logic of rent generation: Contrasting Porter's competitive strategy framework and the resource-based perspective, *Strategic Management Journal,* 22: 907–934.

75. G. Hawawini, V. Subramanian, & P. Verdin, 2003, Is performance driven by industry or firm-specific factors? A new look at the evidence, *Strategic Management Journal,* 24: 1–16.

76. S. Zaheer & A. Zaheer, 2001, Market microstructure in a global b2b network, *Strategic Management Journal,* 22: 859–873.

77. Hitt, Ricart, Costa, & Nixon, The new frontier.

78. Gimeno, Hoskisson, Beal, & Wan, Explaining the clustering of international expansion moves; C. Garcia-Pont & N. Nohria, 2002, Local versus global mimetism: The dynamics of alliance formation in the automobile industry, *Strategic Management Journal,* 23: 307–321.

79. E. D. Jaffe, I. D. Nebenzahl, & I. Schorr, 2005, Strategic options of home country firms faced with MNC entry, *Long Range Planning,* 38(2): 183–196.

80. J. Shamsie, 2003, The context of dominance: An industry-driven framework for exploiting reputation, *Strategic Management Journal,* 24: 199–215; K. C. Robinson & P. P. McDougall, 2001, Entry barriers and new venture performance: A comparison of universal and contingency approaches, *Strategic Management Journal,* 22 (Special Issue): 659–685.

81. R. Makadok, 1999, Interfirm differences in scale economies and the evolution of market shares, *Strategic Management Journal,* 20: 935–952.

82. B. J. Pine II, 2004, Mass customization: The new imperative, *Strategic Direction,* January, 2–3.

83. F. Keenan, S. Holmes, J. Greene, & R. O. Crockett, 2002, A mass market of one, *BusinessWeek,* December 2, 68–72.

84. D. Michaels, 2003, World business (a special report): Victory at sea: How did a French company capture several British naval contracts? Think "multidomestic," *Wall Street Journal Europe,* September 26, R5.

85. J. L. Lunsford & D. Michaels, 2005, New orders: After four years in the rear, Boeing is set to jet past Airbus, *Wall Street Journal,* June 10, A1.

86. J. Angwin & J. T. Hallinan, 2005, Newspaper circulation continues to decline, forcing tough decisions, *Wall Street Journal,* May 2, A1, A6.

87. S. Dutta, O. Narasimhan, & S. Rajiv, 2005, Conceptualizing and measuring capabilities: Methodology and empirical application, *Strategic Management Journal,* 26: 277–285; A. M. Knott, 2003, Persistent heterogeneity and sustainable innovation, *Strategic Management Journal,* 24: 687–705; T. Noda & D. J. Collies, 2001, The evolution of intraindustry firm heterogeneity: Insights from a process study, *Academy of Management Journal,* 44: 897–925.

88. C. Richard, 2005, Small investors rethink auto bonds; Sector starts to recover after GM, Ford downgrades take toll on retail holders, *Wall Street Journal,* June 15, D3.

89. Lunsford & Michaels, New orders: After four years in the rear, Boeing is set to jet past Airbus; C. Matlack & S. Holmes, 2002, Look out, Boeing: Airbus is grabbing market share, but can it make money this way? *BusinessWeek,* October 28, 50–51.

90. D. M. De Carolis, 2003, Competencies and imitability in the pharmaceutical industry: An analysis of their relationship with firm performance, *Journal of Management,* 29: 27–50; D. L. Deephouse, 1999, To be different, or to be the same? It's a question (and theory) of strategic balance, *Strategic Management Journal,* 20: 147–166.

91. K. D. Brouthers, L. E. Brouthers, & S. Werner, 2003, Transaction cost-enhanced entry mode choices and firm performance, *Strategic Management Journal,* 24: 1239–1248.

92. M. E. Porter, 1980, *Competitive Strategy,* New York: Free Press.

93. M. S. Hunt, 1972, Competition in the major home appliance industry, 1960–1970 (doctoral dissertation, Harvard University); Porter, *Competitive Strategy,* 129.

94. G. McNamara, D. L. Deephouse, & R. A. Luce, 2003, Competitive positioning within and across a strategic group structure: The performance of core, secondary, and solitary firms, *Strategic Management Journal,* 24: 161–181.

95. H. R. Greve, 1999, Managerial cognition and the mimetic adoption of market positions: What you see is what you do, *Strategic Management Journal,* 19: 967–988.

96. M. W. Peng, J. Tan, & T. W. Tong, 2004, Ownership types and strategic groups in an emerging economy, *Journal of Management Studies,* 41: 1105–1129; R. K. Reger & A. S. Huff, 1993, Strategic groups: A cognitive perspective, *Strategic Management Journal,* 14: 103–123.

97. M. Peteraf & M. Shanley, 1997, Getting to know you: A theory of strategic group identity, *Strategic Management Journal,* 18 (Special Issue): 165–186.

98. J. Lee, K. Lee, & S. Rho, 2002, An evolutionary perspective on strategic group emergence: A genetic algorithm-based model, *Strategic Management Journal,* 23: 727–746.

99. J. A. Zuniga-Vicente, J. M. de la Fuente Sabate, & I. S. Gonzalez, 2004, Dynamics of the strategic group membership–performance linkage in rapidly changing environments, *Journal of Business Research,* 57: 1378–1390; J. D. Osborne, C. I. Stubbart, & A. Ramaprasad, 2001, Strategic groups and competitive enactment: A study of dynamic relationships between mental models and performance, *Strategic Management Journal,* 22: 435–454.

100. Gimeno, Hoskisson, Beal, & Wan, Explaining the clustering of international expansion moves.

101. Porter, *Competitive Strategy,* 49.

102. G. McNamara, R. A. Luce, & G. H. Tompson, 2002, Examining the effect of complexity in strategic group knowledge structures on firm performance, *Strategic Management Journal,* 23: 153–170.

103. D. B. Montgomery, M. C. Moore, & J. E. Urbany, 2005, Reasoning about competitive reactions: Evidence from executives, *Marketing Science,* 24: 138–149.

104. P. M. Norman, R. D. Ireland, K. W. Artz, & M. A. Hitt, 2000, Acquiring and using competitive intelligence in entrepreneurial teams, paper presented at the Academy of Management, Toronto.

105. A. Afuah, 2000, How much do your co-opetitors' capabilities matter in the face of technological change? *Strategic Management Journal,* 21: 387; A. Brandenburger & B. Nalebuff, 1996, *Co-opetition,* New York: Currency Doubleday.

106. V. Drucker, 1999, Is your computer a sitting duck during a deal? *Mergers & Acquisitions,* July/August, 25–28.

107. A. Crane, 2005, In the company of spies: When competitive intelligence gathering becomes industrial espionage, *Business Horizons,* 48(3): 233–240.

Chapter Four

The Internal Environment: Resources, Capabilities, and Core Competencies

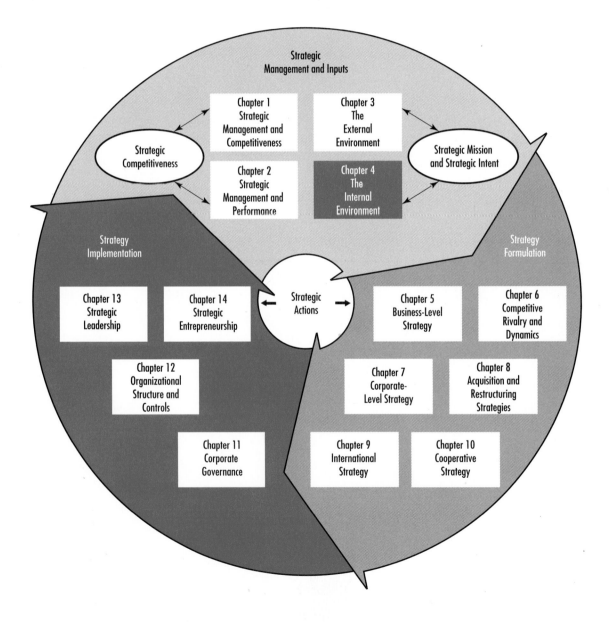

Knowledge Objectives

Studying this chapter should provide you with the strategic management knowledge needed to:

1. Explain the need for firms to study and understand their internal environment.

2. Define value and discuss its importance.

3. Describe the differences between tangible and intangible resources.

4. Define capabilities and discuss how they are developed.

5. Describe four criteria used to determine whether resources and capabilities are core competencies.

6. Explain how value chain analysis is used to identify and evaluate resources and capabilities.

7. Define outsourcing and discuss the reasons for its use.

8. Discuss the importance of identifying internal strengths and weaknesses.

9. Discuss the importance of preventing core competencies from becoming core rigidities.

The Capability to Innovate: A Critical Source of Competitive Advantage

According to the final report on the National Innovation Initiative issued by the U.S. Council on Competitiveness, innovation is the most important factor in determining a company's success in the 21st century. While many firms have become highly efficient in the past 25 years, they must become more innovative in the next 25 years and beyond to develop sustainable competitive advantages. The world is becoming more interconnected and competitive because of increasing globalization. The competitive landscape is becoming more level across countries as firms in some emerging markets are now global competitors. Certainly, firms from China, India, and Russia are competing effectively in global markets.

www.petsmart.com

Enhanced competition has made innovation increasingly important in all types of markets. Incremental improvements in products and processes are no longer enough to sustain a competitive advantage in many industries. In the pet care industry, PetSmart is one the most innovative. PetSmart operates in Canada and the United States and is the leader among retail chains in the sale of specialty pet services and supplies. These services include Doggie Day Care, PetSmart PetsHotel dog and cat boarding facilities, and dog training and grooming. It holds the largest market share in the pet retail industry mainly because it continues to offer consumers greater value than its competitors through innovative services.

Pet ownership is growing at about two times the rate of the human demographic. This demographic fact has led to a growing market for pet care and supplies. PetSmart has 11 percent market share, with its next closest competitor, PETCO, at 6 percent.

The change in name from PETsMart to PetSmart in 2005 represented a change in attitude for the company. The strategy behind this rebranding was to "emphasize its [PetSmart's] evolution from a pet supply store to a solutions-oriented company." In addition to having an extensive list of products, the company now provides many innovative services for pets such as grooming, obedience training, and boarding. Pet-styling salons have become very popular among customers, and the PetsHotel—which offers temperature-controlled rooms for dogs and cats with daily special treats, 24-hour care, and a veterinarian on call—attracts many pet lovers. As of January 2008 PetSmart operated more than 993 stores, with 55 in Canada and the rest in the United States.

According to a report by Citigroup Inc., an American financial services company, PetSmart's service business grew by more than 25 percent on a compound annual basis from 2001 to 2006. This was only 8 percent of sales in 2006 but was expected to grow to over 15 percent of sales by 2011. PetsHotel gave same-store sales at maturity a 25-percent increase and significantly increased each store's operating margins. The addition of PetsHotel started with seven stores in 2004; at the beginning of 2008 there were PetsHotel facilities in more than 87 locations, with two in Ontario. The addition of services such as the PetsHotel is innovative and is helping improve PetSmart's bottom line.

PetSmart is also socially conscious. Since 1994, the independent non-profit animal welfare organization PetSmart Charities, Inc. has kept more than 3 million pets alive through its in-store pet adoption programs and donated over $52 million to animal welfare programs.

SOURCES: 2007, Wikipedia, PetSmart, http://en.wikipedia.org/wiki/PetsMart, accessed November 11; 2006, PETsMART and Petco duke it out for Fido's attention, June 28, http://seekingalpha.com/article/12710-petsmart-and-petco-duke-it-out-for-fido-s-attention-petm-petc, accessed November 11, 2007; 2008, http://phx.corporate-ir.net/phoenix.zhtml?c=93506&p=irol-homeprofile, accessed January 4.

As discussed in Chapter 3, several factors in the global economy, including the rapid development of the Internet's capabilities[1] and of globalization in general, have made it increasingly difficult for firms to develop a competitive advantage that can be sustained for any period of calendar time.[2] In these instances, firms try to create sustained advantages, but they are unlikely to do so unless they continually produce innovative products.[3] As illustrated in the Opening Case, PetSmart has used innovative services to sustain its competitive advantage in the pet goods and services industry.

Another example of continual growth and innovation is Nokia Corporation, the world's largest manufacturer of mobile telephones. As of the third quarter in 2007, Nokia boasted an impressive 39-percent market share in the global device industry.[4] Nokia has made significant internal changes to improve its innovative capabilities, which helps it compete with companies like Motorola, Microsoft, and Apple.

In 2004, Nokia re-organized its corporate structure to encompass four business units: Mobile Phones, Multimedia, Networks, and Enterprise Solutions.[5] By dividing its company into separate business units, each proponent could then receive greater attention and autonomy to innovate. Each division focused on obtaining key consumer insights and developing successful products to help the firm gain and sustain a competitive advantage.

Many firms today are reshaping their business models and restructuring their organizations in ways similar to the changes exemplified by Nokia. In adapting its organizational structure further to make its "product development and manufacturing operations more effective and reduce the time it takes to bring new products to market,"[6] Nokia recently said it was planning another restructuring. According to a 2007 article in *PC World*, an American computer magazine, Nokia will attempt to "fold all its mobile phone development efforts into a single new business unit" because of its growth in Internet-enabled devices and multimedia products.[7] This roll-up in structure means that mobile devices that were previously developed by separate divisions will now be produced under one division. These changes, as well as the creation of two new divisions (Software and Services, and Markets), will comprise the company's new structure. These changes were expected to be in effect by January 1, 2008, according to *PC World*.[8]

Innovative capabilities have become critical in order for companies to remain competitive and maintain market share. Companies such as Procter & Gamble, General Electric (GE), and Johnson & Johnson have been changing their cultures and their business models in order to enhance their innovation output to remain highly competitive in the current environment.[9] Firms must have not only the correct structure, as Nokia has attempted to build, but also the appropriate resources to build innovative capabilities. The probability of developing a sustainable competitive advantage increases when firms use their own *unique* resources, capabilities, and core competencies as a base on which to implement their strategies.[10]

Competitive advantages and the differences they create in firm performance are often strongly related to the resources firms hold and how they are managed.[11] "Resources are the foundation for strategy and unique bundles of resources generate competitive advantages leading to wealth creation."[12] To identify and successfully use their resources over time, leading firms need to think constantly about how to manage them (how to organize to exploit them) to increase the value for customers.[13] As this chapter shows, firms achieve strategic competitiveness and earn above-average returns when their unique core competencies are effectively acquired, bundled, and leveraged to take advantage of opportunities in the external environment.[14]

People are an especially critical resource for producing innovation and gaining a competitive advantage.[15] Even if they are not as critical in some industries as in others, they are necessary for the development and implementation of firms' strategies.[16] In fact, because of the importance of talented employees, a global labour market now exists.

According to "Innovation and Creativity in City Regions," a presentation at the University of Toronto by David Wolfe, the single most important factor for developing innovation is attracting talented people.[17] In agreement with this is American economist Richard Florida, who argues that, "[W]herever talent goes, innovation, creativity, and economic growth are sure to follow."[18] In other words, talented individuals naturally gravitate toward cities and organizations that have more creative thought and innovative projects in the pipeline.[19] And, economic growth follows—a virtuous cycle.

In time, the benefits of any firm's value-creating strategy can be duplicated by competitors; all competitive advantages have a limited life.[20] The question of duplication is not *if* it will happen, but when. In general, the sustainability of a competitive advantage is a function of three factors: (1) the rate of core competency obsolescence because of environmental changes, (2) the availability of substitutes for the core competency, and (3) the imitability of the core competency.[21]

The challenge in all firms is to effectively manage current core competencies while simultaneously developing new ones.[22] Managing effectively (being organized to exploit) means having the right structure, control systems, and reward systems to support each core competency. Only when firms develop a continuous stream of resources and capabilities that are supported through effective structures, control systems, and reward systems, and that contribute to competitive advantages, do they achieve strategic competitiveness, earn above-average returns, and remain ahead of competitors (see Chapter 6).

In Chapter 3, we examined general, industry, and competitor environments to assess what a firm *needs to do*. Armed with this knowledge about the realities and conditions of their external environment, firms have a better understanding of marketplace opportunities and the characteristics of the competitive environment in which they exist. In this chapter, we focus on the firm and its resource and capabilities. By analyzing its internal environment, a firm determines what it *can do*—that is, the actions permitted by its unique resources, capabilities, and core competencies. As discussed in Chapter 1, core competencies are a firm's source of competitive advantage. The magnitude of that competitive advantage is a function primarily of the uniqueness of the firm's core competencies.[23] Matching what a firm can do with what it needs to do (a function of opportunities and threats in the external environment) allows the firm to develop vision, pursue its mission, and select and implement its strategies.

We begin this chapter with a review of the resource-based model of above-average returns. We continue with a discussion of the nature of a firm's internal environment analysis. We then discuss the roles of resources and capabilities in developing core competencies, which are the sources of the firm's competitive advantages. Included in this discussion are the techniques firms can use to identify and evaluate resources and capabilities and the criteria for selecting core competencies from among them. Resources and capabilities are not inherently valuable, but they create value when the firm can use them to perform certain activities that result in a competitive advantage. Accordingly, we also discuss in this chapter the value chain concept and examine four criteria to evaluate core competencies that establish competitive advantage.[24] The chapter closes with cautionary comments about the need for firms to prevent their core competencies from becoming core rigidities. The existence of core rigidities indicates that the firm is too anchored to its past, which prevents it from continuously developing new competitive advantages.

The Resource-Based Model of Above-Average Returns

The resource-based model assumes that each organization is a collection of resources and capabilities, a few of which are unique and provide the basis for a firm's strategy and its primary source of above-average returns. This model suggests that capabilities evolve and must be managed dynamically in pursuit of above-average returns.[25] According to the model, differences in firms' performances across time are due primarily to their unique resources and capabilities rather than the structural characteristics of the industry in which they operate. This model also assumes that firms acquire different resources and develop unique capabilities. Therefore, not all firms competing within a particular industry possess the same resources and capabilities. Additionally, the model assumes that resources may not be highly mobile across firms and that the differences in resources are the basis of competitive advantage.

Resources are inputs into a firm's production process, such as capital equipment, the skills of individual employees, patents, finances, and talented managers. In general, a firm's resources can be classified into three categories: physical, human, and organizational capital. As described later in this chapter, resources are either tangible or intangible in nature.

Individual resources alone may not yield a competitive advantage.[26] In general, competitive advantages are formed through the combination and integration of sets of resources. A **capability** is the capacity for a set of resources to perform a task or an activity in an integrative manner. Through the firm's continued use, capabilities become stronger and more difficult for competitors to understand and imitate. As a source of competitive advantage, a capability "should be neither so simple that it is highly imitable, nor so complex that it defies internal steering and control."[27]

The resource-based model of superior returns is shown in Figure 4.1. Instead of focusing on the accumulation of resources necessary to implement the strategy dictated by

Resources are inputs into a firm's production process, such as capital equipment, the skills of individual employees, patents, finances, and talented managers.

A **capability** is the capacity for a set of resources to perform a task or an activity in an integrative manner.

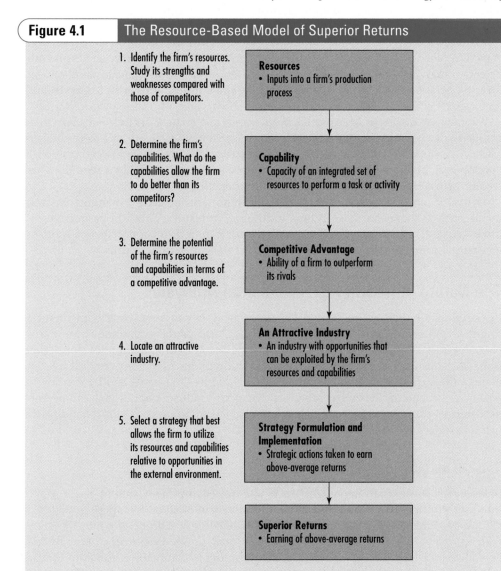

Figure 4.1 | The Resource-Based Model of Superior Returns

1. Identify the firm's resources. Study its strengths and weaknesses compared with those of competitors.

Resources
- Inputs into a firm's production process

2. Determine the firm's capabilities. What do the capabilities allow the firm to do better than its competitors?

Capability
- Capacity of an integrated set of resources to perform a task or activity

3. Determine the potential of the firm's resources and capabilities in terms of a competitive advantage.

Competitive Advantage
- Ability of a firm to outperform its rivals

4. Locate an attractive industry.

An Attractive Industry
- An industry with opportunities that can be exploited by the firm's resources and capabilities

5. Select a strategy that best allows the firm to utilize its resources and capabilities relative to opportunities in the external environment.

Strategy Formulation and Implementation
- Strategic actions taken to earn above-average returns

Superior Returns
- Earning of above-average returns

conditions and constraints in the external environment (see "The I/O Model of Above-Average Returns" in Chapter 3), the resource-based view suggests that a firm's unique resources and capabilities provide the basis for a strategy. The strategy chosen should allow the firm to better exploit its core competencies relative to opportunities in the external environment.

Not all of a firm's resources and capabilities have the potential to be the basis for competitive advantage. This potential is realized when resources and capabilities are valuable, rare, costly to imitate, and organized to be exploited.[28] Resources are *valuable* when they allow a firm to take advantage of opportunities or neutralize threats in its external environment. They are *rare* when possessed by few, if any, current and potential competitors. Resources are *costly to imitate* when other firms either cannot obtain them or are at a cost disadvantage in obtaining them, compared with the firm that already possesses them. Finally, resources are *organized to be exploited* when they have the appropriate structure, control systems, and reward systems that nurture resources and capabilities.

When these four criteria are met, resources and capabilities become core competencies. **Core competencies** are resources and capabilities that serve as a source of sustained competitive advantage for a firm over its rivals. Often related to a firm's functional skills, when developed, nurtured, and applied throughout a firm core competencies may result in strategic competitiveness.

Managerial competencies are important in most firms. For example, they have been shown to be critically important to successful entry into foreign markets.[29] Such competencies may include the capability to effectively organize and govern complex and diverse operations and the capability to create and communicate a strategic vision.[30] Managerial capabilities are critical to a firm's ability to take advantage of its resources.

Another set of important competencies is product-related. Included among these competencies is the capability to develop innovative new products and to re-engineer existing products to satisfy changing consumer tastes.[31] Firms must also continuously develop their competencies to keep them up to date. This development requires a systematic program for updating old skills and introducing new ones.

Dynamic core competencies are especially important in rapidly changing environments, such as those that exist in high-technology industries. Thus, the resource-based model suggests that core competencies are the basis for a firm's competitive advantage, its strategic competitiveness, and its ability to earn above-average returns.

Core competencies are resources and capabilities that serve as a source of sustained competitive advantage for a firm over its rivals.

The Nature of Internal Environmental Analysis

In the global economy, traditional factors such as labour costs, access to financial resources and raw materials, and protected or regulated markets continue to be sources of competitive advantage, but to a lesser degree.[32] One important reason for this decline is that the advantages created by these more traditional sources can be overcome by competitors through an international strategy (discussed in Chapter 9) and by the flow of resources throughout the global economy. The need to identify additional and perhaps new sources of competitive advantage highlights the importance of understanding the firm's resources and capabilities.

The Context of Internal Analysis

Increasingly, those analyzing their firm's internal environment should use a global mind-set. A **global mind-set** is the ability to study an internal environment in ways that are not dependent on the assumptions of a single country, culture, or context.[33] Those with a global mind-set recognize that their firms must possess resources and capabilities that allow understanding of and appropriate responses to competitive situations that are influenced by country-specific factors and unique societal cultures.

A **global mind-set** is the ability to study an internal environment in ways that are not dependent on the assumptions of a single country, culture, or context.

Finally, analysis of the firm's internal environment requires that evaluators examine the firm's portfolio of resources and the bundles of heterogeneous resources and capabilities managers have created.[34] This perspective suggests that individual firms possess at least some resources and capabilities that other companies do not—at least not in the same combination. Resources are the source of capabilities, some of which lead to the development of a firm's core competencies or its competitive advantages.[35] Understanding how to leverage the firm's unique bundle of resources and capabilities is a key outcome decision makers seek when analyzing the internal environment. Figure 4.2 illustrates the relationships among resources, capabilities, and core competencies and shows how firms use them to create strategic competitiveness. Before examining these topics in depth, we describe value and how firms use their resources, capabilities, and core competencies to create it.

Creating Value

By exploiting their core competencies or competitive advantages to at least meet if not exceed the demanding standards of global competition, firms create value for customers.[36] **Value** is measured by a product's performance characteristics and by its attributes for which customers are willing to pay. Firms must provide customers with value that is superior to the value provided by competitors in order to create a competitive advantage.[37] Evidence suggests that increasingly customers perceive higher value in global rather than domestic-only brands.[38] Firms create value by innovatively bundling and leveraging their resources and capabilities.[39] Firms unable to creatively bundle and leverage their resources and capabilities in ways that create value for customers suffer performance declines.

Value is measured by a product's performance characteristics and by its attributes for which customers are willing to pay.

| Figure 4.2 | Components of Internal Analysis Leading to Competitive Advantage and Strategic Competitiveness |

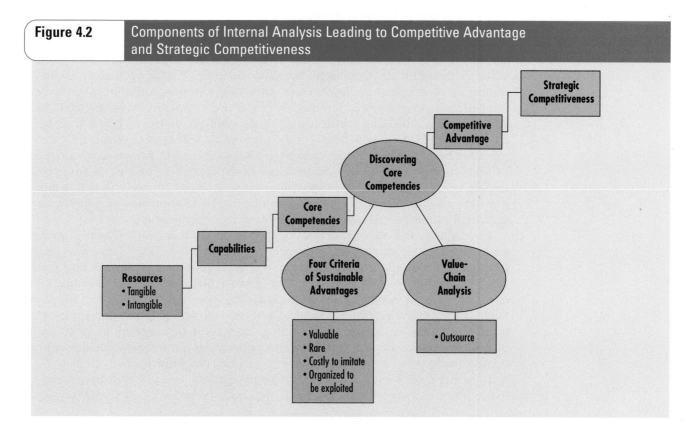

Ultimately, creating value for customers is the source of above-average returns for a firm. What the firm intends regarding value creation affects its choice of business-level strategy (see Chapter 5) and its organizational structure (see Chapter 12).[40] In Chapter 5's discussion of business-level strategies, we note that value is created by a product's low cost, by its highly differentiated features, or by a combination of low cost and high differentiation compared with competitors' offerings. A business-level strategy is effective only when its use is grounded in exploiting the firm's current core competencies. Thus, successful firms continuously examine the effectiveness of current and future core competencies.[41]

At one time, the strategic management process was concerned largely with understanding the characteristics of the industry in which the firm competed and, in light of those characteristics, determining how the firm should be positioned relative to competitors. This emphasis on industry characteristics and competitive strategy underestimated the role of the firm's resources and capabilities in developing competitive advantage. In fact, core competencies, in combination with product-market positions, are the firm's most important sources of competitive advantage.[42] The core competencies of a firm, in addition to results of analyses of its general, industry, and competitor environments, should drive its selection of strategies. Both the resources held by the firm and its environments are important in the formulation of strategy.[43] As Clayton Christensen of the Harvard Business School notes, "Successful strategists need to cultivate a deep understanding of the processes of competition and progress and of the factors that undergird each advantage. Only thus will they be able to see when old advantages are poised to disappear and how new advantages can be built in their stead."[44] By emphasizing core competencies when formulating strategies companies learn to compete primarily on the basis of firm-specific differences, but they must be very aware of how things are changing in the external environment as well.

The Challenge of Internal Analysis

The strategic decisions that managers make in terms of the firm's resources, capabilities, and core competencies are non-routine,[45] have ethical implications,[46] and significantly influence the firm's ability to earn above-average returns.[47] Making these decisions—identifying, developing, deploying, and protecting resources, capabilities, and core competencies—may appear to be relatively easy. However, this task is as challenging and difficult as any other with which managers are involved; moreover, it is increasingly internationalized.[48] Some believe that the pressure on managers to pursue only decisions that help the firm meet the quarterly earnings expected by market analysts makes it difficult to analyze the firm's internal resources accurately.[49] Identifying the firm's core competencies is essential before important strategic decisions are made, including those related to entering or exiting markets, investing in new technologies, building new or additional manufacturing capacity, or forming strategic partnerships.

The challenge and difficulty of making effective decisions are implied by preliminary evidence suggesting that one-half of organizational decisions fail.[50] Sometimes, mistakes are made as the firm analyzes its internal environment. Managers might, for example, identify capabilities as core competencies that do not create a competitive advantage. When a mistake occurs, decision makers must have the confidence to admit it and take corrective actions.[51] A firm can still grow through well-intended errors—the learning generated by making and correcting mistakes can be important to the creation of new competitive advantages.[52] Moreover, firms can learn from the failure resulting from a mistake—that is, what not to do when seeking competitive advantage.[53]

To facilitate developing and using core competencies, managers must have courage, self-confidence, integrity, the capacity to deal with uncertainty and complexity, and a willingness to hold people accountable for their work and to be held accountable themselves. Thus, difficult managerial decisions concerning resources, capabilities, and core competencies are characterized by three conditions: uncertainty, complexity, and intraorganizational conflicts (see Figure 4.3).[54]

Managers face *uncertainty* in terms of new proprietary technologies, rapidly changing economic and political trends, transformations in societal values, and shifts in customer demands.[55] Environmental uncertainty increases the complexity and range of issues to examine when studying the internal environment.[56] Biases about how to cope with uncertainty affect decisions about the resources and capabilities that will become the foundation of the firm's competitive advantage. Finally, intra-organizational conflict surfaces when decisions are made about the core competencies to nurture as well as how to nurture them.

In making decisions affected by these three conditions, judgment is required. *Judgment* is the capability of making successful decisions when no obviously correct model or rule is available or when relevant data are unreliable or incomplete. In this type of situation, decision makers must be aware of possible cognitive biases. Overconfidence, for example, can often lower value when a correct decision is not obvious, such as making a judgment as to whether an internal resource is a strength or weakness.[57]

When exercising judgment, decision makers often take intelligent risks. In the current competitive landscape, executive judgment can be a particularly important source of competitive advantage. One reason is that, over time, effective judgment allows a firm to build a strong reputation and retain the loyalty of stakeholders whose support is linked to above-average returns.[58]

Significant changes in the value-creating potential of a firm's resources and capabilities can occur in a rapidly changing global economy. Because these changes affect a company's power and social structure, inertia or resistance to change may surface. Even though these reactions may happen, decision makers should not deny the changes needed to assure the firm's strategic competitiveness. By denying the need for change,

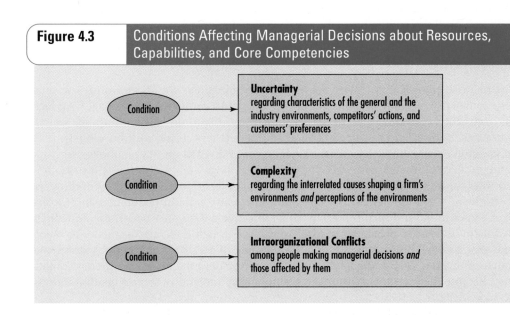

Figure 4.3   Conditions Affecting Managerial Decisions about Resources, Capabilities, and Core Competencies

Condition → **Uncertainty** regarding characteristics of the general and the industry environments, competitors' actions, and customers' preferences

Condition → **Complexity** regarding the interrelated causes shaping a firm's environments *and* perceptions of the environments

Condition → **Intraorganizational Conflicts** among people making managerial decisions *and* those affected by them

SOURCE: Adapted from R. Amit & P.J.H. Schoemaker, 1993, Strategic Assets and Organizational Rent, *Strategic Management Journal*, 14:33.

difficult experiences can be avoided in the short run.[59] However, in the long run, the failure to change when needed leads to performance declines and, in the worst-case scenario, to failure.

Amazon.com, Inc., a pioneer in the e-commerce world,[60] recently made a bold decision to compete head-to-head with Apple Inc. In late September 2007, Amazon launched its own digital music store, very similar to Apple's iTunes. As iTunes is compatible only with the iPod, Amazon will also sell its own music device to play these songs.[61] David Card, an analyst with Jupiter Research, said that "Amazon's entrance into the market represents serious competition for Apple, which can no longer rely solely on the bond between the iPod and iTunes."[62]

Similarly, in 2006 Google Inc. acquired the very popular video sharing Web site YouTube, which has become so pervasive that it now "gets more than half its traffic outside [of its home in] the U.S."[63] and features local-language interfaces for each foreign country. Google is aiming to establish YouTube all around the world, with more distribution channels than the Internet.[64] "This is just the beginning," claims YouTube co-founder Steve Shih Chen. "If we had the resources, we would be launching in 140 countries."[65]

In attempts to increase YouTube's reach "beyond PC screens and onto other video displays: mobile phones, handheld players, and most important, the living room TV," Google recently signed a deal with Apple Inc. to allow YouTube videos to be shown on the new Apple television.[66] Co-founder Chen is excited about this prospect: "the big thing for us in 2007 is accessibility—the goal is to put YouTube on every screen."

Resources, Capabilities, and Core Competencies

Resources, capabilities, and core competencies provide the foundation of competitive advantage. As mentioned earlier in this chapter, resources are the source of a firm's capabilities. Resources are bundled to create organizational capabilities. Capabilities, in turn, are the source of a firm's core competencies, which are the basis of competitive advantages.[67] Later, we explain how some capabilities become core competencies. Figure 4.2 depicts these relationships. In this section, we define and provide examples of these building blocks of competitive advantage.

Resources

Broad in scope, resources cover a spectrum of individual, social, and organizational phenomena.[68] Typically, resources alone do not yield a competitive advantage.[69] In fact, a competitive advantage is generally based on the unique bundling of several resources.[70] For example, Amazon.com combined its service and distribution resources to develop a competitive advantage. Amazon.com started as an online bookstore, shipping orders directly to customers. It quickly grew large and established a distribution network through which it could ship "millions of different items to millions of different customers." Lacking Amazon's combination of resources, traditional bricks-and-mortar companies found it difficult to establish an effective online presence. These difficulties led them to develop partnerships with Amazon. Through these arrangements, Amazon now handles the online presence and the shipping of goods for several book stores and other companies. Arrangements such as these are useful to the bricks-and-mortar companies because they are not accustomed to shipping so much diverse merchandise directly to individuals.[71]

Some of a firm's resources (defined in Chapter 1 as inputs to the firm's production process) are tangible, while others are intangible. **Tangible resources** are assets that can be seen and quantified. Production equipment, manufacturing plants, and formal

Tangible resources are assets that can be seen and quantified. Production equipment, manufacturing plants, and formal reporting structures are examples of tangible resources.

reporting structures are examples of tangible resources. **Intangible resources** include assets that typically are rooted deeply in the firm's history and have accumulated over time. Because they are embedded in unique patterns of routines, intangible resources are relatively difficult for competitors to analyze and imitate. Knowledge, trust between managers and employees, managerial capabilities, organizational routines (the unique ways people work together), scientific capabilities, the capacity for innovation, and the firm's reputation for its goods or services and how it interacts with people (such as employees, customers, and suppliers) are all examples of intangible resources.[72]

The four types of tangible resources are financial, organizational, physical, and technological (see Table 4.1). The three types of intangible resources are human, innovation, and reputational (see Table 4.2).

Intangible resources include assets that typically are rooted deeply in the firm's history and have accumulated over time.

Table 4.1	Tangible Resources
Financial Resources	• The firm's borrowing capacity • The firm's ability to generate internal funds
Organizational Resources	• The firm's formal reporting structure and its formal planning, controlling, and coordinating systems
Physical Resources	• Sophistication and location of a firm's plant and equipment • Access to raw materials
Technological Resources	• Stock of technology, such as patents, trademarks, copyrights, and trade secrets

SOURCES: Adapted from J. B. Barney, 1991, Firm resources and sustained competitive advantage, *Journal of Management*, 17: 101; R. M. Grant, 1991, *Contemporary Strategy Analysis*, Cambridge, U.K.: Blackwell Business, 100–2.

Table 4.2	Intangible Resources
Human Resources	• Knowledge • Trust • Managerial capabilities • Organizational routines
Innovation Resources	• Ideas • Scientific capabilities • Capacity to innovate
Reputational Resources	• Reputation with customers • Brand name • Perceptions of product quality, durability, and reliability • Reputation with suppliers • Efficient, effective, supportive, and mutually beneficial interactions and relationships

SOURCES: Adapted from R. Hall, 1992, The strategic analysis of intangible resources, *Strategic Management Journal*, 13: 136–139; R. M. Grant, 1991, *Contemporary Strategy Analysis*, Cambridge, U.K.: Blackwell Business, 101–104.

Tangible Resources

A firm's borrowing capacity and the status of its plant and equipment are visible, and as such they are tangible resources. The value of many tangible resources can be established through financial statements, but these statements do not account for the value of all of a firm's assets because they disregard some intangible resources.[73] As such, each of the firm's sources of competitive advantage typically is not fully reflected on corporate financial statements. The value of tangible resources is also constrained because they are difficult to leverage—it is difficult to derive additional business or value from a tangible resource. For example, an airplane is a tangible resource or asset, but: "You can't use the same airplane on five different routes at the same time. You can't put the same crew on five different routes at the same time. And the same goes for the financial investment you've made in the airplane."[74]

Although production assets are tangible, many of the processes to use these assets are intangible. Thus, the learning and potential proprietary processes associated with a tangible resource, such as manufacturing equipment, can have unique intangible attributes, such as quality control processes, unique manufacturing processes, and technology that develop over time and create competitive advantage.[75]

Intangible Resources

As suggested above, compared to tangible resources, intangible resources are a superior and more potent source of core competencies.[76] In fact, in the global economy, "the success of a corporation lies more in its intellectual and systems capabilities than in its physical assets. [Moreover], the capacity to manage human intellect—and to convert it into useful products and services—is fast becoming the critical executive skill of the age."[77]

Even though it is difficult to measure the value of intangible assets such as knowledge,[78] there is some evidence that the value of intangible assets is growing relative to that of tangible assets.[79] John Kendrick, a well-known economist studying the main drivers of economic growth, found a general increase in the ratio of intangible business assets to tangible business assets.

Because intangible resources are less visible and more difficult for competitors to understand, purchase, imitate, or substitute for, firms prefer to rely on them rather than on tangible resources as the foundation for their capabilities and core competencies. In fact, the more unobservable (that is, intangible) a resource is, the more sustainable will be the competitive advantage that is based on it.[80] Another benefit of intangible resources is that, unlike most tangible resources, their use can be leveraged. With intangible resources, the larger the network of users the greater the benefit a resource is to each party. For instance, sharing knowledge among employees does not diminish its value for any one person. To the contrary, two people sharing their individualized knowledge sets often can be leveraged to create additional knowledge that, although new to each of them, contributes to performance improvements for the firm.[81]

As shown in Table 4.2, the intangible resource of reputation is an important source of competitive advantage. Earned through the firm's actions as well as its words, a value-creating reputation is a product of years of superior marketplace competence as perceived by stakeholders.[82] A reputation indicates the level of awareness a firm has been able to develop among stakeholders[83] and the degree to which they hold the firm in high esteem.[84] A well-known and highly valued brand name is an application of reputation as a source of competitive advantage.[85] A continuing commitment to innovation and aggressive advertising facilitates firms' efforts to take advantage of the reputation associated with their brands.[86] Because of the desirability of its reputation, the Harley-Davidson brand name, for example, has such status that it adorns a limited-edition Barbie doll, a popular restaurant in New York City, and a line of L'Oréal cologne. Moreover, Harley-Davidson MotorClothes annually generates well in excess of $100 million in revenue for the firm and offers a broad range of clothing items, from black leather jackets to fashions for tots.[87]

Other firms are trying to build their reputations. For example, Li-Ning, a manufacturer and marketer of athletic shoes, competes in the Chinese market against Nike and Adidas, firms with well-known brands. To build its image in preparation for the Olympic Games held in Beijing in 2008, Li-Ning hired a veteran with experience at Procter & Gamble as vice president of marketing. His first initiative was to partner with the National Basketball Association to use its logo on Li-Ning shoes.[88]

A company's competitive strength resides largely in the heads of its most talented employees. In the new century's knowledge economy, the winning companies will be those that can increase their profit per employee by translating this talent into institutional skills, intellectual property, networks, and brands—intangibles that are nearly impossible for their competitors to replicate. By removing barriers that impede knowledge development and by encouraging information sharing, organizations can leverage their most precious asset to ensure lasting competitive advantage in the marketplace.

As noted in the Strategic Focus, many companies espouse the importance of their employees and yet lay them off at the first sign of economic troubles. When they do so, they are more likely to experience longer-term declining performance.[89] Also, firms must make more effective use of their total human capital. Firms that do so, such as Pepsi QTG and Accenture, are the most likely to develop competitive advantages and win competitive battles against their rivals. Reinforcing their efforts, recent research is finding that investments in firm-specific human capital increases learning and, in turn, firm performance.[90] Clearly, some firms are recognizing the value of human capital for their strategic success, placing emphasis on trying to retain older workers because of their knowledge stocks developed over time. Such actions have created interfirm rivalry to acquire and retain high-quality human capital.[91] Emphasizing this rivalry, John Mack, the relatively new CEO of Morgan Stanley, urged his managers to identify and recruit the most talented employees of rival banks because Morgan Stanley had lost significant numbers of top employees who accepted jobs from competitors. He said, "Nothing would underline the regime change more powerfully than pulling in a few big names."[92]

Capabilities

Capabilities exist when resources have been purposely integrated to achieve a specific task or set of tasks. These tasks range from human resource selection to product marketing and research and development activities.[93] Critical to the building of competitive advantages, capabilities are often based on developing, carrying, and exchanging information and knowledge through the firm's human capital.[94] Client-specific capabilities often develop from repeated interactions with clients and the learning about their needs that occurs.[95] As a result, capabilities often evolve and develop over time.[96] The foundation of many capabilities lies in the unique skills and knowledge of a firm's employees[97] and, often, their functional expertise. Hence, the value of human capital in developing and using capabilities and, ultimately, core competencies cannot be overstated.

Global business leaders increasingly support the view that the knowledge possessed by human capital is among the most significant of an organization's capabilities and may ultimately be at the root of all competitive advantages.[98] But firms must also be able to utilize the knowledge that they have and transfer it among their business units.[99] Given this reality, the firm's challenge is to create an environment that allows people to integrate their individual knowledge with that held by others in the firm so that, collectively, the firm has significant organizational knowledge.[100]

As illustrated in Table 4.3, capabilities are often developed in specific functional areas (such as manufacturing, R&D, and marketing) or in a part of a functional area (for example, advertising). Research indicates a relationship between capabilities developed in particular functional areas and the firm's financial performance at both the corporate

Human Capital: Unleashing the Full Potential of Underutilized Assets

Corporations have agreed for many years that their employees are their most valuable asset. Yet corporate decisions are not always in line with this belief. When firms experience performance difficulties or industry downturns, the first cost reductions generally made come through large layoffs of employees. For example, attempting to "reverse sinking profits and regain market share," Intel Corporation eliminated 10,500 jobs in 2006, amounting to about 10 percent of its workforce.

Nevertheless, the data continue to suggest that human capital is the most valuable resource held by most companies. Why is it, then, according to a 2007 report in *The Globe and Mail,* that many companies still do not "unleash" the full potential of their workforce talent?

In the book *Mobilizing Minds: Creating Wealth From Talent in the 21st-Century Organization,* two McKinsey & Co. consultants give advice on how firms can extract the greatest value from their most important yet "most underutilized asset"—their people. One recommended practice is to realign the corporate structure to reduce bureaucracy and corporate politics, and inspire creativity.

Today's business world is driven largely by information and knowledge management, and so it follows that retaining employees with a significant amount of expertise and industry knowledge can pose a significant competitive advantage that trumps even the newest product design or long-term strategic plan. In short, by unleashing a firm's talent and retaining its invaluable knowledge base, you create a competitive advantage that competitors cannot easily duplicate.

Furthermore, it is common for organizations today to invest in sophisticated technology to collect and distribute valuable information across the company. Accenture Ltd., a global management consulting, technology services, and outsourcing company, was recognized for its ability to retain and share knowledge within its organization. For nine years, Accenture was the winner of the Global Most Admired Knowledge Enterprise (Global MAKE) award.

Accenture has integrated one of the largest and most widely used corporate portals, known as the Accenture Knowledge Exchange. This technology solution, based on Microsoft software, has assisted employees in accessing corporate business knowledge and in decreasing costs up to $2 million a year, improving decision-making ability, and helping build a knowledge-sharing culture at Accenture.

Organizational design holds significant influence in exploiting talent in an organization and in encouraging employees to collaborate and exchange knowledge throughout the enterprise. As suggested by a 2007 report in *The Globe and Mail,* employees need to be "evaluated like hockey players and rewarded not just for the goals they score, but for their assists."

In a November 2007 interview with recruiters from Pepsi QTG Canada, one senior student found that the corporate reward structure was designed to attract and retain the best talent. Pepsi QTG and its subsidiaries, like Pepsi QTG Canada, use a reward structure to empower employees. The reward structure is based on 50 percent business performance and 50 percent people performance. The latter criterion is determined for each manager based on how his or her team performs. This ensures that each team's members are led in a way that enhances business performance and individual performance.

SOURCES: 2006, Intel announces massive restructuring, The Associated Press, September 5; 2007, Want a competitive advantage? Unleash your company's hidden talent, *The Globe and Mail,* November 5, B7; L. L. Bryan & C. I. Joyce, 2007, *Mobilizing Minds: Creating Wealth from Talent in the 21st Century Organization,* Toronto: McGraw-Hill; 2007, Global MAKE recognizes organizations which are world leaders in creating shareholder wealth by transforming enterprise knowledge into superior products/services/solutions, http://www.knowledgebusiness.com, accessed November 15; 2006, Global consulting company revamps knowledge system with integrated portal solution, Microsoft Office System Customer Solutions Case Study, Microsoft Corporation, August; 2007, personal interview with A. Orser, November 16.

and business-unit levels,[101] suggesting the need to develop capabilities at both levels. Table 4.3 shows a grouping of organizational functions and the capabilities that some companies are thought to possess in terms of all or parts of those functions.

Core Competencies

Defined in Chapter 1, core competencies are capabilities that serve as a source of competitive advantage for a firm over its rivals. Core competencies distinguish a company competitively and reflect its personality. Core competencies emerge over time through an organizational process of accumulating and learning how to deploy different resources and capabilities.[102] As the capacity to take action, core competencies are "crown jewels of a company," the activities the company performs especially well compared with competitors and through which the firm adds unique value to its goods or services over a long period of time.[103]

Not all of a firm's resources and capabilities are strategic assets—that is, assets that have competitive value and the potential to serve as a source of competitive advantage.[104] Some resources and capabilities may result in incompetence, because they represent competitive areas in which the firm is weaker than its competitors. Thus, some resources or capabilities may stifle or prevent the development of a core competency. Firms with the tangible resource of financial capital—such as Microsoft, which has a

Table 4.3	Examples of Firms' Capabilities	
Functional Areas	**Capabilities**	**Examples of Firms**
Supply chain	Effective use of procurement techniques	Starbucks
Distribution	Effective use of logistics management techniques	Wal-Mart, Dell
Human resources	Motivating, empowering, and retaining employees	Royal Bank of Canada, Microsoft, Dell
Management information systems	Effective and efficient control of inventories through point-of-purchase data collection methods	Wal-Mart, Dell
Marketing	Effective promotion of brand-name products	Procter & Gamble
	Effective customer service	McKinsey & Co.
	Innovative merchandising	Nordstrom Inc.
		Norrell Corporation
		Crate & Barrel
Management	Ability to envision the future of clothing	Lululemon Athletica PepsiCo
	Effective organizational structure	WestJet
	Effective culture	
Manufacturing	Design/production skills yielding reliable products	Komatsu
	Product and design quality	Gap Inc.
	Miniaturization of components and products	Sony
Research & development	Innovative technology	Caterpillar
	Development of sophisticated elevator control solutions	Otis Elevator Co.
	Rapid transformation of technology into new products and processes	Chaparral Steel
	Digital technology	Thomson Consumer Electronics

large amount of cash on hand—may be able to purchase facilities or hire the skilled workers required to manufacture products that yield customer value. However, firms without financial capital have a weakness in that they may be unable to buy or build new capabilities. To be successful, firms must locate external environmental opportunities that can be exploited through their capabilities, while avoiding competition in areas of weakness.[105]

An important question is, "How many core competencies are required for the firm to have a sustained competitive advantage?" Responses to this question vary. McKinsey & Co. recommends that its clients identify three or four competencies around which their strategic actions can be framed.[106] Supporting and nurturing more than four core competencies may prevent a firm from developing the focus it needs to fully exploit its competencies in the marketplace. Firms should take actions that are based on their core competencies. For example, Apple Inc., which is consistently named one of the world's most innovative firms,[107] is considered a business icon today because of its abilities to see around the corner and meet unmet needs.

Of course, not all capabilities are core competencies. And some firms can have weaknesses in important capabilities that detract from their core competencies. For example, Unilever—a global manufacturer of food, personal, and home care products—has its core competency in marketing, but some sources claim that its inability to execute has caused it to lag behind its competitors.[108] According to a 2007 report in *Marketing Week*, when Unilever moved to a more decentralized organization in 2005 its change in structure led to "inefficiency [and] insubordination" and "hinder[ed] new product development."[109] Unilever needs to build up its core competencies to be able to compete better relative to its closest competitors.

Building Core Competencies

Two tools help firms to identify and build core competencies.[110] The first consists of four specific criteria of sustainable competitive advantage that firms can use to determine those capabilities that are core competencies. Because the capabilities shown in Table 4.3 have satisfied these four criteria, they are core competencies. The second tool is the value chain analysis. Firms use this tool to select the value-creating competencies that should be maintained, upgraded, or developed and those that should be outsourced.

Four Criteria of Sustainable Competitive Advantage

As shown in Table 4.4, capabilities that are valuable, rare, costly to imitate, and organized to be exploited are core competencies. In turn, core competencies are sources of competitive advantage for the firm over its rivals. Capabilities failing to satisfy the four criteria of sustainable competitive advantage are not core competencies, meaning that although every core competency is a capability, not every capability is a core competency. In slightly different words, for a capability to be a core competency, it must be valuable and unique from a customer's point of view. For the competitive advantage to be sustainable, the core competency must be inimitable (which also means not duplicable or non-substitutable) from a competitor's point of view and internally organized to be exploited.

A sustained competitive advantage is achieved only when competitors cannot duplicate the benefits of a firm's strategy or when they lack the resources to attempt imitation. For some period of time, the firm may earn a competitive advantage by using capabilities that are, for example, valuable and rare, but imitable.[111] In this instance, the length of time a firm can expect to retain its competitive advantage is a function of how quickly competitors can successfully imitate a good, service, or process. Sustainable competitive advantage results only when all four criteria are satisfied.

Table 4.4	The Four Criteria of Sustainable Competitive Advantage
Valuable Capabilities	Help a firm to reduce costs by neutralizing threats and/or generate revenues by exploiting opportunities
Rare Capabilities	Are not possessed by many other competitors
Costly-to-Imitate Capabilities	Those capabilities that an organization's closest competitors have tried to imitate, duplicate, or substitute for but the costs exceed the benefits. Three reasons a capability may be costly to imitate are: • Historical: A unique and valuable organizational culture or brand name • Ambiguous cause: The causes and uses of a competence are unclear • Social complexity: Interpersonal relationships, trust, and friendship among managers, suppliers, and customers
Organized to Be Exploited	Appropriate structure to support capability Appropriate control systems to support capability Appropriate reward systems to support capability

SOURCE: Barney, Jay B., *Gaining and Sustaining Competitive Advantage*, 3/E, © 2002, pp. 150–159. Adapted by permission of Pearson Education, Inc., Upper Saddle River, NJ.

Valuable

Valuable capabilities allow the firm to exploit opportunities to generate revenues and/or neutralize threats to reduce costs. By effectively using capabilities to exploit opportunities, a firm creates value for customers. Under former CEO Jack Welch's leadership, GE built a valuable competence in financial services. It built this powerful competence largely through acquisitions and its core competency in integrating newly acquired businesses. In addition, to make such competencies as financial services highly successful required placing the right people in the right jobs. As Welch emphasizes, human capital is important in creating value for customers.[112]

> **Valuable capabilities** allow the firm to exploit opportunities to generate revenues and/or neutralize threats to reduce costs.

Rare

Rare capabilities are those capabilities possessed by few, if any, current or potential competitors. A key question to be answered when evaluating this criterion is, "How many rival firms possess these valuable capabilities?" From an economics perspective, a capability is considered rare when the number of competitors possessing the capability is fewer than the number required for perfect competition. Capabilities possessed by many rivals are unlikely to be sources of competitive advantage for any one of them. Instead, valuable but common (i.e., not rare) resources and capabilities are sources of competitive parity.[113] Competitive advantage results only when firms develop and exploit valuable capabilities that differ from those shared with competitors.

> **Rare capabilities** are those capabilities possessed by few, if any, current or potential competitors.

Costly to Imitate

Costly-to-imitate capabilities are capabilities that other firms cannot easily develop. Capabilities that are costly to imitate are created because of one reason or a combination of three reasons (see Table 4.4). First, a firm sometimes is able to develop capabilities because of *unique historical conditions*. "As firms evolve, they pick up skills, abilities and resources that are unique to them, reflecting their particular path through history."[114]

A firm with a unique and valuable organizational culture that emerged in the early stages of the company's history "may have an imperfectly imitable advantage over firms founded in another historical period"[115]—one in which less valuable or less competitively useful values and beliefs strongly influenced the development of the firm's culture. Briefly discussed in Chapter 1, organizational culture is a set of shared values by

> **Costly-to-imitate capabilities** are capabilities that other firms cannot easily develop.

members in the organization. An organizational culture is a source of advantage when employees are held together tightly by their belief in it.[116] WestJet is a Canadian firm that is believed to have a costly-to-imitate organizational culture that is a source of sustained competitive advantage.

UPS has been the prototype in many areas of the parcel delivery business because of its excellence in products, systems, marketing, and other operational business capabilities. "Its fundamental competitive strength, however, derives from the organization's unique culture, which has spanned almost a century, growing deeper all along. This culture provides solid, consistent roots for everything the company does, from skills training to technological innovation."[117]

A second condition of being costly to imitate occurs when the link between the firm's capabilities and its competitive advantage is *causally ambiguous*.[118] In these instances, competitors can't clearly understand how a firm uses its capabilities as the foundation for competitive advantage—competitors do not understand the linkage between a capability and its associated competitive advantage. As a result, firms are uncertain about the capabilities they should develop to duplicate the benefits of a competitor's value-creating strategy. For years, Air Canada has tried to imitate WestJet's low-cost strategy but has been unable to duplicate WestJet's success. WestJet has a unique culture and attracts some of the top talent in the industry. The culture and excellent human capital worked together in implementing WestJet's strategy and are the basis for one of its competitive advantages.

Social complexity is the third reason why capabilities can be costly to imitate. Social complexity means that at least some, and frequently many, of the firm's capabilities are the product of complex social phenomena. Interpersonal relationships, trust, friendships among managers and between managers and employees, and a firm's reputation with suppliers and customers are examples of socially complex capabilities. Vancouver-based retailer Lululemon Athletica holds strong relationships with its customers by seeking out and integrating customer feedback into its design process.[119]

As part of the costly-to-imitate criterion, for a capability to be a source of competitive advantage ". . . there must be no strategically equivalent valuable resources that are themselves either not rare or imitable. Two valuable firm resources (or two bundles of firm resources) are strategically equivalent when they each can be separately exploited to implement the same strategies."[120] In general, the strategic value of capabilities increases as they become more difficult to substitute.[121] The more invisible capabilities are, the more difficult it is for firms to find substitutes and the greater the challenge is to competitors trying to imitate a firm's value-creating strategy. Firm-specific knowledge and trust-based working relationships between managers and nonmanagerial personnel, such as exists at WestJet and at Southwest Airlines, are examples of capabilities that are difficult to identify and for which finding a substitute is challenging. However, causal ambiguity may make it difficult for the firm to learn as well and may stifle progress, because the firm may not know how to improve processes that are not easily codified and thus are ambiguous.[122]

Nonsubstitutable capabilities are capabilities that do not have strategic equivalents. For example, competitors are deeply familiar with Dell Computer's successful direct sales model. However, to date no competitor has been able to imitate Dell's capabilities, as suggested by the following comment: "There's no better way to make, sell, and deliver PCs than the way Dell does it, and nobody executes that model better than Dell."[123] Moreover, no competitor has been able to develop and use substitute capabilities that can duplicate the value Dell creates by using its capabilities. Thus, experience suggests that Dell's direct sales model capabilities are nonsubstitutable.

Organized to Be Exploited

The fourth criterion in our search for core competencies is organized to be exploited. Being **organized to be exploited** means that firms have the correct structure, control systems, and reward systems to support each source of competitive parity, temporary

Nonsubstitutable capabilities are capabilities that do not have strategic equivalents.

Being **organized to be exploited** means that firms have the correct structure, control systems, and reward systems to support each source of competitive parity, temporary competitive advantage, and sustained competitive advantage.

competitive advantage, and sustained competitive advantage. If a firm is pursuing a product differentiation strategy (discussed in Chapter 5) that is difficult for competitors to imitate, it is important that the structure, controls, and rewards be as follows. Appropriate structural characteristics for product differentiation are cross-functional/cross-divisional linkages, a willingness to utilize new structures to take advantage of new opportunities, and a willingness to have isolated areas of intense creative efforts. Control systems need to be flexible in the way they control activities, make allowances for creative people, and allow learning from innovative failures. Reward systems should not punish for failure but reward for risk-taking and creative flair, and be qualitative and subjective in measuring performance.[124]

If a firm wanted to pursue a cost leadership strategy (discussed in Chapter 5) for which competitors would have trouble imitating the structure, control systems and reward systems should be as follows. Structurally, the firm should have few layers in its reporting system, reporting relationships should be simple, and there should be a disciplined focus on a narrow range of business functions. The control system should be one where there is tight cost control; quantitative cost objectives; closely supervised labour, raw material, inventory, and other costs; and a philosophy of cost leadership. Compensation policies should reward for reducing costs, and there should be incentives for all members to be involved in cost reduction.[125]

In summary, sustainable competitive advantage is created only by using valuable, rare, costly-to-imitate, and organized-to-be-exploited capabilities. Table 4.5 shows the competitive consequences and performance implications resulting from combinations of the four criteria of sustainability. The analysis suggested by the table helps managers determine the strategic value of a firm's capabilities. Resources and capabilities falling into the first row in the table (that is, resources and capabilities that are not valuable) should not be emphasized by the firm to formulate and implement strategies. Capabilities yielding competitive parity and either temporary or sustainable competitive advantage should, however, be organized to be exploited. Large competitors such as Coca-Cola and PepsiCo may have capabilities that can yield only competitive parity. In such cases, the firms will nurture these capabilities while simultaneously trying to develop capabilities that can yield either a temporary or sustainable competitive advantage.

Table 4.5	Outcomes from Combinations of the Four Criteria for Sustained Competitive Advantage: The VRIO Framework

Is the resource or capability . . .

Variable?	Rare?	Costly to Imitate?	Organized to Be Exploited?	Competitive Consequences	Performance Implications
No	—	—	No	Competitive Disadvantage	Below-Average Returns
Yes	No	—	Yes	Competitive Parity	Average Returns
Yes	Yes	No	Yes	Temporary Competitive Advantage	Above-Average Returns
Yes	Yes	Yes	Yes	Sustained Competitive Advantage	Above-Average Returns

SOURCE: Barney, Jay B., *Gaining and Sustaining Competitive Advantage*, 1/E, © 1997. Adapted by permission of Pearson Education, Inc., Upper Saddle River, NJ.

Companies like Toyota and Zara (a Spanish textile company) have achieved above-average returns in their industries because of their ability to create a competitive advantage that no competitor is able to replicate.[126] For Toyota, it revolutionized its industry with the Toyota Production System (TPS), which led to greatly reduced lead times, increased cost savings, and quality improvements.[127] Instead of following the retail industry and outsourcing production of its clothes to developing countries, Zara's use of local suppliers enables it to respond quickly to changes in trends, which is integral in the retail industry.[128]

Value Chain Analysis

Primary activities are involved with a product's physical creation, its sale and distribution to buyers, and its service after the sale.

Support activities provide the assistance necessary for the primary activities to take place.

Value chain analysis allows the firm to understand the parts of its operations that create value and those that do not. Understanding these issues is important because the firm earns above-average returns only when the value it creates is greater than the costs incurred to create that value.[129]

The value chain is a template that firms use to understand their cost position and to identify the multiple means that might be used to facilitate implementation of a chosen business-level strategy.[130] As shown in Figure 4.4, a firm's value chain is segmented into primary and support activities. **Primary activities** are involved with a product's physical creation, its sale and distribution to buyers, and its service after the sale. **Support activities** provide the assistance necessary for the primary activities to take place.

The value chain shows how a product moves from the raw-material stage to the final customer. For individual firms, the essential idea of the value chain is to create additional value without incurring significant costs while doing so and to capture the value that has been created. In a globally competitive economy, the most valuable links on the chain are people who have knowledge about customers. This locus of value-creating possibilities applies just as strongly to retail and service firms as to manufacturers. Moreover, for organizations in all sectors, the effects of e-commerce make it increasingly necessary for companies to develop value-adding knowledge processes to compensate for the value and margin that the Internet strips from physical processes.[131]

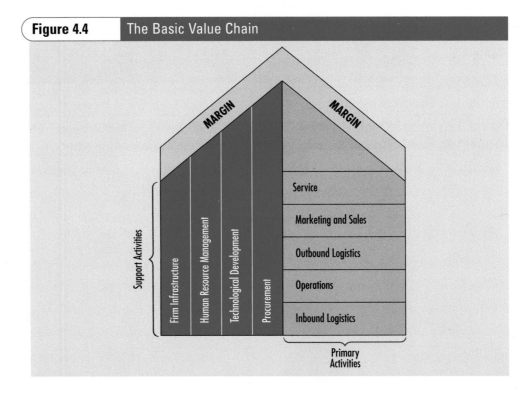

Figure 4.4   The Basic Value Chain

Table 4.6 lists the items that can be evaluated to determine the value-creating potential of primary activities. In Table 4.7, the items for evaluating support activities are shown. All items in both tables should be evaluated relative to competitors' capabilities. To be a source of competitive advantage, a resource or capability must allow the firm (1) to perform an activity in a manner that provides value superior to that provided by competitors, or (2) to perform a value-creating activity that competitors cannot complete. Only under these conditions does a firm create value for customers and have opportunities to capture that value.

Table 4.6	Examining the Value-Creating Potential of Primary Activities
Inbound Logistics	Activities, such as materials handling, warehousing, and inventory control, used to receive, store, and disseminate inputs to a product.
Operations	Activities necessary to convert the inputs provided by inbound logistics into final product form. Machining, packaging, assembly, and equipment maintenance are examples of operations activities.
Outbound Logistics	Activities involved with collecting, storing, and physically distributing the final product to customers. Examples of these activities include finished-goods warehousing, materials handling, and order processing.
Marketing and Sales	Activities completed to provide means through which customers can purchase products and to induce them to do so. To effectively market and sell products, firms develop advertising and promotional campaigns, select appropriate distribution channels, and select, develop, and support their sales force.
Service	Activities designed to enhance or maintain a product's value. Firms engage in a range of service-related activities, including installation, repair, training, and adjustment.

SOURCE: Adapted with permission of The Free Press, a Division of Simon & Schuster Adult Publishing Group, from *Competitive Advantage: Creating and Sustaining Superior Performance*, by Michael E Porter, pp. 39–40. Copyright © 1985, 1998 by Michael E. Porter. All rights reserved.

Table 4.7	Examining the Value-Creating Potential of Support Activities
Procurement	Activities completed to purchase the inputs needed to produce a firm's products. Purchased inputs include items fully consumed during the manufacture of products (e.g., raw materials and supplies, as well as fixed assets—machinery, laboratory equipment, office equipment, and buildings).
Technological Development	Activities completed to improve a firm's product and the processes used to manufacture it. Technological development takes many forms, such as process equipment, basic research and product design, and servicing procedures.
Human Resource Management	Activities involved with recruiting, hiring, training, developing, and compensating all personnel.
Firm Infrastructure	Firm infrastructure includes activities such as general management, planning, finance, accounting, legal support, and governmental relations that are required to support the work of the entire value chain. Through its infrastructure, the firm strives to effectively and consistently identify external opportunities and threats, identify resources and capabilities, and support core competencies.

SOURCE: Adapted with permission of The Free Press, a Division of Simon & Schuster Adult Publishing Group, from *Competitive Advantage: Creating and Sustaining Superior Performance*, by Michael E Porter, pp. 40–43. Copyright © 1985, 1998 by Michael E. Porter. All rights reserved.

Sometimes start-up firms create value by uniquely reconfiguring or recombining parts of the value chain. FedEx changed the nature of the delivery business by reconfiguring outbound logistics (a primary activity) and human resource management (a support activity) to provide overnight deliveries, creating value in the process. As shown in Figure 4.5, the Internet has changed many aspects of the value chain for a broad range of firms. A key reason for this is that the Internet affects how people communicate, locate information, and buy goods and services.

Rating a firm's capability to execute its primary and support activities is challenging. Earlier in the chapter, we noted that identifying and assessing the value of a firm's resources and capabilities requires judgment. Judgment is equally necessary when using value chain analysis. The reason is that there is no obviously correct model or rule available to help in the process.

Figure 4.5   Prominent Applications of the Internet in the Value Chain

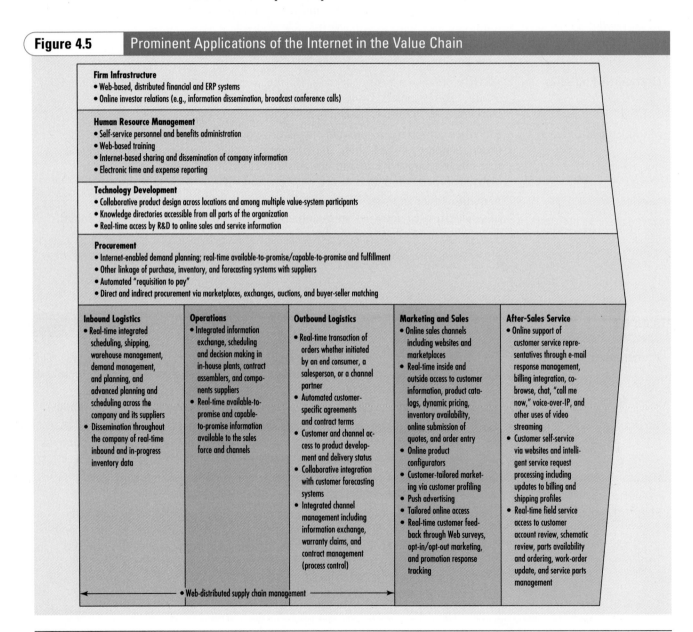

A very valuable activity for senior managers is to take an organization's value chain and perform a VRIO analysis on each primary and support activity. This will give the organization value information as to where something needs to be fixed. For example, it could be that procurement is a source of competitive disadvantage that needs to be fixed internally or outsourced. On the other hand, it may be that outbound logistics is a source of competitive parity but needs to be better organized to be exploited in that the control systems are inappropriate. If this is the case, this source of competitive parity is in danger of becoming a source of competitive disadvantage. Doing an analysis like this also enables senior managers to identify sources of temporary and sustained competitive advantage. If there are more than three or four sources of sustained competitive advantage, those conducting the analysis are probably being too optimistic relative to their competitors.

What should a firm do about primary and support activities in which its resources and capabilities are not a source of at least competitive parity? As mentioned in the previous paragraph, *outsourcing* is one solution to consider.

Outsourcing

Concerned with how components, finished goods, or services will be obtained, **outsourcing** is the purchase of a value-creating activity from an external supplier.[132] Not-for-profit agencies as well as for-profit organizations actively engage in outsourcing.[133] Firms engaging in effective outsourcing increase their flexibility, mitigate risks, and reduce their capital investments.[134] In multiple global industries, the trend toward outsourcing continues at a rapid pace.[135] Moreover, in some industries virtually all firms seek the value that can be captured through effective outsourcing. The auto manufacturing industry and, more recently, the electronics industry are examples of this situation.[136] As with other strategic management process decisions, careful study is required before the firm decides to engage in outsourcing.[137]

Outsourcing is the purchase of a value-creating activity from an external supplier.

Outsourcing can be effective because few, if any, organizations possess the resources and capabilities required to achieve competitive superiority in all primary and support activities. For example, research suggests that few companies can afford to develop internally all the technologies that might lead to competitive advantage.[138] By nurturing a smaller number of capabilities, a firm increases the probability of developing a competitive advantage because it does not become overextended. In addition, by outsourcing activities in which it lacks competence, the firm can fully concentrate on those areas in which it can create value.[139]

Other research suggests that outsourcing does not work effectively without extensive internal capabilities to coordinate external sourcing as well as core competencies.[140] Dell Inc., for example, outsources most of its customer service activities, allowing the firm to concentrate on creating value through its excellent efficiency in its just-in-time inventory system and its online distribution capabilities. In addition, the value generated by outsourcing must be sufficient to cover a firm's costs. For example, research indicates that for European banks outsourcing various information technology activities, "a provider must beat a bank's internal costs by about 40 percent."[141]

To verify that the appropriate primary and support activities are outsourced, four skills are essential for managers involved in outsourcing programs: strategic thinking, deal making, partnership governance, and change management.[142] Managers should understand whether and how outsourcing creates competitive advantage within their company—they need to be able to think strategically.[143] To complete effective outsourcing transactions, these managers must also be deal makers, able to secure rights from external providers that can be fully used by internal managers. They must be able to oversee and govern appropriately the relationship with the company to which the services were outsourced. Because outsourcing can significantly change how an organization operates, managers administering

Outsourcing—Boon or Bane to Competitiveness?

Outsourcing has become a popular strategic action but also has been highly controversial, playing a role in major political debates in some countries. Its popularity is shown by the fact that major electronics companies outsource the manufacturing and often even the design of their products. In fact, 89 percent of the brand-name laptop computers sold by Dell and Hewlett-Packard are manufactured by firms located in other countries. The primary reasons for outsourcing are to lower costs of production and to have a partner with strong expertise in the outsourced area. If the company to which a firm outsources activities is chosen carefully, the product should be manufactured with higher quality and with more efficiency than the outsourcing company could have done. Yet some politicians are concerned about the loss of jobs, while others retort that such actions are necessary for companies to remain competitive in global markets. If firms are not allowed to outsource, they may lose their competitive advantage and be unable to compete in local or global markets. This outcome would most assuredly cost more jobs than outsourcing would.

Outsourcing has reached into all areas of business. For example, medical doctors now often outsource MRI and CT scanning. Such outsourcing saves them from purchasing expensive equipment and from employing people to operate the machines and interpret the data from the scans. An outsourcing organization such as The Center for Diagnostic Imaging, a company controlled by Onex of Toronto, can potentially do the work more cheaply and more accurately. Companies such as The Center for Diagnostic Imaging, the India-based software outsourcer Infosys Technologies, and the Taiwanese computer manufacturing outsourcer Quanta Computer have gained immensely from this outsourcing revolution.

Some firms are now outsourcing functions that previously were considered to be core competencies or critical to their competitive position. Perhaps the most forbidden area of outsourcing in prior years has been research and development, but outsourcing has reached to R&D as well. In some industries, even those where technology is critical, large amounts of R&D are outsourced. For example, large pharmaceutical firms now outsource 40 to 60 percent of their R&D activities. R&D operations can account for 5 to 18 percent of the total costs of major technology companies. To reduce these costs and remain competitive in global markets, many technology firms have been outsourcing parts of their R&D operations to specialized companies in India, China, and Eastern Europe. However, it is critical that they select the appropriate activities to outsource, maintain control, and ensure balance and smooth coordination along the R&D value chain. Essentially, firms must analyze their R&D value chains to identify and keep strategic activities in-house and outsource nonstrategic activities. Care must be taken in the choice of activities to outsource and in selection of the partner to perform the outsourced activities.

One risk of outsourcing is that the partner will gain access to the technical knowledge needed to become a competitor at a future date. For example, Motorola contracted with BenQ Corporation, a Taiwanese company specializing in the manufacturing of computing, communications, and consumer electronics devices, to design and manufacture its mobile phones. But, in 2004, BenQ began to manufacture and market mobile phones in China under its own brand name. Motorola cancelled its contract with BenQ but the damage was done. In addition to this type of risk, Deloitte Consulting found that approximately one-third of the companies that outsourced did not achieve the efficiencies and cost savings expected. Deloitte concluded that outsourcing introduces complexity and some potential coordination costs into the value chain, and recommended that firms take special care in choosing the functions or activities to outsource.

SOURCES: 2008, Onex Web site, The Center for Diagnostic Imaging, retrieved February 18; M. Kanellos, 2005, Outsourcing giant Wipro eyes consulting gigs, *New York Times*, www.nytimes.com, May 3; D. Armstrong, 2005, MRI and CT centers offer doctors way to profit on scans, *Wall Street Journal*, www.wsj.com, May 2; R. Christie, 2005, Outsourcing pitfalls await unwary firms seeking savings, *Wall Street Journal*, www.wsj.com, April 29; T. Hallett, 2005, Outsourcing your core competencies, www.silicon.com, April 28; E. Bellman, 2005, Outsourcing lifts India's Infosys, *Wall Street Journal*, www.wsj.com, April 15; P. Engardio, 2005, Online extra: R&D jobs: Who stays, who goes? *BusinessWeek*, www.businessweek.com, March 21; C. Koch, 2005, Innovation ships out, *CIO*, www.cio.com, January 15; D. Kirkpatrick, 2004, Why outsourcing isn't really the issue, *Fortune*, www.fortune.com, October 29.

these programs must also be able to manage that change, including resolving the employee resistance that accompanies any significant change effort.[144]

There are concerns about the consequences of outsourcing. For the most part, these concerns revolve around the potential loss in firms' innovative ability and the loss of jobs within companies that decide to outsource some of their work activities to others. Thus, innovation and technological uncertainty are two important issues to consider in making outsourcing decisions.[145] Companies should be aware of these issues and be prepared to fully consider the concerns about outsourcing when different stakeholders (e.g., employees) express them. See the Strategic Focus for more on outsourcing.

Competencies, Strengths, Weaknesses, and Strategic Decisions

At the conclusion of the internal analysis, firms must identify their strengths and weaknesses in resources, capabilities, and core competencies. For example, if they have weak capabilities or do not have core competencies in areas required to achieve a competitive advantage, they must acquire those resources and build the capabilities and competencies needed. Alternatively, they could decide to outsource a function or activity where they are weak in order to improve the value that they provide to customers.[146]

Therefore, firms need to have the appropriate resources and capabilities to develop the desired strategy and create value for customers and shareholders as well.[147] Having many resources does not necessarily lead to success. Firms must have the right ones, and the capabilities needed to produce superior value to customers. Undoubtedly, ensuring the appropriate and strong capabilities required for achieving a competitive advantage is a primary responsibility of top-level managers.[148] These important leaders must focus on both the firm's strengths and weaknesses.

Core Competencies and Core Rigidities: Cautions and Reminders

Tools such as outsourcing help the firm focus on its core competencies as the source of its competitive advantages. However, evidence shows that the value-creating ability of core competencies should never be taken for granted. Moreover, the ability of a core competency to be a permanent competitive advantage can't be assumed. The reason for these cautions is that all core competencies have the potential to become *core rigidities*. That is, if a once–core competency continues to be emphasized when it is no longer competitively relevant, it can become a weakness or core rigidity—and a seed of organizational inertia.

Events occurring in the firm's external environment create conditions through which core competencies can become core rigidities, generate inertia, and stifle innovation. "Often the flip side, the dark side, of core capabilities is revealed due to external events when new competitors figure out a better way to serve the firm's customers, when new technologies emerge, or when political or social events shift the ground underneath."[149] However, in the final analysis, changes in the external environment do not cause core competencies to become core rigidities; rather, strategic myopia and inflexibility on the part of managers are the cause.[150]

The Opening Case emphasized the importance of innovation for many firms. How important innovation is to firm success depends partly on the firm's industry and competitive environment as determined through the external environment analysis explained in Chapter 3. If it is important, a firm with strengths in technology development or technological knowledge held can base its strategy on this capability (or competence).[151] We conclude that determining what the firm can do through continuous and effective analyses of its internal environment increases the likelihood of long-term competitive success.

Summary

- In the global landscape, traditional factors (e.g., labour costs and superior access to financial resources and raw materials) can still create a competitive advantage. However, this happens in a declining number of instances. In the new landscape, the resources, capabilities, and core competencies in the firm's internal environment may have a relatively stronger influence on its performance than do conditions in the external environment. The most effective organizations recognize that strategic competitiveness and above-average returns result only when core competencies (identified through the study of the firm's internal environment) are matched with opportunities (determined through the study of the firm's external environment).

- No competitive advantage lasts forever. Over time, rivals use their own unique resources, capabilities, and core competencies to form different value-creating propositions that duplicate the value-creating ability of the firm's competitive advantages. In general, the Internet's capabilities are reducing the sustainability of many competitive advantages. Because competitive advantages are not permanently sustainable, firms must exploit their current advantages while simultaneously using their resources and capabilities to form new advantages that can lead to competitive success in the future.

- Effective management of core competencies requires careful analysis of the firm's resources (inputs to the production process) and capabilities (resources that have been purposely integrated to achieve a specific task or set of tasks). The knowledge possessed by human capital is among the most significant of an organization's capabilities and may ultimately be at the root of all competitive advantages. The firm must create an environment that allows people to integrate their individual knowledge with that held by others so that, collectively, the firm has significant organizational knowledge.

- Individual resources are usually not a source of competitive advantage. Capabilities are a more likely source of competitive advantages, especially relatively sustainable ones. A key reason for this is that the firm's nurturing and support of core competencies that are based on capabilities is less visible to rivals and, as such, is harder to understand and imitate.

- Only when a capability is valuable, rare, costly to imitate, and organized to be exploited is it a core competency and a source of competitive advantage. Over time, core competencies must be supported, but they cannot be allowed to become core rigidities. Core competencies are a source of competitive advantage only when they allow the firm to create value by exploiting opportunities in its external environment. When this is no longer the case, attention shifts to selecting or forming other capabilities that do satisfy the four criteria of sustainable competitive advantage.

- Value chain analysis is used to identify and evaluate the competitive potential of resources and capabilities. By studying their skills relative to those associated with primary and support activities, firms can understand their cost structure and identify the activities through which they can create value. Analyzing an organization's value chain using the VRIO framework is a very valuable activity for a firm's senior managers.

- When the firm cannot create value in either a primary or support activity, outsourcing is considered. Used commonly in the global economy, outsourcing is the purchase of a value-creating activity from an external supplier. The firm must outsource only to companies possessing a competitive advantage in terms of the particular primary or support activity under consideration. In addition, the firm must continuously verify that it is not outsourcing activities from which it could create value.

Review Questions

1. Why is it important for a firm to study and understand its internal environment?

2. What is value? Why is it critical for the firm to create value? How does it do so?

3. What are the differences between tangible and intangible resources? Why is it important for decision makers to understand these differences? Are tangible resources linked more closely to the creation of competitive advantages than are intangible resources, or is the reverse true? Why?

4. What are capabilities? What must firms do to create capabilities?

5. What are the four criteria used to determine which capabilities belonging to a firm are core competencies? Why is it important for these criteria to be used?

6. What is value chain analysis? What does the firm gain when it successfully uses this tool in combination with the VRIO framework?

7. What is outsourcing? Why do firms outsource? Will outsourcing's importance grow in the 21st century? If so, why?

8. How do firms identify internal strengths and weaknesses? Why is it vital that firms base their strategy on such strengths and weaknesses?

IBM entered the personal computer (PC) business in the early 1980s. Determined to get into the business quickly, IBM outsourced almost everything except for what it likely believed was most essential to the operation of the machine: the BIOS (Basic Input/Output System). The BIOS is the built-in software that tells the computer how to receive information from the keyboard, disk drives, and so on and send data to the monitor, printer, etc. Yet it is more likely that the most essential things a computer does are to retrieve, manipulate, and store information (programs, data, entertainment, etc.). To do this the essential part of the system is the Disk Operating System (DOS). IBM designed and copyrighted the BIOS and outsourced the DOS to Bill Gates at Microsoft. IBM has since sold its PC business to Lenovo of China, and Bill Gates is one of the richest people on Earth.

1. It turns out that IBM's BIOS was copied more easily than IBM executives likely thought. One of the first companies to "copy" the IBM BIOS was Phoenix Technologies. Google "How Phoenix copied IBM's BIOS" (without the quotation marks) to find out how this was done. While the actions taken by Phoenix were legal, do you think what the company did was ethical? Why? Why not?

2. Though IBM bought copies of DOS from Microsoft to use on its machines, IBM did not hold the exclusive right to buy the product and Bill Gates was free to sell it to anyone who asked. Did Gates have some obligation to IBM to restrict others from purchasing DOS? Should IBM have made its arrangement with Gates exclusive to them? How would the PC business have been different if this had happened?

3. Apple Computer's Operating System was owned by Apple and efforts to buy or copy it were met with stiff legal opposition. Because of this, Apple's share of the market was limited. Was Apple within its rights to do this? Would allowing freer access to Apple's operating system have been more socially responsible—to customers; to suppliers; or to shareholders?

Competitive Advantage in Athletic Footwear

Athletic footwear is a market where one often thinks of Nike as the dominant firm with clear competitive advantages over its rivals. But if this were true, the other participants would be falling by the wayside. Instead, Nike's rivals continue to do well in this market, although not on the level of Nike. In this exercise you will explore the nature of competitive advantage in the athletic footwear market and the way in which smaller competitors capture and retain one or more competitive advantages, both against a dominant rival (Nike in this instance) and against each other.

In Groups. Find relevant competitive information about the following firms—companies that are competing in the athletic apparel–footwear industry:

- K-Swiss, Inc. (KSWS)

- Adidas-Salomon AG OR (ADDDF.PK)

- Reebok International (RBK)

For each firm, prepare answers to the following questions:

- What is the firm's source of competitive advantage?

- How has the firm been able to sustain this competitive advantage in such a competitive marketplace?

In answering these questions, be certain to use the materials and frameworks appearing in this chapter.

Outsourcing and Competencies

Outsourcing has become increasingly popular. As discussed in this chapter, one of the major concerns firms should have with outsourcing is the relationship between its core competencies and the task or activity being outsourced. In the text and in the Strategic Focus in this chapter that deals with outsourcing, several concerns were raised regarding the negative effects of poor outsourcing decisions on a firm's competitive advantages.

In this exercise, you are presented with three outsourcing opportunities for firms. These are three different situations with various implications flowing from a decision to outsource one or more activities. In each of the three situations, an important consideration is how the outsourced activity relates to the key skills that firms need to develop and retain for a core competency, both now and in the future. The situations do not include firm-specific facts, but an analysis of the industry in each situation will indicate what the critical success factors are in that industry.

Part One. The first step is to think of an industry in which you have an interest. Once you have chosen an industry, obtain an "industry report." Standard & Poor's Industry Surveys or the quarterly industry summaries in the Value Line Investment Survey are good sources to consult to obtain information about the industry that is of interest to you. Study the information in the industry report you have used in order to identify skills you believe a firm would have to possess in order to compete successfully in your chosen industry. Make a list of those skills.

Part Two. With an understanding of the skills that are likely to be critical for success in the industry, evaluate each of the following outsourcing situations. Indicate the advice you would give to the firm as to the wisdom of outsourcing this activity. Be ready to defend your rationale.

- The reservation call centre for an airline
- A software firm's helpline
- A credit card company selling additional services to cardholders

Organizational Resources

The firms listed below have different core competencies. All are clear leaders in their industries, although all also have strong rivals. In the first part of this exercise, you will research one of the firms, identifying its competencies. You will then evaluate those competencies vis-à-vis its rivals. Finally, you will suggest ways in which these competitive advantages could be lost.

Part One—In Groups. Listed below are four firms that have a clear and sustained competitive advantage in their industries. Behind these advantages are core competencies, and that is what you want to first identify. Using online sources, analysts' reports from brokerage houses, or other tools such as the Value Line Investment Survey, identify the core competencies of the firm you have been assigned. Remember that core competencies are a special type of capability, so it is something that a firm does particularly well compared to its rivals. Outcomes of competencies such as market share, reputation, brand, low cost, and the like follow from and are sustained by

core competencies. Thus, these are not the core competencies you are looking for.

- Home Depot
- Starbucks
- Tiffany
- Wal-Mart

Part Two—In Groups. Evaluate each core competency you have identified in Part One for your firm using the criteria of valuable, rare, imperfectly imitable, and organized to be exploited. Remember, if any of these four criteria are not met, then the firm's ability to sustain competitive advantage through this core competency is not present. Be sure that you can defend your selections with respect to each of the four criteria. If you exclude one of the competencies you selected, be able to explain why you changed your mind. Be careful that you apply the concepts correctly by referring back to the material in the text as needed.

Part Three—In Groups. For the core competencies that you retained after completing Part Two of this exercise, identify what the firm has to do in order to sustain these core competencies over time. Put another way, what could the firm do or not do that would lead to the erosion and eventual loss of the competitive advantage that each of those core competencies drives?

Part Four—Whole Class. Each group will present its analysis to the class and the rationale behind its conclusions.

Notes

1. A. Andal-Ancion, P. A. Cartwright, & G. S. Yip, 2003, The digital transformation of traditional businesses, *MIT Sloan Management Review,* 44(4): 34–41.
2. R. R. Wiggins & T. W. Ruefli, 2002, Sustained competitive advantage: Temporal dynamics and the incidence of persistence of superior economic performance, *Organization Science,* 13: 82–105.
3. S. K. McEvily, K. M. Eisenhardt, & J. E. Prescott, 2004, The global acquisition, leverage, and protection of technological competencies, *Strategic Management Journal,* 25: 713–722.
4. Wikipedia, Nokia, http://en.wikipedia.org/wiki/Nokia.
5. 2003, Nokia press release, http://press.nokia.com/PR/200309/918690_5.html, September 26.
6. 2007, Nokia rolls phone groups into single division, http://pcworld.about.com/od/companynews/Nokia-rolls-phone-groups-into.htm, June 20.
7. Ibid.
8. 2007, Nokia rolls phone groups into single division.
9. 2005, Getting an edge on innovation, BusinessWeek Online, www.businessweek.com, March 21.
10. M. Iansiti, F. W. McFarlan, & G. Westerman, 2003, Leveraging the incumbent's advantage, *MIT Sloan Management Review,* 44(4): 58–64; P. W. Roberts & G. R. Dowling, 2002, Corporate reputation and sustained superior financial performance, *Strategic Management Journal,* 23: 1077–1093.
11. S. Dutta, M. J. Zbaracki, & M. Bergen, 2003, Pricing process as a capability: A resource-based perspective, *Strategic Management Journal,* 24: 615–630;

A. M. Knott, 2003, Persistent heterogeneity and sustainable innovation, *Strategic Management Journal,* 24: 687–705.
12. C. G. Brush, P. G. Greene, & M. M. Hart, 2001, From initial idea to unique advantage: The entrepreneurial challenge of constructing a resource base, *Academy of Management Executive,* 15(1): 64–78.
13. T. J. Douglas & J. A. Ryman, 2003, Understanding competitive advantage in the general hospital industry: Evaluating strategic competencies, *Strategic Management Journal,* 24: 333–347; R. Makadok, 2001, Toward a synthesis of the resource-based and dynamic-capability views of rent creation, *Strategic Management Journal,* 22: 387–401.
14. D. G. Sirmon, M. A. Hitt, & R. D. Ireland, 2007, Managing firm resources in dynamic markets to create value: Looking inside the black box, *Academy of Management Review,* in press.
15. G. Hamel & L. Valikangas, 2003, The quest for resilience, *Harvard Business Review,* 81(9): 52–63; S. A. Way, 2002, High-performance work systems and intermediate indicators of firm performance within the U.S. small-business sector, *Journal of Management,* 28: 765–785; M. A. Hitt, L. Bierman, K. Shimizu, & R. Kochhar, 2001, Direct and moderating effects of human capital on strategy and performance in professional service firms: A resource-based perspective, *Academy of Management Journal,* 44: 13–28.
16. M. A. Hitt, C. C. Miller, & A. Colella, 2006. *Organizational Behavior: A Strategic Approach,* New York: John Wiley & Sons.

17. D. A. Wolfe, 2006, Program on Globalization and Regional Innovation Systems: Innovation and Creativity in City Regions, Centre for International Studies, University of Toronto, March 30.
18. R. Florida, 2005, *The Flight of the Creative Class,* New York: HarperBusiness.
19. D. A. Wolfe, 2006, Program on Globalization and Regional Innovation Systems: Innovation and Creativity in City Regions.
20. J. Shamsie, 2003, The context of dominance: An industry-driven framework for exploiting reputation, *Strategic Management Journal,* 24: 199–215; E. Autio, H. J. Sapienza, & J. G. Almeida, 2000, Effects of age at entry, knowledge intensity, and imitability on international growth, *Academy of Management Journal,* 43: 909–924.
21. M. Makhija, 2003, Comparing the resource-based and market-based view of the firm: Empirical evidence from Czech privatization, *Strategic Management Journal,* 24: 433–451; P. L. Yeoh & K. Roth, 1999, An empirical analysis of sustained advantage in the U.S. pharmaceutical industry: Impact of firm resources and capabilities, *Strategic Management Journal,* 20: 637–653.
22. D. F. Abell, 1999, Competing today while preparing for tomorrow, *Sloan Management Review,* 40(3): 73–81; D. Leonard-Barton, 1995, *Wellsprings of Knowledge: Building and Sustaining the Sources of Innovation,* Boston: Harvard Business School Press; R. A. McGrath, J. C. MacMillan, & S. Venkataraman, 1995, Defining and developing competence: A strategic process paradigm, *Strategic Management Journal,* 16: 251–275.
23. H. K. Steensma & K. G. Corley, 2000, On the performance of technology-sourcing partnerships: The interaction between partner interdependence and technology attributes, *Academy of Management Journal,* 43: 1045–1067.
24. J. B. Barney, 2001, Is the resource-based "view" a useful perspective for strategic management research? Yes, *Academy of Management Review,* 26: 41–56.
25. C. Lee, K. Lee, & J. M. Pennings, 2001, Internal capabilities, external networks, and performance: A study on technology-based ventures, *Strategic Management Journal,* 22 (special issue): 615–40; C. C. Markides, 1999, A dynamic view of strategy, *Sloan Management Review,* 40(3): 55–72; Abell, Competing today while preparing for tomorrow.
26. R. L. Priem & J. E. Butler, 2001, Is the resource-based "view" a useful perspective for strategic management research? *Academy of Management Review,* 26: 22–40.
27. P. J. H. Schoemaker & R. Amit, 1994, Investment in strategic assets: Industry and firm-level perspectives, in P. Shrivastava, A. Huff, & J. Dutton (eds.), *Advances in Strategic Management,* Greenwich, CT.: JAI Press, 9.
28. Barney, Is the resource-based "view" a useful perspective for strategic management research? Yes; J. B. Barney, 1995, Looking inside for competitive advantage, *Academy of Management Executive,* 9(4): 49–61
29. A. Madhok, 1997, Cost, value and foreign market entry mode: The transaction and the firm, *Strategic Management Journal,* 18: 39–61.
30. W. Kuemmerle, 2001, Go global—Or not? *Harvard Business Review,* 79(6): 37–49.
31. G. Ahuja & C. M. Lambert, 2001, Entrepreneurship in the large corporation: A longitudinal study of how established firms create breakthrough inventions, *Strategic Management Journal,* 22 (special issue): 521–543; A. Arora & A. Gambardella, 1997, Domestic markets and international competitiveness: Generic and product specific competencies in the engineering sector, *Strategic Management Journal,* 18 (special summer issue): 53–74.
32. M. Subramani & N. Venkataraman, 2003, Safeguarding investments in asymmetric interorganizational relationships: Theory and evidence, *Academy of Management Journal,* 46: 46–62.
33. T. M. Begley & D. P. Boyd, 2003, The need for a corporate global mind-set, *MIT Sloan Management Review,* 44(2): 25–32.
34. Sirmon, Hitt, & Ireland, Managing resources in a dynamic environment.
35. Barney, Is the resource-based "view" a useful perspective for strategic management research? Yes; T. H. Brush & K. W. Artz, 1999, Toward a contingent resource-based theory: The impact of information asymmetry on the value of capabilities in veterinary medicine, *Strategic Management Journal,* 20: 223–250.
36. S. K. McEvily & B. Chakravarthy, 2002, The persistence of knowledge-based advantage: An empirical test for product performance and technological knowledge, *Strategic Management Journal,* 23: 285–305.
37. Sirmon, Hitt, & Ireland, Managing resources in a dynamic environment.
38. J. Benedict, E. M. Steenkamp, R. Batra, & D. L. Alden, 2003, How perceived brand globalness creates brand value, *Journal of International Business Studies,* 34: 53–65.
39. S. Nambisan, 2002, Designing virtual customer environments for new product development: Toward a theory, *Academy of Management Review,* 27: 392–413.
40. J. Wolf & W. G. Egelhoff, 2002, A reexamination and extension of international strategy-structure theory, *Strategic Management Journal,* 23: 181–189; R. Ramirez, 1999, Value co-production: Intellectual origins and implications for practice and research, *Strategic Management Journal,* 20: 49–65.
41. V. Shankar & B. L. Bayus, 2003, Network effects and competition: An empirical analysis of the home video game industry, *Strategic Management Journal,* 24: 375–384; S. W. Floyd & B. Wooldridge, 1999, Knowledge creation and social networks in corporate entrepreneurship: The renewal of organizational capability, *Entrepreneurship: Theory and Practice,* 23(3): 123–143.
42. G. Hawawini, V. Subramanian, & P. Verdin, 2003, Is performance driven by industry- or firm-specific factors? A new look at the evidence, *Strategic Management Journal,* 24: 1–16; M. A. Hitt, R. D. Nixon, P. G. Clifford, & K. P. Coyne, 1999, The development and use of strategic resources, in M. A. Hitt, P. G. Clifford, R. D. Nixon, & K. P. Coyne (eds.), *Dynamic Strategic Resources,* Chichester: John Wiley & Sons, 1–14.
43. M. R. Haas & M. T. Hansen, 2005, When using knowledge can hurt performance: The value of organizational capabilities in a management consulting company, *Strategic Management Journal,* 26: 1–24.
44. C. M. Christensen, 2001, The past and future of competitive advantage, *Sloan Management Review,* 42(2): 105–109.
45. J. R. Hough & M. A. White, 2003, Environmental dynamism and strategic decision-making rationality: An examination at the decision level, *Strategic Management Journal,* 24: 481–489.
46. C. J. Robertson & W. F. Crittenden, 2003, Mapping moral philosophies: Strategic implications for multinational firms, *Strategic Management Journal,* 24: 385–392.
47. C. M. Christensen & M. E. Raynor, 2003, Why hard-nosed executives should care about management theory, *Harvard Business Review,* 81(9): 66–74.
48. N. Checa, J. Maguire, & J. Barney, 2003, The new world disorder, *Harvard Business Review,* 81(8): 70–79; P. Westhead, M. Wright, & D. Ucbasaran, 2001, The internationalization of new and small firms: A resource-based view, *Journal of Business Venturing* 16(4): 333–358.
49. H. J. Smith, 2003, The shareholders vs. stakeholders debate, *MIT Sloan Management Review,* 44(4): 85–90; H. Collingwood, 2001, The earnings game: Everyone plays, nobody wins, *Harvard Business Review,* 79(6): 65–74.
50. P. C. Nutt, 2002, *Why Decisions Fail,* San Francisco: Berrett-Koehler Publishers.
51. J. M. Mezias & W. H. Starbuck, 2003, What do managers know, anyway? *Harvard Business Review,* 81(5): 16–17; M. Keil, 2000, Cutting your losses: Extricating your organization when a big project goes awry, *Sloan Management Review,* 41(3): 55–68.
52. P. G. Audia, E. Locke, & K. G. Smith, 2000, The paradox of success: An archival and a laboratory study of strategic persistence following radical environmental change, *Academy of Management Journal,* 43: 837–853; R. G. McGrath, 1999, Falling forward: Real options reasoning and entrepreneurial failure, *Academy of Management Review,* 24: 13–30.
53. G. P. West III & J. DeCastro, 2001, The Achilles heel of firm strategy: Resource weaknesses and distinctive inadequacies, *Journal of Management Studies,* 38: 417–442; G. Gavetti & D. Levinthal, 2000, Looking forward and looking backward: Cognitive and experimental search, *Administrative Science Quarterly,* 45: 113–137.
54. R. Amit & P. J. H. Schoemaker, 1993, Strategic assets and organizational rent, *Strategic Management Journal,* 14: 33–46.
55. R. E. Hoskisson & L. W. Busenitz, 2001, Market uncertainty and learning distance in corporate entrepreneurship entry mode choice, in M. A. Hitt, R. D. Ireland, S. M. Camp, & D. L. Sexton (eds.), *Strategic Entrepreneurship:*

Creating a New Integrated Mindset, Oxford, UK: Blackwell Publishers, 151–172.

56. C. M. Fiol & E. J. O'Connor, 2003, Waking up! Mindfulness in the face of bandwagons, *Academy of Management Review,* 28: 54–70.

57. N. J. Hiller & D. C. Hambrick, 2005, Conceptualizing executive hubris: The role of (hyper-) core self-evaluations in strategic decision making, *Strategic Management Journal,* 26: 297–319.

58. P. Burrows & A. Park, 2002, What price victory at Hewlett-Packard? *BusinessWeek,* April 1, 36–37.

59. J. M. Mezias, P. Grinyer, & W. D. Guth, 2001, Changing collective cognition: A process model for strategic change, *Long Range Planning,* 34(1): 71–95.

60. Wikipedia, 2007, Amazon Inc., http://en.wikipedia.org/wiki/Amazon.com, accessed November 11.

61. 2007, Amazon launches music download service, September 26, The Associated Press.

62. Ibid.

63. 2007, Google takes YouTube global, *BusinessWeek,* June 19.

64. Ibid.

65. Ibid.

66. Ibid.

67. D. M. De Carolis, 2003, Competencies and imitability in the pharmaceutical industry: An analysis of their relationship with firm performance, *Journal of Management,* 29: 27–50.

68. G. Ahuja & R. Katila, 2004, Where do resources come from? The role of idiosyncratic situations, *Strategic Management Journal,* 25: 887–907.

69. D. L. Deeds, D. De Carolis, & J. Coombs, 2000, Dynamic capabilities and new product development in high-technology ventures: An empirical analysis of new biotechnology firms, *Journal of Business Venturing,* 15: 211–229; T. Chi, 1994, Trading in strategic resources: Necessary conditions, transaction cost problems, and choice of exchange structure, *Strategic Management Journal,* 15: 271–290.

70. Sirmon, Hitt, & Ireland, Managing resources in dynamic environments; S. Berman, J. Down, & C. Hill, 2002, Tacit knowledge as a source of competitive advantage in the National Basketball Association, *Academy of Management Journal,* 45: 13–31.

71. 2003, About Borders Group, www.borders.com, July 18; S. Shepard, 2001, Interview: "The company is not the stock," *BusinessWeek,* April 30, 94–96.

72. K. G. Smith, C. J. Collins, & K. D. Clark, 2005, Existing knowledge, knowledge creation capability, and the rate of new product introduction in high-technology firms, *Academy of Management Journal,* 48: 346–357; S. G. Winter, 2005, Developing evolutionary theory for economics and management, in K. G. Smith and M. A. Hitt (eds.), *Great minds in management: The process of theory development.* Oxford, UK: Oxford University Press, 509–546.

73. Subramani & Venkataraman, Safeguarding investments; R. Lubit, 2001, Tacit knowledge and knowledge management: The keys to sustainable competitive advantage, *Organizational Dynamics,* 29(3): 164–178.

74. A. M. Webber, 2000, New math for a new economy, *Fast Company,* January/February, 214–224.

75. M. Song, C. Droge, S. Hanvanich, & R. Calatone, 2005, Marketing and technology resource complementarity: An analysis of their interaction effect in two environmental contexts, *Strategic Management Journal,* 26: 259–276; R. G. Schroeder, K. A. Bates, & M. A. Junttila, 2002, A resource-based view of manufacturing strategy and the relationship to manufacturing performance, *Strategic Management Journal,* 23: 105–117.

76. M. A. Hitt & R. D. Ireland, 2002, The essence of strategic leadership: Managing human and social capital, *Journal of Leadership and Organization Studies,* 9(1): 3–14.

77. J. B. Quinn, P. Anderson, & S. Finkelstein, 1996, Making the most of the best, *Harvard Business Review,* 74(2): 71–80.

78. S. Tallman, M. Jenkins, N. Henry, & S. Pinch, 2004, Knowledge, clusters and competitive advantage, *Academy of Management Review,* 29: 258–271; A. W. King & C. P. Zeithaml, 2003, Measuring organizational knowledge: A conceptual and methodological framework, *Strategic Management Journal,* 24: 763–772.

79. 2003, Intellectual property, Special Advertising Section, *BusinessWeek,* July 28.

80. K. Funk, 2003, Sustainability and performance, *MIT Sloan Management Review,* 44(2): 65–70.

81. R. D. Ireland, M. A. Hitt, & D. Vaidyanath, 2002, Managing strategic alliances to achieve a competitive advantage, *Journal of Management,* 28: 416–446.

82. D. L. Deephouse, 2000, Media reputation as a strategic resource: An integration of mass communication and resource-based theories, *Journal of Management,* 26: 1091–1112.

83. Shamsie, The context of dominance.

84. Roberts & Dowling, Corporate reputation, 1078.

85. P. Berthon, M. B. Holbrook, & J. M. Hulbert, 2003, Understanding and managing the brand space, *MIT Sloan Management Review,* 44(2): 49–54; D. B. Holt, 2003, What becomes an icon most? *Harvard Business Review,* 81(3): 43–49.

86. J. Blasberg & V. Vishwanath, 2003, Making cool brands hot, *Harvard Business Review,* 81(6): 20–22.

87. 2003, Harley-Davidson MotorClothes Merchandise, www.harleydavidson.com, July 20.

88. D. Roberts & S. Holmes, 2005, China's real sports contest, BusinessWeek Online, www.businessweek.com, March 14.

89. R. D. Nixon, M. A. Hitt, H. Lee, & E. Jeong, 2004, Market reactions to announcements of corporate downsizing actions and implementation strategies, *Strategic Management Journal,* 25: 1121–1129.

90. N. W. Hatch & J. H. Dyer, 2004, Human capital and learning as a source of sustainable competitive advantage, *Strategic Management Journal,* 25: 1155–1178.

91. T. Gardner, 2005, Interfirm competition for human resources: Evidence from the software industry, *Academy of Management Journal,* 48: 237–256; S. J. Peterson & B. K. Spiker, 2005, Establishing the positive contributory value of older workers: A positive psychology perspective, *Organizational Dynamics,* 34(2): 153–167.

92. D. Wighton & D. Wells, 2005, Morgan Stanley to woo talent at rival banks, *Financial Times Online,* www.ft.com, July 4.

93. Sirmon, Hitt, & Ireland, Managing firm resources in dynamic environments; S. Dutta, O. Narasimhan, & S. Rajiv, 2005, Conceptualizing and measuring capabilities: Methodology and empirical application, *Strategic Management Journal,* 26: 277–285.

94. Hitt, Bierman, Shimizu, & Kochhar, Direct and moderating effects of human capital on strategy and performance in professional service firms: A resource-based perspective; M. A. Hitt, R. D. Ireland, & H. Lee, 2000, Technological learning, knowledge management, firm growth and performance: An introductory essay, *Journal of Engineering and Technology Management,* 17: 231–246.

95. S. K. Ethiraj, P. Kale, M. S. Krishnan, & J. V. Singh, 2005, Where do capabilities come from and do they matter? A study in the software services industry, *Strategic Management Journal,* 26: 25–45.

96. M. G. Jacobides & S. G. Winter, 2005, The co-evolution of capabilities and transaction costs: Explaining the institutional structure of production, *Strategic Management Journal,* 26: 395–413.

97. R. W. Coff & P. M. Lee, 2003, Insider trading as a vehicle to appropriate rent from R&D, *Strategic Management Journal,* 24: 183–190.

98. D. L. Deeds, 2003, Alternative strategies for acquiring knowledge, in S. E. Jackson, M. A. Hitt, & A. S. DeNisi (eds.), *Managing Knowledge for Sustained Competitive Advantage,* San Francisco: Jossey-Bass, 37–63.

99. R. A. Noe, J. A. Colquitt, M. J. Simmering, & S. A. Alvarez, 2003, Knowledge management: Developing intellectual and social capital, in S. E. Jackson, M. A. Hitt, & A. S. DeNisi (eds.), *Managing Knowledge for Sustained Competitive Advantage,* San Francisco: Jossey-Bass, 209–242; L. Argote & P. Ingram, 2000, Knowledge transfer: A basis for competitive advantage in firms, *Organizational Behavior and Human Decision Processes,* 82: 150–169.

100. M. J. Tippins & R. S. Sohi, 2003, IT competency and firm performance: Is organizational learning a missing link? *Strategic Management Journal,* 24: 745–761.

101. M. A. Hitt & R. D. Ireland, 1986, Relationships among corporate level distinctive competencies, diversification strategy, corporate structure, and performance, *Journal of Management Studies,* 23: 401–416; M. A. Hitt & R. D. Ireland, 1985, Corporate distinctive competence, strategy, industry, and performance, *Strategic Management Journal,* 6: 273–293; M. A. Hitt, R. D. Ireland, & K. A. Palia, 1982, Industrial firms' grand strategy and functional importance, *Academy of Management Journal,* 25: 265–298; M. A. Hitt, R. D. Ireland, & G. Stadter, 1982, Functional importance and company performance: Moderating effects of grand strategy and industry type, *Strategic Management Journal,* 3: 315–330; C. C. Snow & E. G. Hrebiniak, 1980, Strategy, distinctive competence, and organizational performance, *Administrative Science Quarterly,* 25: 317–336.

102. C. Zott, 2003, Dynamic capabilities and the emergence of intraindustry differential firm performance: Insights from a simulation study, *Strategic Management Journal,* 24: 97–125.

103. K. Hafeez, Y. B. Zhang, & N. Malak, 2002, Core competence for sustainable competitive advantage: A structured methodology for identifying core competence, *IEEE Transactions on Engineering Management,* 49(1): 28–35; C. K. Prahalad & G. Hamel, 1990, The core competence of the corporation, *Harvard Business Review,* 68(3): 79–93.

104. C. Bowman & V. Ambrósini, 2000, Value creation versus value capture: Towards a coherent definition of value in strategy, *British Journal of Management,* 11: 1–15.

105. C. Bowman, 2001, "Value" in the resource-based view of the firm: A contribution to the debate, *Academy of Management Review,* 26: 501–502.

106. C. Ames, 1995, Sales soft? Profits flat? It's time to rethink your business, *Fortune,* June 25, 142–146.

107. 2007, Innovation: Lessons from Apple: What other companies can learn from California's master of innovation, *The Economist,* June 7.

108. R. Thomlinson, 2005, Unilever: One company, two bosses, many problems, Fortune Online, www.fortune.com, January 13.

109. 2007, Strategy: Procter vs Unilever, *Marketing Week,* May 24, 22.

110. J. B. Barney, 1999, How a firm's capabilities affect boundary decisions, *Sloan Management Review,* 40(3): 137–145; J. B. Barney, 1995, Looking inside for competitive advantage, *Academy of Management Executive,* 9(4): 59–60; J. B. Barney, 1991, Firm resources and sustained competitive advantage, *Journal of Management,* 17: 99–120.

111. Barney, Looking inside for competitive advantage.

112. 2005, Jack Welch: It's all in the sauce, Fortune Online, www.fortune.com, April 4.

113. Barney, Looking inside for competitive advantage, 52.

114. Ibid, 53.

115. Barney, Firm resources, 108.

116. L. E. Tetrick & N. Da Silva, 2003, Assessing the culture and climate for organizational learning, in S. E. Jackson, M. A. Hitt, & A. S. DeNisi (eds.), *Managing Knowledge for Sustained Competitive Advantage,* San Francisco: Jossey-Bass, 333–359.

117. L. Soupata, 2001, Managing culture for competitive advantage at United Parcel Service, *Journal of Organizational Excellence,* 20(3): 19–26.

118. A. W. King & C. P. Zeithaml, 2001, Competencies and firm performance: Examining the causal ambiguity paradox, *Strategic Management Journal,* 22: 75–99.

119. Wikipedia, Lululemon Athletica, http://en.wikipedia.org/wiki/Lululemon_athletica.

120. Barney, Firm resources, 111.

121. Amit & Schoemaker, Strategic assets, 39.

122. M. J. Benner & M. L. Tushman, 2003, Exploitation, exploration, and process management: The productivity dilemma revisited, *Academy of Management Review,* 28: 238–256; S. K. McEvily, S. Das, & K. McCabe, 2000, Avoiding competence substitution through knowledge sharing, *Academy of Management Review,* 25: 294–311.

123. A. Serwer, 2002, Dell does domination, *Fortune,* January 21, 70–75.

124. Barney, 2002, *Gaining and Sustaining Competitive Advantage.*

125. Ibid.

126. 2006, Make Operational Innovations: You Must Change Your Way of Thinking, http://wharton.universia.net, September 20.

127. Wikipedia, Toyota Production System, http://en.wikipedia.org/wiki/Toyota_Production_System.

128. 2006, Make Operational Innovations.

129. Sirmon, Hitt, & Ireland, Managing firm resources in dynamic environments; M. E. Porter, 1985, *Competitive Advantage,* New York: Free Press, 33–61.

130. G. G. Dess, A. Gupta, J.-F. Hennart, & C. W. L. Hill, 1995, Conducting and integrating strategy research at the international corporate and business levels: Issues and directions, *Journal of Management,* 21: 376.

131. R. Amit & C. Zott, 2001, Value creation in e-business, *Strategic Management Journal,* 22 (special issue): 493–520; M. E. Porter, 2001, Strategy and the Internet, *Harvard Business Review,* 79(3): 62–78.

132. T. W. Gainey & B. S. Klaas, 2003, The outsourcing of training and development: Factors impacting client satisfaction, *Journal of Management,* 29: 207–229.

133. M. Rola, 2002, Secrets to successful outsourcing management, *Computing Canada,* 28(23): 11.

134. P. Bendor-Samuel, 2003, Outsourcing: Transforming the corporation, *Forbes,* Special Advertising Section, May 26.

135. K. Madigan & M. J. Mandel, 2003, Commentary: Outsourcing jobs: Is it bad? Business Week Online, www.businessweek.com, August 25.

136. J. Palmer, 2003, Auto supplier stands out by focusing on the inside, Wall Street Journal Online, www.wsj.com, August 17; A. Takeishi, 2001, Bridging inter- and intra-firm boundaries: Management of supplier involvement in automobile product development, *Strategic Management Journal,* 22: 403–433; H. Y. Park, C. S. Reddy, & S. Sarkar, 2000, Make or buy strategy of firms in the U.S., *Multinational Business Review,* 8(2): 89–97.

137. M. J. Leiblein, J. J. Reuer, & F. Dalsace, 2002, Do make or buy decisions matter? The influence of organizational governance on technological performance, *Strategic Management Journal,* 23: 817–833.

138. J. C. Linder, S. Jarvenpaa, & T. H. Davenport, 2003, Toward an innovation sourcing strategy, *MIT Sloan Management Review,* 44(4): 43–49.

139. Hafeez, Zhang, & Malak, Core competence for sustainable competitive advantage; B. H. Jevnaker & M. Bruce, 1999, Design as a strategic alliance: Expanding the creative capability of the firm, in M. A. Hitt, P. G. Clifford, R. D. Nixon, & K. P. Coyne (eds.), *Dynamic Strategic Resources,* Chichester: John Wiley & Sons, 266–298.

140. Takeishi, Bridging inter- and intra-firm boundaries.

141. R. Lancellotti, O. Schein, & V. Stadler, 2003, When outsourcing pays off, *The McKinsey Quarterly,* Number 1, 10.

142. M. Useem & J. Harder, 2000, Leading laterally in company outsourcing, *Sloan Management Review,* 41(2): 25–36.

143. R. C. Insinga & M. J. Werle, 2000, Linking outsourcing to business strategy, *Academy of Management Executive,* 14(4): 58–70.

144. M. Katz, 2001, Planning ahead for manufacturing facility changes: A case study in outsourcing, *Pharmaceutical Technology,* March, 160–164.

145. M. J. Mol, P. Pauwels, P. Matthyssens, & L. Quintens, 2004, A technological contingency perspective on the depth and scope of international outsourcing, *Journal of International Management,* 10: 287–305.

146. M. A. Hitt, D. Ahlstrom, M. T. Dacin, E. Levitas, & L. Svobodina, 2004, The institutional effects on strategic alliance partner selection in transition economies: China versus Russia, *Organization Science,* 15: 173–185.

147. Y. Mishina, T. G. Pollock, & J. F. Porac, 2004, Are more resources always better for growth? Resource stickiness in market and product expansion, *Strategic Management Journal,* 25: 1179–1197.

148. D. S. Elenkov & I. M. Manev, 2005, Top management leadership and influence in innovation: The role of sociocultural context, *Journal of Management,* 31: 381–402.

149. Leonard-Barton, *Wellsprings of Knowledge,* 30–31.

150. West & DeCastro, The Achilles heel of firm strategy; Keil, Cutting your losses.

151. D. J. Miller, 2004, Firms' technological resources and the performance effects of diversification: A longitudinal study, *Strategic Management Journal,* 25: 1097–1119.

Part Two

Strategic Actions: Strategy Formulation

Chapter Five

Business-Level Strategy

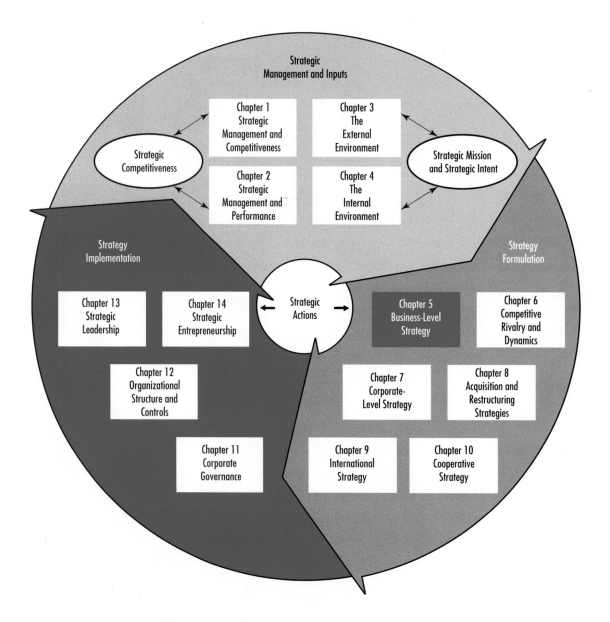

Knowledge Objectives

Studying this chapter should provide you with the strategic management knowledge needed to:

1. Define business-level strategy.

2. Discuss the relationship between customers and business-level strategies in terms of *who*, *what*, and *how*.

3. Explain the differences among business-level strategies.

4. Use the five forces of competition model to explain how above-average returns can be earned through each business-level strategy.

5. Describe the risks of using each of the business-level strategies.

Has Saan Become Surplus?

The headline in the *Peace River Block Daily News* in early 2005 proclaimed "Saturday is SAAN's last day." Saan had been a fixture in rural Canada for over 50 years. The Saan in Dawson Creek, B.C. was one of over 80 stores in the chain that would be closed in the first half of 2005 when the chain underwent bankruptcy protection. Another victim of the Wal-Mart onslaught, the Saan store at the Dawson Mall was closed after the companies in charge of liquidating the chain's inventory decided that continuing the store's clearance sale was not viable. The merchandise was transferred to higher-selling stores. Store manager Tracey Winland noted "It's just not a profitable store."

www.saan.ca/saantoday.html

Saan suffered from a number of problems. The company had weaker than anticipated sales. Saan incurred burdensome costs from sizable overhead expenses related to the company's head office, warehousing, and other support systems. The company also had substantial costs associated with a number of unprofitable and onerous contracts. All of this meant that the company had only two profitable years out of the last six prior to going into bankruptcy.

Saan was founded in 1947 as a war surplus outlet on Winnipeg's Main Street. The chain's name stood for Surplus Army, Airforce, Navy. A bygone equivalent of the five-and-dime in rural Canada, the chain dealt mostly with clothing and footwear. In recent years, Saan had expanded into some department store items like small electronics. Saan's expansion reached its peak in the late 1990s when the chain boasted 350 stores. The chain itself may be surplus to the stock of discount retailers in Canada. Larger chains like Wal-Mart and Giant Tiger had made inroads into Saan's suburban and rural markets.

Carol Baron, a councillor with the municipality of Red Lake in northwestern Ontario—a mining community of 4,900—expressed what could be thought of as a typical response to the bankruptcy filings: "Hopefully, ours is not on the chopping block." She said, "A lot of residents depend on it. . . . It is our most economical type of clothing and variety store." Barton noted that if the Saan store closed, Red Lake residents would either have to drive $2\frac{1}{2}$ hours to the Wal-Mart in Dryden or about $3\frac{1}{2}$ hours to the Zellers in Kenora. She said, "it's a long day down and back."

The company had attempted to expand the format of some stores to match those of its larger competitors. However, it did not make such investments in traditional rural markets. Saan's newer, larger stores were located in suburban "power centres"—locations with vast amounts of retail space and two or three big box stores (like Wal-Mart or Home Depot) clustered together—and where smaller stores like Saan may get overlooked. In its filing under the Companies' Creditors Arrangement Act (CCAA)—Saan's second bankruptcy in under 10 years—company executives noted that this strategy backfired, and "contributed to the financial crisis that has precipitated the need for the CCAA proceedings."

Even though the company came out of bankruptcy and whittled itself down about 120 stores, Saan is far from out of the woods. Debts left over from its 2005 bankruptcy filing still haunt the firm. What caused the downfall of Saan? The answer is perhaps familiar: inefficient, high-cost operations and a failure to stick to the smaller rural markets where Saan could best provide value to customers. From a strategic perspective, the firm's demise resulted from its below-average returns, which was a direct result of its not successfully implementing its business-level strategy.

SOURCES: M. Strauss, 2005, Saan chain gets creditor protection, *The Globe and Mail*, January 7, B4; H. Shaw, 2005, Saan may escape bankruptcy with most stores intact, *National Post*, January 15, FP6; G. Rusak, 2005, Saturday is SAAN's last day, *Peace River Block Daily News*, January 28, 1; M. Strauss, 2007, Struggling Saan seeks financing, *The Globe and Mail*, December 13, B4; Saan Web page, 2007, http://www.saan.ca/2005/ccaa_en.htm, December 18.

Increasingly important to firm success,[1] strategy is concerned with making choices among two or more alternatives.[2] As we noted in Chapter 1, when choosing a strategy the firm decides to pursue one course of action instead of others. The choices made are influenced by opportunities and threats in the firm's external environment (see Chapter 3) as well as the nature and quality of its internal resources, capabilities, and core competencies[3] (see Chapter 4). Historically, Saan used the unique product line and location strategy to take advantage of an opportunity to satisfy the demand from customers in rural areas.

The fundamental objective of using any type of strategy (refer to Figure 1.1) is to gain strategic competitiveness and earn above-average returns.[4] Strategies are purposeful, precede the taking of actions to which they apply, and demonstrate a shared understanding of the firm's vision and mission.[5] An effectively formulated strategy marshals, integrates, and allocates the firm's resources, capabilities, and competencies so that it will be properly aligned with its external environment.[6] A properly developed strategy also rationalizes the firm's vision and mission along with the actions taken to achieve them.[7] Information about a host of variables including markets, customers, technology, worldwide finance, and the changing world economy must be collected and analyzed to properly form and use strategies. Increasingly, Internet technology affects how organizations gather and study data and information that are related to decisions about the choice and use of strategy. In the final analysis, sound strategic choices, ones that reduce uncertainty regarding outcomes,[8] are the foundation on which successful strategies are built.[9]

Business-level strategy, this chapter's focus, is an integrated and coordinated set of commitments and actions the firm uses to gain a competitive advantage by exploiting core competencies in specific product markets.[10] This means that business-level strategy indicates the choices the firm has made about how it intends to compete in individual product markets. The choices are important, as there is an established link between a firm's strategies and its long-term performance.[11] Given the complexity of successfully competing in the global economy, these choices are difficult, often even gut-wrenching.[12] For example, to increase the effectiveness of its differentiation business-level strategy (we define and discuss this strategy later in the chapter), Montreal-based Domtar recently decided to close some manufacturing facilities and to reduce its labour force. Describing his reaction to making these decisions, the firm's CEO said, "Mill closures are very difficult decisions to make . . . The measures . . . are necessary actions that will help the Corporation return to profitability."[13] Decisions made at Saan, such as the closing of the Dawson Creek and 80 other stores, were also difficult.

A **business-level strategy** is an integrated and coordinated set of commitments and actions the firm uses to gain a competitive advantage by exploiting core competencies in specific product markets.

Every firm must form and use a business-level strategy.[14] However, every firm may not use all the strategies—corporate-level, acquisition and restructuring, international, and cooperative—that we examine in Chapters 7 through 10. For example, think of a local dry cleaner with only one location offering a single service (the cleaning and laundering of clothes) in a single storefront. A firm competing in a single–product market area in a single geographic location does not need a corporate-level strategy to deal with product diversity or an international strategy to deal with geographic diversity. In contrast, a diversified firm will use one of the corporate-level strategies as well as choose a separate business-level strategy for each product market area in which the company competes (the relationship between corporate-level and business-level strategies is further examined in Chapter 7). Every firm—from the local dry cleaner to the multinational corporation—chooses at least one business-level strategy. This means that business-level strategy is the *core* strategy—the strategy the firm forms to describe how it intends to compete in a product market.[15]

We discuss several topics to examine business-level strategies. Because customers are the foundation of successful business-level strategies and should never be taken for granted,[16] we offer information about customers that is relevant to choosing a business-level strategy. In terms of customers, when selecting a business-level strategy the firm determines (1) *who* will be served, (2) *what* needs those target customers have that it will satisfy, and (3) *how* those needs will be satisfied. Selecting customers and deciding which of their needs the firm will try to satisfy, as well as how it will do so, are challenging tasks. Global competition, which has created many attractive options for customers, is one reason for this. In the current competitive environment, effective global competitors have become adept at identifying the needs of customers in different cultures and geographic regions as well as learning how to quickly and successfully adapt the functionality of the firms' good or service to meet those needs.

Descriptions of the purpose of business-level strategies and of the five business-level strategies follow the discussion of customers. The five strategies we examine are called *generic* because they can be used in any organization competing in any industry.[17] Our analysis describes how effective use of each strategy allows the firm to favourably position itself relative to the five competitive forces in the industry (see Chapter 3). In addition, we use the value chain (see Chapter 4) to show examples of the primary and support activities that are necessary to implement certain business-level strategies. Because no strategy is risk-free,[18] we also describe the different risks the firm may encounter when using one of these strategies. In Chapter 12, we explain the organizational structures and controls that are linked with the successful use of each business-level strategy.

Customers: Their Relationship with Business-Level Strategies

Strategic competitiveness results only when the firm is able to satisfy a group of customers by using its competitive advantages as the basis for competing in individual product markets. A key reason why firms must satisfy customers with their business-level strategy is that returns earned from relationships with customers are the lifeblood of all organizations.[19] In straightforward language, "Without customers, you don't have a business."[20]

The most successful companies try to find new ways to satisfy current customers and/or to meet the needs of new customers. Dell Inc. does this with an "unrelenting sense of urgency and speed"[21]; Dell believes solutions to customers' needs should be provided quickly and flawlessly. Recently, to meet the needs of home and small-office users and to increase its profitability while doing so, Dell started selling the first sub-$100 laser printer.[22] Dell, similar to other organizations concerned with satisfying customers' needs, manages its relationships with customers in order to understand their current and future needs.[23]

Effectively Managing Relationships with Customers

The firm's relationships with its customers are strengthened when it delivers superior value to them. Strong interactive relationships with customers often provide the foundation for the firm's efforts to profitably serve customers' unique needs.

Calgary-based WestJet is so firmly committed to its customers that it feared that the company's growth would make it more difficult to maintain customer service as its most important priority. Thus, in mid-2006 WestJet established its Guest Experience Committee to review everything the airline does from the customer's viewpoint. "If it has a potential impact on the guest, we look at it," noted Lauri Feser, the airline's VP of marketing. The committee draws members from all the airline's operational areas. Eight core members meet every three weeks, pulling in other employees as required. While it does not have the final say, the committee's recommendations are seen as an important tool in gaining and retaining customers, and are thus given serious consideration by corporate executives.[24]

Importantly, delivering superior value often results in increased customer loyalty. In turn, customer loyalty has a positive relationship with profitability. In the financial services industry, for example, estimates are that companies "can boost profits by almost 100 percent by retaining just five percent more customers."[25] However, more choices and easily accessible information about the functionality of firms' products are creating increasingly sophisticated and knowledgeable customers, making it difficult to earn their loyalty.[26]

A number of companies have become skilled at the art of *managing* all aspects of their relationship with their customers.[27] For example, Amazon.com is an Internet-based venture widely recognized for the quality of information it maintains about its customers, the services it renders, and its ability to anticipate customers' needs.[28] Using the information it has, Amazon tries to serve what it believes are the unique needs of each customer. Based in Mexico, Cemex SA is a "leading global producer and marketer of quality cement and ready-mix concrete."[29] Cemex uses the Internet to link its customers, cement plants, and main control room, allowing the firm to automate orders and optimize truck deliveries in highly congested Mexico City. Analysts believe that Cemex's integration of Web technology with its cost leadership strategy is helping to differentiate it from competitors.[30]

Bank of Montreal (BMO) launched a B2B (business-to-business) e-procurement system called FlexPort. The FlexPort system was designed to ease purchase order, invoicing, and payment problems for customers and suppliers. Actually, FlexPort is more of a B2B2B system—the middle B being the bank. The data captured by FlexPort are translated by the bank and sent back to both buyers and sellers in formats they can each read and tie in to their own accounting and office systems. This reduces problems of trying to adapt the systems of each company to make the B2B transaction work and saving time and money for clients as well as enhancing relationships between customers.[31]

As we discuss next, there are three dimensions of firms' relationships with customers. Companies such as Amazon.com, Cemex, and Bank of Montreal understand these dimensions and manage their relationships with customers in light of them.

Reach, Richness, and Affiliation

The *reach* dimension is about the firm's access and connection to customers. For instance, Canada's largest physical retailer in bookstores, Chapters.Indigo.ca, carries over one million titles to Canadian Internet users and through its hundreds of physical stores (under the Chapters, Indigo, W.H. Smith, and Coles names). By contrast, Amazon.com offers some 4.5 million titles and is located on millions of computer screens. Thus, Amazon.com's reach is significantly magnified relative to that associated with Chapters.Indigo.ca's physical bookstores or likely Internet users.[32]

Richness, the second dimension, is concerned with the depth and detail of the two-way flow of information between the firm and the customer. The potential of the richness dimension to help the firm establish a competitive advantage in its relationship with customers has led traditional financial services brokers, like TD Waterhouse, to offer online services in order to better manage information exchanges with their customers. Broader and deeper information-based exchanges allow firms to better understand their customers and their needs. Such exchanges also enable customers to become more knowledgeable about how the firm can satisfy them. Internet technology and e-commerce transactions have substantially reduced the costs of meaningful information exchanges with current and possible future customers.

Affiliation, the third dimension, is concerned with facilitating useful interactions with customers. The Canadian government's National Research Council independently evaluates all types of innovative construction products, systems, and services through its Institute for Research in Construction (IRC). Its evaluations are based on the latest technical research and expertise. Companies represent their own products, creating a situation in which its financial interests differ substantially from those of builders. Because the IRC's revenues come from sources other than the producer (such as through advertisements in its publications or on its Web site), builders using IRC-evaluated products or services in construction feel they can trust the evaluations. Hence, the IRC provides a service that promotes the user's affiliation with the organization through its independence.[33] Viewing the world through the customer's eyes and constantly seeking ways to create more value for the customer have positive effects in terms of affiliation.

As we discuss next, effective management of customer relationships (along the dimensions of reach, richness, and affiliation) helps the firm answer questions related to the issues of *who, what,* and *how.*

Who: Determining the Customers to Serve

Market segmentation is a process used to cluster people with similar needs into individual and identifiable groups.

Deciding *who* the target customer is that the firm intends to serve with its business-level strategy is an important decision.[34] To make this decision, companies divide customers into groups based on differences in customers' needs (needs are discussed further in the next section). Dividing customers into groups based on their needs is called **market segmentation,** which is a process that clusters people with similar needs into individual and identifiable groups.[35] In the animal health business, for example, the needs for food products of owners of companion pets (e.g., dogs and cats) differ from the needs for food products of those owning production animals (e.g., livestock).[36] As part of its business-level strategy, the firm develops a marketing program to effectively sell products to its particular target customer group.[37]

Almost any identifiable human or organizational characteristic can be used to subdivide a market into segments that differ from one another on a given characteristic. Common characteristics on which customers' needs vary are illustrated in Table 5.1. Based on their internal core competencies and opportunities in the external environment, companies choose a business-level strategy to deliver value to target customers and satisfy their specific needs.

Customer characteristics are often combined to segment markets into specific groups that have unique needs. In the consumer clothing market, for example, Gap learned that its female and male customers want different shopping experiences. In a company official's words, "Research showed that men want to come and go easily, while women want an exploration."[38] In light of these research results, newly developed women's sections in Gap stores are organized by occasion (e.g., work, going out) with accessories for those

Table 5.1	Basis for Customer Segmentation

Consumer Markets
1. Demographic factors (age, income, sex, etc.)
2. Socioeconomic factors (social class, stage in the family life cycle)
3. Geographic factors (cultural, regional, and national differences)
4. Psychological factors (lifestyle, personality traits)
5. Consumption patterns (heavy, moderate, and light users)
6. Perceptual factors (benefit segmentation, perceptual mapping)

Industrial Markets
1. End-use segments (identified by NAICS code)
2. Product segments (based on technological differences or production economics)
3. Geographic segments (defined by boundaries between countries or by regional differences within them)
4. Common buying factor segments (cut across product market and geographic segments)
5. Customer size segments

SOURCE: Adapted from S.C. Jain, 2000, *Marketing Planning and Strategy,* Cincinnati: South-Western College Publishing, p. 120.

occasions scattered throughout the section to facilitate browsing. The men's side of Gap stores is more straightforward, with signs used to direct male customers to clothing items that are commonly stacked by size. Thus, Gap is using its understanding of some of the psychological factors (see Table 5.1) influencing its customers' purchasing intentions to better serve unique groups' needs.

Demographic factors (see Table 5.1 and the discussion in Chapter 3) can also be used to segment markets into generations with unique interests and needs. Evidence suggests, for example, that direct mail is an effective communication medium for the World War II generation (those born before 1932). The Swing generation (those born between 1933 and 1945) values taking cruises and the purchase of second homes. Once financially conservative but now willing to spend money, members of this generation seek product information from knowledgeable sources. The Baby Boom generation (born between 1946 and 1964) desires products that reduce the stress generated by juggling career demands and the needs of older parents with those of their own children. TanJay clothes, known for their consistency of fit and colour, are targeted to Baby Boomer women. More conscious of hype, the millions of people in Generation X (born between 1965 and 1976) want products that deliver as promised. The Xers use the Internet as a primary shopping tool and expect visually compelling marketing. Members of this group are the fastest-growing segment of mutual-fund shareholders, with their holdings overwhelmingly invested in stock funds. As employees, the top priorities of Xers are to work in a creative learning environment, to receive constant feedback from managers, and to be rewarded for using their technical skills.[39] Different marketing campaigns and distribution channels (e.g., the Internet for Generation X customers, direct mail for the World War II generation) affect the implementation of strategies for those companies interested in serving the needs of different generations.

What: Determining Which Customer Needs to Satisfy

After the firm decides *who* it will serve, it must identify the targeted customer group's needs that its goods or services can satisfy. This is important in that successful firms learn how to deliver to customers want they want and when they want it.[40]

In a general sense, *needs (what)* are related to a product's benefits and features.[41] Having close and frequent interactions with both current and potential customers helps the firm identify those individuals' and groups' current and future needs.[42] From a strategic perspective, a basic need of all customers is to buy products that create value for them. The generalized forms of value that goods or services provide are either low cost with acceptable features, or highly differentiated features with acceptable cost. The most effective firms continuously strive to anticipate changes in customers' needs. Failure to do this results in the loss of customers to competitors who are offering greater value in terms of product features and functionalities. For example, some analysts believe that discounters, department stores, and other home furnishing chains are taking customers away from Pier 1 Imports Inc. Recent decisions to launch its first-ever catalogue, to upgrade its Web site, and to improve its marketing programs are possible indicators that Pier 1 has not anticipated changes in its customers' needs in as timely a manner as should be the case.

In any given industry, there is great variety among consumers in terms of their needs.[43] The need some consumers have for fast food may be satisfied by a high-quality, high-end lunch at Montreal brasserie Au Pied de Cochon. Au Pied de Cochon chef Martin Picard revels in pairing the high and the low. His $36 "Duck in a can" is, according to *Maclean's*, "half a mallard duck, foie gras, garlic and balsamic demi-glaze, canned, cooked, then ceremoniously opened at the table and dumped over bread and celeriac purée. He'll do fast-food fare but with top-notch ingredients."[44] In contrast, many large fast-food companies satisfy customer needs for lower-cost food items with

Chapter 5 / Business-Level Strategy

acceptable quality that is delivered quickly.[45] Diversified food and soft-drink producer PepsiCo believes that "any one consumer has different needs at different times of the day." Through its soft drinks (Pepsi products), snacks (Frito-Lay), juices (Tropicana), and cereals (Quaker), PepsiCo is working on developing new products from breakfast bars to healthier potato chips "to make certain that it covers all those needs."[46]

In general, and across multiple product groups (e.g., automobiles, clothing, food), evidence suggests that middle-market consumers in North America want to trade up to higher levels of quality and taste. These customers "are willing to pay premiums of 20% to 200% for the kinds of well-designed, well-engineered, and well-crafted goods—often possessing the artisanal touches of traditional luxury goods—not before found in the mass middle market."[47] These needs represent opportunities for some firms to pursue through their business-level strategies.

To ensure success, a firm must be able to fully understand the needs of the customers in the target group it has selected to serve. In this sense, customer needs are neither right nor wrong, good nor bad. They are simply the desires, in terms of features and performance capabilities, of those customers the firm has targeted to serve. The most effective firms are filled with people committed to understanding the customers' current as well as future needs.

How: Determining Core Competencies Necessary to Satisfy Customer Needs

As explained in Chapters 1 and 4, *core competencies* are resources and capabilities that serve as a source of competitive advantage for the firm over its rivals. Firms use core competency (*how*) to implement value-creating strategies and thereby satisfy customers' needs. Only those firms with the capacity to continuously improve, innovate, and upgrade their competencies can expect to meet and hopefully exceed customers' expectations across time.[48]

Companies draw from a wide range of core competencies to produce goods or services that can satisfy customers' needs. IBM, for example, emphasizes its core competency in technology to rapidly develop new service-related products. Beginning in 1993, CEO Lou Gerstner changed IBM by leveraging its "strength in network integration and consulting to transform [the firm] from a moribund maker of mainframe computers to a sexy services company that can basically design, build, and manage a corporation's entire data system."[49] Longueuil, Quebec's Emergis emphasizes its core competency in e-commerce activities and technologies to develop services for the health care industry. Emergis is involved in some of those "sexy" services of which Gersner spoke; specifically, electronic patient and health records, and the support areas of change management, system integration, consulting, implementation, and managed services.

Another example of a firm that draws upon its technological core competency is the SAS Institute. SAS is the world's largest privately owned software company and is the leader in business intelligence and analytics.[50] Customers use SAS's programs for data warehousing, data mining, and decision support purposes. Allocating over 30 percent of revenues to research and development (R&D), SAS relies on its core competency in R&D to satisfy the data-related needs of such customers as the U.S. Census Bureau and a host of consumer goods firms (e.g., hotels, banks, and catalogue companies).[51] All organizations, including IBM, Emergis, and SAS, must be able to use their core competencies (the *how*) to satisfy the needs (the *what*) of the target group of customers (the *who*) the firm has chosen to serve by using its business-level strategy.

Next, we describe the formal purpose of a business-level strategy and then the five business-level strategies available to all firms.

The Purpose of a Business-Level Strategy

The purpose of a business-level strategy is to create differences between the firm's position and those of its competitors.[52] To position itself differently from competitors, a firm must decide whether it intends to *perform activities differently* or to *perform different activities*.[53] In fact, "choosing to perform activities differently or to perform different activities than rivals" is the essence of business-level strategy.[54] Thus, the firm's business-level strategy is a deliberate choice about how it will perform the value chain's primary and support activities in ways that create unique value. Indeed, in the complex 21st-century competitive landscape, successful use of a business-level strategy results only when the firm learns how to integrate the activities it performs in ways that create competitive advantages that can be used to create value for customers.

Firms develop an activity map to show how they integrate the activities they perform. We show WestJet's activity map in Figure 5.1. The manner in which WestJet has integrated its activities is the foundation for the successful use of its integrated cost leadership/differentiation strategy (we discuss this strategy later in the chapter).[55] In Chapter 6's Opening Case, we describe how WestJet is significantly outperforming the competition. The tight integration among WestJet's activities is a key source of the firm's ability to operate more profitably than the competition.

As shown in Figure 5.1, WestJet has configured the activities it performs such that there are six strategic themes: limited passenger service; unique corporate culture; highly productive ground and gate crews; very low ticket prices; frequent, reliable departures; and high aircraft utilization. Individual clusters of tightly linked activities make it possible for the outcome of a strategic theme to be achieved. For example, no meals included, limited use of travel agents, no connections with other airlines, and no baggage transfers form a cluster of individual activities that support the strategic theme of limited passenger service (see Figure 5.1).

Figure 5.1	WestJet's Activity System

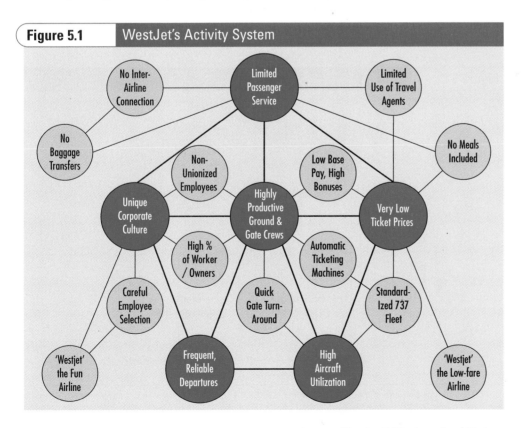

WestJet's tightly integrated activities make it difficult for competitors to imitate the firm's integrated cost leadership/differentiation strategy.[56] The firm's culture influences these activities and their integration and contributes to the firm's ability to continuously identify additional ways to differentiate WestJet's service from its competitors as well as to lower its costs. In fact, the firm's unique culture and customer service, both of which are sources of differentiated customer features, are competitive advantages that its rival has not been able to imitate, although it has tried. Hindsight shows that though Air Canada offered low prices to customers, it was not able to operate at costs close to those of WestJet or to provide customers with any notable sources of differentiation, such as a unique experience while in the air.

Fit among activities is a key to the sustainability of competitive advantage for all firms, including WestJet. As Michael Porter comments, "Strategic fit among many activities is fundamental not only to competitive advantage but also to the sustainability of that advantage. It is harder for a rival to match an array of interlocked activities than it is merely to imitate a particular sales-force approach, match a process technology, or replicate a set of product features. Positions built on systems of activities are far more sustainable than those built on individual activities."[57]

Types of Business-Level Strategies

Firms choose from among five business-level strategies to establish and defend their desired strategic position against competitors: *cost leadership, differentiation, focused cost leadership, focused differentiation,* and *integrated cost leadership/differentiation* (see Figure 5.2). Each business-level strategy helps the firm to establish and exploit a particular *competitive advantage* within a particular *competitive scope.* How firms integrate the activities they perform within each different business-level strategy demonstrates how they differ from one another.[58] Thus, firms have different activity maps—meaning, for example, that WestJet's activity map differs from those of competitor Air Canada and many international carriers.

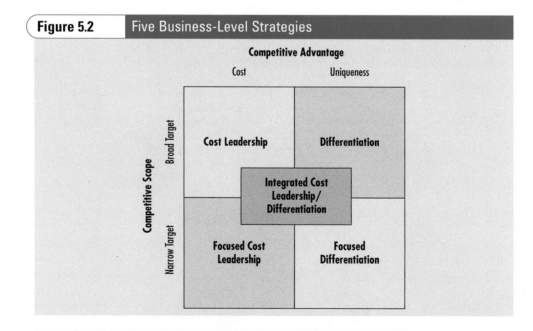

Figure 5.2   Five Business-Level Strategies

SOURCE: Adapted with permission of The Free Press, a Division of Simon & Schuster Adult Publishing Group, from *Competitive Advantage: Creating and Sustaining Superior Performance*, by Michael E Porter, p. 12. Copyright © 1985, 1998 by Michael E. Porter. All rights reserved.

Superior integration of activities increases the likelihood of being able to outperform competitors and to earn above-average returns as a result of doing so.

When selecting a business-level strategy, firms evaluate two types of potential competitive advantage: "lower cost than rivals, or the ability to differentiate and command a premium price that exceeds the extra cost of doing so."[59] Having lower cost derives from the firm's ability to perform activities differently than rivals; being able to differentiate indicates the firm's capacity to perform different (and valuable) activities.[60] Thus, based on the nature and quality of its internal resources, capabilities, and core competencies, a firm seeks to form either a cost competitive advantage or a uniqueness competitive advantage as the basis for implementing a particular business-level strategy.

There are two types of competitive scope—broad target and narrow target (see Figure 5.2). Firms serving a broad target market seek to use their competitive advantage on an industry-wide basis. A narrow competitive scope means that the firm intends to serve the needs of a narrow target customer group. With focus strategies, the firm "selects a segment or group of segments in the industry and tailors its strategy to serving them to the exclusion of others."[61] Buyers with particular needs and buyers located in specific geographic regions are examples of narrow target customer groups. As shown in Figure 5.2, a firm could also strive to develop a combined cost/uniqueness competitive advantage as the foundation for serving a target customer group that is larger than a narrow segment but not as comprehensive as a broad (or industry-wide) customer group. In this instance, the firm uses the integrated cost leadership/differentiation strategy.

None of the five business-level strategies shown in Figure 5.2 is inherently or universally superior to the others.[62] The effectiveness of each strategy is contingent both on the opportunities and threats in a firm's external environment and on the possibilities provided by the firm's unique resources, capabilities, and core competencies. It is critical, therefore, for the firm to select a business-level strategy that is based on a match between the opportunities and threats in its external environment and the strengths of its internal environment as shown by its core competencies.

Cost Leadership Strategy

The **cost leadership strategy** is an integrated set of actions taken to produce goods or services with features that are acceptable to customers at the lowest cost relative to that of competitors.[63] Firms using the cost leadership strategy sell no-frills, standardized goods or services (but with competitive levels of differentiation) to the industry's most typical customers. Cost leaders' goods and services must have competitive levels of differentiation in terms of features that create value for customers. Indeed, emphasizing cost reductions while ignoring competitive levels of differentiation is ineffective. At the extreme, concentrating only on reducing costs could find the firm very efficiently producing products that no customer wants to purchase.

As shown in Figure 5.2, the firm using the cost leadership strategy targets a broad customer segment or group. Cost leaders concentrate on finding ways to lower their costs relative to those of their competitors by constantly rethinking how to complete their primary and support activities to reduce costs still further while maintaining competitive levels of differentiation.[64] Aurora, Ontario's Magna International sells major components to almost every car manufacturer in the world. In an industry where customers are intensely price conscious, Magna has found a way to use employee flexibility, decentralized responsibility, innovation, and employee loyalty to become one of the world's largest parts suppliers.[65]

As primary activities, inbound logistics (e.g., materials handling, warehousing, and inventory control) and outbound logistics (e.g., collecting, storing, and distributing products to customers) often account for significant portions of the total cost to produce

The **cost leadership strategy** is an integrated set of actions taken to produce goods or services with features that are acceptable to customers at the lowest cost, relative to that of competitors.

some goods and services. Research suggests that having a competitive advantage in terms of logistics creates more value when using the cost leadership strategy than when using the differentiation strategy.[66] Thus, cost leaders seeking competitively valuable ways to reduce costs may want to concentrate on the primary activities of inbound logistics and outbound logistics.

Cost leaders also carefully examine all support activities to find additional sources of potential cost reductions. Developing new systems for finding the optimal combination of low cost and acceptable quality in the raw materials required to produce the firm's goods or services is an example of how the procurement support activity can facilitate successful use of the cost leadership strategy.

Calgary-based Liquidation World provides buyers with low-cost items but also takes the view that it provides a service to its vendors by allowing companies with "inventory problems" to maximize the financial recovery from their situation. In some ways, the company views the supplier as a customer too. Thus, Liquidation World specializes in "purchasing and marketing merchandise from distress situations. Inventories are acquired through insurance and freight claims, bankruptcies, receiverships, buybacks, over-production, cancelled orders . . . virtually any kind of problem situation." Because Liquidation World sells items through auctions or low cost/low rent facilities, they can keep the cost of selling goods to a minimum. In the company's warehouses in provinces from Ontario westward, as well as Montana, Alaska, and the U.S. Pacific Northwest, buyers find a sometimes surprising and ever-changing array of low-cost products. Buyers get more for their money, and sellers get more for their goods.[67]

As described in Chapter 4, firms use value-chain analysis to determine the parts of the company's operations that create value and those that do not. Figure 5.3 demonstrates the primary and support activities that allow a firm to create value through the cost leadership strategy. Companies unable to link the activities shown in this figure through the activity map they form typically lack the core competencies needed to successfully use the cost leadership strategy.

Effective use of the cost leadership strategy allows a firm to earn above-average returns in spite of the presence of strong competitive forces (see Chapter 3). The next sections (one for each of the five forces) explain how firms are able to do this.

Rivalry with Existing Competitors

Having the low-cost position is a valuable defence against rivals. Because of the cost leader's advantageous position, rivals hesitate to compete on the basis of price, especially before evaluating the potential outcomes of such competition.[68] Wal-Mart is known for its ability to both control and reduce costs, making it difficult for firms to compete against it on the basis of costs. The discount retailer achieves strict cost control in several ways: "Wal-Mart's 660,000-square-foot main headquarters, with its drab gray interiors and frayed carpets, looks more like a government building than the home of one of the world's largest corporations. Business often is done in the no-frills cafeteria, and suppliers meet with managers in stark, cramped rooms. Employees have to throw out their own garbage at the end of the day and double up in hotel rooms on business trips."[69]

In a cautionary tale for Canadian retailers, the former Kmart's decision to compete against Wal-Mart on the basis of cost contributed to the firm's failure and subsequent bankruptcy filing. Its competitively inferior distribution system—an inefficient and high-cost system compared with Wal-Mart's—is one of the factors that prevented Kmart from having a competitive cost structure.

If the lesson for Canadian retailers is not to compete against Wal-Mart on price, they are not all listening. When Wal-Mart rolled out food products into Ontario stores, Canadian competitors responded. Metro and Sobeys have "aggressive plans" to offer a

Firm Infrastructure	Cost-effective management information systems	Relatively few managerial layers in order to reduce overhead costs	Simplified planning practices to reduce planning costs		
Human Resource Management	Consistent policies to reduce turnover costs		Intense and effective training programs to improve worker efficiency and effectiveness		
Technology Development	Easy-to-use manufacturing technologies		Investments in technologies in order to reduce costs associated with a firm's manufacturing processes		
Procurement	Systems and procedures to find the lowest-cost (with acceptable quality) products to purchase as raw materials		Frequent evaluation processes to monitor suppliers' performances		
	Highly efficient systems to link suppliers' products with the firm's production processes	Use of economies of scale to reduce production costs / Construction of efficient-scale production facilities	A delivery schedule that reduces costs / Selection of low-cost transportation carriers	A small, highly trained sales force / Products priced so as to generate significant sales volume	Efficient and proper product installations in order to reduce the frequency and severity of recalls
	Inbound Logistics	**Operations**	**Outbound Logistics**	**Marketing and Sales**	**Service**

MARGIN

more premium shopping experience at their traditional, non-discount stores. To make itself more competitive, Loblaw is slowly lowering its supply-chain costs. As well, Loblaw entered into a more flexible contract with its union that allows the company to convert 44 of its "conventional" Loblaw or Zehrs stores to lower-cost Real Canadian Superstores. Because it is the biggest grocery chain in Canada (and having the volume discounts that may accompany such a position) and because Loblaw's parent, George Weston, produces a number of food lines for the chain (it owns numerous bakeries and Neilson Dairy, and controls the President's Choice brand name), Loblaw may well, given diligent efforts on the part of the company, have a cost structure that will allow it to compete with Wal-Mart.[70]

Although Wal-Mart is favourably positioned in terms of rivalry with its competitors, there are actions firms can take to successfully compete against this retailing giant. We discuss these actions in the Strategic Focus. Notice that in each instance, competitors able to outperform Wal-Mart complete one or more activities that create value for customers better or differently than Wal-Mart.

Wal-Mart Is Tough to Beat, But It Can Be Done

Wal-Mart's size and success are staggering. Its annual revenue of more than $315 billion is double that of the combined revenue totals of its five largest rivals. Analysts predict that within a decade Wal-Mart's annual revenues will be over half a trillion dollars. If it were a country today, Wal-Mart's revenue would be the third largest economy in the world.

A global powerhouse with locations in multiple countries, Wal-Mart was operating more than 820 million square feet of floor space at the end of 2007—20 percent more acreage than the entire island of Manhattan. However, some believe that Wal-Mart can be "had." The reason for this view is that, as discussed in Chapter 1, no competitive advantage is sustainable forever. In addition, all firms—including Wal-Mart—face savvy competitors who constantly strive to find ways to use their unique capabilities and core competencies to attack even a tough competitor's weaknesses. In one analyst's words, "As with all great powers, Wal-Mart has its imperfections, frailties that wily competitors have learned to exploit." Here are ways some firms have found to compete successfully against Wal-Mart:

1. **Target particular customers and fully understand their needs.** Sure you can get a tent and camping gear at Wal-Mart. But what about the ultra-lightweight, all-season tent and accompanying lightweight all-weather gear for your hike over the Chilkoot Pass as part of your individual re-creation of the Klondike Gold Rush? Mountain Equipment Co-op (MEC) is where you are headed. Because MEC members are very interested in excellent equipment and excellent prices, MEC tends to carry everything for climbing, camping, hiking, biking, kayaking, and mountaineering. The equipment costs more than you would spend at Wal-Mart, but for comparable quality you are likely to spend more almost anywhere else in Canada.

2. **Offer prices lower than Wal-Mart's.** A number of retailers, including Calgary's Liquidation World (mentioned earlier) and Edmonton's XS Cargo, offer prices lower than Wal-Mart on items that may come their way as part of special deals. Stores like Buck or Two have somewhat more consistent inventories at prices far below Wal-Mart. Wal-Mart may sell many of the items carried in Buck or Two, but often at higher prices. All these stores depend on relationships with buyers who search for remainders, discards, and odd-lot or leftover merchandise to provide the lowest cost merchandise. All would be more than happy to take excess inventory off a manufacturer's or retailer's shelves when it can do so at bargain-basement costs.

3. **Re-create customer experiences.** Canadian Tire demonstrates that a large group of Canadian customers value a convenient, attentive, uniquely Canadian retailer with a specialized product line. What could be more convenient than a store within a 15-minute drive for 85 percent of Canadians? Local Canadian Tire stores are fairly attentive to local needs; the organization is a chain of franchises, whose local owners have a better sense of what local customers are demanding. And while Wal-Mart may be the world's third biggest economy, only Canadian Tire prints and distributes its own currency. One sure way to keep customers coming back is to pay them, and when it is done using Canadian Tire "money," the customer has to come back to spend it at the store. The company is also unique in its product assortment. It carries three specialized product lines: automotive, sports and leisure, and home products. The company still has a fairly strong identity with consumers for auto-related needs, and justifiably Canadian Tire has the country's largest selection of auto parts.

4. **Provide superior service.** Wal-Mart's cost leadership strategy finds it offering "everyday low prices" without much service. Firms able to fully understand their customers and "coddle" them with a highly trained sales force can do well competing against Wal-Mart. The greeter at Wal-Mart may point the way to the buggies when you enter and perhaps perform a security check when you leave. Contrast this with an experience at a Black's photography store:

   "We're greeted at the door by a smartly dressed woman who takes the time to qualify us by asking questions to determine our wants. The salesperson calls me by name; easily produces the stack of [my] photos, then pauses and makes eye contact as she presents an alternative to simply paying the bill. She offers to sell me prepaid cards for digital photo processing, an option that would cut the bill considerably, and [she] perfectly describes how. I'm won over by her respectful and knowledgeable approach, and by what's obviously a great deal."

SOURCES: 2007, Good Magazine, http://awesome.goodmagazine.com/transparency/007/trans007storespace.html, December 23; L. Pratt & A. Bygdidyr, 2007, Retail report card, *Profit*, 26(5): 30–34; 2007, Wal-Mart stores, *Fortune 500*, http://money.cnn.com/magazines/fortune/fortune500/snapshots/1551.html, December 21; J. P. Sheppard & S. D. Chowdhury, 2005, Riding the wrong wave: Organizational failure as a failed turnaround, *Long Range Planning*, 38(3): 239–260; 2005, Outsmarting the B2B goliaths, *Re/Think Marketing*, www.rethinkmarketing.com, July 31; S. Hannaford, 2005, Both sides now, *Harvard Business Review*, 83(3): 17; M. Maier, 2005, How to beat Wal-Mart, *Business 2.0*, May, 108–114; D. K. Rigby & D. Haas, 2004, Outsmarting Wal-Mart, *Harvard Business Review*, 82(12): 22; K. Naughton, 2003, Out of the box thinking, *Newsweek*, May 12, 40–44.

Bargaining Power of Buyers (Customers)

Powerful customers can force a cost leader to reduce its prices, but not below the level at which the cost leader's next-most-efficient industry competitor can earn average returns. Although powerful customers might be able to force the cost leader to reduce prices even below this level, they probably would not choose to do so. Prices that are low enough to prevent the next-most-efficient competitor from earning average returns would force that firm to exit the market, leaving the cost leader with less competition and in an even stronger position. Customers would thus lose their power and pay higher prices if they were forced to purchase from a single firm operating in an industry without rivals. Consider Wal-Mart in this regard. Part of the reason why this firm's prices continue to be the lowest available is that, to successfully compete against competitors that are also trying to implement a cost leadership strategy (such as Loblaw or Costco), Wal-Mart continuously searches for ways to reduce its costs relative to competitors. Thus, customers benefit by Wal-Mart having to compete against others trying to use the cost leadership strategy and lowering its prices in the course of engaging in competitive battles.

Bargaining Power of Suppliers

The cost leader operates with margins greater than those of competitors. Among other benefits, higher margins relative to those of competitors make it possible for the cost leader to absorb its suppliers' price increases. When an industry faces substantial increases in the cost of its supplies, only the cost leader may be able to pay the higher prices and continue to earn either average or above-average returns. Alternatively, a powerful cost leader may be able to force its suppliers to hold down their prices, which would reduce suppliers' margins in the process. Wal-Mart and Loblaw both use their power with suppliers (gained because they buy such large quantities from many suppliers) to extract lower prices from them. These savings can then be passed on to customers in the form of lower prices, which further strengthens the organization's position relative to competitors lacking the power to extract lower prices from suppliers.[71]

Potential Entrants

Through continuous efforts to reduce costs to levels lower than competitors', a cost leader becomes highly efficient. Because ever-improving levels of efficiency enhance profit margins, they serve as a significant entry barrier to potential competitors. New entrants must be willing and able to accept no-better-than-average returns until they gain the experience required to approach the cost leader's efficiency. To earn even average returns, new entrants must have the competencies required to match the cost levels of competitors other than the cost leader. The low profit margins (relative to margins earned by firms implementing the differentiation strategy) make it necessary for the cost leader to sell large volumes of its product to earn above-average returns. However, firms striving to be the cost leader must avoid pricing their products so low that their ability to operate profitably is reduced, even though volume increases.

Product Substitutes

Compared with its industry rivals, the cost leader also holds an attractive position in terms of product substitutes. A product substitute becomes an issue for the cost leader when its features and characteristics, in terms of cost and differentiated features, are potentially attractive to the firm's customers. When faced with possible substitutes, the cost leader has more flexibility than its competitors. To retain customers, it can reduce the price of its good or service. With still lower prices and competitive levels of differentiation, the cost leader increases the probability that customers will prefer its product rather than a substitute.

Competitive Risks of the Cost Leadership Strategy

The cost leadership strategy is not risk free. One risk is that the processes used by the cost leader to produce and distribute its good or service could become obsolete because of competitors' innovations. These innovations may allow rivals to produce at costs lower than those of the original cost leader, or to provide additional differentiated features without increasing the product's price to customers.

A second risk is that too much focus by the cost leader on cost reductions may occur at the expense of trying to understand customers' perceptions of "competitive levels of differentiation." As noted earlier, Wal-Mart is well known for constantly and aggressively reducing its costs. At the same time, however, the firm must understand when a cost-reducing decision to eliminate differentiated features (e.g., extended shopping hours, a large number of checkout counters to reduce waits) would create a loss of value for customers.

A final risk of the cost leadership strategy concerns imitation. Using their own core competencies, competitors sometimes learn how to successfully imitate the cost leader's strategy. When this occurs, the cost leader must increase the value that its good or service provides to customers. Commonly, value is increased by selling the current product at an even lower price or by adding differentiated features that customers value while maintaining price. The ultimate example of a cost leader is Wal-Mart. Yet, as the Strategic Focus shows, even Wal-Mart can be beat.

Differentiation Strategy

The **differentiation strategy** is an integrated set of actions taken to produce goods or services (at an acceptable cost) that customers perceive as being different in ways that are important to them.

The **differentiation strategy** is an integrated set of actions taken to produce goods or services (at an acceptable cost) that customers perceive as being different in ways that are important to them.[72] While cost leaders serve an industry's typical customer, differentiators target customers who perceive that value is created for them by the manner in which the firm's products differ from those produced and marketed by competitors.

Firms must be able to produce differentiated products at competitive costs to reduce upward pressure on the price customers pay for them. When a product's differentiated features are produced with non-competitive costs, the price for the product can exceed what the firm's target customers are willing to pay. When the firm has a thorough understanding of what its target customers value, the relative importance they attach to the satisfaction of different needs, and for what they are willing to pay a premium, the differentiation strategy can be successfully used.[73]

Through the differentiation strategy, the firm produces no standardized products for customers who value differentiated features more than they value low cost. For example, superior product reliability and durability and high-performance sound systems are among the differentiated features of Toyota Motor Corporation's Lexus products. The Lexus promotional statement—"We pursue perfection, so you can pursue living"—suggests a strong commitment to overall product quality as a source of differentiation. However, Lexus offers its vehicles to customers at a competitive purchase price. As with Lexus products, a good's or service's unique attributes, rather than its purchase price, provide the value for which customers are willing to pay. For example, Please Mum produces and markets high quality, European-inspired clothing for children under 12 years old. Please Mum's clothes are sold at premium prices to parents who want both the durable, colourful quality and the exceptional sales service. Along with clean, well lit, and well-stocked outlets that provide play areas for young children, Please Mum allows customers to shop online and via individual at-home distributors that bring selections to a parent's home.[74]

Continuous success with the differentiation strategy results when the firm consistently upgrades differentiated features that customers value, without significant cost increases. Because a differentiated product satisfies customers' unique needs, firms following the differentiation strategy are able to charge premium prices. For customers to be willing to pay a premium price, however, a "firm must truly be unique at something or be perceived as unique."[75] The ability to sell a good or service at a price that substantially exceeds the cost of creating its differentiated features allows the firm to outperform rivals and earn above-average returns. For example, Harry Rosen's success rests on its ability to produce and sell differentiated products and excellent service at a price significantly higher than the costs of fabrics, hand-made manufacturing, and excellent fashion advice.

Rather than costs, a firm using the differentiation strategy always concentrates on investing in and developing features that differentiate a good or service in ways that customers value. Harry Rosen's tailors use the finest materials available and will make its customers a true bespoke suit—custom-sewn by hand after more than 20 measurements and details are taken from one single customer. The tailor then uses this personal, hand-drafted pattern cut from scratch to cut and trim the cloth. A single tailor is then given the parts of the garment to sew together. Each suit is completely hand-made, even down to the button holes.[76] It may cost $10,000.[77] More importantly, the company gives great service. Top-level managers spend significant amounts of time analyzing their customers and solving customer problems. The company's information system identifies customers who have not shopped recently, and CEO Rosen will personally call them all to find out why.[78] He has even been known to take a customer call while he is in top-level meetings. Rosen says, "Sometimes I get this silence on the other end of the line and the person says, 'I didn't really expect to get to speak to you'," but I don't live in some ivory tower, I work in our stores. . . ."[79] Spending executive time in this manner sends a strong signal to all employees that "our customers are our greatest concern."[80]

The less similarity between a firm's goods or services and those of competitors, the more buffered it is from rivals' actions. Commonly recognized differentiated goods include Toyota's Lexus, Ralph Lauren's wide array of product lines, and Caterpillar's heavy-duty earth-moving equipment. McKinsey & Co.—thought by some to be the world's most expensive and prestigious consulting firm—is a well-known example of a firm that offers differentiated services.

A good or service can be differentiated in many ways. Unusual features, responsive customer service, rapid product innovations and technological leadership, perceived prestige and status, different tastes, and engineering design and performance are examples of approaches to differentiation. There may be a limited number of ways to reduce costs (as demanded by successful use of the cost leadership strategy). In contrast, virtually anything a firm can do to create real or perceived value is a basis for differentiation. Consider product design as a case in point. Because it can create a positive experience for

Chapter 5 / Business-Level Strategy

customers,[81] design is becoming an increasingly important source of differentiation and, hopefully for firms emphasizing it, of competitive advantage.[82] Product design is being counted on at General Motors (GM), for example, to help the firm deal with the financial performance problems it has recently had to address. Indeed, some analysts believe that newly formed, interactive collaborations between GM designers and engineers are contributing to the development of car designs that are more stylish and visually appealing.[83] Firms using a differentiation strategy should remember that the work being completed in terms of all competitive dimensions (including design) should be oriented to satisfying customers' needs.[84]

A firm's value chain can be analyzed to determine whether the firm is able to link the activities required to create value by using the differentiation strategy. Examples of primary and support activities that are commonly used to differentiate a good or service are shown in Figure 5.4. Companies without the skills needed to link these activities cannot expect to successfully use the differentiation strategy. Next, we explain how firms using the differentiation strategy can successfully position themselves in terms of the five forces of competition (see Chapter 3) to earn above-average returns.

Figure 5.4   Examples of Value-Creating Activities Associated with the Differentiation Strategy

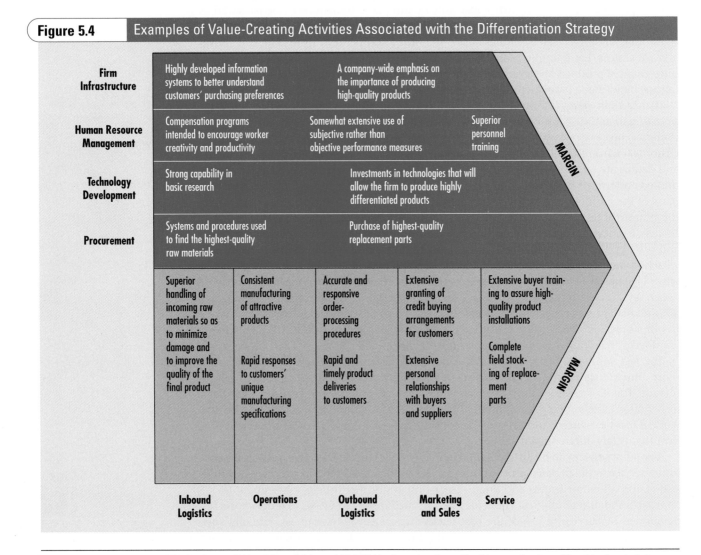

Rivalry with Existing Competitors

Customers tend to be loyal purchasers of products that are differentiated in ways that are meaningful to them. As their loyalty to a brand increases, customers' sensitivity to price increases is reduced. The relationship between brand loyalty and price sensitivity insulates a firm from competitive rivalry. Therefore, the Harry Rosen name has become an icon in high-end men's fashion and is thus insulated from competition, even on the basis of price, as long as the company continues to satisfy the differentiated needs of its customer group. Likewise, a company like Bose is insulated from intense rivalry as long as customers continue to perceive that its stereo equipment offers superior sound quality at a competitive purchase price.

Bargaining Power of Buyers (Customers)

The uniqueness of differentiated goods or services reduces customer sensitivity to price increases. Customers are willing to accept a price increase when a product still satisfies their perceived unique needs better than a competitor's offering can. Thus, the camper whose needs are uniquely satisfied by a Mountain Equipment Co-op tent will likely continue buying those products even if their cost increases. Similarly, the customer who has been highly satisfied with three-year-old gloves from Holt Renfrew will probably replace those gloves with another one made by the same company even though the purchase price is higher than the original one. Purchasers of brand-name food items (e.g., Schneiders meats or Purdy's Chocolates) will accept price increases in those products as long as they continue to perceive that the product satisfies their unique needs at an acceptable cost. Loyal customers of Abercrombie & Fitch Co.'s "preppy but edgy casual clothing at high prices" continue to buy the products even as they become more expensive.[85] In all of these instances, the customers are relatively insensitive to price increases because they do not think that an acceptable product alternative exists.

Bargaining Power of Suppliers

Because the firm using the differentiation strategy charges a premium price for its products, suppliers must provide high-quality components, driving up the firm's costs. However, the high margins the firm earns in these cases partially insulate it from the influence of suppliers in that higher supplier costs can be paid through these margins. Alternatively, because of buyers' relative insensitivity to price increases, the differentiated firm might choose to pass the additional cost of supplies on to the customer by increasing the price of its unique product.

Potential Entrants

Customer loyalty and the need to overcome the uniqueness of a differentiated product present substantial barriers to potential entrants. Entering an industry under these conditions typically demands significant investments of resources and patience while seeking customers' loyalty.

Product Substitutes

Firms selling brand-name goods and services to loyal customers are positioned effectively against product substitutes. In contrast, companies without brand loyalty face a higher probability of their customers switching either to products that offer differentiated features that serve the same function (particularly if the substitute has a lower price) or to products that offer more features and perform more attractive functions.

Competitive Risks of the Differentiation Strategy

As with the other business-level strategies, the differentiation strategy is not risk free. One risk is that customers might decide the price differential between the differentiator's product and the cost leader's product is too large. In this instance, a firm may be offering differentiated features that exceed target customers' needs. The firm then becomes vulnerable to competitors that are able to offer customers a combination of features and price that is more consistent with their needs.

Another risk of the differentiation strategy is that a firm's means of differentiation may cease to provide value for which customers are willing to pay. A differentiated product becomes less valuable if imitation by rivals causes customers to perceive that competitors offer essentially the same good or service, but at a lower price. For example, Walt Disney Company operates different theme parks, including The Magic Kingdom and Epcot Center. Each park offers entertainment and educational opportunities. However, Disney's competitors, such as Canada's Wonderland or Six Flags Corporation, also offer entertainment and educational experiences similar to those available at Disney's locations. To ensure that its facilities create value for which customers are willing to pay, Disney continuously reinvests in its operations to more crisply differentiate them from those of its rivals.[86]

A third risk of the differentiation strategy is that experience can narrow customers' perceptions of the value of a product's differentiated features. For example, customers having positive experiences with generic soft drinks may decide that the differentiated features of Coke or Pepsi are not worth the extra cost. Similarly, while a customer may be impressed with the quality of a Harry Rosen suit, positive experiences with less expensive suits may lead to a conclusion that the price exceeds the benefit. To counter this risk, firms must continue to meaningfully differentiate their product and the service they can provide for customers at a price they are willing to pay.

Counterfeiting is the differentiation strategy's fourth risk. Makers of counterfeit goods—products that attempt to convey a firm's differentiated features to customers at significantly reduced prices—are a concern for many firms using the differentiation strategy. Fakes can damage the reputation of the company. For example, in 2002, children's clothing printed with counterfeit Molson beer logos was seized in Edmonton. A spokesperson for Molson said it was completely inappropriate to have its logos on children's clothing and the company would never authorize such items. Poorly made fakes not only can damage the reputation of the company but also can endanger the health and lives of consumers. In January 2005, the RCMP seized about 5000 household extension cords from one vendor alone. While these devices displayed Underwriters Laboratories (UL) certification markings, when they were tested they melted and caught fire within a matter of minutes.[87] In late 2006, a Vancouver Island woman died after taking pills she purchased from a bogus online pharmacy.

Focus Strategies

Firms choose a focus strategy when they intend to use their core competencies to serve the needs of a particular industry segment or niche to the exclusion of others. Examples of specific market segments that can be targeted by a focus strategy include (1) a particular buyer group (e.g., youth or senior citizens), (2) a different segment of a product line (e.g., products for professional painters or those for "do-it-yourselfers"), or (3) a different geographic market (e.g., the East or the West in Canada, or urban versus rural).[88] Thus, the **focus strategy** is an integrated set of actions taken to produce goods or services that serve the needs of a particular competitive segment.

The **focus strategy** is an integrated set of actions taken to produce goods or services that serve the needs of a particular competitive segment.

To satisfy the needs of its particular buyer group—health-conscious, eco-friendly consumers—Verger Pierre Gingras of Rougemont, Quebec produces a line of high-end artisanal cider vinegar. Pierre Gingras uses only non–genetically modified apples picked directly from the tree and ferments the juice for two years in oak barrels from France to create a cider vinegar with a unique and distinctive flavour.[89] To satisfy its segment of a product line—the needs of world-class competitive figure skaters—Waterloo's Jackson

Ultima Skates produces heat-mouldable, custom-made, flexible-fit skates that need little break-in time (Olympic figure skaters Jeff Buttle, Elvis Stojko, and Surya Bonaly have all worn Jackson skates).[90] To meet the needs of its geographic market—mostly rural small-town customers—B.C.'s Overwaitea Foods locates in small towns around the province. Overwaitea's other store brands (e.g., Save On Foods, Urban Fare) concentrate on more urban markets. By successfully using a focus strategy, firms such as Verger Pierre Gingras, Jackson Ultima Skates, and Overwaitea Foods gain a competitive advantage in specific market niches or segments, even though they do not possess an industry-wide competitive advantage.[91]

Although the breadth of a target is clearly a matter of degree, the essence of the focus strategy "is the exploitation of a narrow target's differences from the balance of the industry."[92] Firms using the focus strategy intend to serve a particular segment of an industry more effectively than can industry-wide competitors. They succeed when they effectively serve a segment whose unique needs are so specialized that broad-based competitors choose not to serve that segment, or when they satisfy the needs of a segment being served poorly by industry-wide competitors.[93] This describes how much of the micro-brew industry in Canada came about.

Focused Cost Leadership Strategy

Based in Sweden, IKEA, a global furniture retailer with locations in 44 countries and sales revenue of about $30 billion in 2007,[94] follows the focused cost leadership strategy.[95] The firm's vision is "Good design and function at low prices."[96] Young buyers desiring style at a low cost are IKEA's target customers.[97] For these customers, the firm offers home furnishings that combine good design, function, and acceptable quality with low prices. According to the firm, "low cost is always in focus. This applies to every phase of our activities."[98] The firm's intentions seem to be realized by customers, who see IKEA as a source of "stuff that's cool and cheap."[99] The firm continues its global expansion, recently opening stores in Russia and China.[100]

IKEA emphasizes several activities to keep its costs low.[101] For example, instead of relying primarily on third-party manufacturers, the firm's engineers design low-cost, modular furniture ready for assembly by customers. To eliminate the need for sales associates or decorators, IKEA positions the products in its stores so that customers can view different living combinations (complete with sofas, chairs, tables, and so forth) in a single roomlike setting, which helps the customer imagine how a grouping of furniture will look in the home. Typically, competitors' furniture stores display multiple varieties of a single item in separate rooms, so their customers examine living room sofas in one room, tables in another room, chairs in yet another location, and accessories in still another area. IKEA's approach requires fewer sales personnel, allowing the company to keep its costs low. A third practice that helps keep IKEA's costs low is requiring customers to transport their own purchases rather than providing delivery service.

Although it is a cost leader, IKEA also offers some differentiated features that appeal to its target customers, including in-store playrooms for children, wheelchairs for customer use, and extended hours. Stores outside those in the home country have "Sweden Shops" that sell Swedish specialties, such as herring, crisp bread, Swedish caviar, and gingerbread biscuits. IKEA believes that these services and products "are uniquely aligned with the needs of [its] customers, who are young, are not wealthy, are likely to have children (but no nanny), and, because they work for a living, have a need to shop at odd hours."[102] Thus, IKEA's focused cost leadership strategy finds the firm offering some differentiated features with its low-cost products.

Focused Differentiation Strategy

Other firms implement the focused differentiation strategy. As noted earlier, firms can differentiate their products in many ways. Vancouver's Straight Line Designs is a custom furniture company that has a reputation for unique style and quality work. The company's whimsical and unusual designs focus on custom products aimed at children and the family. Their furniture is interactive and fun: metre-tall carrots with drawers, beds that look like castles, and cabinets that have no straight lines. While some items are for personal use, many pieces are constructed for trade shows, movies and TV, malls, and retail stores: any place where people feel Straight Line's eye-catching designs may draw in people.[103]

Founded in 1993, Anne Fontaine is a firm specializing in designing, producing, and selling white shirts for women. Started in France, the firm now sells its products in over 70 of its own stores located in major cities across the world. CEO and chief designer Anne Fontaine focuses on white because the colour "represents light and purity, like a breath of fresh air." According to Fontaine, her design style is "eccentric, sensual, and above all feminine." The firm's shirt prices range from $165 to $550. Women desiring a "uniquely feminine" shirt that is made of the highest quality materials are Anne Fontaine's target customer.[104]

With a focus strategy, firms must be able to complete various primary and support activities in a competitively superior manner to develop and sustain a competitive advantage and earn above-average returns. The activities required to use the focused cost leadership strategy are virtually identical to those of the industry-wide cost leadership strategy (Figure 5.3), and activities required to use the focused differentiation strategy are largely identical to those of the industry-wide differentiation strategy (Figure 5.4). Similarly, the manner in which each of the two focus strategies allows a firm to deal successfully with the five competitive forces parallels those of the two broad strategies. The only difference is in the competitive scope, from an industry-wide market to a narrow industry segment. Thus, Figures 5.3 and 5.4 and the text regarding the five competitive forces also describe the relationship between each of the two focus strategies and competitive advantage.

Competitive Risks of Focus Strategies

With either focus strategy, the firm faces the same general risks as does the company using the cost leadership or the differentiation strategy, respectively, on an industry-wide basis. However, focus strategies have three additional risks.

First, a competitor may be able to focus on a more narrowly defined competitive segment and "outfocus" the focuser. There are numerous examples of this in the coffee business. While Starbucks still has huge market share, Canadian competitors from large to small and from east to west seek a segment of their market. Montreal's Van Houtte Coffee, with $300 million in sales, has been producing coffees since 1919 using traditional European small-batch roasting methods to give their coffee a unique flavour. Ontario's Second Cup, with sales of about $200 million, differs from Starbucks in that the chain offers flavoured coffees that customers can brew at home.[105] Small coffee companies in this market "outfocus" Starbucks via their strong support of small third-world farms and excellent coffee taste. For example, Just Us Coffee Roasters Co-operative in Wolfville, Nova Scotia supports small coffee growers through fair trade, as well as roasting small batches of coffee to provide better, fresher coffee to their customers. Toronto's Green Beanery is a Canadian non-profit supporting environment and sustainable development that empowers small farmers and sells green coffees to consumers who roast their own beans for better, fresher flavour. Vancouver's 49th Parallel buys directly from the growers to support fair trade, brews in small batches, and distributes its unique roasts via dealers across Canada.[106]

Second, a company competing on an industry-wide basis may decide that the market segment served by the focus strategy firm is attractive and worthy of competitive pursuit.

For example, consider the possibility that other brewers and marketers of a beer might determine the profit potential in the narrow segment being served by a microbrewery is attractive. Canada has literally hundreds of microbrewers, from Newfoundland's Quidi Vidi Brewing in the east to Vancouver Island's Fat Cat Brewery in the west to Yukon Brewing in the north. Yet if the discerning beer drinker is choosing a brand like Rickards or Creemore Springs to avoid drinking Molson, they will fail; Molson owns those two smaller brands. To drink Alexander Keiths or Kokanee to avoid Labatt is the same problem. These large brewers are increasingly interested in smaller markets.

The third risk involved with a focus strategy is that the needs of customers within a narrow competitive segment may become more similar to those of industry-wide customers as a whole. As a result, the advantages of a focus strategy are either reduced or eliminated. At some point, for example, the needs of IKEA's customers for stylish furniture may dissipate, although their desire to buy relatively inexpensive furnishings may not. If this change in needs were to happen, IKEA's customers might buy from large chain stores that sell somewhat standardized furniture at low costs.

Integrated Cost Leadership/Differentiation Strategy

As stated earlier, many of today's customers have high expectations when purchasing a good or service. In a strategic context, this means that, increasingly, customers want to purchase low-priced, differentiated products. Because of these expectations, a number of firms are trying to perform primary and support activities in ways that allow them to simultaneously pursue low cost and differentiation. Firms seeking to develop this type of activity map use the integrated cost leadership/differentiation strategy. The objective of using this strategy is to efficiently produce products with some differentiated attributes. Efficient production is the source of keeping costs low while some differentiation is the source of unique value. Firms that successfully use the integrated cost leadership/ differentiation strategy have learned to quickly adapt to new technologies and rapid changes in their external environments. The reason for this is that simultaneously concentrating on developing two sources of competitive advantage (cost and differentiation) increases the number of primary and support activities in which the firm must become competent. In turn, having skills in a larger number of activities makes a firm more flexible.

WestJet successfully uses the integrated cost leadership/differentiation strategy, allowing the firm to adapt quickly, learn rapidly, and meaningfully leverage its core competencies while competing against its rivals in the airline industry. To reduce costs, WestJet does a number of things. They benchmark against the best carriers to keep their costs in line. WestJet pays employees below industry average but employ profit sharing and employee share purchase plans to improve performance. To further reduce costs they embrace technology (e.g., WestJet encourages online booking by offering Air Miles and discounts on Web-purchased fares). WestJet maximizes the use of assets. To do this, WestJet reduces downtime by turning its planes around quickly. WestJet flight turnaround time is the fastest in North America. Having a flexible workforce helps in this regard. They can attain quick turnaround by having everyone, from pilots to station agents, picking up garbage, vacuuming carpets, and emptying trash. To improve differentiation, WestJet has an extensive interview process to "find fun and funky people." Applicants are required to tell stories and jokes, and play games. If the process fails, WestJet will quickly fire the person. As a morale boost, top-line management will work along with frontline staff. The company empowers frontline staff to give guest credits to compensate customers for things like late arrivals and overbookings.[107]

Vancouver's Nettwerk Productions began as a music publishing firm and has since expanded into a wide range of music-related ventures. The most visible of these ventures

Chapter 5 / Business-Level Strategy

has been their management of an impressive list of Canadian recording stars—including the Barenaked Ladies and Billy Talent. While music would seem the most differentiated of activities, particularly for a smaller player in the music business, Nettwerk's strategy also includes elements of cost leadership. Frequently Nettwerk will contract with a relatively new artist as a less expensive entry into a relationship with that artist. By handling and developing new artists, the company can gain some loyalty at a very early and less demanding stage of the musician's professional life. The Nettwerk-managed musician Dayna Manning was still wearing braces on her first video. Nettwerk recording artist Sarah McLachlan and Nettwerk-managed star Avril Lavigne were still in their teens when they began their relationships with the company.[108]

Evidence suggests a relationship between successful use of the integrated strategy and above-average returns.[109] Thus, firms able to produce relatively differentiated products at relatively low costs can expect to perform well.[110] Indeed, a researcher found that the most successful firms competing in low–profit-potential industries were integrating the attributes of the cost leadership and differentiation strategies.[111] Other researchers have discovered that "businesses which combined multiple forms of competitive advantage outperformed businesses that only were identified with a single form."[112] The results of another study showed that the highest-performing companies in the Korean electronics industry combined the value-creating aspects of the cost leadership and differentiation strategies.[113] This finding suggests the usefulness of the integrated cost leadership/differentiation strategy in settings outside North America.

Unlike WestJet, which uses the integrated cost leadership/differentiation strategy on an industry-wide basis, Waterloo's Jackson Ultima Skates (discussed above) concentrates on a particular competitive scope. Thus, Jackson is implementing a focused integrated strategy. By producing heat-mouldable skates, Jackson can provide a nearly custom fit at far less cost relative to purely custom-made skates.[114] Thus, the firm's narrowly defined target customers receive some differentiated features (e.g., custom fit) at a low, but not the lowest, cost.

Flexibility is required for firms to complete primary and support activities in ways that allow them to produce somewhat differentiated products at relatively low costs. Flexible manufacturing systems, information networks, and total quality management systems are three sources of flexibility that are particularly useful for firms trying to balance the objectives of continuous cost reductions and continuous enhancements to sources of differentiation as called for by the integrated strategy.

Flexible Manufacturing Systems

A flexible manufacturing system (FMS) increases the "flexibilities of human, physical, and information resources"[115] that the firm integrates to create relatively differentiated products at relatively low costs. A significant technological advance, FMS is a computer-controlled process used to produce a variety of products in moderate, flexible quantities with a minimum of manual intervention.[116]

The goal of an FMS is to eliminate the "low cost versus product variety" trade-off that is inherent in traditional manufacturing technologies. Firms use an FMS to change quickly and easily from making one product to making another.[117] Used properly, an FMS allows the firm to respond more effectively to changes in its customers' needs while retaining low-cost advantages and consistent product quality.[118] Because an FMS also enables the firm to reduce the lot size needed to manufacture a product efficiently, the firm increases its capacity to serve the unique needs of a narrow competitive scope.

The effective use of an FMS is linked with a firm's ability to understand the constraints these systems may create (in terms of materials handling and the flow of supporting resources in scheduling, for example) and to design an effective mix of machines, computer systems, and people.[119] In industries of all types, effective mixes of the firm's tangible assets (e.g., machines) and intangible assets (e.g., people's skills) facilitate implementation of complex competitive strategies, especially the integrated cost leadership/differentiation strategy.[120]

Information Networks

By linking companies with their suppliers, distributors, and customers, information networks provide another source of flexibility. Among other outcomes, these networks, when used effectively,[121] facilitate the firm's efforts to satisfy customer expectations in terms of product quality and delivery speed.[122]

Earlier, we discussed the importance of managing the firm's relationships with its customers in order to understand their needs. Customer relationship management (CRM) is one form of an information-based network process that firms use to do this.[123] An effective CRM system provides a 360-degree view of the company's relationship with customers, encompassing all contact points, business processes, and communication media and sales channels.[124] The firm can then use this information to determine the trade-offs its customers are willing to make between differentiated features and low cost, which is vital for companies using the integrated cost leadership/differentiation strategy.

In addition to determining customers' product needs in terms of cost and differentiated features, effective information networks improve the flow of work and communications among employees producing a firm's good or service.[125] Better work flow and more effective communications allow workers to quickly identify problems and find flexible ways of dealing with them.[126]

Total Quality Management Systems

Total quality management (TQM) is a "managerial innovation that emphasizes an organization's total commitment to the customer and to continuous improvement of every process through the use of data-driven, problem-solving approaches based on empowerment of employee groups and teams."[127] Firms develop and use TQM systems in order to (1) increase customer satisfaction, (2) cut costs, and (3) reduce the amount of time required to introduce innovative products to the marketplace.[128] Ford Motor Company is relying on TQM to help "root out" its quality flaws,[129] while General Motors is "scrambling to narrow the quality gap that its executives say is the main reason consumers shy away from GM."[130] The focus by these firms on TQM to improve product and service quality is appropriate,[131] in that while North American auto manufacturers have made progress, "the Big Three still lag behind some foreign competitors, primarily the Japanese, by most quality measures."[132]

Firms able to simultaneously cut costs while enhancing their ability to develop innovative products increase their flexibility, an outcome that is particularly helpful to firms implementing the integrated cost leadership/differentiation strategy. Exceeding customers' expectations regarding quality is a differentiating feature, and eliminating process inefficiencies to cut costs allows the firm to offer that quality to customers at a relatively low price. Thus, an effective TQM system helps the firm develop the flexibility needed to spot opportunities to simultaneously increase differentiation and reduce costs.

> **Total quality management** is a managerial innovation that emphasizes an organization's total commitment to the customer and to continuous improvement of every process through the use of data-driven, problem-solving approaches based on empowerment of employee groups and teams.

Competitive Risks of the Integrated Cost Leadership/Differentiation Strategy

The potential to earn above-average returns by successfully using the integrated cost leadership/differentiation strategy is appealing. However, this is a risky strategy, as it is difficult for firms to perform primary and support activities in ways that allow them to produce relatively inexpensive products with levels of differentiation that create value for the target customer. Moreover, to properly use this strategy across time, firms must be

Can HBC Get Unstuck from the Middle?

The Hudson's Bay Company is the oldest commercial corporation in North America. As recently as 2005, HBC was making money. Yet HBC's direction is unclear given the very different nature of its two main operating divisions.

With more than $4 billion in sales, HBC's major retailing arm is Zellers. Zellers was Canada's answer to Wal-Mart before there was a Wal-Mart. Since Wal-Mart entered Canada in the mid 1990s, Zellers profits have been less than stable and declining in general. Unable to match the buying power of Wal-Mart, Zellers had to quickly abandon its traditional claim of "Zellers, where the lowest price is the law."

With more than $2.5 billion in sales, HBC's second largest retailing arm is The Bay. The Bay has tried to make a more upscale image and move into some of the market once occupied by Eaton's. At the same time, The Bay has tried not to offend its traditional customers, but has ended up "not precisely positioned" by trying to be all things to all people. "The Bay has designer shops at the same time they have Scratch & Save sales, giving different messages, and the customer is rightly confused." The Bay has been labelled by some as "stuck in the middle." And, while The Bay has tried to avoid extremes in fashion to cater to a wide range of consumers, by doing so it maintained a staid image and created low levels of inventory turnover that made its stores seem less exciting. When international retailers like H&M turned their inventory 12 times per year, The Bay did so only four times per year.

Thus, HBC runs a discount department store chain that has insufficient discounts and a price-conscious upscale department store chain. After losing almost $175 million in 2005, HBC was bought by American Jerry Zucker in early 2006. After Zucker's death in April 2008, the chain was sold to New York–based NRDC Equity Partners. Previously, NRDC had acquired U.S. retail icon Lord & Taylor in 2006. When NRDC bought Lord & Taylor, it took a bottom-up approach to reworking the image of the company and revamping internal operations. Additionally, NRDC owns the Creative Design Studios home-decor chain—a potential good fit with HBC's Home Outfitters. All the entities, including NRDC's Fortunoff jewellery stores, will be folded into a new firm to be known as the Hudson's Bay Trading Company. CEO Richard Baker said that the company will make a new investment of $500 million into HBC.

The new company is likely to make a number of changes. Some 10 to 15 Bay, Zellers, or Home Outfitters locations will become Lord & Taylor locations. The Hudson's Bay Trading Company will also make The Bay a more upscale retailer. Larger Zellers will likely try to become the Canadian version of Target. Target has a reputation for having big, well-stocked stores with relatively low prices, excellent service, and attractive, quality proprietary branded goods. Zellers had already started down this road with exclusive brands like Mossimo, Cherokee, and Delta Burke. If Zellers can become a Canadian Target in the minds of consumers, it may be able to become unstuck from the middle and regain a position of above-average returns.

According to Saatchi & Saatchi CEO Brett Channer, "I think ultimately what they [the Bay stores] are trying to do is deliver a Holt [Renfrew]'s value but for the average Canadian." Richard Talbot, president of Talbot Consultants International, thinks aspiring to Holt's is a good idea. "The biggest mistake was for [the Bay] not to move up into the gap [left by] Eaton's. Instead what they did was move closer to Sears and . . . Wal-Mart. They went into an area where everyone was fighting for the lower-end of the market." By failing to move up, it left Holt Renfrew able to widen its customer reach. "They're morphing into a full size major department store because of the lack of competition." If the new Hudson's Bay Trading Company can successfully exploit the knowledge it gained from operating

Lord & Taylor, and find a Holt Renfrew niche that appeals to the average Canadian, it may be able to get HBC unstuck from the middle and regain a position of above-average returns.

SOURCES: H. Shaw, 2008, American company buys The Bay: Iconic, historic Canadian firm now belongs to Lord & Taylor, *Alberni Valley Times*, July 17, A11; D. Friend, 2008, New American owners plan to freshen up the Bay, Zellers: Retail Lord & Taylor set to launch stores in Canada, fill gap between Bay and Holt Renfrew, *Saint John Telegraph-Journal*, July 17, B5; C. Daniels, 2007, The dawn of a new Bay, *Marketing*, 12(8): 39–41; J. Chidley, 2006, Damned Yankee!, *Canadian Business*, 79(3): 5; J. P. Sheppard & S. D. Chowdhury, 2005, Riding the wrong wave: Organizational failure as a failed turnaround, *Long Range Planning*, 38(3): 239–260.

able to simultaneously reduce costs incurred to produce products (as required by the cost leadership strategy) while increasing products' differentiation (as required by the differentiation strategy).

Firms that fail to perform the primary and support activities in an optimum manner become "stuck in the middle."[133] Being stuck in the middle means that the firm's cost structure is not low enough to allow it to attractively price its products and that its products are not sufficiently differentiated to create value for the target customer. When this happens, the firm will not earn above-average returns and will earn average returns only when the structure of the industry in which it competes is highly favourable.[134] Thus, companies implementing the integrated cost leadership/differentiation strategy must be able to perform the primary and support activities in ways that allow them to produce products that offer the target customer some differentiated features at a relatively low cost/price. As explained earlier, WestJet is able to do this and has avoided becoming stuck in the middle.

Firms can also become stuck in the middle when they fail to successfully implement *either* the cost leadership *or* the differentiation strategy. In other words, industry-wide competitors too can become stuck in the middle. Some speculate that this is what happened at Hewlett-Packard (HP) under former CEO Carly Fiorina's leadership. HP is competing against Dell with a strong low cost position. One analyst suggested that HP was "competing on price one week, service the next, while trying to sell through often conflicting, high-cost channels."[135] As explained in the Strategic Focus, the Hudson's Bay Company (HBC) faced being perceived as stuck in the middle for many years. As you will read, becoming stuck in the middle reduced HBC's ability to earn above-average returns.

Summary

- A business-level strategy is an integrated and coordinated set of commitments and actions the firm uses to gain a competitive advantage by exploiting core competencies in specific product markets. Five business-level strategies (cost leadership, differentiation, focused cost leadership, focused differentiation, and integrated cost leadership/differentiation) are examined in the chapter.

- Customers are the foundation of successful business-level strategies. When considering customers, a firm simultaneously examines three issues: *who, what,* and *how.* These issues, respectively, refer to the customer groups to be served, the needs those customers have that the firm seeks to satisfy, and the core competencies the firm will use to

satisfy customers' needs. Increasing segmentation of markets throughout the global economy creates opportunities for firms to identify increasingly unique customer needs they can try to serve by using one of the business-level strategies.

- Firms seeking competitive advantage through the cost leadership strategy produce no-frills, standardized products for an industry's typical customer. However, these low-cost products must be offered with competitive levels of differentiation. Above-average returns are earned when firms continuously drive their costs lower than those of their competitors while providing customers with products that have low prices and acceptable levels of differentiated features.

- Competitive risks associated with the cost leadership strategy include (1) a loss of competitive advantage to newer technologies, (2) a failure to detect changes in customers' needs, and (3) the ability of competitors to imitate the cost leader's competitive advantage through their own unique strategic actions.

- Through the differentiation strategy, firms provide customers with products that have different (and valued) features. Differentiated products must be sold at a cost that customers believe is competitive given the product's features as compared with the cost/feature combination available through competitors' offerings. Because of their uniqueness, differentiated goods or services are sold at a premium price. Products can be differentiated along any dimension that some customer group values. Firms using this strategy seek to differentiate their products from competitors' goods or services along as many dimensions as possible. The less similarity with competitors' products, the more buffered a firm is from competition with its rivals.

- Risks associated with the differentiation strategy include (1) a customer group's decision that the differences between the differentiated product and the cost leader's good or service are no longer worth a premium price, (2) the inability of a differentiated product to create the type of value for which customers are willing to pay a premium price, (3) the ability of competitors to provide customers with products that have features similar to those associated with the differentiated product, but at a lower cost, and (4) the threat of counterfeiting, whereby firms produce a cheap "knockoff" of a differentiated good or service.

- Through the cost leadership and the differentiated focus strategies, firms serve the needs of a narrow competitive segment (e.g., a buyer group, product segment, or geographic area). This strategy is successful when firms have the core competencies required to provide value to a narrow competitive segment that exceeds the value available from firms serving customers on an industry-wide basis.

- The competitive risks of focus strategies include (1) a competitor's ability to use its core competencies to "outfocus" the focuser by serving an even more narrowly defined competitive segment, (2) decisions by industry-wide competitors to focus on a customer group's specialized needs, and (3) a reduction in differences of the needs between customers in a narrow competitive segment and the industry-wide market.

- Firms using the integrated cost leadership/differentiation strategy strive to provide customers with relatively low-cost products that have some valued differentiated features. Flexibility is required for the firm to learn how to use primary and support activities in ways that allow it to produce somewhat differentiated products at relatively low costs. The primary risk of this strategy is that a firm might produce products that do not offer sufficient value in terms of either low cost or differentiation. When this occurs, the company is "stuck in the middle." Firms stuck in the middle compete at a disadvantage and are unable to earn more than average returns.

Review Questions

1. What is a business-level strategy?

2. What is the relationship between a firm's customers and its business-level strategy in terms of *who, what,* and *how*? Why is this relationship important?

3. What are the differences among the cost leadership, differentiation, focused cost leadership, focused differentiation, and integrated cost leadership/differentiation business-level strategies?

4. How can each one of the business-level strategies be used to position the firm relative to the five forces of competition in a way that helps the firm earn above-average returns?

5. What are the specific risks associated with using each business-level strategy?

Social Responsibility Review

1. WestJet was mentioned several times in the chapter. While the airline is well run, some of its success may come from its information-gathering techniques—or, as some may describe it, corporate espionage. In April 2004, Air Canada launched a $220-million lawsuit accusing senior WestJet executives of heading a scheme to steal confidential information by tapping into Air Canada's Internet site more than 250,000 times. As well, WestJet had used secret passwords belonging to a

former Air Canada employee to retrieve commercially sensitive data about its rival's most profitable routes. To avoid a long legal battle, WestJet paid Air Canada's $5 million in legal fees, donated $10 million to charity, and issued an apology. Should WestJet executives been criminally prosecuted? Why or why not?

2. Earlier in the chapter we noted that Vancouver's Nettwerk Productions will frequently contract with a relatively new artist as a less expensive entry into a relationship with that artist. By doing this, is the company taking advantage of an innocent young talent, or giving them their big break? What should the company do to ensure it is treating its artists fairly? If you were a struggling young artist, what would you think about what Nettwerk does?

3. No discussion of social responsibility is complete without mentioning Wal-Mart. Given that the chapter discusses a number of ways to compete against the giant retailer, is it still fair to say that Wal-Mart's entry into a community will kill small business? Why or why not? What are your concerns as a consumer, community member, and business person?

Experiential Exercises

Differentiation in a Low-Cost World

One competitive reality of the market in the 21st century is that very few firms can succeed by emphasizing only cost or differentiation. When considering the value chain tool developed by Michael Porter, it is important to remember that the capabilities in each activity have the goal of widening the profit margin, whether by positively affecting the cost to produce a good or service, or by the ability to differentiate a good or service from competitors' offerings in ways that customers value, or both. Thus, it is important for firms pursuing differentiation to determine where costs can be cut without damaging the ability to meaningfully differentiate their good or service in ways that will allow them to sell products at a high price. Similarly, low-cost firms need to look for opportunities to add differentiation where they can without increasing average unit costs. In this exercise, you will examine the latter situation.

To complete this exercise, you should visit the firms involved. You are likely familiar with the firms listed below and you probably have some well-developed ideas about what each firm does to find some differentiation opportunities in a low-cost competitive environment. As the first step in this exercise, select one of the industries listed below and conduct the associated research.

Discount Merchandising

Visit a Wal-Mart and a "dollar store," such as Buck or Two. Assess how each of these discount merchandisers pursues differentiation as part of the means of implementing its cost leadership business-level strategy. How does what you observe about these stores' attempts to offer some differentiated features match with the assumptions you had before entering each store? If so, what are the changes? After setting out the ways in which you see these firms differentiating their product offerings and their store presentations, assess and explain how and why these elements make sense.

Fast-Food Hamburgers

Visit a Wendy's, a Burger King, and a Harvey's. Assess how each of these fast-food restaurants pursues differentiation elements as a key part of successfully implementing its cost leadership business-level strategy. Check your assumptions going in about the differentiation approaches of each restaurant. After setting out the ways in which you see these firms differentiating their offerings and store presentations, assess and explain how and why these elements have the potential to help firms create value for customers.

Notes

1. G. Gavetti & J .W. Rivkin, 2005, How strategists really think, *Harvard Business Review,* 83(4): 54–63.
2. G. Gavetti, D. A. Levinthal, & J. W. Rivkin, 2005, Strategy making in novel and complex worlds: The power of analogy, *Strategic Management Journal,* 26: 691–712.
3. J. Tan & D. Tan, 2005, Environment-strategy co-evolution and co-alignment: A staged model of Chinese SOEs under transition, *Strategic Management Journal,* 26: 141–157.
4. G. George, J. Wiklund, & S. A. Zahra, 2005, Ownership and the internationalization of small firms, *Journal of Management,* 31: 210–233.
5. E. Kim, D. Nam, & J. L. Stimpert, 2004, The applicability of Porter's generic strategies in the digital age: Assumptions, conjectures, and suggestions, *Journal of Management,* 30: 569–589; R. D. Ireland, M. A. Hitt, S. M. Camp, & D. L. Sexton, 2001, Integrating entrepreneurship and strategic management actions to create firm wealth, *Academy of Management Executive,* 15(1): 49–63.

6. K. Shimizu & M. A. Hitt, 2004, Strategic flexibility: Organizational preparedness to reverse ineffective strategic decisions, *Academy of Management Executive,* 18(4): 44–59.

7. D. J. Ketchen Jr., C. C. Snow, & V. L. Street, 2004, Improving firm performance by matching strategic decision-making processes to competitive dynamics, *Academy of Management Executive,* 18(4): 29–43.

8. J. J. Janney & G. G. Dess, 2004, Can real-options analysis improve decision-making? Promises and pitfalls, *Academy of Management Executive,* 18(4): 60–75.

9. R. D. Ireland & C. C. Miller, 2005, Decision-making and firm success, *Academy of Management Executive,* 18(4): 8–12.

10. N. Park, J. M. Mezias, & J. Song, 2004, Increasing returns, strategic alliances, and the values of e-commerce firms, *Journal of Management,* 30: 7–27; G. G. Dess, A. Gupta, J. F. Hennart, & C. W. L. Hill, 1995, Conducting and integrating strategy research at the international, corporate, and business levels: Issues and directions, *Journal of Management,* 21: 357–393.

11. M. C. Mankins & R. Steele, 2005, Turning great strategy into great performance, *Harvard Business Review,* 83(7): 65–72; T. J. Douglas & J. A. Ryman, 2003, Understanding competitive advantage in the general hospital industry: Evaluating strategic competencies, *Strategic Management Journal,* 24: 333–347.

12. D. Lei & J. W. Slocum, 2005, Strategic and organizational requirements for competitive advantage, *Academy of Management Executive,* 19(1): 31–45.

13. Z. Patakfalvi, 2007, Domtar: High quality paper at Windsor, *Pulp and Paper Canada,* 108(4): 24–25; 2005, Domtar press release, November 30, retrieved December 18, 2007.

14. J. B. Barney & T. B. Mackey, 2005, Testing resource-based theory, In D. J. Ketchen Jr. & D. D. Bergh (eds.), *Research Methodology in Strategy and Management* (2nd ed.), London: Elsevier, 1–13.

15. C. B. Dobni & G. Luffman, 2003, Determining the scope and impact of market orientation profiles on strategy implementation and performance, *Strategic Management Journal,* 24: 577–585.

16. R. Gulati & J. B. Oldroyd, 2005, The quest for customer focus, *Harvard Business Review,* 83(4): 92–101.

17. M. E. Porter, 1980, *Competitive Strategy,* New York: Free Press.

18. A. J. Slywotzky & J. Drzik, 2005, Countering the biggest risk of all, *Harvard Business Review,* 83(4): 78–88.

19. F. E. Webster Jr., A. J. Malter, & S. Ganesan, 2005, The decline and dispersion of marketing competence, *MIT Sloan Management Review,* 6(4): 35–43.

20. D. Peppers & M. Rogers, 2005, Customers don't grow on trees, *Fast Company,* July, 25–26.

21. B. Breen & M. Aneiro, 2004, Living in Dell time, *Fast Company,* November, 86–95.

22. 2005, Dell selling first laser printer priced below $100, *Dallas Morning News,* www.dallasnews.com, June 21.

23. M. D. Johnson & F. Seines, 2005, Diversifying your customer portfolio, *MIT Sloan Management Review,* 46(3): 11.

24. N. Ramage, 2007, Be our guest, *Marketing,* 112(17): 6.

25. 2005, The customer service center: CSR, www.knowlagent.com, July 23.

26. J. E. Blose, W. B. Tankersley, & L. R. Flynn, 2005, Managing service quality using data envelopment analysis, www.asq.org, June; B. Magura, 2003, What hooks M-commerce customers? *The McKinsey Quarterly,* 44(3): 9.

27. R. Dhar & R. Glazer, 2003, Hedging customers, *Harvard Business Review,* 81(5): 86–92.

28. 2005, Amazon.com, *Standard & Poor's Stock Report,* www.standardandpoors.com, June 25.

29. 2005, About Cemex, Cemex Web Page, www.cemex.com, July 23.

30. 2003, Fitch Mexico assigns AA qualifications to certificates of Cemex, *Emerging Markets Economy,* April 8, 3; L. Walker, 2001, Plugged in for maximum efficiency, *Washington Post,* June 20, G1, G4.

31. N. Sutton, 2002, FlexPort automates purchasing processes, *Computing Canada,* 28(11): 17.

32. 2004, http://asontv.4t.com/chapters.html, March 1; 2007, http://www.chapters.indigo.ca, December 19.

33. 2004, IRC, http://irc.nrc-cnrc.gc.ca/ccmc/home_e.shtml, March 1; P. Evans & T. S. Wurster, 1999, Getting real about virtual commerce, *Harvard Business Review,* 77 (6): 84–94; S. F. Slater & J. C. Narver, 1999, Market-oriented is more than being customer-led, *Strategic Management Journal,* 20: 1165–1168.

34. A. Reed II & L. E. Bolton, 2005, The complexity of identity, *MIT Sloan Management Review,* 46(3): 18–22.

35. C. W. Lamb Jr., J. F. Hair Jr., & C. McDaniel, 2006, *Marketing* (8th ed.), Mason, OH: Thomson South-Western, 224; A. Dutra, J. Frary, & R. Wise, 2004, Higher-order needs drive new growth in mature consumer markets, *Journal of Business Strategy,* 25(5): 26–34.

36. A. Baur, S. P. Hehner, & G. Nederegger, 2003, Pharma for Fido, *The McKinsey Quarterly,* Number 2, 7–10.

37. S. S. Hassan & S. H. Craft, 2005, Linking global market segmentation decisions with strategic positioning options, *Journal of Consumer Marketing,* 22(2/3): 81–88.

38. S. Hamner, 2005, Filling the Gap, *Business 2.0,* July, 30.

39. 2003, Unions and Gen-X: What does the future hold? *HR Focus,* March, 3; F. Marshall, 2003, Storehouse wakes up to Gen-X employees, *Furniture Today,* February 10, 2–3; J. Pereira, 2003, Best on the street, *Wall Street Journal,* May 12, R7; C. Burritt, 2001, Aging boomers reshape resort segment, *Lodging Hospitality,* 57(3): 31–32; J. D. Zbar, 2001, On a segmented dial, digital cuts wire finer, *Advertising Age,* 72(16): S12.

40. J. P. Womack, 2005, Lean consumption, *Harvard Business Review,* 83(3): 58–68.

41. A. Panjwani, 2005, Open source vs. proprietary software: The pluses and minuses, The Financial Express Online, www.financialexpress.com, May 2.

42. M. E. Raynor & H. S. Weinberg, 2004, Beyond segmentation, *Marketing Management,* 13(6): 22–29.

43. W. Reinartz, J. S. Thomas, & V. Kumar, 2005, Balancing acquisition and retention resources to maximize customer profitability, *Journal of Marketing,* 69: 63–85.

44. A. Kingston, 2007, Brilliant, ballsy, it's vegan hell, *Maclean's,* 120(5): 55–56.

45. L. Mazur, 2003, Forget risk-free rules to tap into customer needs, *Marketing,* April 10, 16.

46. D. Foust, F. F. Jespersen, F. Katzenberg, A. Barrett, & R. O. Crockett, 2003, The best performers, BusinessWeek Online, www.businessweek.com, March 24.

47. M. J. Silverstein & N. Fiske, 2003, Luxury for the masses, *Harvard Business Review,* 81(4): 48–57.

48. C. W. L. Hill & F. T. Rothaermel, 2003, The performance of incumbent firms in the face of radical technological innovation, *Academy of Management Review,* 28: 257–274; A. W. King, S. W. Fowler, & C. P. Zeithaml, 2001, Managing organizational competencies for competitive advantage: The middle-management edge, *Academy of Management Executive,* 15(2): 95–106.

49. S. N. Mehta, 2001, What Lucent can learn from IBM, *Fortune,* June 25, 40–44.

50. 2007, IT solutions and consulting, *Emergis,* http://www.emergis.com/solutions/default.aspx, December 20.

51. 2005, www.sas.com, July 25.

52. M. E. Porter, 1985, *Competitive Advantage,* New York: Free Press, 26.

53. M. E. Porter, 1996, What is strategy? *Harvard Business Review,* 74(6): 61–78.

54. Porter, What is strategy?

55. S. Warren & E. Perez, 2005, Southwest's net rises by 41%; Delta lifts cap on some fares, Wall Street Journal Online, www.wsj.com, July 15.

56. E. Souder, 2005, Update: Southwest aims to boost profit 15% in 2006, Wall Street Journal Online, www.wsj.com, July 14.

57. Porter, What is strategy?

58. C. Zott, 2003, Dynamic capabilities and the emergence of intraindustry differential firm performance: Insights from a simulation study, *Strategic Management Journal,* 24: 97–125.

59. M. E. Porter, 1994, Toward a dynamic theory of strategy, in R. P. Rumelt, D. E. Schendel, & D. J. Teece (eds.), *Fundamental Issues in Strategy,* Boston: Harvard Business School Press, 423–461.

60. Porter, What is strategy?, 62.

61. Porter, *Competitive Advantage,* 15.

62. G. G. Dess, G. T. Lumpkin, & J. E. McGee, 1999, Linking corporate entrepreneurship to strategy, structure, and process: Suggested research directions, *Entrepreneurship: Theory & Practice,* 23(3): 85–102; P. M. Wright, D. L. Smart, & G. C. McMahan, 1995, Matches between human resources and strategy among NCAA basketball teams, *Academy of Management Journal,* 38: 1052–1074.

63. Porter, *Competitive Strategy,* 35–40.

64. D. F. Spulber, 2004, *Management Strategy,* New York: McGraw-Hill/Irwin, 175.

65. 2007, Magna International, Investor Information Circular, http://www.magna.com/magna/en/investors/shareholder/spinoffs/pdf/MIDProspectus.pdf, December 21.

66. D. F. Lynch, S. B. Keller, & J. Ozment, 2000, The effects of logistics capabilities and strategy on firm performance, *Journal of Business Logistics,* 21(2): 47–68.

67. 2004, Liquidation World Web page, http://www.liquidationworld.com, March 2.

68. L. K. Johnson, 2003, Dueling pricing strategies, *The McKinsey Quarterly,* 44(3): 10–11.

69. A. D'Innocenzio, 2001, We are paranoid, *Richmond Times-Dispatch,* June 10, E1, E2.

70. Z. Olijnyk, 2006, Food fight, *Canadian Business,* 79(22): 18–19.

71. M. Maier, 2005, How to beat Wal-Mart, *Business 2.0,* May, 108–114.

72. Porter, *Competitive Strategy,* 35–40.

73. Ibid., 65.

74. 2007, Please Mum Web page, http://www.pleasemum.com/, retrieved December 23.

75. Porter, *Competitive Advantage,* 14.

76. 2007, What is bespoke, *English Cut,* http://www.englishcut.com/archives/000004.html, December 24.

77. C. Shulgan, Sew and reap: Behind the irrepressible Harry Rosen, there's a buttoned-down businessman: Larry Rosen, *Report On Business,* 19(5): 30.

78. C. Cornell, 1999, There's something about Harry: After 40 years, Harry Rosen is working harder than ever, *Profit,* April, 44–50.

79. Ibid., 46.

80. Ibid., 44.

81. J. H. Gilmore, 2005, Feedback, *Fast Company,* August, 17.

82. J. A. Byrne, 2005, The power of great design, *Fast Company,* June, 14.

83. D. Welch, 2005, GM's design push picks up speed, *BusinessWeek,* July 18, 40–42.

84. S. Gluskoter, 2005, Let the customer drive design, *Fast Company,* June, 45.

85. R. Berner, 2005, Flip-flops, torn jeans—and control, *BusinessWeek,* May 30, 68–70.

86. Barney, *Gaining and Sustaining Competitive Advantage,* 268.

87. 2007, Police charge two Toronto men with selling dangerous counterfeit electrical products, http://www.rcmp-grc.gc.ca/on/press/2005/2005_mar_30_e.htm, December 24.

88. Porter, *Competitive Strategy,* 98.

89. 2007, Verger Pierre Gingras Web site, http://www.cidervinegar.com/n/en/index.htm, December 25.

90. 2007, Jackson Skates Web page, http://www.jacksonskates.com/html/heat-mold.html, December 25.

91. Porter, *Competitive Advantage,* 15.

92. Ibid.

93. Ibid., 15–16.

94. 2008, IKEA facts and figures Web page, http://franchisor.ikea.com/showContent.asp?swfId=facts1, retrieved February 3; 2008, XE historic currency conversion site, Euro/Canadian dollar exchange rate as of IKEA year end August 31, 2007, http://www.xe.com/ucc/convert.cgi, retrieved February 3; B. Lodge, 2005, Tax incentives debated as IKEA primps, *Dallas Morning News,* July 25, A1, A2.

95. Porter, What is strategy?, 67.

96. 2005, About IKEA, IKEA Web Page, www.ikea.com, July 26.

97. K. Kling & I. Goteman, 2003, IKEA CEO Andres Dahlvig on international growth and IKEA's unique corporate culture and brand identity, *Academy of Management Executive,* 17(1): 31–37.

98. 2005, Our vision, IKEA Web Page, www.ikea.com, July 26.

99. T. Theis, 2005, Explore the store, *Dallas Morning News,* July 29, E1.

100. W. Stewart, 2003, IKEA's flat-pack revolution changing rooms in Russia, *Knight Ridder Tribune Business News,* www.knightridder.com, April 24; 2003, IKEA's RMB 500-million outlet opens in Shanghai, *SinoCast China Business Daily News,* April 18.

101. P. Szuchman, 2005, Can this kitchen be saved? Wall Street Journal Online, www.wsj.com, April 29.

102. G. Evans, 2003, Why some stores strike me as special, *Furniture Today,* 27(24): 91; Porter, What is strategy?, 65.

103. 2007, Straight Line Designs Web page, http://www.straightlinedesigns.com/mframe.htm, December 25.

104. 2005, Anne Fontaine Home Page, www.annefontaine.com, July 26.

105. To do the same thing, the Starbucks customer must add flavouring after brewing to a Starbucks roast; 2007, Van Houtte Web site, http://www.vanhoutte.com/, December 26; 2007, Hoovers Profile of Van Houtte on the Answers.Com Web site, http://www.answers.com/topic/van-houtte-inc?cat=biz-fin, December 26; 2007, Second Cup Income Fund Web site, http://www.secondcupincomefund.com/, December 26.

106. 2007, Just Us Coffee Web site, http://www.justuscoffee.com/AboutJustUs.aspx, December 26; 2007, Green Beanery Web site, http://www.greenbeanery.ca/bean/, December 26; 2007, 49th Parallel Roasters Web site, http://www.49thparallelroasters.com/inside.html, December 26.

107. A. A. Davis, 2004, Sky high, *Profit,* 23(1): 20–23; C. Beddoe, 2003, How much is enough? *Maclean's,* 116(17), 40–41.

108. 2004, Nettwork Management homepage, http://www.nettwerkmanagement.com, March 9; K. Gold, 2003, Music to his ears; Canadian manager Terry McBride, above, is a powerful player in recording industry, *The Windsor Star* (final edition), April 10, B6.

109. Dess, Lumpkin, & McGee, Linking corporate entrepreneurship to strategy, 89.

110. P. Ghemawat, 2001, *Strategy and the Business Landscape,* Upper Saddle River, NJ: Prentice-Hall, 56.

111. W. K. Hall, 1980, Survival strategies in a hostile environment, *Harvard Business Review,* 58(5): 75–87.

112. Dess, Gupta, Hennart, & Hill, Conducting and integrating strategy research, 377.

113. L. Kim & Y. Lim, 1988, Environment, generic strategies, and performance in a rapidly developing country: A taxonomic approach, *Academy of Management Journal,* 31: 802–827.

114. 2007, Jackson Skates Web page, http://www.jacksonskates.com/html/heat-mold.html, December 25.

115. R. Sanchez, 1995, Strategic flexibility in product competition, *Strategic Management Journal,* 16 (Special Issue): 140.

116. A. Faria, P. Fenn, & A. Bruce, 2005, Production technologies and technical efficiency: Evidence from Portuguese manufacturing industry, *Applied Economics,* 37: 1037–1046.

117. J. Baljko, 2003, Built for speed—When putting the reams of supply chain data they've amassed to use, companies are discovering that agility counts, *EBN,* 1352: 25–28.

118. E. K. Bish, A. Muriel, & S. Biller, 2005, Managing flexible capacity in a make-to-order environment, *Management Science,* 51: 167–180.

119. M. Savsar, 2005, Performance analysis of an FMS operating under different failure rates and maintenance policies, *International Journal of Flexible Manufacturing Systems,* 16: 229–249.

120. S. M. Iravani, M. P. van Oyen, & K. T. Sims, 2005, Structural flexibility: A new perspective on the design of manufacturing and service operations, *Management Science,* 51: 151–166.

121. A. McAfee, 2003, When too much IT knowledge is a dangerous thing, *The McKinsey Quarterly,* 44(2): 83–89.

122. F. Mattern, S. Schonwalder, & W. Stein, 2003, Fighting complexity in IT, *The McKinsey Quarterly,* Number 1, 57–65.

123. S. W. Brown, 2003, The employee experience, *Marketing Management,* 12(2): 12–13.

124. S. Isaac & R. N. Tooker, 2001, The many faces of CRM, *LIMRA's MarketFacts Quarterly,* 20(1): 84–89.
125. K. H. Doerr, T. R. Mitchell, C. A. Schriesheim, T. Freed, & X. Zhou, 2002, Heterogeneity and variability in the context of work flows, *Academy of Management Review,* 27: 594–607.
126. G. Edmondson, 2005, BMW keeps the home fires burning, *BusinessWeek,* May 30, 52.
127. J. D. Westphal, R. Gulati, & S. M. Shortell, 1997, Customization or conformity: An institutional and network perspective on the content and consequences of TQM adoption, *Administrative Science Quarterly,* 42: 366–394.
128. V. W. S. Yeung & R. W. Armstrong, 2003, A key to TQM benefits: Manager involvement in customer processes, *International Journal of Services Technology and Management,* 4(1): 14–29.
129. J. Muller, 2001, Ford: Why it's worse than you think, *BusinessWeek,* June 25, 80–89.
130. J. White, G. L. White, & N. Shirouzu, 2001, Soon, the big three won't be, as foreigners make inroads, *Wall Street Journal,* August 13, A1, A12.
131. D. Welch, K. Kerwin, & C. Tierney, 2003, Way to go, Detroit—Now go a lot farther, *BusinessWeek,* May 26, 44.
132. N. Ganguli, T. V. Kumaresh, & A. Satpathy, 2003, Detroit's new quality gap, *The McKinsey Quarterly,* Number 1, 148–151.
133. Porter, *Competitive Advantage,* 16.
134. Ibid., 17.
135. 2005, Three reasons why good strategies fail: execution, execution . . ., *Knowledge@Wharton, http://*knowledge.wharton.upenn.edu, July 30.

Chapter Six

Competitive Rivalry and Competitive Dynamics

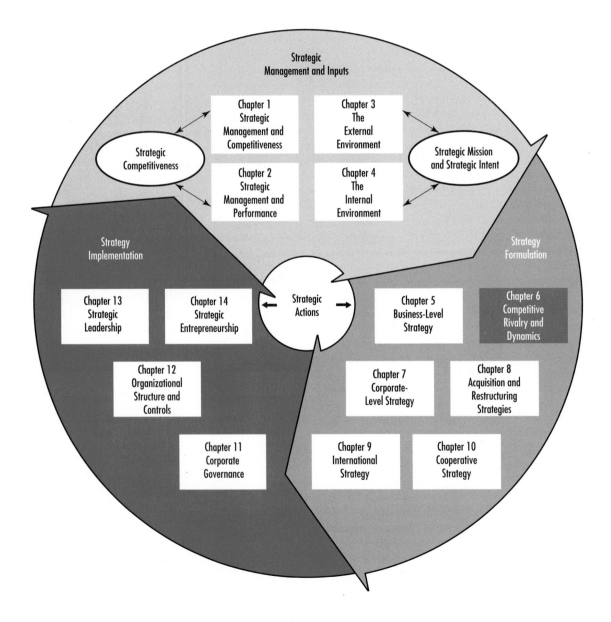

Strategic
Management and Inputs

Chapter 1
Strategic
Management and
Competitiveness

Chapter 3
The
External
Environment

Strategic
Competitiveness

Strategic Mission
and Strategic Intent

Chapter 2
Strategic
Management and
Performance

Chapter 4
The
Internal
Environment

Strategy
Implementation

Strategy
Formulation

Chapter 13
Strategic
Leadership

Chapter 14
Strategic
Entrepreneurship

Strategic
Actions

Chapter 5
Business-Level
Strategy

Chapter 6
Competitive
Rivalry and
Dynamics

Chapter 12
Organizational
Structure and
Controls

Chapter 7
Corporate-
Level Strategy

Chapter 8
Acquisition and
Restructuring
Strategies

Chapter 11
Corporate
Governance

Chapter 9
International
Strategy

Chapter 10
Cooperative
Strategy

Knowledge Objectives

Studying this chapter should provide you with the strategic management knowledge needed to:

1. Define competitors, competitive rivalry, competitive behaviour, and competitive dynamics.

2. Describe market commonality and resource similarity as the building blocks of a competitor analysis.

3. Explain awareness, motivation, and ability as drivers of competitive behaviour.

4. Discuss factors affecting the likelihood a competitor will take competitive actions.

5. Discuss factors affecting the likelihood a competitor will respond to actions taken against it.

6. Explain competitive dynamics in slow-cycle, fast-cycle, and standard-cycle markets.

My Phone Is the Internet: VoIP as a Disruptive Technology

About 40 years ago, comedian Lily Tomlin, in the role of Ernestine the operator, stated a timely but universal truism: *"We're the phone company. We don't care; we don't have to."* If you wanted phone service, you went to the phone company. Even with the deregulation of long-distance years later, you needed to deal with your local phone provider to get service. In early 2004, upstart Primus Telecommunications unveiled a new low-cost local residential phone service. Primus was a long-distance and Internet provider but instantly became another phone company and things were never the same. Of course, you could avoid the phone company by strictly using your cell phone, but the cost was likely to be prohibitive and Primus was offering a better rate than the traditional phone company.

www.primus.ca

www.vonage.ca

www.shaw.ca

Primus's action forced Bell to accelerate technical development of the process Primus employed—voice over Internet protocol (VoIP). Primus's move forced Shaw and Rogers to move into providing local phone service one to two years earlier than planned. Also, the move created an open door for firms like Vonage to enter the market.

How did all this come about? Obviously Primus saw an opportunity to use the technology to expand into a new market, but there is more to the story than a simple market opportunity. How did the technology change come about, and why did the phone company not recognize the opportunity?

Chapter 6 / Competitive Rivalry and Competitive Dynamics

Let's go back to when the phone company was the only game in town. In the second quarter of the last century, economist Joseph Schumpeter coined the term "creative destruction" to describe the process of invention and innovation. He is credited with noting that all advancements are accompanied by the destruction of some previous improvement. This process also has a detrimental effect on the businesses that produce the destroyed technology. The more current version of the term is "disruptive technology," which refers to technologies that undermine the existing way of doing things. The personal computer is a classic example. It destroyed older mainframe computing, and eventually led one of the world's largest companies, IBM, to near failure.

This brings us back to your phone, and a strange set of disruptive technologies and ideas that theoretically include optical fibre, CDs, and the notion that the voice on the phone is not a voice at all. As for the phone, you pick up the receiver, punch in a number, and—through the miracle of electronics and kilometres of wires—someone you want to talk to answers at the other end. At least that is how the phone worked for almost 100 years. Operators gave way to direct dial, the wires became optical fibre, and the voice at the other end became voicemail, but the connection—what the experts call the "public switched telephone network" (PSTN)—remained. With the advent of the cell phone, other companies got involved. However, in many cases the phone company likely still took your call at some point, directed it, and connected you through the PSTN. In many cases, the cell phone provider was the phone company.

Then there was data. Data transmission service was something the phone company could provide, but other companies, like the local cable company, could also provide it. This brought other companies in direct competition with the phone company for the provision of Internet services. But the phone company still provided your phone service via the PSTN.

Thus, with the advent of the CD, voice recording became stored as a digital medium—technically, a series of zeros and ones that was not so much a recording as it was a data stream. Suddenly a voice was no longer a voice, but data. The thing that showed up at your home—which sounded very much like a voice—was actually data.

As early as the mid to late 1990s, computer users could connect two online machines with proper software and headsets and talk for an unlimited time as part of their flat monthly Internet connection charge. If business users with geographically dispersed offices could somehow employ the same technology in a convenient way, they could shave a great deal of money off long-distance phone bills. When businesses and computer-savvy individuals began to realize this, so did companies like Nortel and Cisco, and they began making equipment for voice over Internet protocol. This new and disruptive technology would use the Internet to transmit voice as data in a much less expensive way than PSTN. Anyone who could provide Internet services could potentially be a competitor. Besides the companies mentioned already, some of the major VoIP competitors now include Cogeco, Videotron, AOL Canada, BabyTel, Sprint Canada, and SpectraVoice.

What did the phone company miss? A phone connection had always been a phone connection. There was a dedicated line from one phone to another. This was not the way VoIP worked. It sent small packets of information from one place on the Internet to another by whatever route was possible. It was not an easy concept for engineers who grew up with the PSTN to appreciate. With more than one billion users expected to be using VoIP in 2012, the phone company will have to begin to appreciate the technology. They will care; they'll have to.

SOURCES: I. Cox, 2007, SIP, VoIP will be mainstream in three years, TelecomWeb News Break; H. Reinert & E. S. Reinert, 2006, Creative destruction in economics: Nietzsche, Sombart, Schumpeter, in J. G. Backhaus & W. Drechsler, eds., *Friedrich Nietzsche: Economy, and Society,* New York: Springer; 2005, Leaders: How the internet killed the phone business—Telecoms and the internet, *The Economist,* 376(8444): 11; M. Evans, 2004, Web play targets Bell, Telus . . . , *Financial Post (National Post),* FP1, FP4; D. Ebner, 2004, Internet rings in '04 as new phone . . . , *The Globe and Mail,* January 7, B4; D. Ebner, 2004, Rogers sees healthy improvement in '04 . . . , *The Globe and Mail,* January 6, B21; M. Evans, 2003, Wireless boosts BCE profit 28% . . . , *National Post,* October 30, FP1, FP8; J. A. Schumpeter, 1943, *Capitalism Socialism and Democracy,* London: Unwin University Books.

Basic economics suggests that an organization facing no competition is likely to perform well financially. Such monopolistic organizations have nothing to fear from losing market share from competitors—because there are no competitors. Indeed, the only concern for such a company may essentially be to maximize the value of the firm for the organization's investors.[1] For years, only the phone company could bring you phone service. Even a monopoly like phone service, however, is not protected forever against competition; eventually someone will arrive in the market with a product or service that fulfils the same function the monopolist provides.

Firms operating in the same market, offering similar products, and targeting similar customers are **competitors**.[2] Primus, Shaw, Rogers, Bell, and Vonage are competitors, as are PepsiCo and Coca-Cola. Firms interact with their competitors as part of the broad context within which they operate while attempting to earn above-average returns.[3] The decisions firms make about their interactions with their competitors significantly affect their ability to earn above-average returns.[4] Because 80 to 90 percent of new firms fail, learning how to select the markets in which to compete and how to best compete within them is highly important.[5]

Competitive rivalry is the ongoing set of competitive actions and competitive responses that occur between competitors as they manoeuvre for an advantageous market position. Especially in highly competitive industries, firms constantly jockey for advantage as they launch strategic actions and respond or react to rivals' moves.[6] It is important for those leading organizations to understand competitive rivalry, in that "the central, brute empirical fact in strategy is that some firms outperform others"[7]— meaning that competitive rivalry influences an individual firm's ability to gain and sustain competitive advantages.[8]

A sequence of firm-level moves, rivalry results from firms initiating their own competitive actions and then responding to actions taken by competitors. **Competitive behaviour** is the set of competitive actions and competitive responses the firm takes to build or defend its competitive advantages and to improve its market position.[9] Through competitive behaviour, the firm tries to successfully position itself relative to the five forces of competition (see Chapter 3) and to defend current competitive advantages while building advantages for the future (see Chapter 4). Increasingly, competitors engage in competitive actions and responses in more than one market.[10] Firms competing against each other in several product or geographic markets are engaged in **multimarket competition**.[11] All competitive behaviour—that is, the total set of actions and responses taken by all firms competing within a market—is called **competitive dynamics**. The relationships among these key concepts are shown in Figure 6.1, page 170.

This chapter focuses on competitive rivalry and competitive dynamics. The essence of these important topics is that a firm's strategies are dynamic in nature. Actions taken by one firm elicit responses from competitors that, in turn, typically result in responses from the firm that took the initial action.[12] To the extent possible, other telecommunication companies will need to react to Primus's pricing strategy, as described in the Opening Case.

Another way of highlighting competitive rivalry's effect on the firm's strategies is to say that a strategy's success is determined not only by the firm's initial competitive actions but also by how well it anticipates competitors' responses to them *and* by how well the firm anticipates and responds to its competitors' initial actions (also called attacks).[13] Although competitive rivalry affects all types of strategies (for example, corporate-level, acquisition, and international), its most dominant influence is on the firm's business-level strategy or strategies. Indeed, firms' actions and responses to those of their rivals are the basic building block of business-level strategies.[14] Recall from Chapter 5 that business-level strategy is concerned with what the firm does to successfully use its competitive advantages in specific product markets. In the global economy, competitive rivalry is intensifying,[15] meaning that the significance of its effect on firms'

Competitors are firms operating in the same market, offering similar products and targeting similar customers.

Competitive rivalry is the ongoing set of competitive actions and competitive responses occurring between competitors as they compete against each other for an advantageous market position.

Competitive behaviour is the set of competitive actions and competitive responses the firm takes to build or defend its competitive advantages and to improve its market position.

Multimarket competition occurs when firms compete against each other in several product or geographic markets.

Competitive dynamics refer to all competitive behaviours—that is, the total set of actions and responses taken by all firms competing within a market.

Figure 6.1 From Competitors to Competitive Dynamics

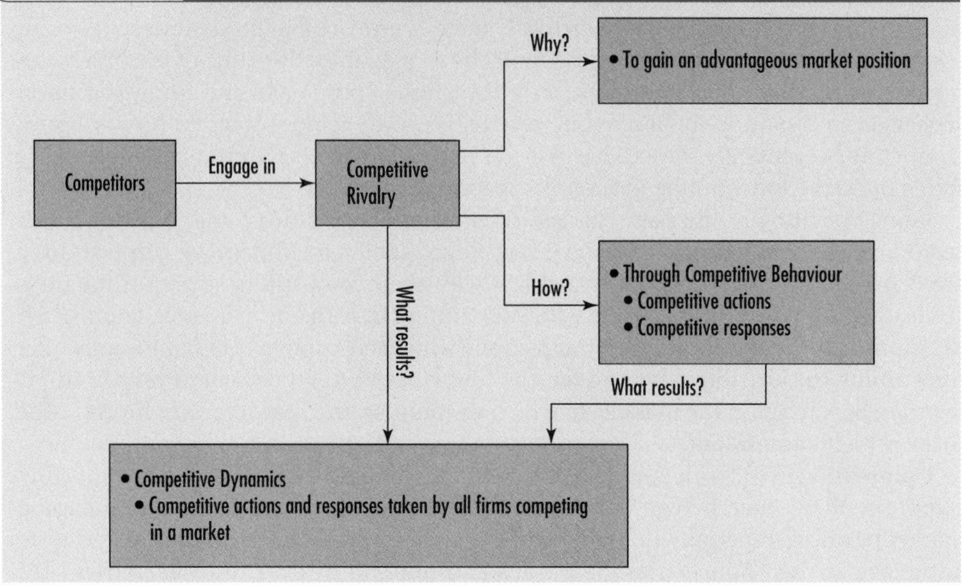

SOURCE: Adapted from M.J. Chen, 1996, Competitor Analysis and Interfirm Rivalry: Toward a Theoretical Integration, *Academy of Management Review*, 21. 100–134.

business-level strategies is increasing. However, firms that develop and use effective business-level strategies tend to outperform competitors in individual product markets, even when experiencing intense competitive rivalry.[16]

An expanding geographic scope contributes to the increasing intensity in the competitive rivalry between firms. Many firms from different parts of the world are beginning to emerge as formidable global competitors. Wipro, the Indian technology firm to which many activities have been outsourced in recent years, entered the global management consulting market in competition with many major firms in this industry. Major Chinese firms made acquisition bids for large international firms in 2005. For example, the Haier Group bid to acquire Maytag, and China's state-owned oil company, CNOOC, made a bid to acquire Unocal.[17]

A Model of Competitive Rivalry

Over time, firms take many competitive actions and responses.[18] As noted earlier, competitive rivalry evolves from this pattern of actions and responses as one firm's competitive actions have noticeable effects on competitors, eliciting competitive responses from them.[19] This pattern shows that firms are mutually interdependent, that they feel each other's actions and responses, and that marketplace success is a function of both individual strategies and the consequences of their use.[20] Increasingly, too, executives recognize that competitive rivalry can have a major and direct effect on the firm's financial performance:[21] Research shows that intensified rivalry within an industry results in decreased average profitability for the competing firms.[22]

Figure 6.2 presents a straightforward model of competitive rivalry at the firm level, but such rivalry is usually dynamic and complex.[23] The competitive actions and responses the firm takes are the foundation for successfully building and using its capabilities and core competencies to gain an advantageous market position.[24] The model in Figure 6.2 presents the sequence of activities commonly involved in competition

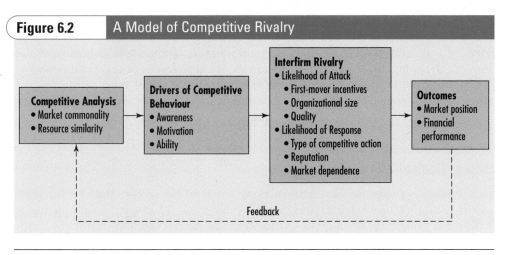

Figure 6.2 A Model of Competitive Rivalry

Competitive Analysis
• Market commonality
• Resource similarity

Drivers of Competitive Behaviour
• Awareness
• Motivation
• Ability

Interfirm Rivalry
• Likelihood of Attack
  • First-mover incentives
  • Organizational size
  • Quality
• Likelihood of Response
  • Type of competitive action
  • Reputation
  • Market dependence

Outcomes
• Market position
• Financial performance

Feedback

SOURCE: Adapted from M.J. Chen, 1996, Competitor Analysis and Interfirm Rivalry: Toward a Theoretical Integration, *Academy of Management Review*, 21: 100–134.

between a particular firm and each of its competitors. Companies can use it to predict competitors' behaviour (actions and responses) and reduce the uncertainty associated with competitors' actions.[25] Being able to predict competitors' actions and responses has a positive effect on the firm's market position and its subsequent financial performance.[26] The sum of all the individual rivalries modelled in Figure 6.2 that occur in a particular market reflects the competitive dynamics in that market.

The remainder of the chapter explains components of the model shown in Figure 6.2. We first describe market commonality and resource similarity as the building blocks of a competitor analysis. Next, we discuss the effects of three organizational characteristics—awareness, motivation, and ability—on the firm's competitive behaviour. We then examine competitive rivalry between firms, or interfirm rivalry, in detail by describing the factors that affect the likelihood a firm will take a competitive action and the factors that affect the likelihood a firm will respond to a competitor's action. In the chapter's final section, we turn our attention to competitive dynamics to describe how market characteristics affect competitive rivalry in slow-cycle, fast-cycle, and standard-cycle markets.

Competitor Analysis

As previously noted, a competitor analysis is the first step the firm takes to be able to predict the extent and nature of its rivalry with each competitor. Recall that a competitor is a firm operating in the same market, offering similar products and targeting similar customers. The number of markets in which firms compete against each other (called market commonality, defined below) and the similarity in their resources (called resource similarity, also defined below) determine the extent to which the firms are competitors. Firms with high market commonality and highly similar resources are "clearly direct and mutually acknowledged competitors."[27] However, being direct competitors does not necessarily mean that the rivalry between the firms will be intense. The drivers of competitive behaviour—as well as factors influencing the likelihood a competitor will initiate competitive actions and will respond to its competitor's competitive actions—influence the intensity of rivalry, even for direct competitors.[28]

In Chapter 3, we discussed competitor analysis as a technique firms use to understand their competitive environment. Together, the general, industry, and competitive environments comprise the firm's external environment. We also described how competitor analysis is used to help the firm *understand* its competitors. This understanding results from studying competitors' future objectives, current strategies, assumptions, and capabilities (refer to Figure 3.3). In this chapter, the discussion of competitor analysis is extended to describe what firms study to be able to *predict* competitors' behaviour in the form of their competitive actions and responses. The discussions of competitor analysis in Chapter 3 and in this chapter are complementary in that firms must first *understand* competitors (Chapter 3) before their competitive actions and competitive responses can be *predicted* (this chapter).

Market Commonality

Each industry is composed of various markets. The financial services industry has markets for insurance, brokerage services, banks, and so forth. To concentrate on the needs of different, unique customer groups, markets can be further subdivided. The insurance market, for example, could be broken into market segments (such as commercial and consumer), product segments (such as health insurance and life insurance), and geographic markets (such as Western Europe and Southeast Asia). In general, the capabilities generated by Internet technologies help to shape the nature of industries' markets along with the competition among firms operating in them.[29] For example, widely available electronic news sources affect how traditional print news distributors such as newspapers conduct their business.

In general, competitors agree about the different characteristics of individual markets that form an industry.[30] For example, in the telecommunications industry there is an understanding that the service providers, like Rogers or Vonage, differ from hardware providers, like Nortel or Cisco. Although differences exist, most industries' markets are somewhat related in terms of technologies used or core competencies needed to develop a competitive advantage.[31] For example, different types of telecommunication companies need to provide reliable and timely service. Service providers like Bell or Shaw must therefore develop service competencies to satisfy their business and residential customers, while Nortel and Cisco must develop such competencies to serve the needs of the companies using their devices to transmit data—VoIP or other.

Firms competing in several markets, some of which may be in different industries, are likely to come into contact with a particular competitor several times,[32] a situation that involves the concept of market commonality. **Market commonality** is concerned with the number of markets with which the firm and a competitor are jointly involved and the degree of importance of the individual markets to each.[33] Firms competing against one another in several or many markets engage in multimarket competition.[34] For example, sportswear retailers Roots Canada and Helly Hanson compete against each other in multiple geographic markets across the world,[35] while Manulife and Sun Life compete against each other in several market segments (institutional and retail) as well as product markets (such as life insurance and wealth management). Airlines, chemicals, pharmaceuticals, and consumer foods are examples of other industries in which firms often simultaneously engage each other in competition in multiple markets.

Firms competing in several markets have the potential to respond to a competitor's actions not only within the market in which the actions are taken, but also in other markets where they compete with the rival. This potential creates a complicated competitive mosaic in which "the moves an organization makes in one market are designed to achieve goals in another market in ways that aren't immediately apparent to its rivals."[36] This potential complicates the rivalry between competitors. In fact, research suggests that "a firm with greater multimarket contact is less likely to initiate an attack, but more likely to move (respond) aggressively when attacked."[37] Thus, in general, multimarket competition reduces competitive rivalry.[38]

Market commonality is concerned with the number of markets with which the firm and a competitor are jointly involved and the degree of importance of the individual markets to each.

Resource Similarity

Resource similarity is the extent to which the firm's tangible and intangible resources are comparable to a competitor's in terms of both type and amount.[39] Firms with similar types and amounts of resources are likely to have similar strengths and weaknesses and use similar strategies.[40] The competition between Sony and Toshiba to establish the standard format for high-definition DVDs demonstrates these expectations. It is similar to the original competition between the two companies in the 1990s regarding DVDs, which ended in a draw with each firm sharing in the royalties from DVD sales. In the current dispute, Sony has considerable support from major consumer electronics firms such as Matsushita, Samsung, Apple, Dell, and entertainment giant Walt Disney. Toshiba has powerful support from Intel, NEC, and many of the movie studios such as Paramount and Warner Bros. Pictures. They could compromise and pool their patents, but each firm would prefer to win the day because of the significant returns their product standing alone would provide.[41] Sony and Toshiba each serve only part of the market; yet establishing one standard requires that one firm wins and one firm loses. In other words, with one standard, one of the firms would serve the whole market. Additionally, they each have strong technological capabilities and the financial resources to develop the technology further as needed. In this case, intangible resources such as firm reputation could play a significant role in deciding the outcome of the competition between these companies.[42]

When performing a competitor analysis, a firm analyzes each of its competitors in terms of market commonality and resource similarity. The results of these analyses can be mapped for visual comparisons. In Figure 6.3, we show different hypothetical intersections between the firm and individual competitors in terms of market commonality and resource similarity. These intersections indicate the extent to which the firm and those with which it is compared are competitors.[43] For example, the firm and its competitor displayed in quadrant I of Figure 6.3 have similar types and amounts of resources (that is, the two firms have a similar portfolio of resources). The firm and its competitor

> **Resource similarity** is the extent to which the firm's tangible and intangible resources are comparable to a competitor's in terms of both type and amount.

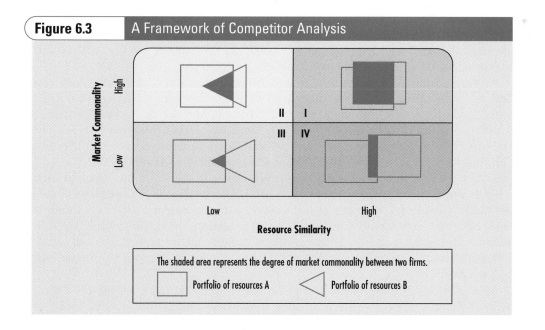

Figure 6.3   A Framework of Competitor Analysis

The shaded area represents the degree of market commonality between two firms.

☐ Portfolio of resources A   ◁ Portfolio of resources B

SOURCE: Adapted from M.J. Chen, 1996, Competitor Analysis and Interfirm Rivalry: Toward a Theoretical Integration, *Academy of Management Review*, 21: 100–134.

in quadrant I would use their similar resource portfolios to compete against each other in many markets that are important to each. These conditions lead to the conclusion that the firms modelled in quadrant I are direct and mutually acknowledged competitors (e.g., Sony and Toshiba). In contrast, the firm and its competitor shown in quadrant III share few markets and have little similarity in their resources, indicating that they are not direct and mutually acknowledged competitors. The firm's mapping of its competitive relationship with rivals is fluid as firms enter and exit markets and as companies' resources change in type and amount. Thus, the companies with which the firm is a direct competitor change across time.

Toyota Motor Corp. and General Motors (GM) have high market commonality, as they compete in many of the same global markets. In years past, the companies also had similar types and quantities of resources. This is changing, though, in that the companies' resources are becoming dissimilar, especially in terms of profitability and sales revenue. In fact, the companies are moving in opposite directions—Toyota's sales and profits are increasing while GM's sales and profits are decreasing. Thus, quadrant II in Figure 6.3 captures the degree to which Toyota and GM are direct competitors. In the Strategic Focus, we suggest the possibility that some of Toyota's recent competitive actions, such as moving into new international markets, are likely to increase the competition between Toyota and GM, hastening GM's decline.

How will GM respond to the possibility of increased competition from Toyota in the global market? The challenge is daunting, in that it is difficult if not impossible to "out-Toyota Toyota."[44] Yet Toyota's chairman, Hiroshi Okuda, is worried about GM's weakness. While Toyota has gone all out to become the world's leading auto manufacturer, its managers are concerned that if GM is hurt too badly there could be a public and political backlash in the United States, leading to restrictions on Toyota's actions in the U.S. market. Most analysts argue, however, that protectionism will only make firms weaker; market competition forces them to strengthen their capabilities. In so doing they will become more competitive over time.[45]

Drivers of Competitive Actions and Responses

As shown in Figure 6.2, market commonality and resource similarity influence the drivers (awareness, motivation, and ability) of competitive behaviour. In turn, the drivers influence the firm's competitive behaviour, as shown by the actions and responses it takes while engaged in competitive rivalry.[46]

Awareness, which is a prerequisite to any competitive action or response taken by a firm, refers to the extent to which competitors recognize the degree of their mutual interdependence that results from market commonality and resource similarity.[47] Awareness tends to be greatest when firms have highly similar resources (in terms of types and amounts) to use while competing against each other in multiple markets. All telecommunications companies are aware of Vonage as a competitor, and certainly Wal-Mart and France's Carrefour, the two largest supermarket groups in the world, are aware of each other as a primary competitor. The last two firms' joint awareness has increased as they use similar resources to compete against each other for dominant positions in multiple European and South American markets.[48] Awareness affects the extent to which the firm understands the consequences of its competitive actions and responses. A lack of awareness can lead to excessive competition, resulting in a negative effect on all competitors' performance.[49]

Motivation, which concerns the firm's incentive to take action or to respond to a competitor's actions, relates to perceived gains and losses. Thus, a firm may be aware of competitors but may not be motivated to engage in rivalry with them if it perceives that its position will not improve or that its market position won't be damaged if it does not respond.[50]

Market commonality affects the firm's perceptions and resulting motivation. For example, all else being equal, the firm is more likely to attack the rival with whom it has low market commonality than the one with whom it competes in multiple markets. The primary reason is that high stakes are involved in trying to gain a more advantageous position over a rival with whom the firm shares many markets. As we mentioned earlier, multimarket competition can find a competitor responding to the firm's action in a market different from the one in which the initial action was taken. Actions and responses of this type can cause both firms to lose focus on core markets and to assail each other with resources that had been allocated for other purposes. Because of the high stakes of competition under the condition of market commonality, there is a high probability that the attacked firm will respond to its competitor's action in an effort to protect its position in one or more markets.[51]

In some instances, the firm may be aware of the large number of markets it shares with a competitor and may be motivated to respond to an action by that competitor, but it lacks the ability to do so. *Ability* relates to each firm's resources and the flexibility they provide. Without available resources (such as financial capital and people), the firm lacks the ability to attack a competitor or respond to its actions. However, similar resources suggest similar abilities to attack and respond. When a firm faces a competitor with similar resources, careful study of a possible attack before initiating it is essential because the similarly resourced competitor is likely to respond to that action.[52]

Resource *dissimilarity* also influences competitive actions and responses between firms, in that "the greater is the resource imbalance between the acting firm and competitors or potential responders, the greater will be the delay in response"[53] by the firm with a resource disadvantage. For example, Wal-Mart initially used a focused cost leadership strategy to compete only in small communities (those with a population of 25,000 or less). Using sophisticated logistics systems and extremely efficient purchasing practices as advantages, among others, Wal-Mart created what was at that time a new type of value (primarily in the form of wide selections of products at the lowest competitive prices) for customers in small retail markets. Local competitors lacked the ability to marshal needed resources at the pace required to respond quickly and effectively. However, even when facing competitors with greater resources (greater ability) or more attractive market positions, firms should eventually respond, no matter how daunting the task seems.[54] Choosing not to respond can ultimately result in failure, as happened with at least some local retailers who didn't respond to Wal-Mart's competitive actions.

As explained in the Strategic Focus, GM was once the market leader but now is having trouble competing in the global auto market. Toyota has long been predicted to exceed GM as the largest auto maker in the world.[55] Some speculate whether GM can survive and compete effectively over time. In a disadvantageous competitive position, firms might best try to serve a special niche in the market to avoid direct competition.[56] Those serving market niches effectively often enjoy positive performance outcomes. Unfortunately, GM attempts to serve the broader market, and so is unlikely to have a positive future unless major changes are made.

Competitive Rivalry

The ongoing competitive action/response sequence between a firm and a competitor affects the performance of both firms[57]; thus, it is important for companies to carefully study competitive rivalry to select and implement successful strategies. Understanding a competitor's awareness, motivation, and ability helps the firm to predict the likelihood of an attack by that competitor and the probability that a competitor will respond to actions taken against it.

As we described earlier, the predictions drawn from studying competitors in terms of awareness, motivation, and ability are grounded in market commonality and resource

Is General Motors Stuck in the 1970s?

At times, it seems that General Motors (GM) operates as if it is still in the 1970s, when its market share was over 50 percent. In 2007, GM finished in almost a dead heat with Toyota as the largest auto manufacturer in the world. It is unlikely to see the top spot again for the foreseeable future. Toyota's competitive actions in recent years to produce exceptionally high-quality and differentiated automobiles, sell them in multiple product segments (e.g., luxury, small fuel efficient, and moderate cost), and expand sales all over the world (e.g., Europe, China) have increased its growth and enhanced its market share. GM's annual sales are the fifth largest in the world across all industries, but the company is faltering. In 2006, its market share was only 25 percent and it was on track to have a net loss of billions of dollars.

GM's problems are many. Importantly, managerial hubris led the firm to use tunnel vision in formulating its strategies, and the firm did not respond effectively (or at all) to major changes in the auto industry. One analyst commented that, "GM has found itself stuck in second gear for a quarter of a century." It did not respond quickly or effectively to the earlier popularity of compact cars or to the more recent trend toward hybrid vehicles. It has negotiated poorly with unions, incurring massive costs and future liabilities. Because of these contractual cost requirements, it has accepted compromises in car design and engineering. The result has been automobiles with outdated designs for the marketplace, unable to compete with more attractive designs from competitors. According to one analyst, "The bedrock principle upon which GM was built—offering a car to feed every market segment—has degraded into a series of contrived brands, most with little identity, and bland, overlapping product lines."

GM has two major assets at present, a well-known brand name and cash. Unfortunately, the brand name has begun to suffer because of poor engineering of introductory-year cars, poor designs, and weak quality relative to competitors. Cash will need to be invested wisely if the company is to be of value, rather than simply keeping a firm out of bankruptcy court. While the decline in sales and profits show the need to shut down plants and reduce production, GM cannot do so. Its union contracts require that all plants be operated at no less than 80 percent capacity.

GM's executives have also shown a penchant for poor strategic decisions and an inability to capitalize on opportunities. For example, GM was an early mover into China. It has invested more than $1 billion in China since 1998, and should be better positioned. Though GM is likely selling more Buicks in China than it still does in North America, Hyundai now outsells them. Sales of GM's entry-level Chevrolet have been less than stellar. Even with five Chevrolet models to choose from, local competitor Chevy did more volume with just one car, its popular QQ. Not only is the local competition hurting GM, but the market has gotten very crowded since GM first arrived—within 10 years of the time it started in China, no fewer than 39 automotive companies with 140 brands have arrived in the market.

Addressing the continuing reductions in performance, GM's CEO, Rick Wagoner, implied that the company was not making the progress needed partly because of the "intense competitive conditions and pricing pressures." With India's Tata Motors's introduction of the $2,500 car, this is likely to get much worse. Further, he suggests that GM must increase its efficiency and productivity. Given the cost structure of Indian and Chinese companies, this is going to be difficult for GM to pull off. A different course might work better. Some experts point to the need for GM to take a quantum technological leap that puts them out front. Moving the company out of the doldrums may take the commercialization of a practical electric car, some other radical new technology like fuel cells, or a miracle.

SOURCES: 2008, The Forbes Global 2000, Forbes Web site, http://www.forbes.com/lists/2007/18/biz_07forbes2000_The-Global-2000_Sales.html, retrieved January 22; 2008, Business: No lakh of daring: The one-lakh car, *The Economist*, 386(8562): 59; J. Anderton, 2007, Domestic shop? Better not be, *SSGM, Service Station & Garage Management*, 37(12): 43; N. Van Praet, 2007, China: GM's next headache?, *Financial Post Business*, July/August, 32–36; 2007, Business: Rising in the East, *The Economist*, 383(8526): 82; J. B. White, 2005, General Motors swings to loss on weakness in North America, *Wall Street Journal*, www.wsj.com, July 20; M. Ihlwan & J. B. Bush, 2005, Hyundai: Crowding into the fast lane, *BusinessWeek*, www.businessweek.com, June 20; D. Welch & D. Beucke, 2005, Why GM's plan won't work, *BusinessWeek*, www.businessweek.com, May 9; D. Roberts, 2005, First-mover disadvantage, *BusinessWeek*, www.businessweek.com, May 9; P. Hjelt, 2005, World's most admired companies, *Fortune*, www.fortune.com, March 1.

similarity. These predictions are fairly general. The value of the final set of predictions the firm develops about each of its competitors' competitive actions and responses is enhanced by studying the "likelihood of attack" factors (such as first-mover incentives and organizational size) and the "likelihood of response" factors (such as the actor's reputation) that are shown in Figure 6.2. Evaluating and understanding these factors allows the firm to refine the predictions it makes about its competitors' actions and responses.

Strategic and Tactical Actions

Firms use both strategic and tactical actions when forming their competitive actions and competitive responses in the course of engaging in competitive rivalry.[58] A **competitive action** is a strategic or tactical action the firm takes to build or defend its competitive advantages or improve its market position. A **competitive response** is a strategic or tactical action the firm takes to counter the effects of a competitor's competitive action. A **strategic action or a strategic response** is a market-based move that involves a significant commitment of organizational resources and is difficult to implement and reverse. A **tactical action or a tactical response** is a market-based move that is taken to fine-tune a strategy; it involves fewer resources and is relatively easy to implement and reverse. Hyundai Motor Co.'s expenditures on research and development and plant expansion to support the firm's desire to be one of the world's largest carmakers in 2010, selling at least one million units annually in North America,[59] are strategic actions. Likewise, Boeing Corp.'s decision to commit the resources required to build the super-efficient 787 midsized jetliner for delivery in 2008[60] demonstrates a strategic action. Changes in airfares are somewhat frequently announced by airlines. As tactical actions that are easily reversed, pricing decisions are often taken by these firms to increase demand in certain markets during certain periods.

Coca-Cola Company, PepsiCo Inc., and Nestlé SA are aware of one another as they compete in the bottled water market. Moreover, this awareness influences the competitive actions and responses these firms initiate as they engage in competitive rivalry. Of course, bottled water isn't the only product category (outside of soft drinks) in which multimarket competitors Coca-Cola and PepsiCo compete against each other. Because of the degree of their market commonality and resource similarity and the fact that they engage in multimarket competition, Coca-Cola and PepsiCo will continue to carefully monitor each other's competitive actions and responses in multiple product areas as part of their competitive rivalry.

> A **competitive action** is a strategic or tactical action the firm takes to build or defend its competitive advantages or improve its market position.
>
> A **competitive response** is a strategic or tactical action the firm takes to counter the effects of a competitor's competitive action.
>
> A **strategic action or a strategic response** is a market-based move that involves a significant commitment of organizational resources and is difficult to implement and reverse.
>
> A **tactical action or tactical response** is a market-based move that is taken to fine-tune a strategy; it involves fewer resources and is relatively easy to implement and reverse.

Likelihood of Attack

In addition to market commonality, resource similarity, and the drivers of awareness, motivation, and ability, other factors affect the likelihood a competitor will use strategic actions and tactical actions to attack its competitors. Three of these factors—first-mover incentives, organizational size, and quality—are discussed next.

First-Mover Incentives

A **first mover** is a firm that takes an initial competitive action in order to build or defend its competitive advantages or to improve its market position. The first-mover concept has been influenced by the work of the famous economist Joseph Schumpeter noted in the Opening Case. He argued that firms achieve competitive advantage by taking innovative actions[61] (innovation is defined and described in detail in Chapter 14). In general, first movers "allocate funds for product innovation and development, aggressive advertising, and advanced research and development."[62]

The benefits of being a successful first mover can be substantial. Especially in fast-cycle markets (discussed later in the chapter), where changes occur rapidly and where it is

> A **first mover** is a firm that takes an initial competitive action in order to build or defend its competitive advantages or to improve its market position.

virtually impossible to sustain a competitive advantage for any length of time, "a first mover may experience five to ten times the valuation and revenue of a second mover."[63] This evidence suggests that although first-mover benefits are never absolute, they are often critical to firm success in industries experiencing rapid technological developments and relatively short product life cycles.[64] In addition to earning above-average returns until its competitors respond to its successful competitive action, the first mover can gain (1) the loyalty of customers who may become committed to the goods or services of the firm that first made them available, and (2) market share that can be difficult for competitors to take during future competitive rivalry.[65] The general evidence that first movers have greater survival rates than later market entrants[66] is perhaps the culmination of first-mover benefits.

The firm trying to predict its competitors' competitive actions might conclude that they will take aggressive strategic actions to gain first movers' benefits. However, while a firm's competitors might be motivated to be first movers, they may lack the ability to do so. First movers tend to be aggressive and willing to experiment with innovation and take higher, yet reasonable, levels of risk.[67] To be a first mover, the firm must have readily available the resources to significantly invest in R&D as well as to rapidly and successfully produce and market a stream of innovative products.[68]

Organizational slack makes it possible for firms to have the ability (as measured by available resources) to be first movers. *Slack* is the buffer or cushion provided by actual or obtainable resources that aren't currently in use and are in excess of the minimum resources needed to produce a given level of organizational output.[69] By the time oil prices began toying with the $100 per barrel mark, many of the large oil companies, such as ExxonMobil, had considerable slack resources: they had significant amounts of cash on hand.

As a liquid resource, slack can quickly be allocated to support the competitive actions that lead to first-mover benefits, such as R&D investments and aggressive marketing campaigns. This relationship between slack and the ability to be a first mover allows the firm to predict that a competitor who is a first mover likely has available slack and will probably take aggressive competitive actions to continuously introduce innovative products. Furthermore, the firm can predict that as a first mover, a competitor will try to rapidly gain market share and customer loyalty in order to earn above-average returns until its competitors are able to effectively respond to its first move.

Firms evaluating their competitors should realize that being a first mover carries risk. For example, it is difficult to accurately estimate the returns that will be earned from introducing product innovations to the marketplace.[70] First movers may also have a difficult time determining the potential uses for a development. The graphic user interface (GUI) for computers was really developed at Xerox. However, Xerox was slow in commercializing the product, and it was not until Steve Jobs took the idea and adopted it for use in Apple computers that the GUI found a market.[71]

Additionally, the first mover's cost to develop a product innovation can be substantial, reducing the slack available to it to support further innovation. Thus, the firm should carefully study the results a competitor achieves as a first mover. Continuous success by the competitor suggests additional product innovations, while lack of product acceptance over the course of the competitor's innovations may indicate less willingness in the future to accept the risks of being a first mover.

A **second mover** is a firm that responds to the first mover's competitive action, typically through imitation. More cautious than the first mover, the second mover studies customers' reactions to product innovations. In the course of doing so, the second mover also tries to find any mistakes the first mover made so that it can avoid them and the problems they created. Often, successful imitation of the first mover's innovations allows the second mover "to avoid both the mistakes and the huge spending of the pioneers [first movers]."[72]

Second movers also have the time to develop processes and technologies that are more efficient than those used by the first mover.[73] Greater efficiencies could result in lower costs for the second mover. Montreal's Mega Brands is a second mover with its construction

A **second mover** is a firm that responds to the first mover's competitive action, typically through imitation.

toys—principally Mega Bloks—and its Rose Art crayons and markers. In an industry where trends and fashions can make or break a company, Mega has found two very viable strategies that work. One is to select toy/play products with a proven track record and consistent sales, then sell them for less; for example, Mega Bloks are compatible with other plastic block construction toys like Lego but sell for less. The other strategy is to team up with the developers of characters like Dora the Explorer or Spiderman and produce and distribute merchandise for them. While the profit is lower, the risk—in an industry where a bad toy season can destroy a firm—is much lower.[74] Overall, the outcomes of the first mover's competitive actions may provide an effective blueprint for second and even late movers as they determine the nature and timing of their competitive responses.[75]

Determining that a competitor is an effective second mover (based on its past actions) allows a first-mover firm to predict that the competitor will respond quickly to successful, innovation-based market entries. The first mover can expect a successful second-mover competitor to study its market entries and to respond with its own new entry into the market within a short time period. As a second mover, the competitor will try to respond with a product that provides greater customer value than does the first mover's product. The most successful second movers are able to rapidly and meaningfully interpret market feedback to respond quickly, yet successfully, to the first mover's successful innovations.

A **late mover** is a firm that responds to a competitive action a significant amount of time after the first mover's action and the second mover's response. Typically, a late response is better than no response at all, although any success achieved from the late competitive response tends to be considerably less than that achieved by first and second movers.

A **late mover** is a firm that responds to a competitive action, but only after considerable time has elapsed after the first mover's action and the second mover's response.

Thus, the firm competing against a late mover can predict that the competitor will likely enter a particular market only after both the first and second movers have achieved success in that market. Moreover, on a relative basis, the firm can predict that the late mover's competitive action will allow it to earn average returns only after the considerable time required for it to understand how to create at least as much customer value as that offered by the first and second movers' products. Although exceptions exist, most of the late mover's competitive actions will be ineffective relative to those initiated by first and second movers.

Late movers can be successful, though. Bill Gates initially introduced Windows years after Apple brought out its graphic user interface (GUI), and Microsoft's GUI was not well accepted until version 3.0—five years after version 1.0 came out. What helped Gates was that he had a lot of slack resources to devote to product development, and he recognized, upon user acceptance of Windows 3.0 (and 3.1 two years later), that the product was, effectively, a disruptive technology. Users had to incur big switching costs to retrain themselves on the new interface. This switching cost was incurred to retrain on both the operating system and all application programs. It mattered little to users what application they moved to because Windows changed the way they did it. Gates used this as an opportunity to move users away from WordPerfect and Lotus 123 (both market leaders in 1990) to Microsoft's Word and Excel. This made the investment in Windows far more profitable because it gave Microsoft entry into a business it had had difficulty getting into—applications software, for example word processing and spreadsheets.

Organizational Size

An organization's size affects the likelihood that it will take competitive actions as well as the types of actions it will take and their timing.[76] In general, small firms are more likely than large companies to launch competitive actions and tend to do it more quickly. Smaller firms are thus perceived as nimble and flexible competitors who rely on speed and surprise to defend their competitive advantages or develop new ones while engaged in competitive rivalry, especially with large companies, to gain an advantageous market position.[77] Small firms' flexibility and nimbleness allow them to develop variety in their competitive actions; large firms tend to limit the types of competitive actions used.[78]

Large firms, however, are likely to initiate more competitive actions along with more strategic actions during a given period.[79] Thus, when studying its competitors in terms of organizational size, the firm should use a measurement such as total sales revenue or total number of employees. The competitive actions the firm likely will encounter from competitors larger than it is will be different than the competitive actions it will encounter from competitors that are smaller.

The organizational-size factor adds another layer of complexity. When engaging in competitive rivalry, the firm often prefers a large number of unique competitive actions. Ideally, the organization has the amount of slack resources held by a large firm to launch a greater *number* of competitive actions and a small firm's flexibility to launch a greater *variety* of competitive actions. Herb Kelleher, co-founder and former CEO of Southwest Airlines, addressed this matter: "Think and act big and we'll get smaller. Think and act small and we'll get bigger."[80]

In the context of competitive rivalry, Kelleher's statement can be interpreted to mean that relying on a limited number or types of competitive actions (which is the large firm's tendency) can lead to reduced competitive success across time, partly because competitors learn how to effectively respond to the predictable. In contrast, remaining flexible and nimble (which is the small firm's tendency) in order to develop and use a wide variety of competitive actions contributes to success against rivals.

Wal-Mart is a large firm that has the flexibility required to take many types of competitive actions. With over $300 billion in sales revenue in 2007, Wal-Mart is one of the world's largest companies. In less than a decade, Wal-Mart has become one of the largest grocery retailers in North America. This accomplishment demonstrates Wal-Mart's ability to successfully compete against its various rivals, even long-established grocers. All of Wal-Mart's 2007 competitors for the top spot—ExxonMobil ($328 billion in sales), Royal Dutch Shell ($307 billion in sales), and British Petroleum ($249 billion in sales)—were large oil companies.[81]

Analysts believe that Wal-Mart's tactical actions are as critical to its success as its strategic actions, and that its tactical actions demonstrate a great deal of flexibility. For example, "every humble store worker has the power to lower the price on any Wal-Mart product if he spots it cheaper elsewhere."[82] Decision-making responsibility and authority have been delegated to the level of the individual worker to make certain the firm's cost leadership business-level strategy always results in the lowest prices for customers. Managers and employees both spend a good deal of time thinking about additional strategic and tactical actions, respectively, that might enhance the firm's performance. Wal-Mart has met the expectation suggested by Kelleher's statement, in that it is a large firm that "remains stuck to its small-town roots" in order to think and act like the small firm capable of using a wide variety of competitive actions. Wal-Mart's competitors might feel confident in predicting that the firm's competitive actions will be a combination of the tendencies shown by small and large companies.

One competitor that has used its "small-town roots" to survive the march of Wal-Mart is Canadian Tire. There is a sense that the local Canadian Tire is a local merchant, since individual stores are, in fact, locally owned franchises. Though they have enlarged their stores to compete with Wal-Mart, the company has kept its product range simple by focusing on its three traditional areas: automotive, sports and leisure, and home products. Canadian Tire has kept customers coming back through identification with their traditional Canadian Tire "money" (bonuses that can be used only at Canadian Tire). It all seems to work. Even with Wal-Mart in the Canadian market, Canadian Tire claims that nine out of ten adult Canadians shop at Canadian Tire at least twice a year, and 40 percent shop there every week.

In the Strategic Focus, we describe how a number of smaller Canadian competitors outperform their larger rivals. Although smaller than their primary competitors, their success has resulted in growth. The competitive challenge for these companies will be to continue thinking and acting as a small firm as they become larger organizations.

Thinking and Acting Small

As we noted earlier, 80 to 90 percent of new firms fail. The vast majority of these firms are small businesses. So what kind of wisdom can we hope to find by looking at them? If the failure rate is so high, much of what they do must be wrong. Not so—many things small businesses do to compete are counterintuitive, but not necessarily wrong. Thus, there may be a couple of lessons here for all firms.

Raise your prices. If you cannot possibly beat Wal-Mart for low prices, then raise them. If most small businesses raised their prices just 5 to 10 percent they could turn failure into success. There is a catch, however—you cannot just raise prices and not do anything. Andy Buyting, president of New Brunswick's Green Village Home & Garden, tried the usual ways to boost profits: cutting costs and smarter buying. But he decided the real benefit lay in raising prices.

Reviewing all the products Green Village sells, he decided about half were price-sensitive. On the other 50 percent, Buyting slowly raised prices by 5 to 20 percent. In spring 2006, Buyting raised the price of his best-selling product, a tray of 12 bedding plants, from $4.99 to $5.99. Not only was there no resistance from customers, but some customers bought more—presuming the higher price meant higher quality. That one price change boosted profit by $16,000. In 2007, Buyting ordered the same plants in trays bearing the Green Village logo, and raised the price to $6.99. They sold out in no time. The lesson: "In retail, we're more scared to raise prices than our customers are to pay higher prices."

The catch is that Buyting did not just boost prices. He invested in staff training, spruced up the facilities, and brought in more specialty merchandise, stealing the funds from his advertising budget. "Once you've provided a better shopping experience, you can raise prices five percent and it will go straight to the bottom line." If a community-based business is perceived as providing good service and quality, people will pay for it.

Honestly, give stuff away. Don't make customers buy something; honestly give things away and make your business part of the community. David Stezenko, co-owner of two Quality Markets in Thunder Bay, Ontario, has a "Cakes for Kids" program. "There are a lot of people in every community who can barely afford to make ends meet and we see such value in a child being able to have a birthday cake," he says, adding that both stores provide a free birthday cake to any child age 10 and under. "There are young mothers coming in here with tears rolling down their faces, they say 'Thank you so much. You have no idea what that meant to my daughter. I can barely pay the rent and keep food on the table and I don't have $14 for a cake.'" In 2006, close to 3,000 birthday cakes were donated to residents of Thunder Bay. Does Quality Markets have loyal customers? They do, and they need them. Unlikely as it may seem, grocery competition in Thunder Bay is fierce. Stezenko says the city has more retail grocery space per capita than any other Canadian city with a population of 100,000 or more.

Mondella Stacey, manager of Coleman's Food Centre in Stephenville, Newfoundland, observed that, "There are a number of people who never have a Christmas party so I thought: 'Why not?'" In addition to live entertainment, decorations throughout the store, and prizes galore, customers can nibble on hors d'oeuvres, cheese, fruitcake, and so on. Santa is there to be photographed with the kids. The major prizes, like last year's fireplace, are giveaways received from suppliers. But the Christmas party, held the Sunday before Christmas, is not just a fun-and-games affair. Guests are welcome to comb the aisles in search of goodies for the holiday season, making it the busiest Sunday of the year.

On the other side of The Rock, Larry Higdon arrived in Baie Verte in 2003 to manage the local Co-op. Higdon was warned of a group of young people in the community who were troublemakers. Seeing them in the parking lot across the street one evening, he was worried they might vandalize the store. He brought out cases of pop and ice cream bars and offered them to the youngsters. "I said, 'There's no catch. Stay and have fun but I want you to do me two

(continued)

favours. Throw the garbage in the garbage cans and don't throw eggs in my windows.' They said, 'No problem, sir,' and that's how it started." Higdon became friends with the group and they became busy holding dances, events for seniors, and fundraising events that allowed them to build a $20,000 playground for the community.

Because of Higdon's ongoing involvement and the community's recognition of what he accomplished, the Baie Verte Co-op went from near bankruptcy to a money-making business. By 2006 its membership had almost doubled from 2003, sales were $4.75 million, and net profit was about $100,000. Another important benefit Higdon sees is a change in the attitude of his staff. "A sense of pride is the biggest thing they now have," he says, "[working here] was almost an embarrassment because they knew the business was going under. Then you become more involved because you feel a little better about what you're doing." Happy employees make happy customers. And happy customers keep coming back.

SOURCES: R. Spence, 2007, Raise your prices!, *Profit*, 26(6): 23; C. Green, 2007, The good neighbour grocer, *Canadian Grocer*, 121(8): 40–42; R. Spence, Bright ideas!, *Profit*, 26(3): 68–72; A. Wahl, 2003, Sierra's smart move, *Canadian Business*, October 14–26, 29; R. Seymour, 2002, Ideas that work: PROFIT 100 CEOs reveal their favourite management tips, *Profit*, June, 66–70.

As described in the Strategic Focus, the firms included demonstrated flexibility in the competitive actions they took. Some of these competitors used strategies that were less than conventional but maintained the small business attitude of being part of the community—as well as looking very carefully at what customers were likely to respond to, and how they were likely to respond.

Quality

Quality has many definitions, including well-established ones relating it to the production of goods or services with zero defects[83] and seeing it as a never-ending cycle of continuous improvement.[84] From a strategic perspective, we consider quality to be an outcome of how the firm completes primary and support activities (see Chapter 4). Thus, **quality** exists when the firm's goods or services meet or exceed customers' expectations. Some evidence suggests that quality may be the most critical component in satisfying the firm's customers.[85]

In the eyes of customers, quality is about doing the right things relative to performance measures that are important to them.[86] Customers may be interested in measuring the quality of a firm's goods and services against a broad range of dimensions. Sample quality dimensions in which customers commonly express an interest are shown in Table 6.1. Quality is possible only when top-level managers support it and when its importance is institutionalized throughout the entire organization.[87] When quality is institutionalized and valued by all, employees and managers alike become vigilant about continuously finding ways to improve quality.[88]

Quality is a universal theme in the global economy and is a necessary but not sufficient condition for competitive success.[89] Without quality, a firm's products lack credibility, meaning that customers don't think of them as viable options. Indeed, customers won't consider buying a product until they believe that it can satisfy at least their base-level expectations in terms of quality dimensions that are important to them. Quality is important for firm performance. For example, innovative new products lead to higher firm performance only when they are of high quality.[90]

Quality affects competitive rivalry. The firm evaluating a competitor whose products suffer from poor quality can predict that the competitor's sales revenue will likely decline until the quality issues are resolved. In addition, the firm can predict that in order to gain credibility with customers the competitor likely won't be aggressive in its

Quality exists when the firm's goods or services meet or exceed customers' expectations.

Table 6.1	Quality Dimensions of Goods and Services

Product Quality Dimensions
1. *Performance*—Operating characteristics
2. *Features*—Important special characteristics
3. *Flexibility*—Meeting operating specifications over some period of time
4. *Durability*—Amount of use before performance deteriorates
5. *Conformance*—Match with preestablished standards
6. *Serviceability*—Ease and speed of repair
7. *Aesthetics*—How a product looks and feels
8. *Perceived quality*—Subjective assessment of characteristics (product image)

Service Quality Dimensions
1. *Timeliness*—Performed in the promised period of time
2. *Courtesy*—Performed cheerfully
3. *Consistency*—Giving all customers similar experiences each time
4. *Convenience*—Accessibility to customers
5. *Completeness*—Fully serviced, as required
6. *Accuracy*—Performed correctly each time

SOURCES: Adapted from J. W. Dean, Jr., & J. R. Evans, 1994, *Total Quality: Management, Organization and Society*, St. Paul, MN: West Publishing Company; H. V. Roberts & B. F. Sergesketter, 1993, *Quality Is Personal*, New York: The Free Press; D. Garvin, 1988, *Managed Quality: The Strategic and Competitive Edge*, New York: The Free Press.

competitive actions until the quality problems are corrected. However, after the problems are corrected, that competitor is likely to take more aggressive competitive actions. Hyundai Motor Co.'s experiences illustrate these expectations.

Immediately upon becoming CEO of Hyundai Motor Co. in March 1999, Mong Koo Chung started touring the firm's manufacturing facilities. Appalled at what he saw, he told workers and managers alike, "The only way we can survive is to raise our quality to Toyota's level."[91] To dramatically improve quality, a quality-control unit was established, and significant resources (over $1 billion annually) were allocated to research and development (R&D) in order to build cars that could compete on price and deliver on quality. Today, quality is still viewed as the firm's number-one priority.[92] In 2003, the director of automotive quality research at J.D. Power observed, "Since 1998, Hyundai is the most improved car in the initial quality survey. They have dropped their number of quality problems by 50 percent."[93] Signalling a strong belief in its products' quality, Hyundai offers a 10-year drive-train warranty in the United States, which the firm has selected as a key market.[94] As noted in the earlier Strategic Focus, Hyundai is taking market share from GM in the Chinese market.[95] Improvements to the quality of Hyundai's products helped the firm to become a more aggressive competitor.

Likelihood of Response

The success of a firm's competitive action is affected by the likelihood that a competitor will respond to it as well as by the type (strategic or tactical) and effectiveness of that response. As noted earlier, a competitive response is a strategic or tactical action the firm takes to counter the effects of a competitor's competitive action. In general, a firm is likely to respond to a competitor's action when (1) the action leads to better use of the competitor's capabilities to gain or produce stronger competitive advantages or an improvement in its market position, (2) the action damages the firm's ability to use its capabilities to create or maintain an advantage, or (3) the firm's market position becomes less defensible.[96]

In addition to market commonality and resource similarity and awareness, motivation, and ability, firms evaluate three other factors—type of competitive action, reputation, and market dependence—to predict how a competitor is likely to respond to competitive actions (see Figure 6.2).

Type of Competitive Action

Competitive responses to strategic actions differ from responses to tactical actions. These differences allow a firm to predict a competitor's likely response to a competitive action that has been launched against it. Generally, strategic actions receive strategic responses and tactical actions receive tactical responses.

In general, strategic actions elicit fewer total competitive responses because strategic responses, such as market-based moves, involve a significant commitment of resources and are difficult to implement and reverse.[97] Moreover, the time needed for a strategic action to be implemented and its effectiveness assessed delays the competitor's response to that action.[98] In contrast, a competitor likely will respond quickly to a tactical action, such as when an airline company almost immediately matches a competitor's tactical action of reducing prices in certain markets. Either strategic actions or tactical actions that target a large number of a rival's customers are likely to elicit strong responses.[99] In fact, if the effects of a competitor's strategic action on the focal firm are significant (e.g., loss of market share, loss of major resources such as critical employees), a response is likely to be swift and strong.[100]

Actor's Reputation

In the context of competitive rivalry, an *actor* is the firm taking an action or a response while *reputation* is "the positive or negative attribute ascribed by one rival to another based on past competitive behaviour."[101] A positive reputation may be a source of above-average returns, especially for consumer goods producers.[102] Thus, a positive corporate reputation is of strategic value[103] and affects competitive rivalry. To predict the likelihood of a competitor's response to a current or planned action, firms evaluate the responses that the competitor has taken previously when attacked—past behaviour is assumed to be a predictor of future behaviour.

Competitors are more likely to respond to strategic or tactical actions when they are taken by a market leader.[104] In particular, evidence suggests that commonly successful actions, especially strategic actions, will be quickly imitated. For example, although a second mover, IBM committed significant resources to enter the PC market. When IBM was immediately successful in this endeavour, competitors such as Dell, Compaq, and Gateway responded with strategic actions to enter the market. IBM's reputation as well as its successful strategic action strongly influenced entry by these competitors. Today, though, Dell is the personal computer market leader and a strong performer.[105] Competitors now target Dell as the market leader.

In contrast to a firm with a strong reputation, such as IBM, competitors are less likely to take responses against a company with a reputation for competitive behaviour that is risky, complex, and unpredictable. The firm with a reputation as a price predator (an actor that frequently reduces prices to gain or maintain market share) generates few responses to its pricing tactical actions because price predators, which typically increase prices once their market share objective is reached, lack credibility with their competitors.[106]

Dependence on the Market

Market dependence denotes the extent to which a firm's revenues or profits are derived from a particular market.[107] In general, firms can predict that competitors with high market dependence are likely to respond strongly to attacks threatening their market position.[108] Interestingly, the threatened firm in these instances may not always respond quickly, although an effective response to an attack on the firm's position in a critical market is very important.

Canada's Bombardier and Brazil's Embraer each have significant shares of the midsize passenger airplane market. When an opportunity is presented to one, the other is likely to be a competitor in the same market and for specific contracts. Given that airlines find it more cost effective to deal with fewer types of aircraft, successful delivery and support of the product by either aircraft maker is likely to create a long-term loyal and lucrative relationship with the customer. These two firms are the primary competitors, so when one receives a contract it normally means that the other one is likely to have lost out. Similarly, there is significant competition in the luxury automobile market. A few years ago, Mercedes introduced a series of new "classes" of its luxury automobile. BMW, whose performance is similar to that of Mercedes and which is substantially dependent on its success in the luxury auto market, followed by introducing its own new series. Mercedes recently announced a new generation of its M-Class autos. Given that the new series of vehicles represents an upgrade, it will be interesting to see whether BMW and other competitors (e.g., Lexus) respond.[109]

Coca-Cola has been losing its competitive capabilities over the last few years. It seems unable to defend its market position against moves made by PepsiCo, even though it is highly dependent on the beverage market. Since the death in 1997 of its highly regarded CEO, Roberto Goizueta, Coca-Cola has struggled through a series of CEOs and other top executives. As a result of this turmoil, and because PepsiCo made the right competitive moves by introducing valued new products, PepsiCo has gained in the market and is earning profits while Coke's profits are falling along with its fortunes. Coke's current CEO, Neville Isdell, is trying to meet the challenge by advertising heavily to support existing brands and by introducing new products.

Competitive Dynamics

Whereas competitive rivalry concerns the ongoing actions and responses between a firm and its competitors for an advantageous market position, competitive dynamics concerns the ongoing actions and responses taking place among *all* firms competing within a market for advantageous positions.

To explain competitive rivalry, we described (1) factors that determine the degree to which firms are competitors (market commonality and resource similarity), (2) drivers of competitive behaviour for individual firms (awareness, motivation, and ability), and (3) factors affecting the likelihood that a competitor will act or attack (first-mover incentives, organizational size, and quality) and respond (type of competitive action, reputation, and market dependence). Building and sustaining competitive advantages are at the core of competitive rivalry, in that advantages are the key to creating value for shareholders.[110]

To explain competitive dynamics, we discuss the effects of varying rates of competitive speed in different markets (called slow-cycle, fast-cycle, and standard-cycle markets, defined below) on the behaviour (actions and responses) of all competitors within a given market. Competitive behaviours as well as the reasons or logic for taking them are similar within each market type, but differ across market type.[111] Thus, competitive dynamics differ in slow-cycle, fast-cycle, and standard-cycle markets. The sustainability of the firm's competitive advantages differs across the three market types.

As noted in Chapter 1, firms want to sustain their competitive advantages for as long as possible, although no advantage is permanently sustainable. The degree of sustainability is affected by how quickly competitive advantages can be imitated and how costly it is to do so.

Slow-Cycle Markets

Slow-cycle markets are markets in which the firm's competitive advantages are shielded from imitation for what are commonly long periods of time and where imitation is costly.

Slow-cycle markets are those in which the firm's competitive advantages are shielded from imitation commonly for long periods of time and where imitation is costly.[112] Thus, competitive advantages are sustainable in slow-cycle markets.

Building a unique and proprietary capability produces a competitive advantage and success in a slow-cycle market. This type of advantage is difficult for competitors to understand. As discussed in Chapter 4, a difficult-to-understand and costly-to-imitate resource or capability usually results from unique historical conditions, causal ambiguity, and/or social complexity. Copyrights, geography, patents, and ownership of an information resource are examples of resources.[113] After a proprietary advantage is developed, the firm's competitive behaviour in a slow-cycle market is oriented to protecting, maintaining, and extending that advantage. Thus, the competitive dynamics in slow-cycle markets usually concentrate on competitive actions and responses that enable firms to protect, maintain, and extend their competitive advantage. Major strategic actions in these markets, such as acquisitions, usually carry less risk than in faster-cycle markets.[114]

Walt Disney Co. continues to extend its proprietary characters, such as Mickey Mouse, Minnie Mouse, and Goofy. These characters have a unique historical development as a result of Walt and Roy Disney's creativity and vision for entertaining people. Products based on the characters seen in Disney's animated films are sold through Disney's theme park shops as well as freestanding retail outlets called Disney Stores. Because copyrights shield it, the proprietary nature of Disney's advantage in terms of animated characters protects the firm from imitation by competitors.

Consistent with another attribute of competition in a slow-cycle market, Disney protects its exclusive rights to its characters and their use as shown by the fact that "the company once sued a day-care center, forcing it to remove the likeness of Mickey Mouse from a wall of the facility."[115] As with all firms competing in slow-cycle markets, Disney's competitive actions (such as building theme parks in France, Japan, and China) and responses (such as lawsuits to protect its right to fully control use of its animated characters) maintain and extend its proprietary competitive advantage while protecting it.

In addition to copyright and patent laws, regulatory requirements (like those administered by the Health Products and Food Branch of Health Canada) are needed to gain approval for new products and to shield pharmaceutical companies' positions.[116] Competitors in this market try to extend patents on their drugs to maintain advantageous positions that patents provide. However, after a patent expires, the firm is no longer shielded from competition, allowing generic imitations and usually leading to a loss of sales.

As is true with Walt Disney Co., pharmaceutical companies aggressively pursue legal actions to protect their patents. This is demonstrated by recent actions taken by Pfizer Inc., the maker and seller of Lipitor, the world's most prescribed cholesterol-lowering drug. Pfizer won British and U.S. lawsuits against Ranbaxy to prohibit the Indian company from making and marketing Lipitor before Pfizer's 1987 patent expires in 2010.[117] The stakes are high in these suits; Pfizer generates more than $10 billion annually on Lipitor sales.[118] Though Pfizer won these cases, the competition is ongoing, global, and disputed at multiple governmental levels. At the global level Pfizer lost a case in 2005 when the Australian patent office eliminated Pfizer's patent protection on Lipitor in a challenge filed by Ranbaxy. While the U.S. courts were kind to the company, at another governmental level the agency that controls patent protection, the U.S. Patent and Trademark Office, was less generous—it ruled that one of Pfizer's several patents on Lipitor was based on invalid arguments.[119]

The competitive dynamics generated by firms competing in slow-cycle markets are shown in Figure 6.4. In slow-cycle markets, firms launch a product (e.g., a new drug) that

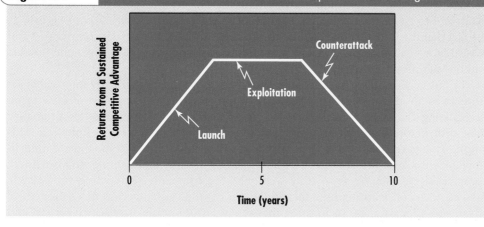

Figure 6.4 Gradual Erosion of a Sustained Competitive Advantage

SOURCE: Adapted from I.C. MacMillan, 1988, Controlling Competitive Dynamics by Taking Strategic Initiative, *Academy of Management Executive*, II(2): 111–118.

has been developed through a proprietary advantage (e.g., R&D) and then exploit it for as long as possible while the product is shielded from competition. Eventually, competitors respond to the action with a counterattack. In markets for drugs, this counterattack commonly occurs as patents expire or are broken through legal means, creating the need for another product launch by the firm seeking a protected market position.

Fast-Cycle Markets

Fast-cycle markets are markets in which the firm's capabilities that contribute to competitive advantages aren't shielded from imitation, and where imitation is often rapid and inexpensive. Thus, competitive advantages aren't sustainable in fast-cycle markets. Firms competing in fast-cycle markets recognize the importance of speed; these companies appreciate that "time is as precious a business resource as money or head count—and that the costs of hesitation and delay are just as steep as going over budget or missing a financial forecast."[120] Such high-velocity environments place considerable pressures on top managers to make strategic decisions quickly, but they must also be effective.[121] The often substantial competition and technology-based strategic focus make the strategic decision complex, increasing the need for a comprehensive approach integrated with decision speed—two often-conflicting characteristics of the strategic decision process.[122]

Reverse engineering and the rate of technology diffusion in fast-cycle markets facilitate rapid imitation. A competitor uses reverse engineering to quickly gain the knowledge required to imitate or improve the firm's products. Technology is diffused rapidly in fast-cycle markets, making it available to competitors in a short period. The technology often used by fast-cycle competitors isn't proprietary, nor is it protected by patents as is the technology used by firms competing in slow-cycle markets. For example, only a few hundred parts, which are readily available on the open market, are required to build a PC. Patents protect only a few of these parts, such as microprocessor chips.[123]

Fast-cycle markets are more volatile than slow-cycle and standard-cycle markets. Indeed, the pace of competition in fast-cycle markets is almost frenzied, as companies rely on innovations as the engines of their growth. Because prices fall quickly in these markets, companies need to profit quickly from their product innovations. Imitation of

Fast-cycle markets are markets in which the firm's competitive advantages aren't shielded from imitation and where imitation happens quickly and perhaps somewhat inexpensively.

Chapter 6 / Competitive Rivalry and Competitive Dynamics many fast-cycle products is relatively easy, as demonstrated by Dell Inc. and Hewlett-Packard, along with a host of local PC vendors, that have partly or largely imitated IBM's PC design to create their products. Continuous declines in the costs of parts, as well as the fact that the information required to assemble a PC isn't especially complicated and is readily available, make it possible for additional competitors to enter this market without significant difficulty.[124]

The fast-cycle market characteristics described above make it virtually impossible for companies in this type of market to develop sustainable competitive advantages. Recognizing this, firms avoid "loyalty" to any of their products, preferring to cannibalize their own before competitors learn how to do so through successful imitation. This emphasis creates competitive dynamics that differ substantially from those found in slow-cycle markets. Instead of concentrating on protecting, maintaining, and extending competitive advantages, as in slow-cycle markets, companies competing in fast-cycle markets focus on learning how to rapidly and continuously develop new competitive advantages that are superior to those they replace. Commonly, they search for fast and effective means of developing new products. For example, it is common in some industries for firms to use strategic alliances to gain access to new technologies and thereby develop and introduce more new products into the market.[125]

The competitive behaviour of firms competing in fast-cycle markets is shown in Figure 6.5. As suggested by the figure, competitive dynamics in this market type entail taking actions and responses that are oriented to rapid and continuous product introductions and the development of a stream of ever-changing competitive advantages. The firm launches a product to achieve a competitive action and then exploits the advantage for as long as possible. However, the firm also tries to develop another temporary competitive advantage before competitors can respond to the first one (see Figure 6.5). Thus, competitive dynamics in fast-cycle markets often result in rapid product upgrades as well as quick product innovations.[126]

As our discussion suggests, innovation plays a key role in the competitive dynamics in fast-cycle markets. For individual firms, this means that innovation is a key source of competitive advantage. Via innovation, the firm can cannibalize its own products before competitors successfully imitate them.

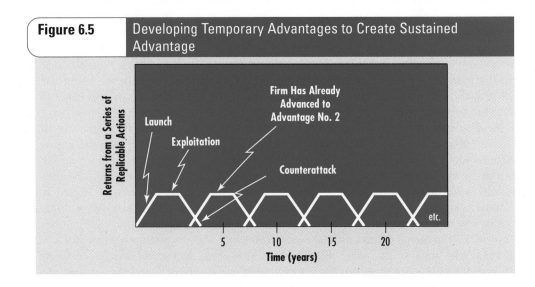

Figure 6.5 | Developing Temporary Advantages to Create Sustained Advantage

SOURCE: Adapted from I.C. MacMillan, 1988, Controlling Competitive Dynamics by Taking Strategic Initiative, *Academy of Management Executive*, II(2): 111–118.

As noted earlier, it is difficult for firms competing in fast-cycle markets to maintain a competitive advantage in terms of their products. Partly because of this, both IBM and Hewlett-Packard (HP) experienced problems in competing effectively over time. In fact, IBM sold its PC business to Lenovo, China's largest PC manufacturer. Changes may be in store for HP's PC business as well. Neither firm has been able to compete effectively with Dell, the current PC market leader.[127]

Standard-Cycle Markets

Standard-cycle markets are markets in which the firm's competitive advantages are moderately shielded from imitation and where imitation is moderately costly. Competitive advantages are partially sustainable in standard-cycle markets, but only when the firm is able to continuously upgrade the quality of its capabilities, making the competitive advantages dynamic. The competitive actions and responses that form a standard-cycle market's competitive dynamics are designed to seek large market shares, to gain customer loyalty through brand names, and to carefully control their operations in order to consistently provide the same positive experience for customers.[128]

Standard-cycle companies serve many customers in competitive markets. Because the capabilities and core competencies on which their competitive advantages are based are less specialized, imitation is faster and less costly for standard-cycle firms than for those competing in slow-cycle markets. However, imitation is slower and more expensive in these markets than in fast-cycle markets. Thus, competitive dynamics in standard-cycle markets rest midway between the characteristics of dynamics in slow-cycle and fast-cycle markets. Imitation comes less quickly and is more expensive for standard-cycle competitors when a firm is able to develop economies of scale by combining coordinated and integrated design and manufacturing processes with a large sales volume for its products.

Because of large volumes, the size of mass markets, and the need to develop scale economies, the competition for market share is intense in standard-cycle markets. This form of competition is readily evident in the competition between Coca-Cola and PepsiCo. They compete in markets all over the world. In recent years, PepsiCo has been winning in domestic and international markets. This outcome is partly due to effective strategic actions by PepsiCo and ineffective actions by Coca-Cola's top management, which evidenced chaos in top management in the period of 1998–2004.

Innovation can also drive competitive actions and responses in standard-cycle markets, especially when rivalry is intense. Some innovations in standard-cycle markets are incremental rather than radical in nature (incremental and radical innovations are discussed in Chapter 14). One of the reasons for Pepsi's success in competition against Coca-Cola has been the innovative new products it has introduced. Coke's CEO in February 2008, Neville Isdell, emphasized heavy advertising to support Coke's strong brand and to support the introduction of a variety of new beverage products in the market. Thus, both Coca-Cola and PepsiCo have emphasized innovation in their competition.

In the final analysis, innovation has a substantial influence on competitive dynamics as it affects the actions and responses of all companies competing within a slow-cycle, fast-cycle, or standard-cycle market. We have emphasized the importance of innovation to the firm's strategic competitiveness in earlier chapters and will do so again in Chapter 14. Our discussion of innovation in terms of competitive dynamics extends the earlier discussions by showing its importance in all types of markets in which firms compete.

Standard-cycle markets are markets in which the firm's competitive advantages are moderately shielded from imitation and where imitation is moderately costly.

Summary

- Competitors are firms competing in the same market, offering similar products, and targeting similar customers. Competitive rivalry is the ongoing set of competitive actions and competitive responses occurring between competitors as they compete against each other for an advantageous market position. The outcomes of competitive rivalry influence the firm's ability to sustain its competitive advantages as well as the level (average, below average, or above average) of its financial returns.

- For the individual firm, the set of competitive actions and responses it takes while engaged in competitive rivalry is called competitive behaviour. Competitive dynamics is the set of actions and responses taken by all firms that are competitors within a particular market.

- Firms study competitive rivalry in order to be able to predict the competitive actions and responses that each of their competitors likely will take. Competitive actions are either strategic or tactical in nature. The firm takes competitive actions to defend or build its competitive advantages or to improve its market position. Competitive responses are taken to counter the effects of a competitor's competitive action. A strategic action or a strategic response requires a significant commitment of organizational resources, is difficult to successfully implement, and is difficult to reverse. In contrast, a tactical action or a tactical response requires fewer organizational resources and is easier to implement and reverse. For an airline company, for example, entering major new markets is an example of a strategic action or a strategic response; changing its prices in a particular market is an example of a tactical action or a tactical response.

- A competitor analysis is the first step the firm takes to be able to predict its competitors' actions and responses. In Chapter 3, we discussed what firms do to *understand* competitors. This discussion is extended in this chapter as we described what the firm does to *predict* competitors' market-based actions. Thus, understanding precedes prediction. Market commonality (the number of markets with which competitors are jointly involved and their importance to each) and resource similarity (how comparable competitors' resources are in terms of type and amount) are studied to complete a competitor analysis. In general, the greater the market commonality and resource similarity, the more that firms acknowledge they are direct competitors.

- Market commonality and resource similarity shape the firm's awareness (the degree to which it and its competitor understand their mutual interdependence), motivation (the firm's incentive to attack or respond), and ability (the quality of the resources available to the firm to attack and respond).

Having knowledge of a competitor in terms of these characteristics increases the quality of the firm's predictions about that competitor's actions and responses.

- In addition to market commonality and resource similarity and awareness, motivation, and ability, three more specific factors affect the likelihood a competitor will take competitive actions. The first of these concerns first-mover incentives. First movers, those taking an initial competitive action, often earn above-average returns until competitors can successfully respond to their action and gain loyal customers. Not all firms can be first movers in that they may lack the awareness, motivation, or ability required to engage in this type of competitive behaviour. Moreover, some firms prefer to be a second mover (the firm responding to the first mover's action). One reason for this is that second movers, especially those acting quickly, can successfully compete against the first mover. By evaluating the first mover's product, customers' reactions to it, and the responses of other competitors to the first mover, the second mover can avoid the early entrant's mistakes and find ways to improve upon the value created for customers by the first mover's good or service. Late movers (those that respond a long time after the original action was taken) commonly are lower performers and are much less competitive.

- Organizational size, the second factor, tends to reduce the variety of competitive actions that large firms launch while it increases the variety of actions undertaken by smaller competitors. Ideally, the firm would like to initiate a large number of diverse actions when engaged in competitive rivalry. The third factor, quality, is a base denominator to successful competition in the global economy. It is a necessary prerequisite to achieve competitive parity. It is a necessary but insufficient condition for gaining an advantage.

- The type of action (strategic or tactical) the firm took, the competitor's reputation for the nature of its competitor behaviour, and that competitor's dependence on the market in which the action was taken are studied to predict a competitor's response to the firm's action. In general, the number of tactical responses taken exceeds the number of strategic responses. Competitors respond more frequently to the actions taken by the firm with a reputation for predictable and understandable competitive behaviour, especially if that firm is a market leader. In general, the firm can predict that when its competitor is highly dependent for its revenue and profitability in the market in which the firm took a competitive action, that competitor is likely to launch a strong response. However, firms that are more diversified across markets are less likely to respond to a particular action that affects only one of the markets in which they compete.

- Competitive dynamics concerns the ongoing competitive behaviour occurring among all firms competing in a market for advantageous positions. Market characteristics affect the set of actions and responses firms take while competing in a given market as well as the sustainability of firms' competitive advantages. In slow-cycle markets, where competitive advantages can be maintained, competitive dynamics finds firms taking actions and responses that are intended to protect, maintain, and extend their proprietary advantages. In fast-cycle markets, competition is almost frenzied as firms concentrate on developing a series of temporary competitive advantages. This emphasis is necessary because firms' advantages in fast-cycle markets are not proprietary and, as such, are subject to rapid and relatively inexpensive imitation. Standard-cycle markets experience competition between slow-cycle and fast-cycle markets; firms are moderately shielded from competition in these markets as they use capabilities that produce competitive advantages that are moderately sustainable. Competitors in standard-cycle markets serve mass markets and try to develop economies of scale to enhance their profitability. Innovation is vital to competitive success in each of the three types of markets. Companies should recognize that the set of competitive actions and responses taken by all firms differs by type of market.

Review Questions

1. Who are competitors? How are competitive rivalry, competitive behaviour, and competitive dynamics defined in the chapter?

2. What is market commonality? What is resource similarity? What does it mean to say that these concepts are the building blocks for a competitor analysis?

3. How do awareness, motivation, and ability affect the firm's competitive behaviour?

4. What factors affect the likelihood a firm will take a competitive action?

5. What factors affect the likelihood a firm will initiate a competitive response to the action taken by a competitor?

6. What competitive dynamics can be expected among firms operating in slow-cycle markets? In fast-cycle markets? In standard-cycle markets?

Social Responsibility Review

1. Microsoft is the perennial second or late mover. Earlier, we mentioned GUIs, word processing, and spreadsheets as examples. Microsoft's Explorer came after Netscape's Internet browser, Microsoft's MSN came after ICQ for instant messaging, and the list goes on. Microsoft's applications always seem to eventually win out. Some have accused the company of trying to monopolize the software market. How would Microsoft do this? If the company is doing this, who could stop it (and how)? Are there legitimate reasons for the Microsoft product always becoming the de facto standard, or is something less savory going on? As a consumer, how do you feel about this?

2. Personal computers are generally an expensive proposition. As such, one criticism of the Internet revolution is that it is leaving the poor behind, both in the developed world and elsewhere. Yet various people, companies, and agencies are trying to make connection to the Internet affordable even in poor countries. One way to do this is by riding down the ever-lowering price of hardware to build lower-priced computers (do a Google search for "the $200 computer"). The other is to reduce cost through use of open source software like Linux. What happens in a decade when Microsoft is faced with millions and millions of young users who grew up on these machines and want nothing to do with Windows? What are the implications of this for technology use in the third world?

3. In an intensely competitive industry the leader may act as if it intends to make a competitive move, when really it is only trying to get the followers to react, wasting time and money. In the late 1990s, Dell Computer set out to produce a monitor that was nearly the size of a big screen TV. The purpose was to allow users to open many windows on one screen without overlap. After much research and analysis, it was decided that it would be more economical for users to purchase multiple small monitors. The plan was scrapped, but Dell "leaked" the secret in hopes one of its main competitors (e.g., Gateway) would undertake the project. After it heard of Dell's plan, Gateway announced it would build the monitor,

and would be the first to do so. Without much research or analysis, the monitor was produced and sold. From the start, sales were slow and half of all units sold were returned for repair. The project was a failure and Gateway realized it had

been set up. Dell knew Gateway longed to be a "first mover" and would seize this opportunity. Was Dell acting in a legitimate way by doing this, or was Gateway simply foolish for not studying the market better?

Experiential Exercises

Candy Fight Coming?

Confectionary is an interesting industry to study. This industry is made up of small firms (e.g., Tootsie Roll [TR] or Winnipeg's Krave's Candy), chewing gum giant Wrigley (WLY), larger candy firms (e.g., M&M Mars [private], Hershey [HSY]), and major food companies such as Cadbury (CSG) and Nestlé (NSRGK.PK). As a private firm, M&M Mars is quite secretive about its operations and its financial performance. Traditionally, Hershey has held strong market positions in North America but weak positions in European markets. In terms of market positions, Cadbury and Nestlé are opposite to Hershey—they hold strong positions in Europe but weak ones in North America. In recent years, these four large firms (Wrigley, M&M Mars, Cadbury, and Hershey) have acquired a number of other companies with the purpose of broadening their product lines and becoming more diversified geographically.

These companies are also emphasizing using their own R&D labs to develop new products. Far more intense competition, in terms of product and geographic variety, is resulting from these efforts. A real "war" for market supremacy has yet to break out, and in fact it may not be in the larger firms' interests to escalate competition. In the meantime, smaller firms such as Tootsie Roll and Krave's are also growing by increasing the diversity of their product lines. Viewed collectively, these firms' actions are increasing the intensity of rivalry among competitors in the confectionary industry.

In this exercise, you will examine the way in which the competitive scope of the firms mentioned above has changed through product line extensions and by increasing their geographic diversity. As a part of your analysis, you will be able to summarize how competitive dynamics are changing. Review Figure 6.1 to recognize the nature of competitive dynamics. Most importantly, to complete this exercise you will be asked to use this information to project future changes in the competitive environment. You will need to access several resources, because part of your challenge is to analyze a private firm and two firms headquartered in Canada (Winnipeg's Krave's, New Brunswick's Ganong Bros., Kitchener's Dare Foods, and Toronto's Kerr Bros. would satisfy both requirements). Standard reports to shareholders will not be available to you for these three firms. Furthermore, some of these firms (e.g., Cadbury and Nestlé) are larger food companies of which confectionaries are but one segment. However, studying

competitors such as the firms competing in the confectionary industry will demonstrate the complexity of competitive dynamics on a global scale or in a global context.

Part One—In Groups. Each member of a group should take two of the firms mentioned above. For each firm, each group member should use the Internet and other sources you find valuable to identify changes in the company's confectionary product line that have occurred since 2000. Look for products that have been acquired as well as those launched from internal R&D. For the same firms, each group member should identify the different geographic areas in which the companies now compete (again using 2000 as the base year). This can be done by looking at changes in sales as well as in statements of managers' intentions to increase positions in weak markets. At the end of this part of the exercise, each group member should have a dynamic view of how the firms he or she is examining have changed their product and geographic profile in the confectionary market since 2000.

Part Two—In Groups. Assemble the members of your group and integrate each person's company-specific information. Share the group's collective information to recognize how the firms have increased their product and geographic diversity. Using the materials in the chapter, as graphically summarized in Figure 6.1, develop the group's expectations about how the firms' product and geographic decisions will affect competitive dynamics in the confectionary industry in the future. What future competitive actions do you think might be taken by a Canadian-based firm relative to firms headquartered elsewhere? What competitive responses might be launched by the firms headquartered outside Canada? Combine your conclusions into a presentation that you could make to a group of investors about the competitive dynamics they could expect to see in the confectionary industry in the future.

Part Three—Whole Class. Present your results to the whole class (the investors) and be prepared to justify your observations.

The Kings of Pill Hill

Companies in the pharmaceutical industry have generally earned above-average profits. However, the rivalry among competitors in this industry is quite intense. As consumers we may miss the basis of this rivalry. The reason for this is that these firms engage in competitive rivalry on dimensions other than price. One way to see the level of competition that managers face is to look at the changes in the sales ranks of the firms over the years and to analyze the industry's characteristics. Studying this information and data should yield a rich picture of the competitive dynamics that take place in this industry as well as an understanding of why firms' success rates relative to their competitors vary across time.

The first three parts of this exercise can be completed as individuals, within assigned groups.

Part One. Use the Internet and/or library sources that are available to you to obtain the sales revenues of firms competing in the Canadian pharmaceutical industry. Begin with the year 1980 or the earliest year available to you to record sales revenues by firm. Using your beginning year as a base, obtain sales revenues for each firm every third year. Prepare a list of the rankings of the firms for each observation year on the basis of sales volumes. What conclusions do you reach as you prepare your list?

Part Two. The purpose of this part of the exercise is for you to identify how each firm tries to compete in the Canadian pharmaceutical industry. Information about a firm's strategy or sought-after industry position should appear in the company's annual reports. In particular, assess the strategies of the firms during certain time periods as reflected below:

- Marion Laboratories in the mid-1980s

- Eli Lilly and Merck in the mid-1990s

- Pfizer in the mid-2000s

These firms were among the sales leaders in the time periods noted above. Note in each case how sales are driven by just a few drugs or compounds. Note specifically the key drugs in each case. What does the information you are finding suggest about competitive dynamics in the pharmaceutical industry? How does this fact impact a company like Toronto's Apotex?

Part Three. Your instructor will assign one of the following characteristics or conditions to you for analysis. Once assigned, use information sources that are available to you to identify the structural characteristics (e.g., entry barriers, power of suppliers, and so forth) that you believe are relatively unique to the pharmaceutical industry. Among the characteristics or conditions you should seek to understand are the following:

- The role of the "prescription-only" requirement for purchase in distorting head-to-head competition.

- The role of patents in protecting firms from identical-compound competition during the patent period.

- How different patent-protected drugs that treat the same condition compete against each other.

- The nature of competition among products that are not covered by patents.

Be sure to obtain information about other structural characteristics that you believe affect or shape competitive dynamics in the industry.

Part Four—Whole Class. Each group or individual will present to the class the information that they collected and the analysis that they did on the part they were assigned from the above list.

Part Five—Individually. Prepare and support an analysis as to why the pharmaceutical industry displays the pattern of leadership changes uncovered in Part One. In looking at the movement of specific firms, use the information you collected in Part Two. Finally, using the knowledge you gained from Part Three, generalize the patterns observed in Parts One and Two to explain the nature of competitive dynamics in the industry.

Notes

1. This does not mean that a monopolist would necessarily charge rapacious prices or provide poor service. A monopolist would not raise prices or low quality past the point where a decline in the number of customers would mean lost profits or draw attention of government to the point that tight regulation or nationalization might occur.
2. D. F. Spulber, 2004, *Management Strategy,* Boston: McGraw-Hill/Irwin, 87–88; M.-J. Chen, 1996, Competitor analysis and interfirm rivalry: Toward a theoretical integration, *Academy of Management Review,* 21: 100–134.
3. T. Galvin, 2002, Examining institutional change: Evidence from the founding dynamics of U.S. health care interest associations, *Academy of Management Journal,* 45: 673–696.
4. B. Pittman, 2003, Leading for value, *Harvard Business Review,* 81(4): 41–46.
5. A. M. Knott & H. E. Posen, 2005, Is failure good? *Strategic Management Journal,* 26: 617–641.
6. A. Nair & L. Filer, 2003, Cointegration of firm strategies within groups: A long-run analysis of firm behavior in the Japanese steel industry, *Strategic Management Journal,* 24: 145–159.
7. T. C. Powell, 2003, Varieties of competitive parity, *Strategic Management Journal,* 24: 61–86.
8. S. Jayachandran, J. Gimeno, & P. R. Varadarajan, 1999, Theory of multimarket competition: A synthesis and implications for marketing strategy, *Journal of Marketing,* 63: 49–66.

9. C. M. Grimm, H. Lee, & K. G. Smith, 2005, *Strategy as Action: Competitive dynamics and competitive advantage,* New York: Oxford University Press; G. Young, K. G. Smith, C. M. Grimm, & D. Simon, 2000, Multimarket contact and resource dissimilarity: A competitive dynamics perspective, *Journal of Management,* 26: 1217–1236.

10. H. A. Haveman & L. Nonnemaker, 2000, Competition in multiple geographic markets: The impact on growth and market entry, *Administrative Science Quarterly,* 45: 232–267.

11. K. G. Smith, W. J. Ferrier, & H. Ndofor, 2001, Competitive dynamics research: Critique and future directions, in M. A. Hitt, R. E. Freeman, & J. S. Harrison (eds.), *Handbook of Strategic Management,* Oxford, UK: Blackwell Publishers, 326.

12. G. Young, K. G. Smith, & C. M. Grimm, 1996, "Austrian" and industrial organization perspectives on firm-level competitive activity and performance, *Organization Science,* 73: 243–254.

13. H. D. Hopkins, 2003, The response strategies of dominant U.S. firms to Japanese challengers, *Journal of Management,* 29: 5–25; G. S. Day & D. J. Reibstein, 1997, The dynamic challenges for theory and practice, in G. S. Day & D. J. Reibstein (eds.), *Wharton on Competitive Strategy,* New York: John Wiley & Sons, 2.

14. M.-J. Chen & D. C. Hambrick, 1995, Speed, stealth, and selective attack: How small firms differ from large firms in competitive behavior, *Academy of Management Journal,* 38: 453–482.

15. D. L. Deeds, D. De Carolis, & J. Coombs, 2000, Dynamic capabilities and new product development in high technology ventures: An empirical analysis of new biotechnology firms, *Journal of Business Venturing,* 15: 211–299.

16. T. J. Douglas & J. A. Ryman, 2003, Understanding competitive advantage in the general hospital industry: Evaluating strategic competencies, *Strategic Management Journal,* 24: 333–347.

17. H. Sender, 2005, Meet China inc.: Topping Japan inc. of 1980s, *Wall Street Journal,* www.wsj.com, June 24.

18. S. J. Marsh, 1998, Creating barriers for foreign competitors: A study of the impact of anti-dumping actions on the performance of U.S. firms, *Strategic Management Journal,* 19: 25–37; K. G. Smith, C. M. Grimm, G. Young, & S. Wally, 1997, Strategic groups and rivalrous firm behavior: Toward a reconciliation, *Strategic Management Journal,* 18: 149–157.

19. W. J. Ferrier, 2001, Navigating the competitive landscape: The drivers and consequences of competitive aggressiveness, *Academy of Management Journal,* 44: 858–877.

20. Smith, Ferrier, & Ndofor, Competitive dynamics research, 319.

21. J. Shamsie, 2003, The context of dominance: An industry-driven framework for exploiting reputation, *Strategic Management Journal,* 24: 199–215; K. Ramaswamy, 2001, Organizational ownership, competitive intensity, and firm performance: An empirical study of the Indian manufacturing sector, *Strategic Management Journal,* 22: 989–998.

22. K. Cool, L. H. Roller, & B. Leleux, 1999, The relative impact of actual and potential rivalry on firm profitability in the pharmaceutical industry, *Strategic Management Journal,* 20: 1–14.

23. D. R. Gnyawali & R. Madhavan, 2001, Cooperative networks and competitive dynamics: A structural embeddedness perspective, *Academy of Management Review,* 26: 431–445.

24. Y. Y. Kor & J. T. Mahoney, 2005, How dynamics, management, and governance of resource deployments influence firm-level performance, *Strategic Management Journal,* 26: 489–496; Young, Smith, Grimm, & Simon, Multimarket contact and resource dissimilarity, 1217.

25. R. L. Priem, L. G. Love, & M. A. Shaffer, 2002, Executives' perceptions of uncertainty scores: A numerical taxonomy and underlying dimensions, *Journal of Management,* 28: 725–746.

26. I. C. MacMillan, A. B. van Putten, & R. S. McGrath, 2003, Global gamesmanship, *Harvard Business Review,* 81(5): 62–71; S. Godin, 2002, Survival is not enough, *Fast Company,* January, 90–94.

27. Chen, Competitor analysis, 108.

28. Ibid., 109.

29. K. Uhlenbruck, M. A. Hitt, & M. Semadeni, 2005, Market value effects of acquisitions of Internet firms: A resource-based analysis, working paper, University of Montana; A. Afuah, 2003, Redefining firm boundaries in the face of the Internet: Are firms really shrinking? *Academy of Management Review,* 28: 34–53.

30. G. K. Deans, F. Kroeger, & S. Zeisel, 2002, The consolidation curve, *Harvard Business Review,* 80(12): 20–21; E. Abrahamson & C. J. Fombrun, 1994, Macrocultures: Determinants and consequences, *Academy of Management Review,* 19: 728–755.

31. C. Salter, 2002, On the road again, *Fast Company,* January, 50–58.

32. Young, Smith, Grimm, & Simon, Multimarket contact, 1219.

33. Chen, Competitor analysis, 106.

34. J. Gimeno & C. Y. Woo, 1999, Multimarket contact, economies of scope, and firm performance, *Academy of Management Journal,* 42: 239–259.

35. 2008, Roots opens flagship store in Beijing, Roots Web site, http://www.roots .com/index.php?/content/view/1551/74/lang,en/, retrieved January 21; Shaw, H., 2001, Roots to open 100 stores in China: "It has managed to create a global brand," *National Post,* October 4, FP1.

36. MacMillan, van Putten, & McGrath, Global gamesmanship, 63.

37. Young, Smith, Grimm, & Simon, Multimarket contact, 1230.

38. J. Gimeno, 1999, Reciprocal threats in multimarket rivalry: Staking out "spheres of influence" in the U.S. airline industry, *Strategic Management Journal,* 20: 101–128; N. Fernandez & P. L. Marin, 1998, Market power and multimarket contact: Some evidence from the Spanish hotel industry, *Journal of Industrial Economics,* 46: 301–315.

39. Jayachandran, Gimeno, & Varadarajan, Theory of multimarket competition, 59; Chen, Competitor analysis, 107.

40. J. Gimeno & C. Y. Woo, 1996, Hypercompetition in a multimarket environment: The role of strategic similarity and multimarket contact on competitive de-escalation, *Organization Science,* 7: 322–341.

41. A. Lashinsky, 2005, Sony vs. Toshiba: A DVD shootout, *Fortune,* www .fortune.com, May 3.

42. K. Lamertz, P. M. Pursey, A. R. Heugens, & L. Calmet, 2005, The configuration of organizational images among firms in the Canadian beer brewing industry, *Journal of Management Studies,* 42: 817–843.

43. Chen, Competitor analysis, 107–108.

44. L. Ulrich, 2003, Outside the box, *Money,* 32(6): 137–138.

45. Toyota's bad memories, 2005, Wall Street Journal Online, www.wsj.com, April 28.

46. Chen, Competitor analysis, 110.

47. Ibid.; W. Ocasio, 1997, Towards an attention-based view of the firm, *Strategic Management Journal,* 18 (Special Issue): 187–206; Smith, Ferrier, & Ndofor, Competitive dynamics research, 320.

48. M. Selva, 2003, Wal-Mart, France's Carrefour set sights on Ahold businesses, *Sunday Business,* April 6, B3; 2001, Wal around the world, *The Economist,* December 8, 55–56.

49. S. Tallman, M. Jenkins, N. Henry, & S. Pinch, 2004, Knowledge, clusters and competitive advantage, *Academy of Management Review,* 29: 258–271; J. F. Porac & H. Thomas, 1994, Cognitive categorization and subjective rivalry among retailers in a small city, *Journal of Applied Psychology,* 79: 54–66.

50. S. H. Park & D. Zhou, 2005, Firm heterogeneity and competitive dynamics in alliance formation, *Academy of Management Review,* 30: 531–554; Smith, Ferrier, & Ndofor, Competitive dynamics research, 320

51. Chen, Competitor analysis, 113.

52. R. Belderbos & L. Sleuwaegen, 2005, Competitive drivers and international plant configuration strategies: A product-level test, *Strategic Management Journal,* 26: 577–593.

53. C. M. Grimm & K. G. Smith, 1997, *Strategy as Action: Industry rivalry and coordination,* Cincinnati: South-Western Publishing Co., 125.

54. 2002, Blue light blues, *The Economist,* January 29, 54; D. B. Yoffie & M. Kwak, 2001, Mastering strategic movement at Palm, *MIT Sloan Management Review,* 43(1): 55–63.

55. N. Bunkley, 2008, Darker 2008 for Detroit's Automakers, *New York Times,* January 1, 157(54176): C1, C4.

56. A. Echols & W. Tsai, 2004, Niche and performance: The moderating role of network embeddedness, *Strategic Management Journal,* 26: 219–238.

57. K. G. Smith, W. J. Ferrier, & C. M. Grimm, 2001, King of the hill: Dethroning the industry leader, *Academy of Management Executive,* 15(2): 59–70.

58. W. J. Ferrier & H. Lee, 2003, Strategic aggressiveness, variation, and surprise: How the sequential pattern of competitive rivalry influences stock market returns, *Journal of Managerial Issues,* 14: 162–180; G. S. Day, 1997, Assessing competitive arenas: Who are your competitors? in G. S. Day & D. J. Reibstein (eds.), *Wharton on Competitive Strategy,* New York: John Wiley & Sons, 25–26.

59. R. Truett, 2003, A chance to shape design destiny, *Automotive News,* April 7, D2; M. Ihlwan, L. Armstrong, & K. Kerwin, 2001, Hyundai gets hot, *BusinessWeek,* December 17, 84–86.

60. 2003, Boeing says to build new 7E7 in United States, Reuters, www.reuters.com, May 16.

61. J. Schumpeter, 1934, *The Theory of Economic Development,* Cambridge, MA: Harvard University Press.

62. J. L. C. Cheng & I. F. Kesner, 1997, Organizational slack and response to environmental shifts: The impact of resource allocation patterns, *Journal of Management,* 23: 1–18.

63. F. Wang, 2000, Too appealing to overlook, *America's Network,* December, 10–12.

64. D. P. Forbes, 2005, Managerial determinants of decision speed in new ventures, *Strategic Management Journal,* 26: 355–366; G. Hamel, 2000, *Leading the Revolution,* Boston: Harvard Business School Press, 103.

65. W. T. Robinson & S. Min, 2002, Is the first to market the first to fail? Empirical evidence for industrial goods businesses, *Journal of Marketing Research,* 39: 120–128.

66. T. Cottrell & B. R. Nault, 2004, *Strategic Management Journal,* 25: 1005–1025; R. Agarwal, M. B. Sarkar, & R. Echambadi, 2002, The conditioning effect of time on firm survival: An industry life cycle approach, *Academy of Management Journal,* 45: 971–994.

67. A. Nerer & P. W. Roberts, 2004, Technological and product-market experience and the success of new product introductions in the pharmaceutical industry, *Strategic Management Journal,* 25: 779–799; A. Srivastava & H. Lee, 2005, Predicting order and timing of new product moves: The role of top management in corporate entrepreneurship, *Journal of Business Venturing,* 20: 459–481.

68. J. W. Spencer & T. P. Murtha, 2005, How do governments matter to new industry creation? *Academy of Management Review,* 30: 321–337.

69. S. W. Geiger & L. H. Cashen, 2002, A multidimensional examination of slack and its impact on innovation, *Journal of Managerial Issues,* 14: 68–84.

70. M. B. Lieberman & D. B. Montgomery, 1988, First-mover advantages, *Strategic Management Journal,* 9: 41–58.

71. J. Reimer, 2005, A history of the GUI, http://arstechnica.com/ articles/paedia/gui.ars/3 and http://arstechnica.com/articles/paedia/gui.ars/ 4, retrieved January 23, 2008.

72. 2001, Older, wiser, webbier, *The Economist,* June 30, 10.

73. M. Shank, 2002, Executive strategy report, IBM business strategy consulting, www.ibm.com, March 14; W. Boulding & M. Christen, 2001, First-mover disadvantage, *Harvard Business Review,* 79(9): 20–21.

74. 2008, *Mega Brands 2006 Annual Report,* Mega Brands Web site, http://www.megabloks.com/en/corpo/pdf/MEGA _Brands_Annual_Report_ 2006.pdf, retrieved January 22.

75. J. Gimeno, R. E. Hoskisson, B. B. Beal, & W. P. Wan, 2005, Explaining the clustering of international expansion moves: A critical test in the U.S. telecommunications industry, *Academy of Management Journal,* 48: 297–319; K. G. Smith, C. M. Grimm, & M. J. Gannon, 1992, *Dynamics of Competitive Strategy,* Newberry Park, CA: Sage Publications.

76. S. D. Dobrev & G. R. Carroll, 2003, Size (and competition) among organizations: Modeling scale-based selection among automobile producers in four major countries, 1885–1981, *Strategic Management Journal,* 24: 541–558; Smith, Ferrier, & Ndofor, Competitive dynamics research, 327.

77. F. K. Pil & M. Hoiweg, 2003, Exploring scale: The advantage of thinking small, *The McKinsey Quarterly,* 44(2): 33–39; Chen & Hambrick, Speed, stealth, and selective attack.

78. D. Miller & M.-J. Chen, 1996, The simplicity of competitive repertoires: An empirical analysis, *Strategic Management Journal,* 17: 419–440.

79. Young, Smith, & Grimm, "Austrian" and industrial organization perspectives.

80. B. A. Melcher, 1993, How Goliaths can act like Davids, *BusinessWeek,* Special Issue, 193.

81. 2008, The Forbes Global 2000, Forbes Web site, http://www.forbes.com/lists/ 2007/18/biz_07forbes2000_The-Global-2000_Sales.html, retrieved January 22.

82. 2001, Wal around the world, 55.

83. P. B. Crosby, 1980, *Quality Is Free,* New York: Penguin.

84. W. E. Deming, 1986, *Out of the Crisis,* Cambridge, MA: MIT Press.

85. L. B. Crosby, R. DeVito, & J. M. Pearson, 2003, Manage your customers' perception of quality, *Review of Business,* 24(1): 18–24.

86. R. S. Kaplan & D. P. Norton, 2001, *The Strategy-Focused Organization,* Boston: Harvard Business School Press.

87. R. Cullen, S. Nicholls, & A. Halligan, 2001, Measurement to demonstrate success, *British Journal of Clinical Governance,* 6(4): 273–278.

88. K. E. Weick & K. M. Sutcliffe, 2001, *Managing the Unexpected,* San Francisco: Jossey-Bass, 81–82.

89. G. Yeung & V. Mok, 2005, What are the impacts of implementing ISOs on the competitiveness of manufacturing industry in China, *Journal of World Business,* 40: 139–157.

90. H.-J. Cho & V. Pucik, 2005, Relationship between innovativeness, quality, growth, profitability, and market value, *Strategic Management Journal,* 26: 555–575.

91. Ihlwan, Armstrong, & Kerwin, Hyundai gets hot, 84.

92. J. C. Armstrong, 2003, Hyundai Motor begins sourcing 2006 Santa Fe, *Automotive News,* April 28, 21.

93. T. Box, 2003, Accelerating quality, *Dallas Morning News,* May 17, D1, D3.

94. The Canadian warranty is still only five years.

95. M. Ihlwan & J. B. Bush, 2005, Hyundai: Crowding into the fast lane, *BusinessWeek,* June 20, www.businessweek.com.

96. J. Schumpeter, 1950, *Capitalism, Socialism and Democracy,* New York: Harper; Smith, Ferrier, & Ndofor, Competitive dynamics research, 323.

97. M.-J. Chen & I. C. MacMillan, 1992, Nonresponse and delayed response to competitive moves, *Academy of Management Journal,* 35: 539–570; Smith, Ferrier, & Ndofor, Competitive dynamics research, 335.

98. M.-J. Chen, K. G. Smith, & C. M. Grimm, 1992, Action characteristics as predictors of competitive responses, *Management Science,* 38: 439–455.

99. M.-J. Chen & D. Miller, 1994, Competitive attack, retaliation and performance: An expectancy-valence framework, *Strategic Management Journal,* 15: 85–102.

100. T. Gardner, 2005, Interfirm competition for human resources: Evidence from the software industry, *Academy of Management Journal,* 48: 237–258; N. Huyghebaert & L. M. van de Gucht, 2004, Incumbent strategic behavior in financial markets and the exit of entrepreneurial start-ups, *Strategic Management Journal,* 25: 669–688.

101. Smith, Ferrier, & Ndofor, Competitive dynamics research, 333.

102. J. Shamsie, 2003, The context of dominance: An industry-driven framework for exploiting reputation, *Strategic Management Journal,* 24: 199–215.

103. P. W. Roberts & G. R. Dowling, 2003, Corporate reputation and sustained superior financial performance, *Strategic Management Journal,* 24: 1077–1093.

104. W. J. Ferrier, K. G. Smith, & C. M. Grimm, 1999, The role of competitive actions in market share erosion and industry dethronement: A study of industry leaders and challengers, *Academy of Management Journal,* 42: 372–388.

105. M. A. Hitt, C. C. Miller, A. Colella, 2006, *Organizational behavior: A strategic approach,* New York: John Wiley & Sons.

106. Smith, Grimm, & Gannon, *Dynamics of Competitive Strategy.*

107. A. Karnani & B. Wernerfelt, 1985, Multiple point competition, *Strategic Management Journal,* 6: 87–97.

108. Smith, Ferrier, & Ndofor, Competitive dynamics research, 330.

109. D. Neil, 2005, It's a step up in class: Mercedes ditches the old M-Class design for sturdy power and southern comfort, *Los Angeles Times,* www.latimes .com, June 15.

110. G. McNamara, P. M. Vaaler, & C. Devers, 2003, Same as it ever was: The search for evidence of increasing hypercompetition, *Strategic Management Journal*, 24: 261–278.

111. A. Kalnins & W. Chung, 2004, Resource-seeking agglomeration: A study of market entry in the lodging industry, *Strategic Management Journal*, 25: 689–699.

112. J. R. Williams, 1992, How sustainable is your competitive advantage? *California Management Review*, 34(3): 29–51.

113. Ibid., 6.

114. N. Pangarkar & J. R. Lie, 2004, The impact of market cycle on the performance of Singapore acquirers, *Strategic Management Journal*, 25: 1209–1216.

115. Ibid., 57.

116. 2008, Health Products and Food Branch Health Canada Web site, http://www.hc-sc.gc.ca/ahc-asc/branch-dirgen/hpfb-dgpsa/index_e.html, retrieved January 22.

117. 2005, Ranbaxy loses Lipitor case—US court favours Pfizer on patent infringement, *Hindu Business Line*, December 18, http://www.thehindubusinessline.com/2005/12/18/stories/2005121802420100.htm, retrieved January 22, 2008.

118. 2005, Pfizer loses Lipitor patent suit, Red Herring, www.redherring.com, March 29; 2003, Pfizer suit is for a blockbuster drug, *Businessline*, February 26, 13.

119. 2005, Pfizer's Lipitor patent rejected on re-examination, Patent Baristas, www.patentbaristas.com, June 23; R. Steyer, 2005, Pfizer contests Lipitor rule, TheStreet.com, www.thestreet.com, March 29.

120. 2003, How fast is your company? *Fast Company*, June, 18.

121. T. Talaulicar, J. Grundei, & A. V. Werder, 2005, Strategic decision making in start-ups: The effect of top management team organization and processes on speed and comprehensiveness, *Journal of Business Venturing*, 20: 519–541.

122. M. Song, C. Droge, S. Hanvanich, & R. Calatone, 2005, Marketing and technology resource complementarity: An analysis of their interaction effect in two environmental contexts, *Strategic Management Journal*, 26: 259–276.

123. R. Williams, 1999, *Renewable Advantage: Crafting Strategy through Economic Time*, New York: Free Press, 8.

124. Ibid.

125. D. Gerwin, 2004, Coordinating new product development in strategic alliances, *Academy of Management Review*, 29: 241–257.

126. R. Sanchez, 1995, Strategic flexibility in production competition, *Strategic Management Journal*, 16 (Special Issue): 9–26.

127. Hitt, Miller, & Colella, *Organizational behavior;* J. Radigan, 2004, The rival visions of IBM and HP, BusinessWeek Online, www.businessweek.com, December 16.

128. Williams, *Renewable Advantage*, 7.

Chapter Seven

Corporate-Level Strategy

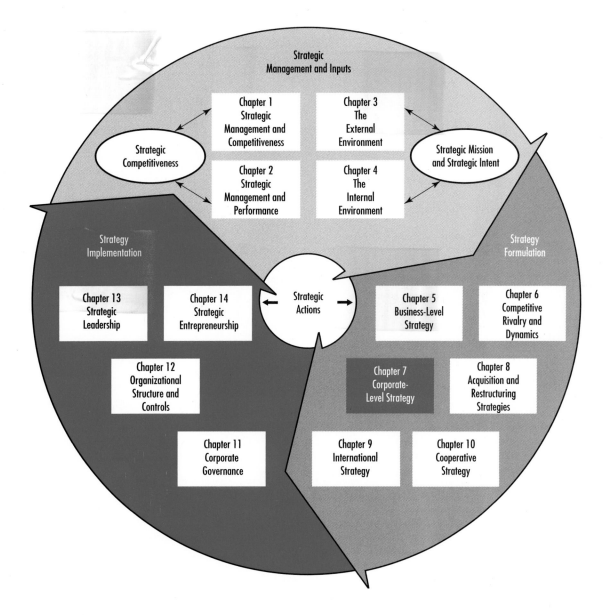

Knowledge Objectives

Studying this chapter should provide you with the strategic management knowledge needed to:

1. Define corporate-level strategy and discuss its purpose.

2. Describe different levels of diversification with different corporate-level strategies.

3. Explain three primary reasons firms diversify.

4. Describe how firms can create value by using a related diversification strategy.

5. Explain the two ways value can be created with an unrelated diversification strategy.

6. Discuss the incentives and resources that encourage diversification.

7. Describe motives that can encourage managers to over-diversify a firm.

Diversification in the Wellness and Restaurant Industries

What do yoga, fitness, green living, and organic products have in common? Yoga mats, Tae Bo videos, and solar panels being sold by the same company. Is this possible? Making a profit while making the world a better place, Gaiam Inc. is making the dream a reality. The name Gaiam (pronounced "guy-um") combines the words "Gaia" and "I am." *Gaia* means mother Earth and comes from the Minoan civilization, which honoured Gaia on the Isle of Crete in ancient Greece around 3000 B.C. The Minoan civilization believed there was a direct connection between the Earth, daily life, and its existence as a civilization. Gaia as a concept suggests the Earth is a living entity.

www.gaiam.com

www.cara.com

Gaiam is positioned as a comprehensive lifestyle company primarily known for its wellness and fitness products, and offers a unique value proposition to its healthy and environmentally conscious customers. It combines "media content, information, experiences and products," and "appeal[s] to consumers interested in any aspect of living more healthfully and lightly on the planet." According to a report in *The Globe and Mail*, Gaiam has "spread its business all over the wellness map," selling a diverse range of products such as organic cotton apparel, household cleaning products, fitness videos, and, yes, solar panels.

Best known for its award-winning yoga DVDs, in 2000 Gaiam made a strategic acquisition of a manufacturer and distributor of solar panels. Through this acquisition, Gaiam expanded its product range to include renewable energy sources and other sustainable living products aimed at helping consumers become more aware of their relationship with the environment.

Gaiam's corporate strategy is to expand its product portfolio through acquisition and to become the market leader in lifestyles, health, and sustainability. By offering a diverse range of products Gaiam is less vulnerable to fluctuations in demand, as it can rely on a diversified revenue stream from a range of diverse products.

Cara Operations Ltd. is a diversified company using a portfolio of food-related concepts to compete in the full-service casual dining segment of the restaurant industry. Casual dining is a segment in which firms offer moderately priced food in casual atmospheres. Analysts believe that demographic trends in North America favour continuing growth in the casual dining segment.

Using its diversified portfolio of casual dining concepts, Cara is able to offer customers dining options that suit almost any appetite and lifestyle. Analysts have observed that this type of "portfolio strategy is difficult to manage." Discussions in this chapter will show that although they can help a firm earn above-average returns, diversification (portfolio) strategies are difficult to successfully use in all industries—not just in the restaurant industry, or in the casual dining segment of that industry.

Although the number of concepts in Cara's portfolio changes in response to each unit's success or lack of success, Cara currently competes with five restaurant concepts and an airport services division. Most of the company's restaurant concepts are ones that a majority of Canadians would recognize, are distinctive, and satisfy a wide range of dining tastes: Milestones Bar & Grill, Harvey's, Swiss Chalet, Kelsey's, and Montana's Cookhouse. These concepts compete in different parts of the casual dining segment: upscale (Milestones); fast food (Harvey's); neighbourhood restaurant (Swiss Chalet); bar and grill (Kelsey's); and speciality barbeque (Montana's). Cara also has maintained its historical presence in airport services through air terminal restaurants and flight kitchens that provide food to airline and rail travellers.

Swiss Chalet generates the largest percentage of Cara's revenue (25 percent). Cara's historical business of airport services provides 15 percent of revenues. With just these six concepts, all in the food services industry, Cara is using a strategy of related-constrained corporate-level diversification strategy (this strategy is defined and discussed later in this chapter).

To successfully use the firm's corporate-level strategy, personnel at Cara constantly evaluate the performance of each dining concept. The organization does its best to offer customers a set of dining options that are complementary rather than competitive. In this way, Cara customers have a chance to eat at a different Cara restaurant every day of the week without overloading on any one cuisine.

Concepts failing to satisfy various performance criteria, including financial expectations and the need to be complementary rather than competitive, have been divested. In 2001 the company sold its interest in Beaver Foods. In 2004, Cara sold off its chain of Bread Garden restaurants. In late 2006, Cara sold its 100-percent interest in the 360-store chain of Second Cup cafés. While Cara had fought hard to acquire a 100-percent interest in Second Cup, the chain fit oddly into its line-up of other chains and was not a large part of Cara sales (about 10 percent). Second Cup's experiences demonstrate how Cara uses its corporate-level strategy to find the best combination of dining concepts. Second Cup is likely to have major competition in the future with Van Houtte expanding out of Montreal, and potential battles with Starbucks. Rather than invest further in a concept encountering stiff competition, Cara decided to sell the chain so the company could concentrate on its other concepts with better growth potential. To successfully use its corporate-level strategy, Cara's upper-level decision makers make decisions about the dining segments in which the firm will compete and how to manage its concepts in those segments.

SOURCES: 2004, SEDAR, Cara announces third quarter results, February 3, http://sedar.com/Display CompanyDocuments .do?lang=EN&issuerNo=00003539, retrieved December 28, 2007; 2007, Cara Web page, http://www.cara.com/cara.html, December 28; 2007, Second Cup Web page, http://www.secondcup.com/eng/about_us.php?about=1#m1, December 28; 2007, Bread Garden Web page, http://www.bgfranchising.com/our_story/, December 28; 2007, Gaiam Green Living, Yoga, Fitness, & Organic Products home page, www.gaiam.com, December 5; 2007, Why Gaiam is stretching its lifestyle options, *The Globe and Mail,* September 10; 2007, Gaiam, http://en.wikipedia.org/wiki/Gaiam, December 5; http://corporate.gaiam.com/crp_aboutBusinessModel.asp?, retrieved January 7, 2008.

Our discussions of business-level strategies (Chapter 5) and the competitive rivalry and competitive dynamics associated with them (Chapter 6) have concentrated on firms competing in a single industry or product market.[1] In this chapter, we introduce you to corporate-level strategies, which are strategies firms use to *diversify* their operations from a single business competing in a single market into several product markets and, most commonly, into several businesses. Thus, a **corporate-level strategy** specifies actions a firm takes to gain a competitive advantage by selecting and managing a group of different businesses competing in different product markets. Corporate-level strategies help firms select new strategic positions—positions that are expected to increase the firm's value.[2]

As outlined in the Opening Case, Gaiam competes in several different markets within the lifestyle, health, and sustainability sector. According to Wikipedia, Gaiam coined the term "lifestyles of health and sustainability," which covers everything from renewable energy solutions to yoga, inspirational films to eco-travel, and organic foods to eco-friendly apparel and furnishings.[3] Each of Gaiam's product offerings (i.e., home, solar, yoga, and fitness) represents a different strategic position in the lifestyle, health, and sustainability segment.

As is the case with Gaiam, firms use corporate-level strategies as a means to grow revenues and profits. But the decision to take actions to pursue growth is never a risk-free choice for firms to make.[4] Indeed, effective firms carefully evaluate their growth options (including the different corporate-level strategies) before committing firm resources to any of them.[5]

Because the diversified firm operates in several different and unique product markets and, in some cases, in several businesses, it forms two types of strategies: corporate-level (or companywide) and business-level (or competitive).[6] Corporate-level strategy is concerned with two key issues: (1) in what product markets/businesses/industries should the firm compete, and (2) how should corporate headquarters manage those businesses.[7] For the diversified corporation, a business-level strategy (see Chapter 5) must be chosen for each of the businesses in which the firm has decided to compete.

As is the case with a business-level strategy, a corporate-level strategy is expected to help the firm earn above-average returns by creating value.[8] Some suggest that few corporate-level strategies actually create value.[9] In fact, the degree to which corporate-level strategies create value beyond the sums of the value created by all of a firm's business units remains an important research question.[10]

Evidence suggests that a corporate-level strategy's value is ultimately determined by the degree to which "the businesses in the portfolio are worth more under the management of the company than they would be under any other ownership."[11] Thus, an effective corporate-level strategy creates, across all of a firm's businesses, aggregate returns that exceed what those returns would be if the business units[12] were stand-alone businesses, and contributes to the firm's strategic competitiveness and its ability to earn above-average returns.[13]

Product diversification, a primary form of corporate-level strategy, concerns the scope of the markets and industries in which the firm competes as well as "how managers buy, create and sell different businesses to match skills and strengths with opportunities presented to the firm."[14] Successful diversification is expected to reduce variability in the firm's profitability as earnings are generated from different businesses. The Opening Case illustrates product diversification in that it shows how a firm like Gaiam can reduce variability in revenue by diversifying its product offerings.

We begin this chapter by examining different levels of diversification (from low to high). After describing the different reasons firms diversify their operations, we focus on two types of related diversification (related diversification signifies a moderate to high level of diversification for the firm). When properly used, these strategies help create value in the diversified firm, either through the sharing of resources (the related-constrained strategy) or the transferring of core competencies across the firm's different

A **corporate-level strategy** specifies actions a firm takes to gain a competitive advantage by selecting and managing a group of different businesses competing in different product markets.

businesses (the related-linked strategy). We then discuss unrelated diversification, which is another corporate-level strategy that can create value. The chapter then shifts to the topic of incentives and resources that may stimulate diversification, although the effects of this type of diversification tend to be value neutral. However, managerial motives to diversify, the final topic in the chapter, can actually destroy some of the firm's value.

Levels of Diversification

Diversified firms vary according to their level of diversification and the connections between and among their businesses. Figure 7.1 lists and defines five categories of businesses according to increasing levels of diversification. The single- and dominant-business categories denote relatively low levels of diversification; more fully diversified firms are classified into related and unrelated categories. A firm is related through its diversification when there are several links among its businesses and between its businesses and corporate headquarters; for example, businesses may share products (goods or services), technologies, or distribution channels. The more links among businesses, the more "constrained" is the relatedness of diversification. Unrelatedness refers to the absence of direct links among businesses.

Low Levels of Diversification

A firm pursuing a low level of diversification uses either a single- or dominant-business corporate-level diversification strategy. A *single-business diversification strategy* is a corporate-level strategy wherein the firm generates 95 percent or more of its sales revenue from its core business area.[15] For example, Wm. Wrigley Jr. Company, the world's largest

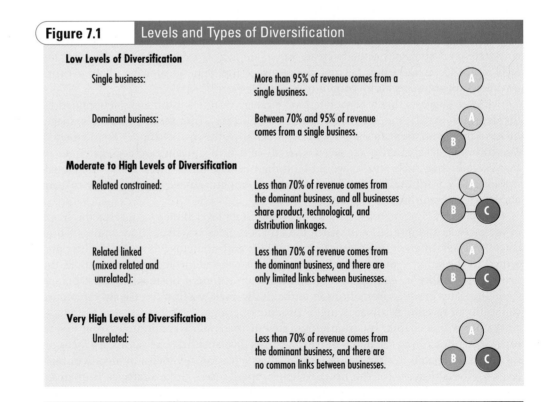

Figure 7.1 — Levels and Types of Diversification

Low Levels of Diversification

Single business: More than 95% of revenue comes from a single business.

Dominant business: Between 70% and 95% of revenue comes from a single business.

Moderate to High Levels of Diversification

Related constrained: Less than 70% of revenue comes from the dominant business, and all businesses share product, technological, and distribution linkages.

Related linked (mixed related and unrelated): Less than 70% of revenue comes from the dominant business, and there are only limited links between businesses.

Very High Levels of Diversification

Unrelated: Less than 70% of revenue comes from the dominant business, and there are no common links between businesses.

SOURCE: Adapted from R.P. Rumelt, 1974, *Strategy, Structure and Economic Performance,* Boston: Harvard Business School.

producer of chewing and bubble gums, historically used a single-business strategy while operating in relatively few product markets. Wrigley's trademark chewing gum brands include Spearmint, Doublemint, and Juicy Fruit, although the firm produces other products as well. Sugar-free Extra, Alpine "throat relief" gum, Orbit White, and Life Saver candies are examples of Wrigley's brands that compete in similar, yet slightly different markets.[16] With the *dominant-business diversification strategy*, Wrigley generates between 70 and 95 percent of its total revenue within a single business area.

Harley-Davidson Motor Company uses this strategy. In 2006, Harley-Davidson's motorcycle sales comprised nearly 78.5 percent of worldwide sales; parts and accessories accounted for nearly 15 percent, and general merchandise 4.8 percent. The remainder of Harley-Davidson's revenue came from bicycle sales from its subsidiary, Buell Motorcycle Company.[17]

Moderate and High Levels of Diversification

A firm generating more than 30 percent of its revenue outside a dominant business and whose businesses are related to each other in some manner uses a related-diversification corporate-level strategy. When the links between the diversified firm's businesses are rather direct, a *related-constrained diversification strategy* is being used.[18] TD Bank Financial Group employs this strategy. TD generated 58 percent of its revenues from its Canadian personal and commercial banking services in 2007. The remaining 42 percent, however, is from the related areas of international, wholesale, and corporate banking.[19] Some large cable companies also use a related-constrained strategy. With a related-constrained strategy, a firm shares resources and activities among its businesses. Cable firms such as Shaw and Rogers in Canada and Comcast and Time Warner in the U.S., for example, share technology-based resources and activities across their television programming, high-speed Internet connection, and phone service businesses. Currently, Shaw and Rogers also offer VoIP phone services via their cable operations.[20] Procter & Gamble (P&G) is also a good example of a company using a related-constrained strategy, as it generates 46 percent of its overall revenue from one business unit called Household Care, and 42 percent of its revenue from its business unit Beauty and Health. The remaining 12 percent of P&G revenues come from its Gillette business.[21]

For example, P&G's paper towel business and baby diaper business both use paper products as a primary input to the manufacturing process. The firm's paper production plant produces inputs for both businesses and is an example of a shared activity, or a way for the two businesses to be related to each other. In addition, because they both produce consumer products, these two businesses are likely to share distribution channels and sales networks.

In 2005 P&G bought The Gillette Company, which in effect created the world's largest consumer products company.[22] P&G has used this scale to enhance its bargaining power (as discussed in Chapter 3) with the likes of Wal-Mart.[23] It also uses this related-constrained diversification strategy to focus its resources in manufacturing and marketing[24] and to reduce duplicate expenditures. Ideally, this structure will help P&G react quickly and strategically in its industries.

In contrast, a diversified company with a portfolio of businesses with only a few links among them is called a mixed related and unrelated firm and is using the *related-linked diversification strategy* (see Figure 7.1). Johnson & Johnson, General Electric (GE), and Canadian Tire use this corporate-level diversification strategy. Compared with related-constrained firms, related-linked firms share and/or transfer fewer resources and assets among their businesses, concentrating instead on transferring knowledge and core competencies between the businesses. As with firms using each type of diversification strategy, companies implementing the related-linked strategy constantly adjust the mix in their portfolio of businesses as well as make decisions about how to manage their businesses.

Since Canadian Tire acquired its bank licence in 2003 it has been expanding its financial services business to the extent that it now accounts for 9 percent of overall revenues.[25] According to a retail analyst at Research Capital, this diversification strategy has been successful in growing Canadian Tire's business.[26]

According to Canadian Tire's 2006 Annual Report, its revenue comprised 64 percent retail, 18 percent petroleum, 9 percent financial services, and 9 percent Mark's Work Wearhouse.[27] According to a report in *The Globe and Mail*, and as indicated in Figure 7.2, Canadian Tire's financial services carry very rich profit margins.[28] Although Canadian Tire's businesses do not share resources to the same degree that P&G's business do, Canadian Tire leverages operational and marketing synergies between its businesses.[29] In its 2006 Annual Report, Canadian Tire attests to reducing costs and increasing competitiveness by sharing resources like brand equity, real estate, supply chain logistics, and marketing spending across the different businesses.[30] According to Canadian Tire, "petroleum plays a strategic role in [its] interrelated network of businesses."[31] Canadian Tire seeks to use gas sales to increase sales at its retail stores and to generate more credit card receivables for its financial services business (see Figure 7.2).[32]

A highly diversified firm that has no relationships among its businesses follows an *unrelated diversification strategy.* Commonly, firms using this type of corporate strategy are called *conglomerates.* The obvious benefits of a conglomerate are the spread of risk and diversified revenues.[33] Others argue that conglomerates provide "management synergies, better support for research and development, and efficient use of capital."[34]

An example of a Canadian conglomerate is Onex Corporation, a Toronto-based investment firm. With about $32 billion in revenue and more than 220,000 employees, Onex Corporation is one of Canada's biggest companies. Onex is a global leader in electronics manufacturing services through its ownership in Celestica. About 20 percent of the company's revenues are aircraft-related. Its Spirit AeroSystems is the world's largest independent supplier of large components for commercial aircraft, and its Hawker Beechcraft division is a leading business and trainer aircraft maker. Another 20 percent of the company's revenues are from health-related activities: emergency medical services, diagnostic and medical imaging, and nursing, assisted living facilities, and support care. Over 10 percent of Onex's revenue comes from activities more involved in the manufacture and support of heavy industry—its Allison Transmission subsidiary manufactures transmissions and hybrid propulsion systems for commercial vehicles; its Tube City IMS subsidiary is a leading provider of outsourced services to steel mills. The remaining companies are among the leaders in their fields. Onex is also one of the world's largest

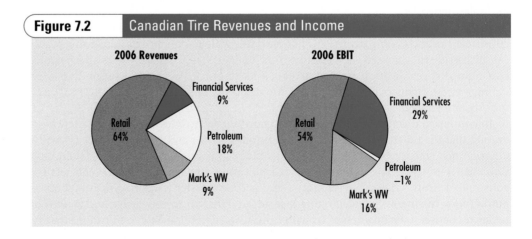

Figure 7.2   Canadian Tire Revenues and Income

2006 Revenues

- Retail 64%
- Financial Services 9%
- Petroleum 18%
- Mark's WW 9%

2006 EBIT

- Retail 54%
- Financial Services 29%
- Petroleum −1%
- Mark's WW 16%

SOURCE: Canadian Tire Corporation, Limited.

integrated underwriters of extended warranties, and a leading global provider of outsourced customer care services. Finally, its Cineplex Entertainment is the largest Canadian movie exhibitor.[35]

Reasons for Diversification

There are many reasons why firms use a corporate-level diversification strategy (see Table 7.1). Typically, a diversification strategy is used to increase the firm's value by improving its overall performance. Value is created either through related diversification or through unrelated diversification when the strategy allows a company's businesses to increase revenues or reduce costs while implementing their business-level strategies.

Other reasons for using a diversification strategy may have nothing to do with increasing the firm's value; in fact, diversification can have neutral effects or even reduce a firm's value, as illustrated in the Strategic Focus on BCE. Value-neutral reasons for diversification include those of a desire to match and thereby neutralize a competitor's market power (such as to neutralize another firm's advantage by acquiring a similar distribution outlet). Decisions to expand a firm's portfolio of businesses to reduce managerial risk can have a negative effect on the firm's value. Greater amounts of diversification reduce managerial risk in that if one of the businesses in a diversified firm fails, the top executive of that business remains employed by the corporation. In addition, because diversification can increase a firm's size and thus managerial compensation, managers have motives to diversify a firm to a level that reduces its value.[36] Diversification rationales that may have a neutral or negative effect on the firm's value are discussed later in this chapter.

Operational relatedness and corporate relatedness are two ways diversification strategies can create value (see Figure 7.3 on page 206). Study of these independent relatedness

Table 7.1	Reasons for Diversification

Value-Creating Diversification
- Economies of scope (related diversification)
- Sharing activities
- Transferring core competencies
- Market power (related diversification)
- Blocking competitors through multipoint competition
- Vertical integration
- Financial economies (unrelated diversification)
- Efficient internal capital allocation
- Business restructuring

Value-Neutral Diversification
- Competition regulation
- Tax laws
- Low performance
- Uncertain future cash flows
- Risk reduction for firm
- Tangible resources
- Intangible resources

Value-Reducing Diversification
- Diversifying managerial employment risk
- Increasing managerial compensation

A Conglomerate Discount at BCE

Bell Canada Enterprises (BCE), Canada's largest communications company, offers a broad range of services—local, long distance, and wireless phone services; high-speed and wireless Internet access; IP–broadband services; information and communications technology services; and direct-to-home satellite and VDSL television services. Other BCE holdings include an interest in CTVglobemedia, Canada's premier media company.

BCE had a history of building up its business portfolio by acquiring interests in other businesses, but it became apparent the investment community didn't appreciate this strategy. When CEO Michael Sabia took charge of BCE in 2002, he shared the investor opinion and relentlessly divested BCE's non-core assets—like its directory business, its satellite unit, and its stake in CGI Group Inc., a technology consulting company. According to a report in *The Globe and Mail,* Sabia was left cleaning up the result of nearly 20 years of diversification that "sent [BCE] down new and disastrous paths—such as the $7.5-billion write-down of overseas long-distance carrier, Teleglobe Inc. five years ago," which filed for bankruptcy protection in 2002.

Although Sabia made changes to refocus BCE on its core telecommunications business, by April 2007 BCE had become an acquisition target for private equity groups and pension funds due to a lack of investor excitement and a "stagnant share price." In determining a purchase price, it became apparent that BCE's investment community valued its diverse business interests less than if they were valued individually. As a result, BCE's share price didn't reflect the true total value of all its businesses—a situation commonly referred to as a "conglomerate discount." On June 30, 2007, BCE accepted a bid from a group led by the Ontario Teachers' Pension Plan.

SOURCES: 2007, About BCE, http://www.bce.ca/en/aboutbce/, retrieved February 26, 2008; 2007, As shareholders gather, the bell tolls for BCE, *The Globe and Mail,* June 4; Bell Canada, http://en.wikipedia.org/wiki/Bell_Canada_Enterprises, retrieved February 26, 2008; 2007, BCE in play, Some possible scenarios, CBC News, June 22.

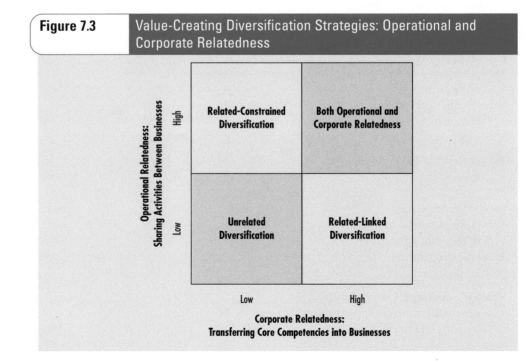

Figure 7.3 Value-Creating Diversification Strategies: Operational and Corporate Relatedness

dimensions shows the importance of resources and key competencies.[37] The figure's vertical dimension depicts opportunities to share operational activities between businesses (operational relatedness), while the horizontal dimension suggests opportunities for transferring corporate-level core competencies (corporate relatedness). The firm with a strong capability in managing operational synergy, especially in sharing assets between its businesses, falls in the upper left quadrant, which also represents vertical sharing of assets through vertical integration. The lower right quadrant represents a highly developed corporate capability for transferring one or more core competencies across businesses. This capability is located primarily in the corporate headquarters office.

Unrelated diversification is also illustrated in Figure 7.3 in the lower left quadrant. Financial economies (discussed later), rather than either operational or corporate relatedness, are the source of value creation for firms using the unrelated diversification strategy.

Value-Creating Diversification: Related-Constrained and Related-Linked Diversification

With the related diversification corporate-level strategy, the firm builds upon or extends its resources and capabilities to create value.[38] The company using the related diversification strategy wants to develop and exploit economies of scope between its businesses.[39] Available to companies operating in multiple product markets or industries,[40] **economies of scope** are cost savings that the firm creates by successfully sharing some of its resources and capabilities or transferring one or more corporate-level core competencies that were developed in one of its businesses to another of its businesses.

As illustrated in Figure 7.3, firms seek to create value from economies of scope through two basic kinds of operational economies: sharing activities (operational relatedness) and transferring corporate-level core competencies (corporate relatedness). The difference between sharing activities and transferring competencies is based on how separate resources are jointly used to create economies of scope. To do so, tangible resources, such as plant and equipment or other business-unit physical assets, often must be shared. Less tangible resources, such as manufacturing know-how, also can be shared.[41] However, know-how transferred between separate activities with no physical or tangible resource involved is a transfer of a corporate-level core competency, not an operational sharing of activities.

Economies of scope are cost savings that the firm creates by successfully sharing some of its resources and capabilities or transferring one or more corporate-level core competencies that were developed in one of its businesses to another of its businesses.

Operational Relatedness: Sharing Activities

Firms can create operational relatedness by sharing either a primary activity (such as inventory delivery systems) or a support activity (such as purchasing practices)—see Chapter 4's discussion of the value chain. Firms using the related-constrained diversification strategy share activities in order to create value. Irving Forest Products (a division of the J. D. Irving conglomerate in Saint John) uses this corporate-level strategy. Irving is the only manufacturer of disposable baby diapers in Canada and sells its product under private label for major North American retailers. The company also produces Majesta and Royale toilet tissue. Irving's toilet tissue and baby diaper business both use paper products as a primary input to the manufacturing process.[42] The firm's paper production plant produces inputs for both businesses and is an example of a shared activity. In addition, because they both produce consumer products, these two businesses are likely to share distribution channels and sales networks.

Irving's businesses share a wider range of activities than what occurs across its disposable diaper and toilet tissue business. Because of its range of activities in the forestry business Irving produces not only paper products but also a range of lumber products. Because it produces lumber, the company is able to supply its own Kent home improvement stores—Atlantic Canada's leading chain of such stores. Additionally, the company can supply lumber to its Kent home construction division—Atlantic Canada's largest builder of residential homes and modularized commercial buildings. To supply Kent, Irving may source products from its own wholesaler, Source Atlantic. Source Atlantic offers an array of products for electrical, plumbing, and heating, as well as industrial piping, valves, bearings, and automation products. Irving also uses its lumber products in its Shamrock Truss division as a source for engineered wood products. Finally, because of concerns about the environment in the pulp and paper industry, Irving has gained expertise in environmental services that it now performs for other organizations.[43] Such value-creating possibilities allow the company to share capture profitable ventures within the organization.

Firms expect activity sharing among units to result in increased strategic competitiveness and improved financial returns.[44] For example, Toronto's Onex Corporation has a subsidiary called ONCAP. ONCAP is essentially a venture capital firm that allows Onex to use its financial wherewithal and management expertise to develop "small and mid-sized North American businesses that offer the opportunity to create significant growth in shareholder value over the long term. Typically, these companies have an enterprise value of between $50 and $500 million." The companies in this group are as diverse as EnGlobe (a leading environmental services firm focused on the beneficial reuse of organic waste), Mister Car Wash (the second-largest full-service car wash chain in the U.S.), and CiCi's Pizza Buffet (a 600-store chain of all-you-want pizza restaurants in the U.S.).[45]

Other issues affect the degree to which activity sharing creates positive outcomes. For example, managers of other businesses in the firm may feel that a newly created business is unfairly receiving assets. Activity sharing is also risky because ties among a firm's businesses create links between outcomes. For instance, if demand for one business's product is reduced, there may not be sufficient revenues to cover the fixed costs required to operate the facilities being shared. Organizational difficulties such as these can reduce activity-sharing success.[46]

Although activity sharing across businesses isn't risk free, research shows that it can create value. For example, studies that examined acquisitions of firms in the same industry (horizontal acquisitions), such as the banking industry, have found that sharing resources and activities and thereby creating economies of scope contributed to post-acquisition increases in performance and higher returns to shareholders.[47] Additionally, firms that sold off related units in which resource sharing was a possible source of economies of scope have been found to produce lower returns than those that sold off businesses unrelated to the firm's core business.[48] Still other research discovered that firms with very closely related businesses had lower risk.[49] These results suggest that gaining economies of scope by sharing activities across a firm's businesses may be important in reducing risk and in creating value. Further, more attractive results are obtained through activity sharing when a strong corporate headquarters office facilitates it.[50]

Corporate Relatedness: Transferring of Core Competencies

Corporate-level core competencies are complex sets of resources and capabilities that link different businesses, primarily through managerial and technological knowledge, experience, and expertise.

Over time, the firm's intangible resources, such as its know-how, become the foundation of core competencies. **Corporate-level core competencies** are complex sets of resources and capabilities that link different businesses, primarily through managerial and technological knowledge, experience, and expertise.[51] The ability to successfully price new products in all of the firm's businesses is an example of what research has shown to be a value-creating, corporate-level competency.[52] Firms seeking to create value through corporate relatedness use the related-linked diversification strategy.

There are at least two ways the related-linked diversification strategy helps firms to create value.[53] First, because the expense of developing a core competency has been incurred in one of the firm's businesses, transferring it to a second business eliminates the need for that second business to allocate resources to develop it. Resource intangibility is a second source of value creation through corporate relatedness. Intangible resources are difficult for competitors to understand and imitate. Because of this difficulty, the unit receiving a transferred corporate-level competency often gains an immediate competitive advantage over its rivals.[54]

To illustrate how diversification can enhance a firm's core capabilities, we should look at one of Canada's largest communications companies, Rogers Communications Inc. Rogers specializes in wireless communications and cable television, but has diversified its business portfolio with additional telecommunications and mass media assets. In particular among its mass media assets, Rogers Communications Inc. made a strategic acquisition of the Toronto Blue Jays Baseball Club in 2000,[55] likely setting itself up for enhanced market power in the future. In July 2001, Rogers Media acquired CTV Sportsnet (and renamed it Rogers Sportsnet); in 2004, Rogers took over the Toronto Skydome[56] (and renamed it the Rogers Centre). Today, these acquisitions are accompanied by many others under the corporate subsidiary Rogers Media Inc., which owns Canada's largest publishing company and owns 51 radio stations and several television properties.[57]

A number of firms have successfully transferred one or more corporate-level core competencies across their businesses. Honda has developed and transferred its competence in engine design and manufacturing to its businesses making products such as motorcycles, lawnmowers, and cars and trucks. With respect to smaller engines, for example, these transfers of the corporate-level competency in terms of engine design and manufacturing have been very successful, in that company officials believe that "Honda has become known as the leader in creating four-stroke engines that are reliable, technologically advanced and easy to start."[58]

One way managers facilitate the transfer of corporate-level core competencies is by moving key people into new management positions.[59] However, the manager of an older business may be reluctant to transfer key people who have accumulated knowledge and experience critical to the business's success. Thus, managers with the ability to facilitate the transfer of a core competency may come at a premium, or the key people involved may not want to transfer. Additionally, the top-level managers from the transferring business may not want the competencies transferred to a new business to fulfill the firm's diversification objectives. To facilitate these transfers requires a strong corporate senior management team, as we mentioned earlier.

Research partly supports some hesitancy on managers' parts when it comes to transfers, in that those studying this activity have found that transferring expertise in manufacturing-based businesses often does not result in improved performance.[60] Moreover, it seems that businesses in which performance does improve often demonstrate a corporate-wide passion for pursuing skill transfer and appropriate coordination mechanisms for realizing economies of scope. See the Strategic Focus for an illustration.

Market Power

Firms using a related diversification strategy may gain market power when successfully using their related-constrained or related-linked strategy. **Market power** exists when a firm is able to sell its products above the existing competitive level, or to reduce the costs of its primary and support activities below the competitive level, or both.[61]

Firms can create market power through multipoint competition[62] and vertical integration. **Multipoint competition** exists when two or more diversified firms simultaneously

Market power exists when a firm is able to sell its products above the existing competitive level or to reduce the costs of its primary and support activities below the competitive level, or both.

Multipoint competition exists when two or more diversified firms simultaneously compete in the same product areas or geographic markets.

What Is the Best Way to Manage Product Diversification at GE?

General Electric (GE) is the epitome of diversification, holding strong positions in markets ranging from technology, media, manufacturing, and financial services. Investors are generally quite pleased with GE's diversification strategy because, according to the business article "GE's Moment," General Electric's "[d]emand for big-ticket items like jet engines, steam turbines and other industrial products . . . go[es] through multiyear cycles," while its other non-related businesses offset some of these cycles. When business is poor in one segment, it could be booming in another.

Using the related-linked corporate-level strategy, GE was organized into 11 core businesses in 2004. As called for by the related-linked strategy, very few resources and activities were shared among these 11 businesses. While little sharing occurred between what were rather independent businesses, activities *were* shared among divisions housed within each business, while corporate headquarters personnel worked to transfer corporate-level core competencies between or among the businesses.

In 2005, things changed in terms of the businesses in GE's portfolio as well as how those businesses were managed. In mid-2005, GE's CEO Jeffery Immelt announced he was reorganizing GE into six, rather than 11, core businesses: Infrastructure, Industrial, Commercial Financial Services, NBC Universal, Healthcare, and Consumer Finance. According to Immelt, "these changes will accelerate GE's growth in key industries." In addition, the reorganization was meant to help GE become a more "customer-focused" organization—one capable of delivering increasingly effective solutions to problems customers wanted solved.

Changes in how GE would manage its portfolio of businesses followed decisions about what businesses would be in the portfolio. The changes in GE's portfolio under Immelt's leadership demonstrate his intention of making GE even more of a high-technology company rather than an industrial firm; in only four years, GE spent over $60 billion to acquire technology-based assets and divested approximately $15 billion of non-technology assets. The newly acquired assets were coupled with GE's remaining assets to batch the firm's operations into six major, technology-oriented businesses. Immelt and his top management team help to manage these six businesses from the corporate headquarters office. These managerial efforts focus on transferring core competencies in different types of technologies from one business to one or more of the remaining five businesses. As in all firms, at GE the skills of top-level managers influence the degree to which the transfers of corporate-level core competencies create value.

SOURCES: V. J. Racanelli, 2007, GE's moment, *Barron's*, June 4; 2007, Imagination at work, GE Home page, www.ge.com, December 6; 2005, GE assigns insurance division to financial services, *Kansas City Star*, www.kansascity.com, June 24; 2005, GE to reorganize into 6 business units, *Wall Street Journal Online*, www.wsj.com, June 23; K. Kranhold & J. S. Lublin, 2005, GE is expected to tap two of its executives as vice chairman, *Wall Street Journal Online*, www.wsj.com, June 17; D. Wakabayashi, 2005, GE streamlines businesses, *Reuter's*, www.reuters.com, June 23; B. Einhorn & R. Tiplady, 2005, What does Li see in this wallflower? *BusinessWeek*, May 23, 58.

Vertical integration exists when a company produces its own inputs (backward integration) or owns its own source of output distribution (forward integration).

compete in the same product areas or geographic markets.[63] The recent acquisition of a digital map information firm, Navteq Corporation, by Nokia Corporation signalled the growth in the mobile GPS and navigation systems market.[64] Subsequent actions taken by Google Inc. to introduce its own version of GPS in smart phones[65] illustrate two diversified firms competing in the same market: mobile navigation devices.

Some firms using a related diversification strategy engage in vertical integration to gain market power. **Vertical integration** exists when a company produces its own inputs (backward integration) or owns its own source of output distribution (forward integration).

In some instances, firms partially integrate their operations, producing and selling their products by using company businesses as well as outside sources.[66]

Vertical integration is commonly used in the firm's core business to gain market power over rivals. Market power is gained as the firm develops the ability to save on its operations, avoid market costs, improve product quality, and, possibly, protect its technology from imitation by rivals.[67] Market power also is created when firms have strong ties between their assets for which no market prices exist. Establishing a market price would result in high search and transaction costs, so firms seek to vertically integrate rather than remain separate businesses.[68]

There are limits to vertical integration. For example, an outside supplier may produce the product at a lower cost. As a result, internal transactions from vertical integration may be expensive and reduce profitability relative to competitors. Also, bureaucratic costs may occur with vertical integration. And, because vertical integration can require substantial investments in specific technologies, it may reduce the firm's flexibility, especially when technology changes quickly. Further, vertically integrating requires that corporate managers must know how to support their potentially very different businesses in their pursuit of value creation and capture. It is possible that the strategic knowledge required across these vertically integrated firms could strain the information-processing capacity of the senior management team. This would result in value destruction. Finally, changes in demand create capacity balance and coordination problems. If one business is building a part for another internal business, but achieving economies of scale requires the first division to manufacture quantities that are beyond the capacity of the internal buyer to absorb, it would be necessary to sell the parts outside the firm as well as to the internal business. Thus, although vertical integration can create value, especially through market power over competitors, it is not without risks and costs.[69]

For example, Canada's major food processing company, Maple Leaf Foods, made the decision to integrate six of its "loosely connected operating companies" to vertically integrate its protein business. It combined its Meat Products Group (consumer foods, pork, poultry, and global operations) with its Agribusiness Group (hog production, feed, and rendering operations). As a result, Maple Leaf Foods can manage the "interlinked nature of the various phases involved in the production of finished pork and poultry products," which it refers to as the "protein value chain."[70] For Maple Leaf, vertical integration is about aligning its hog production, meat processing, and rendering operations to create greater operational efficiencies.[71]

Many manufacturing firms no longer pursue vertical integration as a means of gaining market power.[72] In fact, de-integration is the focus of most manufacturing firms, such as Intel and Dell, and even some large auto companies, such as Ford and General Motors, as they develop independent supplier networks.[73]

Such firms often manage their customers' entire product lines and offer services ranging from inventory management to delivery and after-sales service. Conducting business through e-commerce also allows vertical integration to be changed into "virtual integration."[74] Thus, closer relationships are possible with suppliers and customers through virtual integration or electronic means of integration, allowing firms to reduce the costs of processing transactions while improving their supply-chain management skills and tightening the control of their inventories. This evidence suggests that *virtual integration* rather than *vertical integration* may be a more common source of market power gains for today's firms.

Simultaneous Operational Relatedness and Corporate Relatedness

As Figure 7.3 suggests, some firms simultaneously seek operational and corporate relatedness to create economies of scope.[75] Although difficult, the ability to simultaneously create economies of scope by sharing activities (operational relatedness) and transferring core competencies (corporate relatedness) is very hard for competitors to understand and learn how to imitate. However, firms that fail in their efforts to simultaneously obtain operational and corporate relatedness may create the opposite of what they seek—namely, diseconomies of scope instead of economies of scope.[76]

Walt Disney Company uses a related diversification strategy to simultaneously create economies of scope through operational and corporate relatedness. Encompassing a diverse line of business offerings including theme parks, cruise lines, restaurants, television networks, and movie production, The Walt Disney Company is divided among four business segments: Studio Entertainment, Parks and Resorts, Consumer Products, and Media Networks. Each segment consists of integrated businesses that together maximize exposure and growth worldwide. Within the firm's Studio Entertainment business, for example, Disney can gain economies of scope by sharing activities among its different movie distribution companies such as Touchstone Pictures, Hollywood Pictures, and Miramax. Broad and deep knowledge about its customers is a capability on which Disney relies to develop corporate-level core competencies in terms of advertising and marketing. With these competencies, Disney is able to create economies of scope through corporate relatedness as it cross-sells products that are highlighted in its movies through the distribution channels that are part of its Parks and Resorts and Consumer Products businesses. Thus, characters created in movies (think of those in *The Lion King*) become figures that are marketed through Disney's retail stores (which are part of the Consumer Products business). In addition, themes established in movies become the source of new rides in the firm's theme parks, which are part of the Parks and Resorts business.[77]

As we have described, Walt Disney Company successfully uses related diversification as a corporate-level strategy through which it creates economies of scope by sharing some activities and by transferring core competencies. However, it is difficult for investors to actually observe the value created by a firm (such as Walt Disney Company) as it shares activities and transfers core competencies. Because of this, the value created by a firm using a diversification strategy to create economies of scope in the manner described above tends to be discounted by investors. In general, the reason for this discount is that investors face a "lingering question [about] whether multiple revenue streams will outpace multiple-platform overhead."[78]

Unrelated Diversification

Firms do not seek either operational relatedness or corporate relatedness when using the unrelated diversification corporate-level strategy. An unrelated diversification strategy (see Figure 7.3) can create value through two types of financial economies. We define **financial economies** as cost savings realized through improved allocations of financial resources based on investments inside or outside the firm.[79]

Financial economies are cost savings realized through improved allocations of financial resources based on investments inside or outside the firm.

Efficient internal capital allocations can lead to financial economies. Efficient internal capital allocations reduce risk among the firm's businesses—for example, by leading to the development of a portfolio of businesses with different risk profiles. The second type of financial economy concerns the purchasing of other corporations and then the restructuring of their assets. Here, the diversified firm buys another company, restructures that company's assets in ways that allow it to operate more profitably, and then sells the company for a profit in the external market.[80] Next, we discuss the two types of financial economies in greater detail.

Efficient Internal Capital Market Allocation

In a market economy, capital markets are thought to efficiently allocate capital. Efficiency results as investors take equity positions (ownership) with high expected future cash-flow values. Capital is also allocated through debt as shareholders and debtholders try to improve the value of their investments by taking stakes in businesses with high growth and profitability prospects.

In large diversified firms, the corporate headquarters office distributes capital to its businesses to create value for the overall corporation. The nature of these distributions may generate gains from internal capital market allocations that exceed the gains that would accrue to shareholders as a result of capital being allocated by the external capital market.[81] This happens because while managing the firm's portfolio of businesses those in a firm's corporate headquarters may gain access to detailed and accurate information regarding those businesses' actual and prospective performance.

Compared with corporate office personnel, investors have relatively limited access to internal information and can only estimate the performances of individual businesses and their future prospects. Moreover, although businesses seeking capital must provide information to potential suppliers (such as banks or insurance companies), firms with internal capital markets may have at least two informational advantages. First, information provided to capital markets through annual reports and other sources may not include negative information, instead emphasizing positive prospects and outcomes. External sources of capital have limited ability to understand the operational dynamics of large organizations. Even external shareholders who have access to information have no guarantee of full and complete disclosure.[82] Second, although a firm must disseminate information, that information also becomes simultaneously available to the firm's current and potential competitors. With insights gained by studying such information, competitors might attempt to duplicate a firm's value-creating strategy. Thus, an ability to efficiently allocate capital through an internal market may help the firm protect the competitive advantages it develops while using its corporate-level strategy as well as its various business-unit-level strategies.

If intervention from outside the firm is required to make corrections to capital allocations, only significant changes are possible, such as forcing the firm into bankruptcy or changing the top management team. Alternatively, in an internal capital market, the corporate headquarters office can fine-tune its corrections, such as choosing to adjust managerial incentives or suggesting strategic changes in one of the firm's businesses. Thus, capital can be allocated according to more specific criteria than is possible with external market allocations. Because it has less accurate information, the external capital market may fail to allocate resources adequately to high-potential investments. The corporate headquarters office of a diversified company can more effectively perform such tasks as disciplining underperforming management teams through resource allocations.[83]

Research suggests, however, that in efficient capital markets the unrelated diversification strategy may be discounted.[84] "For years, stock markets have applied a 'conglomerate discount': they value diversified manufacturing conglomerates at 20 percent less, on average, than the value of the sum of their parts. The discount still applies, in good economic times and bad. Extraordinary manufacturers (like GE) can defy it for a while, but more ordinary ones (like Philips and Siemens) cannot."[85] One reason for this discount could be that firms sometimes substitute acquisitions for innovation. In these instances, too many resources are allocated to analyzing and completing acquisitions to further diversify a firm instead of allocating an appropriate amount of resources to nurture internal innovations.

In spite of the associated challenges, a number of corporations continue to use the unrelated diversification strategy.[86] This is certainly the case in Europe, where the use of unrelated diversification is increasing,[87] and in emerging markets as well. The Achilles' heel for firms using the unrelated diversification strategy in a developed economy is that competitors can imitate financial economies more easily than they can replicate the value gained from the economies of scope developed through operational relatedness and corporate relatedness. This is less of a problem in emerging economies, where the

Chapter 7 / Corporate-Level Strategy

absence of a "soft infrastructure" (including effective financial intermediaries, sound regulations, and contract laws) supports and encourages use of the unrelated diversification strategy.[88] In fact, in emerging economies such as in India, diversification increases the performance of firms affiliated with large diversified business groups.[89] The increasing skill levels of people working in corporations located in emerging markets may support the successful use of the unrelated diversification strategy.[90]

Restructuring of Assets

Financial economies can also be created when firms learn how to create value by buying, restructuring, and then selling other companies' assets in the external market.[91] As in the real estate business, buying assets at low prices, restructuring them, and selling them at a price exceeding their cost generates a positive return on the firm's invested capital.[92]

Creating financial economies by acquiring and restructuring other companies' assets requires an understanding of significant trade-offs. Success usually calls for a focus on mature, low-technology businesses because of the uncertainty of demand for high-technology products. In high-technology businesses resource allocation decisions become too complex, creating information-processing overload on the small corporate-headquarters offices that are common in unrelated diversified firms. High-technology businesses are often human-resource dependent; these people can leave or demand higher pay and thus appropriate or deplete the value of an acquired firm.[93]

Buying and then restructuring service-based assets so they can be profitably sold in the external market is also difficult. Here, sales often are a product of close personal relationships between a client and the representative of the firm being restructured. Thus, for both high-technology firms and service-based companies, relatively few tangible assets can be restructured to create value that can be profitably sold. It is difficult to restructure intangible assets such as human capital and effective relationships that have evolved over time between buyers (customers) and sellers (firm personnel).

Value-Neutral Diversification: Incentives and Resources

The objectives firms seek when using related diversification and unrelated diversification strategies all have the potential to help the firm create value by using a corporate-level strategy. However, these strategies, as well as single- and dominant-business diversification strategies, are sometimes used with value-neutral rather than value-creating objectives in mind. As we discuss next, different incentives to diversify sometimes surface and the quality of the firm's resources may permit only diversification that is value neutral rather than value creating.

Incentives to Diversify

Incentives to diversify come from both the external environment and a firm's internal environment. External incentives include competition regulations and tax laws. Internal incentives include low performance, uncertain future cash flows, and the pursuit of synergy and reduction of risk for the firm.

Competition Regulation and Tax Laws

According to a Canadian business law firm Canadian merger and acquisition activity in 2006 was at record levels, with more than 2,800 deals worth approximately $230 billion—the highest level of activity seen since the late 1990s.[94]

Horizontal, vertical, and conglomerate mergers each raise distinctive competitive concerns. Horizontal mergers reduce the number of players in the market, directly affecting competition. Vertical integration by a merger does not reduce the total number of competitors, but it can be anticompetitive because the enhanced market power could impede new businesses from entering the market.[95] A conglomerate merger could create a dominant firm with a decisive competitive advantage, making it difficult for other companies to enter its market.[96]

The tax effects of diversification stem not only from corporate tax changes but also from individual tax rates. Some companies (especially mature ones) generate more cash from their operations than they can reinvest profitably. Some argue that *free cash flows* (liquid financial assets for which investments in current businesses are no longer economically viable) should be redistributed to shareholders as dividends.[97] If the tax rates for dividends are higher than for capital gains, shareholders would prefer that the firm keep the dividend and create value with the free cash. Unfortunately, the projects that can be invested in are only those that have a zero or negative net present value. So, this has the potential to destroy shareholder value. Acquisitions typically increase a firm's depreciable asset allowances. Increased depreciation (a non–cash-flow expense) produces lower taxable income, thereby providing an additional incentive for acquisitions.

Low Performance

Some research shows that low returns are related to greater levels of diversification.[98] If "high performance eliminates the need for greater diversification,"[99] then low performance may provide an incentive for diversification.

Amidst many challenges like reductions in subsidies and considerable price pressures from powerful buyers, the farming industry has been withering away. However, according to the *National Post*, some farmers are responding to these hard times "by diversifying into other areas of expertise."[100] In the United Kingdom, according to a study by the Department for Environment, Food and Rural Affairs, "diversification is widely held to offer considerable scope for improving the economic viability of many farm businesses."[101] Examples of diversification strategies by farms can include producing other foods or crafts, converting to u-pick farms, adding roadside markets, operating bed and breakfasts, and so on.[102]

Research indicates that better performance is more likely when a firm is relatedly diversified rather than pursuing a dominant business strategy or an unrelatedly diversified strategy. This is illustrated in Figure 7.4.

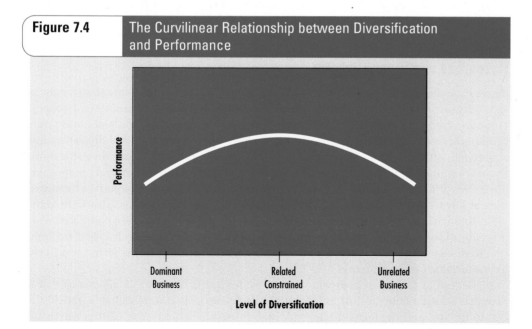

Figure 7.4 The Curvilinear Relationship between Diversification and Performance

Performance

Dominant Business | Related Constrained | Unrelated Business

Level of Diversification

Chapter 7 / Corporate-Level Strategy

Uncertain Future Cash Flows

As a firm's product line matures or is threatened, diversification may be taken as an important defensive strategy.[103] Small firms and companies in mature or maturing industries sometimes find it necessary to diversify for long-term survival.[104] For example, uncertainty was one of the dominant reasons for diversification among railroad firms during the 1960s and 1970s. Railroads diversified primarily because the trucking industry was thought to have the capability to have substantially negative effects on the rail business. The trucking industry created uncertainty for railroad operators regarding the future levels of demand for their services.

Diversifying into other product markets or into other businesses can reduce the uncertainty about a firm's future cash flows. Competing in numerous areas of the lifestyle, health, and sustainability market helps reduce demand uncertainty for Gaiam, for example. While demand for one of Gaiam's products might decline, demand for another might increase during the same period.

Synergy and Firm Risk Reduction

Synergy exists when the value created by business units working together exceeds the value that those same units create working independently.

Diversified firms pursuing economies of scope often have investments that are too inflexible to realize synergy between business units. As a result, a number of problems may arise. **Synergy** exists when the value created by business units working together exceeds the value that those same units create working independently. But as a firm increases its relatedness between business units, it also increases its risk of corporate failure, because synergy produces joint interdependence between/among businesses that constrains the firm's flexibility to respond. This threat may force two basic decisions.

First, the firm may reduce its level of technological change by operating in environments that are more certain. This behaviour may make the firm risk averse and thus uninterested in pursuing new product lines that have potential, but are not proven. Alternatively, the firm may constrain its level of activity sharing and forgo synergy's potential benefits. Either or both decisions may lead to further diversification. The former would lead to related diversification into industries in which more certainty exists. The latter may produce additional, but unrelated, diversification.[105] Research suggests that a firm using a related diversification strategy is more careful in bidding for new businesses, whereas a firm pursuing an unrelated diversification strategy may be more likely to overprice its bid, because an unrelated bidder may not have full information about the acquired firm.[106] However, firms using either a related or an unrelated diversification strategy must understand the consequences of paying large premiums.

Resources and Diversification

As we have discussed, there are several value-neutral incentives for firms to diversify as well as value-creating incentives (such as the ability to create economies of scope). However, even when incentives to diversify exist, a firm must have the types and levels of resources and capabilities needed to successfully use a corporate-level diversification strategy.[107] Although both tangible and intangible resources facilitate diversification, they vary in their ability to create value. Indeed, the degree to which resources are valuable, rare, difficult to imitate, and organized to be exploited (see Chapter 4) influence their ability to create value through diversification. For instance, free cash flows are a tangible, financial resource that may be used to diversify the firm. However, compared with diversification that is grounded in intangible resources, diversification based on only financial resources is more visible to competitors and thus more imitable and less likely to create value on a long-term basis.[108]

Harlequin, a Canadian company owned by TorStar in Toronto, is an example of a firm that added a new product line based on its resources that were valuable, rare, difficult to imitate, and organized to be exploited. It used its authors and editors who were expert in writing and editing books in the romance series industry to become expert in writing and editing single-title books. It took ten years to see appropriate returns, but senior management at Harlequin are very happy they decided to add the Mira line of single-title books to the portfolio.

Tangible resources include the plant and equipment necessary to produce a product and tend to be less-flexible assets. Any excess capacity can be used only for closely related products, especially those requiring highly similar manufacturing technologies. Excess capacity of other tangible resources, such as a sales force, can be used to diversify more easily. Excess capacity in a sales force is more effective with related diversification, because it may sell similar products. The sales force would be more knowledgeable about related-product characteristics, customers, and distribution channels.[109]

Tangible resources may create resource interrelationships in production, marketing, procurement, and technology, defined earlier as activity sharing. On the other hand, intangible resources are more flexible than tangible physical assets in facilitating diversification, especially intangible resources such as tacit knowledge.[110]

Sometimes, however, the benefits expected from using resources to diversify the firm for either value-creating or value-neutral reasons are not gained.[111] For example, Wendy's International decided to sell up to 18 percent of its Canadian doughnut chain, Tim Hortons, through an initial public offering (IPO) that was to be completed by the end of the first quarter of 2006. Influencing this decision was the fact that the doughnut chain had "posted break-even results over the past three years."[112] Thus, use of Wendy's resources to diversify into the doughnut business had created value-neutral results. Wendy's expected to use the resources generated through the IPO to focus on product development improvements in its core restaurants and perhaps to pursue other diversification possibilities that would create value rather than being only value neutral.[113] By the end of 2006, Wendy's had spun off the rest of the chain to its shareholders.[114]

Similarly, Sara Lee Corporation is "embarking on an aggressive strategic plan that will transform the entire enterprise into a tightly focused food, beverage and household products company."[115] Through these efforts, Sara Lee intends to eliminate both the value-creating and value-neutral diversification choices that were not helping the firm substantially improve its financial performance. Under the direction of the firm's new CEO, resources generated by selling off assets were to be redeployed toward strategic acquisitions and product innovation.[116] Of course, keeping its household products division could lead some to question whether it had focused enough. Maybe downscoping to only the food and beverage division would have created even more value for Sara Lee's shareholders.

Value-Reducing Diversification: Managerial Motives to Diversify

Managerial motives to diversify can exist independently of value-neutral reasons (i.e., incentives and resources) and value-creating reasons (e.g., economies of scope). The desire for increased compensation and reduced managerial employment risk are two motives for top-level executives to diversify their firm beyond value-creating and value-neutral levels.[117] In slightly different words, top-level executives may diversify a firm in order to diversify their own employment risk, as long as profitability does not suffer excessively.[118]

Diversification provides additional benefits to top-level managers that shareholders do not enjoy. Research evidence shows that diversification and firm size are highly correlated, and as firm size increases, so does executive compensation.[119] Because large firms are complex, difficult-to-manage organizations, top-level managers commonly receive substantial levels of compensation to lead them.[120] Greater levels of diversification can increase a firm's complexity, resulting in still more compensation for executives to lead an increasingly diversified organization. Governance mechanisms, such as the board of directors, monitoring by owners, executive compensation practices, and the market for corporate control, may limit managerial tendencies to over-diversify. These mechanisms are discussed in more detail in Chapter 11.

In some instances, though, a firm's governance mechanisms may not be strong, resulting in a situation in which executives may diversify the firm to the point that it fails to earn even average returns.[121] The loss of adequate internal governance may result in poor relative performance, thereby triggering a threat of takeover. Although takeovers may improve efficiency by replacing ineffective managerial teams, managers may avoid takeovers through defensive tactics, such as "poison pills," or may reduce their own exposure with "golden parachute" agreements.[122] Therefore, an external governance threat, although restraining managers, does not flawlessly control managerial motives for diversification.[123]

Most large publicly held firms are profitable because the managers leading them are positive stewards of firm resources, and many of their strategic actions, including those related to selecting a corporate-level diversification strategy, contribute to the firm's success.[124] As mentioned, governance mechanisms should be designed to deal with exceptions to the managerial norms of making decisions and taking actions that will increase the firm's ability to earn above-average returns. Thus, it is overly pessimistic to assume that managers usually act in their own self-interest as opposed to their firm's interest.[125]

Top-level executives' diversification decisions may also be held in check by concerns for their reputation. If a positive reputation facilitates development and use of managerial power, a poor reputation may reduce it. Likewise, a strong external market for managerial talent may deter managers from pursuing inappropriate diversification.[126] In addition, a diversified firm may police other firms by acquiring those that are poorly managed in order to restructure its asset base. Knowing that their firms could be acquired if they are not managed successfully encourages executives to use value-creating diversification strategies.

As shown in Figure 7.5, the level of diversification that can be expected to have the greatest positive effect on performance is based partly on how the interaction of resources, managerial motives, and incentives affects the adoption of particular diversification strategies. As indicated earlier, the greater the incentives and the more flexible the resources, the higher the level of expected diversification. Financial resources (the most flexible) should have a stronger relationship to the extent of diversification than either tangible or intangible resources. Tangible resources (the most inflexible) are useful primarily for related diversification.

As discussed in this chapter, firms can create more value by effectively using diversification strategies. However, diversification must be kept in check by corporate governance. We will discuss corporate governance in Chapter 11. Appropriate strategy implementation tools, such as organizational structures, are also important and we will discuss these in Chapter 12.

We have described corporate-level strategies in this chapter. In the next one, we discuss mergers and acquisitions as one of the more prominent means for firms to diversify and to grow profitably while doing so.[127] These trends toward more diversification through acquisitions, which have been partially reversed due to restructuring (see Chapter 8), indicate that learning has taken place regarding corporate-level diversification strategies.[128] Accordingly, firms that diversify should do so cautiously, choosing to focus on relatively few, rather than many, businesses.[129] In fact, research suggests that although unrelated diversification has decreased, related diversification has increased, possibly due to the restructuring that continued into the 1990s and early 21st century.[130] This sequence of diversification followed by restructuring is now taking place in Europe

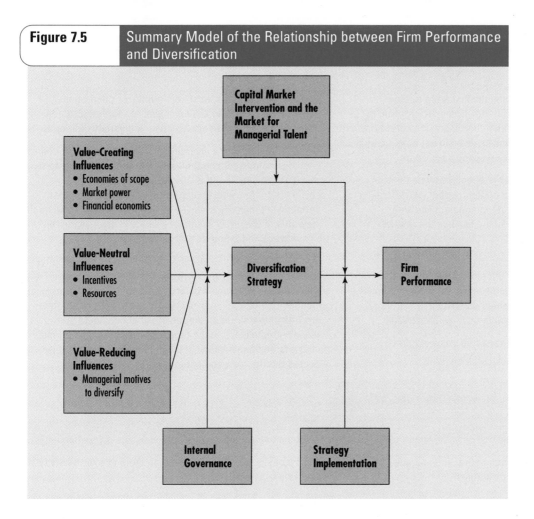

Figure 7.5 Summary Model of the Relationship between Firm Performance and Diversification

and other places such as Korea, mirroring actions of firms in North America and the United Kingdom.[131] Firms can improve their strategic competitiveness when they pursue a level of diversification that is appropriate for their resources (especially financial resources) and core competencies and the opportunities and threats in their country's institutional and competitive environments.[132]

Summary

- The primary reason a firm uses a corporate-level strategy to become more diversified is to create additional value. Using a single- or dominant-business corporate-level strategy may be preferable to seeking a more diversified strategy, unless a corporation can develop economies of scope or financial economies between/among businesses, or unless it can obtain market power through additional levels of diversification. Economies of scope and market power are the main sources of value creation when the firm diversifies by using a corporate-level strategy with moderate to high levels of diversification.

- The corporate-level strategy of related diversification helps the firm to create value by sharing activities or transferring competencies between different businesses in the company's portfolio of businesses.

- Sharing activities usually involves sharing tangible resources between businesses. Transferring core competencies involves transferring competencies developed in one business to another one. It also may involve transferring competencies between the corporate headquarters office and a business unit.

- Sharing activities is usually associated with the related-constrained diversification corporate-level strategy. Activity sharing is costly to implement and coordinate, may create unequal benefits for the divisions involved in the sharing, and may lead to fewer managerial risk-taking behaviours.

- Transferring core competencies is often associated with related-linked (or mixed related and unrelated) diversification, although firms pursuing both sharing activities and transferring core competencies can also use the related-linked strategy.

- Efficiently allocating resources or restructuring a target firm's assets and placing them under rigorous financial controls are two ways to accomplish successful unrelated diversification. Firms using the unrelated diversification strategy focus on creating financial economies to generate value.

- Diversification is sometimes pursued for value-neutral reasons. Incentives from tax and competition government policies, performance disappointments, or uncertainties about future cash flow are examples of value-neutral reasons that senior managers may use to diversify their firms.

- Managerial motives to diversify (including to increase compensation and to reduce their employment risk) can lead to over-diversification and a subsequent reduction in a firm's ability to create value. Evidence suggests, however, that certainly the majority of top-level executives seek to be good stewards of the firm's assets and to avoid diversifying the firm in ways and amounts that destroy value.

- Managers need to pay attention to their firm's internal environment and its external environment when making decisions about the optimum level of diversification for their company. Of course, internal resources are important determinants of the direction that diversification should take. However, conditions in the firm's external environment may facilitate additional levels of diversification, as might unexpected threats from competitors.

Review Questions

1. What is corporate-level strategy and why is it important?

2. What are the levels of diversification firms can pursue by using different corporate-level strategies?

3. What are three reasons causing firms to diversify their operations?

4. How do firms create value when using a related diversification strategy?

5. What are the two ways to obtain financial economies when using an unrelated diversification strategy?

6. What incentives and resources encourage diversification?

7. What motives might encourage managers to over-diversify their firm?

8. What are the ethical implications of senior managers diversifying their firms to increase their compensation and/or reduce their employment risk if such diversification has the potential to destroy shareholder value?

Social Responsibility Review

1. If management's responsibility is to maximize profit, then managers should be building companies that improve the wealth of the shareholders. How, then, can we explain the conglomerate discount? Are managers who create companies subject to a conglomerate discount guilty of stealing the shareholders' money? If so, should they somehow be liable for such losses? If not, why not? Given the knowledge that their company is suffering a conglomerate discount, shouldn't they act before the company gets taken over? Is evidence of a conglomerate discount being socially responsible? To whom? If you argue no, who is being disadvantaged by a conglomerate discount besides the firm's shareholders?

2. In a developed economy competitors can imitate financial economies more easily than they can replicate the value gained from the economies of scope developed through operational or corporate relatedness. So if managers pursue such an easily imitated strategy, are they really adding value to the company? If not, what can the organization legitimately do to address the situation? If so, how sustainable is such a strategy, and is such a strategy in the best interests of shareholders, customers, suppliers, communities, and managers/employees?

3. Shareholders who initially invest in a company do so because they support the business or industry the organization intends to enter. Yet when an organization begins to become widely diversified, is it serving the interests of those shareholders? Do managers owe some obligation to the investors that invested in a business to stay in that business only? Is it being socially responsible to disadvantage shareholders?

Experiential Exercises

Vertical Integration in Beef Production

As mentioned in the text, Maple Leaf Foods made the decision to integrate six of its "loosely connected operating companies" to vertically integrate its protein business. It combined its Meat Products Group (consumer foods, pork, poultry, and global operations) with its Agribusiness Group (hog production, feed, and rendering operations). As a result, Maple Leaf Foods considers that it can manage the interlinked phases involved in its production of finished poultry and pork products, which it calls the protein value chain. For Maple Leaf, vertical integration is about aligning its hog production, meat processing, and rendering operations to create greater operational efficiencies.

Part One. What is the vertical integration logic behind Maple Leaf's decision?

Part Two. Using the Internet, develop a flow chart of the activities in an economic system that take a pig from its pen to the supermarket meat case. Once you have done this, continue your research so that you can answer the following question: Which activities have become vertically integrated in the pork business in the last 15 years, and why?

Onex's Diversity

In the text we describe Onex as an unrelatedly diversified company. In this exercise we want you to determine for yourself what kind of firm Onex is and what you think about the ability of its corporate office to create value for the firm's shareholders.

Part One. First, go to Onex's Web site at www.onex.com and download the firm's most recent annual report. Using the classification scheme set out in Figure 7.1 in this chapter, how do you classify Onex?

Part Two. Examine the explanation that Onex's management gives for how its corporation creates more value for the firm's business units as part of Onex than those would be able to create when operating as stand-alone companies. Follow this up by checking out analysts' reports that you can obtain from the library or a brokerage office. Compare how these independent sources evaluate Onex's ability to create value through its diversified portfolio with that of management. Are the analysts' arguments consistent with the logic advanced by Onex's top-level managers? Why or why not? Provide as much objective evidence as you can to support your assertion.

Part Three. Based on your work in this exercise, would you list Onex as a "buy," "sell," or "hold" if you were a financial analyst? Justify your recommendation.

Notes

1. M. E. Porter, 1980, *Competitive Strategy*, New York: The Free Press, xvi.
2. G. Gavetti, D. A. Levinthal, & J. W. Rivkin, 2005, Strategy making in novel and complex worlds: The power of analogy, *Strategic Management Journal*, 26: 691–712.
3. 2008, Gaiam Web site, http://en.wikipedia.org/wiki/Gaiam, retrieved January 10.
4. G. Probst & S. Raisch, 2005, Organizational crisis: The logic of failure, *Academy of Management Executive*, 19(1): 90–105; S. P. Viguerie & C. Thompson, 2005, The faster they fall, *Harvard Business Review*, 83(3): 22.
5. N. J. Moss, 2005, The relative value of growth, *Harvard Business Review*, 83(4): 102–112.
6. M. E. Porter, 1987, From competitive advantage to corporate strategy, *Harvard Business Review*, 65(3): 43–59.
7. Ibid.; C. A. Montgomery, 1994, Corporate diversification, *Journal of Economic Perspectives*, 8: 163–178.
8. P.-Y. Chu, M.-J. Teng, C.-H. Huang, & H.-S. Lin, 2005, Virtual integration and profitability: Some evidence from Taiwan's IC industry, *International Journal of Technology Management*, 29: 152–172; M. Kwak, 2002, Maximizing value through diversification, *MIT Sloan Management Review*, 43(2): 10.
9. S. A. Mansi & D. M. Reeb, 2002, Corporate diversification: What gets discounted? *Journal of Finance*, 57: 2167–2183; P. Wright, M. Kroll, A. Lado, & B. Van Ness, 2002, The structure of ownership and corporate acquisition strategies, *Strategic Management Journal*, 23: 41–53; C. C. Markides & P. J. Williamson, 1996, Corporate diversification and organizational structure: A resource-based view, *Academy of Management Journal*, 39: 340–367.

10. C. E. Helfat & K. M. Eisenhardt, 2004, Inter-temporal economies of scope organizational modularity, and the dynamics of diversification, *Strategic Management Journal,* 25: 1217–1232.

11. A. Campbell, M. Goold, & M. Alexander, 1995, Corporate strategy: The question for parenting advantage, *Harvard Business Review,* 73(2): 120–132.

12. M. Goold & A. Campbell, 2002, Parenting in complex structures, *Long Range Planning,* 35(3): 219–243; T. H. Brush, P. Bromiley, & M. Hendrickx, 1999, The relative influence of industry and corporation on business segment performance: An alternative estimate, *Strategic Management Journal,* 20: 519–547; T. H. Brush & P. Bromiley, 1997, What does a small corporate effect mean? A variance components simulation of corporate and business effects, *Strategic Management Journal,* 18: 825–835.

13. D. J. Miller, 2004, Firms' technological resources and the performance effects of diversification: A longitudinal study, *Strategic Management Journal,* 25: 1097–1119.

14. D. D. Bergh, 2001, Diversification strategy research at a crossroads: Established, emerging and anticipated paths, in M. A. Hitt, R. E. Freeman, & J. S. Harrison (eds.), *Handbook of Strategic Management,* Oxford, UK: Blackwell Publishers, 363–383.

15. R. P. Rumelt, *Strategy, Structure, and Economic Performance,* Boston: Harvard Business School, 1974; L. Wrigley, 1970, *Divisional Autonomy and Diversification* (Ph.D. dissertation), Harvard Business School.

16. Wm. Wrigley Jr. Company, http://en.wikipedia.org/wiki/Wrigley_Company.

17. 2006 Harley-Davidson Annual Report, http://www.harley-davidson.com/wcm/Content/Pages/Investor_Relations/2006_annual_report_launch.jsp?bmLocale=en_US.

18. R. D. Ireland, R. E. Hoskisson, & M. A. Hitt, 2006, *Understanding Business Strategy,* Mason, OH: Thomson South-Western, 139.

19. 2007, TD Bank 2007 Annual Report, http://www.td.com/ar2007/pdfs/ar2007.pdf, December 28.

20. P. Grant, J. Drucker, & D. K. Berman, 2005, Cable's eyes on wireless prize, Wall Street Journal Online, www.wsj.com, May 18.

21. 2007, P&G Annual Report, http://www.pg.com/investors/annualreports.jhtml, accessed December.

22. The Procter & Gamble Company, Overview, Hoover's Company Information Copyright © 2007, Hoover's, Inc.

23. Ibid.

24. Ibid.

25. 2007, Need a mortgage with those tools?, *The Globe and Mail,* September 5.

26. Ibid.

27. In 2002, Canadian Tire acquired Mark's Work Wearhouse, one of the largest specialty retailers in Canada, offering primarily men's and ladies' casual clothing, footwear, and accessories. Corporate overview, http://investor.relations.canadiantire.ca/ireye/ir_site.zhtml?ticker=ctc.ca&script=2100.

28. Need a mortgage with those tools?

29. 2006, Annual Report, Canadian Tire, http://media.corporate-ir.net/media_files/TOR/CTC.CA/reports/2006AReng.pdf.

30. Ibid.

31. Ibid.

32. Ibid.

33. 2007, Investment spotlight—Conglomerates discount diversity, Frances Hudson, Pensions Management, March 1.

34. Ibid.

35. 2007, Onex Web page, http://www.onex.com, December 31.

36. R. K. Aggarwal & A. A. Samwick, 2003, Why do managers diversify their firms? Agency reconsidered, *Journal of Finance,* 58: 71–118; P. Wright, M. Kroll, & D. Elenkov, 2002, Acquisition returns, increase in firm size, and chief executive officer compensation: The moderating role of monitoring, *Academy of Management Journal,* 45: 599–608.

37. W. S. DeSarbo, C. A. Di Benedetto, M. Song, & I. Sinha, 2005, Revisiting the Miles and Snow strategic framework: Uncovering interrelationships between strategic types, capabilities, environmental uncertainty, and firm performance, *Strategic Management Journal,* 26: 47–74; J. Song, 2002, Firm capabilities and technology ladders, *Strategic Management Journal,* 23: 191–210; J. Lampel & J. Shamsie, 2000, Probing the unobtrusive link: Dominant logic and the design of joint ventures at General Electric, *Strategic Management Journal,* 21: 593–602.

38. M. S. Gary, 2005, Implementation strategy and performance outcomes in related diversification, *Strategic Management Journal,* 26: 643–664; H. Tanriverdi & N. Venkatraman, 2005, Knowledge relatedness and the performance of multibusiness firms, *Strategic Management Journal,* 26: 97–119.

39. M. W. Peng, S.-H. Lee, & D. Y. L. Wang, 2005, What determines the scope of the firm over time? A focus on institutional relatedness, *Academy of Management Review,* 30: 622–633.

40. M. E. Porter, 1985, *Competitive Advantage,* New York: The Free Press, 328.

41. J. W. Lu & P. W. Beamish, 2004, International diversification and firm performance: The S-curve hypothesis, *Academy of Management Journal,* 47: 598–609; R. G. Schroeder, K. A. Bates, & M. A. Junttila, 2002, A resource-based view of manufacturing strategy and the relationship to manufacturing performance, *Strategic Management Journal,* 23: 105–117.

42. 2007, J.D. Irving Web page, http://www.jdirving.com/products-main.aspx?id=516&coll_id=104, December 31.

43. Ibid.

44. D. Gupta & Y. Gerchak, 2002, Quantifying operational synergies in a merger/acquisition, *Management Science,* 48: 517–533.

45. 2007, Onex Corporation: ONCAP, http://www.onex.com/index.taf?pid=63, December 31.

46. M. L. Marks & P. H. Mirvis, 2000, Managing mergers, acquisitions, and alliances: Creating an effective transition structure, *Organizational Dynamics,* 28(3): 35–47.

47. C. Park, 2003, Prior performance characteristics of related and unrelated acquirers, *Strategic Management Journal,* 24: 471–480; G. Delong, 2001, Stockholder gains from focusing versus diversifying bank mergers, *Journal of Financial Economics,* 2: 221–252; T. H. Brush, 1996, Predicted change in operational synergy and post-acquisition performance of acquired businesses, *Strategic Management Journal,* 17: 1–24; H. Zhang, 1995, Wealth effects of U.S. bank takeovers, *Applied Financial Economics,* 5: 329–336.

48. D. D. Bergh, 1995, Size and relatedness of units sold: An agency theory and resource-based perspective, *Strategic Management Journal,* 16: 221–239.

49. M. Lubatkin & S. Chatterjee, 1994, Extending modern portfolio theory into the domain of corporate diversification: Does it apply? *Academy of Management Journal,* 37: 109–136.

50. A. Van Oijen, 2001, Product diversification, corporate management instruments, resource sharing, and performance, *Academy of Management Best Paper Proceedings* (on CD-ROM, Business Policy and Strategy Division); T. Kono, 1999, A strong head office makes a strong company, *Long Range Planning,* 32(2): 225.

51. M. Kotabe, X. Martin, & H. Domoto, 2003, Gaining from vertical partnerships: Knowledge transfer, relationship duration, and supplier performance improvement in the U.S. and Japanese automotive industries, *Strategic Management Journal,* 24: 293–316; L. Capron, P. Dussauge, & W. Mitchell, 1998, Resource redeployment following horizontal acquisitions in Europe and the United States, 1988–1992, *Strategic Management Journal,* 19: 631–661; A. Mehra, 1996, Resource and market based determinants of performance in the U.S. banking industry, *Strategic Management Journal,* 17: 307–322; S. Chatterjee & B. Wernerfelt, 1991, The link between resources and type of diversification: Theory and evidence, *Strategic Management Journal,* 12: 33–48.

52. S. Dutta, M. J. Zbaracki, & M. Bergen, 2003, Pricing process as a capability: A resource-based perspective, *Strategic Management Journal,* 24: 615–630.

53. L. Capron & N. Pistre, 2002, When do acquirers earn abnormal returns? *Strategic Management Journal,* 23: 781–794.

54. J. W. Spencer, 2003, Firms' knowledge-sharing strategies in the global innovation system: Empirical evidence from the flat panel display industry, *Strategic Management Journal,* 24: 217–233.

55. Rogers Communications, Wikipedia, http://en.wikipedia.org/wiki/Rogers_Communications.

56. The Skydome, now known as the Rogers Centre, is the Blue Jays' home venue and largest covered indoor entertainment complex in Canada. http://www.rogerscentre.com/home.jsp.

57. Wikipedia, Rogers Media, http://en.wikipedia.org/wiki/Rogers_Media.

58. 2005, Honda engines, Honda Motor Company Web page, www.honda.com, August 29.

59. G. Stalk Jr., 2005, Rotate the core, *Harvard Business Review*, 83(3): 18–19; C. Zellner & D. Fornahl, 2002, Scientific knowledge and implications for its diffusion, *Journal of Knowledge Management*, 6(2): 190–198.

60. C. St. John & J. S. Harrison, 1999, Manufacturing-based relatedness, synergy, and coordination, *Strategic Management Journal*, 20: 129–145.

61. S. Chatterjee & J. Singh, 1999, Are tradeoffs inherent in diversification moves? A simultaneous model for type of diversification and mode of expansion decisions, *Management Science*, 45: 25–41.

62. Bergh, Diversification strategy research at a crossroads, 369.

63. G. Symeonidis, 2002, Cartel stability with multiproduct firms, *International Journal of Industrial Organization*, 20: 339–352; J. Gimeno & C. Y. Woo, 1999, Multimarket contact, economies of scope, and firm performance, *Academy of Management Journal*, 42: 239–259.

64. 2007, Nokia hopes online maps lead way to riches, *The Globe and Mail*, October 2.

65. 2007, Google introduces system for mobile phone users to automatically indicate location, The Associated Press, November 28.

66. R. Gulati, P. R. Lawrence, & P. Puranam, 2005, Adaptation in vertical relationships: Beyond incentive conflict, *Strategic Management Journal*, 26: 415–440.

67. D. A. Griffin, A. Chandra, & T. Fealey, 2005, Strategically employing natural channels in an emerging market, *Thunderbird International Business Review*, 47(3): 287–311; A. Darr & I. Talmud, 2003, The structure of knowledge and seller-buyer networks in markets for emergent technologies, *Organization Studies*, 24: 443–461.

68. O. E. Williamson, 1996, Economics and organization: A primer, *California Management Review*, 38(2): 131–146.

69. M. G. Jacobides, 2005, Industry change through vertical disintegration: How and why markets emerged in mortgage banking, *Academy of Management Journal*, 48: 465–498.

70. 2006 Annual Report, Maple Leaf Foods Inc., http://library.corporate-ir.net/library/88/884/88490/items/237621/ MLF06AR.pdf.

71. 2007, Investor Relations, Maple Leaf Foods Inc., http://investor.mapleleaf.ca/phoenix.zhtml?c=88490&p=irol-glossary#ver.

72. L. R. Kopczak & M. E. Johnson, 2003, The supply-chain management effect, *MIT Sloan Management Review*, 3: 27–34; K. R. Harrigan, 2001, Strategic flexibility in the old and new economies, in M. A. Hitt, R. E. Freeman, & J. S. Harrison (eds.), *Handbook of Strategic Management*, Oxford, UK: Blackwell Publishers, 97–123.

73. M. R. Subramani & N. Venkatraman, 2003, Safeguarding investments in asymmetric interorganizational relationships: Theory and evidence, *Academy of Management Journal*, 46: 46–62; R. E. Kranton & D. F. Minehart, 2001, Networks versus vertical integration, *Rand Journal of Economics*, 3: 570–601.

74. P. Kothandaraman & D. T. Wilson, 2001, The future of competition: Value-creating networks, *Industrial Marketing Management*, 30: 379–389.

75. K. M. Eisenhardt & D. C. Galunic, 2000, Coevolving: At last, a way to make synergies work, *Harvard Business Review*, 78(1): 91–111.

76. R. Schoenberg, 2001, Knowledge transfer and resource sharing as value creation mechanisms in inbound continental European acquisitions, *Journal of Euro-Marketing*, 10: 99–114.

77. 2007, The Walt Disney Company—Company overview, Walt Disney Web page, http://corporate.disney.go.com, December 6.

78. M. Freeman, 2002, Forging a model for profitability, *Electronic Media*, January 28, 1, 13.

79. D. D. Bergh, 1997, Predicting divestiture of unrelated acquisitions: An integrative model of ex ante conditions, *Strategic Management Journal*, 18: 715–731; C. W. L. Hill, 1994, Diversification and economic performance: Bringing structure and corporate management back into the picture, in R. P. Rumelt, D. E. Schendel, & D. J. Teece (eds.), *Fundamental Issues in Strategy*, Boston: Harvard Business School Press, 297–321.

80. Porter, *Competitive Advantage*.

81. O. E. Williamson, 1975, *Markets and Hierarchies: Analysis and Antitrust Implications*, New York: Macmillan Free Press.

82. J. McTague, 2002, Security in numbers, *Barron's*, December 30, 26; C. Botosan & M. Harris, 2000, Motivations for changes in disclosure frequency and its consequences: An examination of voluntary quarterly segment disclosure, *Journal of Accounting Research*, 38: 329–353; R. Kochhar & M. A. Hitt, 1998, Linking corporate

strategy to capital structure: Diversification strategy, type, and source of financing, *Strategic Management Journal*, 19: 601–610.

83. D. Miller, R. Eisenstat, & N. Foote, 2002, Strategy from the inside out: Building capability-creating organizations, *California Management Review*, 44(3): 37–54; M. E. Raynor & J. L. Bower, 2001, Lead from the center: How to manage divisions dynamically, *Harvard Business Review*, 79(5): 92–100; P. Taylor & J. Lowe, 1995, A note on corporate strategy and capital structure, *Strategic Management Journal*, 16: 411–414.

84. J. M. Campa & S. Kedia, 2002, Explaining the diversification discount, *Journal of Finance*, 57: 1731–1762; M. Kwak, 2001, Spinoffs lead to better financing decisions, *MIT Sloan Management Review*, 42(4): 10; O. A. Lamont & C. Polk, 2001, The diversification discount: Cash flows versus returns, *Journal of Finance*, 56: 1693–1721; R. Rajan, H. Servaes, & L. Zingales, 2001, The cost of diversity: The diversification discount and inefficient investment, *Journal of Finance*, 55: 35–79.

85. 2001, Spoilt for choice, *The Economist*, www.economist.com, July 5.

86. D. J. Denis, D. K. Denis, & A. Sarin, 1999, Agency theory and the reference of equity ownership structure on corporate diversification strategies, *Strategic Management Journal*, 20: 1071–1076; R. Amit & J. Livnat, 1988, A concept of conglomerate diversification, *Journal of Management*, 14: 593–604.

87. Whittington, In praise of the evergreen conglomerate, 4.

88. T. Khanna, K. G. Palepu, & J. Sinha, 2005, Strategies that fit emerging markets, *Harvard Business Review*, 83(6): 63–76.

89. T. Khanna & K. Palepu, 2000, Is group affiliation profitable in emerging markets? An analysis of diversified Indian business groups, *Journal of Finance*, 55: 867–892; T. Khanna & K. Palepu, 2000, The future of business groups in emerging markets: Long-run evidence from Chile, *Academy of Management Journal*, 43: 268–285.

90. S. Sams, 2005, Emerging expertise, *Harvard Business Review*, 83(5): 24–26.

91. R. E. Hoskisson, R. A. Johnson, D. Yiu, & W. P. Wan, 2001, Restructuring strategies and diversified business groups: Differences associated with country institutional environments, in M. A. Hitt, R. E. Freeman, & J. S. Harrison (eds.), *Handbook of Strategic Management*, Oxford, UK: Blackwell Publishers, 433–463; S. J. Chang & H. Singh, 1999, The impact of entry and resource fit on modes of exit by multibusiness firms, *Strategic Management Journal*, 20: 1019–1035.

92. W. Ng & C. de Cock, 2002, Battle in the boardroom: A discursive perspective, *Journal of Management Studies*, 39: 23–49.

93. R. Coff, 2003, Bidding wars over R&D-intensive firms: Knowledge, opportunism, and the market for corporate control, *Academy of Management Journal*, 46: 74–85.

94. Mergers and acquisitions expertise, http://www.osler.com/expertise_mergers.aspx?id=9459.

95. Mergers and Acquisitions—Competitive Concerns, Copyright (c) 2007 Net Industries, http://law.jrank.org/pages/8545 /Mergers-Acquisitions-Competitive-Concerns.html.

96. Ibid.

97. M. C. Jensen, 1986, Agency costs of free cash flow, corporate finance, and takeovers, *American Economic Review*, 76: 323–329.

98. C. Park, 2002, The effects of prior performance on the choice between related and unrelated acquisitions: Implications for the performance consequences of diversification strategy, *Journal of Management Studies*, 39: 1003–1019.

99. Rumelt, *Strategy, Structure and Economic Performance*, 125.

100. 2007, Agriculture: Diversification: Avoid a crash landing, *Post Magazine*, February 22.

101. Ibid.

102. Planning for Farm Diversification, Government of Saskatchewan, http://www.agriculture.gov.sk.ca/Default.aspx? DN=10c63f6a-a3fe-496d-ac01-24494004dd10.

103. A. E. Bernardo & B. Chowdhry, 2002, Resources, real options, and corporate strategy, *Journal of Financial Economics*, 63: 211–234.

104. N. W. C. Harper & S. P. Viguerie, 2002, Are you too focused? *McKinsey Quarterly*, Mid-Summer, 29–38; J. C. Sandvig & L. Coakley, 1998, Best practices in small firm diversification, *Business Horizons*, 41(3): 33–40; C. G. Smith & A. C. Cooper, 1988, Established companies diversifying into young industries: A comparison of firms with different levels of performance, *Strategic Management Journal*, 9: 111–121.

105. N. M. Kay & A. Diamantopoulos, 1987, Uncertainty and synergy: Towards a formal model of corporate strategy, *Managerial and Decision Economics*, 8: 121–130.

106. R. W. Coff, 1999, How buyers cope with uncertainty when acquiring firms in knowledge-intensive industries: Caveat emptor, *Organization Science*, 10: 144–161.

107. S. J. Chatterjee & B. Wernerfelt, 1991, The link between resources and type of diversification: Theory and evidence, *Strategic Management Journal*, 12: 33–48; When the resources do not exist to pursue diversification, research has found diversification to be ill advised: see J. P. Sheppard, 1993, Corporate diversification and survival, *Journal of Financial and Strategic Decisions*, 6(1): 113–132.

108. W. Keuslein, 2003, The Ebitda folly, *Forbes*, March 17, 165–167; Kochhar & Hitt, Linking corporate strategy to capital structure.

109. L. Capron & J. Hulland, 1999, Redeployment of brands, sales forces, and general marketing management expertise following horizontal acquisitions: A resource-based view, *Journal of Marketing*, 63(2): 41–54.

110. A. M. Knott, D. J. Bryce, & H. E. Pose, 2003, On the strategic accumulation of intangible assets, *Organization Science*, 14: 192–207; J. Castillo, 2002, A note on the concept of tacit knowledge, *Journal of Management Inquiry*, 11(1): 46–57; R. D. Smith, 2000, Intangible strategic assets and firm performance: A multi-industry study of the resource-based view, *Journal of Business Strategies*, 17(2): 91–117.

111. K. Shimizu & M. A. Hitt, 2005, What constrains or facilitates divestitures of formerly acquired firms? The effects of organizational inertia, *Journal of Management*, 31: 50–72.

112. 2005, Wendy's announces strategic plan, *Forbes*, www.forbes.com, July 29.

113. 2005, Wendy's to sell part of Tim Hortons chain, *Chicago Tribune*, www.chicagotribune.com, July 29.

114. 2006, Wendy's to spin off rest of Tim Hortons by October 1, CBC News, June 27, http://www.cbc.ca/money/story/ 2006/06/27/timhortons.html, retrieved February 23, 2008.

115. 2005, Sara Lee Corporation announces bold transformation plan to drive long-term growth and performance, Sara Lee Corporation Web page, www.saralee.com, February 21.

116. 2005, Sara Lee cleans out its cupboards, *Fortune*, March 7, 38.

117. J. G. Combs & M. S. Skill, 2003, Managerialist and human capital explanation for key executive pay premiums: A contingency perspective, *Academy of Management Journal*, 46: 63–73; M. A. Geletkanycz, B. K. Boyd, & S. Finkelstein, 2001, The strategic value of CEO external directorate networks: Implications for CEO compensation, *Strategic Management Journal*, 9: 889–898; W. Grossman & R. E. Hoskisson, 1998, CEO pay at the crossroads of Wall Street and Main: Toward the strategic design of executive compensation, *Academy of Management Executive*, 12(1): 43–57; S. Finkelstein & D. C. Hambrick, 1996, *Strategic Leadership: Top Executives and Their Effects on Organizations*, St. Paul, MN: West Publishing Company.

118. W. Shen & A. A. Cannella Jr., 2002, Power dynamics within top management and their impacts on CEO dismissal followed by inside succession, *Academy of Management Journal*, 45: 1195–1206; W. Shen & A. A. Cannella Jr., 2002, Revisiting the performance consequences of CEO succession: The impacts of successor type, postsuccession senior executive turnover, and departing CEO tenure, *Academy of Management Journal*, 45: 717–733; P. J. Lane, A. A. Cannella Jr., & M. H. Lubatkin, 1998, Agency problems as antecedents to unrelated mergers and diversification: Amihud and Lev reconsidered, *Strategic Management Journal*, 19: 555–578; D. L. May, 1995, Do managerial motives influence firm risk reduction strategies? *Journal of Finance*, 50: 1291–1308; Y. Amihud and B. Lev, 1981, Risk reduction as a managerial motive for conglomerate mergers, *Bell Journal of Economics*, 12: 605–617.

119. J. J. Cordeiro & R. Veliyath, 2003, Beyond pay for performance: A panel study of the determinants of CEO compensation, *American Business Review*, 21(1): 56–66; Wright, Kroll, & Elenkov, Acquisition returns, increase in firm size, and chief executive officer compensation; S. R. Gray & A. A. Cannella Jr., 1997, The role of risk in executive compensation, *Journal of Management*, 23: 517–540.

120. R. Bliss & R. Rosen, 2001, CEO compensation and bank mergers, *Journal of Financial Economics*, 1: 107–138; W. G. Sanders & M. A. Carpenter, 1998, Internationalization and firm governance: The roles of CEO compensation, top team composition, and board structure, *Academy of Management Journal*, 41: 158–178.

121. J. J. Janney, 2002, Eat or get eaten? How equity ownership and diversification shape CEO risk-taking, *Academy of Management Executive*, 14(4): 157–158; J. W. Lorsch, A. S. Zelleke, & K. Pick, 2001, Unbalanced boards, *Harvard Business Review*, 79(2): 28–30; R. E. Hoskisson & T. Turk, 1990, Corporate restructuring: Governance and control limits of the internal market, *Academy of Management Review*, 15: 459–477.

122. M. Kahan & E. B. Rock, 2002, How I learned to stop worrying and love the pill: Adaptive responses to takeover law, *University of Chicago Law Review*, 69(3): 871–915.

123. R. C. Anderson, T. W. Bates, J. M. Bizjak, & M. L. Lemmon, 2000, Corporate governance and firm diversification, *Financial Management*, 29(1): 5–22; J. D. Westphal, 1998, Board games: How CEOs adapt to increases in structural board independence from management, *Administrative Science Quarterly*, 43: 511–537; J. K. Seward & J. P. Walsh, 1996, The governance and control of voluntary corporate spin offs, *Strategic Management Journal*, 17: 25–39; J. P. Walsh & J. K. Seward, 1990, On the efficiency of internal and external corporate control mechanisms, *Academy of Management Review*, 15: 421–458.

124. M. Wiersema, 2002, Holes at the top: Why CEO firings backfire, *Harvard Business Review*, 80(12): 70–77.

125. V. Kisfalvi & P. Pitcher, 2003, Doing what feels right: The influence of CEO character and emotions on top management team dynamics, *Journal of Management Inquiry*, 12(10): 42–66; R. Larsson, K. R. Brousseau, M. J. Driver, & M. Homqvist, 2003, International growth through cooperation: Brand-driven strategies, leadership, and career development in Sweden, *Academy of Management Executive*, 17(1): 7–21; W. G. Rowe, 2001, Creating wealth in organizations: The role of strategic leadership, *Academy of Management Executive*, 15(1): 81–94.

126. E. F. Fama, 1980, Agency problems and the theory of the firm, *Journal of Political Economy*, 88: 288–307.

127. F. Vermeulen, 2005, How acquisitions can revitalize companies, *MIT Sloan Management Review*, 46(4): 45–51.

128. M. L. A. Hayward, 2002, When do firms learn from their acquisition experience? Evidence from 1990–1995, *Strategic Management Journal*, 23: 21–39; L. Capron, W. Mitchell, & A. Swaminathan, 2001, Asset divestiture following horizontal acquisitions: A dynamic view, *Strategic Management Journal*, 22: 817–844.

129. W. M. Bulkeley, 1994, Conglomerates make a surprising come-back—with a '90s twist, *Wall Street Journal*, March 1, A1, A6.

130. J. P. H. Fan & L. H. P. Lang, 2000, The measurement of relatedness: An application to corporate diversification, *Journal of Business*, 73: 629–660.

131. Khanna & Palepu, The future of business groups in emerging markets; P. Ghemawat & T. Khanna, 1998, The nature of diversified business groups: A research design and two case studies, *Journal of Industrial Economics*, 46: 35–61.

132. Wan & Hoskisson, Home country environments, corporate diversification strategies, and firm performance.

Chapter Eight

Acquisition and Restructuring Strategies

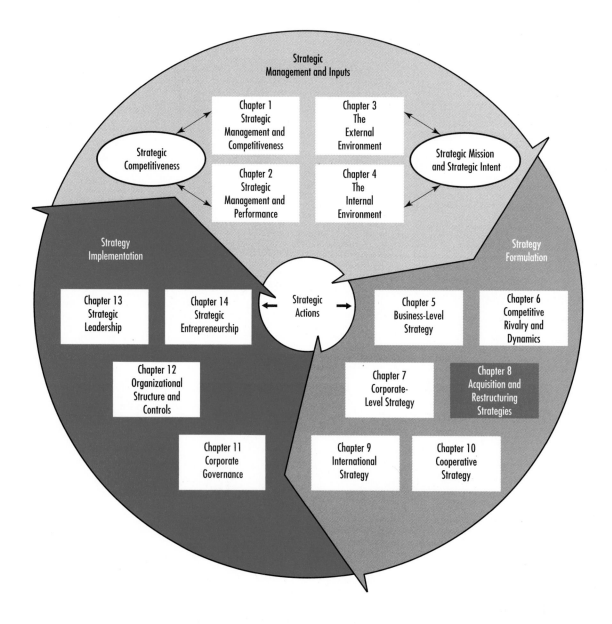

Knowledge Objectives

Studying this chapter should provide you with the strategic management knowledge needed to:

1. Explain the popularity of acquisition strategies in firms competing in the global economy.

2. Discuss reasons why firms use an acquisition strategy to achieve strategic competitiveness.

3. Describe seven problems that work against developing a competitive advantage using an acquisition strategy.

4. Name and describe attributes of effective acquisitions.

5. Define the restructuring strategy and distinguish among its common forms.

6. Explain the short- and long-term outcomes of the different types of restructuring strategies.

Domestic and Cross-Border Acquisitions: Meeting Competitive Challenges and Acquiring Critical Resources

As a firm analyzes its external environment and assesses its internal resources and capabilities to meet environmental challenges, acquisitions as well as adjustments to the firm's set of businesses are often considered. Domestically, a number of Canadian firms have found that horizontal acquisitions (acquisitions of potential competitors) meet their needs to handle these environmental challenges and resource considerations. For example, Rona has been buying up Canadian competitors in order to meet the competitive challenge by Home Depot and an expected entry by U.S. hardware giant Lowes.

www.barrick.com   www.rona.ca

www.mts.mb.ca   www.td.com

    In 2000, Rona was primarily a regional competitor focused mainly in Quebec. In 2000, Rona bought Ontario's 61-store Cashway chain, which increased sales 10 percent—to about $2 billion. In 2001, Rona bought B.C.'s 50-store Revy chain, bringing total sales to about $3 billion. In 2003, Rona bought its provincial rival Reno-Depot, a 20-store chain of mostly big-box stores—the kind that Home Depot ran. This boosted Rona's sales to about $3.7 billion annually, representing a 15-percent share of Canada's home-improvement market. In 2005, Rona bought Alberta's Totem Building Supplies and its sales topped $5 billion. To get to its goal of $7 billion in sales by the end of 2007, Rona picked up 11 stores in B.C. by buying Curtis Lumber, Dick's Lumber, and Mountain Building Centres. At the same time, Rona also bought Ontario's 19-branch Nobal Trade plumbing suppliers, Quebec's 9-store Matériaux Coupal, and Newfoundland's 8-store Chester Dawe Limited.

Phone companies have met aggressive challenges from competitors by making acquisitions. For instance, Manitoba Telecom Services (MTS) acquired Toronto's Allstream, a former AT&T Canada unit. MTS benefited from Allstream's reach outside Manitoba, accessing its extensive broadband fibre-optic network in Canada and through agreements with international service providers like AT&T. This acquisition created a major new national challenger to Montreal's BCE and B.C.'s Telus. The takeover resulted in there being three well-financed national telecoms offering data, wireless, and voice services to corporate clients across most of the country.

Likewise, in order to become the largest dairy processor in Canada—and one of the top 20 dairy processors in the world—Saputo used acquisitions extensively. Saputo has also engaged in some acquisitions to move into the associated area of snack foods. These horizontal acquisitions have been directed at obtaining more efficiency and market power. Others have been directed at diversifying into new areas of business where the competitive challenge is not as significant.

There also have been a number of cross-border acquisitions, especially from Canadian banks seeking a bigger piece of the global market. Toronto-Dominion Bank's announced large-scale acquisition of New Jersey's Commerce Bancorp for $8.5 billion would enable the resulting organization to become the seventh-largest bank in North America—subject, of course, to approval by regulators in both countries. Royal Bank's $2.2-billion acquisition of Trinidad-based RBTT Financial Group would allow Royal a better footing from which to compete against Scotiabank's strong Caribbean presence.

Canadian banks are not the only ones on the move. For instance, Bank of America is now building its share of China Construction Bank, headquartered in Beijing (foreign investors can buy up to 20 percent of a Chinese bank). This deal will give Bank of America a seat on the bank's board. While Europe has lagged in acquiring other banks across borders, things are heating up there as well. In 2005 Italy's UniCredito Italiano SpA established an agreement with Germany's HVB Group AG to create Europe's biggest cross-border banking deal, giving UniCredito branches across a large portion of Western Europe and the former Soviet Union. Both banks have been making acquisitions in Eastern Europe. To preserve the brand names, each bank will maintain its own brand identity in the short term.

As these examples demonstrate, and as will be explained further in this chapter, acquisition strategies are undertaken for a variety of objectives, including creating efficiencies, gaining market power, improving resources necessary to be more competitive, and overcoming entry barriers. A major question, however, is what the net benefits are after the costs of integration are considered. Many acquisitions have led to increased costs and thus have failed, ending in restructuring divestures. It will be interesting to see which of these acquisitions are successful and which create problems for the acquiring firm.

SOURCES: 2007, Rona Web page, http://www.rona.ca, December 28; R. Pulfer, 2007, The Canadians are coming!, *Canadian Business*, 80(21): 15–16; 2007, Saputo Web page, http://www.saputo.com/corpo/client/en/Corpo/Entreprise/Profil.asp#, December 28; 2006, Rona closes Chester Dawe acquisition, *Hardware & Home Centre Magazine*, 30(2): 29; J. Greenwood, 2006, Bigger . . . and better, *Financial Post Business*, February, 15; C. Buckley & J. Creswell, 2005, U.S. bank buys stake in China, *New York Times*, www.nytimes.com, June 17; D. W. Conklin, 2005, Cross-border mergers and acquisitions: A response to environmental transformation, *Journal of World Business*, 40(1): 29–40; T. Gignac, 2004, MTS, Allstream proposal praised: Analysts say merger creates new competition, *Calgary Herald*, March 20, E; 2003, Rona bulks up with purchase of 20-store Reno-Depot chain, *Daily Commercial News and Construction Record*, 76(83): 7; 2001, Rona buys Revy assets, creates Canadian reno giant, *Building*, 51(3): 6–7; J. D'Arcy, 2000, The war for your home: The big-box renovation giants are locked in a death struggle to dominate Canada's suburbs, *Maclean's* (Toronto edition), October 16, 54; 2000, Rona's Cashway deal steps up battle for $8b renovation market, *Daily Commercial News and Construction Record*, 73(27): A1.

In Chapter 7 we studied corporate-level strategies, focusing on types and levels of product diversification strategies that can build core competencies and create competitive advantage. As noted in that chapter, diversification allows a firm to create value by productively using excess resources.[1] In this chapter, we explore mergers and acquisitions, often combined with a diversification strategy, as a prominent strategy employed by firms throughout the world. The acquisitions by Rona described in the Opening Case are horizontal acquisitions that allow Rona to meet the challenge from a significant competitor; these acquisitions have allowed the company to gain the market power needed to meet the competitive challenge presented by Home Depot. This objective is achieved much faster by using this approach than by developing new locations from the ground up.

In the latter half of the 20th century, acquisition became a prominent strategy used by major corporations to achieve growth and meet competitive challenges. Even smaller and more focused firms began employing acquisition strategies to grow and to enter new markets.[2] However, acquisition strategies are not without problems; a number of acquisitions fail. Thus, we focus on how acquisitions can be used to produce value for the firm's stakeholders.[3] Before describing attributes associated with effective acquisitions, we examine the most prominent problems companies experience when using an acquisition strategy. For example, when acquisitions contribute to poor performance, a firm may deem it necessary to restructure its operations. Closing the chapter are descriptions of three restructuring strategies, as well as the short- and long-term outcomes resulting from their use. Setting the stage for these topics is an examination of the popularity of mergers and acquisition and a discussion of the differences among mergers, acquisitions, and takeovers.

The Popularity of Merger and Acquisition Strategies

The acquisition strategy has been a popular strategy among North American firms for many years. Some believe that this strategy played a central role in an effective restructuring of businesses during the 1980s and 1990s and into the 21st century.[4] Increasingly, acquisition strategies are becoming more popular with firms in other nations and economic regions, including Europe. In fact, about 40 to 45 percent of the acquisitions in recent years have been made across country borders (i.e., a firm headquartered in one country acquiring a firm headquartered in another country).[5] For example, 40 percent of Wal-Mart's international growth has come through acquisitions, "and management remains open to further acquisitions."[6] Given the current level of consolidation within the banking industry in Canada, it is more likely that Canadian banks will make cross-border acquisitions in order to grow.[7]

Five waves of mergers and acquisitions took place in the 20th century, with the last two occurring in the 1980s and 1990s.[8] There were 55,000 acquisitions valued at $1.3 trillion in the 1980s, and acquisitions in the 1990s exceeded $11 trillion in value.[9] World economies slowed somewhat in the new millennium, reducing the number of mergers and acquisitions completed.[10] The annual value of mergers and acquisitions for 2000 was about $3.4 trillion and fell to about $1.75 trillion in 2001.[11] However, as the worldwide economy improved, the global volume of announced acquisition agreements was up to $2.7 trillion for 2005, $4 trillion for 2006, and a record $4.5 trillion in 2007.[12] The total for the three years 2005 to 2007 thus exceeded the total for the entire 1990s.

An acquisition strategy is sometimes used because of the uncertainty in the competitive landscape. A firm may make an acquisition to increase its market power because of a competitive threat, to enter a new market because of the opportunity available in that market, or to spread the risk due to the uncertain environment.[13] In addition, as volatility brings undesirable changes to its primary markets, a firm may acquire other companies to shift its core business into different markets.[14]

The strategic management process (refer to Figure 1.1) calls for an acquisition strategy to increase a firm's strategic competitiveness as well as its returns to shareholders. Thus, an acquisition strategy should be used only when the acquiring firm will be able to increase its value through ownership of an acquired firm and the use of its assets.[15]

However, evidence suggests that, at least for the acquiring firms, acquisition strategies may not always result in these desirable outcomes.[16] Researchers have found that shareholders of acquired firms often earn above-average returns from an acquisition while shareholders of acquiring firms are less likely to do so, typically earning returns from the transaction that are close to zero. In the acquisition boom between 1998 and 2000, acquiring-firm shareholders experienced significant losses relative to the losses in all of the 1980s. Acquiring-firm shareholders lost $0.12 on average for the acquisitions between 1998 and 2000, whereas in the 1980s shareholders lost $.016 per dollar spent. This may suggest that for large firms it is now more difficult to create sustainable value by using an acquisition strategy to buy publicly traded companies.[17] In approximately two-thirds of all acquisitions, the acquiring firm's stock price falls immediately after the intended transaction is announced. This negative response is an indication of investors' skepticism about the likelihood that the acquirer will be able to achieve the synergies required to justify the premium.[18]

Mergers, Acquisitions, and Takeovers: What Are the Differences?

A **merger** is a strategy through which two firms agree to integrate their operations on a relatively equal basis. There are few true mergers, because one party is usually dominant in regard to market share or firm size. DaimlerChrysler AG was termed a "merger of equals" and, although Daimler-Benz was the dominant party in the automakers' transaction, Chrysler managers would not allow the business deal to be completed unless it was termed a merger.[19]

An **acquisition** is a strategy through which one firm buys a controlling, or 100 percent, interest in another firm with the intent of making the acquired firm a subsidiary business within its portfolio. In this case, the management of the acquired firm reports to the management of the acquiring firm. While most mergers are friendly transactions, acquisitions can be friendly or unfriendly.

A **takeover** is a special type of an acquisition strategy wherein the target firm does not solicit the acquiring firm's bid. The number of unsolicited takeover bids increased in the economic downturn of 2001–2002, a common occurrence in economic recessions because the poorly managed firms that are undervalued relative to their assets are more easily identified.[20] Such bids may be harder in good times, as Barrick Gold found out with its $1.4-billion unsuccessful offer to take over NovaGold in 2007.[21] Many takeover attempts are not desired by the target firm's managers and are referred to as hostile. In a few cases, unsolicited offers may come from parties familiar and possibly friendly to the target firm.

On a comparative basis, acquisitions are more common than mergers and takeovers. Accordingly, this chapter focuses on acquisitions.

A **merger** is a strategy through which two firms agree to integrate their operations on a relatively equal basis.

An **acquisition** is a strategy through which one firm buys a controlling, or 100 percent, interest in another firm with the intent of making the acquired firm a subsidiary business within its portfolio.

A **takeover** is a special type of an acquisition strategy wherein the target firm does not solicit the acquiring firm's bid.

Reasons for Acquisitions

In this section, we discuss reasons supporting the use of an acquisition strategy—these are summarized in Figure 8.1. For ease of understanding, we have divided these into market and scope concerns versus organizational development concerns. Though each reason can provide a legitimate rationale for an acquisition, such a move may not necessarily lead to a competitive advantage (discussed later in the chapter).

Figure 8.1   Reasons for Acquisitions

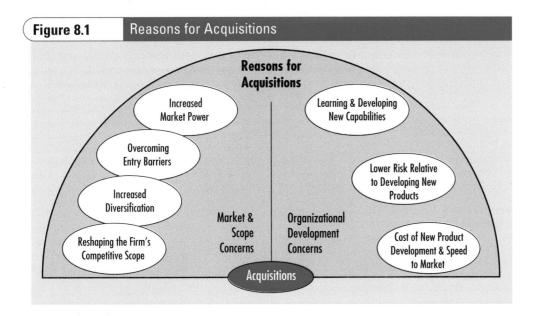

Increased Market Power

A primary reason for acquisitions is to achieve greater market power.[22] As defined in Chapter 7, *market power* exists when a firm is able to sell its goods or services above competitive levels or when the costs of its primary or support activities are below those of its competitors. Market power usually is derived from the size of the firm and its resources and capabilities to compete in the marketplace.[23] It is also affected by the firm's share of the market. Therefore, most acquisitions that are designed to achieve greater market power entail buying a competitor, a supplier, a distributor, or a business in a highly related industry to allow the exercise of a core competency and to gain competitive advantage in the acquiring firm's primary market. One goal in achieving market power is to become a market leader.[24] Again, Barrick Gold is an excellent example of a company that pursued its merger with Placer Dome to become the world's leading gold producer.[25] The performance improvement of the merged firm subsequent to a horizontal acquisition is even more significant than the average potential cost savings if marketing of the combined firms improves economies of scope.[26] To increase their market power, firms often use horizontal, vertical, and related acquisitions.

Horizontal Acquisitions

The acquisition of a company competing in the same industry as the acquiring firm is referred to as a *horizontal acquisition*. Horizontal acquisitions increase a firm's market power by exploiting cost-based and revenue-based synergies.[27] Research suggests that horizontal acquisitions result in higher performance when the firms have similar characteristics.[28] Examples of important similar characteristics include strategy, managerial styles, and resource allocation patterns. Similarities in these characteristics make the integration of the two firms proceed more smoothly.[29]

In 2004, when Roger Hardy was faced with an enticing opportunity to sell his firm at a high price, he made a different choice. "I didn't want to be consolidated," commented Hardy, CEO of Vancouver-based Coastalcontacts.com. "Why not become a global brand instead?" He did just that, by adopting an aggressive acquisition strategy and innovative customer service to build his company into the biggest online seller of contact lenses in Europe and the second-biggest in the world. The firm's total shipments have topped 100 million lenses.[30]

Horizontal acquisitions are often most effective when the acquiring firm integrates the acquired firm's assets with its assets, but only after evaluating and divesting excess capacity and assets that do not complement the newly combined firm's core competencies.[31] As the acquisition of Placer Dome by Barrick illustrates, the merged firm will likely have to divest itself of some facilities in order to reduce costs associated with the acquisition.[32]

Vertical Acquisitions

A *vertical acquisition* refers to a firm acquiring a supplier or distributor of one or more of its goods or services.[33] A firm becomes vertically integrated through this type of acquisition in that it controls additional parts of the value chain (see Chapters 4 and 7). After more than a quarter century of making cheese, Montreal's Saputo entered the fluid milk market, and within a few years had taken over Dairyworld Foods to become a major player in this raw material.[34]

Kodak's acquisition of Creo, a B.C. producer of devices that "convert computer-generated print files directly to plates used for printing," represents a vertical acquisition. Because Kodak's sales of traditional film and developing have been declining as more people turn to digital photography, Kodak has been acquiring firms that move it into the "filmless imaging" area. These acquisitions have included digital printing (as in the Creo acquisition), health care imaging, and consumer photography markets. Although the Creo acquisition is primarily focused on a corporate market, other acquisitions will allow Kodak to sell imaging products across a range of specialty (e.g., health care) and consumer markets.[35]

Vertical acquisitions also occur in service and entertainment businesses. Sony's acquisition of Columbia Pictures in the late 1980s was a vertical acquisition in which Columbia's movie content could be used by Sony's hardware devices. Sony's additional acquisition of CBS Records, a music producer, and development of the PlayStation hardware have formed the bases for more vertical integration. The spread of broadband and the technological shift from analogue to digital hardware require media firms to find new ways to sell their content to consumers. Sony's former CEO Nobuyuki Idei believed that this shift created a new opportunity to sell hardware that integrates this change by selling "televisions, personal computers, game consoles and handheld devices through which all of that wonderful content will one day be streaming."[36]

However, this vision has not functioned well, and Idei was replaced by Howard Stringer as CEO—the first American CEO in Sony's history. Sony's businesses were quite autonomous, and the coordination between them to realize Idei's vision proved difficult to establish. As well, the lack of coordination caused a slowdown in innovation such that "Sony's reputation as an innovator" has suffered as "the snazziest gadgets from competitors, like the iPod and the TiVo digital video recorder, increasingly depend on the specific juggling act that Sony cannot do well: integrating hardware, software and services."[37]

Related Acquisitions

The acquisition of a firm in a highly related industry is referred to as a *related acquisition*. Sun Microsystems Inc.'s main business has been selling computer workstations and servers. However, Sun's performance has suffered because its server business is highly competitive. Because of increased storage needs that are readily accessible by servers, servers and disk storage devices (versus tapes, which are not as accessible) are more often now sold together. In order to take advantage of this growing opportunity, Sun agreed to acquire Storage Technology Corp. for $4.1 billion. "The purchase also will add about 1,000 Storage Technology's sales representatives to sell Sun's disk-based storage systems against tough rivals such as EMC Corp., Hewlett-Packard Co. and International Business Machines Corp."[38] However, because of the difficulty in achieving synergy, related acquisitions are often difficult to value.[39]

Acquisitions intended to increase market power are subject to regulatory review as well as to analysis by financial markets.[40] For example, as noted in the Opening Case, takeovers in the banking industry received a significant amount of government scrutiny as well as close examination by financial analysts. Thus, firms seeking growth and market power through acquisitions must understand the political/legal segment of the general environment (see Chapter 3) in order to successfully use an acquisition strategy.

Overcoming Entry Barriers

Barriers to entry (introduced in Chapter 3) are factors associated with the market or with the firms currently operating in it that increase the expense and difficulty faced by new ventures trying to enter that particular market. For example, well-established competitors may have substantial economies of scale in the manufacture or service of their products. In addition, enduring relationships with customers often create product loyalties that are difficult for new entrants to overcome. When facing differentiated products, new entrants typically must spend considerable resources to advertise their goods or services and may find it necessary to sell at prices below competitors' to entice customers.

Facing the entry barriers created by economies of scale and differentiated products, a new entrant may find acquiring an established company to be more effective than entering the market as a competitor offering a good or service that is unfamiliar to current buyers. In fact, the higher the barriers to market entry, the greater the probability that a firm will acquire an existing firm to overcome them. Although an acquisition can be expensive, it does provide the new entrant with immediate market access.

For example, Toronto's Nortel Networks purchased PEC Solutions for $448 million. Through this acquisition, the new subsidiary, called Nortel PEC Solutions, inherited government contracts in the growing market pertaining to homeland security, intelligence, and defence. This gives Nortel a stronger stake in the federal computer networks market. Although other federal programs have been cut, the budget for information technology increased from the proposed $60 billion in 2005 to $65 billion in 2006. Before the purchase, only 40 of Nortel's 30,000 employees worldwide had security clearances from the U.S. government. Nortel's purchase of PEC significantly increased this number, allowing Nortel to overcome considerable barriers to entry in this growing market. Furthermore, the combined company allows Nortel PEC to compete with the U.S.'s largest contractors such as Lockheed Martin and Northrop Grumman. The acquisition has allowed Nortel to transition into this government service market much more rapidly than it would have been able to without buying a current player in the market. It also has given Nortel improved access to a market for its "large-scale telecommunications equipment."[41]

As in the Nortel example, firms trying to enter international markets often face steep entry barriers. However, acquisitions are commonly used to overcome those barriers.[42] At least for large multinational corporations, another indicator of the importance of entering and then competing successfully in international markets is the fact that five emerging markets (China, India, Brazil, Mexico, and Indonesia) are among the 12 largest economies in the world, with a combined purchasing power that is already one-half that of the Group of Seven industrial nations (Canada, Britain, France, Germany, Italy, Japan, and the U.S.). Furthermore, emerging markets are among the fastest growing economies in the world.[43]

Cross-Border Acquisitions

Acquisitions made between companies with headquarters in different countries are called *cross-border acquisitions* (as exemplified in the Strategic Focus). These acquisitions are often made to overcome entry barriers. In Chapter 10, we examine cross-border alliances and the reason for their use. Compared with a cross-border alliance, a cross-border acquisition gives a firm more control over its international operations.[44]

ArcelorMittal Becomes the Largest Worldwide Steel Producer via a Cross-Border Acquisition Strategy

Mittal Steel Company was formed in 2004 through the combination of Ispat/LNM Holdings and International Steel Group (ISG). At the close of these deals, Lakshmi N. Mittal became CEO of the largest steel company in the world. The company had the capacity to ship 60 million metric tons annually and predicted annual revenues of more than $32 billion. With this combination it outpaced its closest rival, Arcelor SA. Arcelor was formed in 2002 by a merger among Arbed SA of Luxembourg, Usinor SA of France, and Aceraliasa SA of Spain. Early in 2004 Arcelor SA invested $1.2 billion to obtain a 60-percent interest in Companhia Siderurgica de Tubarao, Brazil's second largest crude-steel producer. Thus, significant consolidation in the industry is taking place through cross-border horizontal acquisitions.

The formation of Mittal was no simple arrangement. To create the company, LNM Holdings, privately held by the Mittal family, was acquired by Ipsat, a publicly traded firm. Ipsat was then combined with ISG to form the Mittal Steel Company. Through ISG, Mittal Steel acquired about 40 percent of the North American market in flat-rolled-steel used in automobiles.

ISG—a combination of LTV Steel, Acme Steel, Bethlehem Steel, Weirton Steel, and Georgetown Steel—was created through deals put together by Wilbur Ross, a private equity investor. Most of these ventures had been bankrupt and Ross picked them up rather cheaply during the steel industry downturn of 1999–2000. The bankrupt firms did not have large pension fund liabilities, which would be a drag on earnings.

In 2005, Mittal Steel and Arcelor produced, respectively, 60 million and 44 million metric tons of steel annually. This accounted for less than 10 percent of the total capacity in this global industry. Thus, there was still significant room for additional cross-border and domestic horizontal acquisitions to build more concentration in the globalized steel industry.

Arcelor had been using a cross-border strategy to reduce costs by moving much of its higher-cost European capacity to lower-cost countries such as Brazil, hence the 2004 deal with Siderurgica de Tubarao. Brazil is a great place to manufacture steel because it has plentiful raw materials for steel making and also a surging demand for products that use steel, such as autos. Because the raw product is cheaper to manufacture there, Brazil has become the world's ninth-largest producer of crude steel. Arcelor was seeking to build more value-added products in Brazil. The move allowed Arcelor to make steel at a lower price and add value at its European rolling mills (where the raw product can be converted to higher-quality steel). Thus, the Brazilian operations provided a significant cost advantage for Arcelor through its cross-border acquisition.

Mittal Steel's predecessor company, LNM Holdings, had bought many steel businesses in emerging-market countries, especially in Eastern Europe. LNM sought to consolidate and invest significant amounts to improve productivity in the steel firms. Mittal was similarly looking for deals in Turkey, India, and China.

However, the biggest possible acquisition for Mittal was logically Arcelor. So, in 2006, Mittal made the biggest deal it could—it merged with Arcelor to form ArcelorMittal. The combined company has more than $100 billion in sales and 300,000 employees, who produce more than 100 million tonnes of steel. Though promoted as a merger of equals, Lakshmi N. Mittal is still in charge of the company. Even after the big deal to create the company, ArcelorMittal is still actively acquiring companies. To solidify its presence in Latin America, in 2006 ArcelorMittal acquired Mexico's Sicartsa, the country's leading steel producer, and Grupo Villacero, Mexico's largest steel distributor. In late 2007, ArcelorMittal also bought Cínter S.A., an important stainless steel tube producer located in Uruguay.

All this activity has been supported by high steel prices, a result of the high demand for steel created by the hypergrowth in China and other emerging-market countries. However, China was recently identified as a net exporter, suggesting that the country's domestic demand is slowing. This implies that steel-making capacity around the world may soon grow into oversupply and signal decreasing prices and difficult times in the years ahead. This would be even more problematic because many nations have supported subsidies and loan guarantees to increase production around the world. Thus, besides the consolidation through acquisitions, a significant increase in productive capacity is also being projected. If overcapacity becomes a serious problem in the future larger firms may have a difficult time unless they are much more productive than their competitors and can reduce costs as the price comes down. However, such competition may also lead to further consolidation and additional cross-border acquisitions of companies that are not competitive.

SOURCES: 2008, ArcelorMittal Web page, http://www.arcelormittal.com/index.php?lang=en, July 21; 2007, Mittal press releases, http://www.arcelormittal.com/index.php?lang=en&page=49, December 31; 2005, Mittal completes buy of ISG, *Platt's Metal Week*, April 18, 20; 2005, Business: The wrong worry; steel, *The Economist*, March 12, 80; S. Reed & A. Ashton, 2005, Steel: The mergers aren't over yet, *BusinessWeek*, February 21, 6; P. Barta & P. Glader, 2004, China's steel threat may be excess not shortage, *Wall Street Journal*, December 30, A1, A2; P. Glader, 2004, Mittals see Turkey, Asia as next stops, *Wall Street Journal*, October 28, A3; P. Glader & V. Knight, 2004, Arcelor to invest as much as $1.2 billion in Brazil, *Wall Street Journal*, June 29, A2; M. Pinkham & C. C. Petry, 2004, Merger of Ipsat, ISG forms steel giant, *Metal Standard News*, November, 48–49; S. Reed & M. Arndt, 2004, The raja of steel, *BusinessWeek*, December 20, 50–52; A. Sloan, 2004, The tough deal that saved steel, *Newsweek*, November 8, 46.

Historically, U.S. firms have been the most active acquirers of companies outside their domestic market.[45] However, in the global economy, companies throughout the world are choosing this strategic option with increasing frequency. In recent years, cross-border acquisitions have represented as much as 45 percent of the total number of annual acquisitions.[46] Because of relaxed regulations, the amount of cross-border activity among nations within the European community also continues to increase. The fact that many large European corporations have approached the limits of growth within their domestic markets and thus seek growth in other markets is what some analysts believe accounts for the growth in the range of cross-border acquisitions. Research has indicated that many European and North American firms participated in cross-border acquisitions across Asian countries that experienced a financial crisis due to significant currency devaluations in 1997. These acquisitions, it is argued, facilitated the survival and restructuring of many large Asian companies such that these economies recovered more quickly than they would have without the cross-border acquisitions.[47]

As illustrated in the Strategic Focus, firms in the steel industry are completing a number of large cross-border acquisitions. Although cross-border acquisitions are taking place across a wide variety of industries to overcome entry barriers (see the Opening Case), such acquisitions can be difficult to negotiate and operate because of the differences in foreign cultures.[48]

Increased Diversification

Acquisitions are also used to diversify firms. Based on experience and the insights resulting from it, firms typically find it easier to develop and introduce new products in markets currently served by the firm. In contrast, it is difficult for companies to develop products that differ from their current lines for markets in which they lack experience.[49] Thus, it is uncommon for a firm to develop new products internally to diversify its product lines.[50] Using acquisitions to diversify a firm is the quickest and, typically, the easiest way to change its portfolio of businesses.[51]

With about $32 billion in revenue and more than 220,000 employees, Onex Corporation is one of Canada's biggest companies. Onex is a global leader in electronics manufacturing services (EMS) through its ownership in Celestica. Growing from a single facility in Toronto that the company acquired in 1996, Onex has completed over three dozen acquisitions to build the company into a leading global EMS provider with about 40 facilities spread throughout the Americas, Europe, and Asia. What Onex typically does is to buy into an unrelated business and follow up its initial purchase with related acquisitions in the same or similar lines of business.[52] For example, about 20 percent of Onex's revenues come from health-related activities—a field completely unrelated to Celestica. In January 2005, Onex bought a medical imaging company. In February 2005, Onex acquired a company that provided contracted emergency response services and another that provided outsourced services for hospitals (staffing, management, accreditation, billing, and recordkeeping services). In December 2005, Onex acquired Skilled Healthcare—an organization of nursing and assisted-living-facility operators. In April 2007, Onex acquired another imaging company, Carestream Health, a leading global provider of medical and dental imaging products and services.

Both related diversification and unrelated diversification strategies can be implemented through acquisitions.[53] As shown in the Strategic Focus, Vancouver's Jim Pattison Group has used both types of acquisitions to build a conglomerate. Like Onex, Pattison buys into an unrelated business and follows up its initial purchase with related acquisitions in the same line of business.

Research has shown that the more related the acquired firm is to the acquiring firm, the greater the probability is that the acquisition will be successful.[54] Thus, horizontal acquisitions (through which a firm acquires a competitor) and related acquisitions tend to contribute more to the firm's strategic competitiveness than would the acquisition of a company that operates in product markets quite different from those in which the acquiring firm competes.[55]

Reshaping the Firm's Competitive Scope

As discussed in Chapter 3, the intensity of competitive rivalry is an industry characteristic that affects the firm's profitability.[56] To reduce the negative effect of an intense rivalry on their financial performance, firms may use acquisitions to lessen their dependence on one or more products or markets. Reducing a company's dependence on specific markets alters the firm's competitive scope. As explained in the Strategic Focus, the Jim Pattison Group has used acquisitions extensively to reshape the group's competitive scope—though it can be difficult to see a consistently logical set of businesses.

Learning and Developing New Capabilities

Some acquisitions are made to gain capabilities the firm does not possess. For example, acquisitions may be used to acquire a special technological capability. Research has shown that firms can broaden their knowledge base and reduce inertia through acquisitions.[57] Therefore, acquiring a firm with skills and capabilities that differ from its own helps the acquiring firm to gain access to new knowledge and remain agile.[58] For example, research suggests that firms increase the potential of their capabilities when they acquire diverse talent through cross-border acquisitions. When this is done, greater value is created through the international expansion versus a simple acquisition without such diversity and potential for resource creation.[59] Of course, firms are better able to learn these capabilities if they share some similar properties with the firm's current capabilities. Thus, firms should seek to acquire companies with different but related and complementary capabilities in order to build their own knowledge base.[60]

One of the primary goals at Cisco Systems for its early acquisitions was to gain access to capabilities that it needed to compete in the fast-changing networking equipment industry that connects the Internet. Cisco developed an intricate process to quickly integrate the acquired firms and their capabilities (knowledge). Cisco's processes accounted for its phenomenal success in the latter half of the 1990s. However, it has expanded the goal to include more internal cooperation to "avoid the diving catch."[61] Though it is not acquiring companies at the same rate as it did during the tech boom (Cisco made 23 acquisitions in 2000 alone), it has averaged about 10 per year since 2003. Since 2003,

Making Sense of the Jim Pattison Group

One of Canada's largest privately owned companies, Vancouver's Jim Pattison Group, has more than $6 billion in sales and almost 30,000 employees. It became that size through numerous acquisitions and is still actively seeking acquisitions. If there is a theme to the Jim Pattison Group of products and services, it is that they get things to the customer and they make sure the customer knows those things are there.

The Jim Pattison Group began in 1961 as a car dealership. Pattison still sells cars, though he has acquired dealerships for new Chrysler, Hyundai, Lexus, Suzuki, Toyota, and Volvo sales and leases—13 dealerships in all in southwestern B.C. In other words, Pattison will sell you the car to take you to market. If you live in Alberta or B.C. there is some chance that market is part of the Jim Pattison Group.

Pattison's next big retail purchase was in 1968 when the firm acquired the Overwaitea Foods Group (OFG). He grew the group from there and now OFG includes 111 stores in Alberta and British Columbia under the names Save-On-Foods, Overwaitea, Urban Fare, PriceSmart, Bulkley Valley Wholesale, and Cooper's (acquired in 1999). To back up this growth, in 1995 Pattison bought Buy-Low Foods—the largest food wholesale distributor to independents in Canada. The three companies in the Buy-Low group—Buy-Low Foods, Associated Grocers, and Van-Whole Produce (acquired in 2001)—now service nearly 1,800 supermarkets, convenience, and specialty produce markets along with 24 corporate and franchise stores under the banners Buy-Low, Nesters Market, Shop n' Save, and Budget Foods.

Don't want to cook tonight? Well, Pattison does not run a chain of fast food places! They do, however, make foam-hinged "to go" containers through their packaging division acquired in 1990. So when you get take-out, you may be taking it home in one of the company's containers. Not only does Pattison get you to his markets in the car he sold you, but some of the products in that market may be packaged in containers made by the group. And it goes beyond food product containers. The Group's Montebello subsidiary (also acquired in 1990) manufactures aluminum, laminate, foil, and plastic tubes and cans. These products may be used for pharmaceutical ointments, personal care products, cosmetics, food products, ink markers, adhesives, sealants, or even cigar humidors.

The Jim Pattison Group can very well toot its own horn through its media group. Pattison bought his first radio station in 1965 and in 2000 acquired 13 more, along with 2 television stations. Today Pattison has 19 radio stations throughout British Columbia, and three television stations (two in the B.C. interior and one in Medicine Hat, Alberta). The broadcast group is now Canada's largest private western-based broadcasting company.

Think you can escape Pattison by turning off the radio? Pattison Outdoor's advertising can get the message across with an array of ads in transit shelters and on highway superboards, wall murals, mall posters, and transit and airport advertising. Pattison has been in the billboard business since 1967, when he acquired Seaboard Outdoor Advertising.

One thing the organization might advertise is the unique attractions within Pattison's entertainment group. The organization purchased Ripley's Believe It or Not in 1985. The Ripley's empire now includes over a dozen attractions in eight countries, across four continents. The group's six Guinness World Records Attractions "bring feats of human endeavour to life in six museums that feature the fastest, heaviest, tallest, shortest," and so on. With six locations over three continents, Guinness complements the unusual nature of Pattison's attractions.

Even if the product being touted is not owned by Pattison, Pattison may have a role in its promotion. The Pattison Sign Group manufactures a range of signs to help customers enhance their corporate identity. Some of the company's clients include Rona, CNN, McDonald's Restaurants of Canada, The Source by Circuit City, Movie Gallery, Vancity, Enterprise Rent-a-car, and the North American divisions of Volkswagen, Audi, and Toyota. Pattison began this business when the group acquired Neon Products of Vancouver in 1967.

(continued)

If they did not make the sign for it, Pattison may well have helped deliver the printed advertisement. Beginning with the acquisition of Provincial News of Edmonton in 1969, Pattison has become North America's second-largest magazine and book wholesaler. The firm operates mainly under The News Group name throughout Canada and the U.S. The News Group has captured over 50 percent of the Canadian market and 30 percent of the total North American market. As a periodical supplier, the group distributes more than 4,500 different magazines and well over 10,000 book titles. The News Group receives, processes, delivers, and tracks over 1 billion periodical copies each year.

This does not mean that everything fits perfectly into the mix at the Jim Pattison Group. While most of the company's businesses fit the theme of getting things to customers and making sure that they know they are there, some businesses do not seem to fit. These businesses include canneries and coal shipping. While these interests fit oddly into the Group, it does not mean that they do not have potential for future profitable growth. As part of the food group, Pattison acquired Canfisco in 1984. Canfisco operates three major fish processing plants in Vancouver and Prince Rupert, B.C. The company is the largest supplier of canned salmon to the Canadian market. The group is expanding its nutraceutical market segment with its 100% Pure Wild Sockeye Salmon Oil, a dietary supplement that may have great promise for the future. Pattison's export and investments group includes Westshore Terminals, acquired in 1994. This facility is Canada's leading coal export facility and the West Coast's largest dry bulk terminal. With the growth of the Asian market and a need for all kinds of resources, this operation is likely to have a great future as well.

SOURCES: 2007, Jim Pattison Group Web page, http://www.jimpattison.com, December 30, 2004; A. Biesada, 2004, Jim Pattison Group Profile, Hoover's Online, http://www.hoovers.com/jim-pattison-group/--ID__43507--/free-co-factsheet.xhtml, April 23; A. Biesada, 2004, Overwaitea Food Group Profile, Hoover's Online, http://www. hoovers.com/overwaitea/--ID__107275--/free-co-factsheet.xhtml, accessed April 23; Z. Olijnyk, 2003, Jim Pattison Group, *Canadian Business*, 76(10): 162.

the largest acquisitions have dealt with a range of potential growth areas: wireless, security, and on-demand collaboration. Cisco acquired wireless companies Airespace in 2005 for $450 million and Navini Networks in 2007 for $330 million. In 2007, Cisco also picked up Web security company IronPort for $830 million and collaboration applications market leader WebEx for $3.2 billion.[62]

Lower Risk Relative to Developing New Products

Because the outcomes of an acquisition can be estimated more easily and accurately than the outcomes of an internal product development process, managers may view acquisitions as lowering risk.[63] The difference in risk between an internal product development process and an acquisition can be seen in the results of Pfizer's strategy and that of its competitors described above.[64]

As with other strategic actions discussed in this book, the firm must exercise caution when using a strategy of acquiring new products rather than developing them internally. While research suggests that acquisitions have become a common means of avoiding risky internal ventures (and therefore risky R&D investments), they may also become a substitute for innovation.[65] Thus, acquisitions are not a risk-free alternative to entering new markets through internally developed products.

Cost of New Product Development and Increased Speed to Market

Developing new products internally and successfully introducing them into the marketplace often require significant investments of a firm's resources, including time, making it difficult to quickly earn a profitable return.[66] Also of concern to firms' managers is achieving adequate returns from the capital invested to develop and commercialize new products—an estimated 88 percent of innovations fail to achieve adequate returns. Perhaps contributing to these less-than-desirable rates of return is the successful imitation of approximately 60 percent of innovations within four years after the patents are obtained. Because of outcomes like these, managers often perceive internal product development as a high-risk activity.[67]

Acquisitions are another means a firm can use to gain access to new products and to current products that are new to the firm. Compared with internal product development processes, acquisitions provide more predictable returns as well as faster market entry. Returns are more predictable because the performance of the acquired firm's products can be assessed prior to completing the acquisition.[68] For these reasons, extensive bidding wars and acquisitions are more frequent in high-technology industries.[69]

Acquisition activity is also extensive throughout the pharmaceutical industry, where firms frequently use acquisitions to enter markets quickly, to overcome the high costs of developing products internally, and to increase the predictability of returns on their investments. The cost of bringing a new drug to market was "pushing $900 million and the average time to launch stretched to 12 years." Interestingly, there was one large deal between pharmaceutical firms in 2004, the merger between French firms Sanofi Synthelabo and Avenus that created Sanofi-Avenus. This $67-billion deal accounted for most of the $77.5-billion total value of deals between pharmaceutical firms that year. Although merger activity continued through 2005, 2006, and 2007, the totals were at least 25 percent off the 2004 peak.[70] Most of these deals were smaller, as many companies targeted small acquisitions to supplement market power and reinvigorate or create innovative drug pipelines. Usually it is larger biotech or pharmaceutical firms acquiring smaller biotech firms that have drug opportunities close to market entry.[71]

As indicated previously, compared with internal product development, acquisitions result in more rapid market entries.[72] Acquisitions often represent the fastest means to enter international markets and help firms overcome the liabilities associated with such strategic moves.[73] Acquisitions provide rapid access both to new markets and to new capabilities. Using new capabilities to pioneer new products and to enter markets quickly can create advantageous market positions.[74]

Companies in the medical field, for example, can access new products through acquisitions of other medical manufacturers. In early 2005, MDS—a billion-dollar Toronto-based company engaged in pharmaceutical contract research, medical isotopes, and analytical instruments manufacturing—acquired Molecular Devices. Molecular Devices produces instruments for screening, cellular analysis, and biochemical testing.[75] Pharmaceutical companies can also acquire biotechnology firms both for new products and for new technological capabilities. Pharmaceutical firms often provide the manufacturing and marketing capabilities to take the new products developed by biotechnology firms to the market.[76] For example, in 2005 Pfizer agreed to acquire Angiosyn, Inc., a smaller biotech company that has developed a promising drug to avoid blindness. The deal, valued near $527 million, could extend Pfizer's lead in drugs for eye diseases. This deal "spotlights the interest among the largest pharmaceutical makers to purchasing fledgling biotech concerns."[77]

Problems in Achieving Acquisition Success

Acquisition strategies based on reasons described in this chapter can increase strategic competitiveness and help firms earn above-average returns. However, acquisition strategies are not risk-free. Reasons for the use of acquisition strategies and potential problems with such strategies are shown in Figure 8.2. For ease of understanding, we have divided these into administrative difficulties and strategic difficulties.

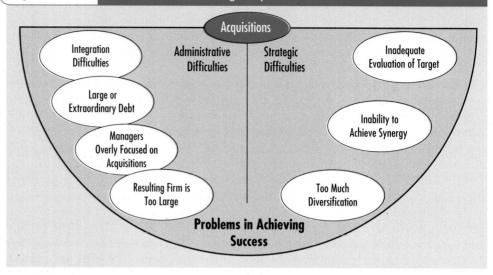

Figure 8.2 Problems in Achieving Acquisition Success

Acquisitions

Integration Difficulties

Large or Extraordinary Debt

Managers Overly Focused on Acquisitions

Resulting Firm is Too Large

Administrative Difficulties

Strategic Difficulties

Inadequate Evaluation of Target

Inability to Achieve Synergy

Too Much Diversification

Problems in Achieving Success

Research suggests that perhaps 20 percent of all mergers and acquisitions are successful, approximately 60 percent produce disappointing results, and the remaining 20 percent are clear failures.[78] Successful acquisitions generally involve having a well-conceived strategy for selecting the target, not paying too high a premium, and employing an effective integration process.[79] As shown in Figure 8.1, several problems may prevent successful acquisitions.

Integration Difficulties

Integrating two companies following an acquisition can be quite difficult. Integration challenges include melding two disparate corporate cultures, linking different financial and control systems, building effective working relationships (particularly when management styles differ), and resolving problems regarding the status of the newly acquired firm's executives.[80]

The importance of a successful integration should not be underestimated.[81] Without it, an acquisition is unlikely to produce positive returns. Thus, as suggested by a researcher studying the process, "managerial practice and academic writings show that the post-acquisition integration phase is probably the single most important determinant of shareholder value creation (and equally of value destruction) in mergers and acquisitions."[82] Integration is complex and involves a large number of activities, which if overlooked can lead to significant difficulties.

It is important to maintain the human capital of the target firm after the acquisition. Much of an organization's knowledge is contained in its human capital.[83] Turnover of key personnel from the acquired firm can have a negative effect on the performance of the merged firm.[84] The loss of key personnel, such as critical managers, weakens the acquired firm's capabilities and reduces its value. If implemented effectively, the integration process can have a positive effect on target firm managers and reduce the probability that they will leave.[85] In the two years after EnCana was created out of Alberta Energy and PanCanadian, their stock rose 14 percent and the company met its goal of reducing annual operating expenses by $250 million. To do this, executives made sure the merged company came together quickly. Within six months after announcing the deal, shareholders and courts had given their approval, EnCana stock was trading in Toronto and

New York, all layoffs of redundant employees had been substantially completed, and employees knew who their supervisors were and what their compensation would be.[86]

Large or Extraordinary Debt

To finance a number of acquisitions completed during the 1980s and 1990s, some companies significantly increased their levels of debt. A financial innovation called junk bonds helped make this increase possible. *Junk bonds* are a financing option through which risky acquisitions are financed with money (debt) that provides a large potential return to lenders (bondholders). Because junk bonds are unsecured obligations that are not tied to specific assets for collateral, interest rates for these high-risk debt instruments sometimes reached between 18 and 20 percent during the 1980s.[87] Some prominent financial economists viewed debt as a means to discipline managers, causing them to act in the shareholders' best interests.[88]

Junk bonds are now used less frequently to finance acquisitions, and the conviction that debt disciplines managers is less strong. Nonetheless, some firms still take on significant debt to acquire companies. For example, when Izzy Asper's CanWest Global Communications acquired the assets of Conrad Black's Hollinger newspaper chain for $3.5 billion in 2000, it was the biggest media deal in Canadian history. While the deal turned CanWest into a dominant media player overnight, it also saddled the company with more than $4 billion in debt.[89] For the better half of a decade the deal's debt restricted the company's acquisition strategy. It was not until 2007 that CanWest even attempted a major acquisition—its $2.3-billion takeover of Alliance Atlantis Communications. Even that deal required significant help from a partnership with New York investment bank Goldman Sachs.[90]

High debt can have several negative effects on the firm. For example, because high debt increases the likelihood of bankruptcy, it can lead to a downgrade in the firm's credit rating by agencies such as Moody's and Standard & Poor's.[91] In addition, high debt may preclude needed investment in activities that contribute to the firm's long-term success, such as R&D, human resource training, and marketing.[92] Still, leverage can be a positive force in a firm's development, allowing it to take advantage of attractive expansion opportunities. However, too much leverage (such as extraordinary debt) can lead to negative outcomes, including postponing or eliminating investments, such as R&D expenditures, that are necessary to maintain strategic competitiveness over the long term.

Managers Overly Focused on Acquisitions

Typically, a considerable amount of managerial time and energy is required for acquisition strategies to contribute to the firm's strategic competitiveness. Activities with which managers become involved include (1) searching for viable acquisition candidates, (2) completing effective due-diligence processes, (3) preparing for negotiations, and (4) managing the integration process after the acquisition is completed.

Top-level managers do not personally gather all of the data and information required to make acquisitions. However, these executives do make critical decisions on the firms to be targeted, the nature of the negotiations, and so forth. Company experiences show that participating in and overseeing the activities required for making acquisitions can divert managerial attention from other matters that are necessary for long-term competitive success, such as identifying and taking advantage of other opportunities and interacting with important external stakeholders.[93]

Both theory and research suggest that managers can become overly involved in the process of making acquisitions.[94] One observer suggested: "The urge to merge is still like an addiction in many companies: doing deals is much more fun and interesting than fixing fundamental problems. So, as in dealing with any other addiction or temptation, maybe it is best to just say no."[95] The over-involvement can be surmounted by learning from mistakes and by not having too much agreement in the board room. Dissent is helpful to make sure that all sides of a question are considered (see Chapter 11).[96] When failure does occur, leaders may be tempted to blame the failure on others and on unforeseen circumstances rather than on their excessive involvement in the acquisition process.[97]

There are a number of examples of being overly focused on making the deal. One more recent example is Hewlett-Packard's (HP) acquisition of Compaq Computer. CEO Carly Fiorina had to battle shareholders to carry out the deal in 2002. In the process, employees and managers at both firms became overly consumed with the deal and lost significant focus on operations. In the end, "HP's shareholders paid $24 billion in stock to buy Compaq and in exchange got relatively little value."[98] Fiorina lost her job and Mark Hurd, the new CEO, has a major job retrenching and reorganizing HP's businesses.[99]

Another interesting case is Japan's Livedoor. By age 32, CEO Takafumi Horie had developed an acquisitive publicly traded company worth about $8 billion. His firm, Livedoor, had acquired 50 other companies including a second-hand car dealer, a securities firm, and an Internet portal. In 2005, Horie made the unheard-of move of launching a hostile takeover bid of another firm: Nippon Broadcasting, an arm of Japan's venerable Fuji TV.[100] The bid failed, but it did attract the attention of regulators. While Horie's obsession with acquisitions had created a sizable enterprise, it did not promote any detailed attention to the firm's finances.[101] In 2006, Horie was arrested and convicted for the financial machinations needed to build Livedoor. The company's stock crashed and parts of it have since been sold off.[102]

The Resulting Firm Is Too Large

Most acquisitions create a larger firm, which should help increase its economies of scale. These economies can then lead to more efficient operations—for example, the two sales organizations can be integrated using fewer sales reps because a sales rep can sell the products of both firms (particularly if the products of the acquiring and target firms are highly related).

Many firms seek increases in size because of the potential economies of scale and enhanced market power (discussed earlier). At some level, the additional costs required to manage the larger firm will exceed the benefits of the economies of scale and additional market power. Additionally, there is an incentive to grow larger because size serves as a takeover defence.[103] Research in the United Kingdom indicates that firms that acquire other firms and grow larger are less likely to be taken over.[104]

The complexities generated by the larger size often lead managers to implement more bureaucratic controls to manage the combined firm's operations. *Bureaucratic controls* are formalized supervisory and behavioural rules and policies designed to ensure consistency of decisions and actions across different units of a firm. However, through time, formalized controls often lead to relatively rigid and standardized managerial behaviour. Certainly, in the long run, the diminished flexibility that accompanies rigid and standardized managerial behaviour may produce less innovation. Because of innovation's importance to competitive success, the bureaucratic controls resulting from a large organization (that is, built by acquisitions) can have a detrimental effect on performance.[105]

Toronto's Brookfield Asset Management, for example, manages about $90 billion in assets. Over three-quarters of these assets are from investment financing and funds, as well as commercial property ownership and management. The remaining parts of the company include the operation of power plants, the administration of power distribution facilities, and the management of timber resources.[106] In early 2008, the company spun off its interests in the electricity transmission and timber operations in Canada, the United States, Chile, and Brazil as Brookfield Infrastructure Partners.[107] The spinoff is designed to give investors a clearer picture of what each company does—that is, the move "is intended to create a pure-play infrastructure investment and make it easier to raise capital."[108]

Inadequate Evaluation of Target

Due diligence is a process through which a potential acquirer evaluates a target firm for acquisition. In an effective due-diligence process, hundreds of items are examined in areas as diverse as the financing for the intended transaction, differences in cultures between the acquiring and target firm, tax consequences of the transaction, and actions that would be necessary to successfully meld the two workforces. Due diligence is commonly performed by investment bankers, accountants, lawyers, and management consultants specializing in that activity, although firms actively pursuing acquisitions may form their own internal due-diligence team.[109]

The failure to complete an effective due-diligence process may easily result in the acquiring firm paying an excessive premium for the target company. In fact, research shows that without due diligence, "the purchase price is driven by the pricing of other 'comparable' acquisitions rather than by a rigorous assessment of where, when, and how management can drive real performance gains. [In these cases], the price paid may have little to do with achievable value."[110] Analysts questioned whether Nortel, for instance, paid too much for PEC Solutions mentioned earlier; PEC's stock price increased by $4.01 to close at $15.32 on the day the acquisition was announced,[111] suggesting the size of the premium Nortel paid.

Many firms once used investment banks to perform their due diligence, but in the post–Enron era the process is increasingly performed in-house. While investment bankers such as Credit Suisse First Boston and Citibank still play a large role in due diligence for large mergers and acquisitions, their role in smaller mergers and acquisitions seems to be decreasing. A growing number of companies are building their own internal operations to offer advice about and to finance mergers. However, although investment banks are playing a lesser role, there will always be the need for an outside opinion for a company's board of directors—to reassure them about a planned merger and reduce their liability.[112]

Inability to Achieve Synergy

Derived from *synergos*, a Greek word that means "working together," *synergy* exists when the value created by units working together exceeds the value those units could create working independently (see Chapter 7). That is, synergy exists when assets are worth more when used in conjunction with each other than when they are used separately.[113] For shareholders, synergy generates gains in their wealth that they could not duplicate or exceed through their own portfolio diversification decisions.[114] Synergy is created by the efficiencies derived from economies of scale and economies of scope and by sharing resources (e.g., human capital and knowledge) across the businesses in the merged firm.[115]

A firm develops a competitive advantage through an acquisition strategy only when a transaction generates private synergy. *Private synergy* is created when the combination and integration of the acquiring and acquired firms' assets yields capabilities and core competencies that could not be developed by combining and integrating either firm's assets with another company. Private synergy is possible when firms' assets are complementary in unique ways; that is, the unique type of asset complementarity is not possible by combining either company's assets with another firm's assets.[116] Because of its uniqueness, private synergy is difficult for competitors to understand and imitate. However, private synergy is difficult to create.

A firm's ability to account for costs that are necessary to create anticipated revenue- and cost-based synergies affects the acquisition's success. Firms experience several expenses when trying to create private synergy through acquisitions. Called transaction costs, these expenses are incurred when firms use acquisition strategies to create synergy.[117] Transaction costs may be direct or indirect. Direct costs include legal fees and charges from investment bankers who complete due diligence for the acquiring firm. Indirect costs include managerial time to evaluate target firms and then to complete negotiations, as well as the loss of key managers and employees following an acquisition.[118] Firms tend to underestimate the sum of indirect costs when the value of the synergy that may be created by combining and integrating the acquired firm's assets with the acquiring firm's assets is calculated.

Monsanto is one of the leading firms in developing strains of seed for basic food sources such as corn and soy beans. To pursue additional opportunities it purchased Seminis for $1.4 billion.[119] This deal "marks Monsanto's entry into the market for non-genetically modified fruits and vegetable seeds." Seminis has significant market share in these basic seed areas. For example, it has 36 percent of cucumber, 34 percent of hot pepper, and 23 percent of the tomato seed market shares. However, Monsanto's stock fell 10 percent in the few days after announcement of the deal. Analysts indicated "the acquisition could pose integration problems and results in few immediate synergies."[120] The concern is that more direct biotechnology shaping of fruits and vegetables sold in grocery stores will not be accepted by the public, although consumers have accepted indirect shaping of corn and soy bean seeds.

Too Much Diversification

As explained in Chapter 7, diversification strategies can lead to strategic competitiveness and above-average returns. In general, firms using related diversification strategies outperform those employing unrelated diversification strategies. However, conglomerates formed by using an unrelated diversification strategy also can be successful, as demonstrated by Onex Corporation.

At some point, however, firms can become over-diversified. The level at which over-diversification occurs varies across companies because each firm has different capabilities to manage diversification. Recall from Chapter 7 that related diversification requires more information processing than does unrelated diversification. Because of this additional information processing, related diversified firms become over-diversified with a smaller number of business units than do firms using an unrelated diversification strategy.[121] Regardless of the type of diversification strategy implemented, however, over-diversification results in declines in performance, after which business units are often divested.[122] The pattern of excessive diversification followed by divestments of under-performing business units acquired earlier is currently taking place in the media industry. We discuss this later in a Strategic Focus. Many firms in the media industry have been seeking to divest businesses bought in the boom era of the late 1990s through 2001, when the Internet economy collapsed.[123] These cycles were also frequent among U.S. firms during the 1960s through the 1980s.[124]

Even when a firm is not over-diversified, a high level of diversification can have a negative effect on the firm's long-term performance. For example, the scope created by additional amounts of diversification often causes managers to rely on financial rather than strategic controls to evaluate business units' performances (financial and strategic controls are defined and explained in Chapters 12 and 13). Top-level executives often rely on financial controls to assess the performance of business units when they do not have a rich understanding of business units' objectives and strategies. Use of financial controls, such as return on investment (ROI), causes individual business-unit managers to focus on short-term outcomes at the expense of long-term investments. When long-term investments are reduced to increase short-term profits, a firm's overall strategic competitiveness may be harmed.[125]

Another problem resulting from too much diversification is the tendency for acquisitions to become substitutes for innovation. Typically, managers do not intend acquisitions to be used in that way. However, a reinforcing cycle evolves. Costs associated with acquisitions may result in fewer allocations to activities, such as R&D, that are linked to innovation. Without adequate support, a firm's innovation skills begin to atrophy.

Without internal innovation skills, the only option available to a firm to gain access to innovation is to complete still more acquisitions. Evidence suggests that a firm using acquisitions as a substitute for internal innovations eventually encounters performance problems.[126]

Effective Acquisitions

Earlier in the chapter, we noted that acquisition strategies do not consistently produce above-average returns for the acquiring firm's shareholders.[127] Nonetheless, some companies are able to create value when using an acquisition strategy.[128] For example, few companies have grown so successfully by acquisition as Cisco has. A number of other network companies tried to pursue acquisitions to build up their ability to sell into the network equipment binge, but only Cisco retained much of its value in the post-bubble era. Many firms, such as Nortel, Lucent, and Ericsson, teetered on the edge of bankruptcy after the Internet bubble burst. When it makes an acquisition, "Cisco has gone much further in its thinking about integration. Not only is retention important, but Cisco also works to minimize the distractions caused by an acquisition. This is important, because the speed of change is so great, that even if the target firm's product development teams are distracted, they will be slowed contributing to acquisition failure. So, integration must be rapid and reassuring."[129]

Results from a research study shed light on the differences between unsuccessful and successful acquisition strategies and suggest that there is a pattern of actions that can improve the probability of acquisition success.[130] The study shows that when the target firm's assets are complementary to the acquired firm's assets, an acquisition is more successful. With complementary assets, integrating two firms' operations has a higher probability of creating synergy. In fact, integrating two firms with complementary assets frequently produces unique capabilities and core competencies.[131] With complementary assets, the acquiring firm can maintain its focus on core businesses and leverage the complementary assets and capabilities from the acquired firm. Often, targets were selected and "groomed" by establishing a working relationship prior to the acquisition.[132] As discussed in Chapter 10, strategic alliances are sometimes used to test the feasibility of a future merger or acquisition between the involved firms.[133]

The study's results also show that friendly acquisitions facilitate integration of the firms involved in an acquisition. Through friendly acquisitions, firms work together to find ways to integrate their operations to create synergy.[134] In hostile takeovers, animosity often results between the two top-management teams, a condition that in turn affects working relationships in the newly created firm. As a result, more key personnel in the acquired firm may be lost, and those who remain may resist the changes necessary to integrate the two firms.[135] With effort, cultural clashes can be overcome, and fewer key managers and employees will become discouraged and leave.[136]

Additionally, effective due-diligence processes involving the deliberate and careful selection of target firms and an evaluation of the relative health of those firms (financial health, cultural fit, and the value of human resources) contribute to successful acquisitions.[137] Financial slack in the form of debt equity or cash, in both the acquiring and acquired firms, also has frequently contributed to success in acquisitions. While financial slack provides access to financing for the acquisition, it is still important to maintain a low or moderate level of debt after the acquisition to keep debt costs low. When substantial debt was used to finance the acquisition companies with successful acquisitions reduced the debt quickly, partly by selling off assets from the acquired firm, especially noncomplementary or poorly performing assets. For these firms, debt costs do not prevent long-term investments such as R&D, and managerial discretion in the use of cash flow is relatively flexible.

Another attribute of successful acquisition strategies is an emphasis on innovation, as demonstrated by continuing investments in R&D activities. Significant R&D investments show a strong managerial commitment to innovation, a characteristic that is increasingly important to overall competitiveness, as well as acquisition success.

Flexibility and adaptability are the final two attributes of successful acquisitions. When executives of both the acquiring and the target firms have experience in managing change and learning from acquisitions, they will be more skilled at adapting their capabilities to new environments.[138] As a result, they will be more adept at integrating the two organizations, which is particularly important when firms have different organizational cultures. Efficient and effective integration may quickly produce the desired synergy in the newly created firm. Effective integration allows the acquiring firm to keep valuable human resources in the acquired firm from leaving.[139]

The attributes and results of successful acquisitions are summarized in Table 8.1. Managers seeking acquisition success should emphasize the seven attributes that are listed. The Irving Companies are a conglomerate holding group for the Irving family—one of Canada's richest families. The group of companies operates in the oil industry and also has stakes in related convenience stores, shipbuilding, and forestry. The company owns an interest in transportation, lumber products, home improvement, residential building, automation products, food, and environment services companies. The group has grown through a combination of internal growth, acquisitions, and acquisition of joint venture partners' interests.[140] Their acquisition strategy in these businesses has been successful because they have followed many of the suggestions in Table 8.1.

As we have learned, some acquisitions enhance strategic competitiveness. However, the majority of acquisitions that took place from the 1970s through the 1990s did not enhance firms' strategic competitiveness. In fact, "history shows that anywhere between

Table 8.1	Attributes of Successful Acquisitions

Attributes	Results
1. Acquired firm has assets or resources that are complementary to the acquiring firm's core business	1. High probability of synergy and competitive advantage by maintaining strengths
2. Acquisition is friendly	2. Faster and more effective integration and possibly lower premiums
3. Acquiring firm conducts effective due diligence to select target firms and evaluate the target firm's health (financial, cultural, and human resources)	3. Firms with strongest complementarities are acquired and overpayment is avoided
4. Acquiring firm has financial slack (cash or a favourable debt position)	4. Financing (debt or equity) is easier and less costly to obtain
5. Merged firm maintains low to moderate debt position	5. Lower financing cost, lower risk (e.g., of bankruptcy), and avoidance of trade-offs that are associated with high debt
6. Acquiring firm has sustained and consistent emphasis on R&D and innovation	6. Maintain long-term competitive advantage in markets
7. Acquiring firm manages change well and is flexible and adaptable	7. Faster and more effective integration facilitates achievement of synergy

one-third [and] more than half of all acquisitions are ultimately divested or spun-off."[141] Thus, firms often use restructuring strategies to correct for the failure of a merger or an acquisition.

Restructuring

Defined formally, **restructuring** is a strategy through which a firm changes its set of businesses or its financial structure.[142] From the 1970s into the 2000s, divesting businesses from company portfolios and downsizing accounted for a large percentage of firms' restructuring strategies. Restructuring has become a global phenomenon.[143]

The need to execute a restructuring strategy often follows an acquisition. For example, British/Australian metals giant Rio Tinto took on billions in debt to buy Canada's Alcan Aluminium. In order to offload some of this debt, Rio Tinto said it had planned to divest more than $10 billion in assets—including Alcan's packaging business.[144] Yet, as Rio Tinto was completing its acquisition of Alcan in late 2007, Australian mining behemoth BHP Billiton made an offer to buy Rio Tinto.[145] While the initial offer involves no cash, it does include a share buyback clause that would cost BHP some money.[146] Thus, even with no cash initially changing hands, BHP may need to divest itself of some assets in the course of the acquisition. The most likely sales are one or both of its Canadian diamond mines (BHP's Ekati, and Rio's Diavik).[147]

In other instances, however, firms use a restructuring strategy because of changes in their external and internal environments. For example, opportunities sometimes surface in the external environment that are particularly attractive to the diversified firm in light of its core competencies. In such cases, restructuring may be appropriate to position the firm to create more value for stakeholders, given the environmental changes.[148]

As discussed next, there are three restructuring strategies that firms use: downsizing, downscoping, and leveraged buyouts.

Downsizing

Once thought to be an indicator of organizational decline, downsizing is now recognized as a legitimate restructuring strategy.[149] *Downsizing* is a reduction in the number of a firm's employees and, sometimes, in the number of its operating units, but it may or may not change the composition of businesses in the company's portfolio. Thus, downsizing is an intentional proactive management strategy, whereas "decline is an environmental or organizational phenomenon that occurs involuntarily and results in erosion of an organization's resource base."[150]

In the late 1980s, early 1990s, and early 2000s, thousands of jobs were lost in private and public organizations in North America. One study estimates that 85 percent of *Fortune* 1000 firms have used downsizing as a restructuring strategy.[151] Moreover, *Fortune* 500 firms laid off more than one million employees, or 4 percent of their collective workforce, in 2001 and into the first few weeks of 2002.[152] This trend continues in many industries. For instance, in 2006 GM signalled that it would lay off 30,000 people through 2008 due to poor competitive performance, especially as a result of the improved performance of foreign competitors.[153]

Downscoping

Downscoping has a more positive effect on firm performance than downsizing does.[154] *Downscoping* refers to divestiture, spin-off, or some other means of eliminating businesses unrelated to a firm's core businesses. Commonly, downscoping is described as a set of actions that causes a firm to strategically refocus on its core businesses.[155] Brookfield Asset Management, as mentioned, is spinning off its infrastructure business.

Restructuring is a strategy through which a firm changes its set of businesses or its financial structure.

A firm that downscopes often also downsizes simultaneously. However, it does not eliminate key employees from its primary businesses in the process, because such action could lead to a loss of one or more core competencies. Instead, a firm that is simultaneously downscoping and downsizing becomes smaller by reducing the diversity of businesses in its portfolio.[156]

By refocusing on its core businesses, the firm can be managed more effectively by the top management team. Managerial effectiveness increases because the firm has become less diversified, allowing the top management team to better understand and manage the remaining businesses.[157]

In general, North American firms use downscoping as a restructuring strategy more frequently than European companies do, while the trend in Europe, Latin America, and Asia has been to build conglomerates. In Latin America, these conglomerates are called *grupos*. Many Asian and Latin American conglomerates have begun to adopt Western corporate strategies in recent years and have been refocusing on their core businesses. This downscoping has occurred simultaneously with increasing globalization and with more open markets that have greatly enhanced the competition. By downscoping, these firms have been able to focus on their core businesses and improve their competitiveness.[158]

Downscoping has been practised recently by many emerging-market firms. For example, the Tata Group, founded by Jamsetji Nusserwanji Tata in 1868 as a private trading firm and now India's largest business group, includes 91 firms in a wide range of industries. The group covers chemicals, communications, consumer products, energy, engineering, information systems, materials, and services industries. The group's revenue in 2003–2004 was $14.25 billion, about 2.6 percent of India's GDP. Tata's member companies employ about 220,000 people and export their products to 140 countries. However, as India has changed, Tata executives have sought to restructure its member businesses to "build a more focused company without abandoning the best of Tata's manufacturing tradition."[159] Over a 10-year period Tata has restructured from 250 businesses to its current set.

Leveraged Buyouts

Leveraged buyouts are commonly used as a restructuring strategy to correct for managerial mistakes or because the firm's managers are making decisions that primarily serve their own interests rather than those of shareholders.[160] A *leveraged buyout* (LBO) is a restructuring strategy whereby a party buys all of a firm's assets in order to take the firm private. Once the transaction is completed, the company's stock is no longer traded publicly. Firms that facilitate or engage in taking public firms or a business unit of a firm private are called *private equity firms*.

Usually, significant amounts of debt are incurred to finance a buyout; hence the term "leveraged" buyout. To support debt payments and to downscope the company to concentrate on the firm's core businesses, the new owners may immediately sell a number of assets.[161] It is not uncommon for those buying a firm through an LBO to restructure the firm to the point that it can be sold at a profit within a five- to eight-year period.

Management buyouts (MBOs), employee buyouts (EBOs), and whole-firm buyouts, in which one company or partnership purchases an entire company instead of a part of it, are the three types of LBOs. In part because of managerial incentives, MBOs, more so than EBOs and whole-firm buyouts, have been found to lead to downscoping, increased strategic focus, and improved performance.[162] Research has shown that management buyouts can also lead to greater entrepreneurial activity and growth.[163]

While there may be different reasons for a buyout, one is to protect against a capricious financial market, allowing the owners to focus on developing innovations and bringing them to the market.[164] As such, buyouts can represent a form of firm rebirth to facilitate entrepreneurial efforts and stimulate strategic growth.[165]

Restructuring Outcomes

The short-term and long-term outcomes resulting from the three restructuring strategies are shown in Figure 8.3. As indicated, downsizing does not commonly lead to a higher firm performance.[166] Still, in free-market-based societies at large, downsizing has generated an incentive for individuals who have been laid off to start their own businesses.

Research has shown that downsizing contributed to lower returns for both North American and Japanese firms. The stock markets in the firms' respective nations evaluated downsizing negatively. Investors concluded that downsizing would have a negative effect on companies' ability to achieve strategic competitiveness in the long term. Investors also seem to assume that downsizing occurs as a consequence of other problems in a company.[167] This assumption may be caused by a firm's diminished corporate reputation when a major downsizing is announced.[168] This is clear in the GM layoffs mentioned above. An unintentional outcome of downsizing, however, is that laid-off employees often start new businesses in order to live through the disruption in their lives. Accordingly, downsizing has generated a host of entrepreneurial new ventures.

As shown in Figure 8.3, downsizing tends to result in a loss of human capital in the long term. Losing employees with many years of experience with the firm represents a major loss of knowledge. As noted in Chapter 4, knowledge is vital to competitive success in the global economy. Thus, in general, research evidence and corporate experience suggest that downsizing may be of more tactical (or short-term) value than strategic (or long-term) value.[169]

Downscoping generally leads to more positive outcomes in both the short and the long term than does downsizing or engaging in a leveraged buyout (see Figure 8.3). Downscoping's desirable long-term outcome of higher performance is a product of reduced debt costs and the emphasis on strategic controls derived from concentrating on the firm's core businesses. In so doing, the refocused firm should be able to increase its ability to compete.[170]

While whole-firm LBOs have been hailed as a significant innovation in the financial restructuring of firms, there can be negative trade-offs.[171] First, the resulting large debt

---

Figure 8.3 Restructuring and Outcomes

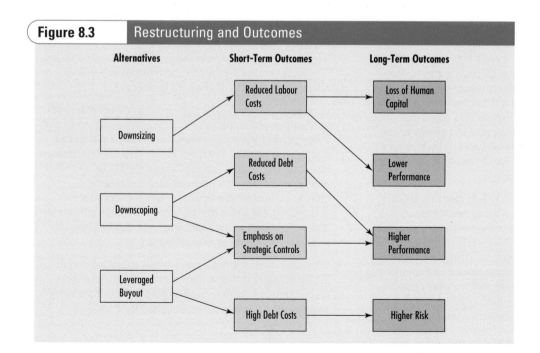

increases the financial risk of the firm, as is evidenced by the number of companies that filed for bankruptcy in the 1990s after executing a whole-firm LBO. Sometimes, the intent of the owners to increase the efficiency of the bought-out firm and then sell it within five to eight years creates a short-term and risk-averse managerial focus.[172] As a result, these firms may fail to invest adequately in R&D or take other major actions designed to maintain or improve the company's core competency.[173] Research also suggests that in firms with an entrepreneurial mind-set buyouts can lead to greater innovation, especially if the debt load is not too great.[174] However, because buyouts more often result in significant debt, most LBOs have taken place in mature industries where stable cash flows are possible. This enables the buyout firm to meet the recurring debt payments, as exemplified by buyouts in the steel industry described in this chapter's Strategic Focus dealing with Mittal Steel.

Summary

- Acquisition strategies are increasingly popular. Because of globalization, deregulation of multiple industries in many different economies, and favourable legislation, the number and size of domestic and cross-border acquisitions continues to increase.

- Firms use acquisition strategies to (1) increase market power, (2) overcome entry barriers to new markets or regions, (3) avoid the costs of developing new products and increase the speed of new market entries, (4) reduce the risk of entering a new business, (5) become more diversified, (6) reshape their competitive scope by developing a different portfolio of businesses, and (7) enhance their learning, thereby adding to their knowledge base.

- Among the problems associated with the use of an acquisition strategy are (1) the difficulty of effectively integrating the firms involved, (2) incorrectly evaluating the target firm's value, (3) creating debt loads that preclude adequate long-term investments (e.g., R&D), (4) overestimating the potential for synergy, (5) creating a firm that is too diversified, (6) creating an internal environment in which managers devote increasing amounts of their time and energy to analyzing and completing the acquisition, and (7) developing a combined firm that is too large, necessitating extensive use of bureaucratic, rather than strategic, controls.

- Effective acquisitions have the following characteristics: (1) the acquiring and target firms have complementary resources that can be the basis of core competencies in the newly created firm, (2) the acquisition is friendly thereby facilitating integration of the two firms' resources, (3) the target firm is selected and purchased based on thorough due diligence, (4) the acquiring and target firms have considerable slack in the form of cash or debt capacity, (5) the merged firm maintains a low or moderate level of debt by selling off portions of the acquired firm or some of the acquiring firm's poorly performing units, (6) the acquiring and acquired firms have experience in terms of adapting to change, and (7) R&D and innovation are emphasized in the new firm.

- Restructuring is used to improve a firm's performance by correcting for problems created by ineffective management. Restructuring by downsizing involves reducing the number of employees and hierarchical levels in the firm. Although it can lead to short-term cost reductions, they may be realized at the expense of long-term success because of the loss of valuable human resources (and knowledge) and overall corporate reputation.

- The goal of restructuring through downscoping is to reduce the firm's level of diversification. Often, the firm divests unrelated businesses to achieve this goal. Eliminating unrelated businesses makes it easier for the firm and its top-level managers to refocus on the core businesses.

- Leveraged buyouts (LBOs) represent an additional restructuring strategy. Through an LBO, a firm is purchased so that it can become a private entity. LBOs usually are financed largely through debt. There are three types of LBOs: management buyouts (MBOs), employee buyouts (EBOs), and whole-firm LBOs. Because they provide clear managerial incentives, MBOs have been the most successful of the three. Often, the intent of a buyout is to improve efficiency and performance to the point where the firm can be sold successfully within five to eight years.

- Commonly, restructuring's primary goal is gaining or reestablishing effective strategic control of the firm. Of the three restructuring strategies, downscoping is aligned the most closely with establishing and using strategic controls.

1. Why are acquisition strategies popular in many firms competing in the global economy?

2. What reasons account for firms' decisions to use acquisition strategies as one means of achieving strategic competitiveness?

3. What are the seven primary problems that affect a firm's efforts to successfully use an acquisition strategy?

4. What are the attributes associated with a successful acquisition strategy?

5. What is the restructuring strategy and what are its common forms?

6. What are the short- and long-term outcomes associated with the different restructuring strategies?

Social Responsibility Review

1. Irving Oil, mentioned earlier, is an example of a company that, because it is privately owned, can quickly make important decisions for the long-run health of the organization. This allowed the company to invest in the production of low-sulphur refined products long before required by law and carve out a very successful niche in the market. Some have argued that leveraged buyouts serve a similar function in that LBOs restore corporate governance mechanisms by making the managers owners who will strive for the highest financial return (rather than employees who simply try for a satisfactory profit). On the other hand, leveraged buyouts expose the company to huge amounts of risky debt that have the potential to endanger jobs, workplace safety, and community health. Under what conditions do you believe a leveraged buyout would be proper? Are such buyouts good for the companies that employ them? Are they good for the communities in which these companies do business?

2. Earlier we discussed Japanese conglomerate Livedoor. Many have labelled the company the Enron of Japan because a number of people lost their life's savings in the collapse of the company. On the other hand, investors entrusted their money to what some in the press labelled a 32-year-old ex–computer geek—CEO Takafumi Horie. As

well, Horie had the audacity to take on a venerated company, headed by well respected managers twice his age. He did this in a country where age, tradition, and a propriety about the way things are done are of critical importance. Should investors have seen this result coming in advance? Are there cultural limits to a strategy—that is, is it prudent to launch an unfriendly takeover in Japan?

3. As discussed earlier, a BHP Billiton–Rio Tinto merger could result in the creation of a corporation with a market capitalization that would likely reach at least $400 billion and allow the combined company to control about 40 percent of the world's uranium. This amount would rank it in the Exxon or Microsoft range. How big is too big? If absolute power corrupts absolutely, how much does $400 billion corrupt? With this kind of concentrated wealth and power, are some companies just too big relative to the national governments that are supposed to regulate their behaviour? Why or why not? Frighteningly, we cannot even rank where a market cap of $400 billion would put BHP because the rankings change by the minute (do a Google search for "largest market capitalization," and check the Yahoo! Finance—Stock Screener for an update).

Experiential Exercises

Determining the Best Path to Firm Growth

You are on the executive board of an information technology firm that provides trafficking software to the trucking industry. One of the firm's managers feels the company should grow and has suggested expanding by creating trafficking services

online. You know your firm is in a position to expand, but you are not sure about the best way to do so.

Part One. Should the firm consider a merger with or an acquisition of a firm that offers the suggested services, or should it develop them internally? List the advantages and disadvantages of each strategic option.

Part Two. Based on your findings and other information, assume that your firm decides to obtain trafficking software for rail shipments through an acquisition of an existing firm. Predict some general problems your firm might encounter in an acquisition and how they might be resolved.

Mergers and Acquisitions

Merger and acquisition activity is increasingly common, both domestically and internationally. However, such activity does not always result in the intended outcomes. In general, shareholders of acquired firms often enjoy above-average returns, while shareholders of acquiring firms are less likely to do so. Identify a recent major merger or acquisition, such as one that made the front page of the *Financial Post* or the *Wall Street Journal* or was a feature story in a business periodical such as *Fortune* or *The Economist*. Then find two or three other comprehensive articles about this merger or acquisition from more than one source, especially over a period of several weeks as the merger/acquisition events unfolded. This process of triangulation will provide a better understanding of any business activity and its results, as well as help substantiate the facts of the case.

1. What are the primary reasons for the merger or acquisition of study? Is this a horizontal, vertical, or related integration? How do you know? How is the firm's market power affected?

2. Was the merger or acquisition a success? To what extent do analysts anticipate problems in achieving success with this merger or acquisition? What issues appear to be of concern?

3. What happened to the stock prices of the involved firms before, during, and after the merger/acquisition? What actions could have been taken to make the integration more efficient and effective in achieving the acquiring firm's goals?

Notes

1. J. Anand, 2004, Redeployment of corporate resources: A study of acquisition strategies in the US defense industries, 1978–1996, *Managerial and Decision Economics,* 25: 383–400; L. Capron & N. Pistre, 2002, When do acquirers earn abnormal returns? *Strategic Management Journal,* 23: 781–794.

2. R. A. Krishnan, S. Joshi, & H. Krishnan, 2004, The influence of mergers on firms' product-mix strategies, *Strategic Management Journal,* 25: 587–611.

3. H. Shahrur, 2005, Industry structure and horizontal takeovers: Analysis of wealth effects on rivals, suppliers, and corporate customers, *Journal of Financial Economics,* 76: 61–98; K. Fuller, J. Netter, & M. Stegemoller, 2002, What do returns to acquiring firms tell us? Evidence from firms that make many acquisitions, *Journal of Finance,* 57: 1763–1793; M. A. Hitt, J. S. Harrison, & R. D. Ireland, 2001, *Mergers and Acquisitions: A Guide to Creating Value for Stakeholders,* New York: Oxford University Press.

4. B. E. Chappuis, K. A. Frick, & P. J. Roche, 2004, High-tech mergers take shape, *McKinsey Quarterly* (1): 60–69; G. K. Deans, F. Kroeger, & S. Zeisel, 2002, The consolidation curve, *Harvard Business Review,* 80(12): 20–21; 2000, How M&As will navigate the turn into a new century, *Mergers and Acquisitions,* January, 29–35.

5. J. A. Schmidt, 2002, Business perspective on mergers and acquisitions, in J. A. Schmidt (ed.), *Making Mergers Work,* Alexandria, VA: Society for Human Resource Management, 23–46.

6. 2005, Wal-Mart open to more international acquisitions, *Forbes,* www.forbes.com, June 14.

7. M. A. Hitt, R. D. Ireland, R. E. Hoskisson, R. G. Rowe & J. P. Sheppard, 2002, Strategic Focus: The Decade of Europe: 2000–2010, *Strategic Management: Competitiveness and Globalization—Concepts,* 1st Canadian ed., Toronto: Thomson Nelson, 230.

8. E. R. Auster & M. L. Sirower, 2002, The dynamics of merger and acquisition waves: A three-stage conceptual framework with implications for practice, *Journal of Applied Behavioral Science,* 38: 216–244.

9. M. A. Hitt, R. D. Ireland, & J. S. Harrison, 2001, Mergers and acquisitions: A value creating or a value destroying strategy? in M. A. Hitt, R. E. Freeman, & J. S. Harrison, *Handbook of Strategic Management,* Oxford, UK: Blackwell Publishers, 385–408.

10. L. Saigol, 2002, Thin pickings in dismal year for dealmaking, *Financial Times,* www.ft.com, January 2; 2001, Waiting for growth, *The Economist,* www.economist.com, April 27.

11. 2002, Mergers snapshot: 2001 deal volume, *Wall Street Journal,* January 4, C12; 2001, The great merger wave breaks, *The Economist,* January 27, 59–60.

12. G. Platt, 2008, Corporate financing focus: Cross border mergers set record as global consolidation continues, Allbusiness.com, February 1, http://www .allbusiness.com/company-activities-management/company-structures/ 10203339-1.html, retrieved July 21; 2008, Zurich Financial Services news release, July 18, 2007, http://www.zurich.com/main/investorrelations/ news/2007/english/2007_0718_01_article.htm, January 2; International Financial Law Review, 2006, The 2006 Guide to Mergers and Acquisitions, http://www.iflr.com/store/product.asp?PositionID=4507&ProductID=5986, retrieved January 2, 2008; D. K. Berman, 2005, Lots of merger activity—A few big deals, *Wall Street Journal,* July 1, C12; D. K. Berman, 2005, Year-end review of markets & finance 2004; simmering M&A sector reaches a boil; Crush of December activity signals M&A is heating up; Will "deals beget deals"? *Wall Street Journal,* January 5, R10.

13. R. Coff, 2003, Bidding wars over R&D-intensive firms: Knowledge, opportunism, and the market for corporate control, *Academy of Management Journal,* 46: 74–85; P. Chattopadhyay, W. H. Glick, & G. P. Huber, 2001, Organizational actions in response to threats and opportunities, *Academy of Management Journal,* 44: 937–955.

14. J. J. Reuer & T. W. Tong, 2005, Real options in international joint ventures, *Journal of Management,* 31: 403–423; A. E. M. A. Schilling & H. K. Steensma, 2002, Disentangling the theories of firm boundaries: A path model and empirical test, *Organization Science,* 13: 387–401; H. T. J. Smit, 2001, Acquisition strategies as option games, *Journal of Applied Corporate Finance,* 14(2): 79–89.

15. G. Cullinan, J.-M. Le Roux, & R.-M. Weddigen, 2004, When to walk away from a deal, *Harvard Business Review,* 82(4): 96–104; L. Selden & G. Colvin, 2003, M&A needn't be a loser's game, *Harvard Business Review,* 81(6): 70–73.

16. J. J. Reuer, 2005, Avoiding lemons in M&A deals, *MIT Sloan Management Review,* 46(3): 15–17; M. C. Jensen, 1988, Takeovers: Their causes and consequences, *Journal of Economic Perspectives,* 1(2): 21–48.

17. Moleller, Schlingemann, & Stulz, Wealth destruction on a massive scale.

18. D. K. Berman, 2005, Mergers horror II: The rhetoric, *Wall Street Journal*, May 24, C1; T. Wright, M. Kroll, A. Lado, & B. Van Ness, 2002, The structure of ownership and corporate acquisition strategies, *Strategic Management Journal*, 23: 41–53; A. Rappaport & M. L. Sirower, 1999, Stock or cash? *Harvard Business Review*, 77(6): 147–158.

19. A. Keeton, 2003, Class-action is approved against DaimlerChrysler, *Wall Street Journal*, June 13, B2.

20. E. Thornton, F. Keesnan, C. Palmeri, & L. Himelstein, 2002, It sure is getting hostile, *BusinessWeek*, January 14, 28–30.

21. 2007, Barrick backs off hostile bid for NovaGold, *The Northern Miner*, 93(10): 4.

22. P. Haspeslagh, 1999, Managing the mating dance in equal mergers, "Mastering Strategy" (Part Five), *Financial Times*, October 25, 14–15.

23. P. Wright, M. Kroll, & D. Elenkov, 2002, Acquisition returns, increase in firm size and chief executive officer compensation: The moderating role of monitoring, *Academy of Management Journal*, 45: 599–608.

24. G. Anders, 2002, Lessons from WaMu's M&A playbook, *Fast Company*, January, 100–107.

25. 2008, Mining Watch Canada Web page, http://www.miningwatch.ca/index.php?/Barrick, January 2.

26. C. Hamburg, M. Bucerius, & M. Bucerius, 2005, A marketing perspective on mergers and acquisitions: How marketing integration affects post-merger performance, *Journal of Marketing*, 69: 95–113.

27. Capron & Pistre, When do acquirers earn abnormal returns?; L. Capron, 1999, Horizontal acquisitions: The benefits and risks to long-term performance, *Strategic Management Journal*, 20: 987–1018.

28. C. E. Fee & S. Thomas, 2004, Sources of gains in horizontal mergers: Evidence from customer, supplier, and rival firms, *Journal of Financial Economics*, 74: 423–460.

29. M. Lubatkin, W. S. Schulze, A. Mainkar, & R. W. Cotterill, 2001, Ecological investigation of firm effects in horizontal mergers, *Strategic Management Journal*, 22: 335–357; K. Ramaswamy, 1997, The performance impact of strategic similarity in horizontal mergers: Evidence from the U.S. banking industry, *Academy of Management Journal*, 40: 697–715.

30. J. McElgunn, 2007, Seize the day!, *Profit*, 26(3): 33–38.

31. L. Capron, W. Mitchell, & A. Swaminathan, 2001, Asset divestiture following horizontal acquisitions: A dynamic view, *Strategic Management Journal*, 22: 817–844.

32. 2008, Mining Watch Canada Web page, http://www.miningwatch.ca/index.php?/Barrick, January 2.

33. M. R. Subramani & N. Venkatraman, 2003, Safeguarding investments in asymmetric interorganizational relationships: Theory and evidence, *Academy of Management Journal*, 46: 46–62; T. S. Gabrielsen, 2003, Conglomerate mergers: Vertical mergers in disguise? *International Journal of the Economics of Business*, 10(1): 1–16.

34. B. Branswell, 2001, A big cheese gets bigger, *Maclean's*, 114(11): 38–39.

35. W. M. Bulkeley & S. Weinberg, 2005, Kodak to buy printing supplier for $980 million, *Wall Street Journal*, February 1, B5.

36. 2003, Special report: The complete home entertainer? Sony, *The Economist*, March 1, 62–64.

37. P. Dvorak, 2005, Out of tune: At Sony, rivalries were encouraged; Then came iPod, *Wall Street Journal*, June 29, A1, A6.

38. D. Clark & C. Forelle, 2005, Sun Microsystems to buy Storagetek for $4.1 billion, *Wall Street Journal*, June 3, A3.

39. D. Gupta & Y. Gerchak, 2002, Quantifying operational synergies in a merger/acquisition, *Management Science*, 48: 517–533.

40. D. E. M. Sappington, 2003, Regulating horizontal diversification, *International Journal of Industrial Organization*, 21: 291–315.

41. G. Witte, 2005, Nortel to buy PEC Solutions for $448 million, *Washington Post*, April 27, E01.

42. S.-F. S. Chen & M. Zeng, 2004, Japanese investors' choice of acquisitions vs. startups in the US: The role of reputation barriers and advertising outlays, *International Journal of Research in Marketing*, 21(2): 123–136; S. J. Chang &

43. P. M. Rosenzweig, 2001, The choice of entry mode in sequential foreign direct investment, *Strategic Management Journal*, 22: 747–776.

44. 2004, Leaders: Grow up emerging economies, *The Economist*, October 16, 12; N. Dawar & A. Chattopadhyay, 2002, Rethinking marketing programs for emerging markets, *Long Range Planning*, 35(5): 457–474; J. A. Gingrich, 1999, Five rules for winning emerging market consumers, *Strategy & Business*, 15: 19–33.

44. K. Shimizu, M. A. Hitt, D. Vaidyanath, & V. Pisano, 2004, Theoretical foundations of cross-border mergers and acquisitions: A review of current research and recommendations for the future, *Journal of International Management*, 10: 307–353; J. A. Doukas & L. H. P. Lang, 2003, Foreign direct investment, diversification and firm performance, *Journal of International Business Studies*, 34: 153–172; Hitt, Harrison, & Ireland, *Mergers and Acquisitions*, Chapter 10.

45. A. Seth, K. P. Song, & R. R. Pettit, 2002, Value creation and destruction in cross-border acquisitions: An empirical analysis of foreign acquisitions of U.S. firms, *Strategic Management Journal*, 23: 921–940.

46. Schmidt, Business perspective on mergers and acquisitions.

47. A. M. Agami, 2002, The role that foreign acquisitions of Asian companies played in the recovery of the Asian financial crisis, *Multinational Business Review*, 10(1): 11–20.

48. P. Quah & S. Young, 2005, Post-acquisition management: A phases approach for cross-border M&As, *European Management Journal*, 17(1), 65–75; J. K. Sebenius, 2002, The hidden challenge of cross-border negotiations, *Harvard Business Review*, 80(3): 76–85.

49. Hill & Rothaermel, The performance of incumbent firms in the face of radical technological innovation.

50. M. A. Hitt, R. E. Hoskisson, R. D. Ireland, & J. S. Harrison, 1991, Effects of acquisitions on R&D inputs and outputs, *Academy of Management Journal*, 34: 693–706.

51. Capron, Mitchell, & Swaminathan, Asset divestiture following horizontal acquisitions; D. D. Bergh, 1997, Predicting divestiture of unrelated acquisitions: An integrative model of ex ante conditions, *Strategic Management Journal*, 18: 715–731.

52. M. A. Hitt, R. D. Ireland, R. E. Hoskisson, W. G. Rowe, & J. P. Sheppard, 2002, Strategic Focus: The Decade of Europe: 2000–2010, *Strategic Management: Competitiveness and Globalization—Concepts*, 1st Canadian ed., Toronto: Thomson Nelson, 235.

53. C. E. Helfat & K. M. Eisenhardt, 2004, Inter-temporal economies of scope, organizational modularity, and the dynamics of diversification, *Strategic Management Journal*, 25: 1217–1232; C. Park, 2003, Prior performance characteristics of related and unrelated acquirers, *Strategic Management Journal*, 24: 471–480.

54. Hitt, Harrison, & Ireland, *Mergers and Acquisitions*.

55. J. Anand & H. Singh, 1997, Asset redeployment, acquisitions and corporate strategy in declining industries, *Strategic Management Journal*, 18 (Special Issue): 99–118.

56. Helfat & Eisenhardt, Inter-temporal economies of scope, organizational modularity, and the dynamics of diversification; W. J. Ferrier, 2001, Navigating the competitive landscape: The drivers and consequences of competitive aggressiveness, *Academy of Management Journal*, 44: 858–877.

57. J. Anand & A. Delios, 2002, Absolute and relative resources as determinants of international acquisitions, *Strategic Management Journal*, 23(2): 119–134; F. Vermeulen & H. Barkema, 2001, Learning through acquisitions, *Academy of Management Journal*, 44: 457–476.

58. F. Vermeulen, 2005, How acquisitions can revitalize firms, *MIT Sloan Management Review*, 46(4): 45–51; J. Gammelgaard, 2004, Access to competence: An emerging acquisition motive, *European Business Forum*, Spring, 44–48; M. L. A. Hayward, 2002, When do firms learn from their acquisition experience? Evidence from 1990–1995, *Strategic Management Journal*, 23: 21–39.

59. J. Anand, L. Capron, & W. Mitchell, 2005, Using acquisitions to access multinational diversity: Thinking beyond the domestic versus cross-border M&A comparison, *Industrial and Corporate Change*, 14(2): 191–224.

60. J. S. Harrison, M. A. Hitt, R. E. Hoskisson, & R. D. Ireland, 2001, Resource complementarity in business combinations: Extending the logic to organizational alliances, *Journal of Management,* 27: 679–690.

61. J. Chatman, C. O'Reilly, & V. Chang, 2005, Cisco Systems: Developing a human capital strategy, *California Management Review,* 47(2): 137–167; S. Thurm, 2003, After the boom: A go-go giant of Internet age, Cisco is learning to go slow, *Wall Street Journal,* May 7, A1.

62. 2008, Cisco Acquisitions Web site, http://www.cisco.com/web/about/ac49/ ac0/ac1/about_cisco_acquisition_years_list .html, January 3; S. Thurm, 2005, Cisco to acquire wi-fi company for $450 million technology from Airespace may help company remain leader in corporate market, *Wall Street Journal,* January 13, B4.

63. L.-F. Hsieh; Y.-T. Tsai, 2005, Technology investment mode of innovative technological corporations: M & A strategy intended to facilitate innovation, *Journal of American Academy of Business,* 6(1): 185–194; G. Ahuja & R. Katila, 2001, Technological acquisitions and the innovation performance of acquiring firms: A longitudinal study, *Strategic Management Journal,* 22: 197–220; M. A. Hitt, R. E. Hoskisson, & R. D. Ireland, 1990, Mergers and acquisitions and managerial commitment to innovation in M-form firms, *Strategic Management Journal,* 11 (Special Issue): 29–47.

64. J. Whalen & A. L. Abboud, 2005, Big pharma, flush with cash, is looking acquisitive, *Wall Street Journal,* February 16, C1, C4.

65. Hitt, Hoskisson, Johnson, & Moesel, The market for corporate control.

66. V. Bannert & H. Tschirky, 2004, Integration planning for technology intensive acquisitions, *R&D Management,* 34(5): 481–494; W. Vanhaverbeke, G. Duysters, & N. Noorderhaven, 2002, External technology sourcing through alliances or acquisitions: An analysis of the application-specific integrated circuits industry, *Organization Science,* 6: 714–733.

67. H. Gatignon, M. L. Tushman, W. Smith, & P. Anderson, 2002, A structural approach to assessing innovation: Construct development of innovation locus, type, and characteristics, *Management Science,* 48: 1103–1122; Hitt, Harrison, & Ireland, *Mergers and Acquisitions.*

68. M. A. Hitt, R. E. Hoskisson, R. A. Johnson, & D. D. Moesel, 1996, The market for corporate control and firm innovation, *Academy of Management Journal,* 39: 1084–1119.

69. Coff, Bidding wars over R&D-intensive firms: Knowledge, opportunism, and the market for corporate control.

70. 2007, Dollars and deals, *Pharmaceutical Executive,* 27(11): 126.

71. L. Jarvis, 2005, Pharma M&A cooling slightly in 2005, *Chemical Market Reporter,* Jun 6–12, 20–21.

72. P. Kale & P. Puranam, 2004, Choosing equity stakes in technology-sourcing relationships: An integrative framework, *California Management Review,* 46(3): 77–99; T. Yoshikawa, 2003, Technology development and acquisition strategy, *International Journal of Technology Management,* 25(6,7): 666–674.

73. Y. Luo, O. Shenkar, & M.-K. Nyaw, 2002, Mitigating liabilities of foreignness: Defensive versus offensive approaches, *Journal of International Management,* 8: 283–300; J. W. Lu & P. W. Beamish, 2001, The internationalization and performance of SMEs, *Strategic Management Journal,* 22 (Special Issue): 565–586.

74. C. W. L. Hill & F. T. Rothaermel, 2003, The performance of incumbent firms in the face of radical technological innovation, *Academy of Management Review,* 28: 257–274; G. Ahuja & C. Lampert, 2001, Entrepreneurship in the large corporation: A longitudinal study of how established firms create breakthrough inventions, *Strategic Management Journal,* 22 (Special Issue): 521–543.

75. 2007, MDS in deal to buy Molecular Devices, *Chemical and Engineering News,* 85(6): 17.

76. F. Rothaermel, 2001, Incumbent's advantage through exploiting complementary assets via interfirm cooperation, *Strategic Management Journal,* 22 (Special Issue): 687–699.

77. A. Grimes & S. Hensley, 2005, Pfizer nears a deal to acquire Angiosyn, pad eye-drug roster, *Wall Street Journal,* January 20, C1, C5.

78. Schmidt, Business perspective on mergers and acquisitions.

79. M. Zollo & H. Singh, 2004, Deliberate learning in corporate acquisitions: Post-

acquisition strategies and integration capability in U.S. bank mergers, *Strategic Management Journal,* 25: 1233–1256; P. Mallette, C. L. Fowler, & C. Hayes, 2003, The acquisition process map: Blueprint for a successful deal, *Southern Business Review,* 28(2): 1–13; Hitt, Harrison, & Ireland, *Mergers and Acquisitions.*

80. R. A. Weber & C. F. Camerer, 2003, Cultural conflict and merger failure: An experimental approach, *Management Science,* 49: 400–415; J. Vester, 2002, Lessons learned about integrating acquisitions, *Research Technology Management,* 45(3): 33–41; D. K. Datta, 1991, Organizational fit and acquisition performance: Effects of post-acquisition integration, *Strategic Management Journal,* 12: 281–297.

81. J. R. Carleton & C. S. Lineberry, 2004, *Achieving Post-Merger Success,* New York: John Wiley & Sons; Y. Weber & E. Menipaz, 2003, Measuring cultural fit in mergers and acquisitions, *International Journal of Business Performance Management,* 5(1): 54–72.

82. M. Zollo, 1999, M&A—The challenge of learning to integrate, "Mastering Strategy" (Part Eleven), *Financial Times,* December 6, 14–15.

83. M. A. Hitt, L. Bierman, K. Shimizu, & R. Kochhar, 2001, Direct and moderating effects of human capital on strategy and performance in professional service firms, *Academy of Management Journal,* 44: 13–28.

84. J. A. Krug, 2003, Why do they keep leaving? *Harvard Business Review,* 81(2): 14–15; H. A. Krishnan & D. Park, 2002, The impact of workforce reduction on subsequent performance in major mergers and acquisitions: An exploratory study, *Journal of Business Research,* 55(4): 285–292; G. G. Dess & J. D. Shaw, 2001, Voluntary turnover, social capital and organizational performance, *Academy of Management Review,* 26: 446–456.

85. J. A. Krug & H. Hegarty, 2001, Predicting who stays and leaves after an acquisition: A study of top managers in multinational firms, *Strategic Management Journal,* 22: 185–196.

86. Verberg, Watson & Kirby, You win some, Op cit.

87. G. Yago, 1991, *Junk Bonds: How High Yield Securities Restructured Corporate America,* New York: Oxford University Press, 146–148.

88. M. C. Jensen, 1986, Agency costs of free cash flow, corporate finance, and takeovers, *American Economic Review,* 76: 323–329.

89. J. Gray, 2000, Izzy's next move, *Canadian Business,* 73(15): 47–49.

90. J. Gatehouse, 2007, Living up to Izzy: How dad's dreams are still the Aspers' biggest problem, *Maclean's,* 120(44): 42–49.

91. M. A. Hitt & D. L. Smart, 1994, Debt: A disciplining force for managers or a debilitating force for organizations? *Journal of Management Inquiry,* 3: 144–152.

92. Hitt, Harrison, & Ireland, *Mergers and Acquisitions.*

93. Hughes, Lang, Mester, Moon, & Pagano, Do bankers sacrifice value to build empires? Managerial incentives, industry consolidation, and financial performance; Hitt, Hoskisson, Johnson, & Moesel, The market for corporate control; Hitt, Hoskisson, & Ireland, Mergers and acquisitions and managerial commitment to innovation in M-form firms.

94. M. L. A. Hayward & D. C. Hambrick, 1997. Explaining the premiums paid for large acquisitions: Evidence of CEO hubris, *Administrative Science Quarterly,* 42: 103–127; R. Roll, 1986, The hubris hypothesis of corporate takeovers, *Journal of Business,* 59: 197–216.

95. J. Pfeffer, 2003, The human factor: Curbing the urge to merge, *Business 2.0,* July, 58.

96. Hayward, When do firms learn from their acquisition experience?

97. Weber & Camerer, Cultural conflict and merger failure: An experimental approach.

98. C. J. Loomis, 2005, Why Carly's big bet is failing, *Fortune,* February 7, 50–59.

99. P. Burrows & P. Elgin, 2005, The un-Carly unveils his plan, *BusinessWeek,* www.businessweek.com, June 16.

100. 2005, Business: Shaking up corporate Japan; Hostile takeovers, *The Economist,* 374(8419): 79; 2005, Business: Livedoor cuts a deal; Japanese takeovers, *The Economist,* 375(8423): 79; 2006, Special report: From hero to zero: Japan after Livedoor, *The Economist,* 378(8463): 70.

101. 2006, Humbled former CEO denies he knew of fraud, *Toronto Star,* November 8, C2.

102. Special report: From hero to zero; 2006, Business: Still livin' on the edge; Face value, *The Economist*, 378(8461): 66; 2007, Business: Hostility, of sorts; Takeovers in Japan, *The Economist*, 385(8560): 110.

103. R. M. Cyert, S.-H. Kang, & P. Kumar, 2002, Corporate governance, takeovers, and top-management compensation: Theory and evidence, *Management Science*, 48: 453–469.

104. A. P. Dickerson, H. D. Gibson, & E. Tsakalotos, 2003, Is attack the best form of defence? A competing risks analysis of acquisition activity in the UK, *Cambridge Journal of Economics*, 27: 337–357.

105. Hitt, Harrison, & Ireland, *Mergers and Acquisitions*.

106. 2007, Brookfield Asset Management, May 2007 Corporate Brochure, http://www.brookfield.com/investorcenter/investorpresentations/resources/ BAM_Brochure.pdf, December 29; 2007, Brookfield Asset Management, 2007 Annual Report, http://www.brookfield.com/investorcenter/financialreports/annualreports/resources/2005/2005%20AR.pdf.

107. 2008, Brookfield unit spinoff confirmed for Jan. 14, *The Globe and Mail*, January 4, B6.

108. 2008, Brookfield Asset Management infrastructure spinoff confirmed for Jan. 14, Canadian Press NewsWire, January 3.

109. G. Cullinan, J.-M. Le Roux, & R.-M. Weddigen, 2004, When to walk away from a deal, *Harvard Business Review*, 82(4): 96–104.

110. Rappaport & Sirower, Stock or cash? 149.

111. Witte, Nortel to buy PEC Solutions for $448 million.

112. E. Thornton, 2003, Bypassing the street, *BusinessWeek*, June 2, 79.

113. T. N. Hubbard, 1999, Integration strategies and the scope of the company, "Mastering Strategy" (Part Eleven), *Financial Times*, December 6, 8–10.

114. Hitt, Harrison, & Ireland, *Mergers and Acquisitions*.

115. T. Saxton & M. Dollinger, 2004, Target reputation and appropriability: Picking and deploying resources in acquisitions, *Journal of Management*, 30: 123–147.

116. Harrison, Hitt, Hoskisson, & Ireland, Resource complementarity in business combinations; J. B. Barney, 1988, Returns to bidding firms in mergers and acquisitions: Reconsidering the relatedness hypothesis, *Strategic Management Journal*, 9 (Special Issue): 71–78.

117. O. E. Williamson, 1999, Strategy research: Governance and competence perspectives, *Strategic Management Journal*, 20: 1087–1108.

118. Hitt, Hoskisson, Johnson, & Moesel, The market for corporate control.

119. S. Killman, 2005, Monsanto Co. to pay $1 billion for produce-seed firm Seminis, *Wall Street Journal*, January 25, A3.

120. K. Sissell, 2005, Monsanto acquires seeds firm for $1.4 billion, *Chemical Week*, February 2, 9.

121. C. W. L. Hill & R. E. Hoskisson, 1987, Strategy and structure in the multiproduct firm, *Academy of Management Review*, 12: 331–341.

122. R. A. Johnson, R. E. Hoskisson, & M. A. Hitt, 1993, Board of director involvement in restructuring: The effects of board versus managerial controls and characteristics, *Strategic Management Journal*, 14 (Special Issue): 33–50; C. C. Markides, 1992, Consequences of corporate refocusing: Ex ante evidence, *Academy of Management Journal*, 35: 398–412.

123. G. Garai, 2002, Take our outfit—Please! How do you start a small business? Maybe by relieving a corporation of a rashly acquired division, as our expert explains, BusinessWeek Online, www.businessweek.com, December 18.

124. D. Palmer & B. N. Barber, 2001, Challengers, elites and families: A social class theory of corporate acquisitions, *Administrative Science Quarterly*, 46: 87–120.

125. Hitt, Harrison, & Ireland, *Mergers and Acquisitions*; R. E. Hoskisson & R. A. Johnson, 1992, Corporate restructuring and strategic change: The effect on diversification strategy and R&D intensity, *Strategic Management Journal*, 13: 625–634.

126. Hitt, Harrison, & Ireland, *Mergers and Acquisitions*.

127. A. P. Dickerson, H. D. Gibson, & E. Tsakalotos, 2002. Takeover risk and the market for corporate control: The experience of British firms in the 1970s and 1980s, *International Journal of Industrial Organization*, 20: 1167–1195.

128. Reuer, Avoiding lemons in M&A deals; R. M. Di Gregorio, 2003, Making

129. D. Mayer & M. Kenney, 2004, Economic action does not take place in a vacuum: Understanding Cisco's acquisition and development strategy, *Industry and Innovation*, 11(4): 299–325.

130. M. A. Hitt, R. D. Ireland, J. S. Harrison, & A. Best, 1998, Attributes of successful and unsuccessful acquisitions of U.S. firms, *British Journal of Management*, 9: 91–114.

131. Harrison, Hitt, Hoskisson, & Ireland, Resource complementarity in business combinations.

132. J. Hagedoorn & G. Dysters, 2002, External sources of innovative capabilities: The preference for strategic alliances or mergers and acquisitions, *Journal of Management Studies*, 39: 167–188.

133. P. Porrini, 2004, Can a previous alliance between an acquirer and a target affect acquisition performance? *Journal of Management*, 30: 545–562; J. Reuer, 2001, From hybrids to hierarchies: Shareholder wealth effects of joint venture partner buyouts, *Strategic Management Journal*, 22: 27–44.

134. R. J. Aiello & M. D. Watkins, 2000, The fine art of friendly acquisition, *Harvard Business Review*, 78(6): 100–107.

135. P. Gwynne, 2002, Keeping the right people, *MIT Sloan Management Review*, 43(2): 19; D. D. Bergh, 2001, Executive retention and acquisition outcomes: A test of opposing views on the influence of organizational tenure, *Journal of Management*, 27: 603–622; J. P. Walsh, 1989, Doing a deal: Merger and acquisition negotiations and their impact upon target company top management turnover, *Strategic Management Journal*, 10: 307–322.

136. M. L. Marks & P. H. Mirvis, 2001, Making mergers and acquisitions work: Strategic and psychological preparation, *Academy of Management Executive*, 15(2): 80–92.

137. Cullinan, Le Roux, & Weddigen, When to walk away from a deal; S. Rovit & C. Lemire, 2003, Your best M&A strategy, *Harvard Business Review*, 81(3): 16–17.

138. Hitt, Harrison, & Ireland, *Mergers and Acquisitions*; Q. N. Huy, 2001, Time, temporal capability and planned change, *Academy of Management Review*, 26: 601–623; L. Markoczy, 2001, Consensus formation during strategic change, *Strategic Management Journal*, 22: 1013–1031.

139. R. W. Coff, 2002, Human capital, shared expertise, and the likelihood of impasse in corporate acquisitions, *Journal of Management*, 28: 107–128.

140. 2005, Irving empire: Wagons to oil tankers, *The Brunswickan*, November 2: 4; 2007, J. D. Irving Web page, http://www.jdirving.com/products-main.aspx?id=516&coll_id=104, December 31; 2008, Irving Oil Web page, http://www.irvingoil.com/company/wwa.asp, January 4.

141. J. Anand, 1999, How many matches are made in heaven, Mastering Strategy (Part Five), *Financial Times*, October 25, 6–7.

142. R. A. Johnson, 1996, Antecedents and outcomes of corporate refocusing, *Journal of Management*, 22: 437–481; J. E. Bethel & J. Liebeskind, 1993, The effects of ownership structure on corporate restructuring, *Strategic Management Journal*, 14 (Special Issue): 15–31.

143. R. E. Hoskisson, A. A. Cannella, L. Tihanyi, & R. Faraci, 2004. Asset restructuring and business group affiliation in French civil law countries, *Strategic Management Journal*, 25: 525–539; R. E. Hoskisson, R. A. Johnson, D. Yiu, & W. P. Wan, 2001, Restructuring strategies of diversified groups: Differences associated with country institutional environments, in M. A. Hitt, R. E. Freeman, & J. S. Harrison (eds.), *Handbook of Strategic Management*, Oxford, UK: Blackwell Publishers, 433–463.

144. C. French, 2007, BHP-Rio deal might rattle diamond sector; Diavik and Ekati mines could be sold, analysts say, *National Post*, November 21, FP4.

145. While it is not our intention to be the last word on definitions, it seems that the difference between "giant" and "behemoth" is about $55 billion in assets— "giant" Rio Tinto having about $150 billion in assets and "behemoth" BHP having about $205 billion in assets; see BHP Billiton news release, November 12, 2007, http://www.bhpbilliton.com/bbContentRepository/071112Nr3307ProposedCombinationWithRioTinto.pdf, retrieved January 4, 2008.

146. As well, the initial offer, at $140 billion, is almost10 percent less than Rio's current market capitalization and is thus likely to be increased, possibly with some cash involved; see C. French, 2007, BHP-Rio deal might rattle diamond sector.

147. C. French, 2007, BHP-Rio deal might rattle diamond sector.

148. J. L. Morrow Jr., R. A. Johnson, & L. W. Busenitz, 2004, The effects of cost and asset retrenchment on firm performance: The overlooked role of a firm's competitive environment, *Journal of Management,* 30: 189–208; T. A. Kruse, 2002, Asset liquidity and the determinants of asset sales by poorly performing firms, *Financial Management,* 31(4): 107–129.

149. R. D. Nixon, M. A. Hitt, H.-U. Lee, & E. Jeong, 2004, Market reactions to announcements of corporate downsizing actions and implementation strategies, *Strategic Management Journal,* 25: 1121–1129.

150. G. J. Castrogiovanni & G. D. Bruton, 2000, Business turnaround processes following acquisitions: Reconsidering the role of retrenchment, *Journal of Business Research,* 48: 25–34; W. McKinley, J. Zhao, & K. G. Rust, 2000, A sociocognitive interpretation of organizational downsizing, *Academy of Management Review,* 25: 227–243.

151. W. McKinley, C. M. Sanchez, & A. G. Schick, 1995, Organizational downsizing: Constraining, cloning, learning, *Academy of Management Executive,* 9(3): 32–44.

152. P. Patsuris, 2002, Forbes.com layoff tracker surpasses 1M mark, *Forbes,* www.forbes.com, January 16.

153. T. Ventis, 2006, GM plant closures shake up Canadian auto-parts suppliers, 64(1): 8–9.

154. Hoskisson & Hitt, *Downscoping.*

155. L. Dranikoff, T. Koller, & A. Schneider, 2002, Divestiture: Strategy's missing link, *Harvard Business Review,* 80(5): 74–83.

156. M. Rajand & M. Forsyth, 2002, Hostile bidders, long-term performance, and restructuring methods: Evidence from the UK, *American Business Review,* 20(1): 71–81.

157. Johnson, Hoskisson, & Hitt, Board of director involvement; R. E. Hoskisson & M. A. Hitt, 1990, Antecedents and performance outcomes of diversification: A review and critique of theoretical perspectives, *Journal of Management,* 16: 461–509.

158. R. E. Hoskisson, R. A. Johnson, L. Tihanyi, & R. E. White, 2005, Diversified business groups and corporate refocusing in emerging economies, *Journal of Management,* forthcoming.

159. M. Kripalani, 2004, Ratan Tata: No one's doubting now, *BusinessWeek,* July 26, 50–51.

160. D. D. Bergh & G. F. Holbein, 1997, Assessment and redirection of longitudinal analysis: Demonstration with a study of the diversification and divestiture relationship, *Strategic Management Journal,* 18: 557–571; C. C. Markides & H. Singh, 1997, Corporate restructuring: A symptom of poor governance or a solution to past managerial mistakes? *European Management Journal,* 15: 213–219.

161. M. F. Wiersema & J. P. Liebeskind, 1995, The effects of leveraged buyouts on corporate growth and diversification in large firms, *Strategic Management Journal,* 16: 447–460.

162. R. Harris, D. S. Siegel, & M. Wright, 2005, Assessing the impact of management buyouts on economic efficiency: Plant-level evidence from the United Kingdom, *Review of Economics and Statistics,* 87: 148–153; A. Seth & J. Easterwood, 1995, Strategic redirection in large management buyouts: The evidence from post-buyout restructuring activity, *Strategic Management Journal,* 14: 251–274; P. H. Phan & C. W. L. Hill, 1995, Organizational restructuring and economic performance in leveraged buyouts: An ex-post study, *Academy of Management Journal,* 38: 704–739.

163. C. M. Daily, P. P. McDougall, J. G. Covin, & D. R. Dalton, 2002, Governance and strategic leadership in entrepreneurial firms, *Journal of Management,* 3: 387–412.

164. M. Wright, R. E. Hoskisson, L. W. Busenitz, & J. Dial, 2000, Entrepreneurial growth through privatization: The upside of management buyouts, *Academy of Management Review,* 25: 591–601.

165. M. Wright, R. E. Hoskisson, & L. W. Busenitz, 2001, Firm rebirth: Buyouts as facilitators of strategic growth and entrepreneurship, *Academy of Management Executive,* 15(1): 111–125.

166. Bergh, Executive retention and acquisition outcomes: A test of opposing views on the influence of organizational tenure.

167. H. A. Krishnan & D. Park, 2002, The impact of work force reduction on subsequent performance in major mergers and acquisitions: An exploratory study, *Journal of Business Research,* 55(4): 285–292; P. M. Lee, 1997, A comparative analysis of layoff announcements and stock price reactions in the United States and Japan, *Strategic Management Journal,* 18: 879–894.

168. D. J. Flanagan & K. C. O'Shaughnessy, 2005, The effect of layoffs on firm reputation, *Journal of Management,* 31: 445–463.

169. N. Mirabal & R. DeYoung, 2005, Downsizing as a strategic intervention, *Journal of American Academy of Business,* 6(1): 39–45.

170. K. Shimizu & M. A. Hitt, 2005, What constrains or facilitates divestitures of formerly acquired firms? The effects of organizational inertia, *Journal of Management,* 31: 50–72.

171. S. Toms & M. Wright, 2005, Divergence and convergence within Anglo-American corporate governance systems: Evidence from the US and UK, 1950–2000, *Business History,* 47(2): 267–295.

172. P. Desbrieres & A. Schatt, 2002, The impacts of LBOs on the performance of acquired firms: The French case, *Journal of Business Finance & Accounting,* 29(5,6): 695–729.

173. G. D. Bruton, J. K. Keels, & E. L. Scifres, 2002, Corporate restructuring and performance: An agency perspective on the complete buyout cycle, *Journal of Business Research,* 55: 709–724; W. F. Long & D. J. Ravenscraft, 1993, LBOs, debt, and R&D intensity, *Strategic Management Journal,* 14 (Special Issue): 119–135.

174. Wright, Hoskisson, Busenitz, & Dial, Entrepreneurial growth through privatization; S. A. Zahra, 1995, Corporate entrepreneurship and financial performance: The case of management leveraged buyouts, *Journal of Business Venturing,* 10: 225–248.

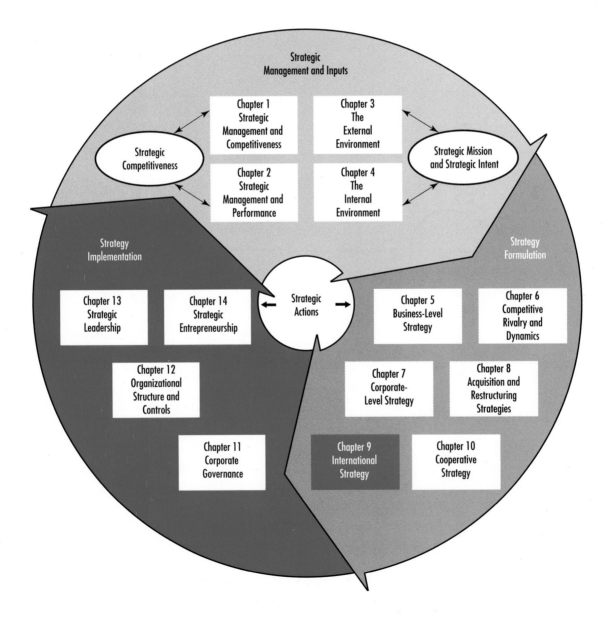

Chapter Nine

International Strategy

Knowledge Objectives

Studying this chapter should provide you with the strategic management knowledge needed to:

1. Explain traditional and emerging motives for firms to pursue international diversification.

2. Explore the four factors that lead to a basis for international business-level strategies.

3. Define the three international corporate-level strategies: multidomestic, global, and transnational.

4. Discuss the environmental trends affecting international strategy, especially liability of foreignness and regionalization.

5. Name and describe the five alternative modes for entering international markets.

6. Explain the effects of international diversification on firm returns and innovation.

7. Name and describe two major risks of international diversification.

8. Explain why the positive outcomes from international expansion are limited.

Chinese Firms' Incentives for Foreign Acquisitions

In 2007, China's foreign-exchange reserves—assets of the Chinese government that are held in different hard currencies such as the dollar, euro, and yen—increased over one-half trillion dollars to reach $1.4 trillion by year end. These reserves result from China's trade surplus with businesses in foreign countries, including Canada. Because of this trade imbalance, other governments have pressured China to increase the value of its currency, the yuan, which would reduce the competitive position of export-related businesses in China. One way the Chinese government can reduce this pressure is by encouraging Chinese companies to reduce the trade imbalance by buying assets overseas. Goods produced by Chinese firms in other nations have the potential to reduce the trade surplus.

www.lenovo.com

www.minmetals.com

www.cnooc.com.cn/yyww

From 2004 onward, Chinese companies dramatically increased bidding for foreign assets. In early 2004, TCL Corp., a large television manufacturer, purchased the television operations of France's Thomson SA and the mobile handset operations of France's Alcatel SA. In 2005, Lenovo Group, the largest personal computer manufacturer in

China, acquired the PC assets of IBM. Lenovo was allowed to use the IBM label for five years as it built its brand in North America.

As the world's largest consumer of mineral raw materials, it is not surprising that China's resource companies are on the hunt for overseas resources. In 2004, China's largest metals and minerals trading group, Minmetals, bid nearly $6 billion for Canada's Noranda. The bid ultimately failed due to time-consuming details that could not be ironed out. The China National Offshore Oil Corporation (CNOOC), a large producer of oil and natural gas in China, made a bid to take over Unocal Corp. for $18.5 billion in 2005 after Chevron and Unocal had agreed for the firms to merge at $16.5 billion. Chevron offered a counter bid that was ultimately successful, even though it was lower than the CNOOC bid. Although the Minmetals and CNOOC transactions were not successfully completed, they demonstrated the incentive of Chinese firms to engage in foreign entry, in part due to the excessive foreign reserves incentive.

These foreign reserves are also being invested domestically and abroad in the steel industry. Although China does not have the largest steel firm in the world—that honour belongs to Netherlands-based Mittal Steel, which, as described in Chapter 8, has the capacity to produce 130 million metric tons of steel per year—Chinese mills turned out nearly half a billion tons of crude steel in 2007. This is about the same amount of steel produced in all of the Americas, Africa, the European Union, and Japan combined—more than one-third of the world's total production.

Neither Minmetals nor CNOOC has walked away from the acquisition path. Minmetals has entered a joint venture with Chile's state-owned copper concern, Codelco, set up a comprehensive co-operation framework with the government of Jamaica for joint exploration and development of bauxite resources on that island, created a joint exploration company with Century Aluminum of the U.S. for a number of exploration projects, and contracted with Bolivia's Mining Resources and Metallurgical Department to jointly develop mineral resources. CNOOC purchased Canadian-based PetroKazakhstan for $4 billion in 2005.

Minmetals and CNOOC are not the only resource companies actively acquiring. China Nonferrous Metal Mining Group invested $150 million in copper mining in Zambia. Aluminum Corp. of China (also known as Chinalco) invested $2.2 billion in a bauxite mine in Australia, and bought Peru Copper for about $800 million.

SOURCES: International Iron & Steel Institute, 2008, Steel statistics, http://www.worldsteel.org/?action=stats&type=steel& period=latest&month=11&year=2007, January 7; 2007, Chinability Web site, China's foreign exchange reserves 1977–2007, http://www. chinability.com/Reserves.htm, December 31; J. Sanford, 2007, Petro politics, *Canadian Business*, 78(22): 90–91; T. Saywell, 2007, Resource security high on China's agenda, *The Northern Miner*, 93(41): 1–2; 2007, Canada's trade surplus at 13-month high, CBC News, March 9, http://www.cbc.ca/money/story/2007/03/09/trade.html; 2007, ArcelorMittal announces partnership for a seamless tube mill in Saudi Arabia, ArcelorMittal press release, February 15, http://www.dofascotube.com/interim/pdfs/tube_saudi_announcement.pdf, retrieved January 8, 2008; A. Browne, O. Brown, S. Yang, & V. Ruan, 2005, China's reserves of foreign money surged last year, *Wall Street Journal*, January 12, A2; S. Lohr, 2005, The big tug of war over Unocal, *New York Times*, www.nytimes.com, July 6; D. Normile, 2005, Branded in China, *Electronic Business*, March, 61–65; E. B. Smith, 2005, Chinese snap up brand-name U.S. firms, *USA Today*, www.usatoday.com, June 21; C. Chandler, 2004, TV's Mr. Big, *Fortune*, February 9, 84–87.

As the Opening Case indicates, China's firms are exercising their financial muscle due to high levels of foreign reserves from a huge trade surplus by entering other markets through foreign direct investment by acquisitions and other modes of entry. China's entrance into the World Trade Organization (WTO) has brought change not only to China and its trading partners but also to industries and firms throughout the world. Despite its underdeveloped market and institutional environment, China is taking advantage of the size of its market with its foreign direct investment. Many firms choose direct investment over indirect investment because it provides better protection for the assets invested.[1] Domestic firms are becoming more competitive and building up capacity. As indicated by the overall capacity of Chinese firms in the steel industry and overall demand for steel as China builds up its infrastructure and manufacturing capacity (for instance, in the auto industry), the potential global market power of China is astounding.[2]

As foreign firms enter China and as Chinese firms enter into other foreign markets, both opportunities and threats for firms competing in global markets are exemplified. This chapter examines opportunities facing firms as they seek to develop and exploit core competencies by diversifying into global markets. In addition, we discuss different problems, complexities, and threats that might accompany a firm's international strategy.[3] Although national boundaries, cultural differences, and geographical distances all pose barriers to entry into many markets, significant opportunities draw businesses into the international arena. A business that plans to operate globally must formulate a successful strategy to take advantage of these global opportunities.[4] Furthermore, to mould their firms into truly global companies, managers must develop global mind-sets.[5] Especially in regard to managing human resources, traditional means of operating with little cultural diversity and without global sourcing are no longer effective.[6]

As firms move into international markets, they develop relationships with suppliers, customers, and partners, and then learn from these relationships. Such activity is evident in the pharmaceuticals industry as firms compete against each other in global markets and invest in all areas of the world in order to learn about new markets and new potential drugs.[7]

In this chapter, as illustrated in Figure 1.1, we discuss the importance of international strategy as a source of strategic competitiveness and above-average returns. The chapter focuses on the incentives to internationalize. Once a firm decides to compete internationally, it must select its strategy and choose a mode of entry into international markets. It may enter international markets by exporting from domestic-based operations, licensing some of its products or services, forming joint ventures with international partners, acquiring a foreign-based firm, or establishing a new subsidiary. Such international diversification can extend product life cycles, provide incentives for more innovation, and produce above-average returns. These benefits are tempered by political and economic risks and the problems of managing a complex international firm with operations in multiple countries.

Figure 9.1 provides an overview of the various choices and outcomes of strategic competitiveness. The relationships among international opportunities, the resources and capabilities that result in strategies, and the modes of entry that are based on core competencies are explored in this chapter.

An **international strategy** is a strategy through which the firm sells its goods or services outside its domestic market.[8] One of the primary reasons for implementing an international strategy (as opposed to a strategy focused on the domestic market) is that international markets yield potential new opportunities.[9]

An **international strategy** is a strategy through which the firm sells its goods or services outside its domestic market.

Figure 9.1 Opportunities and Outcomes of International Strategy

Identify International Opportunities	Explore Resources & Capabilities	Use Core Competency		Strategic Competitiveness Outcomes
	International Strategies	Modes of Entry		
Increased market size	International business-level strategy	Exporting	Management Problems, Risk, and First Steps	Better performance
Return on investment	Multidomestic strategy	Licensing		
Economies of scale & learning	Global strategy	Strategic alliances		Innovation
		Acquisition	Management Problems, Risk, and First Steps	
Location advantages	Transnational strategy	Establishment of a new subsidiary		

Identifying International Opportunities: Incentives to Use an International Strategy

Raymond Vernon captured the classic rationale for international diversification.[10] He suggested that typically a firm discovers an innovation in its home-country market, especially in an advanced economy such as that of Canada or the United States. Some demand for the product may then develop in other countries, and exports are provided by domestic operations. Increased demand in foreign countries justifies direct foreign investment in production capacity abroad, especially because foreign competitors also organize to meet increasing demand. As the product becomes standardized, the firm may rationalize its operations by moving production to a region with low manufacturing costs.[11] Vernon, therefore, observed that one reason why firms pursue international diversification is to extend a product's life cycle.

Another traditional motive for firms to become multinational is to secure needed resources. Key supplies of raw material—especially minerals and energy—are important in some industries, as illustrated in the Opening Case by the acquisitions by Minmetals and CNOOC. For instance, aluminum producers need a supply of bauxite, tire firms need rubber, and oil companies scour the world to find new petroleum reserves. Other industries, such as clothing, electronics, watch-making, and many others, have moved portions of their operations to foreign locations in pursuit of lower production costs.

Although these traditional motives persist, other emerging motivations also drive international expansion (see Chapter 1). For instance, pressure has increased for a global integration of operations, mostly driven by more universal product demand. As nations industrialize, the demand for some products and commodities appears to become more similar. This "nationless," or borderless, demand for globally branded products may be due to similarities in lifestyle in developed nations. Increases in global communication media also facilitate the ability of people in different countries to visualize and model lifestyles in different cultures.[12] IKEA, for example, has become a global brand by selling furniture in 44 countries through about 300 stores that it owns and operates through franchisees. It generated about $30 billion in sales in 2007. All of its furniture is sold in components that can be packaged in flat packs and assembled by the consumer after purchase. This arrangement has allowed for easier shipping and handling than fully assembled units and has facilitated the development of the global brand.[13]

In some industries, technology drives globalization because the economies of scale necessary to reduce costs to the lowest level often require an investment greater than that needed to meet domestic market demand. Korean car maker Hyundai certainly found this to be true; accordingly, it has sought to enhance its operations worldwide.[14] There is also pressure for cost reductions, achieved by purchasing from the lowest-cost global suppliers. For instance, research and development expertise for an emerging business start-up may not exist in the domestic market.[15]

New, large-scale emerging markets, such as China and India, provide a strong internationalization incentive because of their high potential demand for consumer products and services.[16] Because of currency fluctuations, firms may also choose to distribute their operations across many countries, including emerging ones, in order to reduce the risk of devaluation in one country.[17] However, the uniqueness of emerging markets presents both opportunities and challenges.[18] While India, for example, differs from Western countries in many respects, including culture, politics, and the precepts of its economic system, it also offers a huge potential market and its government is becoming more supportive of foreign direct investment.[19] However, the differences between China and India and Western countries pose serious challenges to Western competitive paradigms that emphasize the skills needed to manage financial, economic, and political risks.[20]

The large majority of Canadian-based companies' international business is, as one may expect, in the U.S. market, where 43 percent of Canadian firms' assets are located outside Canada. We will discuss the typical, critical, first move most Canadian businesses make in moving into the U.S. market later in the chapter. The trend, however, is moving away from U.S. investment. Twenty-five years ago, about 70 percent of Canadian direct investment abroad was devoted to the U.S. During the same 25-year period, Canadian direct investment into Europe rose from 14 percent to almost 30 percent.[21] While subtle regional differences in the U.S. should not be ignored, companies seeking to internationalize their operations in Europe face far more complex pressures to respond to greatly differing local, national, or regional customs.[22] This is especially important where goods or services require customization because of cultural differences, or effective marketing to entice customers to try a different product.[23]

The need for local repair and service capabilities, for example, influences a firm to be responsive to local country conditions through its internationalization strategy.[24] This localization may affect even industries that are seen as needing more global economies of scale, as in the white goods industry (i.e., home appliances, like refrigerators).

Employment contracts and labour forces differ significantly in international markets. For example, it is more difficult to lay off employees in Europe than in North America because of employment contract differences. In many cases, host governments demand joint ownership with a local company in order to invest in local operations. This allows the foreign firm to avoid tariffs. Also, host governments frequently require a high percentage of procurements, manufacturing, and R&D to use local sources.[25] These issues increase the need for local investment and responsiveness as opposed to seeking global economies of scale.

We've discussed incentives that influence firms to use international strategies. When these strategies are successful, firms can derive four basic benefits: (1) increased market size; (2) greater returns on major capital investments or on investments in new products and processes; (3) greater economies of scale, scope, or learning; and (4) a competitive advantage through location (for example, access to low-cost labour, critical resources, or customers). We examine these benefits in terms of both their costs (such as higher coordination expenses and limited access to knowledge about host country political influences[26]) and their managerial challenges.

Increased Market Size

Firms can expand the size of their potential market—sometimes dramatically—by moving into international markets. The need to go international is particularly obvious for Canadian companies—given the close presence of a single market ten times the size of the domestic one, the potential for quick growth is huge. Pharmaceutical firms have been doing significant foreign direct investment into China due to the size of the market. One researcher who sampled 117 pharmaceutical firms found that "ninety-nine firms (84.6 percent) chose a joint venture entry operation with a local Chinese partner as their entry mode for the Chinese market and the remaining firms (15.4 percent) established a 100 percent foreign-owned venture operation in China."[27]

Although changing consumer tastes and practices linked to cultural values or traditions are not simple, following an international strategy is a particularly attractive option to firms competing in domestic markets that have limited growth opportunities. For example, firms in the beer industry lack significant growth opportunities in their domestic markets. Accordingly, most large global brewers have pursued a strategy of acquiring other brewers, both in developed markets and in emerging economies. For instance, in just two years (2004–2005) Heineken NV purchased five breweries in Russia and almost tripled its market share in that region from 5.4 percent to 15 percent. The Dutch brewer is now the third largest shareholder of the Russian beer market, behind Baltic Beverages Holdings (a joint venture between Copenhagen-based Carlsberg AS and Edinburgh-based Scottish and Newcastle PLC) and Belgian brewer InBev, which have about 35 percent and 17 percent, respectively.[28]

The size of an international market also affects a firm's willingness to invest in R&D to build competitive advantages in that market.[29] Larger markets usually offer higher potential returns and thus pose less risk for a firm's investments. The strength of the science base in the country in question also can affect a firm's foreign R&D investments. Most firms prefer to invest more heavily in those countries with the scientific knowledge and talent to produce value-creating products and processes from their R&D activities.[30] Research suggests that German multinationals are increasingly investing in international R&D opportunities for resource development and learning purposes as opposed to market-seeking motives.[31]

Return on Investment

Large markets may be crucial for earning a return on significant investments, such as plant and capital equipment or R&D. Therefore, most R&D-intensive industries such as electronics are international. In addition to the need for a large market to recoup heavy investment in R&D, the development pace for new technology is increasing. New products become obsolete more rapidly, and therefore investments need to be recouped more quickly. Moreover, firms' abilities to develop new technologies are expanding, and because of different patent laws across country borders imitation by competitors is more likely. Through reverse engineering, competitors are able to take apart a product, learn the new technology, and develop a similar product. Because their competitors can imitate the new technology relatively quickly, firms need to recoup new product development costs even more rapidly. Consequently, the larger markets provided by international expansion are particularly attractive in industries such as pharmaceuticals because they expand the opportunity for the firm to recoup significant capital investments and large-scale R&D expenditures.[32]

Regardless of other issues, however, the primary reason for investing in international markets is to generate above-average returns on investments. Still, firms from different countries have different expectations and use different criteria to decide whether to invest in international markets.[33] Turkey, for example, has experienced significant growth since 2001 due to foreign direct investment and better management. Companies are noticing its fairly large market and entry point for other markets in the Middle East. In 2004 Turkey drew in less than $2.5 billion in foreign direct investment (FDI); in 2005 this number rose to over $9.5 billion, and over $20 billion in 2006.[34]

Economies of Scale and Learning

By expanding their markets, firms may be able to enjoy economies of scale, particularly in their manufacturing operations. To the extent that a firm can standardize its products across country borders and use the same or similar production facilities, thereby coordinating critical resource functions, it is more likely to achieve optimal economies of scale.[35]

Economies of scale are critical in the global auto industry. China's decision to join the World Trade Organization will allow carmakers from other countries to enter the country and lower tariffs to be charged (in the past, Chinese carmakers have had an advantage over foreign carmakers due to tariffs). Ford, Honda, General Motors, and Volkswagen are each producing an economy car to compete with the existing cars in China. Because of global economies of scale (allowing them to price their products competitively) and local investments in China, all of these companies are likely to obtain significant market share in China. Shanghai Automotive Industry Corp. (SAIC) is one of the local Chinese firms that has helped these foreign car companies achieve their significant success in manufacturing cars in China. SAIC has joint ventures, for instance, with both GM and Volkswagen and produced 1.34 million vehicles in 2006. Furthermore, SAIC is seeking to develop opportunities for exporting vehicles overseas. It aspires to be one of the six largest automakers in the world by 2020.[36]

Firms may also be able to exploit core competencies in international markets through resource and knowledge sharing between units across country borders.[37] This sharing generates synergy, which helps the firm produce higher-quality goods or services at lower cost. In addition, working across international markets provides the firm with new learning opportunities.[38] Multinational firms have substantial occasions to learn from the different practices they encounter in separate international markets. However, research finds that to take advantage of the international R&D investments, firms need to already have a strong R&D system in place to absorb the knowledge.[39]

Location Advantages

Firms may locate facilities in other countries to lower the basic costs of the goods or services they provide. These facilities may provide easier access to lower-cost labour, energy, and other natural resources. Other location advantages include access to critical supplies and to customers.[40] Once positioned favourably with an attractive location, firms must manage their facilities effectively to gain the full benefit of a location advantage.

Such location advantages can be influenced by costs of production and transportation requirements as well as by the needs of the intended customers. Cultural influences may also affect location advantages and disadvantages. If there is a strong match between the cultures in which international transactions are carried out, the liability of foreignness is lower than if there is high cultural distance.[41]

Research also suggests that regulation distances influence the ownership positions of multinational firms as well as their strategies for managing expatriate resources.[42] For example, a little known business fact is that Canada is really closer to Cuba than the United States. Before you grab your drink and head outside to the pool note that we mean this in a political sense, not a geographic one. In the early 1960s, after Castro came to power in Cuba, a series of events took place that eventually ended in Cuba nationalizing all U.S. assets and the U.S. slapping a full trade embargo on Cuba.[43] This embargo has lasted well over a half-century and is supposed to include trade in any U.S. goods or property. The result has been closer Canadian ties to Cuba—which has allowed Canadian businesses, like Sherritt International, to be a big presence in the country.

Cuban operations made up about 30 percent of Sherritt's nearly billion-dollar revenue. Because of Cuba, Sherritt mines one of the world's least expensive sources of nickel, operates Cuban oil wells and a soya factory, holds a 25-percent indirect stake in a popular Havana hotel, and via its power unit produces more than 10 percent of Cuba's electricity. Similarly, a lack of U.S. competitors has likely allowed Leisure Canada to become a leading developer of luxury resorts in Cuba. Leisure Canada has multiple properties currently under development, including five-star hotels, over 4,200 hotel rooms in Cuba, and PGA championship golf courses.[44]

International Strategies

Firms choose to use one or both of two basic types of international strategies: business-level international strategy and corporate-level international strategy. At the business level, firms follow generic strategies: cost leadership, differentiation, focused cost leadership, focused differentiation, or integrated cost leadership/differentiation. There are three corporate-level international strategies: multidomestic, global, or transnational (a combination of multidomestic and global). To create competitive advantage, each strategy must realize a core competency based on difficult-to-duplicate resources and capabilities.[45] As discussed in Chapters 5 and 7, firms expect to create value through the implementation of a business-level strategy and a corporate-level strategy.[46]

International Business-Level Strategy

Each business must develop a competitive strategy focused on its own domestic market. We discussed business-level strategies in Chapter 5 and competitive rivalry and competitive dynamics in Chapter 6. International business-level strategies have some unique features. In an international business-level strategy, the home country of operation is often the most important source of competitive advantage.[47] The resources and capabilities established in the home country frequently allow the firm to pursue the strategy into markets located in other countries. However, research indicates that as a firm continues its growth into multiple international locations, the country of origin is less important for competitive advantage.[48] Michael Porter's model, illustrated in Figure 9.2,

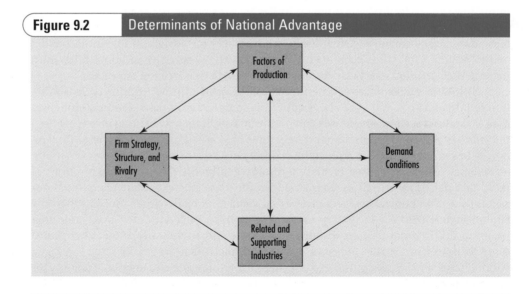

Figure 9.2   Determinants of National Advantage

describes the factors contributing to the advantage of firms in a dominant global industry and associated with a specific home country or regional environment.[49] The first dimension in Porter's model is *factors of production*. This dimension refers to the inputs necessary to compete in any industry—labour, land, natural resources, capital, and infrastructure (such as transportation, postal, and communication systems). There are basic factors (for example, natural and labour resources) and advanced factors (such as digital communication systems and a highly educated workforce). Other production factors are generalized (highway systems and the supply of debt capital) and specialized (skilled personnel in a specific industry, such as the workers in a port who specialize in handling bulk chemicals). If a country has both advanced and specialized production factors, it is likely to serve an industry well by spawning strong home-country competitors that also can be successful global competitors.

Ironically, countries often develop advanced and specialized factors because they lack critical basic resources. For example, some Asian countries, such as South Korea, lack abundant natural resources but offer a strong work ethic, a large number of engineers, and systems of large firms to create an expertise in manufacturing. Similarly, Germany developed a strong chemical industry, partially because Hoechst and BASF spent years creating a synthetic indigo dye to reduce their dependence on imports, unlike Britain, whose colonies provided large supplies of natural indigo.[50]

The second dimension in Porter's model, *demand conditions,* is characterized by the nature and size of buyers' needs in the home market for the industry's goods or services. The sheer size of a market segment can produce the demand necessary to create scale-efficient facilities.

Chinese manufacturing companies have spent years focused on building their businesses in China, and only recently are beginning to look at markets beyond their borders. As the opening case suggests, companies such as Lenovo (personal computers) and Haier (small appliances) have begun the difficult process of building their brand equity in other countries, beginning in the Far East and seeking to make subsequent moves into the West. These companies have been helped by China's entry to the World Trade Organization and are looking to overseas markets to increase market share and profits. The efficiency built in a large-scale market could help lead to ultimate domination of the industry in other countries, although this could be difficult for firms coming from an emerging economy.

Specialized demand may also create opportunities beyond national boundaries. For example, Swiss firms have long led the world in tunnelling equipment because of the need to tunnel through mountains for rail and highway passage in Switzerland. Japanese firms have created a niche market for compact, quiet air conditioners, which are important in Japan because homes are often small and close together.[51]

Related and supporting industries are the third dimension in Porter's model. Italy has become the leader in the shoe industry because of related and supporting industries; a well-established leather-processing industry provides the leather needed to construct shoes and related products. Also, many people travel to Italy to purchase leather goods, providing support in distribution. Supporting industries in leather-working machinery and design services also contribute to the success of the shoe industry. In fact, the design services industry supports its own related industries, such as ski boots, fashion apparel, and furniture. In Japan, cameras and copiers are related industries. Similarly, it is argued that the "creative resources nurtured by [the] popular cartoons and animation sector, combined with technological knowledge accumulated in the consumer electronics industry, facilitated the emergence of a successful video game industry in Japan."[52]

Firm strategy, structure, and rivalry make up the final country dimension and also foster the growth of certain industries. The dimension of strategy, structure, and rivalry among firms varies greatly from nation to nation. Because of the excellent technical training

Chapter 9 / International Strategy

system in Germany, there is a strong emphasis on methodical product and process improvements. In Japan, unusual cooperative and competitive systems have facilitated the cross-functional management of complex assembly operations. In Italy, the national pride of the country's designers has spawned strong industries in sports cars, fashion apparel, and furniture. In North America, competition among computer manufacturers and software producers has favoured the development of these industries.

The four basic dimensions of the "diamond" model in Figure 9.2 emphasize the environmental or structural attributes of a national economy that contribute to national advantage. Government policy also clearly contributes to the success and failure of many firms and industries. We can see the impact of government policy, as well as all the determinants of national advantage—factors of production, related and supporting industries, rivalry, and demand—play out in the aluminum industry.

Aluminum production requires bauxite (the ore from which alumina is made) and large amounts of electricity—about $2 billion worth per year.[53] Though most electricity is produced by coal,[54] the most economical way to produce it is via hydro. Most large hydroelectric projects are either built by governments or require extensive government approvals. The seven largest producers of aluminum are China, Russia, the U.S., Canada, Australia, Brazil, and Norway.[55] Six of these seven countries (all except Australia) are the world's largest producers of hydroelectricity. China is the world's largest producer of coal[56]—from which it generates electricity. Canada, the U.S., and Russia have a long history of government involvement in publicly owned hydroelectric projects.[57] Two of the industry's largest competitors historically (Alcan and Alcoa) were headquartered in North America, where there are inexpensive government-owned hydro power supplies.[58] Firms like Australia's Rio Tinto and BHP have been able to create a presence in the industry because about one-third of the world's bauxite is mined in Australia and the country is in close proximity to China, where demand for alumina products is high.[59]

Although each firm must create its own success, not all firms will survive to become global competitors—not even those operating with the same country factors that spawned the successful firms. The actual strategic choices managers make may be the most compelling reason for success or failure. Accordingly, the factors illustrated in Figure 9.2 are likely to produce competitive advantages only when the firm develops and implements an appropriate strategy that takes advantage of distinct country factors. Thus, these distinct country factors are necessary to consider when analyzing the business-level strategies (i.e., cost leadership, differentiation, focused cost leadership, focused differentiation, and integrated cost leadership/differentiation, discussed in Chapter 5) in an international context. However, pursuing an international strategy leads to more adjustment and learning as the firm adjusts to competition in the host country.

International Corporate-Level Strategy

The international business-level strategies are based at least partially on the type of international corporate-level strategy the firm has chosen. Some corporate strategies give individual country units the authority to develop their own business-level strategies; other corporate strategies dictate the business-level strategies in order to standardize the firm's products and sharing of resources across countries.[60]

International corporate-level strategy focuses on the scope of a firm's operations through both product and geographic diversification. International corporate-level strategy is required when the firm operates in multiple industries and multiple countries or regions.[61] The headquarters unit guides the strategy, although business- or country-level managers can have substantial strategic input depending on the type of international corporate-level strategy followed. The three international corporate-level strategies are multidomestic, global, and transnational, as shown in Figure 9.3.

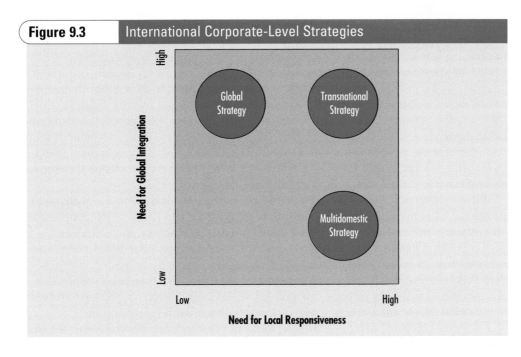

Figure 9.3 International Corporate-Level Strategies

Multidomestic Strategy

A **multidomestic strategy** is an international strategy in which strategic and operating decisions are decentralized to the strategic business unit in each country so as to allow that unit to tailor products to the local market.[62] A multidomestic strategy focuses on competition within each country. It assumes that the markets differ and therefore are segmented by country boundaries. The multidomestic strategy uses a highly decentralized approach, allowing each division to focus on a geographic area, region, or country.[63] In other words, consumer needs and desires, industry conditions (e.g., the number and type of competitors), political and legal structures, and social norms vary by country. With multidomestic strategies, the firm can customize its products to meet the specific needs and preferences of local customers. Therefore, these strategies should maximize a firm's competitive response to the idiosyncratic requirements of each market.[64]

The use of multidomestic strategies usually expands the firm's local market share because the firm can pay attention to the needs of the local clientele.[65] However, the use of these strategies results in more uncertainty for the corporation as a whole, because of the differences across markets and thus the different strategies employed by local country units.[66] Moreover, multidomestic strategies do not allow for the achievement of economies of scale and can be more costly. As a result, firms employing a multidomestic strategy decentralize their strategic and operating decisions to the business units operating in each country. Historically, Unilever, a large European consumer products firm, has had a very decentralized approach to managing its international operations.[67] The French defence contractor French Thomson-CSF has transformed into a new global defence and aerospace electronics group called Thales SA. Thales has won contracts worldwide by using a multidomestic strategy. It has become a local player in six countries outside France: Britain, the Netherlands, Australia, South Africa, South Korea, and Singapore.[68] It implemented its strategy with a series of joint ventures and acquisitions of local players in each of these markets. The multidomestic strategy has been commonly used by European multinational firms because of the variety of cultures and markets found in Europe.[69]

A **multidomestic strategy** is an international strategy in which strategic and operating decisions are decentralized to the strategic business unit in each country so as to allow that unit to tailor products to the local market.

Global Strategy

In contrast to a multidomestic strategy, a global strategy assumes more standardization of products across country markets. As a result, a global strategy is centralized and controlled by the home office. The strategic business units operating in each country are assumed to be interdependent, and the home office attempts to achieve integration across these businesses.[70] A **global strategy** is an international strategy through which the firm offers standardized products across country markets, with competitive strategy being dictated by the home office. Thus, a global strategy emphasizes economies of scale and offers greater opportunities to take innovations developed at the corporate level or in one country and utilize them in other markets. Improvements in global accounting and financial reporting standards are facilitating this strategy.[71]

While a global strategy produces lower risk, it may cause the firm to forgo growth opportunities in local markets, either because those markets are less likely to be identified as opportunities or because the opportunities require that products be adapted to the local market.[72] The global strategy is not as responsive to local markets and is difficult to manage because of the need to coordinate strategies and operating decisions across country borders. Vodafone, in implementing a global strategy, has had difficulty in Japan: "By focusing too much on building a globally oriented brand, Vodafone failed to give Japanese customers what they wanted, chiefly a wide line-up of phones with fancy features."[73]

Achieving efficient operations with a global strategy requires sharing resources and facilitating coordination and cooperation across country boundaries, which in turn require centralization and headquarters control. Furthermore, research suggests that the performance of the global strategy is enhanced if it deploys in areas where regional integration among countries is occurring, such as the European Union. Many Japanese firms have successfully used the global strategy.[74]

Cemex is the third largest cement company in the world, behind France's Lafarge and Switzerland's Holcim, and is the largest producer of ready mix, a prepackaged product that contains all the ingredients needed to make localized cement products. In 2005, Cemex acquired RMC for $4.1 billion. RMC is a large U.K. cement producer with two-thirds of its business in Europe. Cemex was already the number-one producer in Spain through its acquisition of a Spanish company in 1992. In 2000 Cemex acquired Southdown, a large manufacturer in the United States. Accordingly, Cemex has strong market power in the Americas as well as in Europe. Because Cemex pursues a global strategy effectively, its integration of its centralization process has resulted in a quick payoff for its merger integration process. To integrate its businesses globally, Cemex uses the Internet as one way of increasing revenue and lowering its cost structure. By using the Internet to improve logistics and manage an extensive supply network, Cemex can significantly reduce costs. Connectivity between the operations in different countries and universal standards dominates its approach.[75]

Transnational Strategy

A **transnational strategy** is an international strategy through which the firm seeks to achieve both global efficiency and local responsiveness. Realizing these goals is difficult: one requires close global coordination while the other requires local flexibility. "Flexible coordination"—building a shared vision and individual commitment through an integrated network—is required to implement the transnational strategy. Such integrated networks allow a firm to manage its connections with customers, suppliers, partners, and other parties more efficiently than using arm's-length transactions.[76] The transnational strategy is difficult to use because of its conflicting goals (see Chapter 12 for more on the implementation of this and other corporate-level international strategies). On the positive side, the effective implementation of a transnational strategy often produces higher performance than does the implementation of either the multidomestic or global international corporate-level strategies.[77]

A **global strategy** is an international strategy through which the firm offers standardized products across country markets, with competitive strategy being dictated by the home office.

A **transnational strategy** is an international strategy through which the firm seeks to achieve both global efficiency and local responsiveness.

Renault has used this strategy to reinvigorate Nissan, in which Renault bought a controlling interest in 1999. Since then, Carlos Ghosn, CEO of Nissan, has brought Nissan back from being a very poor performer to being one of the top performers in the industry. The business units of Renault cooperate to achieve global and regional efficiencies and adapt to local market conditions successfully.[78]

Canadian company Bombardier's rail operations suggest that it also pursuing a transnational strategy. Passenger rail transport has significant pressures for local responsiveness—for example, government demands for local employment. To meet this demand, Bombardier has numerous plants and maintenance facilities around the globe. Concurrently, the company faces global pressures for world-class computerized scheduling, vehicle programming for driverless systems, project design, and construction engineering. These tasks are done at fewer locations to provide a critical mass of engineering and programming expertise at each.[79]

Environmental Trends

Although the transnational strategy is difficult to implement, emphasis on global efficiency is increasing as more industries begin to experience global competition. To add to the problem, there is also an increased emphasis on local requirements: global goods and services often require some customization to meet government regulations within particular countries or to fit customer tastes and preferences. In addition, most multinational firms desire coordination and sharing of resources across country markets to hold down costs, as illustrated by the Cemex example above.[80] Furthermore, some products and industries may be more suited than others for standardization across country borders.

As a result, most large multinational firms with diverse products employ a multidomestic strategy with certain product lines and a global strategy with others. Many multinational firms may require this type of flexibility if they are to be strategically competitive, in part due to trends that change over time. For small and medium-sized firms, the research suggests that their managers are influenced by the strategy they implement (those with a differentiation strategy are more positively disposed to the agreement than are those pursuing a cost leadership strategy) and by their experience and rivalry with exporting firms.[81] Two important environmental conditions that impact international strategy are the liability of foreignness and regionalization.

Liability of Foreignness

The dramatic success of Japanese firms such as Toyota and Sony in North America and other international markets in the 1980s was a powerful jolt to North American managers and awakened them to the importance of global competition. In the 21st century, China, India, Brazil, and Eastern Europe represent potential major international market opportunities for firms from many countries, including Canada, Japan, the European Union, and the U.S.[82] However, there are legitimate concerns about the relative attractiveness of global strategies. This is illustrated by the experience of Walt Disney Company in opening theme parks in foreign countries. For example, Disney suffered "lawsuits in France, at Disneyland Paris, because of the lack of fit between its transferred personnel policies and the French employees charged to enact them."[83]

Research shows that global strategies are not as prevalent as once thought and are very difficult to implement, even when using Internet-based strategies.[84] As such, firms may focus less on truly global markets and more on regional adaptation. Although parallel developments in the Internet and mobile telecommunication facilitate communications across the globe, as noted earlier, the implementation of Web-based strategies also requires local adaptation.

The globalization of businesses with local strategies is demonstrated by Victoria, B.C.–based AbeBooks. Since launching its Web site one year after its founding in 1995, AbeBooks has gone on to become the world's largest online marketplace for books. The company can access over 100 million new and used books from more than 13,500 book-sellers from 57 countries. While one can access all these books through the company's main Web site (www.abebooks.com), there are also local sites for the German, French, and U.K. markets. These came online after AbeBooks acquired European leader JustBooks in 2001. In 2004, AbeBooks added a Spanish-language site when it acquired Iberlibro.com.[85]

With word of mouth and limited online advertising, a Web site business can be built in a foreign country without a lot of initial marketing expenses. Once the online busi-ness is large enough, a catalogue business can be launched with mailings targeted to cus-tomers who have used the business online. This is how mail-order clothier Lands' End developed markets for its wares in the U.K., France, Italy, Ireland, and Germany. Thus, even smaller firms can sell their goods and services globally when facilitated by elec-tronic infrastructure without having significant (brick-and-mortar) facilities outside of their home location. Lands' End and other retailers are going further by creating per-sonal customization for fitting apparel sizes over the Internet. Service can be enhanced by being able to order online and pick up at a store. Even with custom ordering systems, significant local adaptation is still needed in each country or region.[86]

Regionalization

Regionalization is a second trend that has become more common in global markets. Because a firm's location can affect its strategic competitiveness,[87] it must decide whether to compete in all or many global markets, or to focus on a particular region or regions. Competing in all markets provides economies that can be achieved because of the combined market size. Research suggests that firms that compete in risky emerging markets can also have higher performance.[88]

However, a firm that competes in industries where the international markets differ greatly (in which it must employ a multidomestic strategy) may wish to narrow its focus to a particular region of the world. In so doing, it can better understand the cultures, legal and social norms, and other factors that are important for effective competition in those markets. For example, a firm may focus on Far East markets rather than competing simultaneously in the Middle East, Europe, and the Far East. Or, the firm may choose a region of the world where the markets are more similar and some coordination and sharing of resources would be possible. In this way, the firm may be able not only to better understand the markets in which it competes, but also to achieve some economies, even though it may have to employ a multidomestic strategy. For instance, research suggests that most large retailers are better at focusing on a particular region rather than being truly global.[89]

Countries that develop trade agreements to increase the economic power of their regions may promote regional strategies. The European Union (EU) and South America's Organization of American States (OAS) are associations that developed trade agreements to promote the flow of trade across country boundaries within their respective regions.[90] Many European firms acquire and integrate their businesses in Europe to better coordi-nate pan-European brands as the EU creates more unity in European markets. With this process likely to continue as new countries are added to the agreement, some interna-tional firms may prefer to pursue regional strategies versus global strategies because the size of the market is increasing.[91]

The North American Free Trade Agreement (NAFTA), signed by Canada, the United States, and Mexico, facilitates free trade across country borders in North America. NAFTA loosens restrictions on international strategies within this region and provides greater

The First International Step: To the U.S.

The U.S. should be a good place for Canadians to do business; we share one of the world's longest borders and we are each other's main trading partner. Yet developing profitable operations in the U.S. is a challenge. Canadian businesses—like Second Cup, Canadian Tire, and E.D. Smith—all fared poorly when they went south of the border. "Whenever you go cross-border," says Donald Chu, a senior analyst at Standard & Poor's Corp., "the biggest difficulty is that people think it's the same marketplace, but it's not. When companies come from the U.S. up to Canada, they often get their heads handed to them on a platter, and the same goes for Canadian companies going down to the U.S."

We like to think of America and Americans as different from Canada and Canadians. Yet when Canadian businesses consider the U.S., they tend to view it as pretty much like the home market. It is not, in three significant ways: the market, the competitive environment, and the people.

In the U.S. market, consumers demand better service and lower prices; Canadians have tended to be more brand-loyal to national chains. The Keg steakhouse chain of Vancouver recognized this when it began opening restaurants in the U.S. northwest. Food portions had to be larger—not because Americans really ate more, but because they wanted to "be sure they're getting value." There were, of course, those other pesky subtle differences. U.S. customers preferred local wines; Canadian wine tastes were more diverse. The Keg in the U.S. does a bigger Thanksgiving business, and its bars do a bigger Halloween business.

Though regional differences exist in both markets, Canadian executives have generally found regional differences in buying behaviour in the U.S. to be much greater than in Canada. Canada was seen to be more homogeneous politically, economically, and socially. Doing business in the United States required knowledge of each individual region, because the differences between them could be large. Montreal convenience store operator Alimentation Couche-Tard (which operates Mac's, Becker's, and Provi-Soir in Canada) has been careful to recognize regional differences by decentralizing and customizing store designs and merchandise offerings to local tastes in its 5,000 stores.

Couche-Tard has also made sure its move into the U.S. has been fast and significant. The company had pursued a strategy to move into the American heartland first, where it had purchased the 225-store Bigfoot convenience store chain in 2001 and the 400-store Dairy Mart chain in 2002. Couche-Tard's 2003 acquisition of America's 1,600-store Circle-K chain made it the fourth-largest convenience store operator in North America. The Circle-K purchase, along with the other chains picked up along the way, gave the company a strong base of operations from which it has expanded into the U.S. south (four acquisitions totalling more than 360 stores from 2004 to 2006).

The U.S. competitive environment, like any other, involves building new relationships with new suppliers. Business research has also found that Americans are more competitive than Canadians. U.S. executives will describe actions in their market as a battlefield, as though it was "all out war" with their competitors. With this comes a higher propensity for risk. This was certainly the case when Toronto's Manulife purchased Boston's John Hancock Insurance to become North America's second-largest life insurance company. Hancock had a greater penchant for risk; speculative-grade securities made up 8 to 10 percent of Hancock's investment portfolio. This was more than double the average for most Canadian insurers. Hancock also carried some riskier and unfamiliar product lines—like long-term care and fixed annuities. Thus, developing a consistent approach to risk management—critical for any insurance company—has been vital to this successful combination.

People's attitudes, values, and behaviours are different between the two countries. American employees have been described as possessing a greater desire for independence than Canadian employees, and to be much less interested in unions. American employees

(continued)

were generally perceived to be more conscientious about productivity. American employees' strong work orientation created an expectation that they would be rewarded based on merit. American managers tended to have a higher level of experience in the retail industry and their executives were expected to live up to higher performance standards (not meeting goals was more likely to lead to termination in the U.S. than in Canada).

However, the above points are over-generalizations one must be careful about. For example, because of regional differences, E. D. Smith found that workers in its Winona, Ontario plant were far more productive and conscientious than employees in its Byhalia, Mississippi plant. For the Canadian maker of jams, pie fillings, and sauces, conscientious employees were those who could produce defect-free products with zero shortages. After four years of trying to get the American plant to meet E. D. Smith's demanding product standards, the company finally closed the plant because of the consistent inability of workers to achieve the required degree of quality.

SOURCES: R. L. Tung, 2008, The cross-cultural research imperative: The need to balance cross-national and intra-national diversity, *Journal of International Business Studies*, 39: 41–46; 2008, Couche-Tard History Web site, http://www.couche-tard.com/history.html, retrieved January 12; J. Valorzi, 2006, Canadian companies generate mixed results in competitive U.S. market, *Nelson Daily News*, August 28, 5; 2004, Manulife press release, http://www.manulife.com/corporate/corporate2.nsf/Public/corporate042804.html, retrieved January 12, 2008; K. Kalawsky, 2003, Dominic finally gets his big catch. Now what? . . . , *National Post*, November 10, DM3; S. Silcoff & R. Gibbens, 2003, Couche-Tard grows in U.S. on $1.1B deal . . . , *National Post*, October 7, FP1; 1999, How to succeed in the U.S. market by really really trying, *National Post*, June 3, 76; T. Belford & K. Vermond, 1999, Mr. Smith goes to Mississippi . . . , *National Post*, December 15, E14; S. O'Grady & H. W. Lane, 1996, The psychic distance paradox, *Journal of International Business Studies*, 27, 309–333.

opportunity for regional international strategies. Though not as high profile, Canada also has free trade agreements with Costa Rica, Chile, and Israel, as well as a completed negotiation for a free trade agreement with the European Free Trade Association (Iceland, Norway, Switzerland, and Liechtenstein). Free trade negotiations are underway for a free trade area to cover 34 democratic countries in the Americas. In addition, Canada has "foreign protection and promotion agreements" dealing with investor and property rights with nine other countries in the Americas (as well as ten European, four Asian, and two African countries).[92]

Most firms enter regional markets sequentially, beginning in markets with which they are more familiar. They also introduce their largest and strongest lines of business into these markets first, followed by their other lines of business once the first lines are successful. They also usually invest in the same area as their original investment location.[93]

This suggests that the most logical place for Canadian organizations to start a global expansion would be the United States. However, even with a regional approach, unrecognized subtle cultural differences can often trip up otherwise well-run organizations.[94] As discussed in the Strategic Focus, these differences may explain the experience of numerous Canadian organizations that competitors that have difficulties when entering the U.S. market.

After the firm selects its international strategies and decides whether to employ them in regional or world markets, it must choose a market entry mode.[95]

Choice of International Entry Mode

International expansion is accomplished by exporting products, participating in licensing arrangements, forming strategic alliances, making acquisitions, and establishing new wholly owned subsidiaries. These means of entering international markets and their characteristics are shown in Table 9.1. Each means of market entry has its advantages and disadvantages. Thus, choosing the appropriate mode or path to enter international markets affects the firm's performance in those markets.[96]

Table 9.1	Global Market Entry: Choice of Entry
Type of Entry	**Characteristics**
Exporting	High cost, low control
Licensing	Low cost, low risk, little control, low returns
Strategic alliances	Shared costs, shared resources, shared risks, problems of integration (e.g., two corporate cultures)
Acquisition	Quick access to new market, high cost, complex negotiations, problems of merging with domestic operations
New wholly owned subsidiary	Complex, often costly, time consuming, high risk, maximum control, potential above-average returns

Exporting

Many industrial firms begin their international expansion by exporting goods or services to other countries.[97] Exporting does not require the expense of establishing operations in the host countries, but exporters must establish some means of marketing and distributing their products. Usually, exporting firms develop contractual arrangements with host-country firms.

The disadvantages of exporting include the often high costs of transportation and possible tariffs placed on incoming goods. Furthermore, the exporter has less control over the marketing and distribution of its products in the host country and must either pay the distributor or allow the distributor to add to the price to recoup its costs and earn a profit.[98] As a result, it may be difficult to market a competitive product through exporting or to provide a product that is customized to each international market.[99] However, evidence suggests that cost leadership strategies enhance the performance of exports in developed countries, whereas differentiation strategies are more successful in emerging economies.[100]

Firms export mostly to countries that are closest to their facilities because of the lower transportation costs and the usually greater similarity between geographic neighbours. For example, Canadian NAFTA partners Mexico and the U.S. account for more than three-quarters of the goods exported from Ontario. The Internet has also made exporting easier. Even small firms can access critical information about foreign markets, examine a target market, research the competition, and find lists of potential customers.[101] Governments also use the Internet to facilitate applications for export and import licences.

Small businesses are most likely to use the exporting mode of international entry. Currency exchange rates are one of the most significant problems small businesses face. The U.S. administration has supported a weak dollar against other currencies, which makes exporting to the United States more expensive for U.S. consumers and U.S. goods less costly to Canadian buyers. On the one hand, this has put great pressure on Canadian exporters to run very efficient operations to be more competitive (and it has put pressure on Canadian retailers to compete against U.S. retailers and exporting U.S. mail-order houses). On the other hand, in spite of the high dollar, worldwide demand has pushed commodity prices and the value of Canadian mining products being exported to exceptional levels.[102]

Licensing

Licensing is an increasingly common form of organizational network, particularly among smaller firms. A licensing arrangement allows a foreign company to purchase the right to manufacture and sell the firm's products within a host country or set of countries.[103] The licenser is normally paid a royalty on each unit produced and sold. The licensee takes the risks and makes the monetary investments in facilities for manufacturing, marketing, and distributing the goods or services. As a result, licensing is possibly the least costly form of international expansion.

Corus Entertainment's animation division, Nelvana, produces children's T.V. shows like *Max and Ruby, Franklin, Babar, Pippi Longstocking,* and a long list of others. While Nelvana produces animation, it must license the rights to broadcast it outside of Canada internationally. More importantly, it does not produce the merchandising that goes along with the programming—toys, puzzles, games, dolls, and so on. Nelvana licenses the right to produce these products to avoid the expensive investment in product manufacturing and distribution facilities. Interestingly, Nelvana is the beneficiary of licensing from others as it also licenses the rights to produce the characters developed by authors elsewhere.[104]

Licensing is also a way to expand returns based on previous innovations.[105] Even if product life cycles are short, licensing may be a useful tool. For instance, because the toy industry faces relentless change and an unpredictable buying public, licensing is used and contracts are often completed in foreign markets where labour may be less expensive.[106]

Licensing also has disadvantages. For example, it gives the firm very little control over the manufacture and marketing of its products in other countries. Thus, licence deals must be structured properly.[107] In addition, licensing provides the least potential returns, because returns must be shared between the licenser and the licensee. Worse, the international firm may learn the technology and produce and sell a similar competitive product after the licence expires. Komatsu, for example, first licensed much of its technology from International Harvester, Bucyrus-Erie, and Cummins Engine to compete against Caterpillar in the earthmoving equipment business. Komatsu then dropped these licences and developed its own products using the technology it had gained from these U.S. companies.[108]

Richmond, B.C.'s Boston Pizza expanded throughout Canada over the course of 25 years by being a franchise licenser of restaurants. About a dozen years ago, the chain decided to expand into the U.S. market. Using the name *Boston's, The Gourmet Pizza,* it has licensed the concept to U.S. franchisees who have opened scores of locations. Boston's now has locations in more than 25 states.[109] Although Boston Pizza has used franchise licensing successfully, if a firm wants to move to a different ownership arrangement licensing may create some inflexibility. Thus, it is important that a firm think ahead and consider sequential forms of entry in international markets.[110]

Strategic Alliances

In recent years, strategic alliances have become a popular means of international expansion.[111] Strategic alliances allow firms to share the risks and the resources required to enter international markets.[112] Moreover, strategic alliances can facilitate the development of new core competencies that contribute to the firm's future strategic competitiveness.[113]

Begun in late 1996, Manulife-Sinochem is a joint venture company between Toronto's Manulife International and the Sinochem group (a Fortune 500 company and one of China's biggest foreign trading companies). Today the venture, 51 percent owned by Manulife, has more than 8,000 staff and agents serving more than 300,000 clients in Shanghai, Beijing, and 23 other cities. Manulife has successfully used this joint venture to develop the Chinese market. While about 20 percent of Manulife's life insurance polices are in Asia—Manulife has been in the region since the 1890s—the growth of this joint venture likely means that this percentage will increase.[114]

As in the Manulife example, most strategic alliances are formed with a host-country firm that knows and understands the competitive conditions, legal and social norms, and cultural idiosyncrasies of the country, which should help the expanding firm manufacture and market a competitive product. Often, firms in emerging economies want to form international alliances and ventures to gain access to sophisticated technologies that are new to them. This type of arrangement can benefit the non–emerging-economy firm as well, in that it gains access to a new market and does not have to pay tariffs to do so (because it is partnering with a local company).[115] In return, the host-country firm may find its new access to the expanding firm's technology and innovative products attractive. Each partner in an alliance brings knowledge or resources to the partnership.[116] Indeed, partners often enter an alliance with the purpose of learning new capabilities. Common among those desired capabilities are technological skills.[117] Managing these expectations can facilitate improved performance.

The alliance mentioned earlier in the chapter between Renault, a French automaker, and its Japanese partner, Nissan, has been successful over the years because of the way it was managed. Research suggests that company executives need to know their own firm well, understand factors that determine the norms in different countries, know how the firm is seen by other partners in the venture, and learn to adapt while remaining consistent with their own company cultural values. Such a multi-faceted and versatile approach has helped the Renault and Nissan alliance succeed over the years.[118]

Not all alliances are successful; in fact, many fail.[119] The primary reasons for failure include incompatible partners and conflict between the partners.[120] International strategic alliances are especially difficult to manage.[121] Several factors may cause a relationship to sour. Trust between the partners is critical and is affected by at least four fundamental issues: the initial condition of the relationship, the negotiation process to arrive at an agreement, partner interactions, and external events.[122] Trust is also influenced by the country cultures involved in the alliance or joint venture.[123]

Research has shown that equity-based alliances, over which a firm has more control, tend to produce more positive returns (strategic alliances are discussed in greater depth in Chapter 10). However, if trust is required to develop new capabilities in a research collaboration, equity can serve as a barrier to the necessary relationship building.[124] If conflict in a strategic alliance or joint venture will not be manageable, an acquisition may be a better option.[125] Research suggests that alliances are more favourable in the face of high uncertainty and where cooperation is needed to share knowledge between partners and where strategic flexibility is important, such as with small and medium-sized firms. However, acquisitions are better in situations with less need for strategic flexibility and when the transaction is used to maintain economies of scale or scope.[126] Alliances can also lead to an acquisition, which is discussed next.

Acquisitions

As free trade has continued to expand in global markets, cross-border acquisitions have also been increasing significantly. In recent years, cross-border acquisitions have comprised more than 45 percent of all acquisitions completed worldwide.[127] As explained in Chapter 8, acquisitions can provide quick access to a new market. In fact, acquisitions may provide the fastest, and often the largest, initial international expansion of any of the alternatives.[128] Thus, entry is much quicker than by other modes. For example, Wal-Mart has entered Germany and the United Kingdom by acquiring local firms.[129] Also, acquisitions are the mode used by many firms to enter Eastern European markets.

When Unicredito Italiano SPA bought Germany's HVB Group AG, the rationale behind the acquisition was that the market for banking will ultimately be unified for financial services across European Union country boundaries. Both of these firms have also been buying banks in other parts of Europe, especially in Eastern Europe. Therefore, the combination allows for better market power within Western Europe and emerging economies in Eastern Europe.[130]

Although acquisitions have become a popular mode of entering international markets, they are not without costs. International acquisitions carry some of the disadvantages of domestic acquisitions, as indicated in the Opening Case (also see Chapter 8). In addition, they can be expensive and also often require debt financing, which carries an extra cost. International negotiations for acquisitions can be exceedingly complex and are generally more complicated than domestic acquisitions. For example, it is estimated that only 20 percent of cross-border bids lead to a completed acquisition, compared with 40 percent of bids for domestic acquisitions.[131] Dealing with the legal and regulatory requirements in the target firm's country and obtaining appropriate information to negotiate an agreement often presents significant problems. Finally, the problems of merging the new firm into the acquiring firm often are more complex than in domestic acquisitions. The acquiring firm must deal not only with different corporate cultures, but also with potentially different social cultures and practices. Therefore, while international acquisitions have been popular because of the rapid access to new markets they provide, they also carry with them important costs and multiple risks.

China is home to several large energy companies that are finally forming a global strategy. China's increasing petroleum needs and dependence on the Middle East are spurring the companies to seek foreign oil sources. This is illustrated by the acquisition intentions of CNOOC described in the Opening Case. SAIC, a China-based automobile producer, acquired the assets of MG Rover Group, a British auto producer that was in insolvency. This acquisition gives the Chinese firm an entry point into Europe and an opportunity to establish its own brand through the MG Rover label. SAIC had previously considered a joint venture but has now fully funded the bid, worth $104 million.[132]

New Wholly Owned Subsidiary

Establishment of a new wholly owned subsidiary is referred to as a **greenfield venture.**

The establishment of a new wholly owned subsidiary is referred to as a **greenfield venture.** This process is often complex and potentially costly, but it affords maximum control to the firm and has the most potential to provide above-average returns. This potential is especially true of firms with strong intangible capabilities that might be leveraged through a greenfield venture. A firm maintains full control of its operations with a greenfield venture. More control is especially advantageous if the firm has proprietary technology. Research also suggests that "wholly-owned subsidiaries and expatriate staff are preferred" in service industries where "close contacts with end customers" and "high levels of professional skills, specialized know-how, and customization" are required.[133] Other research suggests that greenfield investments are more prominent where physical capital-intensive plants are planned and that acquisitions are more likely preferred when a firm is human capital intensive—that is, where a strong local degree of unionization and high cultural distance would cause difficulty in transferring knowledge to a host nation through a greenfield approach.[134]

The risks are also high, however, because of the costs of establishing a new business operation in a new country. The firm may have to acquire the knowledge and expertise of the existing market by hiring either host-country nationals, possibly from competitors, or consultants, which can be costly. Still, the firm maintains control over the technology, marketing, and distribution of its products. Furthermore, the company must build new manufacturing facilities, establish distribution networks, and learn and implement appropriate marketing strategies to compete in the new market.[135] Research also suggests that if a policy change emerges, firms prefer to move toward a wholly owned approach. For instance, after the Asian financial crisis many countries had to change their institutional policy to allow more foreign ownership. As the institutional policy changed, many firms chose to go with a wholly owned approach rather than a joint venture.[136]

The globalization of the air cargo industry has implications for companies such as UPS and FedEx. The impact of this globalization is especially pertinent to the China and Asia Pacific region. China's air cargo market is expected to grow 11 percent per year through 2023. Accordingly, all have opened cargo hubs in the region. DHL opened its Central Asia hub in 2000. In 2008, UPS and FedEx completed the building of their hubs in Shanghai and Guangzhou, respectively. Not to be outdone, DHL is developing a cargo hub for North Asia in Shanghai. These investments will be wholly owned because these firms need to maintain the integrity of their IT and logistics systems in order to maximize efficiency. Greenfield ventures also help the firms to maintain the proprietary nature of their systems.[137]

Dynamics of Mode of Entry

A firm's choice of mode of entry into international markets is affected by a number of factors.[138] Initially, market entry will often be achieved through export, which requires no foreign manufacturing expertise and investment only in distribution. Licensing can facilitate the product improvements necessary to enter foreign markets, as in the Komatsu example. Strategic alliances have been popular because they allow a firm to connect with an experienced partner already in the targeted market. Strategic alliances also reduce risk through the sharing of costs. Therefore, all three modes—export, licensing, and strategic alliance—are good tactics for early market development. Also, the strategic alliance is often used in more uncertain situations, such as an emerging economy.[139] However, if intellectual property rights in the emerging economy are not well protected, the number of firms in the industry is growing fast, and the need for global integration is high, the wholly owned entry mode is preferred.[140]

To secure a stronger presence in international markets, acquisitions or greenfield ventures may be required. Large aerospace firms Airbus and Boeing have used joint ventures.[141] Bombardier's Chinese joint venture activity has helped it secure contracts for rail cars—including a $1.5-billion order for 640 high-speed cars from the Chinese Ministry of Railways in 2007.[142] Military equipment firms such as Thales SA, as noted above, have used acquisitions to build a global presence.[143] Many Japanese auto manufacturers, such as Honda, Nissan, and Toyota, have gained a presence in the United States through both greenfield ventures and joint ventures.[144] Toyota, for example, has two advantages that must be maintained internally: efficient manufacturing techniques using a team approach, and a reputation for producing high-quality automobiles.[145] These advantages for Toyota are based on effective management; if Toyota outsourced manufacturing, it would likely lose these advantages. Therefore, Toyota uses some form of foreign direct investment (e.g., greenfield ventures, joint ventures) rather than another mode of entry. Both acquisitions and greenfield ventures are likely to come at later stages in the development of an international strategy. In addition, both strategies tend to be more successful when the firm making the investment possesses valuable core competencies.[146] Large diversified business groups, often found in emerging economies, not only gain resources through diversification but also have specialized abilities in managing differences in inward and outward flows of foreign direct investment. In particular, Korean *chaebols* have been adept at making acquisitions in emerging economies.[147]

Thus, to enter a global market, a firm selects the entry mode that is best suited to the situation at hand. In some instances, the various options will be followed sequentially, beginning with exporting and ending with greenfield ventures.[148] In other cases, the firm may use several, but not all, of the different entry modes, each in different markets. The decision regarding which entry mode to use is primarily a result of the industry's competitive conditions, the country's situation and government policies, and the firm's unique set of resources, capabilities, and core competencies.

Strategic Competitiveness Outcomes

Once its international strategy and mode of entry have been selected, the firm turns its attention to implementation issues (see Chapter 12). It is important to do this because, as explained next, international expansion is risky and may not result in a competitive advantage (see Figure 9.1). The probability the firm will achieve success by using an international strategy increases when that strategy is effectively implemented.

International Diversification and Returns

International diversification is a strategy through which a firm expands the sales of its goods or services across the borders of global regions and countries into different geographic locations or markets.

As noted earlier, firms have numerous reasons to diversify internationally. **International diversification** is a strategy through which a firm expands the sales of its goods or services across the borders of global regions and countries into different geographic locations or markets. Because of its potential advantages, international diversification should be related positively to firms' returns. Research has shown that, as international diversification increases, firms' returns decrease and then increase as firms learn to manage international expansion.[149] In fact, the stock market is particularly sensitive to investments in international markets. Firms that are broadly diversified into multiple international markets usually achieve the most positive stock returns, especially when they diversify geographically into core business areas.[150] There are also many reasons for the positive effects of international diversification, such as potential economies of scale and experience, location advantages, increased market size, and the opportunity to stabilize returns. Stabilization of returns helps reduce a firm's overall risk.[151] All of these outcomes can be achieved by smaller and newer ventures, as well as by larger and established firms. New ventures can also enjoy higher returns when they learn new technologies from their international diversification.[152]

Firms in the Japanese auto industry, particularly Toyota, have found that international diversification may allow them to better exploit their core competencies, because sharing knowledge resources between operations can produce synergy. Also, a firm's returns may affect its decision to diversify internationally. For example, poor returns in a domestic market may encourage a firm to expand internationally in order to enhance its profit potential. In addition, internationally diversified firms may have access to more flexible labour markets, as the Japanese do in North American markets, and may thereby benefit from global scanning for competition and market opportunities. Also, through global networks with assets in many countries, firms can develop more flexible structures to adjust to changes that might occur. "Offshore outsourcing" has created significant value-creation opportunities for firms engaged in it, especially as firms move into markets with more flexible labour markets. Furthermore, offshoring increases exports to firms that receive the offshoring contract.[153]

The Malaysian oil company Petronas, like China's CNOOC, is state-owned. However, Petronas's operations are profitable, which is usually counter to most state-owned monopolies. Because Malaysia's oil reserves have dwindled and because few domestic opportunities exist to drill for new reserves, Petronas expanded its operations abroad to fill the potentially growing reserve challenge. It has done so successfully and has operations in 32 countries.[154] It has gone to Iraq and the Sudan, among other places where more technologically developed Western rivals have been apprehensive to venture. Although multinational firms such as Petronas can produce above-average returns, international diversification can be carried too far, as explained later.

International Diversification and Innovation

In Chapter 1, we indicated that the development of new technology is at the heart of strategic competitiveness. As noted in Porter's model (see Figure 9.2), a nation's competitiveness depends, in part, on the capacity of its industry to innovate. Eventually, and inevitably, competitors outperform firms that fail to innovate and improve their operations and products. Therefore, the only way to sustain a competitive advantage is to upgrade it continually.[155]

International diversification provides the potential for firms to achieve greater returns on their innovations (through larger or more numerous markets) and lowers the often substantial risks of R&D investments. Therefore, international diversification provides incentives for firms to innovate.[156]

In addition, international diversification may be necessary to generate the resources required to sustain a large-scale R&D operation. An environment of rapid technological obsolescence makes it difficult to invest in new technology and the capital-intensive operations required to take advantage of such investment. Firms operating solely in domestic markets may find such investments problematic because of the length of time required to recoup the original investment. If the time is extended, it may not even be possible to recover the investment before the technology becomes obsolete.[157] As a result, international diversification improves a firm's ability to appropriate additional and necessary returns from innovation before competitors can overcome the initial competitive advantage created by the innovation.

For instance, research suggests that Japanese foreign direct investment in developing countries is focused more on market-seeking and labour cost–saving purposes, whereas investment in developed economies is more focused on strategy development as well as market-seeking purposes. In these firms, a relatively strong ownership advantage is evident versus in developing economies.[158] In addition, firms moving into international markets are exposed to new products and processes. If they learn about those products and processes and integrate this knowledge into their operations, further innovation can be developed.[159] Research, however, finds that to take advantage of R&D investment, knowledge-absorptive capacity needs to be in place as well.[160]

The relationship among international diversification, innovation, and returns is complex. Some level of performance is necessary to provide the resources to generate international diversification, which in turn provides incentives and resources to invest in research and development. The latter, if done appropriately, should enhance the returns of the firm, which then provides more resources for continued international diversification and investment in R&D.[161]

Because of the potential positive effects of international diversification on performance and innovation, such diversification may even enhance returns in product-diversified firms. International diversification would increase market potential in each of these firms' product lines, but the complexity of managing a firm that is both product-diversified and internationally diversified is significant. Research indicates that media firms gain from both product and geographic diversification. However, international diversification often contributes more than product diversification in developed countries.[162] Research also suggests that firms in less developed countries gain more from being product-diversified than firms in developed countries. This is especially true when partnering with multinational firms from a more developed country that are looking to enter a less developed country in pursuit of increased international diversification.[163]

Evidence suggests that more culturally diverse top-management teams often have a greater knowledge of international markets and their idiosyncrasies[164] (top-management teams are discussed further in Chapter 13). Moreover, an in-depth understanding of diverse markets among top-level managers facilitates intrafirm coordination and the use of long-term, strategically relevant criteria to evaluate the performance of managers and their units.[165] In turn, this approach facilitates improved innovation and performance.[166]

Complexity of Managing Multinational Firms

Although firms can realize many benefits by implementing an international strategy, doing so is complex and can produce greater uncertainty.[167] For example, multiple risks are involved when a firm operates in several different countries. Firms can grow only so large and diverse before becoming unmanageable, or before the costs of managing them exceed their benefits.[168] For example, The Body Shop has retail outlets in over 50 countries. One of the difficulties it has is coordinating the different IT platforms and managing the different accounting and reporting standards used in each country.[169] Other complexities include the highly competitive nature of global markets, multiple cultural environments, potentially rapid shifts in the value of different currencies, and the instability of some national governments.

Risks in an International Environment

International diversification carries multiple risks.[170] Because of these risks, international expansion is difficult to implement and manage. The chief risks are political and economic. Taking these risks into account, highly internationally diversified firms are accustomed to market conditions yielding competitive situations that differ from what was predicted. Sometimes, these situations contribute to the firm's strategic competitiveness; on other occasions, they have a negative effect on the firm's efforts. Specific examples of political and economic risks are shown in Figure 9.4.

Figure 9.4	Risk in the International Environment

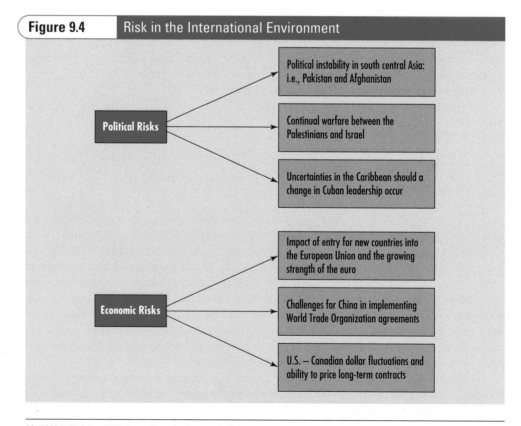

SOURCES: K. Whitelaw, 2008, A mourning nation faces a volatile future . . . , *U.S. News & World Report,* 144(1): 29; M. B. Zuckerman, 2008, Hopes for peace, *U.S. News & World Report,* 143(20): 70; 2007, The Americas: Not gone yet: Cuba and the United States, *The Economist,* 380(8491): 44; 2008, Finance and economics: Déjà vu: The Euro area, *The Economist,* 386(8561): 64; 2007, Lost in translation: China and US trade, *The Economist,* 383(8529): 80; N. Stewart, 2007, Canadian dollar: Canadian exporters struggle with parity, *Northern Ontario Business,* 28(2): 22.

Political Risks

Political risks are risks related to instability in national governments and to war, both civil and international. Instability in a national government creates numerous problems, including economic risks and uncertainty created by government regulation; the existence of many, possibly conflicting, legal authorities or corruption; and the potential nationalization of private assets.[171] Foreign firms that invest in another country may have concerns about the stability of the national government and what might happen to their investments or assets because of unrest and government instability.[172]

In addition to the items listed in Figure 9.4, Russia has reduced foreign direct investment by prosecuting powerful private firm executives as well as seeking to gain state control of firm assets. For example, Yukos, a thriving oil and gas firm, was penalized for alleged tax fraud and broken up. The CEO was jailed because of the accusations. As a result, the assets of Yukos were partly assimilated into Gazprom, a government-owned oil and gas enterprise. Furthermore, other acquisitions of Russian businesses such as by Seimens AG were not approved by the Russian government. This trend has given pause to some firms considering significant foreign direct investment in Russia. Although the Russian government has tried to create more reassurance with regard to property rights, firms are still leery of investing in Russia given the current trend toward more government control over the private sector.[173] As the Strategic Focus notes, property rights issues extend far beyond Russia and the energy sector.

Economic Risks

As illustrated in the example of Russia and property rights, economic risks are interdependent with political risks. As discussed in the Strategic Focus, if firms cannot protect their intellectual property, they will not make foreign direct investments. Countries therefore need to create and sustain strong intellectual property rights and their enforcement, or they risk losing their reputation in the eyes of potential investing firms and might also risk sanctions from international political bodies such as the WTO.

In addition to the items listed in Figure 9.4, another economic risk is the security risk posed by terrorism. For instance, concerns about terrorism in Indonesia have kept firms from investing in that economy. Although many foreign investors in the energy and mining sectors have stuck with Indonesia through political and economic instability, the nation needs to attract new investors to sustain economic growth. Indonesia, with the world's biggest Muslim population, has a hard time competing for investment against the comparatively faster growth in China and India, which have fewer security risks.[174]

As noted earlier, foremost among the economic risks of international diversification are the differences and fluctuations in the value of different currencies.[175] The value of the dollar relative to other currencies determines the value of the international assets and earnings of Canadian firms; for example, an increase in the value of the Canadian dollar can reduce the value of Canadian multinational firms' international assets and earnings in other countries. Furthermore, the value of different currencies can also, at times, dramatically affect a firm's competitiveness in global markets because of its effect on the prices of goods manufactured in different countries.[176]

An increase in the value of the dollar can harm Canadian firms' exports to international markets because of the price differential of the products. Although the dollar has been weak over the last quarter century, it has gained substantial strength—particularly against the currency of Canada's main trading partner, the U.S. As such, not only do profits from a Canadian firm's American operations not look as good as they might otherwise, but also exporting becomes more difficult. However, it makes the assets of firms where the currency is higher look stronger but weakens the pricing power of their exports.

Are China and India Changing Their Approach to Intellectual Property Enforcement?

The lack of intellectual property protection in large nations such as China and India has made it difficult for Western innovation-oriented firms to be successful there. This problem exists for a large variety of industries, from movies and music to software and pharmaceuticals. However, as China and India open their markets, government officials in these countries are reconsidering their current laws and enforcement arrangements for intellectual property rights.

Interestingly, many of India's most innovative companies are welcoming the possibility of stronger patent protections for scientific intellectual property. In the early stages of a country's economic development, lax intellectual property laws allow the imitation of more highly developed countries' intellectual property. India's previous patent system, for example, allowed Indian pharmaceutical companies to copy drug patents created abroad by merely changing the manufacturing process. This allowed a local pharmaceutical industry focused on generic drug manufacturing to keep medicines quite inexpensive for local consumers— as little as one-tenth of original prices.

However, as Indian companies consider foreign direct investment and developing multinational enterprises in the pharmaceutical industry outside of India, stronger international patent protection becomes more reasonable. For instance, Indian pharmaceutical companies applied for nearly 800 patents at the World Intellectual Property Organization (WIPO) in 2004, twice as many as were applied for in the previous four years combined. Accordingly, stronger intellectual property laws and enforcement create a better environment for Indian pharmaceutical, software, and other knowledge-industry participants to retain profits for their product innovations.

Similar experiences are being encountered in the Chinese market. There are few recent cases in which the Chinese courts have protected a foreign firm's intellectual property. North American, Asian, and European business groups have been cajoling Beijing to do a better job of marshalling intellectual property protection. Fostering better intellectual property protection is important for any firm considering locating a new R&D and manufacturing facility in China. Microsoft has claimed that 90 percent of the Microsoft-labelled software used in China is actually counterfeit. Philips Electronics NV has continually faced counterfeiting in its compact disc sales with little recourse in the Chinese courts, especially in remote parts of the country. Honda confronted a company producing a scooter that it called a "Hongda."

Of course, China has taken on more intellectual property rights obligations with its entrance into the World Trade Organization. However, the culture in China is a difficult one to overcome. Because during the Communist era in China property belonged "collectively" to the state and to the people and not to individuals or to enterprises, intellectual property ownership is a difficult concept to adjust to for the Chinese. Some commentators have suggested that, instead of imposing fines for people caught violating patents, trademarks, and copyrights, China should launch criminal actions against counterfeiters. Such an enforcement approach, it has been argued, would send a stronger signal to counterfeiters.

However, others argue that the government ownership and control of intellectual property rights in the economy undermines private property rights, especially intangible knowledge such as that associated with patents and copyrights. If successful, new invention and innovation that would take place in private laboratories and start-up companies throughout the country may undermine the power and employment opportunities associated with state-owned firms. Thus, China's state-owned firms' political interests are potentially in conflict with its private enterprises' commercial and entrepreneurial interests.

However, as Chinese firms enter world markets, there needs to be a shift in managerial mind-set in moving from an orientation of imitation toward innovation. It will be a significant strategic leap when state-owned firms move from a focus on products "made in China" to "created in China." If other nations begin to pirate their hard-earned innovations and wisdom, it is likely to follow that the government will implement stronger structural safeguards protecting intellectual property rights. One analyst concluded, "Such enlightened self-interest can be the only driver for the true cultural change needed." Furthermore, to create an incentive for increased foreign direct investment of high–value added investment of technology companies such as research and development centres, China will need to change its anti–intellectual-property-rights culture.

SOURCES: 2005, Official questions China piracy claims, *Managing Intellectual Property*, May, 1; F. M. R. Armbrecht, 2005, "Created in China" should speed its respect for IP rights, *Research Technology Management*, 48(2): 2–5; E. Bellman, 2005, India senses patent appeal: Local companies envision benefits in stronger protections, *Wall Street Journal*, April 21, A20; P. Choate, 2005, *Hot Property: The Stealing of Ideas in an Age of Globalization*, New York: Alfred A. Knopf; I. P. Mahmood & C. Rufin, 2005, Government's dilemma: The role of government in imitation and innovation, *Academy of Management Review*, 30: 338–360; A. Stevenson-Yang & K. DeWoskin, 2005, China destroys the IP paradigm, *Far Eastern Economic Review*, March, 9–18.

Limits to International Expansion: Management Problems

Firms tend to earn positive returns on early international diversification, but the returns often level off and become negative as the diversification increases past some point.[177] There are several reasons for the limits to the positive effects of international diversification. First, greater geographic dispersion across country borders increases the costs of coordination between units and the distribution of products. Second, trade barriers, logistical costs, cultural diversity, and other differences by country (e.g., access to raw materials and different employee skill levels) greatly complicate the implementation of an international diversification strategy.[178]

Institutional and cultural factors can present strong barriers to the transfer of a firm's competitive advantages from one country to another.[179] Marketing programs often have to be redesigned and new distribution networks established when firms expand into new countries. In addition, firms may encounter different labour costs and capital charges. In general, it is difficult to effectively implement, manage, and control a firm's international operations.

Wal-Mart made significant mistakes in markets around the world as it internationalized. For example, its first Mexican stores carried ice skates, riding lawn mowers, fishing tackle—even clay pigeons for skeet shooting. To get rid of the clay pigeons, the stores would radically discount them, "only to have automated inventory systems linked to Wal-Mart's corporate headquarters in Bentonville, Arkansas, order a fresh batch."[180] As Wal-Mart began to get the right mix of products, it became very successful in Latin America, especially in Mexico, and elsewhere in the world. The company has accelerated growth through international acquisitions; 40 percent of the international sales growth from 2001 to 2005 has come from foreign-acquired retailers. In November 2007, Wal-Mart opened its 3,000th international store in São Paulo. Mitch Slape, senior vice president of Wal-Mart's International Business Development, noted that, "In just 16 years, Wal-Mart has gone from just one international retail location to 3,000, with nearly 600,000 associates serving 49 million international customers each week. In the last seven years, we've had a compound annual growth rate of 27.4 percent.[181]

The amount of international diversification that can be managed varies from firm to firm and is according to the abilities of each firm's managers. The problems of central coordination and integration are mitigated if the firm diversifies into more friendly countries that are geographically close and have cultures similar to its own country's culture. In that case, there are likely to be fewer trade barriers, the laws and customs are better understood, and the product is easier to adapt to local markets.[182] For example, Canadian firms may find it less difficult to expand their operations into the U.S., Mexico, and Western European countries than into Asian countries.

Management must also be concerned with the relationship between the host government and the multinational corporation.[183] Although government policy and regulations are often barriers, many firms, such as Toyota and General Motors, have turned to strategic alliances to overcome those barriers.[184] By forming interorganizational networks, such as strategic alliances (see Chapter 10), firms can share resources and risks but also build flexibility. However, large networks can be difficult to manage.[185]

Summary

- The use of international strategies is increasing not only because of traditional motivations, but also for emerging reasons. Traditional motives include extending the product life cycle, securing key resources, and having access to low-cost labour. Emerging motivations focus on the combination of the Internet and mobile telecommunications, which facilitates global transactions. Also, there is increased pressure for global integration as the demand for commodities becomes borderless, and yet pressure is also increasing for local country responsiveness.

- An international strategy usually attempts to capitalize on four benefits: increased market size; the opportunity to earn a return on large investments; economies of scale and learning; and advantages of location.

- International business-level strategies are usually grounded in one or more home-country advantages, as Porter's diamond model suggests. The diamond model emphasizes four determinants: factors of production; demand conditions; related and supporting industries; and patterns of firm strategy, structure, and rivalry.

- There are three types of international corporate-level strategies. A multidomestic strategy focuses on competition within each country in which the firm competes. Firms using a multidomestic strategy decentralize strategic and operating decisions to the business units operating in each country, so that each unit can tailor its goods and services to the local market. A global strategy assumes more standardization of products across country boundaries; therefore, competitive strategy is centralized and controlled by the home office. A transnational strategy seeks to combine aspects of both multidomestic and global strategies in order to emphasize both local responsiveness and global integration and coordination. This strategy is difficult to implement, requiring an integrated network and a culture of individual commitment.

- Although the transnational strategy's implementation is a challenge, environmental trends are causing many multinational firms to consider the need for both global efficiency and local responsiveness. Many large multinational firms—particularly those with many diverse products—use a multidomestic strategy with some product lines and a global strategy with others.

- Furthermore, research suggests that the liability of foreignness is more difficult to overcome than once thought.

- Some firms decide to compete only in certain regions of the world, as opposed to viewing all markets in the world as potential opportunities. Competing in regional markets allows firms and managers to focus their learning on specific markets, cultures, locations, resources, and so on.

- Firms may enter international markets in one of several ways, including exporting, licensing, forming strategic alliances, making acquisitions, and establishing new wholly owned subsidiaries, often referred to as greenfield ventures. Most firms begin with exporting or licensing, because of their lower costs and risks, but later may expand to strategic alliances and acquisitions. The most expensive and risky means of entering a new international market is through the establishment of a new wholly owned subsidiary. On the other hand, such subsidiaries provide the advantages of maximum control by the firm and, if they are successful, the greatest returns.

- International diversification facilitates innovation in a firm, because it provides a larger market to gain more and faster returns from investments in innovation. In addition, international diversification may generate the resources necessary to sustain a large-scale R&D program.

- In general, international diversification is related to above-average returns, but this assumes that the diversification is effectively implemented and that the firm's international operations are well managed. International diversification provides greater economies of scope and learning, which, along with greater innovation, help produce above-average returns.

- Several risks are involved with managing multinational operations. Among these are political risks (e.g., instability of national governments) and economic risks (e.g., fluctuations in the value of a country's currency).

- There are also limits to the ability to manage international expansion effectively. International diversification increases coordination and distribution costs, and management problems are exacerbated by trade barriers, logistical costs, and cultural diversity, among other factors.

1. What are the traditional and emerging motives that cause firms to expand internationally?

2. What four factors provide a basis for international business-level strategies?

3. What are the three international corporate-level strategies? How do they differ from each other? What factors lead to their development?

4. What environmental trends are affecting international strategy?

5. What five modes of international expansion are available, and what is the normal sequence of their use?

6. What is the relationship between international diversification and innovation? How does international diversification affect innovation? What is the effect of international diversification on a firm's returns?

7. What are the risks of international diversification? What are the challenges of managing multinational firms?

8. What factors limit the positive outcomes of international expansion?

Social Responsibility Review

1. Asian countries represent a large and growing market for cigarettes, while markets in the West are shrinking due to health concerns. In many cases, Western firms have had trouble entering markets like China and Korea because of state control of the tobacco industry and the revenues that governments can gain from tobacco sales. As such, cigarette firms have an incentive to form a deal with state-owned firms. The state-owned firms would get access to famous brands and the associated revenues and cigarette firms would tap a new market with little need for direct investment. Strategically, this all makes sense—so where's the harm?

2. The European Union began as a series of free trade agreements. Is NAFTA the beginning of the same thing for the Americas? What would be the pros and cons for businesses, governments, and consumers of a free trade zone that would encompass all of the Americas?

3. One way to create a premium price for your product is to create a well recognized, quality brand. However, if you personally want something that, on minimal inspection, can pass for the real thing, what's wrong with buying it?

Experiential Exercises

Bombardier's Overseas Entry

Montreal's Bombardier Transportation realized that succeeding in the rail transit industry meant that markets outside North America were critical to the firm's long-term growth in sales and profitability. Some local production capabilities in the markets of governments the company wished to sell rail cars to would be a competitive advantage on which the company's future success depended. Executives felt that being able to duplicate these competitive advantages would be critical to its efforts to effectively compete in economies other than its domestic market. In considering how to do this, Bombardier's top-level managers decided that different modes of entry would be used to enter different markets. This decision found Bombardier Transportation using multiple modes of entry rather than a single mode of entry into international markets.

Part One. For this part of the exercise, use the Internet and other sources of information available to you to research

Bombardier Transportation's international operations in the countries appearing in the following list. Sales revenue, market share, number of stores, competitive challenges, and plans regarding how the company intends to compete in the future in each country are examples of the information you should gather for each country. Most importantly, for each country you should determine the entry mode Bombardier Transportation used to enter the market (use the entry modes discussed in this chapter to make this determination).

- Germany   • United Kingdom
- United States   • China

Part Two. Using materials in this chapter, prepare answers to the following questions with respect to each of the countries listed in Part One of the exercise.

- What factors and conditions influenced Bombardier to select the entry mode it used to enter each of the four countries?

- In your view and given your understanding of the material in this chapter, what made each country-specific entry mode superior to the other entry modes?

- In each country, did Bombardier make any significant changes in terms of ownership and control of its stores after it entered the market? If so, what were those changes and what factors influenced their occurrence? Were these changes successful? Why or why not?

National Champions

Michael Porter's determinants of national advantage diamond (Figure 9.2) captures the many factors on which strong national industries are based. It is logical that when competing against firms from these countries in international markets, rivals from other countries may be starting from a weaker competitive position in general. As with the five forces model in Chapter 3, Porter's diamond captures many elements in each of its components. Those elements can work to increase or decrease a particular nation's advantage, and they can have an interactive effect among themselves. In this exercise, your group will analyze a particular country and an advantaged industry from that country in order to understand why firms from that industry are able to successfully compete in economies outside their domestic market.

Each group will be assigned one of the following sets of country, industry, and firm.

Country	Industry	Firm
Canada	Newsprint	Abitibi-Price
France	Fashion clothing	Guy Laroche
Italy	Footwear	Bruno Magli
Japan	Automobiles	Toyota
Korea	Shipbuilding	Hyundai Heavy Industries Co., Ltd
Switzerland	Pharmaceuticals	Novartis
United Kingdom	Whiskey	William Grant & Sons
United States	Airframes	Boeing
Canada	Passenger rail cars	Bombardier

Given your assignment, complete the following tasks: Research your assigned country and industry with respect to each of the components of Porter's diamond that deals with the determinants of national advantage. To do this, you may use sources such as the U.S. CIA's and State Department's Web sites. In addition, *The Economist* and the *Financial Times* have Web sites that offer a great deal of information that can be useful to examine countries and industries. Use the tools from Chapter 9 and the concepts of core competencies and competitive advantage that are explained in other chapters to analyze the information you have obtained through your research. Note that core competencies and competitive advantage exist at the level of individual firms. However, when analyzing a country's national advantage, those advantages become transferred to the firm and help many firms from that country compete against rivals from other countries. Be careful to note that national advantage is not necessarily equated with market share or with creating large firms. Prepare a presentation of your analysis for presentation to the class.

Notes

1. S. Li, 2005, Why a poor governance environment does not deter foreign direct investment: The case of China and its implications for investment protection, *Business Horizons*, 48(4): 297–302.
2. E. Kurtenbach, 2005, Steel heating up in China; industry, demand booming, *The Arizona Republic*, July 3, D3.
3. W. P. Wan, 2005, Country resource environments, firm capabilities, and corporate diversification strategies. *Journal of Management Studies*, 42: 161–182; S. Werner, 2002, Recent developments in international management research: A review of 20 top management journals, *Journal of Management*, 28: 277–305.
4. R. E. Hoskisson, H. Kim, R. E. White, & L. Tihanyi, 2004, A framework for understanding international diversification by business groups from emerging economies. In M. A. Hitt & J. L. C. Cheng (eds.), Theories of the multinational enterprise: Diversity, complexity, and relevance. *Advances in International Management*, Oxford, UK: Elsevier/JAI Press, 137–163; A. K. Gupta & V. Govindarajan, 2001, Converting global presence into global competitive advantage, *Academy of Management Executive*, 15(2): 45–57.
5. T. M. Begley & D. P. Boyd, 2003, The need for a corporate global mind-set, *MIT Sloan Management Review*, 44(2): 25–32; A. K. Gupta & V. Govindarajan, 2002, Cultivating a global mindset, *Academy of Management Executive*, 16(1): 116–126.
6. V. Mok & G. Yeung, 2005, Employee motivation, external orientation and the technical efficiency of foreign-financed firms in China: A stochastic frontier analysis, *Managerial and Decision Economics*, 26(3): 175–190; R. L. Mecham III, 2003, Success for the new global manager: What you need to know to work across distances, countries, and cultures, *Leadership Quarterly*, 14: 347–352; A. McWilliams, D. D. Van Fleet, & P. M. Wright, 2001, Strategic management of human resources for global competitive advantage, *Journal of Business Strategies*, 18(1): 1–24.
7. D. M. De Carolis, 2003, Competencies and imitability in the pharmaceutical industry: An analysis of their relationship with firm performance, *Journal of Management*, 29: 27–50; J. S. Childers Jr., R. L. Somerly, & K. E. Bass, 2002, Competitive environments and sustained economic rents: A theoretical examination of country-specific differences within the pharmaceutical industry, *International Journal of Management*, 19(1): 89–98; G. Bottazzi, G. Dosi, M. Lippi, F. Pammolli, & M. Riccaboni, 2001, Innovation and corporate growth in the evolution of the drug industry, *International Journal of Industrial Organization*, 19: 1161–1187.

8. L. Tongli, E. J. Ping, & W. K. C. Chiu, 2005, International diversification and performance: Evidence from Singapore, *Asia Pacific Journal of Management,* 22: 65–88; S. Tallman & K. Fladmoe-Lindquist, 2002, Internationalization, globalization, and capability-based strategy, *California Management Review,* 45(1): 116–135; S. Tallman, 2001, Global strategic management, in M. A. Hitt, R. E. Freeman, & J. S. Harrison (eds.), *Handbook of Strategic Management,* Oxford, UK: Blackwell Publishers, 462–490.

9. J. E. Ricart, M. J. Enright, P. Ghemawat, S. L. Hart, & T. Khanna, 2004, New frontiers in international strategy, *Journal of International Business Studies,* 35: 175–200; W. Hejazi & P. Pauly, 2003, Motivations for FDI and domestic capital formation, *Journal of International Business Studies,* 34: 282–289.

10. R. Vernon, 1996, International investment and international trade in the product cycle, *Quarterly Journal of Economics,* 80: 190–207.

11. J. M.-S. Cheng, C. Blankson, P. C. S. Wu, & S. S. M. Chen, 2005, A stage model of an international brand development: The perspectives of manufacturers from two newly industrialized economies—South Korea and Taiwan, *Industrial Marketing Management,* 34: 504–514; S. Andersson, 2004, Internationalization in different industrial contexts, *Journal of Business Venturing,* 19: 851–875; H. F. Lau, C. C. Y. Kwok, & C. F. Chan, 2000, Filling the gap: Extending international product life cycle to emerging economies, *Journal of Global Marketing,* 13(4): 29–51.

12. L. Yu, 2003, The global-brand advantage, *MIT Sloan Management Review,* 44(3): 13.

13. Store numbers include 270 open stores plus 23 expected store openings in 2008, http://www.ikea-group.ikea.com/?ID=11, retrieved January 8, 2008; Revenues of $18.9 billion euros for the IKEA fiscal year ended August 31, 2007 at the exchange rate at the time of $1.45 per euro, http://www.ikea-group.ikea.com/?ID=10, http://www.oanda.com/convert/fxhistory, retrieved January 8, 2008; 2005, IKEA, a household name, *Journal of Commerce,* May 30, 1.

14. 2005, Business: A better drive; Hyundai Motor, *The Economist,* May 21, 75; Y. S. Pak, J. Lee, & J. M. An, 2002, Lessons learned from Daewoo Motors' experience in emerging markets, *Multinational Business Review,* 10(2): 122–128; B. Kim & Y. Lee, 2001, Global capacity expansion strategies: Lessons learned from two Korean carmakers, *Long Range Planning,* 34(3): 309–333.

15. D. Rigby & C. Zook, 2003, Open-market innovation, *Harvard Business Review,* 89(10): 80–89; J.-R. Lee & J.-S. Chen, 2003, Internationalization, local adaptation and subsidiary's entrepreneurship: An exploratory study on Taiwanese manufacturing firms in Indonesia and Malaysia, *Asia Pacific Journal of Management,* 20: 51–72; K. Macharzina, 2001, The end of pure global strategies? *Management International Review,* 41(2): 105.

16. Y. Luo, 2003, Market-seeking MNEs in an emerging market: How parent-subsidiary links shape overseas success, *Journal of International Business Studies,* 34: 290–309; 2003, Special Report: Two systems, one grand rivalry—India and China, *The Economist,* June 21, 66–68; Y. Luo, 2000, Entering China today: What choices do we have? *Journal of Global Marketing,* 14(2): 57–82.

17. C. C. Y. Kwok & D. M. Reeb, 2000, Internationalization and firm risk: An upstream-downstream hypothesis, *Journal of International Business Studies,* 31: 611–629; J. J. Choi & M. Rajan, 1997, A joint test of market segmentation and exchange risk factor in international capital markets, *Journal of International Business Studies,* 28: 29–49.

18. M. Wright, I. Filatotchev, R. E. Hoskisson, & M. W. Peng, 2005, Strategy research in emerging economies: Challenging the conventional wisdom, *Journal of Management Studies,* 42: 1–30; T. London & S. Hart, 2004, Reinventing strategies for emerging markets: Beyond the transnational model, *Journal of International Business Studies,* 35: 350–370; R. E. Hoskisson, L. Eden, C. M. Lau, & M. Wright, 2000, Strategy in emerging economies, *Academy of Management Journal,* 43: 249–267.

19. H. Sender, 2005, The economy; the outlook: India comes of age, as focus on returns lures foreign capital, *Wall Street Journal,* June 6, A2.

20. M. W. Peng, S.-H. Lee, & D. Y. L. Wang, 2005, What determines the scope of the firm over time? A focus on institutional relatedness, *Academy of Management Review,* 30: 622–633; M. Peng, 2003, Institutional transitions and strategic choices, *Academy of Management Review,* 28: 275–296.

21. 2007, StatsCan, Foreign Direct Investment, The Daily, May 9, http://www.statcan.ca/Daily/English/070509/d070509a.htm; 2003, StatsCan, Foreign Direct Investment, The Daily, March 26, http://www.statcan.ca/Daily/English/030326/d030326a.htm; 2001, StatsCan, *Special Report: Canadian Foreign Direct Investment Trends in the 1990s,* http://strategis.ic.gc.ca/epic/internet/ineas-aes.nsf/vwapj/srmei199807e.PDF/$FILE/srmei199807e.PDF; all retrieved January 8, 2008.

22. 2005, EU economy: Building transatlantic bridges, *EIU ViewsWire,* May 27; T. Aeppel, 2003, Manufacturers spent much less abroad last year—U.S. firms cut investing overseas by estimated 37 percent; The "high-wage paradox," *Wall Street Journal,* May 9, A8.

23. T. Stein, 2005, Globe trotters: Venture firms are increasingly looking beyond U.S. shores, encouraged by the explosive growth, low development costs and surging entrepreneurship in emerging markets. But can U.S.-style venture capital be exported successfully? *Venture Capital Journal,* May 2, 1; W. Kuemmerle, 2001, Go global—or not? *Harvard Business Review,* 79(6): 37–49; Y. Luo & M. W. Peng, 1999, Learning to compete in a transition economy: Experience, environment and performance, *Journal of International Business Studies,* 30: 269–295.

24. O. Gadiesh, 2004, Risk-proofing your brand, *European Business Forum,* Summer, 82; Lee & Chen, Internationalization, local adaptation and subsidiary's entrepreneurship.

25. J. W. Spencer, T. P. Murtha, & S. A. Lenway, 2005, How governments matter to new industry creation, *Academy of Management Review,* 30: 321–337; I. P. Mahmood & C. Rufin, 2005, Government's dilemma: The role of government in imitation and innovation, *Academy of Management Review,* 30: 338–360.

26. L. Eden & S. Miller, 2004, Distance matters: Liability of foreignness, institutional distance and ownership strategy, In M. Hitt & J. L. Cheng (eds.), *Advances in International Management,* Oxford, UK: Elsevier/JAI Press, 187–221; T. Kostova & S. Zaheer, 1999, Organizational legitimacy under conditions of complexity: The case of the multinational enterprise, *Academy of Management Review,* 24: 64–81; S. Zaheer & E. Mosakowski, 1997, The dynamics of the liability of foreignness: A global study of survival in financial services, *Strategic Management Journal,* 18: 439–464.

27. F. Jiang, 2005, Driving forces of international pharmaceutical firms' FDI into China, *Journal of Business Research,* 22(1): 21–39.

28. D. Ter-Sakarian, 2006, Opening time, *Business Eastern Europe,* 35(5): 6–7; C. Mercer & A. Drujinina, 2005, Heineken, Inbev snap up "last Russian breweries," CEE Food Industry.com Web site, http://www.cee-foodindustry.com/news/ng.asp?id=61347-heineken-inbev-beer, retrieved January 8, 2008; W. Echikson, 2005, Beer makers want to tap Russia, an increasingly frothy market, *Wall Street Journal,* September 14, B3; 2005, Heineken NV: Russian brewer is acquired, lifting marketshare to 8.3 percent, *Wall Street Journal,* May 9, A1.

29. K. Asakawa & M. Lehrer, 2003, Managing local knowledge assets globally: The role of regional innovation relays, *Journal of World Business,* 38: 31–42.

30. Cantwell, Dunning, & Janne, Towards a technology-seeking explanation of U.S. direct investment in the United Kingdom; W. Chung & J. Alcacer, 2002, Knowledge seeking and location choice of foreign direct investment in the United States, *Management Science,* 48(12): 1534–1554.

31. B. Ambos, 2005, Foreign direct investment in industrial research and development: A study of German MNCs, *Research Policy,* 34: 395–410.

32. Jiang, Driving forces of international pharmaceutical firms' FDI into China.

33. W. Chung, 2001, Identifying technology transfer in foreign direct investment: Influence of industry conditions and investing firm motives, *Journal of International Business Studies,* 32: 211–229.

34. 2007, MENA region gets a quarter of all investment in the developing world, November 12, ANIMA Investment Network Web site, retrieved January 8, 2008; M. Demirsar, 2006, Major League FDI recipient, *Banker,* 156(963): 74–76; J. C. Cooper & K. Madigan, 2005, Turkey: Leaving the bloom-bust cycle behind, *BusinessWeek,* May 23, 34.

35. K. J. Petersen, R. B. Handfield, & G. L. Ragatz, 2005, Supplier integration into new product development: Coordinating product, process and supply chain design, *Journal of Operations Management*, 23: 371–388; S. Prasad, J. Tata, & M. Madan, 2005, Build to order supply chains in developed and developing countries, *Journal of Operations Management*, 23: 551–568; A. J. Mauri & A. V. Phatak, 2001, Global integration as inter-area product flows: The internalization of ownership and location factors influencing product flows across MNC units, *Management International Review*, 41(3): 233–249.

36. 2008, SAIC and Yuejin Auto merger creates Chinese car colossus, *People's Daily Online*, December 26, 2007, http://english.people.com.cn/90001/90778/6327992.html, retrieved January 9, 2008; A. Taylor, 2004, Shanghai Auto wants to be the world's next great car company, *Fortune*, October 4, 103–109.

37. W. Kuemmerle, 2002, Home base and knowledge management in international ventures, *Journal of Business Venturing*, 2: 99–122; H. Bresman, J. Birkinshaw, & R. Nobel, 1999, Knowledge transfer in international acquisitions, *Journal of International Business Studies*, 30: 439–462; J. Birkinshaw, 1997, Entrepreneurship in multinational corporations: The characteristics of subsidiary initiatives, *Strategic Management Journal*, 18: 207–229.

38. J. Cantwell, J. Dunning, & O. Janne, 2004, Towards a technology-seeking explanation of U.S. direct investment in the United Kingdom, *Journal of International Management*, 10, 5–20; S. Makino, C. M. Lau, & R. S. Yeh, 2002, Asset-exploitation versus asset-seeking: Implications for location choice of foreign direct investment from newly industrialized economies, *Journal of International Business Studies*, 33(3): 403–421.

39. J. Penner-Hahn & J. M. Shaver, 2005, Does international research increase patent output? An analysis of Japanese pharmaceutical firms, *Strategic Management Journal*, 26: 121–140.

40. K. Ito & E. L. Rose, 2002, Foreign direct investment location strategies in the tire industry, *Journal of International Business Studies*, 33(3): 593–602.

41. R. Tahir & J. Larimo, 2004, Understanding the location strategies of the European firms in Asian countries, *Journal of American Academy of Business*, 5: 102–110; D. Xu & O. Shenkar, 2004, Institutional distance and the multinational enterprise, *Academy of Management Review*, 27: 608–618.

42. D. Xu, Y. Pan, & P. W. Beamish, 2004, The effect of regulative and normative distances on MNE ownership and expatriate strategies, *Management International Review*, 44(3): 285–307.

43. A clearer timeline of what happened can be found at PBS: http://www.pbs.org/wgbh/amex/castro/timeline/index.html, Timeline: Post-Revolution Cuba, PBS Web site, retrieved January 9, 2008; A short version of this is that Castro created closer ties with Russia's communist government. This included a trade deal that sent Cuban sugar to Russia and Russian oil to Cuba. To show its displeasure regarding this arrangement, the U.S. slapped Cuba with a partial trade embargo. When Russian oil arrived in Cuba, American-owned refineries refused to process it. Castro responded by nationalizing the refineries. The U.S. issued a full trade embargo and Castro then nationalized all U.S. assets in Cuba.

44. P. Diekmeyer, 2004, Castro's capitalist, *Canadian Business*, 77(13): 24; 2007, Dubai's Profile Group to acquire big stake in resort developer Leisure Canada, *Prince George Citizen*, December 21, http://www.princegeorgecitizen.com/index.php?option=com_content&task=view&id=109366&Itemid=167, retrieved January 9, 2008.

45. Tallman & Fladmoe-Lindquist, Internationalization, globalization, and capability-based strategy; D. A. Griffith & M. G. Harvey, 2001, A resource perspective of global dynamic capabilities, *Journal of International Business Studies*, 32: 597–606; Y. Luo, 2000, Dynamic capabilities in international expansion, *Journal of World Business*, 35(4): 355–378.

46. D. Tan & J. T. Mahoney, 2005, Examining the Penrose effect in an international business context: The dynamics of Japanese firm growth in U.S. industries, *Managerial and Decision Economics*, 26(2): 113–127; K. Uhlenbruck, 2004, Developing acquired foreign subsidiaries: The experience of MNEs for multinationals in transition economies, *Journal of International Business Studies*, 35: 109–123.

47. J. Gimeno, R. E. Hoskisson, B. D. Beal, & W. P. Wan, 2005, Explaining the clustering of international expansion moves: A critical test in the U.S. telecommunications industry, *Academy of Management Journal*, 48: 297–319.

48. L. Nachum, 2001, The impact of home countries on the competitiveness of advertising TNCs, *Management International Review*, 41(1): 77–98.

49. M. E. Porter, 1990, *The Competitive Advantage of Nations*, New York: The Free Press.

50. Ibid., 84.

51. Porter, *The Competitive Advantage of Nations*, 89.

52. Y. Aoyama & H. Izushi, 2003, Hardware gimmick or cultural innovation? Technological, cultural, and social foundations of the Japanese video game industry, *Research Policy*, 32: 423–443.

53. Wikipedia, 2008, Aluminium Oxide, http://en.wikipedia.org/wiki/Aluminium_oxide, retrieved January 9; 2008, Industry Overview, The Aluminum Association, Inc. Web site, http://www.aluminum.org/Content/NavigationMenu/The_Industry/Overview/Overview.htm, retrieved January 9.

54. 2008, International Energy Outlook 2007, Energy Information Administration Web site, Report #:DOE/EIA-0484(2007), http://www.eia.doe.gov/oiaf/ieo/electricity.html, retrieved January 9.

55. 2008, Aluminum: 2004–2005 production, European Association of Mining Industries Web site, http://www.euromines.org/mm.html, retrieved January 9; Wikipedia, 2008, List of countries by aluminium production, http://en.wikipedia.org/wiki/List_of_countries_by_aluminium_production, retrieved January 9.

56. 2008, Facts About Hydropower, The Wisconsin Valley Improvement Company Web site, http://www.wvic.com/hydro-facts.htm, retrieved January 9; 2008, World Coal Production 2005, Energy Information Administration Web site, *International Energy Annual 2005*, http://www.eia.doe.gov/pub/international/iea2005/table51.xls, retrieved January 9.

57. All territories and most provinces have government-owned power authorities (Nova Scotia and PEI have investor-owned providers and Alberta has both investor- and municipally owned providers), and a great deal this of power is generated via hydro; the U.S. has two large federal hydro-generating power companies, the Bonneville Power Administration, covering four western states, and the Tennessee Valley Authority, covering six southern states; there are also about 2,000 publicly owned power utilities in the U.S. (including ones in Puerto Rico, Los Angeles, Long Island, and Seattle (see http://www.appanet.org/); Russia, by virtue of over 75 years of Communist rule, had numerous publicly owned power generators.

58. 2007, Business: Gimme smelter: Aluminium, *The Economist*, 384(8538): 66.

59. Ibid; 2008, Reuters, Factbox—World bauxite reserves and production, February 15, 2007, http://www.alertnet.org/thenews/newsdesk/L15774125.htm, retrieved January 9.

60. P. Ghemawat, 2004, Global standardization vs. localization: A case study and model, in J. A. Quelch & R. Deshpande (eds.), *The Global Market: Developing a Strategy to Manage Across Borders*, New York: Jossey-Bass; J. Birkinshaw, 2001, Strategies for managing internal competition, *California Management Review*, 44(1): 21–38.

61. W. P. Wan & R. E. Hoskisson, 2003, Home country environments, corporate diversification strategies and firm performance, *Academy of Management Journal*, 46: 27–45; J. M. Geringer, S. Tallman, & D. M. Olsen, 2000, Product and international diversification among Japanese multinational firms, *Strategic Management Journal*, 21: 51–80; M. A. Hitt, R. E. Hoskisson, & R. D. Ireland, 1994, A mid-range theory of the interactive effects of international and product diversification on innovation and performance, *Journal of Management*, 20: 297–326.

62. L. Li, 2005, Is regional strategy more effective than global strategy in the U.S. service industries?, *Management International Review*, 45: 37–57; B. B. Alred & K. S. Swan, 2004, Global versus multidomestic: Culture's consequences on innovation, *Management International Review*, 44: 81–105; A.-W. Harzing, 2000, An empirical analysis and extension of the Bartlett and Ghoshal typology of multinational companies, *Journal of International Business Studies*, 32: 101–120.

63. A. Ferner, P. Almond, I. Clark, T. Colling, & T. Edwards, 2004, The dynamics of central control and subsidiary anatomy in the management of human resources: Case study evidence from US MNCs in the UK, *Organization Studies,* 25: 363–392.

64. L. Nachum, 2003, Does nationality of ownership make any difference and if so, under what circumstances? Professional service MNEs in global competition, *Journal of International Management,* 9: 1–32; Sheth, From international to integrated marketing; J. Taggart & N. Hood, 1999, Determinants of autonomy in multinational corporation subsidiaries, *European Management Journal,* 17: 226–236.

65. Y. Luo, 2001, Determinants of local responsiveness: Perspectives from foreign subsidiaries in an emerging market, *Journal of Management,* 27: 451–477.

66. M. Geppert, K. Williams, & D. Matten, 2003, The social construction of contextual rationalities in MNCs: An Anglo-German comparison of subsidiary choice, *Journal of Management Studies,* 40: 617–641; M. Carpenter & J. Fredrickson, 2001, Top management teams, global strategic posture, and the moderating role of uncertainty, *Academy of Management Journal,* 44: 533–545; T. T. Herbert, 1999, Multinational strategic planning: Matching central expectations to local realities, *Long Range Planning,* 32: 81–87.

67. G. Jones, 2002, Control, performance, and knowledge transfers in large multinationals: Unilever in the United States, 1945–1980, *Business History Review,* 76(3): 435–478.

68. D. Michaels, 2003, World business (a special report): Victory at sea: How did a French company capture several British naval contracts? Think "multidomestic," *Wall Street Journal Europe,* September 26, R5.

69. A. W. Harzing & A. Sorge, 2003, The relative impact of country of origin and universal contingencies in internationalization strategies and corporate control in multinational enterprises: Worldwide and European perspectives, *Organization Studies,* 24: 187–214.

70. Li, Is regional strategy more effective than global strategy in the U.S. service industries?; Alred & Swan, Global versus multidomestic: Culture's consequences on innovation; Harzing, An empirical analysis and extension of the Bartlett and Ghoshal typology; I. C. MacMillan, A. B. van Putten, & R. G. McGrath, 2003, Global gamesmanship, *Harvard Business Review,* 81(5): 62–7.

71. R. G. Barker, 2003, Trend: Global accounting is coming, *Harvard Business Review,* 81(4): 24–25.

72. A. Yaprak, 2002, Globalization: Strategies to build a great global firm in the new economy, *Thunderbird International Business Review,* 44(2): 297–302; D. G. McKendrick, 2001, Global strategy and population level learning: The case of hard disk drives, *Strategic Management Journal,* 22: 307–334.

73. G. Parker, 2005, Going global can hit snags, Vodafone finds, *Wall Street Journal,* June 16, B1.

74. A. Delios & P. W. Beamish, 2005, Regional and global strategies of Japanese firms, *Management International Review,* 45: 19–36; H. D. Hopkins, 2003, The response strategies of dominant US firms to Japanese challengers, *Journal of Management,* 29: 5–25; S. Massini, A. Y. Lewin, T. Numagami, & A. Pettigrew, 2002, The evolution of organizational routines among large Western and Japanese firms, *Research Policy,* 31(8,9): 1333–1348; J. K. Johansson & G. S. Yip, 1994, Exploiting globalization potential: U.S. and Japanese strategies, *Strategic Management Journal,* 15: 579–601.

75. K. A. Garrett, 2005, Cemex, *Business Mexico,* April, 23.

76. T. B. Lawrence, E. A. Morse, & S. W. Fowler, 2005, Managing your portfolio of connections, *MIT Sloan Management Review,* 46(2): 59–65; Y. Doz, J. Santos, & P. Williamson, 2001, *From Global to Metanational: How Companies Win in the Knowledge Economy,* Boston: Harvard Business School Press; C. A. Bartlett & S. Ghoshal, 1989, *Managing across Borders: The Transnational Solution,* Boston: Harvard Business School Press.

77. A. Abbott & K. Banerji, 2003, Strategic flexibility and firm performance: The case of US based transnational corporations, *Global Journal of Flexible Systems Management,* 4(1/2): 1–7; J. Child & Y. Yan, 2001, National and transnational effects in international business: Indications from Sino-foreign joint ventures, *Management International Review,* 41(1): 53–75.

78. J. P. Millikin & D. Fu, 2005, The global leadership of Carlos Ghosn at Nissan, *Thunderbird International Business Review,* 47(1): 121–137; B. James, 2003, Ghosn's local vision plays on a world stage, *International Herald Tribune,* May 3, 9.

79. 2004, Bombardier Web page, http://www.bombardier.com, accessed February 11; 2004, Rail Control Solutions of Bombardier Transportation Web page, http://www.ria.connect.co.uk/directory/bombrcsolutions.php, accessed February 11.

80. A. M. Rugman & A. Verbeke, 2003, Extending the theory of the multinational enterprise: Internalization and strategic management perspectives, *Journal of International Business Studies,* 34: 125–137.

81. T. L. Pett & J. A. Wolff, 2003, Firm characteristic and managerial perceptions of NAFTA: An assessment of export implications for U.S. SMEs, *Journal of Small Business Management,* 41(2): 117–132.

82. Wright, Filatotchev, Hoskisson, & Peng, Strategy research in emerging economies: Challenging the conventional wisdom.

83. N. Y. Brannen, 2004, When Mickey loses face: Recontextualization, semantic fit and Semiotics of foreignness, *Academy of Management Review,* 29: 593–616.

84. S. Zaheer & A. Zaheer, 2001, Market microstructure in a global B2B network, *Strategic Management Journal,* 22: 859–873.

85. 2008, AbeBooks Fact Sheet, http://www.abebooks.com/docs/CompanyInformation/factSheet.shtml, January 11.

86. J. Schlosser, 2004, Cashing in on the new world of Me, *Fortune,* December 13, 244–248.

87. A. Rugman & A. Verbeke, 2004, A perspective on regional and global strategies of multinational enterprises, *Journal of International Business Studies,* 35: 3–18; B. Elango, 2004, Geographic scope of operations by multinational companies: An exploratory study of regional and global strategies, *European Management Journal,* 22(4): 431–441.

88. C. Pantzalis, 2001, Does location matter? An empirical analysis of geographic scope and MNC market valuation, *Journal of International Business Studies,* 32: 133–155.

89. A. Rugman & S. Girod, 2003, Retail multinationals and globalization: The evidence is regional, *European Management Journal,* 21(1): 24–37.

90. R. D. Ludema, 2002, Increasing returns, multinationals and geography of preferential trade agreements, *Journal of International Economics,* 56: 329–358; L. Allen & C. Pantzalis, 1996, Valuation of the operating flexibility of multinational corporations, *Journal of International Business Studies,* 27: 633–653.

91. Delios & Beamish, Regional and global strategies of Japanese firms.

92. 2008, Foreign Affairs and International Trade Canada, Negotiations and Agreements Web Site, http://www.international.gc.ca/trade-agreements-accords-commerciaux/agr-acc/index.aspx?menu_id=15&menu=, retrieved January 12.

93. W. Chung & J. Song, 2004, Sequential investment, firm motives, and agglomeration of Japanese electronics firms in the United States, *Journal of Economics and Management Strategy,* 13: 539–560; D. Xu & O. Shenkar, 2002, Institutional distance and the multinational enterprise, *Academy of Management Review,* 27(4): 608–618; J. Chang & P. M. Rosenzweig, 1998, Industry and regional patterns in sequential foreign market entry, *Journal of Management Studies,* 35: 797–822.

94. S. O'Grady & H. W. Lane, 1996, The Psychic Distance Paradox, *Journal of International Business Studies,* 27, 309–333.

95. K. D. Brouthers, L. E. Brouthers, & S. Werner, 2003, Industrial sector, perceived environmental uncertainty and entry mode strategy, *Journal of Business Research,* 55: 495–507; S. Zahra, J. Hayton, J. Marcel, & H. O'Neill, 2001, Fostering entrepreneurship during international expansion: Managing key challenges, *European Management Journal,* 19: 359–369.

96. H. Zhao, Y. Luo, & T. Suh, 2004, Transaction costs determinants and ownership-based entry mode choice: A meta-analytical review, *Journal of International Business Studies,* 35: 524–544; K. D. Brouthers, 2003, Institutional, cultural and transaction cost influences on entry mode choice

and performance, *Journal of International Business Studies,* 33: 203–221; R. Konopaske, S. Werner, & K. E. Neupert, 2002, Entry mode strategy and performance: The role of FDI staffing, *Journal of Business Research,* 55: 759–770.

97. C. Lages, C. R. Lages, & L. F. Lages, 2005, The RELQUAL scale: A measure of relationship quality in export market ventures, *Journal of Business Research,* 58: 1040–1048; R. Isaak, 2002, Using trading firms to export: What can the French experience teach us? *Academy of Management Executive,* 16(4): 155–156; M. W. Peng, C. W. L. Hill, & D. Y. L. Wang, 2000, Schumpeterian dynamics versus Williamsonian considerations: A test of export intermediary performance, *Journal of Management Studies,* 37: 167–184.

98. Y. Chui, 2002, The structure of the multinational firm: The role of ownership characteristics and technology transfer, *International Journal of Management,* 19(3): 472–477.

99. Luo, Determinants of local responsiveness.

100. L. E. Brouthers & K. Xu, 2002, Product stereotypes, strategy and performance satisfaction: The case of Chinese exporters, *Journal of International Business Studies,* 33: 657–677; M. A. Raymond, J. Kim, & A. T. Shao, 2001, Export strategy and performance: A comparison of exporters in a developed market and an emerging market, *Journal of Global Marketing,* 15(2): 5–29; P. S. Aulakh, M. Kotabe, & H. Teegen, 2000, Export strategies and performance of firms from emerging economies: Evidence from Brazil, Chile and Mexico, *Academy of Management Journal,* 43: 342–361.

101. 2008, Ontario Exports Web site, http://www.2ontario.com/welcome/ooit_300.asp and http://www.2ontario.com/welcome/ooit_317.asp, retrieved January 12; W. Dou, U. Nielsen, & C. M. Tan, 2003, Using corporate Websites for export marketing, *Journal of Advertising Research,* 42(5): 105–115; A. Haahti, V. Madupu, U. Yavas, & E. Babakus, 2005, Cooperative strategy, knowledge intensity and export performance of small and medium sized enterprises, *Journal of World Business,* 40(2): 124–138.

102. P. Westhead, M. Wright, & D. Ucbasaran, 2001, The internationalization of new and small firms: A resource-based view, *Journal of Business Venturing,* 16: 333–358; 2007, Profile: Quebec pulley maker boosts productivity to stay competitive, *Machinery & Equipment.* 23(2): 14; 2007, Business: A nation of angry shoppers: Cross-border shopping, *The Economist,* 385(8554): 96; 2006, Coal and copper fuel BC's mining boom, *The Northern Miner.* 92(14): 5.

103. D. Kline, 2003, Sharing the corporate crown jewels, *MIT Sloan Management Review,* 44(3): 83–88; M. A. Hitt & R. D. Ireland, 2000, The intersection of entrepreneurship and strategic management research, in D. L. Sexton & H. Landstrom (eds.), *Handbook of Entrepreneurship,* Oxford, UK: Blackwell Publishers, 45–63; A. Arora & A. Fosfuri, 2000, Wholly-owned subsidiary versus technology licensing in the worldwide chemical industry, *Journal of International Business Studies,* 31: 555–572.

104. 2008, Nelvana Web site, http://www.nelvana.com/shows/index.asp, retrieved January 15; K. Damsell, 2000, Corus swallows Nelvana, Broadcaster's $540 million acquisition of animation house part of global ambition, *The Globe and Mail,* September 19, B1, B11.

105. Y. J. Kim, 2005, The impact of firm and industry characteristics on technology licensing, *S. A. M. Advanced Management Journal,* 70(1): 42–49.

106. M. Johnson, 2001, Learning from toys: Lessons in managing supply chain risk from the toy industry, *California Management Review,* 43(3): 106–124.

107. Rigby & Zook, Open-market innovation.

108. C. A. Bartlett & S. Rangan, 1992, Komatsu limited, in C. A. Bartlett & S. Ghoshal (eds.), *Transnational Management: Text, Cases and Readings in Cross-Border Management,* Homewood, IL: Irwin, 311–326.

109. 2008, Boston Pizza Web site, http://www.bostonpizza.com/, and Boston's, The Gourmet Pizza Web site, http://www.bostonsgourmet.com/, retrieved Janurary 15.

110. J. J. Reuer & T. W. Tong, 2005, Real options in international joint ventures, *Journal of Management,* 31: 403–423; B. Petersen, D. E. Welch, & L. S. Welch, 2000, Creating meaningful switching options in international operations, *Long Range Planning,* 33(5): 688–705.

111. R. Larsson, K. R. Brousseau, M. J. Driver, & M. Homqvist, 2003, International growth through cooperation: Brand-driven strategies, leadership, and career

development in Sweden, *Academy of Management Executive,* 17(1): 7–21; J. W. Lu & P. W. Beamish, 2001, The internationalization and performance of SMEs, *Strategic Management Journal,* 22 (Special Issue): 565–586; M. Koza & A. Lewin, 2000, Managing partnerships and strategic alliances: Raising the odds of success, *European Management Journal,* 18(2): 146–151.

112. J. S. Harrison, M. A. Hitt, R. E. Hoskisson, & R. D. Ireland, 2001, Resource complementarity in business combinations: Extending the logic to organization alliances, *Journal of Management,* 27: 679–690; T. Das & B. Teng, 2000, A resource-based theory of strategic alliances, *Journal of Management,* 26: 31–61.

113. M. A. Hitt, D. Ahlstrom, M. T. Dacin, E. Levitas, & L. Svobodina, 2004, The institutional effects on strategic alliance partner selection in transition economies: China versus Russia, *Organization Science,* 15: 173–185; M. Peng, 2001, The resource-based view and international business, *Journal of Management,* 27: 803–829.

114. Manulife press release, 2007, Manulife-Sinochem expands business in Shandong Province with a new sales office licence in Yantai, http://www.manulife.com/corporate/corporate2.nsf/Public/china122007.html, retrieved January 15, 2008; 2006 Manulife Annual Report, 2007, http://www.manulife.com/corporate/corporate2.nsf/LookupFiles/DownloadableFile2006AnnualReport/$File/2006AnnualReport.pdf, retrieved January 15, 2008; 2008, Manulife History Web page, http://www.manulife.com/corporate/corporate2.nsf/Public/history.html, retrieved January 15, 2008.

115. J. Bamford, D. Ernst, & D. G. Fubini, 2004, Launching a world-class joint venture, *Harvard Business Review,* 82(2): 91–100.

116. E. W. K. Tsang, 2002, Acquiring knowledge by foreign partners for international joint ventures in a transition economy: Learning-by-doing and learning myopia, *Strategic Management Journal,* 23(9): 835–854; P. J. Lane, J. E. Salk, & M. A. Lyles, 2002, Absorptive capacity, learning, and performance in international joint ventures, *Strategic Management Journal,* 22: 1139–1161; B. L. Simonin, 1999, Transfer of marketing know-how in international strategic alliances: An empirical investigation of the role and antecedents of knowledge ambiguity, *Journal of International Business Studies,* 30: 463–490.

117. A. T. Mohr & J. F. Puck, 2005, Managing functional diversity to improve the performance of international joint ventures, *Long Range Planning,* 38(2): 163–182; P. Almeida, J. Song, & R. M. Grant, 2002, Are firms superior to alliances and markets? An empirical test of cross-border knowledge building, *Organization Science,* 13(2): 147–161; M. A. Hitt, M. T. Dacin, E. Levitas, J. L. Arregle, & A. Borza, 2000, Partner selection in emerging and developed market contexts: Resource based and organizational learning perspectives, *Academy of Management Journal,* 43: 449–467.

118. R. Pooley, 2005, The model alliance of Renault and Nissan, *Human Resource Management International Digest,* 13(2): 29–32.

119. M. W. Peng & O. Shenkar, 2002, Joint venture dissolution as corporate divorce, *Academy of Management Executive,* 16(2): 92–105; O. Shenkar & A. Yan, 2002, Failure as a consequence of partner politics: Learning from the life and death of an international cooperative venture, *Human Relations,* 55: 565–601.

120. J. A. Robins, S. Tallman, & K. Fladmoe-Lindquist, 2002, Autonomy and dependence of international cooperative ventures: An exploration of the strategic performance of U.S. ventures in Mexico, *Strategic Management Journal,* 23(10): 881–901; Y. Gong, O. Shenkar, Y. Luo, & M.-K. Nyaw, 2001, Role conflict and ambiguity of CEOs in international joint ventures: A transaction cost perspective, *Journal of Applied Psychology,* 86: 764–773.

121. P. K. Jagersma, 2005, Cross-border alliances: Advice from the executive suite, *Journal of Business Strategy,* 26(1): 41–50; D. C. Hambrick, J. Li, K. Xin, & A. S. Tsui, 2001, Compositional gaps and downward spirals in international joint venture management groups, *Strategic Management Journal,* 22: 1033–1053; M. T. Dacin, M. A. Hitt, & E. Levitas, 1997, Selecting partners for successful international alliances: Examination of U.S. and Korean firms, *Journal of World Business,* 32: 3–16.

122. J. Child & Y. Yan, 2003, Predicting the performance of international joint ventures: An investigation in China, *Journal of Management Studies,* 40(2):

283–320; J. P. Johnson, M. A. Korsgaard, & H. J. Sapienza, 2002, Perceived fairness, decision control, and commitment in international joint venture management teams, *Strategic Management Journal,* 23(12): 1141–1160; A. Arino, J. de la Torre, & P. S. Ring, 2001, Relational quality: Managing trust in corporate alliances, *California Management Review,* 44(1): 109–131.

123. L. Huff & L. Kelley, 2003, Levels of organizational trust in individualist versus collectivist societies: A seven-nation study, *Organization Science,* 14(1): 81–90.

124. Y. Pan & D. K. Tse, 2000, The hierarchical model of market entry modes, *Journal of International Business Studies,* 31: 535–554; Y. Pan, S. Li, & D. K. Tse, 1999, The impact of order and mode of market entry on profitability and market share, *Journal of International Business Studies,* 30: 81–104; J. J. Reuer & M. Zollo, 2005, Termination outcomes of research alliances, *Research Policy,* 34(1): 101–115.

125. P. Porrini, 2004, Can a previous alliance between an acquirer and a target affect acquisition performance? *Journal of Management,* 30: 545–562; J. J. Reuer, 2002, Incremental corporate reconfiguration through international joint venture buyouts and selloffs, *Management International Review,* 42: 237–260.

126. J. J. Reuer, 2005, Avoiding lemons in M&A deals, *MIT Sloan Management Review,* 46(3): 15–17; G. A. Knight & P. W. Liesch, 2002, Information internalisation in internationalising the firm, *Journal of Business Research,* 55(12): 981–995; J. H. Dyer, P. Kale, & H. Singh, 2004, When to ally and when to acquire, *Harvard Business Review,* 82(7): 108–117; W. H. Hoffmann & W. Schaper-Rinkel, 2001, Acquire or ally? A strategy framework for deciding between acquisition and cooperation, *Management International Review,* 41(2): 131–159.

127. K. Shimizu, M. A. Hitt, D. Vaidyanath, & V. Pisano, 2004, Theoretical foundations of cross-border mergers and acquisitions: A review of current research and recommendations for the future, *Journal of International Management,* 10: 307–353; M. A. Hitt, J. S. Harrison, & R. D. Ireland, 2001, *Mergers and Acquisitions: A Guide to Creating Value for Stakeholders,* New York: Oxford University Press.

128. M. A. Hitt & V. Pisano, 2003, The cross-border merger and acquisition strategy, *Management Research,* 1: 133–144.

129. J. Levine, 2004, Europe: Gold mines and quicksand, *Forbes,* April 12, 76.

130. J. Singer, C. Mollenkamp, & E. Taylor, 2005, Unicredito agrees to acquire HVB: Deal totaling $18.8 billion would create huge leader spanning European borders, *Wall Street Journal,* June 13, A3; G. Edmondson & M. Kline, 2005, An Italian bank pulls the trigger, *BusinessWeek,* June 27, 34.

131. 1999, French dressing, *The Economist,* July 10, 53–54.

132. C. Buckley, 2005, SAIC to fund MG Rover bid, *The Times of London,* www.timesonline.co.uk, July 18.

133. A.-W. Harzing, 2002, Acquisitions versus greenfield investments: International strategy and management of entry modes, *Strategic Management Journal,* 23: 211–227; K. D. Brouthers & L. E. Brouthers, 2000, Acquisition or greenfield start-up? Institutional, cultural and transaction cost influences, *Strategic Management Journal,* 21: 89–97; C. Bouquet, L. Hebert, & A. Delios, 2004, Foreign expansion in service industries: Separability and human capital intensity, *Journal of Business Research,* 57: 35–46.

134. D. Elango, 2005, The influence of plant characteristics on the entry mode choice of overseas firms, *Journal of Operations Management,* 23(1): 65–79.

135. P. Deng, 2003, Determinants of full-control mode in China: An integrative approach, *American Business Review,* 21(1): 113–123; R. Belderbos, 2003, Entry mode, organizational learning, and R&D in foreign affiliates: Evidence from Japanese firms, *Strategic Management Journal,* 34: 235–259.

136. K. E. Meyer & H. V. Nguyen, 2005, Foreign investment strategies in subnational institutions in emerging markets: Evidence from Vietnam, *Journal of Management Studies,* 42: 63–93; J. Reuer, O. Shenkar, & R. Ragozzino, 2004, Mitigating risks in international mergers and acquisitions: The role of contingent payouts, *Journal of International Business Studies,* 35: 19–32.

137. A. Bartram, 2007, DHL makes Shanghai its North Asia hub, *China Economic Review,* November 28, http://www.china economicreview.com/logistics/2007/11/28/dhl-makes-shanghai-its-north-asia-hub/, retrieved January 15,

2008; B. Stanley, 2005, United Parcel Service to open a hub in Shanghai, *Wall Street Journal,* July 8, B2; B. Stanley, 2005, FedEx plans hub in Guangzhou: Facility to begin operation in 2008 as cargo industry tries to claim turf in Asia, *Asian Wall Street Journal,* July 14, A3.

138. V. Gaba, Y. Pan, & G. R. Ungson, 2002, Timing of entry in international market: An empirical study of U.S. Fortune 500 firms in China, *Journal of International Business Studies,* 33(1): 39–55; S.-J. Chang & P. Rosenzweig, 2001, The choice of entry mode in sequential foreign direct investment, *Strategic Management Journal,* 22: 747–776.

139. K. E. Myer, 2001, Institutions, transaction costs, and entry mode choice in Eastern Europe, *Journal of International Business Studies,* 32: 357–367.

140. S. Li, 2004, Why are property rights protections lacking in China? An institutional explanation, *California Management Review,* 46(3): 100–115; Y. Luo, 2001, Determinants of entry in an emerging economy: A multilevel approach, *Journal of Management Studies,* 38: 443–472.

141. A. Antoine, C. B. Frank, H. Murata, & E. Roberts, 2003, Acquisitions and alliances in the aerospace industry: An unusual triad, *International Journal of Technology Management,* 25(8): 779–790.

142. 2007, Bombardier Joint Venture Awarded Contract for 40 High-Speed Trainsets in China, *Marketwire,* October 31, http://www.marketwirecanada.com/mw/release.do?id=786830&k=, retrieved January 15, 2008.

143. A. Antoine, C. B. Frank, H. Murata, & E. Roberts, 2003, Acquisitions and alliances in the aerospace industry.

144. L. J. Howell & J. C. Hsu, 2002, Globalization within the auto industry, *Research Technology Management,* 45(4): 43–49; A. Takeishi, 2001, Bridging inter- and intra-firm boundaries: Management of supplier involvement in automobile product development, *Strategic Management Journal,* 22: 403–433.

145. S. J. Spear, 2004, Learning to lead at Toyota, *Harvard Business Review,* 82(5): 78–86.

146. J. Hagedoorn & G. Dysters, 2002, External sources of innovative capabilities: The preference for strategic alliances or mergers and acquisitions, *Journal of Management Studies,* 39: 167–188; H. Chen, 1999, International performance of multinationals: A hybrid model, *Journal of World Business,* 34: 157–170.

147. J. E. Garten, 2005, A new threat to America, Inc., *BusinessWeek,* July 25, 114; Hoskisson, Kim, Tihanyi, & White, A framework for understanding international diversification by business groups from emerging economies.

148. J. Song, 2002, Firm capabilities and technology ladders: Sequential foreign direct investments of Japanese electronics firms in East Asia, *Strategic Management Journal,* 23: 191–210.

149. J. W. Lu & P. W. Beamish, 2004, International diversification and firm performance: The S-curve hypothesis, *Academy of Management Journal,* 47: 598–609.

150. S. E. Christophe & H. Lee, 2005, What matters about internationalization: A market-based assessment, *Journal of Business Research,* 58: 536–643; J. A. Doukas & L. H. P. Lang, 2003, Foreign direct investment, diversification and firm performance, *Journal of International Business Studies,* 34: 153–172.

151. Kwok & Reeb, 2000, Internationalization and firm risk; J. M. Geringer, P. W. Beamish, & R. C. daCosta, 1989, Diversification strategy and internationalization: Implications for MNE performance, *Strategic Management Journal,* 10: 109–119; R. E. Caves, 1982, *Multinational Enterprise and Economic Analysis,* Cambridge, MA: Cambridge University Press.

152. Zahra, Ireland, & Hitt, International expansion by new venture firms.

153. D. Farrell, 2005, Offshoring: Value creation through economic change, *Journal of Management Studies,* 42: 675–683; J. P. Doh, 2005, Offshore outsourcing: Implications for international business and strategic management theory and practice, *Journal of Management Studies,* 42: 695–704.

154. L. Lopez, 2005, Petronas's net soared in year; high oil, petroleum prices fueled 41 percent rise in revenue; widening global stature, *Asian Wall Street Journal,* July 1, A3; L. Lopez, 2003, A well-oiled money machine, *Far Eastern Economic Review,* March 13, 40–43.

155. J. Penner-Hahn & J. M. Shaver, 2005, Does international research and development increase patent output? An analysis of Japanese pharmaceutical firms, *Strategic Management Journal,* 26: 121–140; Hagedoorn & Dysters,

External sources of innovative capabilities; G. Hamel, 2000, *Leading the Revolution,* Boston: Harvard Business School Press.

156. L. Tihanyi, R. A. Johnson, R. E. Hoskisson, & M. A. Hitt, 2003, Institutional ownership differences and international diversification: The effects of board of directors and technological opportunity, *Academy of Management Journal,* 46: 195–211.

157. Ambos, Foreign direct investment in industrial research and development; F. Bradley & M. Gannon, 2000, Does the firm's technology and marketing profile affect foreign market entry? *Journal of International Marketing,* 8(4): 12–36; M. Kotabe, 1990, The relationship between off-shore sourcing and innovativeness of U.S. multinational firms: An empirical investigation, *Journal of International Business Studies,* 21: 623–638.

158. S. Makino, P. W. Beamish, & N. B. Zhao, 2004, The characteristics and performance of Japanese FDI in less developed and developed countries, *Journal of World Business,* 39(4): 377–392.

159. Asakawa & Lehrer, Managing local knowledge assets globally: The role of regional innovation relays; I. Zander & O. Solvell, 2000, Cross border innovation in the multinational corporation: A research agenda, *International Studies of Management and Organization,* 30(2): 44–67.

160. Penner-Hahn & Shaver, Does international research increase patent output?

161. O. E. M. Janne, 2002, The emergence of corporate integrated innovation systems across regions: The case of the chemical and pharmaceutical industry in Germany, the UK and Belgium, *Journal of International Management,* 8: 97–119; N. J. Foss & T. Pedersen, 2002, Transferring knowledge in MNCs: The role of sources of subsidiary knowledge and organizational context, *Journal of International Management,* 8: 49–67.

162. J. Jung & S. M. Chan-Olmsted, 2005, Impacts of media conglomerates' dual diversification on financial performance, *Journal of Media Economics,* 18(3): 183–202.

163. Wan & Hoskisson, Home country environments, corporate diversification strategies and firm performance.

164. D. S. Elenkov, W. Judge, & P. Wright, 2005, Strategic leadership and executive innovation influence: An international multi-cluster comparative study, *Strategic Management Journal,* 26: 665–682; P. Herrmann, 2002, The influence of CEO characteristics on the international diversification of manufacturing firms: An empirical study in the United States, *International Journal of Management,* 19(2): 279–289.

165. H. A. Krishnan & D. Park, 2003, Power in acquired top management teams and post-acquisition performance: A conceptual framework, *International Journal of Management,* 20: 75–80; A. McWilliams, D. D. Van Fleet, & P. M. Wright, 2001, Strategic management of human resources for global competitive advantage, *Journal of Business Strategies,* 18(1): 1–24.

166. M. A. Hitt, R. E. Hoskisson, & H. Kim, 1997, International diversification: Effects on innovation and firm performance in product-diversified firms, *Academy of Management Journal,* 40: 767–798.

167. Y. Li, L. Li, Y. Liu, & L. Wang, 2005, Linking management control system with product development and process decisions to cope with environment complexity. *International Journal of Production Research,* 43: 2577–2591; J. Child, L. Chung, & H. Davies, 2003, The performance of cross-border units in China: A test of natural selection, strategic choice and contingency theories, *Journal of International Business Studies,* 34: 242–254.

168. Y.-H. Chiu, 2003, The impact of conglomerate firm diversification on corporate performance: An empirical study in Taiwan, *International Journal of Management,* 19: 231–237; Luo, Market-seeking MNEs in an emerging market: How parent-subsidiary links shape overseas success.

169. 2005, Keeping IT together, *Chain Store Age,* June, 48.

170. Y. Paik, 2005, Risk management of strategic alliances and acquisitions between western MNCs and companies in central Europe, *Thunderbird International Business Review,* 47(4): 489–511; A. Delios & W. J. Henisz, 2003, Policy uncertainty and the sequence of entry by Japanese firms, 1980–1998, *Journal of International Business Studies,* 34: 227–241; D. M. Reeb, C. C. Y. Kwok, & H. Y. Baek, 1998, Systematic risk of the multinational corporation, *Journal of International Business Studies,* 29: 263–279.

171. P. Rodriguez, K. Uhlenbruck, & L. Eden, 2005, Government corruption and the entry strategies of multinationals, *Academy of Management Review,* 30: 383–396; J. H. Zhao, S. H. Kim, & J. Du, 2003, The impact of corruption and transparency on foreign direct investment: An empirical analysis, *Management International Review,* 43(1): 41–62.

172. P. S. Ring, G. A. Bigley, T. D'aunno, & T. Khanna, 2005, Perspectives on how governments matter, *Academy of Management Review,* 30: 308–320; S. Globerman & D. Shapiro, 2003, Governance infrastructure and US foreign direct investment, *Journal of International Business Studies,* 34(1): 19–39.

173. G. Chazan, 2005, Putin pledges to help foreign investors, *Wall Street Journal,* June 27, A13.

174. T. Mapes, 2005, Terror still keeps foreign investors out of Indonesia, *Wall Street Journal,* May 31, A14.

175. T. Vestring, T. Rouse, & U. Reinert, 2005, Hedging your offshoring bets, *MIT Sloan Management Review,* 46(3): 26–29; L. L. Jacque & P. M. Vaaler, 2001, The international control conundrum with exchange risk: An EVA framework, *Journal of International Business Studies,* 32: 813–832.

176. T. G. Andrews & N. Chompusri, 2005, Temporal dynamics of crossvergence: Institutionalizing MNC integration strategies in post-crisis ASEAN, *Asia Pacific Journal of Management,* 22(1): 5–22; S. Mudd, R. Grosse, & J. Mathis, 2002, Dealing with financial crises in emerging markets, *Thunderbird International Business Review,* 44(3): 399–430.

177. Lu & Beamish, International diversification and firm performance: The s-curve hypothesis; Wan & Hoskisson, Home country environments, corporate diversification strategies and firm performance; Hitt, Hoskisson, & Kim, International diversification; S. Tallman & J. Li, 1996, Effects of international diversity and product diversity on the performance of multinational firms, *Academy of Management Journal,* 39: 179–196.

178. F. J. Contractor, S. K. Kundu, & C. C. Hsu, 2003, A three-stage theory of international expansion: The link between multinationality and performance in the service sector, *Journal of International Business Studies,* 34(1), 5–19; A. K. Rose & E. van Wincoop, 2001, National money as a barrier to international trade: The real case for currency union, *American Economic Review,* 91: 386–390.

179. I. Bjorkman, W. Barner-Rasmussen, & L. Li, 2004, Managing knowledge transfer in MNCs: The impact of headquarters control mechanisms, *Journal of International Business Studies,* 35: 443–455.

180. D. Luhnow, 2001, How NAFTA helped Wal-Mart transform the Mexican market. *Wall Street Journal,* August 31, A1, A2.

181. 2008, Wal-Mart to Open its 3000th International Store, Wal-Mart Web page, http://www.walmartfacts.com/articles/5500.aspx, retrieved January 16.

182. P. S. Barr & M. A. Glynn, 2004, Cultural variations in strategic issue interpretation: Relating cultural uncertainty avoidance to controllability in discriminating threat and opportunity, *Strategic Management Journal,* 25: 59–67; V. Miroshnik, 2002, Culture and international management: A review, *Journal of Management Development,* 21(7,8): 521–544.

183. W. P. J. Henisz & B. A. Zelner, 2005, Legitimacy, interest group pressures and change in emergent institutions, the case of foreign investors and host country governments, *Academy of Management Review,* 30: 361–382; T. P. Blumentritt & D. Nigh, 2002, The integration of subsidiary political activities in multinational corporations, *Journal of International Business Studies,* 33: 57–77.

184. N. Shirouzu, 2005, Mean but lean, Toyota seeks outside help, *Wall Street Journal,* July 14, B4.

185. J. W. Lu & P. W. Beamish, 2004, Network development and firm performance: A field study of internationalizing Japanese firms, *Multinational Business Review,* 12(3): 41–61; U. Andersson, M. Forsgren, & U. Holm, 2002, The strategic impact of external networks: Subsidiary performance and competence development in the multinational corporation, *Strategic Management Journal,* 23: 979–996; S. J. Chang & S. Park, 2005, Types of firms generating network externalities and MNCs' co-location decisions, *Strategic Management Journal,* 26: 595–616.

Chapter Ten

Cooperative Strategy

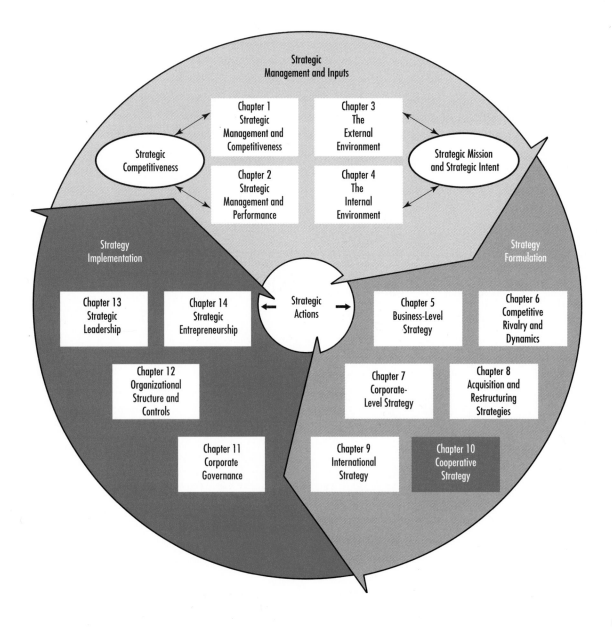

Knowledge Objectives

Studying this chapter should provide you with the strategic management knowledge needed to:

1. Define cooperative strategies and explain why firms use them.

2. Define and discuss three types of strategic alliances.

3. Name the business-level cooperative strategies and describe their use.

4. Discuss the use of corporate-level cooperative strategies in diversified firms.

5. Understand the importance of cross-border strategic alliances as an international cooperative strategy.

6. Explain cooperative strategies' risks.

7. Describe two approaches used to manage cooperative strategies.

Using Alliances to Build Greater Value

Strategic alliances have become an essential ingredient in companies' strategies. There are many reasons for this, but the bottom line is that when firms form appropriate alliances and manage them effectively, they help create value. For example, Fujitsu has developed a number of successful strategic alliances that have played a major role in the firm's success in recent years. Fujitsu has had a successful partnership with Siemens AG for over 20 years. One outcome of the partnership was the merger of the two companies' European computer operations into a joint venture (JV) named Fujitsu Siemens Computers. This JV manufactures and sells a variety of information systems products.

www.fujitsu-siemens.com

www.staralliance.com

www.lenovo.com

In 1993, Fujitsu and Advanced Micro Devices (AMD) formed a JV, Fujitsu AMD Semiconductor Ltd., to design, develop, and sell flash memory chips. These chips are sold to each of the parent firms, which then use them in products sold in international markets. In 1997, Fujitsu formed a strategic alliance with Computer Associates to develop and market Jasmine, a software product offered as a standard for global solutions. In 1998, Fujitsu formed a strategic alliance with Cisco Systems to provide sales and support for Cisco products in Europe. Fujitsu has developed alliances with other firms such as Dell, EDS, Intel, Microsoft, Novell, Oracle, Sun Microsystems, and Veritas.

Thus, strategic alliances have served as a critical means of populating international markets for Fujitsu.

Strategic alliances have been critically important to other firms as well. For example, Air Canada was one of the founding members of the Star Alliance in 1997—along with Lufthansa AG, Scandinavian Airlines Systems, Thai Airways International, and United Airlines. The alliance has expanded to a total of 20 airlines. The alliance allows passengers to more seamlessly transfer between airlines on longer trips that may route them through more than one carrier. Thus, it puts passengers in Air Canada seats that might not otherwise be there—both because Air Canada's passengers can more easily connect with other airlines, and because other airlines' passengers now fly on Air Canada.

While Fujitsu and Air Canada apparently developed strategic alliances to take advantage of opportunities, others may form alliances out of necessity. For example, many computer manufacturers have formed alliances with foreign manufacturers in order to hold down costs, allowing them to compete more effectively in the global markets for PCs. In 2004 Dell, Apple, Gateway, and Acer outsourced 100 percent of the manufacturing of their laptop computers. IBM outsourced only 40 percent, lost money on its laptops, and sold the business to Lenovo, the leading Chinese PC company. Thus, computer firms must find ways to keep their costs down in order to compete in the industry and do so by developing strategic alliances with foreign manufacturers. Now 80 percent of laptop computers are manufactured by Taiwanese companies, mostly in mainland China, where costs are even lower.

Strategic alliances are critical in Europe's information technology (IT) services industry as well. The industry has become highly competitive in recent years with the entry of global IT service providers such as IBM and the growth of others such as Siemens. An example of the competitive challenge is IBM's acquisition of the IT group from the Danish firm Maersk and another smaller Danish firm for $575 million. As a part of the deal, IBM will provide IT services to these companies. Siemens did the same with BBC Technology in a 10-year deal worth $3.7 billion. In this way the services firms entered the market and shut out competition from these potentially lucrative deals. The stakes are high; analysts estimate the market for IT services in Europe is $212 billion annually, with the global market at $636 billion annually. Thus, strategic alliances can be highly important to individual firms, and they are critical to certain industries (e.g., IT services).

SOURCES: 2008, Star Alliance Web site, http://www.staralliance.com/en/meta/airlines/index.html, retrieved January 25; 2005, Strategic alliances, Fujitsu, www.fujitsu.com, July 23; J. Dean & P. Tam, 2005, The laptop trail, Wall Street Journal Online, www.wsj.com, June 9; A. Reinhardt, 2005, Europe's tech outfits hurry to the altar, BusinessWeek Online, wwwbusinessweek.com, May 9; P. Fitzpatrick, Air Canada forms alliance with four other airlines, *Financial Post*, 10(58): 10.

In previous chapters, we examined important strategies for achieving growth, innovation, and strategic execution (internal growth) and acquisitions (external growth). In this chapter, we examine cooperative strategies, which are another means by which firms grow and differentiate themselves from competitors to develop value-creating competitive advantages.[1]

A **cooperative strategy** is a strategy in which firms work together to achieve a shared objective.[2] Thus, cooperating with other firms is another strategy that is used to create value for a customer that exceeds the cost of providing that value and to establish a favourable position relative to competition (see Chapters 3, 5, 6, and 9).[3] While the Opening Case examines joint ventures, there are several types of strategic alliances that we explore in this chapter. Fujitsu forms equity-based alliances designed to take advantage of market opportunities. Air Canada has had a valuable nonequity strategic alliance through the Star Alliance that appears to offer its members a competitive advantage. They all derive substantial revenue from the alliance each year. The increasing importance of cooperative strategies as a growth engine should not be underestimated. Increasingly, cooperative strategies are formed by competitors, as shown by the Star Alliance. Because members reach many destinations that others do not, the alliance provided greater value to each airline's customers; the companies' cooperation created more value than their competition.[4]

The alliances formed by Dell and Hewlett-Packard with foreign computer manufacturers were a competitive necessity. They also drove IBM out of the laptop computer business. We refer to this form of alliance as outsourcing.[5] The competition for IT alliances in Europe is fierce, as evidenced by the acquisition of IT groups by Siemens and IBM as a means of obtaining IT services contracts with major European firms. This means that effective competition in the 21st-century landscape results when firms learn how to cooperate with others and use this cooperation as a means of competing.[6]

Because they are the primary type of cooperative strategy used by firms, strategic alliances are this chapter's focus. Although not frequently used, collusive strategies are another type of cooperative strategy discussed in this chapter. In a collusive strategy, two or more firms cooperate to increase prices above the fully competitive level.[7]

We examine several topics in this chapter. First, we define and offer examples of different strategic alliances as primary types of cooperative strategies. Next, we discuss the extensive use of cooperative strategies in the global economy and reasons for this use. In succession, we then describe business-level (including collusive strategies), corporate-level, international, and network cooperative strategies—most in the form of strategic alliances. The chapter closes with discussion of the risks of using cooperative strategies as well as how effective management of them can reduce those risks.

> A **cooperative strategy** is a strategy in which firms work together to achieve a shared objective.

Strategic Alliances as a Primary Type of Cooperative Strategy

A **strategic alliance** is a cooperative strategy in which firms combine some of their resources and capabilities to create a competitive advantage.[8] Thus, as linkages between them, strategic alliances involve firms with some degree of exchange and sharing of resources and capabilities to co-develop or distribute goods or services.[9] Strategic alliances allow firms to leverage their existing resources and capabilities while working with partners to develop additional resources and capabilities as the foundation for new competitive advantages.[10]

Many firms, especially large global competitors, establish multiple strategic alliances. This is evident in the Opening Case, with Fujitsu forming alliances with AMD, Cisco, Dell, and Microsoft, among others. Focusing on developing advanced technologies, Lockheed Martin has formed over 250 alliances with firms in more than 30 countries as it concentrates on its primary business of defence modernization.[11] In general, strategic alliance success requires cooperative behaviour from all partners. Actively solving

> A **strategic alliance** is a cooperative strategy in which firms combine some of their resources and capabilities to create a competitive advantage.

problems, being trustworthy, and consistently pursuing ways to combine partners' resources and capabilities to create value are examples of cooperative behaviour known to contribute to alliance success.[12]

A competitive advantage developed through a cooperative strategy often is called a collaborative or relational advantage.[13] As previously discussed, particularly in Chapter 5, competitive advantages enhance the firm's marketplace success.[14] Rapid technological changes and the global economy are examples of factors challenging firms to constantly upgrade current competitive advantages while they develop new ones to maintain strategic competitiveness.[15]

Three Types of Strategic Alliances

There are three major types of strategic alliances: joint venture, equity strategic alliance, and nonequity strategic alliance.

A **joint venture** is a strategic alliance in which two or more firms create a legally independent company to share some of their resources and capabilities to develop a competitive advantage. Joint ventures are effective in establishing long-term relationships and in transferring tacit knowledge. Because it can not be codified, tacit knowledge is learned through experiences[16] such as those taking place when people from partner firms work together in a joint venture. As discussed in Chapter 3, tacit knowledge is an important source of competitive advantage for many firms.[17]

Typically, partners in a joint venture own equal percentages and contribute equally to its operations. In China, Shui On Construction and entrepreneur Paul S. P. Tung created a 50–50 joint venture called TH Group to invest in cement factories. Cement is big business in China as the government seeks to develop the infrastructure (ports, highways, etc.) of the western provinces. Mr. Tung contributed the money and Shui On the expertise necessary to develop a large, well-run cement company.[18] Overall, evidence suggests that a joint venture may be the optimal alliance when firms need to combine their resources and capabilities to create a competitive advantage that is substantially different from any they possess individually and when the partners intend to enter highly uncertain markets.[19]

An **equity strategic alliance** is an alliance in which two or more firms own different percentages of the company they have formed by combining some of their resources and capabilities to create a competitive advantage. Many foreign direct investments, such as those made by Japanese and U.S. companies in China, are completed through equity strategic alliances.[20] The Strategic Focus addresses the wide range of fields where one can find equity strategic alliances.

A **nonequity strategic alliance** is an alliance in which two or more firms develop a contractual relationship to share some of their unique resources and capabilities to create a competitive advantage. In this type of strategic alliance, firms do not establish a separate independent company and therefore do not take equity positions. Because of this, nonequity strategic alliances are less formal and demand fewer partner commitments than do joint ventures and equity strategic alliances.[21] The relative informality and lower commitment levels characterizing nonequity strategic alliances make them unsuitable for complex projects where success requires effective transfers of tacit knowledge between partners.[22]

However, firms today increasingly use this type of alliance in many different forms, such as licensing agreements, distribution agreements, and supply contracts.[23] For example, Waterloo, Ontario's Research In Motion (RIM; discussed in Chapter 1) has a range of alliances that allow various parts of RIM's BlackBerry services to be used on wireless devices worldwide. RIM's software includes features that automatically deliver e-mail and other data to and from a range of wireless devices. RIM's list of alliance partners includes Sony Ericsson, Nokia, Samsung, and Motorola.[24] A key reason for

A **joint venture** is a strategic alliance in which two or more firms create a legally independent company to share some of their resources and capabilities to develop a competitive advantage.

An **equity strategic alliance** is an alliance in which two or more firms own different percentages of the company they have formed by combining some of their resources and capabilities to create a competitive advantage.

A **nonequity strategic alliance** is an alliance in which two or more firms develop a contractual relationship to share some of their unique resources and capabilities to create a competitive advantage.

Equity Alliances from Bread to Read

An alliance is a lot like a potluck dinner—you bring the salad, I bring the main course, he brings the drinks, she brings dessert . . . everyone brings something to the table and we end up with something complete. Okay, now that we're hungry let's all go to Tim Hortons—but we can still talk about alliances. While Timmy's is not any kind of joint venture, you may not realize that the sandwich and Timbits you pick up there are the product of one. In 2001, in a $155-million, 50–50 joint venture with Cuisine de France (a subsidiary of Ireland's IAWS Group), the company opened Maidstone Bakeries—a 300,000-square-foot par-baking facility in Brantford, Ontario. Yes, they partially bake and then freeze your Timbits. The last 15 minutes or so of baking occur at the store—the product still tastes fresh, and it is a really fast way to make baked goods. And, because products can be made quickly in small batches, they do not have to stay on the shelf for long. Tim Hortons had never done par-baking before, and rather than sacrifice quality they brought in Cuisine de France to help them do it right.

Joint ventures may be undertaken to meet a competitive challenge. In late 2007, SABMiller, one of the world's bigger brewers—and America's second largest—formed a joint venture in the U.S. and Puerto Rico with Molson Coors, North America's third biggest brewer. The pair teamed up to take on Anheuser-Busch—North America's leading brewer. Because of anemic growth in demand, neither SABMiller nor Molson Coors was likely to expand sales without taking on Anheuser-Busch. However, together the combined operation will have about $7 billion in revenue and almost 30 percent of the market. The savings from combining operations may be as much as $500 million annually.

In order to break into the Chinese market, firms will often partner with Chinese competitors. As noted in Chapter 9, Toronto's Manulife joined with Sinochem group (one of China's biggest foreign trading companies) to form a joint venture with more than 8,000 staff and agents who serve more than 300,000 clients in more than 25 cities in China. Manulife has successfully used this joint venture to develop the Chinese market for insurance services and has become one of the few, if not the only, profitable insurance ventures in China.

Often, a project requires a range of expertise and resources, and numerous partners are brought in to help. The world's longest bridge over sometimes-frozen salt water is the Confederation Bridge connecting Borden, P.E.I. to Aulac, N.B. The 13-kilometre span was built by a consortium that included constructors and engineers from Canada, France, and Holland (SCI, VINCI, and Ballast Nedam, respectively) and financing from the Ontario Municipal Employees Retirement System (OMERS). OMERS is one of the masters of joint ventures. The organization not only supplied the financing for the Confederation Bridge but also has a major stake in the company that manages, maintains, and operates the bridge until 2032, when that task is turned over to the Government of Canada.

Perhaps OMERS's most interesting joint ventures are in communications. Through Borealis, OMERS has a majority interest in the Ciel consortium—a communications company that contracted with International Launch Services (ILS) to put up a satellite at 129° west longitude. ILS is also a joint venture incorporated in the U.S. whose owners include Russia's Khrunichev State Research and Production Space Center and RSC Energia of Moscow. However, OMERS's most vital joint venture is with Apax Partners, one of the largest private equity firms in the U.S. In 2007 OMERS and Apax teamed up and bought Nelson Education Ltd. for almost $8 billion. In the scheme of world events this is perhaps not vital, but it does strike close to home—while Nelson publishes hundreds of titles its most important one, for our purposes, is this book.

SOURCES: Reuters, 2008, Tim Hortons Inc. THI Web site, http://stocks.us.reuters.com/stocks/fullDescription.asp?rpc=66& symbol=THI; 2008, City of Brantford Economic Development Web site, http://www.brantfordbrant.com/sectors/food.php; 2008, Confederation Bridge Web site, http://www.confederationbridge.com/en/about_the_bridge/; 2008, Borealis Infrastructure Web site, http://www.borealisinfrastructure .com/assets.aspx; 2008, Ciel Satellite Web site, http://www.cielsatellite.ca/ about.html; J. Milliot, 2007, Educational segment dominates M&A dollars, purchases topped $13 billion in 2007, *Publishers Weekly*, http://www.publishersweekly.com/article/CA6515076.html, December 24;

(continued)

2007, SABMiller and Molson Coors sign definitive agreement to form MillerCoors U.S. Joint Venture, *Wall Street Journal*, http://online .wsj.com/public/article/PR-CO-20071221-901564.html?mod=crnews, December 21; 2007, Business: Another round? Beer mergers, *The Economist*, 385(8550): 89; L. Bobak, 2007, Thomson sells Learning textbook division to Apax and OMERS for US$7.75B, http://finance. sympatico.msn.ca/investing/news/businessnews/article.aspx?cp-documentid=4855035, May 11, 2008; D. Mavin, 2007, Into the maelstrom, *Financial Post Business*, October, 52–57; Manulife press release, 2007, Manulife-Sinochem expands business in Shandong Province with a new sales office license in Yantai, http://www.manulife.com/ corporate/corporate2.nsf/Public/china122007.html; information from all Web sites retrieved January 24, 2008.

the growth in types of cooperative strategies is the complexity and uncertainty that characterize most global industries, making it difficult for firms to be successful without partnerships.[25]

Typically, outsourcing commitments take the form of a nonequity strategic alliance.[26] Outsourcing (discussed in Chapter 4) is the purchase of a value-creating primary or support activity from another firm. Dell and most other computer firms outsource most or all of their production of laptop computers, as discussed in the Opening Case. Another form of nonequity alliance would be the ongoing relationship Cirque du Soleil has with fellow Montreal creator Sid Lee. Sid Lee is what can best be described as a creative consultant; the Web site introduction at www.sidlee.com explains what the company does without using any words at all.[27] Sid Lee cooperates with Cirque on numerous projects—for example Web site design, coming up with the visual identities for shows, and developing branded retail environments, such as a Cirque-themed spa or restaurant concept. While Sid Lee may add its creativity to Cirque, the relationship is a two-way street. Sid Lee chairman Bertrand Cesvet notes that "These guys [Cirque] have the most incredible network around the world, and they enable us to stumble onto amazing opportunities that would have been unheard of in our industry in Canada."[28]

Reasons Why Firms Develop Strategic Alliances

Cooperative strategies have become an integral part of the competitive landscape and are quite important to many companies. For example, surveyed executives of technology companies stated that strategic alliances are central to their firms' success.[29] Speaking directly to the issue of technology acquisition and development for these firms, a manager noted that, "you have to partner today or you will miss the next wave. You cannot possibly acquire the technology fast enough, so partnering is essential."[30]

Among other benefits, strategic alliances allow partners to create value that they couldn't develop by acting independently,[31] and to enter markets more quickly.[32] Moreover, most (if not all) firms lack the full set of resources and capabilities needed to reach their objectives, which indicates that partnering with others will increase the probability of reaching them.[33]

The effects of the greater use of cooperative strategies—particularly in the form of strategic alliances—are noticeable. In large firms, for example, alliances account for more than 20 percent of revenue.[34] Supporting this expectation is the belief of many senior-level executives that alliances are a prime vehicle for firm growth.[35] In some industries, alliance versus alliance is becoming more prominent than firm versus firm as a point of competition. In the global airline industry, for example, competition is increasingly between large alliances rather than between airlines.[36]

Essentially, firms form strategic alliances to reduce competition, enhance their competitive capabilities, gain access to resources, take advantage of opportunities, and build strategic flexibility. To do so means that they must select the right partners and develop trust.[37] Thus, firms attempt to develop a network portfolio of alliances in which they create social capital that affords them flexibility.[38] Because of the social capital, they can call on their partners for help when needed. Of course, social capital means reciprocity exists: Partners can ask them for help as well (and they are expected to provide it).[39]

The individually unique competitive conditions of slow-cycle, fast-cycle, and standard-cycle markets[40] cause firms using cooperative strategies to achieve slightly different objectives (see Table 10.1). We discussed these three market types in Chapter 6, on competitive rivalry and competitive dynamics. Slow-cycle markets are markets where the firm's competitive advantages are shielded from imitation for relatively long periods of time and where imitation is costly. These markets are close to monopolistic conditions. Railroads and, historically, telecommunications, utilities, and financial services are examples of industries characterized as slow-cycle markets. In fast-cycle markets, the firm's competitive advantages aren't shielded from imitation, preventing their long-term sustainability. Competitive advantages are moderately shielded from imitation in standard-cycle markets, typically allowing them to be sustained for a longer period of time than in fast-cycle market situations but for a shorter period of time than in slow-cycle markets.

Table 10.1	Reasons for Strategic Alliances by Market Type
Market	**Reason**
Slow-Cycle	• Gain access to a restricted market • Establish a franchise in a new market • Maintain market stability (e.g., establishing standards)
Fast-Cycle	• Speed up development of new goods or services • Speed up new market entry • Maintain market leadership • Form an industry technology standard • Share risky R&D expenses • Overcome uncertainty
Standard-Cycle	• Gain market power (reduce industry overcapacity) • Gain access to complementary resources • Establish better economies of scale • Overcome trade barriers • Meet competitive challenges from other competitors • Pool resources for very large capital projects • Learn new business techniques

Slow-Cycle Markets

Firms in slow-cycle markets often use strategic alliances to enter restricted markets or to establish franchises in new markets. For example, due to consolidating acquisitions, the North American steel industry has three major players: Mittal Steel, Nucor, and U.S. Steel (in recent years these companies have bought Canadian producers Dofasco, Harris Steel, and Stelco, respectively). In an effort to compete in a global steel market, these companies are focused on obtaining international partners and foreign markets. They have made strategic alliances in Europe and Asia and are invested in ventures in South America and Australia. For example, Nucor is investing in joint ventures in Brazil and Australia. While the global consolidation continues, these companies are increasing their competitiveness through their strategic alliances overseas.[41]

Slow-cycle markets are becoming rare in the 21st-century competitive landscape for several reasons, including the privatization of industries and economies, the rapid expansion of the Internet's capabilities for the quick dissemination of information, and the speed with which advancing technologies make quickly imitating even complex products possible.[42] Firms competing in slow-cycle markets should recognize the future likelihood that they'll encounter situations in which their competitive advantages become partially sustainable (in the instance of a standard-cycle market) or unsustainable (in the case of a fast-cycle market). Cooperative strategies can be helpful to firms making the transition from relatively sheltered markets to more competitive ones.[43]

Fast-Cycle Markets

Fast-cycle markets tend to be unstable, unpredictable, and complex.[44] Combined, these conditions virtually preclude establishing long-lasting competitive advantages, forcing firms to constantly seek sources of new competitive advantages while creating value by using current ones. Alliances between firms with current excess resources and capabilities and those with promising capabilities help companies competing in fast-cycle markets to make an effective transition from the present to the future and also to gain rapid entry to new markets.

The information technology (IT) industry is a fast-cycle market. The IT landscape continues to change rapidly as businesses are becoming more focused on selecting a handful of strategic partners to help drive down costs, integrate technologies that provide significant business advantages or productivity gains, and aggressively look for applications that can be shifted to more flexible and cost-effective platforms. We learned about the highly competitive European IT market in the Opening Case. In fact, IBM's and Siemens's actions exemplify the aggressiveness with which firms try to obtain and solidify a market position. Dell, also mentioned in the Opening Case, strives to maintain its market leadership through responsiveness to customers. As a result of customers' requests, it has made servers and storage more modular and more customizable. Dell's connection to customers also helped it to identify wireless technology as critical for corporations, and thus made it a standard feature on all corporate laptops as early as 2004. Dell's strategic partners incorporate much of this technology into the machines manufactured for and sold by Dell.[45]

Standard-Cycle Markets

In standard-cycle markets, which are often large and oriented toward economies of scale (e.g., commercial aerospace), alliances are more likely to be made by partners with complementary resources and capabilities. While airline alliances were originally set up to increase revenue, airlines have realized that they could also be used to reduce costs. SkyTeam (which includes Russia's Aeroflot, AeroMexico, Delta, and Air France) developed an internal Web site to speed joint buying and let member carriers swap tips on pricing. Managers at Oneworld (which includes American Airlines, British Airways, Cathay Pacific, and Japan Airlines,) claim alliance members have saved up to $200 million through joint purchasing. Star Alliance (which includes Air Canada, United, and Lufthansa) estimates that its member airlines save up to 25 percent on joint orders. Star Alliance members have gone even further and set up joint specifications on regional and long-distance jetliners. Such agreements include standards for items ranging from galleys and toilets, to cargo holds and avionics, as well as aircraft procurement and disposal. This allows manufactures and maintenance personnel to reduce their costs in a way that should help the member airlines reduce their costs.[46]

Companies also may cooperate in standard-cycle markets to gain market power. As discussed in Chapter 7, market power allows the firm to sell its product above the existing competitive level or to reduce its costs below the competitive level, or both.

Paris-based Areva Group maintains numerous mining joint ventures with Saskatoon's Cameco.[47] Cameco's expertise as one of the world's leading uranium miners and Areva's processing capabilities as a world leader in nuclear power make them an excellent match.[48] It also doesn't hurt that Canada is the world's biggest producer of uranium ore and that France gets almost 80 percent of its electrical needs from nuclear power.[49] Because Areva has an assured resource of known quality and Cameco has a confirmed buyer, long-term efficient scale investments can be made by both. Thus, as leading producers in their respective areas, the joint ventures give each firm substantial market power.

Business-Level Cooperative Strategy

A **business-level cooperative strategy** is used to help the firm improve its performance in individual product markets. As discussed in Chapter 5, business-level strategy details what the firm intends to do to gain a competitive advantage in specific product markets. Thus, the firm forms a business-level cooperative strategy when it believes that combining its resources and capabilities with those of one or more partners will create competitive advantages that it can't create by itself and that will lead to success in a specific product market. There are four business-level cooperative strategies (see Figure 10.1).

A **business-level cooperative strategy** is used to help the firm improve its performance in individual product markets.

Complementary Strategic Alliances

Complementary strategic alliances are business-level alliances in which firms share some of their resources and capabilities in complementary ways to develop competitive advantages.[50] There are two types of complementary strategic alliances—vertical and horizontal (see Figure 10.1).

Complementary strategic alliances are business-level alliances in which firms share some of their resources and capabilities in complementary ways to develop competitive advantages.

Vertical Complementary Strategic Alliance

In a vertical complementary strategic alliance, firms share their resources and capabilities from different stages of the value chain to create a competitive advantage (see Figure 10.2).[51] Oftentimes, vertical complementary alliances are formed in reaction to environmental changes. In other words, they serve as a means of adaptation to the environmental changes.[52] The alliances formed by Dell, Hewlett-Packard, and other computer firms with Taiwanese manufacturers represent this type of cooperative arrangement. Personal computers had become more of a commodity product with little differentiation among them. As a result, price became a major competitive factor, requiring firms to control their costs. To substantially reduce the cost of manufacturing

Figure 10.1 Business-Level Cooperative Strategies

- Complementary strategic alliances
  - Vertical
  - Horizontal
- Competition response strategy
- Uncertainty-reducing strategy
- Competition-reducing strategy

Figure 10.2 Vertical and Horizontal Complementary Strategic Alliances

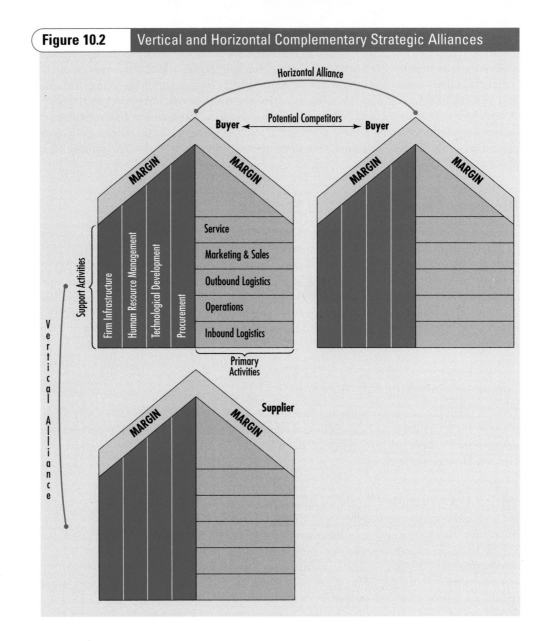

each unit, many of the computer firms turned to outsourcing. As noted earlier, IBM outsourced only about 40 percent of its manufacturing and could not control its costs as well as its competitors. IBM essentially left the market, selling its laptop business to Lenovo. As exemplified in the computer industry, these types of changes in industries and in the global competitive environments have led to vertical disintegration.[53] Dell and several other computer firms outsource 100 percent of their laptop computer manufacturing rather than performing it in-house. The Taiwanese manufacturers have the technological capabilities *and* access to low-cost labour, thereby providing complementary capabilities. A critical issue for firms is how much technological knowledge they should share with their partner. They need the partners to have adequate knowledge to perform the task effectively and to be complementary to their capabilities. Part of this decision depends on the trust and social capital developed between the partners.[54]

Horizontal Complementary Strategic Alliance

A horizontal complementary strategic alliance is an alliance in which firms share some of their resources and capabilities from the same stage of the value chain to create a competitive advantage (see Figure 10.2). Commonly, firms use this type of alliance to focus on long-term product development and distribution opportunities.[55] Bell Canada and Microsoft Canada entered into an alliance to provide Internet services in Canada through a new portal. Although they share the day-to-day operations of the portal, Bell Canada is responsible for content development and for customer support, billing, and marketing. Microsoft provides access to its portal infrastructure and to online services such as Hotmail and MSN Messenger.[56]

Importantly, horizontal alliances may require equal investments of resources by the partners but they rarely provide equal benefits to the partners. There are several potential reasons for the imbalance in benefits.[57] Frequently, the partners have different opportunities as a result of the alliance. Partners may learn at different rates and have different capabilities to leverage the complementary resources provided in the alliance. Some firms are more effective in managing alliances and in deriving the benefits from them. The partners may have different reputations in the market thus differentiating the types of actions firms can legitimately take in the marketplace. For example, Mitsubishi Motors experienced a decrease in global sales revenues by about 50 percent during 2004–2005. This is because of major management blunders in which loans were made to young and highly risky consumers, producing a large number of bad loans, and because of defects in its vehicles that were believed to result in fatalities. Managers covered up this defect problem rather than trying to correct it. To bolster its productivity and capacity utilization rates, Mitsubishi Motors developed an alliance with Peugeot to manufacture new SUVs to be sold under Peugeot's brand name. This alliance will help Mitsubishi to reduce the overall cost per unit of its own vehicles.[58]

Competition-Response Strategy

As discussed in Chapter 6, competitors initiate competitive actions to attack rivals and launch competitive responses to their competitors' actions. Strategic alliances can be used at the business level to respond to competitors' attacks. Because they can be difficult to reverse and expensive to operate, strategic alliances are primarily formed to respond to strategic rather than tactical actions.

France Telecom and Microsoft announced the formation of an alliance with two initial major projects. The first project is intended to develop a series of phones based on Microsoft technology that uses the Internet services. The phones will be designed to use as traditional cell phones or to access the Internet while at home or on the road. This project is in response to the announcement by BT Group PLC of a new hybrid fixed-line and mobile phone service using short-range wireless technology called Bluetooth. The France Telecom–Microsoft alliance will use the more powerful Wireless Fidelity (Wi-Fi) technology. Didier Lombard, CEO of France Telecom, stated that the telecom industry is undergoing rapid changes and current members must also act rapidly to adapt. The partnership with Microsoft is designed to respond to these changes.[59]

Uncertainty-Reducing Strategy

Particularly in fast-cycle markets, business-level strategic alliances are used to hedge against risk and uncertainty.[60] They also are used when entering new product markets or emerging economies. For example, Dutch bank ABN-AMRO developed a venture called ShoreCap International involving a multisector partnership of organizations including private businesses, financial institutions, development funds, and foundations. ShoreCap invests capital in and advises local financial institutions that do small and microbusiness lending in developing economies, targeting Asia, Africa, and Central and

Eastern Europe. The venture's leading sponsor, ShoreBank Corporation, is a for-profit community development and environmental bank. It has a history of collaboration with financial institutions and other partners, including the World Bank. Through this cooperative strategy with other financial institutions, ShoreBank's goal is to reduce the risk of providing credit to smaller borrowers in disadvantaged regions. It also hopes to reduce poverty in the regions where it invests.[61]

In other instances, firms form business-level strategic alliances to reduce the uncertainty associated with developing new products or establishing a technology standard.[62] Interestingly, the alliance between France Telecom and Microsoft is a competition-response alliance for France Telecom but it is an uncertainty-reducing alliance for Microsoft. Microsoft is using the alliance to learn more about the telecom industry and business. It wants to learn how it can develop software to satisfy needs in this industry. By partnering with a firm in this industry, it is reducing its uncertainty about the market and software needs. And, the alliance is clearly designed to develop new products so the alliance reduces the uncertainty for both firms by combining their knowledge and capabilities.

Competition-Reducing Strategy

Used to reduce competition, collusive strategies differ from strategic alliances in that collusive strategies are often an illegal type of cooperative strategy. There are two types of collusive strategies: explicit collusion and tacit collusion.

Explicit collusion "exists when firms directly negotiate production output and pricing agreements in order to reduce competition."[63] Explicit collusion strategies are illegal in most developed economies (except in regulated industries).

Firms that use explicit collusion strategies may face litigation and may be found guilty of non-competitive actions. For instance, in late 2007, the Canadian Competition Bureau served search warrants on several major chocolate bar makers requiring them to turn over documents on pricing arrangements. John Pecman, the bureau's assistant deputy commissioner in the criminal matters branch, noted that an Ontario court had "granted search warrants based on the evidence that there are reasonable grounds to believe that a number of the suppliers in the chocolate industry have engaged in activities contrary to the conspiracy provisions—that's a cartel. . . ." Pecman added that, "The volume of commerce affected here is definitely potentially in the billions of dollars per year." Nestle Canada, Cadbury Adams Canada, Hershey, and Mars Canada were among the firms contacted by the Competition Bureau. These are serious charges affecting the future of the companies charged and thus their current market values.[64]

Tacit collusion exists when several firms in an industry indirectly coordinate their production and pricing decisions by observing each other's competitive actions and responses.[65] Tacit collusion results in below fully competitive production output and above fully competitive prices. Unlike explicit collusion, firms engaging in tacit collusion do not directly negotiate output and pricing decisions.

Mutual forbearance is a form of tacit collusion "in which firms avoid competitive attacks against those rivals they meet in multiple markets." Rivals learn a great deal about each other when engaging in multimarket competition, including how to deter the effects of their rival's competitive attacks and responses. Given what they know about each other as a competitor, firms choose not to engage in what could be destructive competitions in multiple product markets.[66]

AOL dominates the instant-messaging (IM) business, with almost 60 million users. Yahoo! and MSN also operate IM services, but unlike e-mail instant messages cannot cross over programs and this irritates many users. AOL and Microsoft quietly announced in 2003 that they would integrate their IM services for consumers. MSN has the next largest group of IM users (23.6 million) and through this strategic agreement with AOL was able to reduce the level of competition.[67]

Tacit collusion tends to be used as a business-level competition-reducing strategy in highly concentrated industries, such as breakfast cereals. Firms in these industries recognize that they are interdependent and that their competitive actions and responses significantly affect competitors' behaviour toward them. Understanding this interdependence and carefully observing competitors because of it tends to lead to tacit collusion.

Canada's six major banks (Royal Bank, TD Canada Trust, Scotiabank, BMO, CIBC, and National) hold about 90 percent of bank assets.[68] Some believe that this high degree of concentration results in higher prices for bank services. A similar argument has been raised regarding branded cereals in the U.S. Four firms (Kellogg, General Mills, Post, and Quaker) have accounted for as much as 80 percent of sales volume in the ready-to-eat segment and their price is "well above [the] costs of production."[69] Prices above the competitive level in an industry suggest the possibility that dominant firms use a tacit-collusion cooperative strategy.

In general, governments in free-market economies need to determine how rivals can collaborate to increase their competitiveness without violating established regulations.[70] However, this is challenging when evaluating collusive strategies, particularly tacit ones. For example, regulation of pharmaceutical and biotech firms which must collaborate to meet global competition might lead to too much price fixing; regulation is required to make sure the balance is right, although sometimes the regulation gets in the way of efficient markets.[71] Individual companies must analyze the effect of a competition-reducing strategy on their performance and competitiveness.

While most tacit collusion is legal, some tacit collusion may be considered illegal. Researcher Jay Barney argues that, "firms that consciously make price and output decisions in order to reduce competition may be engaging in what the courts call conscious parallelism and thus be subject to antitrust laws and penalties."[72] He recommends that firms contemplating tacit collusion should receive competent legal counsel to assess whether the signals sent to indicate cooperation are within legal guidelines.

Assessment of Business-Level Cooperative Strategies

Firms use business-level strategies to develop competitive advantages that can contribute to successful positions and performance in individual product markets. To develop a competitive advantage using an alliance, the particular set of resources and capabilities that are integrated through the alliance must be valuable, rare, imperfectly imitable, and organized to be exploited (see Chapter 4).

Evidence suggests that complementary business-level strategic alliances, especially vertical ones, have the greatest probability of creating a sustainable competitive advantage.[73] Horizontal complementary alliances are sometimes difficult to maintain because they are often between rivalrous competitors. As noted earlier, the international airline industry, in an effort to avoid laws blocking international mergers, has been forming global partnerships for a number of years. Yet the industry has ultrathin margins and not-infrequent bankruptcies. Between 2001 and 2005, Air Canada, Australia's Ansett, Belgium's national carrier, Sabena, and four of the top seven U.S. carriers filed for bankruptcy protection (US Airways, United Airlines, Northwest Airlines, and Delta). The logical consequence of these conditions is likely to be a consolidation of carriers—some which may belong to different alliances. For example, if either SkyTeam members Northwest or Delta merged into United—a Star Alliance member—which airline would quit which alliance? Because of the high rivalry among partners in the airline industry, the horizontal alliances that have formed may well be unstable in the near term.[74]

Although strategic alliances designed to respond to competition and to reduce uncertainty can also create competitive advantages, these advantages often are more temporary than those developed through complementary (both vertical and horizontal) strategic alliances. The primary reason is that complementary alliances have a stronger focus on creating value than do competition-reducing and uncertainty-reducing alliances, which are formed to respond to competitors' actions or reduce uncertainty rather than to attack competitors.

Of the four business-level cooperative strategies, the competition-reducing strategy has the lowest probability of creating a sustainable competitive advantage. For example, research suggests that firms following a foreign direct investment strategy using alliances as a follow-the-leader imitation approach may not have strong strategic or learning goals. Thus, such investment could be attributable to tacit collusion among the participating firms rather than intended to obtain a competitive advantage.[75] Companies using such competition-reducing business-level strategic alliances should carefully monitor the degree to which they are facilitating the creation of competitive advantages.

Corporate-Level Cooperative Strategy

A **corporate-level cooperative strategy** is used by a firm to help it diversify in terms of products offered or markets served, or both.

A firm uses a **corporate-level cooperative strategy** to help it diversify in terms of products offered or markets served, or both. Diversifying alliances, synergistic alliances, and franchising are the most commonly used corporate-level cooperative strategies (see Figure 10.3).

Firms use diversifying alliances and synergistic alliances to grow and diversify their operations through a means other than a merger or an acquisition.[76] When a firm seeks to diversify into markets in which the host nation's government prevents mergers and acquisitions, alliances become an especially appropriate option. Corporate-level strategic alliances are also attractive compared with mergers and particularly acquisitions, because they require fewer resource commitments[77] and permit greater flexibility in terms of efforts to diversify partners' operations.[78] An alliance can be used as a way to determine whether the partners might benefit from a future merger or acquisition between them. This "testing" process often characterizes alliances formed to combine firms' unique technological resources and capabilities.[79]

Diversifying Strategic Alliance

A **diversifying strategic alliance** is a corporate-level cooperative strategy in which firms share some of their resources and capabilities to diversify into new product or market areas.

A **diversifying strategic alliance** is a corporate-level cooperative strategy in which firms share some of their resources and capabilities to diversify into new product or market areas. Much of the activity of the Ontario Municipal Employees Retirement System (OMERS) noted in the earlier Strategic Focus has been to diversify its holdings into a wide range of infrastructure projects. On a larger international scale, Shell Petrochemicals and China National Offshore Oil Corp. (CNOOC) formed a joint venture to construct a $4.3-billion petrochemicals complex in southern China. The venture's goal is to make products for "high-consumption areas along the country's coastal economic zones."[80] CNOOC's business has been mainly upstream offshore oil production. The joint venture represents CNOOC's continuing diversification from its core upstream business. After the venture began, the partners experienced some tense times. CNOOC's bid to acquire Unocal was discouraged by Shell because Unocal was a

Figure 10.3   Corporate-Level Cooperative Strategies

• Diversifying alliances
• Synergistic alliances
• Franchising

competitor. Fortunately for Shell, CNOOC's bid was rejected by Unocal in favour of a bid by Chevron.[81]

It should be noted that highly diverse networks of alliances can lead to poorer performance by partner firms.[82] However, cooperative ventures are also used to reduce diversification in firms that have over-diversified.[83] Japanese chipmakers Fujitsu, Mitsubishi Electric, Hitachi, NEC, and Toshiba have been using joint ventures to consolidate and then spin off diversified businesses that were performing poorly. For example, Fujitsu, realizing that memory chips were becoming a financial burden, dumped its flash memory business into a joint venture company controlled by Advanced Micro Devices. This alliance helped Fujitsu to refocus on its core businesses.[84]

Synergistic Strategic Alliance

A **synergistic strategic alliance** is a corporate-level cooperative strategy in which firms share some of their resources and capabilities to create economies of scope. Similar to the business-level horizontal complementary strategic alliance, synergistic strategic alliances create synergy across multiple functions or multiple businesses between partner firms.

The Public Sector Pension Investment Board (a Canadian Crown corporation) and Loral Space and Communications Inc. developed a joint venture in which they purchased satellite operator Telesat from BCE. Since regulations favour Canadian control, the pension plan holds a 36 percent economic stake in Telesat, but holds voting control and a majority of seats on the company's board. Loral holds a 64 percent economic stake. The move allows Telesat to launch a new high-power, direct broadcast satellite called Nimiq 5. Nimiq 5's manufacturer is Loral Space and Communications. Nimiq 5's entire payload is under contract to Bell ExpressVu, to be used for a wide range of digital television services. By doing this as a joint venture, all the parties gain—it is synergistic because it gives Bell cash and a new satellite; it gives the pension fund a revenue-producing asset; and, while it gives Loral an interest in a satellite, it also gives it the contract for manufacturing Nimiq 5.[85]

The Strategic Focus suggests that franchises are a major means of growth for some firms, such as Jugo Juice and most major pizza chains. By contrast, Outback Steakhouse has used franchises to a much lesser extent. Because franchising helps firms grow faster it simultaneously helps firms build their brand if they closely control the quality of franchise operations.

Franchising

Franchising is a corporate-level cooperative strategy in which a firm (the franchisor) uses a franchise as a contractual relationship to describe and control the sharing of its resources and capabilities with partners (the franchisees).[86] A franchise is a "contractual agreement between two legally independent companies whereby the franchisor grants the right to the franchisee to sell the franchisor's product or do business under its trademarks in a given location for a specified period of time."[87]

Franchising is a popular strategy; companies using it account for $1 trillion in annual North American retail sales and compete in more than 75 industries. Already frequently used in developed nations, franchising is expected to account for significant portions of growth in emerging economies in the 21st century's first two decades. As with diversifying and synergistic strategic alliances, franchising is an alternative to pursuing growth through mergers and acquisitions.

McDonald's, Mr. Sub, and Hilton International are well-known examples of firms that use the franchising corporate-level cooperative strategy. The convenience store company Couche-Tard has successfully used franchising in its expansion both domestically and internationally. The chain now has more than 4,300 franchised outlets worldwide under

A **synergistic strategic alliance** is a corporate-level cooperative strategy in which firms share some of their resources and capabilities to create economies of scope.

Franchising is a corporate-level cooperative strategy in which a firm (the franchisor) uses a franchise as a contractual relationship to describe and control the sharing of its resources and capabilities with partners (the franchisees).

Franchising Fast Food

While franchise operations can often be seen as being dominated by the big U.S. chains like McDonald's and Subway, Canada has some serious contenders of its own. To survive, they rely on unique market positioning. A quick survey gives one a better idea of the distinctiveness of some of these operations.

First, let's have a drink, or at a minimum go to the pub. The Firkin Group has more than 30 pubs in the Toronto area, more than a handful in the U.S., and scores of franchises likely to be opening across North America in the next five years. At Firkin (which is not something obscene—it's an old name for a nine-gallon wooden ale barrel) of course there's pub food to go with the beer. Firkins average about 300 square metres, with bar seating for 80 to 100. The concept for the franchise is based on generating an inviting pub environment and combining an individual name, like an animal, with "Firkin." So there's a Frog and Firkin, a Fox and Firkin, a Phoenix and Firkin, a Frigate and Firkin, and so on. This creates individual "Firkins" where, as the company's motto states, "Every one's a little different; one's just right for you." So, if you like some of the aspects of your local Firkin but not others, there's likely to be one just down the road that fits your style.

If you want something healthier to drink, why not go to a Jugo Juice? For a society on the go, the "on-the-go" choices are often fatty foods or high-sugar, caffeine-heavy drinks. The Jugo philosophy is the notion of a coffee break without coffee, and a lunch without eating. The founders thought people would prefer a healthy and delicious alternative. Rather than a fancy coffee drink, people can have a healthy "meal in a cup." Since opening the first Jugo Juice in late 1998 in Calgary, and franchising in 2002, Jugo Juice has grown to more than 80 locations across North America. Interestingly "Jugo" means juice in Spanish, so the name of the franchise is, literally, Juice Juice.

Jugo Juice is not the only Canadian franchisor riding the trend toward healthier, fresher, non-additive foods—and that likes a good play on words. Ho-Lee-Chow is an Ontario-centred fast food and delivery chain of restaurants serving Asian food. About half of the chain's 18 stores are in Toronto. A somewhat larger operation is Manchu Wok. Founded in Peterborough in 1980, the chain now has more than 200 stores, found mostly in mall locations across North America. Though the chain is now owned by Hong Kong's Café de Coral, local ownership—in the form of franchisees—still accounts for 75 percent of the stores.

Another chain that focuses on fresh, quality ingredients is Sarpino's Pizzeria. Accordingly, Sarpino's touts that its pizzas are made from authentic ingredients, cheeses made from 100 percent real mozzarella, fresh sauces, a choice of high-quality meats, fresh vegetable toppings, and dough that is hand kneaded each day in the Italian tradition at every location. Sarpino's founder Gerry Koutougos knows his pizza, having started the Pizza 2 for 1 franchise.

With hundreds of locations around the world, and hundreds of millions of dollars in resources, one might think that Canada's pizza business would be dominated by Pizza Hut, Domino's, and Little Caesars. It's not. Canadian-based pizza franchise chains abound. This may have something to do with the ability of regional players to create products uniquely adapted to their geographic area and to spread out successfully from that base.

Thus, Boston Pizza and Panago were able to expand from their base in the west; Greco Pizza and Pizza Delight are expanding from their base in Atlantic Canada, Quebec, and Ontario; and Ontario's Pizza Nova is moving into Quebec. These are just some of the pizza chains with more than 100 stores. With more than 500 locations, Toronto's Pizza Pizza is simply unavoidable in Ontario. All these pizza vendors have some unique features to their menus. So, give me a Boston Pizza Thai chicken wrap, a Pizza Delight French onion soup, a Greco donair, some Pizza Nova chicken wings, a Panago Memphis slow-roasted pork pizza, and a Pizza Pizza tikka masala pizza. Follow all that with up one additional franchise opportunity from Toronto: U Weight Loss Clinic. . . .

SOURCES: 2008, The Firkin Group of Pubs Web site information sheet, http://www.firkinpubs.com/render/rendermedia.aspx?id=228; 2008, Jugo Juice Web site, http://www.jugojuice.com/content/view/1/15/; 2008, Ho-Le-Chow Web site, http://www.holeechow.com/about/; 2008,

Manchu Wok Web site, http://www.manchuwok.com/; 2008, Sarpino's Pizza Web site, http://www.sarpinos.com/pages/story/; 2008, Canadian Businesses for Sale Web site, Pizza, http://canadian.businessesforsale.com/canadian/C1037-1/Pizza-Franchises.aspx; 2008, Boston Pizza Web site, http://www.bostonpizza.com; 2008, Panago Pizza Web site, http://www.panago.com/; 2008, 241 Pizza Web site, http://www.241pizza .com; 2008, Pizza Delight Web site, http://www.pizzadelight.com/corporate; 2008, Pizza Nova Web site, http://www.pizzanova.com/home.aspx; 2008, Pizza Pizza Web site, http://www.pizzapizza.ca; 2008, Greco Pizza Web site, http://www.greco.ca/aboutus.asp; 2008, U Weight Loss Clinic Web site, http://www.uweightloss.com/index.aspx; S. L. Jameson, 2003, Sarpino's Pizzeria brings a new flavor to Willow Glen, *Willow Glen Resident*, http://www.community-newspapers.com/archives/wgresident/20030305/wg-taste.shtml, March 5; information from all Web sites retrieved January 28, 2008.

the Circle K banner. Convenience stores are especially popular in Asia, where stores like Circle K and 7-Eleven are more like pantries for city dwellers short on space.[88] Thus, Circle K has 24 stores per million people in Japan, far more than Couche-Tard's 17 per million in North America.[89]

In the most successful franchising strategy, the partners (the franchisor and the franchisees) closely work together.[90] A primary responsibility of the franchisor is to develop programs to transfer to the franchisees the knowledge and skills that are needed to successfully compete at the local level.[91] In return, franchisees should provide feedback to the franchisor regarding how their units could become more effective and efficient.[92] Working cooperatively, the franchisor and its franchisees find ways to strengthen the core company's brand name, which is often the most important competitive advantage for franchisees operating in their local markets.[93]

Franchising is a particularly attractive strategy to use in fragmented industries, such as retailing and commercial printing. In fragmented industries, a large number of small and medium-sized firms compete as rivals; however, no firm or small set of firms has a dominant share, making it possible for a company to gain a large market share by consolidating independent companies through contractual relationships.[94] That is why franchising is a common strategy used by food chains, as described in the Strategic Focus.

Assessment of Corporate-Level Cooperative Strategies

Costs are incurred with each type of cooperative strategy.[95] Compared with those at the business level, corporate-level cooperative strategies commonly are broader in scope and more complex, making them relatively more costly. Organizations forming and using cooperative strategies, especially corporate-level ones, should be aware of alliance costs and carefully monitor them. In spite of these costs, firms can create competitive advantages and value when they effectively form and use corporate-level cooperative strategies.[96] The likelihood of this being the case increases when successful alliance experiences are internalized. In other words, those involved with forming and using corporate-level cooperative strategies can also use them to develop useful knowledge about how to succeed in the future. To gain maximum value from this knowledge, firms should organize it and verify that it is always properly distributed to those involved with the formation and use of alliances.[97]

We explained in Chapter 7 that firms answer two questions to form a corporate-level strategy: In which businesses will the diversified firm compete, and How will those businesses be managed? These questions are also answered as firms form corporate-level cooperative strategies. Thus, firms able to develop corporate-level cooperative strategies and manage them in ways that are valuable, rare, imperfectly imitable, and organized to be exploited (see Chapter 4) develop a competitive advantage that is in addition to advantages gained through the activities of individual cooperative strategies. Later in the chapter, we further describe alliance management as a source of competitive advantage.

International Cooperative Strategy

A **cross-border strategic alliance** is an international cooperative strategy in which firms with headquarters in different nations combine some of their resources and capabilities to create a competitive advantage.

A **cross-border strategic alliance** is an international cooperative strategy in which firms with headquarters in different nations combine some of their resources and capabilities to create a competitive advantage. For example, British Petroleum (BP) invested over $6 billion in a joint venture with Russian oil company Tyumen Oil. The venture combined BP's Russian assets, a stake in Russian oil company Sidanco, with Tyumen. The new company is the 10th-largest oil producer in the world, increasing its competitive advantage against other, smaller oil companies.[98] Taking place in virtually all industries, the number of cross-border alliances being completed continues to increase,[99] in some cases at the expense of mergers and acquisitions.[100] However, as the Strategic Focus on franchising suggests, there is a significant amount of international cooperative activity.

While cross-border alliances can be complex, they may be necessary to improve technology—as demonstrated by the international alliance among IBM, Sony, and Toshiba to develop a new microprocessor. In 2005, IBM, Sony, and Toshiba announced the development of a microprocessor called the Cell and the introduction to the market of new products using the Cell. The Cell represents a major breakthrough in architectural design, resulting in a small but powerful microprocessor. Engineers from the three companies have been collaborating at a joint design centre since 2001. The Cell's ultra–high-speed communication capabilities are especially suited for entertainment and media applications. The alliance partners describe it as a "supercomputer on a chip." The Cell incorporates many of the positive attributes of IBM's sophisticated servers, Sony's computer entertainment systems, and Toshiba's advanced semiconductor technology. Sony and Toshiba expect to use the Cell in a broad range of new products including digital televisions, home servers, and supercomputers.[101]

There are several reasons for the increasing use of cross-border strategic alliances. In general, multinational corporations outperform domestic-only firms.[102] Thus, to expand into international markets a firm may form cross-border strategic alliances to leverage core competencies that are the foundation of its domestic success.[103] Nike has used its core competency with celebrity marketing as it expands overseas, especially because its North American business growth has slowed. It has sought to duplicate its marketing strategy in international markets, signing big-name athletes to sell shoes and apparel. Nike has alliance agreements with Brazilian soccer star Ronaldo and the world's most popular soccer team, Manchester United. The firm also has alliance agreements with two world-famous athletes, golfer Tiger Woods and cyclist Lance Armstrong, who won seven straight Tour de France events. These alliances have helped Nike achieve considerable financial success over time.[104]

Limited domestic growth opportunities and foreign-government economic policies are additional reasons why firms use cross-border alliances. As discussed in Chapter 9, local ownership is an important national policy objective in some nations. In India and China, for example, governmental policies reflect a strong preference to license local companies. Thus, in some countries, the full range of entry mode choices that we described in Chapter 9 may not be available to firms wishing to internationally diversify. Indeed, investment by foreign firms in these instances may be allowed only through a partnership with a local firm, such as in a cross-border alliance. Especially important, strategic alliances with local partners can help firms overcome certain liabilities of moving into a foreign country, such as lack of knowledge of the local culture or institutional norms.[105] A cross-border strategic alliance can also be helpful to foreign partners from an operational perspective, because the local partner has significantly more information about factors contributing to competitive success such as local markets, sources of capital, legal procedures, and politics.[106]

Firms also use cross-border alliances to help transform themselves or to better use their advantages to benefit from opportunities surfacing in the rapidly changing global economy. In these cases, the firm leverages its distinctive capabilities through the alliance. This is the case in the alliance among IBM, Sony, and Toshiba mentioned earlier. Sony and Toshiba plan to use their Cell microprocessor in high-definition televisions that they developed using their knowledge of the consumer electronics market. The microprocessor takes advantage of IBM's strong technological capabilities.

In general, cross-border alliances are more complex and risky than domestic strategic alliances.[107] However, the fact that firms competing internationally tend to outperform domestic-only competitors suggests the importance of learning how to diversify into international markets. Compared with mergers and acquisitions, cross-border alliances may be a better way to learn this process, especially in the early stages of firms' geographic diversification efforts. When Starbucks was looking to expand overseas, it wanted to do so quickly in order to keep its first-mover advantage. Thus, it agreed to a complex series of joint ventures in many countries in the interest of speed. While the company receives a percentage of the revenues and profits as well as licensing fees for supplying its coffee, controlling costs abroad is more difficult than in its home market.[108] However, as noted above, the firm hopes to learn a great deal from serving multiple markets. Careful and thorough study of a proposed cross-border alliance contributes to success,[109] as do precise specifications of each partner's alliance role.[110] These points are explored later in our discussion of how to best manage alliances.

Network Cooperative Strategy

Increasingly, firms use several cooperative strategies. In addition to forming their own alliances with individual companies, a growing number of firms are joining forces in multiple networks.[111] A **network cooperative strategy** is a cooperative strategy wherein several firms agree to form multiple partnerships to achieve shared objectives.

A network cooperative strategy is particularly effective when it is formed by firms clustered together,[112] as with Silicon Valley in California, Ottawa's Silicon Valley North tech sector, B.C.'s Silicon Delta,[113] and Singapore's Silicon Island.[114] Effective social relationships and interactions among partners while sharing their resources and capabilities make it more likely that a network cooperative strategy will be successful,[115] as does having a productive strategic centre firm (discussed further in Chapter 12). Firms involved in networks gain information and knowledge from multiple sources. They can use these heterogeneous knowledge sets to produce more and better innovation. As a result, firms involved in networks of alliances tend to be more innovative.[116] Research evidence suggests that the positive financial effects of network cooperative strategies make these strategies important contributors to the 21st-century success of both supplier and buyer partners involved.[117] However, there are disadvantages to participating in networks in that a firm can be locked in to its partners, precluding the development of alliances with others. In certain types of networks, such as Japanese *keiretsus,* firms in the network are expected to help other firms in the network whenever they need aid. Such expectations can become a burden and reduce the focal firm's performance over time.[118]

Alliance Network Types

An important advantage of a network cooperative strategy is that firms gain access "to their partners' partners."[119] Having access to multiple collaborations increases the likelihood that additional competitive advantages will be formed as the set of shared resources and capabilities expands.[120] In turn, development of new capabilities further stimulates the development of product innovations that are so critical to strategic competitiveness in the global economy.[121]

The set of strategic alliance partnerships resulting from the use of a network cooperative strategy is commonly called an *alliance network.* The alliance networks that companies

A **network cooperative strategy** is a cooperative strategy wherein several firms agree to form multiple partnerships to achieve shared objectives.

develop vary by industry conditions. A stable alliance network is formed in mature industries where demand is relatively constant and predictable. Through a stable alliance network, firms try to extend their competitive advantages to other settings while continuing to profit from operations in their core, relatively mature industry. Thus, stable networks are built for exploitation of the economies (scale and/or scope) available between firms.[122] Dynamic alliance networks are used in industries characterized by frequent product innovations and short product life cycles.[123] For instance, the pace of innovation in the information technology (IT) industry is too fast for any one company to maintain success over time. Thus, the ability to develop and nurture strategic partnerships can make the difference between success and failure. As such, independent software vendors earn more than 40 percent of their revenue through successful partnering. After IBM's "near-death experience" in the early 1990s, the power of its alliances with more than 90,000 business partners helped shape its turnaround. By partnering, companies play on "teams," fielding the best players at every position and thus providing stamina and flexibility for customers. Through partnerships, a company can offer a broader range of IT solutions and improve the probability of market success.[124]

Thus, dynamic alliance networks are primarily used to stimulate rapid, value-creating product innovations and subsequent successful market entries, demonstrating that their purpose is often exploration of new ideas.[125] Often, large firms in such industries as software and pharmaceuticals create networks of smaller entrepreneurial start-up firms to accomplish this goal.[126] Small firms also build credibility faster by being engaged in such joint network relationships.[127]

Firms regularly use strategic alliances to enter international markets; they help these firms survive in those markets early and to be competitive later. In fact, as noted earlier, firms are increasingly participating in international network alliances. IBM has alliances with Sony and Toshiba to develop the Cell microprocessor, and another alliance with Microsoft and Markham, Ontario's ATI Technologies to develop a different chip. However, Microsoft and ATI gain value indirectly from IBM's other alliance because it adds to IBM's technological capabilities.

While these alliances appear to be successful, there are risks with alliances as well.

Competitive Risks with Cooperative Strategies

Stated simply, many cooperative strategies fail.[128] In fact, evidence shows that two-thirds of cooperative strategies have serious problems in their first two years and that as many as 70 percent of them fail. This failure rate suggests that even when the partnership has potential complementarities and synergies, alliance success is elusive.[129]

Although failure is undesirable, it can be a valuable learning experience. Companies need to carefully study a cooperative strategy's failure to gain insights that can be used to successfully develop future cooperative strategies.[130] Companies should work hard to avoid cooperative strategy failure and to learn from failure if it occurs. In the construction industry, cooperation on a project between the main contractor and subcontractors is very important. Without managing areas of mistrust, including suspected incompetence and potential dishonesty, success can be elusive, and failure of the alliance can be very costly.[131] Prominent cooperative strategy risks are shown in Figure 10.4.

One cooperative strategy risk is that a partner may act opportunistically. Opportunistic behaviours surface either when formal contracts fail to prevent them or when an alliance is based on a false perception of partner trustworthiness. Not infrequently, the opportunistic firm wants to acquire as much of its partner's tacit knowledge as it can.[132] Full awareness of what a partner wants in a cooperative strategy reduces the likelihood a firm will suffer from another's opportunistic actions.[133]

In January 2004, Hewlett-Packard and Apple made a surprise announcement of an alliance for HP to distribute Apple's iPod devices to retail outlets. HP explained that the

Figure 10.4 Managing Competitive Risks in Cooperative Strategies

Competitive Risks	Risk and Asset Management Approaches	Desired Outcome
• Inadequate contracts • Misrepresentation of competencies • Partners fail to use their complementary resources • Holding alliance partner's specific investments hostage	• Detailed contracts and monitoring • Developing trusting relationships	• Creating value

iPod would become the centre of its digital entertainment strategy. It was a surprise because the two firms are strong competitors in the personal computer market. However, in July 2005 HP announced that selling the iPod no longer fit its digital media strategy. HP accounted for about 5 percent of iPod's sales, slightly over 6 million units valued at over $4 billion in revenue to Apple annually. HP did not profit greatly from these sales and it had to use the Apple name, though the firms originally stated that iPods sold by HP would carry the HP logo. Furthermore, it was reported that Apple had control of the financial characteristics of the deal. It appears that the partnership favoured Apple and that HP decided it was not gaining adequate value from the alliance for it to continue. Therefore, the alliance was dissolved.[134]

Some cooperative strategies fail when it is discovered that a firm has misrepresented the competencies it can bring to the partnership. The risk of competency misrepresentation is more common when the partner's contribution is grounded in some of its intangible assets. Superior knowledge of local conditions is an example of an intangible asset that partners often fail to deliver. Asking the partner to provide evidence that it does possess the resources and capabilities (even when they are largely intangible) it is to share in the cooperative strategy may be an effective way to deal with this risk.

Another risk is that a firm will not actually make available to its partners the resources and capabilities (like its most sophisticated technologies) that it committed to the cooperative strategy. This risk surfaces most commonly when firms form an international cooperative strategy.[135] In these instances, different cultures and languages can cause misinterpretations of contractual terms or trust-based expectations.

A final risk is that one firm may make investments specific to the alliance while its partner does not. For example, the firm might commit resources and capabilities to develop manufacturing equipment that can be used only to produce items coming from the alliance. If the partner isn't also making alliance-specific investments, the firm is at a relative disadvantage in terms of returns earned from the alliance compared with investments made to earn the returns.

Pixar and Disney partnered to develop and market several computer-animated features, including *Toy Story, Monsters Inc., A Bug's Life, Finding Nemo,* and *The Incredibles,* all which have been box-office hits. However, Disney perceived risks in its partnership with Pixar. Pixar had significant bargaining power to strike another deal—with Disney or with another company. All of Pixar's films have done better at the box office than Disney's recent animated features, and Pixar had contributed to a third of Disney's operating profits in recent years. Yet talks to extend the deal turned sour, with allegations flying between Apple Computer founder Steve Jobs (who is also Pixar's CEO) and Disney's then-CEO Michael Eisner. In January 2004, Pixar announced it was breaking off talks with Disney and would look elsewhere for a studio partner. Yet given the long and positive results of the arrangement it was not easy for either party to walk away, and by

January 2006 Disney announced it would buy Pixar for $7.4 billion in stock and Steve Jobs would get a seat on the Disney board.[136]

Managing Cooperative Strategies

As our discussion has shown, cooperative strategies represent important strategic alternatives for firms competing in the global economy.[137] However, our study of cooperative strategies also shows that they are complex and challenging to manage successfully.[138]

Firms gain the most benefit from cooperative strategies when they are effectively managed. The firm that learns how to manage cooperative strategies better than its competitors may develop a competitive advantage in terms of this activity.[139] Because the ability to effectively manage cooperative strategies is unevenly distributed across organizations in general, assigning managerial responsibility for a firm's cooperative strategies to a high-level executive or to a team improves the likelihood the strategies will be well managed.

Those responsible for managing the firm's set of cooperative strategies coordinate activities, categorize knowledge learned from previous experiences, and make certain that what the firm knows about how to effectively form and use cooperative strategies is in the hands of the right people at the right time. Firms use one of two primary approaches to manage cooperative strategies—cost minimization and opportunity maximization[140] (see Figure 10.4). This is the case whether or not the firm has formed a separate cooperative strategy management function.

In the cost-minimization management approach, the firm develops formal contracts with its partners. These contracts specify how the cooperative strategy is to be monitored and how partner behaviour is to be controlled. The goal of this approach is to minimize the cooperative strategy's cost and to prevent opportunistic behaviour by a partner. The focus of the second managerial approach—opportunity maximization—is on maximizing a partnership's value-creation opportunities. In this case, partners are prepared to take advantage of unexpected opportunities to learn from each other and to explore additional marketplace possibilities. Less formal contracts, with fewer constraints on partners' behaviours, make it possible for partners to explore how their resources and capabilities can be shared in multiple value-creating ways.

Firms can successfully use both approaches to manage cooperative strategies. However, the costs to monitor the cooperative strategy are greater with cost minimization in that writing detailed contracts and using extensive monitoring mechanisms is expensive, even when the approach is intended to reduce alliance costs. Although monitoring systems may prevent partners from acting in their own best interests, they also often preclude positive responses to new opportunities that surface to use the alliance's competitive advantages. Thus, formal contracts and extensive monitoring systems tend to stifle partners' efforts to gain maximum value from their participation in a cooperative strategy and require significant resources to put into place and use.[141]

For example, Sony Ericsson Mobile Communications was a joint venture formed by Sony and Ericsson to become the top seller of multimedia mobile-phone handsets. Although it was growing at three times the overall market rate in its core areas, the venture posted a loss. Notably, the loss was attributed to costs from job cuts and closing units, such as research parks in Munich, Germany, and North Carolina. Such cost-cutting activities may create difficulties for strategic alliances built to explore opportunities.[142]

The relative lack of detail and formality that is a part of the contract developed by firms using the second management approach of opportunity maximization means that firms need to trust each other to act in the partnership's best interests. A psychological state, *trust* is a willingness to be vulnerable because of the expectations of positive behaviour from the firm's alliance partner.[143] When partners trust each other, there is less need to write detailed formal contracts to specify each firm's alliance behaviours,[144] and the cooperative relationship tends to be more stable.[145] On a relative basis, trust tends to be more difficult to establish in international cooperative strategies compared with domestic ones. Differences in trade policies, cultures, laws, and politics that are part of cross-border alliances account for the increased difficulty. When trust exists, partners' monitoring costs are reduced and opportunities to create value are maximized. Essentially, in these cases, the firms have built social capital as described earlier in the chapter.[146]

Research showing that trust between partners increases the likelihood of alliance success seems to highlight the benefits of the opportunity maximization approach to managing cooperative strategies. Trust may also be the most efficient way to influence and control alliance partners' behaviours.[147] Research indicates that trust can be a capability that is valuable, rare, and imperfectly imitable.[148] Thus, firms known to be trustworthy can have a competitive advantage in terms of how they develop and use cooperative strategies both internally and externally.[149] One reason is that it is impossible to specify all operational details of a cooperative strategy in a formal contract. Confidence that its partner can be trusted reduces the firm's concern about the inability to contractually control all alliance details.

In 2005, CapitaLand Ltd. of Singapore signed a contract to acquire a 65 percent ownership in 15 malls in which Wal-Mart is the anchor. The deal represented an extension of Wal-Mart's partnership with Shenzhen International Trust & Investment Co. (Szitic). The malls are managed by a joint venture between CapitaLand and Szitic. The agreement among the parties allows CapitaLand an option to invest in 17 other malls to be anchored by Wal-Mart. This deal suggests that the partners have built a level of trust and social capital in prior relationships. Otherwise they would not have extended the relationship with further partnerships nor would they have agreed to grant options for future joint activities. With China's substantial growth potential and Wal-Mart's significant expansion plans, the social capital among these partners may have valuable benefits for all parties over time.[150]

Summary

- A cooperative strategy is one in which firms work together to achieve a shared objective. Strategic alliances, in which firms combine some of their resources and capabilities to create a competitive advantage, are the primary form of cooperative strategies. Joint ventures (where firms create and own equal shares of a new venture that is intended to develop competitive advantages), equity strategic alliances (where firms own different shares of a newly created venture), and nonequity strategic alliances (where firms cooperate through a contractual relationship) are the three basic types of strategic alliances. Outsourcing, discussed in Chapter 4, commonly occurs as firms form nonequity strategic alliances.

- Collusive strategies are the second type of cooperative strategies. In many economies and certainly in developed ones, explicit collusive strategies are illegal unless sanctioned by government policies. With increasing globalization, fewer government-sanctioned situations of

explicit collusion exist. Tacit collusion, also called mutual forbearance, is a cooperative strategy through which firms tacitly cooperate to reduce industry output below the potential competitive output level, thereby raising prices above the competitive level. Firms using tacit collusion need to ensure they do not fall into the trap of conscious parallelism.

- The reasons why firms use cooperative strategies vary by slow-cycle, fast-cycle, and standard-cycle market conditions. To enter restricted markets (slow-cycle), to move quickly from one competitive advantage to another (fast-cycle), and to gain market power (standard-cycle) are among the reasons by market type for use of cooperative strategies.

- There are four business-level cooperative strategies (a business-level cooperative strategy is used to help the firm improve its performance in individual product markets). Through vertical and horizontal complementary alliances, companies combine their resources and capabilities to create value in different parts (vertical) or the same parts (horizontal) of the value chain. Competition-responding strategies are formed to respond to competitors' actions, especially strategic ones. Competition-reducing strategies are used to avoid excessive competition while the firm marshals its resources and capabilities to improve its competitiveness. Uncertainty-reducing strategies are used to hedge against risks created by the conditions of uncertain competitive environments (such as new product markets). Complementary alliances have the highest probability of yielding a sustainable competitive advantage; competition-reducing alliances have the lowest probability of doing so.

- Corporate-level cooperative strategies are used when the firm wants to pursue product and/or geographic diversification. Through diversifying strategic alliances, firms agree to share some of their resources and capabilities to enter new markets or produce new products. Synergistic alliances are ones where firms share resources and capabilities to develop economies of scope. This alliance is similar to the business-level horizontal complementary alliance in which firms try to develop operational synergy, except that synergistic alliances are used to develop synergy at the corporate level. Franchising is a corporate-level cooperative strategy where the franchisor uses a franchise as a contractual relationship to specify how resources and capabilities will be shared with franchisees.

- As an international cooperative strategy, a cross-border alliance is used for several reasons, including the performance superiority of firms competing in markets outside their domestic market and governmental restrictions on growth through mergers and acquisitions. Cross-border alliances tend to be riskier than their domestic counterparts,

particularly when partners aren't fully aware of each other's purpose for participating in the partnership.

- A network cooperative strategy is one wherein several firms agree to form multiple partnerships to achieve shared objectives. One of the primary benefits of a network cooperative strategy is the firm's opportunity to gain access "to its partner's other partnerships." When this happens, the probability greatly increases that partners will find unique ways to share their resources and capabilities to form competitive advantages. Network cooperative strategies are used to form either a stable alliance network or a dynamic alliance network. Used in mature industries, partners use stable networks to extend competitive advantages into new areas. In rapidly changing environments where frequent product innovations occur, dynamic networks are primarily used as a tool of innovation.

- Cooperative strategies are not risk free. If a contract is not developed appropriately, or if a partner misrepresents its competencies or fails to make them available, failure is likely. Furthermore, a firm may be held hostage through asset-specific investments made in conjunction with a partner, which may be exploited.

- Trust is an increasingly important aspect of successful cooperative strategies. Firms recognize the value of partnering with companies known for their trustworthiness. When trust exists, a cooperative strategy is managed to maximize the pursuit of opportunities between partners. Without trust, formal contracts and extensive monitoring systems are used to manage cooperative strategies. In this case, the interest is to minimize costs rather than to maximize opportunities by participating in a cooperative strategy. The key is to build trust and social capital.

Review Questions

1. What is the definition of cooperative strategy and why is this strategy important to firms competing in the 21st-century competitive landscape?

2. What is a strategic alliance? What are the three types of strategic alliances firms use to develop a competitive advantage?

3. What are the four business-level cooperative strategies and what are the differences among them?

4. What are the three corporate-level cooperative strategies?

How do firms use each one to create a competitive advantage?

5. Why do firms use cross-border strategic alliances?

6. What risks are firms likely to experience as they use cooperative strategies?

7. What are the differences between the cost-minimization approach and the opportunity-maximization approach to managing cooperative strategies?

1. Canada is home to many great inventions: the paint roller, road lines, and time itself (well, at least time zones). Perhaps Canada's greatest invention is the five-cent chocolate bar—invented by the Ganong Brothers in 1898. That price stayed the same for almost 50 years—the only thing better than a five-cent candy bar was hockey! And then, one day in 1947, it was gone! In what we would describe here as a perfect example of tacit price collusion, candy bar makers had raised the price to eight cents!

   A great hue and cry arose, and children across the nation boycotted the price increases. Sales fell 80 percent virtually overnight. In Victoria, the legislature was shut down when children swarmed its halls demanding the return of nickel bars. Manufacturers argued that the end of wartime contracts and the elimination of labour and price controls meant they had no choice but to raise the price of candy bars. Candy makers were demonized in the press, and the public, frustrated with rising postwar prices, cheered the children on. At the height of its popularity, the movement became a victim to the times. The *Toronto Telegram* labelled the protestors communists and the movement disintegrated.

   Through all of this, not one candy company did what many would do with later price increases: shrink the size of the bar. Was this really just inflation or collusion? If it was not collusion, why would no candy maker shrink the bar, lower the price, and likely take advantage of the gain in market share? Were the candy companies being socially responsible by raising prices? Were the protestors being socially responsible? What about the press? The government?

2. Apple's iPhone was a huge success and demand for the product has been great. However, when the product first came out consumers could get an iPhone in the U.S., Britain, and Germany—but not in Canada. Well, at least not one made by Apple. Toronto-based Comwave Telecom Inc. has been marketing a collection of voice-over-internet services and products under the registered trademark iPhone since 2004, including a product called iPhone Mobile. What are Apple's rights regarding use of the product's name versus those of Comwave? Does the public's demand for the product make any difference in Comwave's rights to the name?

3. Every time there is a drastic rise in gas prices, there is a call for an investigation regarding collusion among oil companies. Why does this happen? If it is tacit collusion, isn't that still collusion? Are such practices socially responsible on the part of the oil companies? What, if anything, can or should the public and/or government do about such practices?

What's In It for Cameco?

In 2005, construction began on the Cigar Lake Uranium Mine in Saskatchewan. Cigar Lake is the world's largest undeveloped high-grade uranium deposit. The mine is a strategic alliance between Saskatoon's Cameco, Paris-based Areva Resources, and two Japanese companies, Idemitsu Kosan (Japan's largest independent oil company) and Tokyo Electric Power Company (TEPCO). The purpose of this alliance was, most directly, to develop the mine. To complete this exercise, you will be asked to carefully examine this alliance to determine the purposes it serves for each firm.

Part One—In Groups of Four. Use the Internet and archives of business periodicals such as the *Financial Post* and the *Canadian Mining Journal* to identify the terms of this strategic alliance. In addition, gain access to information detailing the specifications of the mine. While completing this part of the exercise, be certain to examine only the terms of the alliance to which the four partners agreed.

Part Two—Individually. As individuals within your four-person groups, you will be assigned one of the four partners to this alliance—either Cameco, Areva, Idemitsu Kosan, or TEPCO. Based on each person's understanding of the terms of the alliance, your task is to describe the motivations or reasons why your assigned firm chose to participate in this strategic alliance. You should be able to locate a number of discussions describing the reasons each firm decided to enter this project. Anticipate that writers will offer different perspectives regarding each of the four firms. When reading the commentaries, carefully assess the appropriateness of the writers' views given what you learned by completing the first part of this exercise. Once you have identified what you believe are the actual reasons why your firm decided to participate in this particular alliance, use the material on attributes of a successful alliance from Chapter 10 to evaluate the degree to which you think this alliance will be successful. Be prepared to discuss your work with your group members.

Part Three—In Groups of Four. Your next task is to discuss your findings about each firm as a group. Do the purposes of participating in the alliance vary among the partners? If so, what factors or conditions might create those differences? How important are those differences for the alliance's success? As a group, reach a consensus about the purposes of each firm with respect to participating in this strategic alliance. In reaching these conclusions, do not let current events regarding this alliance influence your thinking. Your task is to understand the purposes of each firm at the time the alliance was formed. Be prepared to present your group's conclusions to the entire class.

Part Four—Whole Class. In this part of the exercise, each team will present its assessment of the purposes supporting or driving each firm's decision to participate in the strategic alliance. After all the teams have presented their assessments, discuss the differences among the groups' inputs and what may have caused those differences. Be prepared to decide whether your group would change its assessments in light of hearing peers discuss their perspectives. Finally, as a class, obtain current information about the status of this alliance. Is the alliance reaching its anticipated success? Does each firm seem to be making progress toward reaching the purposes it sought when deciding to participate in the alliance? In the view of the class and given the current status of this alliance, what is likely to happen with this alliance in the future and why?

Alliance Strategy

Assume you are the CEO of Century Pharmaceuticals, Inc., and that you are seeking a strategic alliance with Excel Research, an independent, full-service research organization. Excel Research specializes in working with pharmaceutical companies to efficiently and effectively navigate the regulatory approval process and bring new drug therapies to market. Excel will help Century with the three-stage clinical trials process for its submissions to regulators for new drug products. Excel will also help with Century's projects working on investigational new drugs (IND) that are not ready for clinical trials. As CEO, you believe that Century Pharmaceuticals and Excel Research can successfully work together to create novel therapies to fill unmet needs in dermatology and other therapeutic arenas with greater speed and at lower cost.

In pharmaceuticals, as elsewhere, firms have one year from invention to apply for a patent. The patent life begins to run at that time, but unlike other inventors the pharmaceutical firms have to further develop the drug target as an IND and then go through a series of tests to show that the drug is safe and effective prior to marketing before they can exploit their patent. This can eat up several years of the effective patent life. Upon expiration of the patent generic firms can quickly enter the market, as the drugs are well understood combinations of basic chemicals. Delays in the approval process can cost firms billions of dollars a year in unrealized revenue during the patent period.

You expect that the strategic alliance between Century Pharmaceuticals and Excel Research will provide enhanced benefits for both companies. Under your leadership, Century is committed to continuing to grow by implementing its differentiation strategy, which specifies the objectives of acquiring new products and introducing new indications (regulator-approved uses for which limited patent extension can be given) for therapies in specific markets. Excel Research has an established and proven track record of success in supporting and providing the evaluation required to bring new therapies and new uses for existing therapies to market.

Based on this information, determine answers to the following questions using the concepts in Chapter 10, and make a brief presentation to the class as the board of directors.

1. Is the above case a complementary strategic alliance? If so, what kind of complementary strategic alliance?

2. Is it a competition-response strategy? If so, who are the competitors and what are they doing?

3. Is it an uncertainty-reducing strategy? If so, how can the uncertainty be reduced?

4. Is it a competition-reducing strategy? If so, explain how it works.

Notes

1. S. J. Chang, 2004, Venture capital financing, strategic alliances, and the initial public offerings of Internet startups, *Journal of Business Venturing,* 19: 721–741; J. Hagedoorn & G. Dysters, 2002, External sources of innovative capabilities: The preference for strategic alliances or mergers and acquisitions, *Journal of Management Studies,* 39: 167–188.
2. T. A. Hemphill, 2003, Cooperative strategy, technology innovation and competition policy in the United States and the European Union, *Technology Analysis & Strategic Management,* 15(1): 93–101; J. B. Barney, 2002, *Gaining and Sustaining Competitive Advantage,* 2nd ed., Upper Saddle River, NJ: Prentice-Hall, 339.
3. K. Singh & W. Mitchell, 2005, Growth dynamics: The bidirectional relationship between interfirm collaboration and business sales in entrant and incumbent alliances, *Strategic Management Journal,* 26: 497–521; C. Young-Ybarra & M. Wiersema, 1999, Strategic flexibility in information technology alliances: The influence of transaction cost economics and social exchange theory, *Organization Science,* 10: 439–459.

4. J. Bowser, 2001, Strategic co-opetition: The value of relationships in the networked economy, IBM Business Strategy Consulting, www.ibm.com, March 12.

5. M. J. Mol, P. Pauwels, P. Matthyssens, & L. Quintens, 2004, A technological contingency perspective on the depth and scope of international outsourcing, *Journal of International Management*, 10: 287–305.

6. C. Hardy, T. B. Lawrence, & D. Grant, 2005, Discourse and collaboration: The role of conversations and collective identity, *Academy of Management Review*, 30: 58–77; A. Haahti, V. Madupu, U. Yavas, & E. Babakus, 2005, Cooperative strategy, knowledge intensity and export performance of small and medium sized enterprises, *Journal of World Business*, 40: 124–138; R. Vassolo, J. Anand, & T. B. Folta, 2004, Non-additivity in portfolios of exploration activities: A real options-based analysis of equity alliances in biotechnology, *Strategic Management Journal*, 25: 1045–1061.

7. Barney, *Gaining and Sustaining Competitive Advantage*, 339.

8. R. D. Ireland, M. A. Hitt, & D. Vaidyanath, 2002, Alliance management as a source of competitive advantage, *Journal of Management*, 28: 413–446; J. G. Coombs & D. J. Ketchen, 1999, Exploring interfirm cooperation and performance: Toward a reconciliation of predictions from the resource-based view and organizational economics, *Strategic Management Journal*, 20: 867–888.

9. M. R. Subramani & N. Venkatraman, 2003, Safeguarding investments in asymmetric interorganizational relationships: Theory and evidence, *Academy of Management Journal*, 46(1): 46–62.

10. P. Kale, J. H. Dyer, & H. Singh, 2002, Alliance capability, stock market response, and long-term alliance success: The role of the alliance function, *Strategic Management Journal*, 23: 747–767; D. F. Kuratko, R. D. Ireland, & J. S. Hornsby, 2001, Improving firm performance through entrepreneurial actions: Acordia's corporate entrepreneurship strategy, *Academy of Management Executive*, 15(4): 60–71.

11. A. Antoine, C. B. Frank, H. Murata, & E. Roberts, 2003, Acquisitions and alliances in the aerospace industry: An unusual triad, *International Journal of Technology Management*, 25(8): 779–790; 2002, Lockheed Martin, Responsive global partnerships, www.lockheedmartin.com, retrieved March 17.

12. D. Gerwin, 2004, Coordinating new product development in strategic alliances, *Academy of Management Review*, 29: 241–257; Ireland, Hitt, & Vaidyanath, Alliance management as a source of competitive advantage.

13. M. Harvey, M. B. Myers, & M. M. Novicevic, 2003, The managerial issues associated with global account management: A relational contract perspective, *Journal of Management Development*, 22(1,2): 103–129; T. K. Das & B.-S. Teng, 2001, A risk perception model of alliance structuring, *Journal of International Management*, 7: 1–29.

14. A. Afuah, 2002, Mapping technological capabilities into product markets and competitive advantage: The case of cholesterol drugs, *Strategic Management Journal*, 23: 171–179; A. Arino, 2001, To do or not to do? Noncooperative behavior by commission and omission in interfirm ventures, *Group & Organization Management*, 26(1): 4–23; C. Holliday, 2001, Sustainable growth, the DuPont way, *Harvard Business Review*, 79(8): 129–134.

15. Y. Kim & K. Lee, 2003, Technological collaboration in the Korean electronic parts industry: Patterns and key success factors, *R&D Management*, 33(1): 59–77; M. A. Geletkanycz & S. S. Black, 2001, Bound by the past? Experience-based effects on commitment to the strategic status quo, *Journal of Management*, 27: 3–21.

16. S. L. Berman, J. Down, & C. W. L. Hill, 2002, Tacit knowledge as a source of competitive advantage in the National Basketball Association, *Academy of Management Journal*, 45: 13–31.

17. H. Hoang & F. T. Rothaermel, 2005, The effect of general and partner-specific alliance experience on joint R&D project performance, *Academy of Management Journal*, 48: 332–345.

18. M. Clifford, 2003, Concrete lessons in reform, BusinessWeek Online, www.businessweek.com, retrieved June 16.

19. R. E. Hoskisson & L. W. Busenitz, 2002, Market uncertainty and learning distance in corporate entrepreneurship entry mode choice, in M. A. Hitt, R. D. Ireland, S. M. Camp, & D. L. Sexton (eds.), *Strategic Entrepreneurship: Creating a New Mindset*, Oxford, UK: Blackwell Publishers, 151–172.

20. A.-W. Harzing, 2002, Acquisitions versus greenfield investments: International strategy and management of entry modes, *Strategic Management Journal*, 23: 211–227; S.-J. Chang & P. M. Rosenzweig, 2001, The choice of entry mode in sequential foreign direct investment, *Strategic Management Journal*, 22: 747–776.

21. S. Das, P. K. Sen, & S. Sengupta, 1998, Impact of strategic alliances on firm valuation, *Academy of Management Journal*, 41: 27–41.

22. P. Bierly & E. Kessler, 1999. The timing of strategic alliances. In M. A. Hitt, P. G. Clifford, R. D. Nixon, & K. P. Coyne (eds.), *Dynamic Strategic Resources*, West Sussex, England: John Wiley & Sons, 299–321.

23. T. B. Folta & K. D. Miller, 2002, Real options in equity partnerships, *Strategic Management Journal*, 23: 77–88; Barney, *Gaining and Sustaining Competitive Advantage*, 339; S. D. Hunt, C. J. Lambe, & C. M. Wittmann, 2002, A theory and model of business alliance success, *Journal of Relationship Marketing*, 1(1): 17–35.

24. 2004, Research In Motion press release, http://www.rim.com/news/press/index.shtml, retrieved May 1.

25. A. Hinterhuber, 2002, Value chain orchestration in action and the case of the global agrochemical industry, *Long Range Planning*, 35(6): 615–635; A. C. Inkpen, 2001, Strategic alliances, in M. A. Hitt, R. E. Freeman, & J. S. Harrison (eds.), *Handbook of Strategic Management*, Oxford, UK: Blackwell Publishers, 409–432.

26. M. Delio, 1999, Strategic outsourcing, *Knowledge Management*, 2(7): 62–68.

27. While Web site introductions can be annoyances that delay getting to some piece of sought-after information, the one at the Sid Lee Web site (http://www.sidlee.com) is one we happily watched all the way through. It is an eye-catching display that, without using words, explains perfectly what the company does.

28. M. Dickie, 2007, Sid Lee & Cirque: From marcom input to creative partner: New roles for agencies, *Strategy*, August, 51.

29. M. J. Kelly, J.-L. Schaan, & H. Jonacas, 2002, Managing alliance relationships: Key challenges in the early stages of collaboration, *R&D Management*, 32(1): 11–22.

30. A. C. Inkpen & J. Ross, 2001, Why do some strategic alliances persist beyond their useful life? *California Management Review*, 44(1): 132–148.

31. C. Hardy, N. Phillips, & T. B. Lawrence, 2003, Resources, knowledge and influence: The organizational effects of interorganizational collaboration, *Journal of Management Studies*, 40(2): 321–347; Inkpen, Strategic alliances, 411.

32. L. Fuentelsaz, J. Gomez, & Y. Polo, 2002, Followers' entry timing: Evidence from the Spanish banking sector after deregulation, *Strategic Management Journal*, 23: 245–264.

33. K. R. Harrigan, 2001, Strategic flexibility in the old and new economies, in M. A. Hitt, R. E. Freeman, & J. S. Harrison (eds.), *Handbook of Strategic Management*, Oxford, UK: Blackwell Publishers, 97–123.

34. G. W. Dent, Jr., 2001, Gap fillers and fiduciary duties in strategic alliances, *Business Lawyer*, 57(1): 55–104.

35. M. Gonzalez, 2001, Strategic alliances, *Ivey Business Journal*, 66(1): 47–51.

36. M.-J. Oesterle & K. Macharzina, 2002, Editorial: De-regulation, liberalization, and concentration in the airline industry, *Management International Review*, 42(2): 115–119; M. Johnson, 2001, Airlines rush for comfort alliances, *Global Finance*, 15(11): 119–120.

37. M. A. Hitt, D. Ahlstrom, M. T. Dacin, E. Levitas, & L. Svobodina, 2004, The institutional effects of strategic alliance partner selection in transition economies: China versus Russia, *Organization Science*, 15: 173–185; P. A. Saparito, C. C. Chen, & H. J. Sapienza, 2004, The role of relational trust in bank-small firm relationships, *Academy of Management Journal*, 47: 400–410.

38. A. C. Inkpen & E. W. K. Tsang, 2005, Social capital, networks and knowledge transfer, *Academy of Management Review*, 30: 146–165.

39. A. Bollingtoft & J. P. Ulhoi, 2005, The networked business incubator—Leveraging entrepreneurial agency, *Journal of Business Venturing*, 20: 265–290; T. G. Pollock, J. F. Porac, & J. B. Wade, 2004, Constructing deal networks: Brokers as network "architects" in the U.S. IPO market and other examples, *Academy of Management Review*, 29: 50–72.

40. J. R. Williams, 1998, *Renewable Advantage: Crafting Strategy through Economic Time*, New York: The Free Press.

41. M. Arndt, 2003, Up from the scrap heap, BusinessWeek Online, www.businessweek.com, July 21.

42. S. A. Zahra, R. D. Ireland, I. Gutierrez, & M. A. Hitt, 2000, Privatization and entrepreneurial transformation: Emerging issues and a future research agenda, *Academy of Management Review*, 25: 509–524.

43. I. Filatotchev, M. Wright, K. Uhlenbruck, L. Tihanyi, & R. E. Hoskisson, 2003, Governance, organizational capabilities, and restructuring in transition economies, *Journal of World Business*, 38(4): 331–347.

44. K. M. Eisenhardt, 2002, Has strategy changed? *MIT Sloan Management Review*, 43(2): 88–91.

45. M. Dell, 2003, Collaboration equals innovation, *InformationWeek*, January 27, 24–26; H. D'Antoni, 2003, Behind the numbers: Business alliances merit closer examination, *InformationWeek*, January 27, 88.

46. S. Lekic, 2004, Star Alliance mulls jet standards, *The Montreal Gazette*, February 24, B7.

47. 2008, Areva Joint Ventures Web site, http://www.cogema.ca/uranium/index.html, retrieved January 26.

48. 2008, Cameco Investor Relations Web site, http://www.cameco.com/investor_relations/about_us/; 2008, Areva Operations Web site, http://www.areva.com/servlet/operations-en.html, retrieved January 26.

49. D. DuBois, 2007, Energy Priorities, May 3, http://energypriorities.com/entries/2007/05/france_78_nuclear.php; retrieved January 26, 2008; 2007, *World Uranium Mining, Nuclear Issues Briefing Paper 41*, July, http://www.uic.com.au/nip41.htm, retrieved January 26, 2008.

50. D. R. King, J. G. Covin, & H. Hegarty, 2003, Complementary resources and the exploitation of technological innovations, *Journal of Management*, 29: 589–606; J. S. Harrison, M. A. Hitt, R. E. Hoskisson, & R. D. Ireland, 2001, Resource complementarity in business combinations: Extending the logic to organizational alliances, *Journal of Management*, 27: 679–699.

51. Subramani & Venkatraman, Safeguarding investments in asymmetric interorganizational relationships.

52. R. Gulati, P. R. Lawrence, & P. Puranam, 2005, Adaptation in vertical relationships beyond incentive conflict, *Strategic Management Journal*, 26: 415–440.

53. M. G. Jacobides, 2005, Industry change through vertical disintegration: How and why markets emerged in mortgage banking, *Academy of Management Journal*, 48: 465–498.

54. G. Hoetker, 2005, How much you know versus how well I know you: Selecting a supplier for a technically innovative component, *Strategic Management Journal*, 26: 75–96.

55. M. Kotabe & K. S. Swan, 1995, The role of strategic alliances in high technology new product development, *Strategic Management Journal*, 16: 621–636.

56. J. Li, 2003, Bell Canada, Microsoft in Internet service alliance, Wall Street Journal Online, www.wsj.com, June 16.

57. P. Dussauge, B. Garrette, & W. Mitchel, 2004, Asymmetric performance: The market share impact of scale and link alliances in global auto industry, *Strategic Management Journal*, 25: 701–711.

58. 2005, Peugeot in pact with Mitsubishi for new SUVs, Wall Street Journal Online, www.wsj.com, July 12; 2004, Mitsubishi Motors truck scandal reaches court, *Sydney Morning Herald*, June 12, http://www.smh.com.au/articles/2004/06/11/1086749899114.html?from=storyrhs, retrieved July 22, 2008.

59. C. Bryan-Low & B. Lagrotteria, 2005, France Telecom and Microsoft forge product alliance, Wall Street Journal Online, www.wsj.com, July 7.

60. J. J. Reuer & T. W. Tong, 2005, Real options in international joint ventures, *Journal of Management*, 31: 403–423; S. Chatterjee, R. M. Wiseman, A. Fiegenbaum, & C. E. Devers, 2003, Integrating behavioural and economic concepts of risk into strategic management: The twain shall meet, *Long Range Planning*, 36(1): 61–80; Hitt, Ireland, Camp, & Sexton, *Strategic Entrepreneurship*, 9.

61. Dow Jones, 2003, ABN, ShoreBank set up co to invest in developing economies, Wall Street Journal Online, www.wsj.com, July 10.

62. Hoetker, How much you know versus how well I know you, 75.

63. Barney, *Gaining and Sustaining Competitive Advantage*, 339.

64. 2007, Cadbury in chocolate price-fixing probe, *The Australian*, November 29, http://www.theaustralian.news.com.au/story/0,25197,22840706-12377,00.html, retrieved January 26, 2008.

65. D. Leahy & S. Pavelin, 2003, Follow-my-leader and tacit collusion, *International Journal of Industrial Organization*, 21(3): 439–454.

66. B. R. Golden & H. Ma, 2003, Mutual forbearance: The role of intrafirm integration and rewards, *Academy of Management Review*, 28: 479–493.

67. 2003, AOL, Microsoft vow messaging cooperation, *New York Times*, www.nytimes.com, June 4.

68. 2008, The Canadian Financial System, Canada's Chartered Banks Web site, Government of Canada, Department of Finance, http://www.fin.gc.ca/toce/1995/fctshtsum95-e.html, retrieved January 27.

69. G. K. Price & J. M. Connor, 2003, Modeling coupon values for ready-to-eat breakfast cereals, *Agribusiness*, 19(2): 223–244; G. K. Price, 2000, Cereal sales soggy despite price cuts and reduced couponing, *Food Review*, 23(2): 21–28.

70. S. B. Garland & A. Reinhardt, 1999, Making antitrust fit high tech, *BusinessWeek*, March 22, 34–36.

71. E. G. Rogoff & H. S. Guirguis, 2002, Legalized price-fixing, *Forbes*, December 9, 48.

72. J. B. Barney, 2007, *Gaining and Sustaining Competitive Advantage* (3rd ed.), Upper Saddle River, NJ: Pearson, Prentice-Hall, 287.

73. Jacobides, Industry change through vertical disintegrations; Dussauge, Garrette, & Mitchell, Asymmetric performance.

74. 2008, The Airline Blog, http://theairlineblog.blogspot.com/2008_01_01_archive.html, retrieved January 27; 2005, Northwest could lose its lucrative pact with KLM, Wall Street Journal Online, www.wsj.com, July 18; 2003, Who gains if United should die? *The Economist*, May 10, 56.

75. Leahy & Pavelin, Follow-my-leader and tacit collusion.

76. Harrison, Hitt, Hoskisson, & Ireland, Resource complementarity, 684–685; S. Chaudhuri & B. Tabrizi, 1999, Capturing the real value in high-tech acquisitions, *Harvard Business Review*, 77(5): 123–130.

77. A. E. Bernardo & B. Chowdhry, 2002, Resources, real options, and corporate strategy, *Journal of Financial Economics*, 63: 211–234; Inkpen, Strategic alliances, 413.

78. J. L. Johnson, R. P.-W. Lee, A. Saini, & B. Grohmann, 2003, Market-focused strategic flexibility: Conceptual advances and an integrative model, *Academy of Marketing Science Journal*, 31: 74–90; Young-Ybarra & Wiersema, Strategic flexibility, 439.

79. Folta & Miller, Real options in equity partnerships, 77.

80. A. R. Sorkin, 2005, Bid by Chevron in big oil deal thwarts China, *New York Times*, www.nytimes.com, July 20; 2005, Shell may discourage CNOOC from purchasing American Unocal, *China Chemical Reporter*, www.highbeam.com, March 6; 2002, CNOOC adds petrochemicals to downstream strategy, *Petroleum Economist*, December, 39.

81. Ibid.

82. A. Goerzen & P. W. Beamish, 2005, The effect of alliance network diversity on multinational enterprise performance, *Strategic Management Journal*, 333–354.

83. M. V. Shyam Kumar, 2005, The value from acquiring and divesting a joint venture: A real options approach, *Strategic Management Journal*, 26: 321–331.

84. J. Yang, 2003, One step forward for Japan's chipmakers, Business Week Online, www.businessweek.com, July 7.

85. 2008, Knet Web site, http://media.knet.ca/node/2425, retrieved January 27; 2008, Loral Skynet Web site, http://www.loralskynet.com/pdf/Telesat-Loral-Closed-FINAL.pdf, retrieved January 27.

86. J. G. Combs & D. J. Ketchen Jr., 2003, Why do firms use franchising as an entrepreneurial strategy? A meta-analysis, *Journal of Management*, 29: 427–443.

87. F. Lafontaine, 1999, Myths and strengths of franchising, "Mastering Strategy" (Part Nine), *Financial Times*, November 22, 8–10.

88. 2005, 7-Eleven, Inc., www.entrepreneur.com, July 28; J. Wilgoren, 2003, In the urban 7-Eleven, the Slurpee looks sleeker, *New York Times*, www.nytimes.com, July 13.

89. 2008, Couche-Tard Web page, http://www.couche-tard.com/index.php?module=CMS&func=view&id=31; 2008, Circle-K Web site, http://www.circlek.com/CircleK/AboutUs/AroundTheWorld.htm; 2008, CIA Factbook, Canada, https://www.cia.gov/library/publications/the-world-factbook/print/ca.html; 2008, CIA Factbook, Japan, https://www.cia.gov/library/publications/the-world-factbook/print/ja.html; 2008, CIA Factbook, US, https://www.cia.gov/library/publications/the-world-factbook/print/us.html; all Web sites retrieved January 28.

90. S. C. Michael, 2002, Can a franchise chain coordinate? *Journal of Business Venturing*, 17: 325–342.

91. M. Gerstenhaber, 2000, Franchises can teach us about customer care, *Marketing*, March 16, 18.

92. P. J. Kaufmann & S. Eroglu, 1999, Standardization and adaptation in business format franchising, *Journal of Business Venturing*, 14: 69–85.

93. S. C. Michael, 2002, First mover advantage through franchising, *Journal of Business Venturing*, 18: 61–81.

94. Barney, *Gaining and Sustaining Competitive Advantage*, 110–111.

95. M. Zollo, J. J. Reuer, & H. Singh, 2002, Interorganizational routines and performance in strategic alliances, *Organization Science*, 13: 701–714.

96. Ireland, Hitt, & Vaidyanath, Alliance management.

97. P. Almeida, G. Dokko, & L. Rosenkopf, 2003, Startup size and the mechanisms of external learning: Increasing opportunity and decreasing ability? *Research Policy,* 32(2): 301–316; B. L. Simonin, 1997, The importance of collaborative know-how: An empirical test of the learning organization, *Academy of Management Journal,* 40: 1150–1174.

98. H. Timmons, 2003, BP signs deal with Russian firm for venture in oil and gas, *New York Times,* June 27, W1.

99. R. Narula & G. Duysters, 2004, Globalization and trends in international R&D alliances, *Journal of International Management,* 10: 199–218; M. A. Hitt, M. T. Dacin, E. Levitas, J.-L. Arregle, & A. Borza, 2000, Partner selection in emerging and developed market contexts: Resource-based and organizational learning perspectives, *Academy of Management Journal,* 43: 449–467.

100. D. Kovaleski, 2003, More firms shaking hands on strategic partnership agreements, *Pensions & Investments,* February 3, 20; A. L. Velocci Jr., 2001, U.S.–Euro strategic alliances will outpace company mergers, *Aviation Week & Space Technology,* 155(23): 56.

101. S. Hamm, 2005, IBM discovers the power of one, *BusinessWeek,* February 14, 80; D. Clark & R. A. Guth, 2005, Sony, IBM, Toshiba to offer first peek of "Cell" chip design, *Wall Street Journal,* February 7, B1; 2005, IBM, Sony, Sony Computer Entertainment Inc., and Toshiba disclose key details of the Cell chip, press release, Sony Corporation, February 7; D. Hug, 2004, IBM, Sony, SCEI, and Toshiba to unveil next-generation cell processor, *JCNN News Summaries,* December 1.

102. I. M. Manev, 2003, The managerial network in a multinational enterprise and the resource profiles of subsidiaries, *Journal of International Management,* 9: 133–152; M. A. Hitt, R. E. Hoskisson, & H. Kim, 1997, International diversification: Effects on innovation and firm performance in product diversified firms, *Academy of Management Journal,* 40: 767–798.

103. H. K. Steensma, L. Tihanyi, M. A. Lyles, & C. Dhanaraj, 2005, The evolving value of foreign partnerships in transitioning economies, *Academy of Management Journal,* 48: 213–235; L. Nachum & D. Keeble, 2003, MNE linkages and localized clusters: Foreign and indigenous firms in the media cluster of Central London, *Journal of International Management,* 9: 171–192.

104. 2005, Tiger Woods leads the charge for Nike Golf as an outstanding year unfolds, Yahoo! Finance, biz.yahoo.com, July 18; C. Noon, 2005, Armstrong, sets the pace in the Alps, Forbes.com, July 15; S. Holmes, 2003, The real Nike news is happening abroad, BusinessWeek Online, www.businessweek.com, July 21.

105. Y. Luo, O. Shenkar, & M.-K. Nyaw, 2002, Mitigating the liabilities of foreignness: Defensive versus offensive approaches, *Journal of International Management,* 8: 283–300.

106. S. R. Miller & A. Parkhe, 2002, Is there a liability of foreignness in global banking? An empirical test of banks' x-efficiency, *Strategic Management Journal,* 23: 55–75; Y. Luo, 2001, Determinants of local responsiveness: Perspectives from foreign subsidiaries in an emerging market, *Journal of Management,* 27: 451–477.

107. J. E. Oxley & R. C. Sampson, 2004, The scope and governance of international R&D alliances, *Strategic Management Journal,* 25: 723–749.

108. S. Holmes, 2003, For Starbucks, there's no place like home, BusinessWeek Online, www.businessweek.com, June 9.

109. H. J. Teegen & J. P. Doh, 2002, US–Mexican alliance negotiations: Impact of culture on authority, trust, performance, *Thunderbird International Business Review,* 44(6): 749–775; P. Ghemawat, 2001, Distance matters: The hard reality of global expansion, *Harvard Business Review,* 79(8): 137–147.

110. J. K. Sebenius, 2002, The hidden challenge of cross-border negotiations, *Harvard Business Review,* 80(3): 76–85.

111. Z. Zhao, J. Anand, & W. Mitchell, 2005, A dual networks perspective on interorganizational transfer of R&D capabilities: International joint ventures in the Chinese automotive industry, *Journal of Management Studies,* 42: 127–160.

112. C. B. Copp & R. L. Ivy, 2001, Networking trends of small tourism businesses in Post-Socialist Slovakia, *Journal of Small Business Management,* 39: 345–353.

113. E. Beauchesne, 2004, TD predicts solid growth for Ottawa, *The Ottawa Citizen,* January 16, E3; W. Hanley, 1999, Growing up in Silicon Delta . . . , *National Post,* November 24, D1; S. S. Cohen & G. Fields, 1999, Social capital and capital gains in Silicon Valley, *California Management Review,* 41(2): 108–130; M. E. Porter, 1998, Clusters and the new economics of competition, *Harvard Business Review,* 78(6):

77–90; R. Pouder & C. H. St. John, 1996, Hot spots and blind spots: Geographical clusters of firms and innovation, *Academy of Management Review,* 21: 1192–1225.

114. M. Ferrary, 2003, Managing the disruptive technologies life cycle by externalising the research: Social network and corporate venturing in the Silicon Valley, *International Journal of Technology Management,* 25(1,2): 165–180; S. S. Cohen & G. Fields, 1999, Social capital and capital gains in Silicon Valley, *California Management Review,* 41(2): 108–130; J. A. Matthews, 1999, A silicon island of the east: Creating a semiconductor industry in Singapore, *California Management Review,* 41(2): 55–78.

115. A. C. Cooper, 2002, Networks, alliances, and entrepreneurship, in M. A. Hitt, R. D. Ireland, S. M. Camp, & D. L. Sexton (eds.), *Strategic Entrepreneurship: Creating a New Mindset,* Oxford, UK: Blackwell Publishers, 203–222.

116. G. G. Bell, 2005, Clusters, networks, and firm innovativeness, *Strategic Management Journal,* 26: 287–295.

117. A. Echols & W. Tsai, 2005, Niche and performance: The moderating role of network embeddedness, *Strategic Management Journal,* 26: 219–238; S. Chung & G. M. Kim, 2003, Performance effects of partnership between manufacturers and suppliers for new product development: The supplier's standpoint, *Research Policy,* 32: 587–604.

118. H. Kim, R. E. Hoskisson, & W. P. Wan, 2004, Power, dependence, diversification strategy and performance in keiretsu member firms, *Strategic Management Journal,* 25: 613–636.

119. R. S. Cline, 2001, Partnering for strategic alliances, *Lodging Hospitality,* 57(9): 42.

120. M. Rudberg & J. Olhager, 2003, Manufacturing networks and supply chains: An operations strategy perspective, *Omega,* 31(1): 29–39.

121. G. J. Young, M. P. Charns, & S. M. Shortell, 2001, Top manager and network effects on the adoption of innovative management practices: A study of TQM in a public hospital system, *Strategic Management Journal,* 22: 935–951.

122. E. Garcia-Canal, C. L. Duarte, J. R. Criado, & A. V. Llaneza, 2002, Accelerating international expansion through global alliances: A typology of cooperative strategies, *Journal of World Business,* 37(2): 91–107; F. T. Rothaermel, 2001, Complementary assets, strategic alliances, and the incumbent's advantage: An empirical study of industry and firm effects in the biopharmaceutical industry, *Research Policy,* 30: 1235–1251.

123. V. Shankar & B. L. Bayus, 2003, Network effects and competition: An empirical analysis of the home video game industry, *Strategic Management Journal,* 24: 375–384.

124. B. Duncan, 2003, Five steps to successful strategic partnering, *Information Week,* www.informationweek.com, July 21.

125. Z. Simsek, M. H. Lubatkin, & D. Kandemir, 2003, Inter-firm networks and entrepreneurial behavior: A structural embeddedness perspective, *Journal of Management,* 29: 401–426; H. W. Volberda, C. Baden-Fuller, & F. A. J. van den Bosch, 2001, Mastering strategic renewal: Mobilising renewal journeys in multi-unit firms, *Long Range Planning,* 34(2): 159–178.

126. King, Covin, & Hegarty, Complementary resources and the exploitation of technological innovations.

127. A. I. Goldberg, G. Cohen, & A. Fiegenbaum, 2003, Reputation building: Small business strategies for successful venture development, *Journal of Small Business Management,* 41(2): 168–186; S. Das, P. K. Sen, & S. Sengupta, 2003, Strategic alliances: A valuable way to manage intellectual capital? *Journal of Intellectual Capital,* 4(1): 10–19.

128. D. C. Hambrick, J. Li, K. Xin, & A. S. Tsui, 2001, Compositional gaps and downward spirals in international joint venture management groups, *Strategic Management Journal,* 22: 1033–1053; T. K. Das & B.-S. Teng, 2000, Instabilities of strategic alliances: An internal tensions perspective, *Organization Science,* 11: 77–101.

129. Ireland, Hitt, & Vaidyanath, Alliance management; A. Madhok & S. B. Tallman, 1998, Resources, transactions and rents: Managing value through interfirm collaborative relationships, *Organization Science,* 9: 326–339.

130. D. De Cremer & D. van Knippenberg, 2002, How do leaders promote cooperation? The effects of charisma and procedural fairness, *Journal of Applied Psychology,* 87: 858–867.

131. S.-O. Cheung, T. S. T. Ng, S.-P. Wong, & H. C. H. Suen, 2003, Behavioral aspects in construction partnering, *International Journal of Project Management,* 21: 333–344.

132. P. M. Norman, 2002, Protecting knowledge in strategic alliances—Resource and relational characteristics, *Journal of High Technology Management Research,* 13(2):

177–202; P. M. Norman, 2001, Are your secrets safe? Knowledge protection in strategic alliances, *Business Horizons,* November/December, 51–60.

133. M. A. Hitt, M. T. Dacin, B. B. Tyler, & D. Park, 1997, Understanding the differences in Korean and U.S. executives strategic orientations, *Strategic Management Journal,* 18: 159–168.

134. N. Wingfield & P.-W. Tam, 2005, H-P to stop reselling iPods, unwinding a high-profile deal, Wall Street Journal Online, www.wsj.com, July 29.

135. R. Abratt & P. Motlana, 2002, Managing co-branding strategies: Global brands into local markets, *Business Horizons,* 45(5): 43–50; P. Lane, J. E. Salk, & M. A. Lyles, 2001, Absorptive capacity, learning, and performance in international joint ventures, *Strategic Management Journal,* 22: 1139–1161.

136. I. Fried & J. Borland, 2006, Walt Disney announced Tuesday that it's paying $7.4 billion in stock to acquire Pixar Animation Studios—A deal that puts Apple Computer CEO Steve Jobs on Disney's board of directors, CNET News.com, January 24, http://www.news.com/2100-1026_3-6030607.html, retrieved January 2008; R. Grover, 2003, Is Steve about to move his cheese? *BusinessWeek,* February 10, 72.

137. R. Larsson, K. R. Brousseau, M. J. Driver, & M. Homqvist, 2003, International growth through cooperation: Brand-driven strategies, leadership, and career development in Sweden, *Academy of Management Executive,* 17(1): 7–21; R. Larsson, L. Bengtsson, K. Henriksson, & J. Sparks, 1998, The interorganizational learning dilemma: Collective knowledge development in strategic alliances, *Organization Science,* 9: 285–305.

138. Ireland, Hitt, & Vaidyanath, Alliance management.

139. J. H. Dyer, P. Kale, & H. Singh, 2001, How to make strategic alliances work, *MIT Sloan Management Review,* 42(4): 37–43.

140. J. H. Dyer, 1997, Effective interfirm collaboration: How firms minimize transaction costs and maximize transaction value, *Strategic Management Journal,* 18: 535–556.

141. J. H. Dyer & C. Wujin, 2003, The role of trustworthiness in reducing transaction costs and improving performance: Empirical evidence from the United States, Japan, and Korea, *Organization Science,* 14: 57–69.

142. 2003, Sony Ericsson venture to close sites and cut 500 jobs, *New York Times,* www.nytimes.com, June 25; J. L. Schenker, 2003, Sony Ericsson posts loss despite sales gain, *New York Times,* www.nytimes.com, July 16.

143. Hutt, Stafford, Walker, & Reingen, Case study: Defining the social network, 53.

144. D. L. Ferrin & K. T. Dirks, 2003, The use of rewards to increase and decrease trust: Mediating processes and differential effects, *Organization Science,* 14(1): 18–31; D. F. Jennings, K. Artz, L. M. Gillin, & C. Christodouloy, 2000, Determinants of trust in global strategic alliances: Amrad and the Australian biomedical industry, *Competitiveness Review,* 10(1): 25–44.

145. V. Perrone, A. Zaheer, & B. McEvily, 2003, Free to be trusted? Boundary constraints on trust in boundary spanners, *Organization Science,* 14: 422–439; H. K. Steensma, L. Marino, & K. M. Weaver, 2000, Attitudes toward cooperative strategies: A cross-cultural analysis of entrepreneurs, *Journal of International Business Studies,* 31: 591–609.

146. Inkpen and Tsang, Social capital; L. Huff & L. Kelley, 2003, Levels of organizational trust in individualist versus collectivist societies: A seven-nation study, *Organization Science,* 14(1): 81–90.

147. Dyer & Wujin, The role of trustworthiness in reducing transaction costs and improving performance.

148. J. H. Davis, F. D. Schoorman, R. C. Mayer, & H. H. Tan, 2000, The trusted general manager and business unit performance: Empirical evidence of a competitive advantage, *Strategic Management Journal,* 21: 563–576.

149. B. Hillebrand & W. G. Biemans, 2003, The relationship between internal and external cooperation: Literature review and propositions, *Journal of Business Research,* 56: 735–744.

150. K. Lim, 2005, CapitaLand will boost its presence in China, Wall Street Journal Online, www.wsj.com, July 11.

Part Three

Strategic Actions: Strategy Implementation

3

Chapter Eleven

Corporate Governance

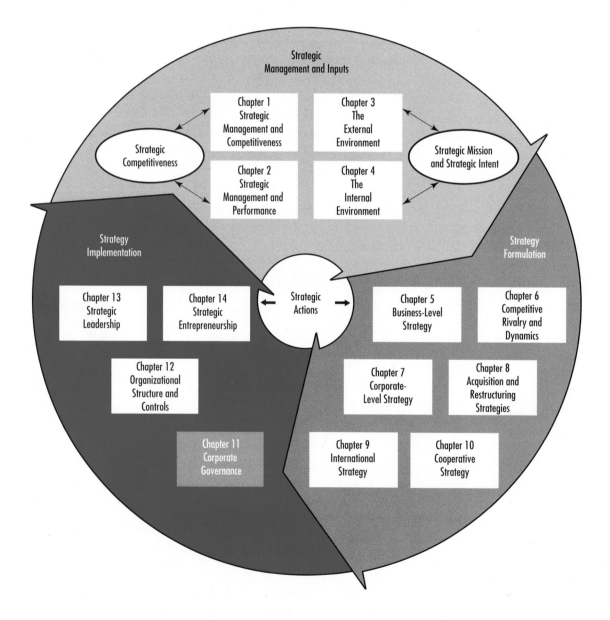

Knowledge Objectives

Studying this chapter should provide you with the strategic management knowledge needed to:

1. Define corporate governance and explain why it is used to monitor and control managers' strategic decisions.

2. Explain why ownership has been largely separated from managerial control in the modern corporation.

3. Define an agency relationship and managerial opportunism and describe their strategic implications.

4. Explain how three internal governance mechanisms—ownership concentration, the board of directors, and executive compensation—are used to monitor and control managerial decisions.

5. Discuss the types of compensation executives receive and their effects on strategic decisions.

6. Describe how the external corporate governance mechanism—the market for corporate control—acts as a restraint on top-level managers' strategic decisions.

7. Discuss the use of corporate governance in international settings.

8. Describe how corporate governance fosters ethical strategic decisions and the importance of such behaviours on the part of top-level executives.

Sentenced for Poor Corporate Governance

Following a four-month criminal trial, Conrad Black—the Canadian-born member of the British House of Lords—stood before a federal judge on December 10, 2007 in Chicago to receive his 6.5-year prison sentence and his $125,000 fine.

www.macleans.ca

Conrad Black's primary conviction was for "swindling" shareholders of his former Hollinger International newspaper group out of money. Black had been Chairman of the Hollinger media conglomerate, but was forced to resign after an internal committee found that non-compete payments which should have gone to his company were made to Black and others without proper approval or authorization. According to *Maclean's* magazine, this went on for some time due to Black's "convoluted pretzel" of a corporate structure, which was "designed to make the internal money trail virtually impossible to follow."

Through the Canadian holding company Ravelston Corporation Limited, Hollinger International paid Black and his senior executives US$203 million during 1995 to 2002, making Black's compensation more than that of the CEOs of the *New York Times,* the *Washington Post,* and the *Chicago Tribune* combined.

Speaking directly to Conrad Black, the federal judge said on December 10, "I frankly cannot understand how somebody of your stature—on top of the media empire that you were on top of—could engage in the conduct that you engaged in, and put everything at risk, including your reputation and your integrity."

Black may have had regrets for breaking the law, or he might have been remorseful about getting caught. However, Black may have simply viewed his monetary shenanigans as a cat and mouse game with his fellow shareholders. One in which he simply lost out to people who were more interested and angrier than he had expected. Black admitted that he had "clearly misjudged the strength of the corporate governance movement."

SOURCE: 2007, Conrad Black quick facts, *Saint John Telegraph-Journal,* December 11; 2003, Conrad Black's fall, *Maclean's,* December 1; 2007, Conrad Black's shabby downfall, *Fortune,* December 11; 2007, Conrad Black vows he'll be back, CBC News, November 30.

As the Opening Case illustrates, control over executive compensation is an increasingly important part of the strategic management process.[1] If the board makes the wrong decision in compensating the firm's strategic leader (e.g., CEO), or, in the case of Hollinger International, is unaware, shareholders and the firm suffer. Compensation is used to motivate CEOs to act in the best interests of the firm—in particular, the shareholders. When they do so, the firm's value should increase.

What are a CEO's actions worth? The Opening Case suggests that they are increasingly worth a significant amount. However, some research suggests that firms with a smaller pay gap between the CEO and other top executives perform better, especially when collaboration among top management team members is more important.[2] The performance improvement is attributed to better cooperation among the top management team members. Other research suggests that CEOs receive excessive compensation when corporate governance is the weakest,[3] as was the case with Hollinger International.

Corporate governance is the set of mechanisms used to manage the relationships among stakeholders that is used to determine and control the strategic direction and performance of organizations.[4] At its core, corporate governance is concerned with identifying ways to ensure that strategic decisions are made effectively.[5] Governance can also be thought of as a means corporations use to establish order between parties (the firm's owners and its top-level managers) whose interests may conflict. Thus, corporate governance reflects and enforces the company's values.[6] In modern corporations, a primary objective of corporate governance is to ensure that the interests of top-level managers are aligned with the interests of the shareholders. This was a lesson learned by Henry Ford in 1916.[7]

Ford believed that he should pay his workers well and reward customers with annual price cuts. Of course, this meant fewer dividends to pay out to shareholders. Two of his shareholders were the brothers John Dodge and Horace Dodge. John was also a member of the board of directors. They were ambitious, and John quit the board so they could develop their own car company. Their idea was to finance their car company using the quarterly dividends they earned on their shares in Ford. Their plans were derailed when Ford stopped paying dividends in order to proceed with further price reductions for his customers. The Dodge brothers sued Ford, arguing that profits belonged to shareholders and that it was not Ford's right to give profits to customers in the form of price reductions. The judge in the case agreed and reinstated the dividend. In addition, he rebuked Ford for forgetting that "a business corporation is organized and carried on primarily for the profit of the stockholders." The judge further stated that an organization could not be operated "for the merely incidental benefit of shareholders and for the primary purpose of benefiting others."[8]

According to Joel Bakan in his classic book *The Corporation*, the ruling in the *Dodge versus Ford* case "still stands for the legal principle that managers and directors have a legal duty to put shareholders' interests above all others and no legal authority to serve any other interests—what has become known as 'the best interests of the corporation principle.'" This principle, now fixed in the corporate laws of most countries such as Canada, the United States, and the United Kingdom, compels senior managers and members of boards of directors to act in the best interests of the organization, especially its owners—that is, its shareholders.[9]

Since the famous *Dodge versus Ford* case, corporate governance has come to involve oversight in areas where owners, managers, and members of boards of directors may have conflicts of interest. These areas include the election of directors, the general supervision of CEO pay (like in the Conrad Black case) and more focused supervision of director pay, and the corporation's overall structure and strategic direction.[10]

Corporate governance has been emphasized in recent years because, as the Opening Case illustrates, corporate governance mechanisms occasionally fail to adequately monitor and control senior managers' decisions. This situation has resulted in changes in

Corporate governance is the set of mechanisms used to manage the relationship among stakeholders that is used to determine and control the strategic direction and performance of organizations.

governance mechanisms in corporations throughout the world, especially with respect to efforts intended to improve the performance of boards of directors. These changes often cause confusion about the proper role of the board. According to one observer, "Depending on the company, you get very different perspectives: Some boards are settling for checking the boxes on compliance regulations, while others are thinking about changing the fundamental way they govern, and some worry that they've gotten themselves into micromanaging the CEO and company. There's a fair amount of turmoil and collective searching going on."[11] A second and more positive reason for this interest is that evidence suggests that a well-functioning corporate governance and control system can create a competitive advantage for an individual firm.[12] For example, one governance mechanism—the board of directors—has been suggested to be rapidly evolving into a major strategic force in business.[13] Thus, in this chapter, we describe actions designed to implement strategies that focus on monitoring and controlling mechanisms, which can help to ensure that top-level managerial actions contribute to the firm's strategic competitiveness and its ability to earn above-average returns.

Effective corporate governance is also of interest to nations.[14] As stated by one scholar, "Every country wants the firms that operate within its borders to flourish and grow in such ways as to provide employment, wealth, and satisfaction, not only to improve standards of living materially but also to enhance social cohesion. These aspirations cannot be met unless those firms are competitive internationally in a sustained way, and it is this medium- and long-term perspective that makes good corporate governance so vital."[15]

Unethical behaviour at Bre-X Minerals Ltd, a Calgary-based mining company, impacted more than just its firm and its direct shareholders. In the 1990s Bre-X reported that it had discovered a large deposit of gold in Indonesia, and this had an unprecedented impact on its stock price: originally a penny stock, Bre-X eventually climbed to $286.50 on the Toronto Stock Exchange (TSX) and achieved a market capitalization of over C$6 billion.[16]

However, Bre-X's gold find in Indonesia turned out to be the "most elaborate fraud in the history of mining."[17] Crushed samples had been falsified by "salting" with real gold. This deceitful act was revealed in 1997, and Bre-X had to face a number of very angry investors who had lost billions—and, of course, the many lawsuits that followed.[18] Some investors, like the Ontario Teachers' Pension Plan, lost up to $100 million from this fraudulent behaviour. Bre-X also may have compromised the reputation of the entire Toronto Stock Exchange, as John Carson, senior vice president for market regulation at the Toronto exchange, suggested it would "take time for Canada to regain its credibility in the prospecting business" as a result of Bre-X's behaviour.[19]

Corporate governance, then, reflects company standards, which in turn collectively reflect societal standards.[20] In many corporations, shareholders hold top-level managers accountable for their decisions and the results these decisions generate. As with these firms and their boards, nations that effectively govern their corporations may gain a competitive advantage over rival countries. Today, the fundamental goal for most businesses is to maximize shareholder value.[21] Traditionally, shareholders are treated as the firm's key stakeholders, because they are the company's legal owners. The firm's owners expect top-level managers and others influencing the corporation's actions (for example, the board of directors) to make decisions that will result in the maximization of the company's value and, hence, of the owners' wealth.[22]

In the first section of this chapter, we describe the relationship that is the foundation on which the modern corporation is built: the relationship between owners and managers. The majority of this chapter is used to explain various mechanisms owners use to govern managers and to ensure that they comply with their responsibility to maximize shareholder value. Three internal governance mechanisms and a single external one are used in the modern corporation. The three internal governance mechanisms we describe in this chapter are (1) ownership concentration, as represented by types of shareholders and their different incentives to monitor managers; (2) the board of directors; and (3) executive compensation. We then consider the market for corporate control, an external corporate governance mechanism. Essentially, this market is a set of potential owners seeking to acquire undervalued firms and earn above-average returns on their investments by replacing ineffective top-level management teams.[23]

The chapter's focus then shifts to the issue of international corporate governance. We outline the differences between governance approaches in Canada compared to the United States. This discussion suggests that, in part due to globalization, the structures used to govern global companies in many different countries—including Germany, Japan, the United Kingdom, the United States, and Canada—are becoming more, rather than less, similar.

Closing our analysis of corporate governance is a consideration of the need for these control mechanisms to encourage and support ethical behaviour in organizations. Importantly, the mechanisms discussed in this chapter can positively influence the governance of the modern corporation, which has placed significant responsibility and authority in the hands of top-level managers. The most effective managers understand their accountability for the firm's performance and respond positively to corporate governance mechanisms.[24] In addition, the firm's owners should not expect any single mechanism to remain effective over time. Rather, the use of several mechanisms allows owners to govern the corporation in ways that maximize strategic competitiveness and increase the financial value of their firm. With multiple governance mechanisms operating simultaneously, however, it is also possible for some of the governance mechanisms to be in conflict.[25] Later, we review how these conflicts can occur.

Separation of Ownership and Managerial Control

Historically, North American firms have been managed by the founder-owners and their descendants. In these cases, corporate ownership and control resided in the same persons. As firms grew larger, "the managerial revolution led to a separation of ownership and control in most large corporations, where control of the firm shifted from entrepreneurs to professional managers while ownership became dispersed among thousands of unorganized stockholders who were removed from the day-to-day management of the firm."[26] These changes created the modern public corporation, which is based on the efficient separation of ownership and managerial control. Supporting the separation is a basic legal premise suggesting that the primary objective of a firm's activities is to increase the corporation's profit and, thereby, the financial gains of the owners (the shareholders).[27]

The separation of ownership and managerial control allows shareholders to purchase stock, which entitles them to income (residual returns) from the firm's operations after paying expenses. This right, however, requires that they also take a risk that the firm's expenses may exceed its revenues. To manage this investment risk, shareholders maintain a diversified portfolio by investing in several companies to reduce their overall risk.[28] The idea is that poor performance or failure of any one firm in which they invest has less overall effect on their personal wealth. To summarize, this means that shareholders, especially dispersed shareholders, specialize in managing their investment risk and not in managing the corporation.

On the other hand, in small firms, managers often are high-percentage owners, so there is less separation between ownership and managerial control. In fact, there are a large number of family-owned firms in which ownership and managerial control are not separated. In terms of choosing a CEO for a family-owned firm, research suggests that firm performance is better when a member of the family is the CEO than when the CEO is an outsider.[29] In many countries, such as Latin America, Asia, some European countries, and even Canada, family-owned firms represent the dominant form.[30] When compared to the U.S., Canada has a larger concentration of corporate ownership, and a higher percentage of family-based businesses.[31] In 2007, a study reported in the *Toronto Star* suggested that family businesses in Canada generate 55 percent of the nation's GDP.[32] The primary purpose of most of these firms is to increase the family's wealth, which explains why a family CEO often is better than an outside CEO.[33]

There are at least two critical issues for family-controlled firms. First, as they grow, they may not have access to all of the skills needed to effectively manage the firm and maximize its returns for the family. Thus, they may need outsiders. Also as they grow, they may need to seek outside capital and thus give up some of the ownership. In these cases, protection of the minority owners' rights becomes important.[34] To avoid these potential problems, when these firms grow and become more complex their owner-managers may contract with managerial specialists. These managers make major decisions in the owner's firm and are compensated on the basis of their decision-making skills. As decision-making specialists, managers are agents of the firm's owners and are expected to use their skills to operate the owners' firm in ways that will maximize the return on their investment.[35]

Without owner (shareholder) specialization in risk bearing and management specialization in decision making, a firm may be limited by the abilities of its owners to manage and make effective strategic decisions. Thus, the separation and specialization of ownership (risk bearing) and managerial control (decision making) should produce the highest returns for the firm's owners.

Agency Relationships

An **agency relationship** exists when one or more persons (the principal or principals) hire another person or persons (the agent or agents) as decision-making specialists to perform a service.

The separation between owners and managers creates an agency relationship. An **agency relationship** exists when one or more persons (the principal or principals) hire another person or persons (the agent or agents) as decision-making specialists to perform a service.[36] Thus, an agency relationship exists when one party delegates decision-making responsibility to a second party for compensation (see Figure 11.1).[37] In addition to

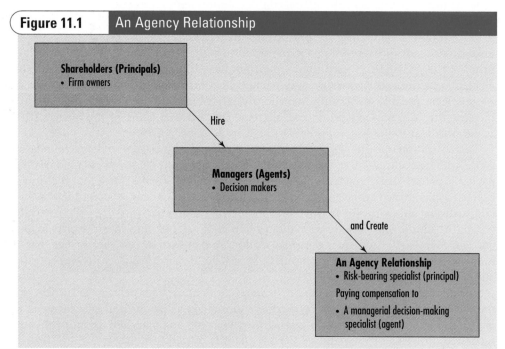

Figure 11.1 An Agency Relationship

Shareholders (Principals)
• Firm owners

Hire

Managers (Agents)
• Decision makers

and Create

An Agency Relationship
• Risk-bearing specialist (principal)

Paying compensation to

• A managerial decision-making specialist (agent)

shareholders and top executives, other examples of agency relationships are consultants and clients and insured and insurer. Moreover, within organizations an agency relationship exists between managers and their employees, as well as between the firm's owners and top executives.[38] In the modern corporation, managers must understand the links between these relationships and the firm's effectiveness.[39] Although the agency relationship between managers and their employees is important, in this chapter we focus on the agency relationship between the firm's owners (the principals) and top-level managers (the principals' agents), because this relationship is related directly to how the firm's strategies are implemented.

The separation between ownership and managerial control can be problematic. Research evidence documents a variety of agency problems in the modern corporation.[40] Problems can surface because the principal and the agent have different interests and goals, or because shareholders lack direct control of large publicly traded corporations. Problems also arise when an agent makes decisions that result in the pursuit of goals that conflict with those of the principals. Thus, the separation of ownership and control potentially allows divergent interests (between principals and agents) to surface, which can lead to managerial opportunism.

Managerial opportunism is the seeking of self-interest with guile (i.e., cunning or deceit).[41] Opportunism is both an attitude (e.g., an inclination) and a set of behaviours (i.e., specific acts of self-interest).[42] It is not possible for principals to know beforehand which agents will or will not act opportunistically. The reputations of top executives are an imperfect predictor, and opportunistic behaviour cannot be observed until it has occurred. Thus, principals establish governance and control mechanisms to prevent agents from acting opportunistically, even though only a few are likely to do so.[43] Any time that principals delegate decision-making responsibilities to agents, the opportunity for conflicts of interest exists. Top executives, for example, may make strategic decisions that maximize their personal welfare and minimize their personal risk.[44] Decisions such as these prevent the maximization of shareholder wealth. Decisions regarding product diversification demonstrate these possibilities.

Managerial opportunism is the seeking of self-interest with guile (i.e., cunning or deceit).

Product Diversification as an Example of an Agency Problem

As explained in Chapter 7, a corporate-level strategy to diversify the firm's product lines can enhance a firm's strategic competitiveness and increase its returns, both of which serve the interests of shareholders and the top executives. However, product diversification to a greater degree than necessary can result in two benefits to managers that shareholders do not enjoy, so top executives may prefer a greater degree of product diversification more than shareholders do.[45]

First, diversification usually increases the size of a firm, and size is positively related to executive compensation. Also, diversification increases the complexity of managing a firm and its network of businesses and may thus require more pay because of this complexity.[46] Thus, increased product diversification provides an opportunity for top executives to increase their compensation.[47]

Second, product diversification and the resulting diversification of the firm's portfolio of businesses can reduce top executives' employment risk. Managerial employment risk is the risk of job loss, loss of compensation, and loss of managerial reputation.[48] These risks are reduced with increased diversification, because a firm and its upper-level managers are less vulnerable to the reduction in demand associated with a single or limited number of product lines or businesses. This greater than necessary diversification may reduce the firm's ability to generate above-average returns.

Another concern that may represent an agency problem is a firm's free cash flows, over which top executives have control. Free cash flows are defined as that cash and/or access to cash that is available to the firm after the firm has invested in all projects that have a positive net present value within its current businesses.[49] In anticipation of positive returns, managers may decide to invest these funds in products that are not associated with the firm's current lines of business to increase the firm's level of diversification. The managerial decision to use free cash flows to diversify the firm beyond the level necessary for best returns to its owners is an example of self-serving and opportunistic managerial behaviour. In contrast to managers, shareholders may prefer that free cash flows be distributed to them as dividends, so they can control how the cash is invested.[50] And, of course, this level of diversification adds a second level of diversification to a shareholder's portfolio that is even more expensive than the first level of diversification available to shareholders when they diversify their stock portfolio as mentioned earlier.

Curve *S* in Figure 11.2 depicts the shareholders' optimal level of diversification. Owners seek the level of diversification that reduces the risk of the firm's total failure while simultaneously increasing the company's value through the development of economies of scale and scope (see Chapter 7). Of the four corporate-level diversification strategies shown in Figure 11.2, shareholders likely prefer the diversified position noted by point *A* on curve *S*—a position that is located between the dominant business and related-constrained diversification strategies. Of course, the optimum level of diversification owners seek varies from firm to firm.[51] Factors that affect shareholders' preferences include the firm's primary industry, the intensity of rivalry among competitors in that industry, and the top management team's experience with implementing diversification strategies.

As do principals, upper-level executives—as agents—also seek an optimal level of diversification. Declining performance resulting from too much product diversification increases the probability that corporate control of the firm will be acquired in the market. After a firm is acquired, the employment risk for the firm's top executives increases substantially. Furthermore, a manager's employment opportunities in the external managerial labour market (discussed in Chapter 13) are affected negatively by a firm's poor performance. Therefore, top executives prefer diversification, but not to a

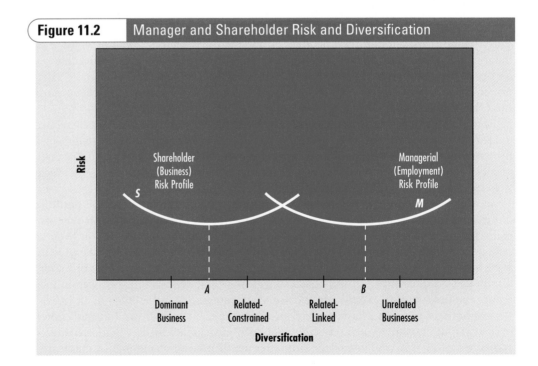

Figure 11.2   Manager and Shareholder Risk and Diversification

point that it increases their employment risk and reduces their employment opportunities.[52] Curve *M* in Figure 11.2 shows that executives prefer higher levels of product diversification than do shareholders. Top executives might prefer the level of diversification shown by point *B* on curve *M*.

In general, shareholders prefer riskier strategies and more focused diversification. They reduce their risk through holding a diversified portfolio of equity investments. Alternatively, managers obviously cannot balance their employment risk by working for a diverse portfolio of firms. Therefore, top executives may prefer a level of diversification that maximizes firm size and their compensation and that reduces their employment risk. Product diversification, therefore, is a potential agency problem that could result in principals incurring costs to control their agents' behaviours.

Agency Costs and Governance Mechanisms

The potential conflict illustrated by Figure 11.2, coupled with the fact that principals do not know which managers might act opportunistically, demonstrates why principals establish governance mechanisms. However, the firm incurs costs when it uses one or more governance mechanisms. **Agency costs** are the sum of incentive costs, monitoring costs, enforcement costs, and individual financial losses incurred by principals because governance mechanisms cannot guarantee total compliance by the agent. If a firm is diversified, governance costs increase because it is more difficult to monitor what is going on inside the firm.[53]

In general, managerial interests may prevail when governance mechanisms are weak, as is exemplified by allowing managers a significant amount of autonomy to make strategic decisions. If, however, the board of directors controls managerial autonomy, or if other strong governance mechanisms are used, the firm's strategies should better reflect the interests of the shareholders. More recently, governance observers have been concerned about more egregious behaviour beyond inefficient corporate strategy.

Due to fraudulent behaviour that was found in the Hollinger and Bre-X cases, concerns regarding corporate governance have been on the rise. In the United States in particular, this movement has been driven by a series of corporate governance failures beginning in 2002, when shareholders from a large number of firms experienced fraud due to internal control failures allowing unethical executives in firms such as Enron, WorldCom, Adelphia, and Tyco too much discretion. In response to this perceived crisis in governance, the U.S. Congress enacted the Sarbanes-Oxley Act in 2002.[54]

The Sarbanes-Oxley Act has "introduced a new era of corporate governance, including requirements for auditor independence, the restriction of firms engaging in accounting from both auditing and consulting services, independence of firms' board committees, management assessment of internal controls and personal certification of financial reports by firms' CEOs and CFOs."[55] Although a U.S. Congress Act, Sarbanes-Oxley has impacted many Canadian firms because of the interrelated nature of many U.S. firms who own Canadian subsidiaries and many Canadian firms who own U.S. subsidiaries.

Research suggests that more intensive application of governance mechanisms may produce significant changes in strategies. William Donaldson, former chairman of the SEC in the United States, argued that the collapse of investor confidence after the Enron and other scandals suggests that corporate America needs more intense governance in order for continued investment in the stock market to facilitate growth. Donaldson said that "the short-term costs of compliance, particularly efforts to improve internal control and corporate governance over financial reporting, should be viewed as an investment."[56]

However, others argue that the indirect costs of Sarbanes-Oxley—the impact on strategy formulation and implementation—are even more influential.[57] One observer noted: "Many boards have been vigilant in their oversight role in regard to corporate value. However, CEOs and directors have been distracted from more important strategic

Agency costs are the sum of incentive costs, monitoring costs, enforcement costs, and individual financial losses incurred by principals because governance mechanisms cannot guarantee total compliance by the agent.

issues in order to meet detailed compliance deadlines provided by the Sarbanes-Oxley Act. Boards need to refocus on three critical strategic processes: strategic planning, risk assessment and renewal which include succession planning."[58] In Canada, some believe that some aspects of what is called for in "good governance" may be too costly. One business writer reported that while top Canadian executives are willing to accept new corporate governance rules, many also believe that the gains may be minimal. The majority of these executives expected the cost of higher governance standards to increase. Many believe that balancing the costs versus the perceived benefits to be gained is a grave concern for corporations. Paul Desmarais, the chairman and co-CEO of the Power Corporation of Canada, considers that corporate governance concerns have reached hysterical proportions, and he is convinced many directors will not be willing to take the risks necessary to make their firms grow and prosper.[59]

Next, we explain the effects of different governance mechanisms on the decisions managers make about the choice and the use of the firm's strategies.

Ownership Concentration

Both the number of large-block shareholders and the total percentage of shares they own define **ownership concentration.**

Large-block shareholders typically own at least 10 percent of a corporation's issued shares.

Both the number of large-block shareholders and the total percentage of shares they own define **ownership concentration. Large-block shareholders** typically own at least 10 percent of a corporation's issued shares (in the U.S. it is 5 percent). Ownership concentration as a governance mechanism has received considerable interest because large-block shareholders are increasingly active in their demands that corporations adopt effective governance mechanisms to control managerial decisions.[60]

In general, diffuse ownership (a large number of shareholders with small holdings and few, if any, large-block shareholders) produces weak monitoring of managers' decisions. Among other problems, diffuse ownership makes it difficult for owners to effectively coordinate their actions. Diversification of the firm's product lines beyond the shareholders' optimum level can result from ineffective monitoring of managers' decisions. Higher levels of monitoring could encourage managers to avoid strategic decisions that harm shareholder value. In fact, research evidence shows that ownership concentration is associated with lower levels of firm product diversification.[61] Thus, with high degrees of ownership concentration, the probability is greater that managers' strategic decisions will be intended to maximize shareholder value.

As noted, such concentration of ownership has an influence on strategies and firm value. Interestingly, research in Spain showed a curvilinear relationship between shareholder concentration and firm value. At moderate levels of shareholder concentration, firm value increased; at high levels of concentration, firm value decreased for shareholders, especially minority shareholders.[62] When large shareholders have a high degree of wealth, they have power relative to minority shareholders in extracting wealth from the firm, especially when they are in managerial positions. The importance of boards of directors in mitigating expropriation of minority shareholder value has been found relative to strong family ownership who have incentives to appropriate shareholder wealth to an extent that it is detrimental to minority shareholders.[63] Such expropriation is often found in countries such as Korea where minority shareholder rights are not as protected as they are in Canada and the United States.[64] However, in Canada and the United States much of this concentration has come from increasing equity ownership by institutional investors.

The Growing Influence of Institutional Owners

A classic work published in the 1930s argued that the "modern" corporation had become characterized by a separation of ownership and control.[65] This change occurred primarily because growth prevented founders-owners from maintaining their dual positions in their increasingly complex companies. More recently, another shift has occurred: Ownership of many modern corporations is now concentrated in the hands of institutional investors rather than individual shareholders.[66]

Institutional owners are financial institutions such as stock mutual funds and pension funds that control large-block shareholder positions. Because of their prominent ownership positions, institutional owners, as large-block shareholders, are a powerful governance mechanism. Institutions of these types now own more than 50 percent of the stock in large corporations, and of the top 1,000 corporations they own, on average, 56 percent of the stock. Pension funds control at least one-half of corporate equity.[67]

These ownership percentages suggest that as investors institutional owners have both the size and the incentive to discipline ineffective top-level managers, and can significantly influence a firm's choice of strategies and overall strategic decisions.[68] Research evidence indicates that institutional and other large-block shareholders are becoming more active in their efforts to influence a corporation's strategic decisions. Initially, these shareholder activists and institutional investors concentrated on the performance and accountability of CEOs and contributed to the ouster of a number of them. They are now targeting what they believe are ineffective boards of directors.[69]

> **Institutional owners** are financial institutions such as stock mutual funds and pension funds that control large-block shareholder positions.

Board of Directors

Typically, shareholders monitor the managerial decisions and actions of a firm through the board of directors. Shareholders elect members to their firm's board. Those who are elected are expected to oversee managers and to ensure that the corporation is operated in ways that will maximize shareholders' wealth while also paying close attention to the interests of other stakeholders such as customers, suppliers, employees, and communities. Even with large institutional investors having major equity ownership, diffuse ownership continues to exist in most firms, which means that in large corporations monitoring and control of managers by individual shareholders is limited. Furthermore, large financial institutions, such as banks, are prevented from directly owning stock in firms and from having representatives on companies' boards of directors, although this is not the case in Europe and elsewhere.[70] These conditions highlight the importance of the board of directors for corporate governance.

Unfortunately, over time, boards of directors have not been highly effective in monitoring and controlling top management's actions.[71] Boards are experiencing increasing pressure from shareholders, lawmakers, and regulators to become more forceful in their oversight role and thereby forestall inappropriate actions by top executives. If changes are instituted, boards will have even more power to influence the actions of managers and the directions of their companies. Furthermore, boards not only serve a monitoring role, but they also provide resources to firms. These resources include their personal knowledge and expertise as well as their access to resources of other firms through their external contacts and relationships.[72]

The **board of directors** is a group of elected individuals whose primary responsibility is to act in the owners' and other stakeholders' interests by formally monitoring and controlling the corporation's top-level executives.[73] Boards have the power to direct the affairs of the organization, punish and reward managers, and protect shareholders' rights and interests.[74] Thus, an appropriately structured and effective board of directors protects owners from managerial opportunism such as that found in the case of Hollinger International and Bre-X. Board members are seen as potential stewards of their company's resources, and the way they carry out these responsibilities affects the society in which their firm operates.[75]

> The **board of directors** is a group of elected individuals whose primary responsibility is to act in the owners' interests by formally monitoring and controlling the corporation's top-level executives.

Generally, board members (often called directors) are classified into one of three groups (see Table 11.1). *Insiders* are active top-level managers in the corporation who are elected to the board because they are a source of information about the firm's day-to-day operations.[76] *Related outsiders* have some relationship with the firm, contractual or

Table 11.1	Classifications of Board of Directors Members
Insiders	The firm's CEO and other top-level managers
Related Outsiders	Individuals not involved with the firm's day-to-day operations, but who have a relationship with the company
Outsiders	Individuals who are independent of the firm in terms of day-to-day operations and other relationships

otherwise, that may create questions about their independence, but these individuals are not involved with the corporation's day-to-day activities. *Outsiders* provide independent counsel to the firm and may hold top-level managerial positions in other companies or may have been elected to the board prior to the beginning of the current CEO's tenure.[77]

Historically boards of directors were primarily dominated by inside managers. A widely accepted view is that a board with a significant percentage of its membership drawn from the firm's top executives tends to provide relatively weak monitoring and control of managerial decisions.[78] Managers have been suspected of using their power to select and compensate directors and exploiting their personal ties with them. Two strategy researchers consider that a good board will have a balance of power between inside directors and outside directors. They argue that the insiders would have the rich strategic knowledge required for board-level discussion, while the outsiders would have the objectivity necessary to question the strategic decisions being recommended by the insiders. They suggested that an imbalance of power on either side would lead to an inappropriate lack of strategic knowledge or an overemphasis on objective measures of performance with little regard to the strategic nature of the decisions necessary to grow and prosper.[79] See the Strategic Focus for an illustration.

Contrary to the balance of power argument, some governance experts advocate reforms to ensure that independent outside directors represent a significant majority of the total membership of a board.[80] In Canada, the Dey Report on Corporate Governance suggested establishing a separate audit committee composed only of outsiders.[81] Alternatively, others argue that having outside directors is not enough to resolve the problems; it depends on the power of the CEO. In some cases, the CEO is powerful enough to reduce the effectiveness of outside board members.[82]

Recent corporate scandals have increased overall interest in reforming the CEO and chairperson relationship; that is, separating the roles so that the CEO's power relative to the board is diluted. However, some argue that it might be useful for a CEO to concurrently serve as board chairperson, if the firm is in crisis and needs to have a consistent message. In regard to governance oversight and evaluation of strategic proposals, however, it's rather like the fox guarding the hen house. In other words, the chairperson of the board has effective control of the oversight of corporate management, which likely will lead to continued governance problems.

An alternative proposal to this is to have a lead independent outside director (LID) chosen from the ranks of the outside independent board members. The LID serves as a liaison between corporate management and the outside board members. Thus, the outside directors no longer have direct contact with the CEO if an evaluation of the CEO's performance is required. This allows for more arm's-length evaluation of the CEO and also protects the CEO from being unnecessarily distracted, especially when only routine matters are brought up. Of course, the effectiveness of any position rests upon the ability and character of the person in the position. No amount of structural independence can overcome a desire or intent to be fraudulent and/or to escape accountability. Either of

How Independent Is "Independent"?

According to a report by *The Globe and Mail,* Canadian companies are becoming more aware of the need for independent board members. This indicates improvement since the first *Globe and Mail* study by the *Report on Business* (ROB) that set out to examine our nation's corporate governance practices. In 2002, the ROB study found that most of the companies surveyed had practices that would not meet the U.S. governance standards. The ROB team surveyed 207 Canadian companies in the S&P/TSX index and examined, among a range of other factors, the level of board independence from management.

To evaluate a company's board of directors and the separation of ownership, in its surveys the ROB team uses strict criteria to describe what a "related" board member is. The ROB's definition is "anyone who earns compensation from the company (or whose firm does) beyond director fees." The study also considers previously employed executives, as well as close family members of management, to be "related."

The ROB study found that 20 percent of the surveyed companies held a "majority of related directors," and of the audit committees, "43 per cent included related directors." These findings indicated that many of the Canadian companies not only would fail to satisfy U.S. governance standards, but also did not meet the Toronto Stock Exchange's voluntary standards that recommend companies have a majority of independent board members and fully independent audit committees. The study also found that 31 percent of the companies had "related directors" as Chairs.

Companies across Canada frequently claim that their boards primarily comprise directors who are "unrelated" to management. This of course suggests that their boards are objective in their dealings with executives. However, the ROB examination of corporate governance practices in 2006 discovered that many Canadian publicly held companies make this declaration despite having directors with "close ties to management," "family members of senior management," "professional advisers like lawyers," and ex-managers. Some companies also refer to board members from their parent company as "unrelated" directors.

SOURCES: 2007, Board games 2007: The new realities of corporate governance, *The Globe and Mail,* November 26; 2006, Independent has many meanings: Determining directors' connection to management is all over the board, *The Globe and Mail,* October 23; 2002, Board games, *The Globe and Mail,* October 7; 2006, Corporate Canada opens up, *The Globe and Mail,* October 23.

these approaches, splitting the roles or creating the role of the LID, increases the scrutiny of the CEO and the strategic decisions that he or she makes. Thus, either approach intensifies the governance associated with board of director monitoring.

In short, much research suggests that boards need to reduce the power of the CEO by separating the chairperson of the board's role and the CEO's role on the board so that the same person does not hold both positions.[83] It is believed by these advocates that separating the roles of the CEO and the chairperson provides more power and independence to independent outside directors relative to CEOs. Because of recent problems associated with egregious use of CEO power, CEOs who have recently been appointed by boards generally have to meet tougher standards. As a result, often the selection process takes longer.

Alternatively, having a large number of outside board members can also create some problems. Outsiders do not have contact with the firm's day-to-day operations and typically do not have easy access to the level of information about managers and their skills that is required to effectively evaluate managerial decisions and initiatives.[84] Outsiders can, however, obtain valuable information through frequent interactions with inside board members, during board meetings and otherwise. Insiders possess such information by virtue of their organizational positions. Thus, boards with a critical mass of insiders typically are better informed about intended strategic initiatives, the reasons for the initiatives, and the outcomes expected from them.[85] As mentioned earlier, without this type of information, outsider-dominated boards may emphasize the use of financial, as opposed to strategic, controls to gather performance information to evaluate managers' and business units' performances.

A virtually exclusive reliance on financial evaluations shifts risk to top-level managers, who, in turn, may make decisions to maximize their interests and reduce their employment risk. Reductions in R&D investments, additional diversification of the firm, and the pursuit of greater levels of compensation are some of the results of managers' actions to achieve financial goals set by outsider-dominated boards.[86]

Enhancing the Effectiveness of the Board of Directors

Because of the importance of boards of directors in corporate governance and as a result of increased scrutiny from shareholders—in particular, large institutional investors—the performances of individual board members and of entire boards are being evaluated more formally and with greater intensity.[87] Given the demand for greater accountability and improved performance, many boards have initiated voluntary changes. Among these changes are (1) increases in the diversity of the backgrounds of board members (for example, a greater number of directors from public service, academic, and scientific settings; a greater percentage of ethnic minorities and women; and members from different countries), (2) the strengthening of internal management and accounting control systems, and (3) the establishment and consistent use of formal processes to evaluate the board's performance.[88]

Additional changes include (4) the creation of a "lead director" role that has strong powers with regard to the board agenda and oversight of nonmanagement board member activities, and (5) modification of the compensation of directors, especially reducing or eliminating stock options as a part of the package. Fishery Products International, headquartered in St. John's, Newfoundland and Labrador, had a member of the Fish, Food and Allied Workers' Union on its board from 1987 to the early 2000s. Father Desmond McGrath was the education officer for the union.

Boards have become more involved in the strategic decision-making process, so they must work collaboratively. Some argue that improving the processes used by boards to make decisions and monitor managers and firm outcomes is the key to increasing board effectiveness.[89] Moreover, because of the increased pressure from owners and the potential conflict among board members, procedures are necessary to help boards function effectively in facilitating the strategic decision-making process.[90]

Increasingly, outside directors are being required to own significant equity stakes as a prerequisite to holding a board seat. In fact, some research suggests that firms perform better if outside directors have such a stake.[91]

Other research suggests that diverse boards help firms make more effective strategic decisions and perform better over time.[92] One activist concludes that boards need three foundational characteristics to be effective: director stock ownership, executive meetings to discuss important strategic issues, and a serious nominating committee that truly controls the nomination process to strongly influence the selection of new board members.[93] Once on the job, the outside director needs to seek effectiveness through three linked sets of behaviours that suggest the non-executive director should be "engaged but non-executive" (not seek to micromanage), "challenging but supportive" (help improve decisions and then support the decision made), and "independent but involved" (make independent evaluation of important decisions and be involved in the strategic decision processes of the board).[94]

An issue surfacing in Canada in recent years is whether high-quality candidates are going to continue to be willing to serve on boards. One business writer reported that Jay

Taylor, former CEO of Placer Dome Ltd., was not keen on being a director after he stepped down as CEO. Taylor apparently saw the role as 90 percent governance and stated that he did not have the traffic cop mentality to do the job. He said that, "Watching people and looking for infractions and fraud and embezzlement is not what it's all about for me."[95]

Executive Compensation

The compensation of top-level managers, and especially of CEOs, generates a great deal of interest and strongly held opinions. One reason for this widespread interest can be traced to a natural curiosity about extremes and excesses. Another stems from a more substantive view, that CEO pay is tied in an indirect but tangible way to the fundamental governance processes in large corporations: Who has power? What are the bases of power? How and when do owners and managers exert their relative preferences? How vigilant are boards? Who is taking advantage of whom?[96]

Executive compensation is a governance mechanism that seeks to align the interests of managers and owners through salaries, bonuses, and long-term incentive compensation, such as stock awards and options.[97] Long-term incentive plans have become a critical part of compensation packages. The use of longer-term pay helps firms cope with or avoid potential agency problems by linking managerial wealth to the wealth of common shareholders.[98] Because of this, the stock market generally reacts positively to the introduction of a long-range incentive plan for top executives.[99]

Sometimes the use of a long-term incentive plan prevents major shareholders (e.g., institutional investors) from pressing for changes in the composition of the board of directors, because they assume the long-term incentives will ensure that top executives will act in shareholders' best interests. Alternatively, shareholders largely assume that top-executive pay and the performance of a firm are more closely aligned when firms have boards that are dominated by outside members.[100]

However, sometimes the persistence of institutional investors pays off in regard to questioning actions by boards regarding pay packages. This is certainly the case at Hollinger International, Inc., where the persistent questions of Christopher H. Browne, a managing director of Tweedy, Browne Company, Hollinger's largest shareholder, led to the CEO's dismissal. Browne simply asked the important question as to the background of the pay being provided to Conrad Black and others. A report sponsored by the board found that over $400 million between 1997 and 2003 had been transferred to Hollinger's key managers, including Black. This amounted to approximately 95 percent of the company's entire net income during this period. Browne's questions led to key managers losing their positions and the firm being broken up into pieces. Consequently, the collective share price went from $7.70 in March 2003 to around $17.00 in late 2004.[101]

Effectively using executive compensation as a governance mechanism is particularly challenging to firms implementing international strategies. For example, the interests of owners of multinational corporations may be best served when there is less uniformity among the firm's foreign subsidiaries' compensation plans.[102] Developing an array of unique compensation plans requires additional monitoring and increases the firm's potential agency costs. Importantly, levels of pay vary by regions of the world. For example, managerial pay is highest in the United States, somewhat lower in Canada, and much lower in Asia. Compensation is lower in India partly because many of the largest firms have strong family ownership and control.[103] As corporations acquire firms in other countries, the managerial compensation puzzle becomes more complex and may cause additional executive turnover.[104] See the Strategic Focus for an illustration of how CEO pay links to performance.

Executive compensation is a governance mechanism that seeks to align the interests of managers and owners through salaries, bonuses, and long-term incentive compensation, such as stock awards and options.

How Does CEO Pay Link to Performance?

The Ontario Securities Commission (OSC), the largest securities regulator in Canada, requires that all public companies disclose a statement in their annual proxy circulars explaining their executive compensation policies. Companies must inform investors of the criteria used to calculate executives' compensation, and the relative weighting assigned to each criterion. Companies are supposed to discuss "the specific relationship of corporate performance to executive compensation," and are required to inform shareholders if and why a CEO received bonus pay even when they may have not met the performance criteria.

Although these are so-called "requirements" of the OSC, many public companies in Canada are not abiding by these rules. According to *The Globe and Mail*'s *Report on Business* (ROB), some companies neglected to provide any details on how executives were compensated in 2006. The portion of the ROB study conducted in 2006 to examine compensation reports that of 207 Canadian companies on the S&P/TSX index, 14 percent of the companies surveyed did not mention the performance criteria they use to set executive bonuses. Only 6 percent of the 207 companies offered complete compensation statements outlining all criteria and relative weighting used. In 2005, the OSC examined the compensation statements for 76 large companies and found "defects in 75 of them." The OSC subsequently contacted the companies asking for improvements.

This lack of information leaves shareholders "scratching their heads about how much senior managers are actually being paid." This was the case in the Hollinger International example. Moreover, executive compensation structures are far from straightforward; "It seems like no one is just paid a straight salary anymore," says David Wilson, Chair of the Ontario Securities Commission. Good corporate governance means being completely transparent and divulging all information so that investors can make an informed decision. The OSC is working on creating and monitoring strict reporting rules for executive compensation policies.

Believing that CEOs of public companies are overpaid is certainly not new. A recent Web survey by COMPAS Inc. "found that many CEOs themselves think pay is excessive." COMPAS surveyed 127 CEOs of SMEs in response to a report published by the Canadian Centre for Policy Alternatives. This report argued that the 100 highest-paid CEOs earn $38,998 for a little more than one day's work. This amount approximately equals the average earned by Canadians in a year.

Interestingly, the CEOs were divided on the effect of this income inequality. Fifty percent consider it inappropriate to have such diverse income disparities, while the other 50 percent consider that income inequality may not be a problem. "I cannot understand why Canadians think there is something wrong with being successful and earning a lot of money," wrote one. "CEO compensation only becomes an issue when CEOs do not provide acceptable value to the shareholders," wrote another. These CEOs believe that high-income earners cause their firms and their communities to achieve economic growth.

SOURCES: 2006, Firms break pay disclosure rules: 14% of companies didn't give details of the performance criteria boards consider, *The Globe and Mail*, October 23; 2006, Shareholders will know what managers earn, *Montreal Gazette*, May 30; J. Castaldo, 2008, The CEO poll: Excessive executive compensation, Canadian Business Online, http://www. canadianbusiness.com/managing/strategy/article.jsp?content= 20080110_123134_7700, January 10, accessed February 14, 2008.

A Complicated Governance Mechanism

Executive compensation—especially long-term incentive compensation—is complicated for several reasons. First, the strategic decisions made by top-level managers are typically complex and non-routine, so direct supervision of executives is inappropriate for judging the quality of their decisions. The result is a tendency to link the compensation of top-level managers to measurable outcomes, such as the firm's financial performance. Second, an executive's decision often affects a firm's financial outcomes over an extended period, making it difficult to assess the effect of current decisions on the corporation's performance. In fact, strategic decisions are more likely to have long-term, rather than short-term, effects on a company's strategic outcomes. Third, a number of other factors affect a firm's performance besides top-level managerial decisions and behaviour. Unpredictable economic, social, or legal changes (see Chapter 3) make it difficult to discern the effects of strategic decisions. Thus, although performance-based compensation may provide incentives to top management teams to make decisions that best serve shareholders' interests,[105] such compensation plans alone are imperfect in their ability to monitor and control managers.[106] Still, incentive compensation represents a significant portion of many executives' total pay.

Although incentive compensation plans may increase the value of a firm in line with shareholder expectations, such plans are subject to managerial manipulation. For instance, as firms are being forced to expense stock options, *Forbes* magazine has reported that many firms are using "creative accounting" to reduce the expense associated with these options by changing the "expectations of volatility." The idea is that the value of options increases as the stock price varies. If the stock price does not vary as much, then stock options are valued lower. This creates a lower expense for firms using options simply by changing the accounting formula.[107]

Additionally, annual bonuses may provide incentives to pursue short-run objectives at the expense of the firm's long-term interests. Supporting this conclusion, some research has found that bonuses based on annual performance were negatively related to investments in R&D when the firm was highly diversified, which may affect the firm's long-term strategic competitiveness.[108] However, research has found a positive relationship between investments in R&D and long-term compensation in non-family firms.[109]

Although long-term, performance-based incentives may reduce the temptation to underinvest in the short run, they increase executive exposure to risks associated with uncontrollable events, such as market fluctuations and industry decline. The longer term is the focus of incentive compensation, the greater the long-term risks borne by top-level managers. Also, because long-term incentives tie a manager's overall wealth to the firm in a way that is inflexible, such incentives and ownership may not be valued as highly by a manager as by outside investors who have the opportunity to diversify their wealth in a number of other financial investments.[110] Thus, firms may have to overcompensate managers using long-term incentives, as the next section suggests.

The Effectiveness of Executive Compensation

The compensation received by some top-level managers, especially CEOs, has angered many stakeholders, especially shareholders. Table 11.2 lists the compensation received by the highest paid Canadian CEOs in 2006, and shows the largest value of stock options for Canadian CEOs in that same year. As the table shows, James Balsillie had both the highest stock options and the highest total compensation. Among the ten CEOs listed, Bradley Langille (at Gammon Lake) had the lowest base salary at $300,308, with James Balsillie and Michael Lazaridis (both at Research In Motion) having the second lowest base salary at $561,032. This suggests that the high compensation comes from contingent long-term compensation, such as the exercise of stock options. This trend is likely to continue in this 21st century, partly because of the long-term incentive plans most companies now use to have CEOs do their jobs as if they were owners.

Table 11.2	Highest Paid Canadian CEOs, 2006		
Name	**Company**	**Total Compensation**	**Options**
James Balsillie	Research In Motion Ltd.	$54,709,465	$54,148,433
Glenn Murphy	Shoppers Drug Mart Corp	$34,441,947	$31,694,010
Michael Lazaridis	Research In Motion Ltd.	$32,990,309	$32,429,277
Paul Desmarais Jr.	Power Corp. of Canada	$23,992,660	$21,366,170
John Lederer	Loblaw Cos. Ltd.	$21,666,256	$ 3,391,593
Dominic D'Alessandro	Manulife Financial Corp.	$20,294,064	$10,573,210
Bradley Langille	Gammon Lake Resources Inc.	$19,946,318	$19,282,500
Ian Telfer	Goldcorp Inc.	$17,180,097	$14,878,250
Edward Rogers	Rogers Communication Inc.	$16,376,229	$10,723,980
Andre Desmarais	Power Corp. of Canada	$16,231,764	$13,477,274

Note: Compensation includes base salary, annual bonus, other (e.g., insurance premiums, car and housing allowances), and option gains.

SOURCE: From 2007, Our annual report on executive compensation, *Globe and Mail Report on Business*, June 4, B4.

The primary reason for compensating executives in stock is that the practice affords them an incentive to keep the stock price high and hence aligns managers' interests with shareholders' interests. However, there may be some unintended consequences. Managers who own more than 1 percent of their firm's stock may be less likely to be forced out of their jobs, even when the firm is performing poorly.[111]

Furthermore, a review of the research suggests that over time firm size has accounted for more than 50 percent of the variance in total CEO pay, while firm performance has accounted for less than 5 percent of the variance.[112] Thus, the effectiveness of pay plans as a governance mechanism is suspect.

While some stock option–based compensation plans are well designed with option strike prices substantially higher than current stock prices, too many have been designed simply to give executives more wealth that will not immediately show up on the balance sheet. Research of stock option repricing where the strike price value of the option has been lowered from its original position suggests that action is taken more frequently in high-risk situations.[113] However, repricing also happens when firm performance was poor, to restore the incentive effect for the option. Evidence also suggests that politics are often involved.[114] Additionally, research has found that repricing stock options does not appear to be a function of management entrenchment or ineffective governance. These firms often have had sudden and negative changes to their growth and profitability. They also frequently lose their top managers.[115] Interestingly, institutional investors prefer compensation schemes that link pay with performance, including the use of stock options.[116] Again, this evidence shows that no internal governance mechanism is perfect.

While stock options became highly popular as a means of compensating top executives and linking pay with performance, they also have become controversial.[117] It seems that option awards became a means of providing large compensation packages and the options awarded did not relate to the firm's performance, particularly when boards showed a propensity to reprice options at a lower strike price when stock prices fell precipitously.[118] The large number of options granted in recent years and the increasingly common practice of repricing them was one of the reasons for the pressure to expense options. This action is quite costly to many firms' stated profits and appears to have dampened the excessive use of options.

Market for Corporate Control

The **market for corporate control** is an external governance mechanism that becomes active when a firm's internal controls fail.[119] The market for corporate control is composed of individuals and firms that buy ownership positions in or take over potentially undervalued corporations so they can form new divisions in established diversified companies or merge two previously separate firms. Because the undervalued firm's executives are assumed to be responsible for formulating and implementing the strategy that led to poor performance, they are usually replaced. Thus, when the market for corporate control operates effectively, it ensures that managers who are ineffective or act opportunistically are disciplined.[120]

The market for corporate control is often viewed as a "court of last resort."[121] This suggests that the takeover market as a source of external discipline is used only when internal governance mechanisms are relatively weak and have proven to be ineffective. Alternatively, other research suggests that the rationale for takeovers as a corporate governance strategy is not as strong as the rationale for takeovers as an ownership investment in target candidates where the firm is performing well and does not need discipline.[122] Additionally, a study of active corporate raiders in the 1980s showed that takeover attempts often were focused on above-average-performance firms in an industry.[123] Taken together, this research suggests that takeover targets are not always low performers with weak governance. As such, this research suggests that the market for corporate control may not be as efficient a governance device as theory suggests. At the very least, internal governance controls would be much more precise relative to this external control mechanism.

Although the market for corporate control may be a blunt instrument as far as corporate governance is concerned, the takeover market has continued to be very active. In fact, research suggests that more intense governance environments may have fostered an increasingly active takeover market. Because institutional investors have more concentrated ownership, they may be interested in firms that are targeted for acquisition. Target firms earn a substantial premium over the acquiring firm. At the same time, managers who have ownership positions or stock options are likely to gain in making a transaction with an acquiring firm. There is even more evidence that this may be the case given the increasing number of firms that have golden parachutes allowing up to three years of additional compensation plus other incentives if a firm is taken over. These compensation contracts reduce the risk for managers if a firm is taken over. In fact, research suggests that there was a friendlier environment in the 1990s for takeovers due to these ownership and governance arrangements.[124] Although the 1980s had more defences put up against hostile takeovers, the current environment has been much more friendly, most likely due to the increased intensity of the governance devices on both the buyer (institutional investor) side and the corporate management side. The idea that CEOs who have substantial ownership or stock options in the target firm do well in the friendly transactions in the 1990s and into the 21st century is also supported by research.[125]

The market for corporate control governance mechanism should be triggered by a firm's poor performance relative to industry competitors. A firm's poor performance, often demonstrated by the firm's earning below-average returns, is an indicator that internal governance mechanisms have failed; that is, their use did not result in managerial decisions that maximized shareholder value. This market has been active for some time. As noted in Chapter 8, the decade of the 1990s produced the largest number and value of mergers and acquisitions. The major reduction in the stock market resulted in a significant drop in acquisition activity in the first part of the 21st century. However, the number of mergers and acquisitions began to increase and the market for corporate control has become increasingly international, with over 40 percent of merger and acquisition activity involving two firms from different countries.[126]

The **market for corporate control** is an external governance mechanism that becomes active when a firm's internal controls fail.

While some acquisition attempts are intended to obtain resources important to the acquiring firm, most of the *hostile* takeover attempts are due to the target firm's poor performance.[127] Therefore, target firm managers and members of the boards of directors are highly sensitive about hostile takeover bids. It frequently means that they have not done an effective job in managing the company. If they accept the offer, they are likely to lose their jobs; the acquiring firm will insert its own management. If they reject the offer and fend off the takeover attempt, they must improve the performance of the firm or risk losing their jobs as well.[128]

Managerial Defence Tactics

Hostile takeovers are the major activity in the market for corporate control governance mechanism. Not all hostile takeovers are prompted by poorly performing targets, and firms targeted for hostile takeovers may use multiple defence tactics to fend off the takeover attempt. Historically, the increased use of the market for corporate control has enhanced the sophistication and variety of managerial defence tactics that are used to reduce the influence of this governance mechanism. The market for corporate control tends to increase risk for managers. As a result, managerial pay is often augmented indirectly through golden parachutes (wherein, as mentioned, a CEO can receive up to three years' salary if his or her firm is taken over). Golden parachutes, similar to most other defence tactics, are controversial.

Among other outcomes, takeover defences increase the costs of mounting a takeover, causing the incumbent management to become entrenched, while reducing the chances of introducing a new management team.[129] For example, when Oracle launched a hostile takeover bid for PeopleSoft, PeopleSoft's management succumbed to the takeover, but used a takeover defence strategy that allowed it to hold Oracle at bay for roughly a year and a half. As one observer noted, "PeopleSoft had a number of defence mechanisms, including a board with staggered terms. In addition, its board was authorized to increase or decrease its own size without shareholder approval, and its directors could only be removed for cause and only by a vote of 66.67 percent of entitled voters."[130] In addition, PeopleSoft had a poison pill in place "entitling holders of its common stock to buy any acquirer's shares at a very cheap price in the event of a hostile takeover. That provision forced Oracle to take it to court in an effort to avoid the hefty dilution that might be triggered by the poison pill."[131]

Table 11.3 lists a number of takeover defence strategies. Some defence tactics necessitate only changes in the financial structure of the firm, such as repurchasing shares of the firm's outstanding stock.[132] Some tactics (e.g., reincorporation of the firm in another state) require shareholder approval, but the greenmail tactic, wherein money is used to repurchase stock from a corporate raider to avoid the takeover of the firm, does not. These defence tactics are controversial, and the research on their effects is inconclusive. Alternatively, most institutional investors oppose the use of defence tactics.

Some acquiring institutions take actions to have firms' poison pills eliminated. Many institutional investors have also been opposed to severance packages (golden parachutes), and the opposition is growing significantly in Europe as well.[133] But there can be advantages to severance packages, because they may encourage executives to accept takeover bids that are attractive to shareholders.[134]

A potential problem with the market for corporate control is that it may not be totally efficient. A study of several of the most active corporate raiders in the 1980s showed that approximately 50 percent of their takeover attempts targeted firms with above-average performance in their industry—corporations that were neither undervalued nor poorly managed.[135] The targeting of high-performance businesses may lead to acquisitions at premium prices and to decisions by managers of the targeted firm to

Table 11.3 Hostile-Takeover Defence Strategies

Defence Strategy	Category	Popularity among Firms	Effectiveness as a Defence	Stockholder Wealth Effects
Poison pill Preferred stock in the merged firm offered to shareholders at a highly attractive rate of exchange.	Preventive	High	High	Positive
Corporate charter amendment An amendment to stagger the elections of members to the board of directors of the attacked firm so that all are not elected during the same year, which prevents a bidder from installing a completely new board in the same year.	Preventive	Medium	Very low	Negative
Golden parachute Lump-sum payments of cash that are distributed to a select group of senior executives when the firm is acquired in a takeover bid.	Preventive	Medium	Low	Negligible
Litigation Lawsuits that help a target company stall hostile attacks; areas may include antitrust, fraud, inadequate disclosure.	Reactive	Medium	Low	Positive
Greenmail The repurchase of shares of stock that have been acquired by the aggressor at a premium in exchange for an agreement that the aggressor will no longer target the company for takeover.	Reactive	Very low	Medium	Negative
Standstill agreement Contract between the parties in which the pursuer agrees not to acquire any more stock of the target firm for a specified period of time in exchange for the firm paying the pursuer a fee.	Reactive	Low	Low	Negative
Capital structure change Dilution of stock, making it more costly for a bidder to acquire; may include employee stock option plans (ESOPs), recapitalization, new debt, stock selling, share buybacks.	Reactive	Medium	Medium	Inconclusive

SOURCE: J.A. Pearce II and R.B. Robinson, Jr., 2004, Hostile Takeover Defenses that Maximize Shareholder Wealth, *Business Horizons*, 47(5): 15–24. Permission by CCC.

establish what may prove to be costly takeover defence tactics to protect their corporate positions.[136]

Although the market for corporate control lacks the precision of internal governance mechanisms, the fear of acquisition and influence by corporate raiders is an effective constraint on the managerial-growth motive. The market for corporate control has been responsible for significant changes in many firms' strategies and, when used appropriately, has served shareholders' interests. But this market and other means of corporate governance vary by region of the world and by country. Accordingly, we next address the topic of international corporate governance.

International Corporate Governance

Understanding the corporate governance structure of one's own country is not enough for multinational firms in today's global economy.[137] There are distinct differences among governance standards and regulations across countries. Announced on December 7, 2007, our Canadian government imposed strict rules on foreign takeovers, "implementing new guidelines around buyers' corporate governance, transparency and commerciality."[138] This could have been initiated because of the increased international investment by foreign state–owned companies that may have non-commercial objectives with negligent reporting and corporate governance standards.[139]

Corporate Governance in Canada Relative to the United States

Canada maintains a largely "voluntary, principles-based" approach to corporate governance, with standards that tend to be more lenient than those in the United States, where companies must follow a strict "rules-based" approach to governance under the Sarbanes-Oxley Act.[140] A major reason for the different approaches, some believe, is because when compared to the United States corporate ownership in Canada is highly concentrated,[141] and there are far fewer public companies in Canada.

However, some Canadian companies are voluntarily responding to the increasing demand for corporate governance. For example, Jay Hennick, controlling shareholder and CEO of FirstService Corporation (a leader in commercial real estate, residential property management, integrated security, and property improvement services), has said his company is looking to establish a more independent board of directors because of pressure from U.S. investors.[142] But Hennick explained that although "governance is very much a big issue . . . it's not so much driven by Canada."[143]

While the stability associated with German and Japanese governance structures has historically been viewed as an asset, the governance systems in these countries are changing as well, just as they are in other parts of the world.[144] These changes are partly the result of multinational firms operating in many different countries and attempting to develop a more global governance system.[145] While the similarity is increasing, differences remain evident, and firms employing an international strategy must understand these differences in order to operate effectively in different international markets.[146]

Global Corporate Governance

The 21st-century competitive landscape is fostering the creation of a relatively uniform governance structure that will be used by firms throughout the world.[147] For example, as markets become more global and customer demands more similar, shareholders are becoming the focus of managers' efforts in an increasing number of companies in Korea and Taiwan.[148] Investors are becoming more and more active throughout the world, as evidenced by the growing shareholder outrage at severance packages given to executives in Europe.

Changes in governance are evident in many countries and are moving the governance models closer to that of the United States.[149] Firms in Europe, especially in France and the United Kingdom, are developing boards of directors with more independent members. Similar actions are occurring in Japan, where boards are being reduced in size and foreign members added.

Even in transitional economies, such as those of China and Russia, changes in corporate governance are occurring.[150] However, changes are implemented more slowly in these economies. Chinese firms have found it helpful to use stock-based compensation plans, thereby providing an incentive for foreign companies to invest in China.[151] Because Russia has reduced controls on the economy and on business activity much faster than China has, the country needs more effective governance systems to control its managerial activities. In fact, research suggests that ownership concentration leads to lower performance in Russia, primarily because minority shareholder rights are not well protected through adequate governance controls.[152]

Governance Mechanisms and Ethical Behaviour

The governance mechanisms described in this chapter are designed to ensure that the agents of the firm's owners—the corporation's top executives—make strategic decisions that best serve the interests of the entire group of stakeholders, as described in Chapter 1. In North America, shareholders are recognized as a company's most significant stakeholder. Thus, governance mechanisms focus on the control of managerial decisions to ensure that shareholders' interests will be served, but product market stakeholders (e.g., customers, suppliers, and host communities) and organizational stakeholders (e.g., managerial and nonmanagerial employees) are important as well.[153] Therefore, at least the minimal interests or needs of all stakeholders must be satisfied through the firm's actions. Otherwise, dissatisfied stakeholders will withdraw their support from one firm and provide it to another (for example, customers will purchase products from a supplier offering an acceptable substitute).

The firm's strategic competitiveness is enhanced when its governance mechanisms take into consideration the interests of all stakeholders. Although the idea is subject to debate, some believe that ethically responsible companies design and use governance mechanisms that serve all stakeholders' interests. There is, however, a more critical relationship between ethical behaviour and corporate governance mechanisms. The Conrad Black and the Bre-X cases illustrate the devastating effects of poor ethical behaviour not only on a firm's stakeholders, but also on other firms. This issue is being taken seriously in other countries, such as Japan, as well.[154]

In addition to the aforementioned scandals, other examples—like Enron, WorldCom, and Tyco—demonstrate that all corporate owners are vulnerable to unethical behaviours by their employees, including top-level managers—the agents who have been hired to make decisions that are in shareholders' best interests. The decisions and actions of a corporation's board of directors can be an effective deterrent to these behaviours. In fact, some believe that the most effective boards participate actively to set boundaries for their firms' business ethics and values.[155] Once formulated, the board's expectations related to ethical decisions and actions of all of the firm's stakeholders must be clearly communicated to its top-level managers. Moreover, as shareholders' agents, these managers must understand that the board will hold them fully accountable for the development and support of an organizational culture that increases unethical decisions and behaviours. As explained in Chapter 13, CEOs can be positive role models for improved ethical behaviour.

Only when the proper corporate governance is exercised can strategies be formulated and implemented that will help the firm achieve strategic competitiveness and earn above-average returns. As the discussion in this chapter suggests, corporate governance mechanisms are a vital, yet imperfect, part of firms' efforts to select and successfully use strategies.

Summary

- Corporate governance is a relationship among stakeholders that is used to determine a firm's direction and control its performance. How firms monitor and control top-level managers' decisions and actions affects the implementation of strategies. Effective governance that aligns managers' decisions with shareholders' interests can help produce a competitive advantage.

- There are three internal governance mechanisms in the modern corporation—ownership concentration, the board of directors, and executive compensation. The market for corporate control is the single external governance mechanism influencing managers' decisions and the outcomes resulting from them.

- Ownership is separated from control in the modern corporation. Owners (principals) hire managers (agents) to make decisions that maximize the firm's value. As risk-bearing specialists, owners diversify their risk by investing in multiple corporations with different risk profiles. As decision-making specialists, owners expect their agents (the firm's top-level managers) to make decisions that will lead to maximization of the value of their firm. Thus, modern corporations are characterized by an agency relationship that is created when one party (the firm's owners) hires and pays another party (top-level managers) to use its decision-making skills.

- Separation of ownership and control creates an agency problem when an agent pursues goals that conflict with principals' goals. Principals establish and use governance mechanisms to control this problem.

- Ownership concentration is based on the number of large-block shareholders and the percentage of shares they own. With significant ownership percentages, such as those held by large mutual funds and pension funds, institutional investors often are able to influence top executives' strategic decisions and actions. Thus, unlike diffuse ownership, which tends to result in relatively weak monitoring and control of managerial decisions, concentrated ownership produces more active and effective monitoring. Institutional investors are an increasingly powerful force in corporate America and actively use their positions of concentrated ownership to force managers and boards of directors to make decisions that maximize a firm's value.

- In North America and the United Kingdom, a firm's board of directors, composed of insiders, related outsiders, and outsiders, is a governance mechanism expected to represent shareholders' collective interests. The percentage of outside directors on many boards now exceeds the percentage of inside directors. Outsiders are expected to be more independent of a firm's top-level managers compared with directors selected from inside the firm.

- Executive compensation is a highly visible and often criticized governance mechanism. Salary, bonuses, and long-term incentives are used to strengthen the alignment between managers' and shareholders' interests. A firm's board of directors is responsible for determining the effectiveness of the firm's executive compensation system. An effective system elicits managerial decisions that are in shareholders' best interests.

- In general, evidence suggests that shareholders and boards of directors have become more vigilant in their control of managerial decisions. Nonetheless, these mechanisms are insufficient to govern managerial behaviour in many large companies. Therefore, the market for corporate control is an important governance mechanism. Although it, too, is imperfect, the market for corporate control has been effective in causing corporations to combat inefficient diversification and to implement more effective strategic decisions.

- Corporate governance structures used in Germany and Japan differ from each other and from those used in Canada and the United States, where governance structure has historically focused on maximizing shareholder value. In Germany, employees, as a stakeholder group, have a more prominent role in governance. By contrast, until recently, Japanese shareholders played virtually no role in the monitoring and control of top-level managers. However, all of these systems are becoming increasingly similar, as are many governance systems both in developed countries, such as France and Spain, and in transitional economies, such as Russia and China.

- Effective governance mechanisms ensure that the interests of all stakeholders are served. Thus, long-term strategic success results when firms are governed in ways that permit at least minimal satisfaction of capital market stakeholders (e.g., shareholders), product market stakeholders (e.g., customers and suppliers), and organizational stakeholders (managerial and nonmanagerial employees). Moreover, effective governance produces ethical behaviour in the formulation and implementation of strategies.

1. What is corporate governance? What factors account for the considerable amount of attention corporate governance receives from several parties, including shareholder activists, business press writers, and academic scholars? Why is governance necessary to control managers' decisions?

2. What does it mean to say that ownership is separated from managerial control in the modern corporation? Why does this separation exist?

3. What is an agency relationship? What is managerial opportunism? What assumptions do owners of modern corporations make about managers as agents?

4. How is each of the three internal governance mechanisms—ownership concentration, boards of directors, and executive compensation—used to align the interests of managerial agents with those of the firm's owners?

5. What trends exist regarding executive compensation? What is the effect of the increased use of long-term incentives on executives' strategic decisions?

6. What is the market for corporate control? What conditions generally cause this external governance mechanism to become active? How does the mechanism constrain top executives' decisions and actions?

7. How can corporate governance foster ethical strategic decisions and behaviours on the part of managers as agents?

1. How and when do owners and managers exert their relative preferences? Do you believe that boards are vigilant in exercising oversight? What is the fiduciary responsibility of boards to owners, customers, suppliers, communities, employees?

2. Who has power? What are the bases of power? Does it make sense that in a democracy, people with so much power (CEOs) are unelected by the people who grant the rights for the corporation to exist? Is it being socially responsible to allow one vote per share, or should it be one vote per shareholder?

3. When things are going bad economically, people blame the government. Yet it is the CEOs who control the businesses that fuel the economy. Find out what the pay is for your premier, members of Parliament, and the prime minister. Now look again at the total compensation of the top ten highest paid CEOs in Canada noted in this chapter. Do you think executive pay is too high? Should we start blaming CEOs when there's an economic downturn? It could be argued that paying the best compensation possible is necessary to get the best CEO and top management team possible and that it is being socially responsible in that this gives the firm the best chance to provide value for customers, suppliers, communities, employees, and shareholders. What would you say to someone who argued for high compensation based on this point?

Institutional Power

As discussed in the chapter, institutional investors now play a significant role in terms of corporate governance. In particular, institutional investors have taken what are often substantial ownership positions in some of the largest public companies in Canada and the United States. One reason for this is that these investors have large sums of capital that they need to invest to maximize the return to their shareholders. Thus, institutional investors such as large mutual fund companies, insurance companies, and retirement funds often own billions of dollars worth of stock in a company. Along with this large stock ownership comes the potential to influence board of directors' elections and shareholder resolutions. But is this large concentration of stock ownership something that really creates shareholder power? In this exercise, you will explore the extent of some institutional holdings and then consider the effects of those holdings on shareholders, board members, executives, and corporate governance in general.

Part One. The Ontario Teachers' Pension Plan (OTPP) has over $106 billion in assets. Visit OTPPs' Web site (www.otpp.com/web/website.nsf/web) and assess in which publicly traded companies they have significant amounts of shares.

OR

The Ontario Municipal Employees Retirement System (OMERS) has over $48 billion in assets. Visit OMERS' Web site (www.omers.com) and assess in which publicly traded companies they have significant amounts of shares.

Part Two. Using the information you obtained in Part One and the discussions about corporate governance in the chapter, prepare answers to the following questions:

- What is the degree of power that an investor such as OTPP and OMERS has with respect to the board and top managers of firms such as Royal Bank of Canada or Manulife Financial Corp?

- What limits the amount of power an institutional investor such as OTPP and OMERS has on firms in which it holds ownership positions such as Royal Bank of Canada or Manulife Financial Corp?

- How much have shareholders (such as those holding positions in Royal Bank of Canada or Manulife Financial Corp) benefited from the rise of institutional shareholdings?

CEO Compensation

In Chapter 11, we listed the total compensation of the top ten highest paid CEOs in Canada in 2006. Several business publications have suggested that Canadian CEOs are paid much less than their United States counterparts. Find a list of the highest paid CEOs in the United States and compare the amounts with those for Canadian CEOs. Are Canadian CEOs paid less? If the answer is yes, this could have ramifications for Canadian businesses if future CEOs decide to pursue their business careers in the United States rather than in Canada. Given the comparative compensations, come to class prepared to discuss whether you will pursue a business career in Canada or in the United States, and why.

Notes

1. K. Hendry & G. C. Kiel, 2004, The role of the board in firm strategy: Integrating agency and organisational control perspectives, *Corporate Governance,* 12(4): 500–520; M. Carpenter & J. Westphal, 2001, Strategic context of external network ties: Examining the impact of director appointments on board involvement in strategic decision making, *Academy of Management Journal,* 44: 639–660.
2. A. Henderson & J. Fredrickson, 2001, Top management team coordination needs and the CEO pay gap: A competitive test of economic and behavioral views, *Academy of Management Journal,* 44: 96–117.
3. S. Werner, H. L. Tosi, & L. Gomez-Mejia, 2005, Organizational governance and employee pay: How ownership structure affects the firm's compensation strategy, *Strategic Management Journal,* 26: 377–384; J. E. Core, R. W. Holthausen, & D. F. Larcker, 1999, Corporate governance, chief executive officer compensation, and firm performance, *Journal of Financial Economics,* 51: 371–406.
4. M. D. Lynall, B. R. Golden, & A. J. Hillman, 2003, Board composition from adolescence to maturity: A multitheoretic view, *Academy of Management Review,* 28: 416–431; A. J. Hillman, G. D. Keim, & R. A. Luce, 2001, Board composition and stakeholder performance: Do stakeholder directors make a difference? *Business and Society,* 40: 295–314.
5. A. Desai, M. Kroll, & P. Wright, 2005, Outside board monitoring and the economic outcomes of acquisitions: A test of the substitution hypothesis, *Journal of Business Research,* 58, 926–934; C. M. Daily, D. R. Dalton, & A. A. Cannella, 2003, Corporate governance: Decades of dialogue and data, *Academy of Management Review,* 28: 371–382; P. Stiles, 2001, The impact of the board on strategy: An empirical examination, *Journal of Management Studies,* 38: 627–650.
6. M. S. Schwartz, T. W. Dunfee, & M. J. Kline, 2005, Tone at the top: An ethics code for directors? *Journal of Business Ethics,* 58: 79–100; D. Finegold, E. E. Lawler III, & J. Conger, 2001, Building a better board, *Journal of Business Strategy,* 22(6): 33–37.
7. J. Bakan, 2004, *The Corporation,* Toronto: Penguin, Canada, 36–37.
8. J. Bakan, 2004, *The Corporation,* Toronto: Penguin Canada, 36–37; C. Gelderman, 1981, *Henry Ford: The Wayward Capitalist,* New York: Dial Press, 83; D. G. Smith, 1998, The shareholder primacy norm, *The Journal of Corporation Law,* 23, 277.
9. Bakan, 36–37.
10. E. F. Fama & M. C. Jensen, 1983, Separation of ownership and control, *Journal of Law and Economics,* 26: 301–325.
11. C. Hymowitz, 2004, Corporate Governance (a special report); Experiments in corporate governance: Finding the right way to improve board oversight isn't easy, but plenty of companies are trying, *Wall Street Journal,* June 21, R1.
12. M. Carney, 2005, Corporate governance and competitive advantage in family-controlled firms, *Entrepreneurship Theory and Practice,* 29: 249–265; R. Charan, 1998, *How Corporate Boards Create Competitive Advantage,* San Francisco: Jossey-Bass.
13. G. J. Nicholson & G. C. Kiel, 2004, Breakthrough board performance: How to harness your board's intellectual capital, *Corporate Governance,* 4(1): 5–23; A. Cannella Jr., A. Pettigrew, & D. Hambrick, 2001, Upper echelons: Donald Hambrick on executives and strategy, *Academy of Management Executive,* 15(3): 36–52; J. D. Westphal & E. J. Zajac, 1997, Defections from the inner circle: Social exchange, reciprocity and diffusion of board independence in U.S. corporations, *Administrative Science Quarterly,* 42: 161–212.
14. X. Wu, 2005, Corporate governance and corruption: A cross-country analysis, *Governance,* 18(2): 151–170; J. McGuire & S. Dow, 2002, The Japanese keiretsu system: An empirical analysis, *Journal of Business Research,* 55: 33–40.
15. J. Charkham, 1994, *Keeping Good Company: A Study of Corporate Governance in Five Countries,* New York: Oxford University Press, 1.
16. Bre-X, http://en.wikipedia.org/wiki/Bre-X, December 17, 2007.
17. Ibid.
18. Ibid.
19. 1998, The saga of Bre-X is a cautionary tale: Canadian exchanges: Both small and volatile, *International Herald Tribune,* June 27.
20. R. E. Hoskisson, D. Yiu, & H. Kim, 2004, Corporate governance systems: Effects of capital and labor market congruency on corporate Innovation and global competitiveness, *Journal of High Technology Management,* 15: 293–315.
21. R. Aguilera & G. Jackson, 2003, The cross-national diversity of corporate governance: Dimensions and determinants, *Academy of Management Review,*

28: 447–465; Cadbury Committee, 1992, *Report of the Cadbury Committee on the Financial Aspects of Corporate Governance,* London: Gee.

22. R. P. Wright, 2004, Top managers' strategic cognitions of the strategy making process: Differences between high and low performing firms, *Journal of General Management,* 30(1): 61–78.

23. T. Moeller, 2005, Let's make a deal! How shareholder control impacts merger payoffs, *Journal of Financial Economics,* 76(1): 167–190; M. A. Hitt, R. E. Hoskisson, R. A. Johnson, & D. D. Moesel, 1996, The market for corporate control and firm innovation, *Academy of Management Journal,* 39: 1084–1119.

24. K. Berryman & T. Stephenson, 2004, A new era in corporate governance, www.mckinseyquarterly.com, April 15; K. Ramaswamy, M. Li, & R. Veliyath, 2002, Variations in ownership behavior and propensity to diversify: A study of the Indian context, *Strategic Management Journal,* 23: 345–358.

25. R. E. Hoskisson, M. A. Hitt, R. A. Johnson, & W. Grossman, 2002, Conflicting voices: The effects of ownership heterogeneity and internal governance on corporate strategy, *Academy of Management Journal,* 45: 697–716.

26. G. E. Davis & T. A. Thompson, 1994, A social movement perspective on corporate control, *Administrative Science Quarterly,* 39: 141–173.

27. R. Bricker & N. Chandar, 2000, Where Berle and Means went wrong: A reassessment of capital market agency and financial reporting, *Accounting, Organizations and Society,* 25: 529–554; M. A. Eisenberg, 1989, The structure of corporation law, *Columbia Law Review,* 89(7): 1461, as cited in R. A. G. Monks & N. Minow, 1995, *Corporate Governance,* Cambridge, MA: Blackwell Business, 7.

28. R. M. Wiseman & L. R. Gomez-Mejia, 1999, A behavioral agency model of managerial risk taking, *Academy of Management Review,* 23: 133–153.

29. R. C. Anderson & D. M. Reeb, 2004, Board composition: Balancing family influence in S&P 500 firms, *Administrative Science Quarterly,* 49: 209–237.

30. Carney, Corporate governance and competitive advantage in family-controlled firms; N. Anthanassiou, W. F. Crittenden, L. M. Kelly, & P. Marquez, 2002, Founder centrality effects on the Mexican family firm's top management group: Firm culture, strategic vision and goals and firm performance, *Journal of World Business,* 37: 139–150.

31. L. V. Ryan, 2005, Corporate governance and business ethics in North America: The state of the art, *Business and Society,* March, 44, 1; ABI/INFORM Global.

32. 2007, Handing over the keys to the kids not that easy, *Toronto Star,* October 11.

33. G. Redding, 2002, The capitalist business system of China and its rationale, *Asia Pacific Journal of Management,* 19: 221–249.

34. T.-S. Lee & Y.-H. Yeh, 2004, Corporate governance and financial distress: Evidence from Taiwan, *Corporate Governance,* 12(3): 378–388; M. Carney & E. Gedajlovic, 2003, Strategic innovation and the administrative heritage of East Asian family business groups, *Asia Pacific Journal of Management,* 20: 5–26; D. Miller & I. Le Breton-Miller, 2003, Challenge versus advantage in family business, *Strategic Organization,* 1: 127–134.

35. E. E. Fama, 1980, Agency problems and the theory of the firm, *Journal of Political Economy,* 88: 288–307.

36. D. Dalton, C. Daily, T. Certo, & R. Roengpitya, 2003, Meta-analyses of financial performance and equity: Fusion or confusion? *Academy of Management Journal,* 46: 13–26; M. Jensen & W. Meckling, 1976, Theory of the firm: Managerial behavior, agency costs, and ownership structure, *Journal of Financial Economics,* 11: 305–360.

37. D. C. Hambrick, S. Finkelstein, & A. C. Mooney, 2005, Executive job demands: New insights for explaining strategic decisions and leader behaviors, *Academy of Management Review,* 30: 472–491; L. R. Gomez-Mejia, M. Nunez-Nickel, & I. Gutierrez, 2001, The role of family ties in agency contracts, *Academy of Management Journal,* 44: 81–95.

38. M. G. Jacobides & D. C. Croson, 2001, Information policy: Shaping the value of agency relationships, *Academy of Management Review,* 26: 202–223.

39. H. E. Ryan Jr. & R. A. Wiggins III, 2004, Who is in whose pocket? Director compensation, board independence, and barriers to effective monitoring, *Journal of Financial Economics,* 73: 497–524.

40. M. W. Peng, 2004, Outside directors and firm performance during institutional transitions, *Strategic Management Journal,* 25: 453–471; A. J. Hillman & T. Dalziel, 2003, Boards of directors and firm performance: Integrating agency and resource dependence perspectives, *Academy of Management Review,* 28: 383–396.

41. Hoskisson, Hitt, Johnson, & Grossman, Conflicting voices; O. E. Williamson, 1996, *The Mechanisms of Governance,* New York: Oxford University Press, 6.

42. R. W. Coff & P. M. Lee, 2003, Insider trading as a vehicle to appropriate rent from R&D, *Strategic Management Journal,* 24: 183–190; C. C. Chen, M. W. Peng, & P. A. Saparito, 2002, Individualism, collectivism, and opportunism: A cultural perspective on transaction cost economics, *Journal of Management,* 28: 567–583; S. Ghoshal & P. Moran, 1996, Bad for practice: A critique of the transaction cost theory, *Academy of Management Review,* 21: 13–47.

43. K. H. Wathne & J. B. Heide, 2000, Opportunism in interfirm relationships: Forms, outcomes, and solutions, *Journal of Marketing,* 64(4): 36–51.

44. T. Yoshikawa, P. H. Phan, & J. Linton, 2004, The relationship between governance structure and risk management approaches in Japanese venture capital firms, *Journal of Business Venturing,* 19: 831–849; L. Tihanyi, R. A. Johnson, R. E. Hoskisson, & M. A. Hitt, 2003, Institutional ownership differences and international diversification: The effects of boards of directors and technological opportunity, *Academy of Management Journal,* 46: 195–211; Y. Amihud & B. Lev, 1981, Risk reduction as a managerial motive for conglomerate mergers, *Bell Journal of Economics,* 12: 605–617.

45. R. C. Anderson, T. W. Bates, J. M. Bizjak, & M. L. Lemmon, Corporate governance and firm diversification, *Financial Management,* 29(1): 5–22; R. E. Hoskisson & T. A. Turk, 1990, Corporate restructuring: Governance and control limits of the internal market, *Academy of Management Review,* 15: 459–477.

46. R. Bushman, Q. Chen, E. Engel, & A. Smith, 2004, Financial accounting information, organizational complexity and corporate governance systems, *Journal of Accounting & Economics,* 7: 167–201; M. A. Geletkanycz, B. K. Boyd, & S. Finkelstein, 2001, The strategic value of CEO external directorate networks: Implications for CEO compensation, *Strategic Management Journal,* 9: 889–898.

47. Y. Grinstein & P. Hribar, 2004, CEO compensation and incentives: Evidence from M&A bonuses, *Journal of Financial Economics,* 73: 119–143; P. Wright, M. Kroll, & D. Elenkov, 2002, Acquisition returns, increase in firm size and chief executive officer compensation: The moderating role of monitoring, *Academy of Management Journal,* 45: 599–608; S. Finkelstein & D. C. Hambrick, 1989, Chief executive compensation: A study of the intersection of markets and political processes, *Strategic Management Journal,* 16: 221–239.

48. Gomez-Mejia, Nunez-Nickel, & Gutierrez, The role of family ties in agency contracts.

49. M. S. Jensen, 1986, Agency costs of free cash flow, corporate finance, and takeovers, *American Economic Review,* 76: 323–329.

50. M. Jensen & E. Zajac, 2004, Corporate elites and corporate strategy: How demographic preferences and structural position shape the scope of the firm, *Strategic Management Journal,* 25: 507–524; T. H. Brush, P. Bromiley, & M. Hendrickx, 2000, The free cash flow hypothesis for sales growth and firm performance, *Strategic Management Journal,* 21: 455–472.

51. K. Ramaswamy, M. Li, & B. S. P. Petitt, 2004, Who drives unrelated diversification? A study of Indian manufacturing firms, *Asia Pacific Journal of Management,* 21: 403–423; Ramaswamy, Li, & Veliyath, Variations in ownership behavior and propensity to diversify.

52. A. Desai, M. Kroll, & P. Wright, 2005, Outside board monitoring and the economic outcomes of acquisitions: A test of the substitution hypothesis, *Journal of Business Research,* 58: 926–934; P. Wright, M. Kroll, A. Lado, & B. Van Ness, 2002, The structure of ownership and corporate acquisition strategies, *Strategic Management Journal,* 23: 41–53.

53. T. K. Mukherjee, H. Kiymaz, & H. K. Baker, 2004, Merger motives and target valuation: A survey of evidence from CFOs, *Journal of Applied Finance,* 14(2): 7–24; R. Rajan, H. Servaes, & L. Zingales, 2001, The cost of diversity: The diversification discount and inefficient investment, *Journal of Finance,* 55: 35–79; A. Sharma, 1997, Professional as agent: Knowledge asymmetry in agency exchange, *Academy of Management Review,* 22: 758–798.

54. A. Borrus, L. Lavelle, D. Brady, M. Arndt, & J. Weber, 2005, Death, taxes and Sarbanes-Oxley? Executives may be frustrated with the law's burdens, but corporate performance is here to stay, *BusinessWeek,* January 17, 28–31.

55. D. R. Dalton & C. M. Dalton, 2005, Sarbanes-Oxley legislation and the private company: If not a marriage, then certainly an engagement, *Journal of Business Strategy,* 26(2): 7–8

56. R. Marden & R. Edwards, 2005, The Sarbanes-Oxley "axe," *CPA Journal,* April, 6–10.

57. J. Fox, 2005, Calling off the dogs, *Fortune,* June 27, 27–29.

58. W. J. Hass & S. G. Pryor IV, 2005, The board's role in corporate renewal, *Journal of Private Equity,* 8(2): 12.

59. P. Fitzpatrick, 2003, Is good governance too costly? Many CEOs say yes, *National Post, Financial Post,* December 3, FP1; Silcoff, 2004, Governance run amok: DesMarais, *National Post, Financial Post,* May 13, FP1.

60. A. de Miguel, J. Pindado, & C. de la Torre, 2004, Ownership structure and firm value: New evidence from Spain, *Strategic Management Journal,* 25: 1199–1207; J. Coles, N. Sen, & V. McWilliams, 2001, An examination of the relationship of governance mechanisms to performance, *Journal of Management,* 27: 23–50.

61. M. Singh, I. Mathur, & K. C. Gleason, 2004, Governance and performance implications of diversification strategies: Evidence from large U.S. firms, *Financial Review,* 39: 489–526; S.-S. Chen & K. W. Ho, 2000, Corporate diversification, ownership structure, and firm value: The Singapore evidence, *International Review of Financial Analysis,* 9: 315–326; R. E. Hoskisson, R. A. Johnson, & D. D. Moesel, 1994, Corporate divestiture intensity in restructuring firms: Effects of governance, strategy, and performance, *Academy of Management Journal,* 37: 1207–1251.

62. De Miguel, Pindado, & de la Torre, Ownership structure and firm value: New evidence from Spain.

63. R. C. Anderson & D. M. Reeb, 2004, Board composition: Balancing family influence in S&P 500 firms, *Administrative Science Quarterly,* 49: 209–237.

64. S. J. Chang, 2003, Ownership structure, expropriation and performance of group-affiliated companies in Korea, *Academy of Management Journal,* 46: 238–253.

65. A. Berle & G. Means, 1932, *The Modern Corporation and Private Property,* New York: Macmillan.

66. B. Ajinkya, S. Bhojraj, & P. Sengupta, 2005, The association between outside directors, institutional investors and the properties of management earnings forecasts, *Journal of Accounting Research,* 43: 343–376; P. A. Gompers & A. Metrick, 2001, Institutional investors and equity prices, *Quarterly Journal of Economics,* 116: 229–259; M. P. Smith, 1996, Shareholder activism by institutional investors: Evidence from CalPERS, *Journal of Finance,* 51: 227–252.

67. Hoskisson, Hitt, Johnson, & Grossman, Conflicting voices; C. M. Dailey, 1996, Governance patterns in bankruptcy reorganizations, *Strategic Management Journal,* 17: 355–375.

68. Hoskisson, Hitt, Johnson, & Grossman, Conflicting voices; R. E. Hoskisson & M. A. Hitt, 1994, *Downscoping: How to Tame the Diversified Firm,* New York: Oxford University Press.

69. K. Rebeiz, 2001, Corporate governance effectiveness in American corporations: A survey, *International Management Journal,* 18(1): 74–80.

70. S. Thomsen & T. Pedersen, 2000, Ownership structure and economic performance in the largest European companies, *Strategic Management Journal,* 21: 689–705.

71. R. V. Aguilera, 2005, Corporate governance and director accountability: An institutional comparative perspective, *British Journal of Management,* 16(S1), S39–S53; E. H. Fram, 2004, Governance reform: It's only just begun, *Business Horizons,* 47(6): 10–14.

72. Hillman & Dalziel, Boards of directors and firm performance.

73. Rebeiz, Corporate governance effectiveness in American corporations; J. K. Seward & J. P Walsh, 1996, The governance and control of voluntary corporate spinoffs, *Strategic Management Journal,* 17: 25–39.

74. S. Young, 2000, The increasing use of non-executive directors: Its impact on UK board structure and governance arrangements, *Journal of Business Finance & Accounting,* 27(9/10): 1311–1342; P. Mallete & R. L. Hogler, 1995, Board composition, stock ownership, and the exemption of directors from liability, *Journal of Management,* 21: 861–878.

75. C. Caldwell & R. Karri, 2005, Organizational governance and ethical systems: A covenantal approach to building trust, *Journal of Business Ethics,* 58: 249–259; J. Chidley, 2001, Why boards matter, *Canadian Business,* October 29, 6; D. P. Forbes & F. J. Milliken, 1999, Cognition and corporate governance: Understanding boards of directors as strategic decision-making groups, *Academy of Management Review,* 24: 489–505.

76. Hoskisson, Hitt, Johnson, & Grossman, Conflicting voices; B. D. Baysinger & R. E. Hoskisson, 1990, The composition of boards of directors and strategic control: Effects on corporate strategy, *Academy of Management Review,* 15: 72–87.

77. Carpenter & Westphal, Strategic context of external network ties: Examining the impact of director appointments on board involvement in strategic decision making; E. J. Zajac & J. D. Westphal, 1996, Director reputation, CEO-board power, and the dynamics of board interlocks, *Administrative Science Quarterly,* 41: 507–529.

78. J. Westphal & L. Milton, 2000, How experience and network ties affect the influence of demographic minorities on corporate boards, *Administrative Science Quarterly,* June, 45(2): 366–398.

79. W. G. Rowe & D. Rankin, 2002, Insiders or outsiders: Who should have more power on a board? *Ivey Business Journal,* http://cases.ivey.uwo.ca/ Cases/Pages/PreviewPDF.aspx?prod=9B02TF09, accessed February 14, 2008.

80. 2003, The hot seat, Wall Street Journal Online, www.wsj.com, February 24; 2001, The fading appeal of the boardroom series, *The Economist,* February 10 (Business Special): 67–69.

81. R. M. Corbin, 1999, *Report on Corporate Governance, Five Years to the Dey,* Toronto Stock Exchange, 35.

82. H. L. Tosi, W. Shen, & R. J. Gentry, 2003, Why outsiders on boards can't solve the corporate governance problem, *Organizational Dynamics,* 32: 180–192.

83. J. W. Lorsch & A. Zelleke, 2005, Should the CEO be the Chairman, *MIT Sloan Management Review,* 46(2): 71–74.

84. J. Roberts, T. McNulty, P. Stiles, 2005, Beyond agency conceptions of the work of the non-executive director: Creating accountability in the boardroom, *British Journal of Management,* 16(S1): S5–S26.

85. J. Coles & W. Hesterly, 2000, Independence of the chairman and board composition: Firm choices and shareholder value, *Journal of Management,* 26: 195–214; S. Zahra, 1996, Governance, ownership and corporate entrepreneurship among the Fortune 500: The moderating impact of industry technological opportunity, *Academy of Management Journal,* 39: 1713–1735.

86. Yoshikawa, Phan, & Linton, The relationship between governance structure and risk management approaches in Japanese venture capital firms; Hoskisson, Hitt, Johnson, & Grossman, Conflicting voices.

87. E. E. Lawler III & D. L. Finegold, 2005, The changing face of corporate boards, *MIT Sloan Management Review,* 46(2): 67–70; A. Conger, E. E. Lawler, & D. L. Finegold, 2001, *Corporate Boards: New Strategies for Adding Value at the Top,* San Francisco: Jossey-Bass; J. A. Conger, D. Finegold, & E. E. Lawler III, 1998, Appraising boardroom performance, *Harvard Business Review,* 76(1): 136–148.

88. J. Marshall, 2001, As boards shrink, responsibilities grow, *Financial Executive,* 17(4): 36–39.

89. S. Finkelstein & A. C. Mooney, 2003, Not the usual suspects: How to use board process to make boards better, *Academy of Management Executive,* 17: 101–113.

90. Hoskisson, Hitt, Johnson, & Grossman, Conflicting voices.

91. W. Shen, 2005, Improve board effectiveness: The need for incentives, *British Journal of Management,* 16(S1): S81–S89; M. Gerety, C. Hoi, & A. Robin, 2001, Do shareholders benefit from the adoption of incentive pay for directors? *Financial Management,* 30: 45–61; D. C. Hambrick & E. M. Jackson, 2000, Outside directors with a stake: The linchpin in improving governance, *California Management Review,* 42(4): 108–127.

92. I. Filatotchev & S. Toms, 2003, Corporate governance, strategy and survival in a declining industry: A study of UK cotton textile companies, *Journal of Management Studies,* 40: 895–920.

93. J. Kristie, 2001, The shareholder activist: Nell Minow, *Directors and Boards,* 26(1): 16–17.

94. Roberts, McNulty, & Stiles, Beyond agency conceptions of the work of the non-executive director: Creating accountability in the boardroom.

95. D. Hasselback, 2004, Placer's Taylor snubs governance "cop" job: Refuses directorships, *National Post, Financial Post,* May 6, FP1.

96. L. A. Bebchuk & J. M Fried, 2004, *Pay Without Performance: The Unfulfilled Promise of Executive Compensation,* Cambridge, MA: Harvard University Press; M. A. Carpenter & W. G. Sanders, 2002, Top management team compensation: The missing link between CEO pay and firm performance, *Strategic Management Journal,* 23: 367–375; D. C. Hambrick & S. Finkelstein, 1995, The effects of ownership structure on conditions at the top: The case of CEO pay raises, *Strategic Management Journal,* 16: 175.

97. J. S. Miller, R. M. Wiseman, & L. R. Gomez-Mejia, 2002, The fit between CEO compensation design and firm risk, *Academy of Management Journal,* 45: 745–756; L. Gomez-Mejia & R. M. Wiseman, 1997, Reframing executive compensation: An assessment and outlook, *Journal of Management,* 23: 291–374.

98. J. McGuire & E. Matta, 2003, CEO stock options: The silent dimension of ownership, *Academy of Management Journal,* 46: 255–265; W. G. Sanders & M. A. Carpenter, 1998, Internationalization and firm governance: The roles of CEO compensation, top team composition and board structure, *Academy of Management Journal,* 41: 158–178.

99. N. T. Hill & K. T. Stevens, 2001, Structuring compensation to achieve better financial results, *Strategic Finance,* 9: 48–51; J. D. Westphal & E. J. Zajac, 1999, The symbolic management of stockholders: Corporate governance reform and shareholder reactions, *Administrative Science Quarterly,* 43: 127–153.

100. L. Gomez-Mejia, M. Larraza-Kintana, & M. Makri, 2003, The determinants of executive compensation in family-controlled public corporations, *Academy of Management Journal,* 46: 226–237; F. Elloumi & J. P. Gueyie, 2001, CEO compensation, IOS and the role of corporate governance, *Corporate Governance,* 1(2): 23–33; M. J. Conyon & S. I. Peck, 1998, Board control, remuneration committees, and top management compensation, *Academy of Management Journal,* 41: 146–157.

101. N. Byrnes, 2004, Not so fast, Lord Black, *BusinessWeek,* September 27, 104.

102. S. O'Donnell, 2000, Managing foreign subsidiaries: Agents of headquarters, or an interdependent network? *Strategic Management Journal,* 21: 521–548; K. Roth & S. O'Donnell, 1996, Foreign subsidiary compensation: An agency theory perspective, *Academy of Management Journal,* 39: 678–703.

103. K. Ramaswamy, R. Veliyath, & L. Gomes, 2000, A study of the determinants of CEO compensation in India, *Management International Review,* 40(2): 167–191.

104. J. Krug & W. Hegarty, 2001, Predicting who stays and leaves after an acquisition: A study of top managers in multinational firms, *Strategic Management Journal,* 22: 185–196.

105. Carpenter & Sanders, Top management team compensation.

106. Werner, Tosi, & Gomez-Mejia, Organizational governance and employee pay: How ownership structure affects the firm's compensation strategy; S. Bryan, L. Hwang, & S. Lilien, 2000, CEO stock-based compensation: An empirical analysis of incentive-intensity, relative mix, and economic determinants, *Journal of Business,* 73: 661–693.

107. E. MacDonald, 2005, A volatile brew: Companies have found how to ease the impact of strict new stock option rules, *Forbes,* August 15, 70–71.

108. R. E. Hoskisson, M. A. Hitt, & C. W. L. Hill, 1993, Managerial incentives and investment in R&D in large multiproduct firms, *Organization Science,* 4: 325–341.

109. Gomez-Mejia, Larraza-Kintana, & Makri, 2003, The determinants of executive compensation in family-controlled public corporations.

110. L. K. Meulbroek, 2001, The efficiency of equity-linked compensation: Understanding the full cost of awarding executive stock options, *Financial Management,* 30(2): 5–44.

111. J. Dahya, A. A. Lonie, & D. A. Power, 1998, Ownership structure, firm performance and top executive change: An analysis of UK firms, *Journal of Business Finance & Accounting,* 25: 1089–1118.

112. L. Gomez-Mejia, 2003, What should be done about CEO pay? *Academy of Management Issues Forum,* July; H. Tosi, S. Werner, J. Katz, & L. Gomez-Mejia, 2000, How much does performance matter? A meta-analysis of CEO pay studies, *Journal of Management,* 26: 301–339.

113. J. C. Bettis, J. M. Biziak, & M. L. Lemmon, 2005, Exercise behavior, valuation and the incentive effects of employee stock options, *Journal of Financial Economics,* 76: 445–470.

114. T. G. Pollock, H. M. Fischer, & J. B. Wade, 2002, The role of politics in repricing executive options, *Academy of Management Journal,* 45: 1172–1182; M. E. Carter & L. J. Lynch, 2001, An examination of executive stock option repricing, *Journal of Financial Economics,* 59: 207–225; D. Chance, R. Kumar, & R. Todd, 2001, The "repricing" of executive stock options, *Journal of Financial Economics,* 59: 129–154.

115. N. K. Chidambaran & N. R. Prabhala, 2003, Executive stock option repricing, internal governance mechanisms and management turnover, *Journal of Financial Economics,* 69: 153–189.

116. J. C. Hartzell & L. T. Starks, 2003, Institutional investors and executive compensation, *Journal of Finance,* 58: 2351–2374.

117. P. T. Chingos, 2004, *Responsible Executive Compensation for a New Era of Accountability,* Hoboken, NJ: Wiley.

118. M. A. Chen, 2004, Executive option repricing, incentives, and retention, *Journal of Finance,* 59: 1167–1199; P. Brandes, R. Dharwadkar, & G. V. Lemesis, 2003, Effective stock option design: Reconciling stakeholder, strategic and motivational factors, *Academy of Management Executive,* 17(1): 77–93.

119. Moeller, Let's make a deal! How shareholder control impacts merger payoffs; R. Coff, 2002, Bidding wars over R&D intensive firms: Knowledge, opportunism and the market for corporate control, *Academy of Management Journal,* 46: 74–85; Hitt, Hoskisson, Johnson, & Moesel, The market for corporate control and firm innovation.

120. R. Sinha, 2004, The role of hostile takeovers in corporate governance, *Applied Financial Economics,* 14: 1291–1305; D. Goldstein, 2000, Hostile takeovers as corporate governance? Evidence from 1980s, *Review of Political Economy,* 12: 381–402

121. O. Kini, W. Kracaw, & S. Mian, 2004, The nature of discipline by corporate takeovers, *Journal of Finance,* 59: 1511–1551.

122. R. Sinha, 2004, The role of hostile takeovers in corporate governance, *Applied Financial Economics,* 14: 1291–1305.

123. J. P. Walsh & R. Kosnik, 1993, Corporate raiders and their disciplinary role in the market for corporate control, *Academy of Management Journal,* 36: 671–700.

124. Moeller, Let's make a deal! How shareholder control impacts merger payoffs.

125. J. Hartzell, E. Ofek, & D. Yermack, 2004, What's in it for me? CEOs whose firms are acquired, *Review of Financial Studies,* 17: 37–61.

126. K. Shimizu, M. A. Hitt, D. Vaidyanath, & P. Vincenzo, 2004, Theoretical foundations of cross-border mergers and acquisitions: A review of current research and recommendations for the future, *Journal of International Management,* 10: 307–353; M. A. Hitt & V. Pisano, 2003, The cross-border merger and acquisition strategy, *Management Research,* 1: 133–144.

127. Sinha, The role of hostile takeovers in corporate governance; J. Anand & A. Delios, 2002, Absolute and relative resources as determinants of international acquisitions, *Strategic Management Journal,* 23: 119–134.

128. J. Harford, 2003, Takeover bids and target directors' incentives: The impact of a bid on directors' wealth and board seats, *Journal of Financial Economics,* 69: 51–83; S. Chatterjee, J. S. Harrison, & D. D. Bergh, 2003, Failed takeover attempts, corporate governance and refocusing, *Strategic Management Journal,* 24: 87–96.

129. C. Sundaramurthy, J. M. Mahoney, & J. T. Mahoney, 1997, Board structure, antitakeover provisions, and stockholder wealth, *Strategic Management Journal,* 18: 231–246.

130. B. E. Tunick, 2005, The Oracle from Oracle: Will other tech giants follow the M&A call? *Investment Dealers' Digest,* February 7, 1.

131. Ibid.

132. W. G. Sanders & M. A. Carpenter, 2003, Strategic satisficing? A behavioral-agency theory perspective on stock repurchase program announcements, *Academy of Management Journal,* 46: 160–178; J. Westphal & E. Zajac, 2001, Decoupling policy from practice: The case of stock repurchase programs, *Administrative Science Quarterly,* 46: 202–228.

133. A. Cala, 2005, Carrying golden parachutes; France joins EU trend to reign in executive severance deals, *Wall Street Journal,* June 8, A13.

134. J. A. Pearce II & R. B. Robinson Jr., 2004, Hostile takeover defenses that maximize shareholder wealth, *Business Horizons,* 47(5): 15–24.

135. Walsh & Kosnik, Corporate raiders.

136. A. Chakraborty & R. Arnott, 2001, Takeover defenses and dilution: A welfare analysis, *Journal of Financial and Quantitative Analysis,* 36: 311–334.

137. C. C. J. M. Millar, T. I. Eldomiaty, C. J. Choi, & B. Hilton, 2005, Corporate governance and institutional transparency in emerging markets, *Journal of Business Ethics,* 59: 163–174; D. Norburn, B. K. Boyd, M. Fox, & M. Muth, 2000, International corporate governance reform, *European Business Journal,* 12(3): 116–133; M. Useem, 1998, Corporate leadership in a globalizing equity market, *Academy of Management Executive,* 12(3): 43–59.

138. Canada strengthens rules on foreign takeovers, CanWest News, December 8, 2007.

139. Ibid.

140. The Sarbanes-Oxley Act is legislation that established new or enhanced standards for all U.S. public company boards, management, and public accounting firms, Sarbanes-Oxley Act, Wikipedia, http://en.wikipedia.org/wiki/Sarbanes-Oxley_Act.

141. L. V. Ryan, 2005, Corporate governance and business ethics in North America: The state of the art, *Business and Society,* March 2005, 44, 1; ABI/INFORM Global.

142. Board games, *The Globe and Mail,* October 7, 2002.

143. Ibid.

144. S. M. Jacoby, 2004, *The Embedded Corporation: Corporate Governance and Employment Relations in Japan and the United States,* Princeton, NJ: Princeton University Press.

145. P. Witt, 2004, The competition of international corporate governance systems—A German perspective, *Management International Review,* 44: 309–333; L. Nanchum, 2003, Does nationality of ownership make any difference and if so, under what circumstances? Professional service MNEs in global competition, *Journal of International Management,* 9: 1–32.

146. Aguilera & Jackson, The cross-national diversity of corporate governance: Dimensions and determinants.

147. J. B. White, 2000, The company we'll keep, Wall Street Journal Online, www.wsj.com, January 17.

148. J.-S. Baek, J.-K. Kang, & K. S. Park, 2004, Corporate governance and firm value: Evidence from the Korean financial crisis, *Journal of Financial Economics,* 71: 265–313; T.-S. Lee & Y.-H. Yeh, 2004, Corporate governance and financial distress: Evidence from Taiwan, *Corporate Governance,* 12: 378–388.

149. T. Edwards, 2004, Corporate governance, industrial relations and trends in company-level restructuring in Europe: Convergence towards the Anglo-American model? *Industrial Relations Journal,* 35: 518–535.

150. N. Boubarkri, J.-C. Cosset, & O. Guedhami, 2004, Postprivatization corporate governance: The role of ownership structure and investor protection, *Journal of Financial Economics,* 76: 369–399; K. Uhlenbruck, K. E. Meyer, & M. A. Hitt, 2003, Organizational transformation in transition economies: Resource-based and organizational learning perspectives, *Journal of Management Studies,* 40: 257–282; P. Mar & M. Young, 2001, Corporate governance in transition economies: A case study of 2 Chinese airlines, *Journal of World Business,* 36(3): 280–302.

151. J. Li, K. Lam, & J. W. Moy, 2005, Ownership reform among state firms in China and its implications, *Management Decision,* 43: 568–588; L. Chang, 1999, Chinese firms find incentive to use stock-compensation plans, *Wall Street Journal,* November 1, A2; T. Clarke & Y. Du, 1998, Corporate governance in China: Explosive growth and new patterns of ownership, *Long Range Planning,* 31(2): 239–251.

152. M. A. Hitt, D. Ahlstrom, M. T. Dacin, E. Levitas, & L. Svobodina, 2004, The institutional effects on strategic alliance partner selection in transition economies: China versus Russia, *Organization Science,* 15: 173–185; I. Filatotchev, R. Kapelyushnikov, N. Dyomina, & S. Aukutsionek, 2001, The effects of ownership concentration on investment and performance in privatized firms in Russia, *Managerial and Decision Economics,* 22(6): 299–313; E. Perotti & S. Gelfer, 2001, Red barons or robber barons? Governance and investment in Russian financial-industrial groups, *European Economic Review,* 45(9): 1601–1617.

153. S. Sharma & I. Henriques, 2005, Stakeholder influences on sustainability practices in the Canadian Forest products industry, *Strategic Management Journal,* 26: 159–180; Hillman, Keim, & Luce, Board composition and stakeholder performance; R. Oliver, 2000, The board's role: Driver's seat or rubber stamp? *Journal of Business Strategy,* 21: 7–9.

154. N. Demise, 2005, Business ethics and corporate governance in Japan, *Business and Society,* 44: 211–217.

155. Caldwell & Karri, Organizational governance and ethical systems: A covenantal approach to building trust; A. Felo, 2001, Ethics programs, board involvement, and potential conflicts of interest in corporate governance, *Journal of Business Ethics,* 32: 205–218.

Chapter Twelve

Organizational Structure and Controls

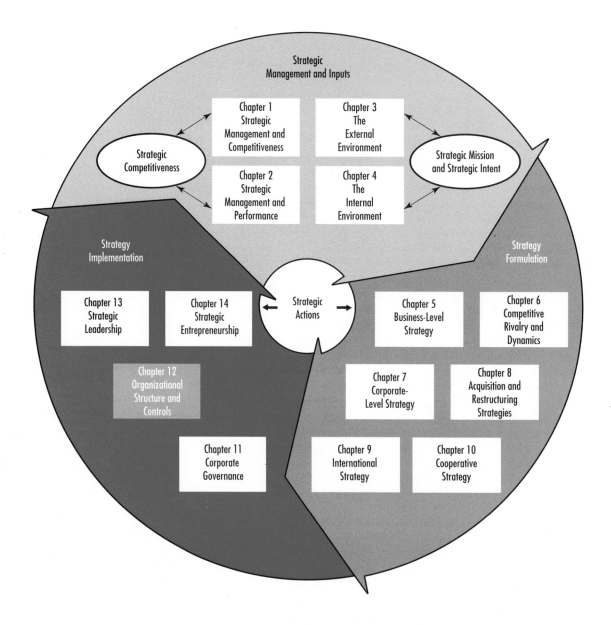

Knowledge Objectives

Studying this chapter should provide you with the strategic management knowledge needed to:

1. Define organizational structure and controls and discuss the difference between strategic and financial controls.

2. Describe the relationship between strategy and structure.

3. Discuss the functional structures used to implement business-level strategies.

4. Explain the use of three versions of the multidivisional (M-form) structure to implement different diversification strategies.

5. Discuss the organizational structures used to implement three international strategies.

6. Define strategic networks and discuss how strategic centre firms implement such networks at the business, corporate, and international levels.

Sony's Online Music Business: Organization and Cooperation Difficulties

Sony has been quite successful in implementing its strategy worldwide in consumer electronics. Its Sony Walkman and Sony PlayStation products have been exemplary in this regard. However, Sony has experienced difficulty in pursuing its competitive strategy with its online music business. In part, this problem is caused by the same organizational structure that helped to create its past successes.

www.sony.com

Sony's decentralized product divisions have fostered innovation through an entrepreneurial spirit within its separate divisions. The organizational structure encourages competition, so that, for example, engineers in separate divisions are encouraged to outdo each other. This approach created "monster hits" that turned Sony into one of the most successful global brands in consumer products over the past few decades.

However, Sony's reputation as an innovator has suffered because it has been beaten by the competition with products such as the iPod and TiVo digital video recorders. These products require the integration of hardware, software, and online services—but Sony's structure has worked against it, causing the divisions to be competitive at product efforts that require more coordination.

Sony has used a strategic business unit (SBU) multidivisional structure (defined later in the chapter), which allows strong decentralization in each product group or division. These groups compete with each other for resources but are highly autonomous business units focused on a particular set of related businesses. Using this structure has made it difficult to "communicate with everybody when you have that many silos." This is exemplified by Sony's CONNECT Music service, which was created in an attempt to enter the digital music market that has been dominated by Apple's iTunes.

The CONNECT Music service was met by opposition from Sony's music group, which was concerned that it would lose power to control its copyrighted music through free music downloads that might be initiated through CONNECT Music. To make matters worse, the PC and Walkman groups had each developed competing digital music players that they wished to promote. Theoretically, given Sony's market presence and prowess in these separate areas, it could out-compete Apple's iPod and iTunes. However, the CONNECT Music service required coordination with the PC and Walkman groups as well as with the music-business group, which was reluctant to participate.

This coordination problem, combined with severe competition from Apple Inc., led to the eventual demise of Sony's CONNECT Music service in North America. Sony announced that by 2008 it planned to switch over to Windows Media technology for its Walkman products, and to shift resources to focus on its PlayStation division.

Given that the competition between divisions that once helped Sony develop highly successful new products is now hurting its reputation for innovation, we believe that this example of Sony illustrates how important the organizational structure can be when seeking to implement a firm's newly chosen strategy.

SOURCES: 2005, With Sony trailing, can anything stop Samsung?, Marketing Week, July 28, 9; B. Carter, 2005, Sony seeks new beginning, Marketing, March 16, 16; P. Dvorak, 2005, Out of tune: At Sony, rivalries were encouraged: Then came iPod, Wall Street Journal, A1, A6; P. Dvorak, 2005, Stringer takes control at Sony with plans to streamline firm, Wall Street Journal, June 23, B4; K. Kelly & E. Smith, 2005, Past as prologue: New CEO to seek synergies, Wall Street Journal, March 8, B1; A. Lashinsky, 2005, Saving face at Sony, Fortune, February 21, 79–83; CONNECT™ music service phase out FAQ, http://esupport.sony.com/perl/news-item.pl?template=EN&news_id=215; 2007, Sony to unplug Connect digital music service, www.reghardware.co.uk/2007/08/30/sony_to_kill_connect/, August 30; 2007, Sony pulls the plug on Connect, refocuses on PlayStation, www.engadget.com, June 17.

As described in Chapter 5, all firms use one or more business-level strategies. In Chapters 7 to 10, we discuss the other strategies that might be used (corporate-level, acquisition and restructuring, international, and cooperative). Once selected, strategies can't be implemented in a vacuum. Organizational structure and controls, this chapter's topic, provide the framework within which strategies are used in both for-profit organizations and not-for-profit agencies.[1] However, as we explain, separate structures and controls are required to successfully implement different strategies. For example, Sony uses a form of the multidivisional structure (M-form) to support the use of its related-linked corporate-level strategy, while each of its business units employs a version of the functional structure (U-form) to effectively implement the differentiation business-level strategy. Top-level managers have the final responsibility for ensuring that the firm has matched each of its strategies with the appropriate organizational structure and that changes to structure take place when strategies are changed. The match or degree of fit between strategy and structure influences the firm's attempts to earn above-average returns.[2] Thus, the ability to select an appropriate strategy and match it with the appropriate structure is an important characteristic of effective strategic leadership.[3]

This chapter opens with an introduction to organizational structure and controls. We then provide more details about the need for the firm's strategy and structure to be properly matched. As the Opening Case exemplifies, a firm's efforts to match strategy and structure is affected by the fact that they influence each other.[4] As we discuss, strategy has a more important influence on structure, although once in place, structure influences strategy.[5]

The chapter describes the relationship between growth and structural change that successful firms experience. This is followed with discussions of the different organizational structures that firms use to implement the separate business-level, corporate-level, international, and cooperative strategies. A series of figures highlights the different structures firms match with strategies. Across time and based on their experiences, organizations, especially large and complex ones, customize these general structures to meet their unique needs.[6] Typically, the firm tries to form a structure that is complex enough to facilitate use of its strategies but simple enough for all parties to understand and implement.[7]

Organizational Structure and Controls

Research shows that organizational structure and the controls that are a part of the structure affect firm performance.[8] In particular, evidence suggests that performance declines when the firm's strategy is not matched with the most appropriate structure and controls.[9] As the Opening Case illustrates, an ineffective match between strategy and structure is thought to account for Sony's failure in creating a successful online music business. Even though mismatches between strategy and structure do occur, such as the one at Sony, research evidence suggests that managers try to act rationally when forming or changing their firm's structure.[10]

Organizational Structure

Organizational structure specifies the firm's formal reporting relationships, procedures, controls, and authority and decision-making processes.[11] Developing an organizational structure that effectively supports the firm's strategy is difficult,[12] especially given the uncertainty (unpredictable variation)[13] about cause–effect relationships in the global economy's dynamic competitive environments.[14] When a structure's elements (i.e., reporting relationships, procedures, and so forth) are properly aligned with one another, this structure facilitates effective implementation of the firm's strategies.[15] Thus, organizational structure is a critical component of effective strategy implementation processes.[16]

Organizational structure specifies the firm's formal reporting relationships, procedures, controls, and authority and decision-making processes.

A firm's structure specifies the work to be done and how to do it, given the firm's strategy or strategies.[17] Thus, organizational structure influences how managers work and the decisions resulting from that work.[18] Supporting the implementation of strategies, structure is concerned with processes used to complete organizational tasks.[19] Effective structures provide the stability a firm needs to successfully implement its strategies and maintain its current competitive advantages, while simultaneously providing the flexibility to develop competitive advantages that will be needed for its future strategies.[20] Thus, *structural stability* provides the capacity the firm requires to consistently and predictably manage its daily work routines,[21] while *structural flexibility* provides the opportunity to explore competitive possibilities and then allocate resources to activities that will shape the competitive advantages the firm will need to be successful in the future.[22] An effective organizational structure allows the firm to *exploit* current competitive advantages while *developing* new ones.[23]

Modifications to the firm's current strategy or selection of a new strategy call for changes to its organizational structure. However, research shows that once in place, organizational inertia often inhibits efforts to change structure, even when the firm's performance suggests that it is time to do so.[24] In his pioneering work, Alfred Chandler, a well-known business professor at Harvard University, found that organizations change their structures only when inefficiencies force them to do so.[25] Firms seem to prefer the structural status quo and its familiar working relationships until the firm's performance declines to the point where change is absolutely necessary.[26] In addition, top-level managers hesitate to conclude there are problems with the firm's structure (or its strategy, for that matter), because doing so suggests that their previous choices weren't the best ones.[27] Because of these inertial tendencies, structural change is often induced instead by the actions of stakeholders who are no longer willing to tolerate the firm's performance. For example, continuing losses of customers who have become dissatisfied with the value created by the firm's products could force change, as could reactions from capital market stakeholders.

Appropriate timing of structural change happens when top-level managers recognize that a current organizational structure no longer provides the coordination and direction needed for the firm to implement its strategies successfully.[28]

Organizational Controls

Organizational controls guide the use of strategy, indicate how to compare actual results with expected results, and suggest corrective actions to take when the difference between actual and expected results is unacceptable.

Strategic controls are largely subjective criteria intended to verify that the firm is using appropriate strategies for the conditions in the external environment and the company's competitive advantages.

Organizational controls are an important aspect of structure.[29] **Organizational controls** guide the use of strategy, indicate how to compare actual results with expected results, and suggest corrective actions to take when the difference is unacceptable. When there are fewer differences between actual and expected outcomes, the organization's controls are more effective.[30] It is difficult for the company to successfully exploit its competitive advantages without effective organizational controls.[31] Properly designed organizational controls provide clear insights regarding behaviours that enhance firm performance.[32] Firms rely on strategic controls and financial controls as part of their structures to support use of their strategies.

Strategic controls are largely subjective criteria intended to verify that the firm is using appropriate strategies for the conditions in the external environment and the company's competitive advantages. Thus, strategic controls are concerned with examining the fit between what the firm *might do* (as suggested by opportunities in its external environment) and what it *can do* (as indicated by its competitive advantages). Effective strategic controls help the firm understand what it takes to be successful.[33] Strategic controls demand rich communications between top managers who use them to judge the firm's performance and middle- and first-level managers with primary responsibility for implementing the firm's strategies. These frequent exchanges are both formal and informal in nature.[34]

Strategic controls are also used to evaluate the degree to which the firm focuses on the requirements to implement its strategies. For a business-level strategy, for example, the strategic controls are used to study primary and support activities to verify that those activities critical to successful implementation of the business-level strategy are being properly emphasized and executed. With related corporate-level strategies, strategic controls are used to verify the sharing of appropriate strategic factors such as knowledge, markets, and technologies across businesses. To effectively use strategic controls when evaluating related diversification strategies, executives must have a deep, rich strategic understanding of each unit's business-level strategy.[35] As we discuss more fully below, the use of strategic controls does not negate the need for financial controls, but the emphasis needs to be on strategic controls when both are capable of being used.

For example, in attempts to improve its strategic control over operations, Intel Corporation's CEO, Paul Otellini, shifted the chip maker's organization and control systems to focus employees on different product platforms.[36] As such, Otellini reorganized Intel into five market-focused units: corporate computing, the digital home, mobile computing, health care, and channel products (PCs produced by smaller manufacturers).[37] Each platform brings engineers, software writers, and marketers together to focus on creating and selling platform products for particular market-oriented customer groups. In doing so, Intel's CEO has facilitated improved strategic control by having more executives and affiliated functional teams control each market platform.

Partly because strategic controls are difficult to use with extensive diversification,[38] financial controls are emphasized to evaluate the performance of the firm using the unrelated diversification strategy. The unrelated diversification strategy's focus on financial outcomes (see Chapter 7) requires the use of standardized financial controls to compare performances between units and managers.[39]

Financial controls are largely objective criteria used to measure the firm's performance against previously established quantitative standards. Accounting-based measures, such as return on investment and return on assets, and market-based measures, such as economic value added, are examples of financial controls.

When using financial controls, firms evaluate their current performance against previous outcomes as well as against competitors and industry averages. In the global economy, technological advances are being used to develop highly sophisticated financial controls, making it possible for firms to analyze their performance results more thoroughly and to ensure compliance with regulations. For example, companies such as Oracle Corp. and SAP develop software tools that automate processes firms can use to meet the international financial reporting requirements specified, for example, by the Sarbanes-Oxley Act from the U.S.[40]

Both strategic and financial controls are important aspects of each organizational structure, and any structure's effectiveness is determined by using a combination of strategic and financial controls. However, the relative use of controls varies by type of strategy. For example, companies and business units of large diversified firms using the cost leadership strategy emphasize financial controls (such as quantitative cost goals), while companies and business units using the differentiation strategy emphasize strategic controls (such as subjective measures of the effectiveness of product development teams).[41] As explained above, a corporate-wide emphasis on sharing among business units (as called for by related diversification strategies) results in an emphasis on strategic controls, while financial controls are emphasized for strategies in which activities or capabilities are not shared (e.g., in an unrelated diversification). Table 12.1 contains characteristics of strategic and financial controls.

Financial controls are largely objective criteria used to measure the firm's performance against previously established quantitative standards.

| Table 12.1 | Characteristics of Strategic and Financial Control Systems |

Strategic Controls
- High level of interaction among divisions
- High level of interaction between corporate HQ and divisions
- Ability to share resources and capabilities among divisions
- Ability to transfer core competencies among divisions
- Information sharing among divisions
- Corporate managers with an in-depth knowledge of the work being done in divisions
- A long-term perspective and a willingness to accept risky ventures
- Relatively more is spent on:
  - Research and development
  - Managerial/employee training and development
  - Capital and equipment
  - Market research
- A good system to monitor product market/operational/financial data
- Open communication between corporate and divisional managers
- Employees evaluated on the basis of an open, subjective appraisal of what was done to achieve financial results

Financial Controls
- A least-cost behaviour approach
- Capital funds are channelled to divisions that yield higher financial returns— and financial returns are the only criterion used
- A short-term perspective and risk avoidance
- Corporate managers have a superficial knowledge of divisional operations
- Competition among divisions
- Managers and employees evaluated on the basis of short-term financial criteria
- Relatively less is spent on:
  - Research and development
  - Managerial/employee training and development
  - Capital and equipment
  - Market research
- Focus is on:
  - Short-term ROI (return on investment)
  - Cash flow
  - Revenue growth
  - Market share

Relationships between Strategy and Structure

Strategy and structure have a reciprocal relationship.[42] This relationship highlights the interconnectedness between strategy formulation (Chapter 5 and Chapters 7 to 10) and strategy implementation (Chapters 11 to 14). In general, this reciprocal relationship finds structure flowing from or following the selection of the firm's strategy. Once in place, structure can influence current strategic actions as well as choices about future strategies. The general nature of the strategy/structure relationship means that changes to the firm's strategy create the need to change how the organization completes its work. In the "structure influences strategy" direction, firms must be vigilant in their efforts to verify that how their structure calls for work to be completed remains consistent with the implementation requirements of chosen strategies. Research shows, however, that "strategy has a much more important influence on structure than the reverse."[43]

Corporate Structure May Limit Google's Success in the Middleware Market

The pervasive search engine Google Inc. is said to attract more than 380 million people worldwide. It generates revenue primarily through its advertising business, both online and radio. Google also offers an online application suite that includes e-mail, word processing, spreadsheets, and calendar management, at a substantially lower price than Microsoft. In addition, Google has partnered with Motorola and Samsung to create "Google-powered wireless phones." Tests of the phone show that Google is concerned principally with ease of use, reminiscent of products like Apple's iPod and iPhone.

Many of Google's features have resulted from "employee pet projects," where Google allows its engineers 20 percent of their time to work on things they are passionate about. This informal and decentralized structure at Google has helped stimulate creativity and in turn has resulted in many innovative product offerings. In fact, there are Google applications that allow users to create documents, crunch numbers, build Web sites, and more (e.g., Google Docs, Google Spreadsheets, Google Page Creator).

However, as one Harvard professor suggests, Google's attempt to break into the office application market may require a significantly different organizational structure. Professor Thomas Eisenmann suggests that for Google to be successful in this market would require "old-fashioned leadership from the top and a disciplined hierarchy to carry out big tasks." In addition, Eisenmann proposes that Google's autonomous teams may "start bumping into one another as they try to push their projects to prominence." This competition has the potential to limit Google's success in the software application market, which demands reliable and compatible systems and strong customer support. These success factors generally require a large degree of collaboration, so whether Google's extreme decentralization and entrepreneurial culture can support success in this market is uncertain.

SOURCES: 2007, Google: Hoover's Company Information; 2007, Google: Twenty percent time, Wikipedia, December 20; 2007, Business: Why Google inspires diverging case studies, *Wall Street Journal*, August 15; 2008, Video review: Google-powered phone: A prototype phone running on Google's Android operating system is quick and easy to use, Times Online, http://technology.timesonline.co.uk/tol/news/tech_and_web/article3362693.ece, February 13, retrieved March 3, 2008; J. L. Ledford, 2007, *Google Powered: Productivity with Online Tools*, New York: Wiley.

Regardless of the strength of the reciprocal relationships between strategy and structure, those choosing the firm's strategy and structure should be committed to matching each strategy with a structure that provides the stability needed to use current competitive advantages as well as the flexibility required to develop future advantages. This means, for example, that when changing strategies the firm should simultaneously consider the structure that will be needed to support use of the new strategy. A proper strategy/structure match can be a competitive advantage and contribute to a firm's earning above-average returns. See the Strategic Focus for an illustration of the relationship between strategy and structure.

Evolutionary Patterns of Strategy and Organizational Structure

Research suggests that most firms experience a certain pattern of relationships between strategy and structure. Chandler[44] found that firms tended to grow in somewhat predictable patterns: "first by volume, then by geography, then integration (vertical, horizontal) and finally through product/business diversification"[45] (see Figure 12.1). Chandler interpreted his findings to indicate that the firm's growth patterns determine its structural form.

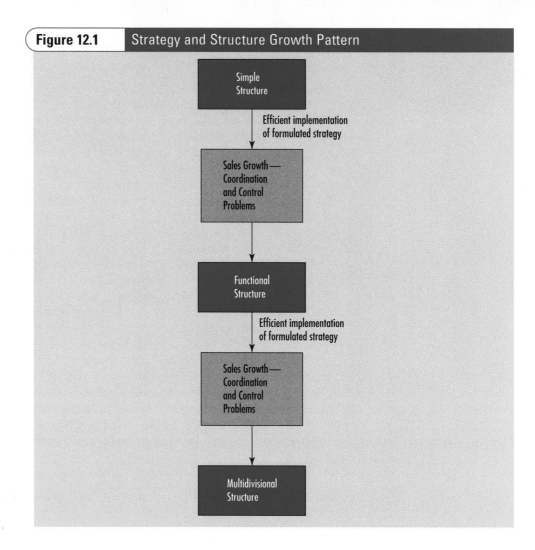

Figure 12.1   Strategy and Structure Growth Pattern

Simple
Structure

Efficient implementation
of formulated strategy

Sales Growth—
Coordination
and Control
Problems

Functional
Structure

Efficient implementation
of formulated strategy

Sales Growth—
Coordination
and Control
Problems

Multidivisional
Structure

As shown in Figure 12.1, sales growth creates coordination and control problems that the existing organizational structure cannot efficiently handle. Organizational growth creates the opportunity for the firm to change its strategy to try to become even more successful. However, the existing structure's formal reporting relationships, procedures, controls, and authority and decision-making processes lack the sophistication required to support use of the new strategy.[46] A new structure is needed to help decision makers gain access to the knowledge and understanding required to effectively integrate and coordinate actions to implement the new strategy.[47]

Three major types of organizational structures are used to implement strategies: simple structure, functional structure, and multidivisional structure.

Simple Structure

The **simple structure** is a structure in which the owner-manager makes all major decisions and monitors all activities while staff members serve as an extension of the manager's supervisory authority.[48] Typically, the owner-manager actively works in the business on a daily basis. Informal relationships, few rules, limited task specialization, and unsophisticated information systems characterize the simple structure. Frequent and informal communications between the owner-manager and employees make it relatively

The **simple structure** is a structure in which the owner-manager makes all major decisions and monitors all activities while the staff serve as an extension of the manager's supervisory authority.

easy to coordinate the work that is to be done. The simple structure is matched with focus strategies and business-level strategies, as these firms commonly compete by offering a single product line in a single geographic market. Local restaurants, repair businesses, and other specialized enterprises are examples of firms relying on the simple structure to implement their strategy.

As the small firm grows larger and becomes more complex, managerial and structural challenges emerge. For example, the amount of competitively relevant information requiring analysis substantially increases, placing significant pressure on the owner-manager. Additional growth and success may cause the firm to change its strategy. Even if the strategy remains the same, the firm's larger size dictates the need for more sophisticated workflows and integrating mechanisms. At this evolutionary point, firms tend to move from the simple structure to a functional organizational structure.[49]

Casketfurniture.com, an example of a company using the focus differentiation strategy, may soon move from the simple structure to a functional structure. Family-owned and -managed, this venture is a part of MHP Enterprises Ltd., a small family firm operating out of Nelson, British Columbia. MHP has long been managed through a simple structure, and in 1997 MHP decided to expand its distribution to mortuaries by selling products related to death and funerals by establishing Casketfurniture.com. Using the Internet, this venture sells what it believes are creative products throughout the world. The continuing success of Casketfurniture.com could create coordination and control problems for MHP that may be solved only by the firm changing from the simple to the functional structure.[50]

Functional Structure

The **functional structure** consists of a chief executive officer and a limited corporate staff, with functional line managers in dominant organizational areas such as production, accounting, marketing, R&D, engineering, and human resources.[51] This U-form structure allows for functional specialization,[52] thereby facilitating active sharing of knowledge within each functional area. Knowledge sharing facilitates career paths as well as the professional development of functional specialists. However, a functional orientation can have a negative effect on communication and coordination among those representing different organizational functions. Because of this, the CEO must work hard to verify that the decisions and actions of individual business functions promote the entire firm rather than a single function.[53] The functional structure supports implementation of business-level strategies and some corporate-level strategies (e.g., single or dominant business) with low levels of diversification.

The **functional structure** consists of a chief executive officer and a limited corporate staff, with functional line managers in dominant organizational areas, such as production, accounting, marketing, R&D, engineering, and human resources.

Multidivisional Structure

With continuing growth and success, firms often consider greater levels of diversification. However, successful diversification requires analysis of substantially greater amounts of data and information when the firm offers the same products in different markets (market or geographic diversification) or offers different products in several markets (product diversification). In addition, trying to manage high levels of diversification through functional structures creates serious coordination and control problems.[54] Thus, greater diversification leads to a new structural form.[55]

The **multidivisional (M-form) structure** consists of operating divisions, each representing a separate business or profit centre in which the top corporate officer delegates responsibilities for day-to-day operations and business-unit strategy to division managers. Each division represents a distinct, self-contained business with its own functional hierarchy.[56] As initially designed, the M-form was thought to have three major benefits: "(1) it enabled corporate officers to more accurately monitor the performance of each business, which simplified the problem of control; (2) it facilitated comparisons

The **multidivisional (M-form) structure** consists of operating divisions, each representing a separate business or profit centre in which the top corporate officer delegates responsibilities for day-to-day operations and business-unit strategy to division managers.

between divisions, which improved the resource allocation process; and (3) it stimulated managers of poorly performing divisions to look for ways of improving performance."[57] Active monitoring of performance through the M-form increases the likelihood that decisions made by managers heading individual units will be in shareholders' best interests. Because diversification is a dominant corporate-level strategy used in the global economy, the M-form is a widely adopted organizational structure.[58]

Used to support implementation of related and unrelated diversification strategies, the M-form helps firms successfully manage the many demands (including those related to processing vast amounts of information) of diversification.[59] Partly because of its value to diversified corporations, some consider the multidivisional structure to be one of the 20th century's most significant organizational innovations.[60]

None of the organizational structures described (simple, functional, or multidivisional) is inherently superior to the others.[61] In legendary management consultant Peter Drucker's words, "There is no one right organization. . . . Rather, the task . . . is to select the organization for the particular task and mission at hand."[62] In our context, Drucker is saying that the firm must select a structure that is "right" for the particular strategy that has been selected to pursue the firm's vision and mission. Because no single structure is optimal in all instances, managers concentrate on developing proper matches between strategies and organizational structures rather than searching for an "optimal" structure. We now describe the strategy/structure matches that evidence shows positively contribute to firm performance.

Matches between Business-Level Strategies and the Functional Structure

Different forms of the functional organizational structure are used to support implementation of the cost leadership, differentiation, and integrated cost leadership/differentiation strategies. The differences in these forms are accounted for primarily by different uses of three important structural characteristics or dimensions: *specialization* (concerned with the type and number of jobs required to complete work[63]), *centralization* (the degree to which decision-making authority is retained at higher managerial levels[64]), and *formalization* (the degree to which formal rules and procedures govern work[65]).

Using the Functional Structure to Implement the Cost Leadership Strategy

Firms using the cost leadership strategy want to sell large quantities of standardized products to an industry's or a segment's typical customer. Simple reporting relationships, few layers in the decision-making and authority structure, a centralized corporate staff, and a strong focus on process improvements through the manufacturing function rather than the development of new products by emphasizing product R&D characterize the cost leadership form of the functional structure[66] (see the top portion of Figure 12.2). This structure contributes to the emergence of a low-cost culture—a culture in which all employees constantly try to find ways to reduce the costs incurred to complete their work.

In terms of centralization, decision-making authority is centralized in a staff function to maintain a cost-reducing emphasis within each organizational function (engineering, marketing, etc.). While encouraging continuous cost reductions, centralized staff members also verify that further cuts in costs in one function won't adversely affect productivity levels in other functions.[67]

Jobs are highly specialized in the cost leadership functional structure. Job specialization is accomplished by dividing work into homogeneous subgroups. Organizational functions are the most common subgroup, although work is sometimes batched on the basis of products produced or clients served. Specializing in their work allows employees to increase their efficiency, reducing the firm's costs as a result. Highly formalized rules

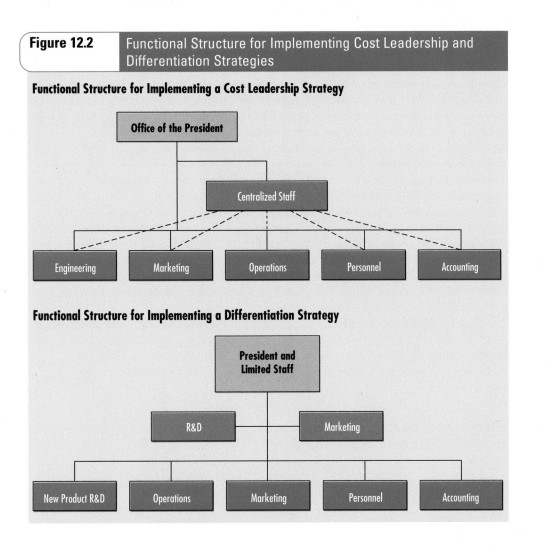

Figure 12.2 Functional Structure for Implementing Cost Leadership and Differentiation Strategies

Functional Structure for Implementing a Cost Leadership Strategy

- Office of the President
  - Centralized Staff
    - Engineering
    - Marketing
    - Operations
    - Personnel
    - Accounting

Functional Structure for Implementing a Differentiation Strategy

- President and Limited Staff
  - R&D
  - Marketing
    - New Product R&D
    - Operations
    - Marketing
    - Personnel
    - Accounting

and procedures, often emanating from the centralized staff, guide the work completed in the cost leadership form of the functional structure. Predictably, following formal rules and procedures creates cost-reducing efficiencies.

Known for its commitment to "everyday low prices," Wal-Mart's organizational structure helps it to drive costs continuously lower.[68] Its procurement is such an important function to Wal-Mart in terms of cost savings that it created an organization-wide division dedicated solely to global procurement; this results in Wal-Mart being able to purchase in bulk to obtain lower prices. As discussed in the opening case in Chapter 3, competitors' efforts to duplicate the success of Wal-Mart's cost leadership strategies have failed, partly because they have not been able to gain the degree of scale that Wal-Mart boasts.

Using the Functional Structure to Implement the Differentiation Strategy

Firms using the differentiation strategy produce products that customers perceive as being different in ways that create value for them. With this strategy, the firm wants to sell nonstandardized/customized products to customers with unique needs. Relatively complex and flexible reporting relationships, frequent use of cross-functional product development teams, and a strong focus on marketing and product R&D rather than manufacturing and process R&D (as with the cost leadership form of the functional structure) characterize the differentiation form of the functional structure (see the bottom portion of Figure 12.2). This structure contributes to the emergence of a development-oriented culture—a culture in which employees try to find ways to further differentiate current products and to develop new, highly differentiated products.[69]

A good example is the development of the BlackBerry, a wireless e-mail solution. Canada's leader in the wireless e-mail market is Research In Motion (RIM). Known for its innovation, RIM uses product-functional teams to develop new and successful products like its BlackBerry.[70] Moreover, due to its informal corporate culture, RIM has successfully stimulated a creative and development-focused atmosphere.[71]

Continuous product innovation demands that people throughout the firm be able to interpret and take action based on information that is often ambiguous, incomplete, and uncertain. With a strong focus on the external environment to identify new opportunities, employees often gather this information from people outside the firm, such as customers and suppliers. Commonly, rapid responses to the possibilities indicated by the collected information are necessary, suggesting the need for decision-making responsibility and authority to be decentralized. To support creativity and the continuous pursuit of new sources of differentiation and new products, jobs in this structure are not highly specialized. This lack of specialization means that workers have a relatively large number of tasks in their job descriptions. Few formal rules and procedures are also characteristics of this structure.

Low formalization, decentralization of decision-making authority and responsibility, and low specialization of work tasks combine to create a structure in which people interact frequently to exchange ideas about how to further differentiate current products while developing ideas for new products that can be differentiated to create value for customers.

Using the Functional Structure to Implement the Integrated Cost Leadership/Differentiation Strategy

Firms using the integrated cost leadership/differentiation strategy want to sell products that create value because of their relatively low cost and reasonable sources of differentiation. The cost of these products is low "relative" to the cost leader's prices, while their differentiation is "reasonable" compared with the clearly unique features of the differentiator's products.

The integrated cost leadership/differentiation strategy is used frequently in the global economy, although it is difficult to successfully implement. This difficulty is due largely to the fact that different primary and support activities (see Chapter 4) must be emphasized when using the cost leadership and differentiation strategies. To achieve the cost leadership position, production and process engineering are emphasized, with infrequent product changes. To achieve a differentiated position, marketing and new product R&D are emphasized while production and process engineering are not. Thus, effective use of the integrated strategy results when the firm successfully combines activities intended to reduce costs with activities intended to create additional differentiation features. As a result, the integrated form of the functional structure must have decision-making patterns that are partially centralized and partially decentralized. Additionally, jobs are semi-specialized, and rules and procedures call for some formal and some informal job behaviour.

While the strategies of differentiation and cost leadership may seem mutually exclusive, this is not always the case. For example, Mountain Equipment Co-op (MEC), a Canadian-based outdoor sports retailer, differentiates itself by having a strong commitment to environmental friendliness. The retailer builds its stores from 97 percent[72] recycled material and operates on significantly less energy. This environmental commitment has helped build the MEC brand while resulting in up to $30,000 to $40,000 in annual cost savings in some stores.[73] The decision for environmental consciousness gives evidence to the effectiveness of an integrated differentiation/cost leadership strategy.

Matches between Corporate-Level Strategies and the Multidivisional Structure

As explained earlier, Chandler's research showed that the firm's continuing success leads to product or market diversification or both.[74] The firm's level of diversification is a function of decisions about the number and type of businesses in which it will compete, as well as how it will manage the businesses (see Chapter 7). Geared to managing individual organizational functions, increasing diversification eventually creates information processing, coordination, and control problems that the functional structure cannot handle. Thus, use of a diversification strategy requires the firm to change from the functional structure to the multidivisional structure to develop an appropriate strategy/structure match.

As defined in Figure 7.1 in Chapter 7, corporate-level strategies have different degrees of product and market diversification. The demands created by different levels of diversification highlight the need for a unique organizational structure to effectively implement each strategy (see Figure 12.3).

Using the Cooperative Form of the Multidivisional Structure to Implement the Related-Constrained Strategy

The **cooperative form** is a structure in which horizontal integration is used to bring about interdivisional cooperation.[75] The divisions in the firm using the related-constrained diversification strategy commonly are formed around products, markets, or both. As the Opening Case illustrates, Sony would likely experience better coordination among its divisions if it were to implement the cooperative form of the multidivisional structure, given the lack of divisional coordination in its poorly executed online music strategy. In Figure 12.4, we use product divisions as part of the representation of the cooperative form of the multidivisional structure, although market divisions could be used instead of or in addition to product divisions to develop the figure.

All of the related-constrained firm's divisions share one or more corporate strengths. Production competencies, marketing competencies, and channel dominance are examples of strengths that the firm's divisions might share.[76] Production expertise is one of the strengths of Sony's divisions. However, as the Opening Case illustrates, Sony has had difficulties in coordinating across divisions to create joint products in online music.

Magna International, Canada's largest automobile parts manufacturer,[77] has two main operating divisions: manufacturing and assembly. Each is a separate profit centre under the

> The **cooperative form** is a structure in which horizontal integration is used to bring about interdivisional cooperation.

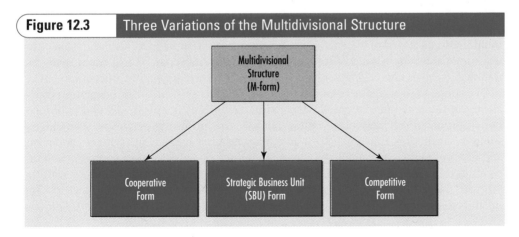

Figure 12.3 Three Variations of the Multidivisional Structure

Multidivisional Structure (M-form)
→ Cooperative Form
→ Strategic Business Unit (SBU) Form
→ Competitive Form

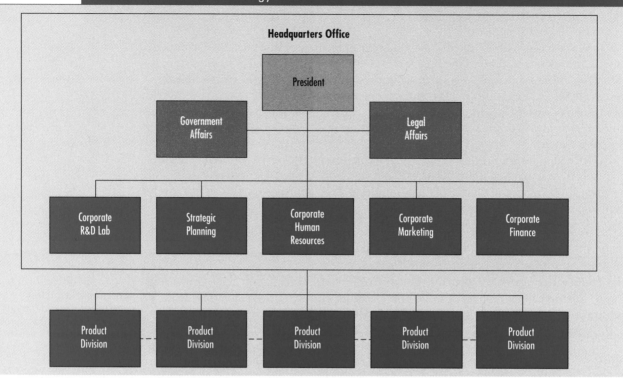

authority of a different general manager. Magna's divisions are aligned by geographic region and then by product division (i.e., metal body systems, exterior trim components, etc).[78]

Largely due to Magna's multidivisional structure, it has been able to capitalize on one of the biggest trends in the automotive industry—namely, outsourcing low-volume, niche vehicle engineering, development, and assembly. Magna has achieved success in this regard because its divisions work together to accomplish the engineering, manufacturing and assembly, or any combination thereof, to provide a total manufacturing solution.[79]

The sharing of divisional competencies facilitates the corporation's efforts to develop economies of scope. As explained in Chapter 7, economies of scope (cost savings resulting from the sharing of competencies developed in one division with another division) are linked with successful use of the related-constrained strategy. Interdivisional sharing of competencies depends on cooperation, suggesting the use of the cooperative form of the multidivisional structure.[80] Increasingly, it is important that the links resulting from effective use of integration mechanisms support the cooperative sharing of both intangible resources (such as knowledge) and tangible resources (such as facilities and equipment).[81]

The cooperative structure uses different characteristics of structure as integrating mechanisms to facilitate interdivisional cooperation. Defined earlier in the discussion of functional organizational structures, centralization is one of these mechanisms. Centralizing some organizational functions (such as human resource management, R&D, marketing, and finance) at the corporate level allows the linking of activities among divisions. Work completed in these centralized functions is managed by the firm's central office with the purpose of exploiting common strengths among divisions by sharing competencies.[82] The intent is to develop competitive advantages in the divisions as they implement their cost leadership, differentiation, or integrated cost leadership/differentiation business-unit strategies, which allows the firm to create more value compared to the value that is created by nondiversified rivals' use of business-level strategies.[83]

Frequent and direct contact between division managers, used as another integrating mechanism, encourages and supports cooperation and the sharing of competencies or resources that could be used to create new advantages. Sometimes, liaison roles are established in each division to reduce the time division managers spend integrating and coordinating their unit's work with the work occurring in other divisions. Temporary teams or task forces may be formed around projects whose success depends on sharing competencies that are embedded within several divisions. Formal integration departments might be established in firms frequently using temporary teams or task forces. Ultimately, **a matrix organization** may evolve in firms implementing the related-constrained strategy.[84] Although complicated, an effective matrix structure can lead to improved coordination among a firm's divisions (see Figure 12.5).[85]

The success of the cooperative multidivisional structure is significantly affected by how well information is processed among divisions. But because cooperation among divisions implies a loss of managerial autonomy, division managers may not readily commit themselves to the type of integrative information-processing activities that this structure demands. Moreover, coordination among divisions sometimes results in an unequal flow of positive outcomes to divisional managers. In other words, when managerial rewards are

A **matrix organization** is an organizational structure in which there is a dual structure combining both functional specialization and business product or project specialization.

Figure 12.5	A Typical Product and Matrix Structure

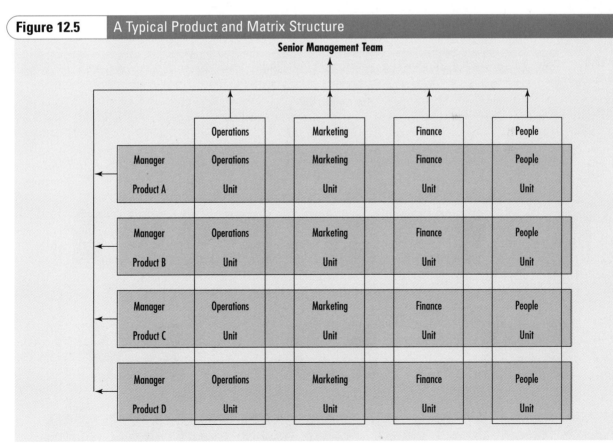

based at least in part on the performance of individual divisions, the manager of the division that is able to benefit the most by the sharing of corporate competencies might be viewed as receiving relative gains at others' expense. Strategic controls (see Table 12.1) are important in these instances, as divisional managers' performance can be evaluated at least partly on the basis of how well they have facilitated interdivisional cooperative efforts. Furthermore, using reward systems that emphasize overall company performance, besides outcomes achieved by individual divisions, helps overcome problems associated with the cooperative form.

Using the Strategic Business Unit Form of the Multidivisional Structure to Implement the Related-Linked Strategy

When the firm has fewer links, or less constrained links among its divisions, the related-linked diversification strategy is used. The strategic business unit form of the multidivisional structure supports implementation of this strategy. The **strategic business unit (SBU) form** consists of three levels: corporate headquarters, strategic business units (SBUs), and SBU divisions (see Figure 12.6).

The divisions within each SBU are related in terms of shared products or markets or both, but the divisions of one SBU have little in common with the divisions of the other SBUs. Divisions within each SBU share product or market competencies to develop economies of scope and possibly economies of scale. The integration mechanisms used by the divisions in a cooperative structure can be equally well used by the divisions within the individual strategic business units that are part of the SBU form of the multidivisional structure. In this structure, each SBU is a profit centre that is controlled and

The **strategic business unit (SBU) form** consists of three levels: corporate headquarters, strategic business units (SBUs), and SBU divisions.

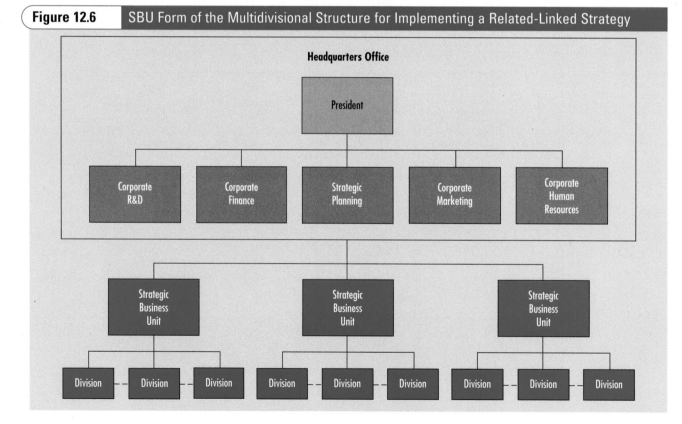

Figure 12.6 SBU Form of the Multidivisional Structure for Implementing a Related-Linked Strategy

evaluated by the headquarters office. Although both financial and strategic controls are important, on a relative basis financial controls (see Table 12.1) are vital to headquarters' evaluation of each SBU; strategic controls are critical when the heads of SBUs evaluate their divisions' performance. Strategic controls are also critical to the headquarters' efforts to determine whether the company has chosen an effective portfolio of businesses and whether those businesses are being successfully managed.

The SBU structure is used by large firms and can be complex, with the complexity reflected by the organization's size and product and market diversity. The Goodyear Tire & Rubber Company employs five strategic business units that are unique in the geography they serve, but are identical in the products they offer.[86] Sony used the related-linked strategy but it needed to pursue the related-constrained strategy accompanied by the cooperative M-form structure, as exemplified in the Opening Case about its difficulty in getting separate SBUs to cooperate in creating an online music business.

In general, each SBU has several related businesses that are coordinated by SBU managers. The sharing of competencies among units within an SBU is an important characteristic of this form of the M-form structure (see the notes to Figure 12.6). In addition, each SBU receives strategic help from corporate headquarters on contracting/training new franchised businesses, and running fee-for-service businesses using more centralized functions. One drawback to the SBU structure is that multifaceted businesses often have difficulties in communicating this complex business model to shareholders.[87] Furthermore, if coordination among SBUs is needed, problems can arise because the SBU structure, similar to the competitive form discussed next, does not easily foster cooperation across SBUs.

Using the Competitive Form of the Multidivisional Structure to Implement the Unrelated Diversification Strategy

Firms using the unrelated diversification strategy want to create value through efficient internal capital allocations or by restructuring, buying, and selling businesses.[88] The competitive form of the multidivisional structure supports implementation of this strategy.

The **competitive form** is a structure in which there is complete independence among the firm's divisions (see Figure 12.7). Unlike the divisions included in the cooperative

The **competitive form** is a structure in which there is complete independence among the firm's divisions.

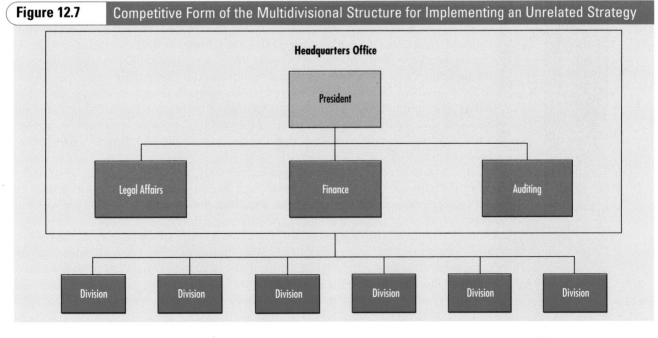

Figure 12.7   Competitive Form of the Multidivisional Structure for Implementing an Unrelated Strategy

structure, the divisions that are part of the competitive structure do not share common corporate strengths (e.g., marketing competencies or channel dominance). Because strengths aren't shared, integrating devices aren't developed for use by the divisions included in the competitive structure.

The efficient internal capital market that is the foundation for use of the unrelated diversification strategy requires organizational arrangements that emphasize divisional competition rather than cooperation.[89] Three benefits are expected from the internal competition that the competitive form of the multidivisional structure facilitates. First, internal competition creates flexibility—corporate headquarters can have divisions working on different technologies to identify those with the greatest potential, for example. Resources can then be allocated to the division that is working with the most promising technology to fuel the entire firm's success. Second, internal competition challenges the status quo and inertia, because division heads know that future resource allocations are a product of excellent current performance as well as superior positioning of their division in terms of future performance. Last, internal competition motivates effort. The challenge of competing against internal peers can be as great as the challenge of competing against external marketplace competitors.[90]

Independence among divisions, as shown by a lack of sharing of corporate strengths and the absence of integrating devices, allows the firm using the unrelated diversification strategy to form specific profit performance expectations for each division to stimulate internal competition for future resources, especially financial resources. The benefits of internal capital allocations or restructuring cannot be fully realized unless divisions are held accountable for their own independent performance. In the competitive structure, organizational controls (primarily financial controls; see Table 12.1) are used to emphasize and support internal competition among separate divisions and as the basis for allocating corporate capital based on divisions' performances.

Textron, a global multi-industry company, has a portfolio of well-known brands that it researches thoroughly before acquiring. Following a strict set of criteria, it selects businesses to integrate into its company in an attempt to enhance its portfolio. It runs a number of independent businesses including units that manufacture fasteners, golf carts, and Bell helicopters. Textron uses return on invested capital (ROIC) as the "compass for guiding" the evaluation of its diversified set of businesses as they compete internally for resources.[91]

To emphasize competitiveness among divisions, the headquarters office generally maintains an arm's-length relationship with each division, intervening in affairs only to audit operations and discipline managers whose divisions perform poorly. In emphasizing competition among divisions, the headquarters office relies on financial controls to set rate-of-return targets and to monitor divisional performance relative to those targets. The headquarters office then allocates cash flow on a competitive basis, rather than automatically returning cash to the division that produced it. Thus, the focus of the headquarters' work is on performance appraisal, resource allocation, and long-range planning to verify that the firm's portfolio of businesses will lead to financial success.[92]

The three major forms of the multidivisional structure should each be paired with a particular corporate-level strategy. Table 12.2 shows these structures' characteristics. Differences are seen in the degree of centralization, the focus of the performance appraisal, the horizontal structures (integrating mechanisms), and the incentive compensation schemes. The most centralized and most costly structural form is the cooperative structure. The least centralized, with the lowest bureaucratic costs, is the competitive structure. The SBU structure requires partial centralization and involves some of the mechanisms necessary to implement the relatedness between divisions. Also, the divisional incentive compensation awards are allocated according to both SBUs and corporate performance.

| | **Table 12.2** | **Characteristics of the Structures Necessary to Implement the Related-Constrained, Related-Linked, and Unrelated Diversification Strategies** | |

	Overall Structural Form		
Structural Characteristics	Cooperative M-form (related-constrained strategy)[a]	SBU M-form (related-linked strategy)[a]	Competitive M-form (unrelated diversification strategy)[a]
Centralization of operations	Centralized at corporate office	Partially centralized (in SBUs)	Decentralized to divisions
Use of integration mechanisms	Extensive	Moderate	Nonexistent
Divisional performance appraisals	Emphasize subjective (strategic) criteria	Use a mixture of subjective (strategic) and objective (financial) criteria	Emphasize objective (financial) criteria
Divisional incentive compensation	Linked to overall corporate performance	Mixed linkage to corporate, SBU, and divisional performance	Linked to divisional performance

[a]Strategy implemented with structural form.

Matches between International Strategies and Worldwide Structures

As explained in Chapter 9, international strategies are becoming increasingly important for long-term competitive success.[93] Among other benefits, international strategies allow the firm to search for new markets, resources, core competencies, and technologies as part of its efforts to outperform competitors.[94]

As with business-level and corporate-level strategies, unique organizational structures are necessary to successfully implement the different international strategies.[95] Forming proper matches between international strategies and organizational structures facilitates the firm's efforts to effectively coordinate and control its global operations.[96] More importantly, research findings confirm the validity of the international strategy/structure matches we discuss here.[97]

Using the Worldwide Geographic Area Structure to Implement the Multidomestic Strategy

The *multidomestic strategy* decentralizes the firm's strategic and operating decisions to business units in each country so that product characteristics can be tailored to local preferences. Firms using this strategy try to isolate themselves from global competitive forces by establishing protected market positions or by competing in industry segments that are most affected by differences among local countries. The worldwide geographic area structure is used to implement this strategy. The **worldwide geographic area structure** emphasizes national interests and facilitates the firm's efforts to satisfy local or cultural differences (see the left side of Figure 12.8 on page 382). Because using the multidomestic strategy requires little coordination between different country markets, integrating mechanisms among divisions in the worldwide geographic area structure are not needed. Hence, formalization is low, and coordination among units in a firm's worldwide geographic area structure is often informal.

The **worldwide geographic area structure** emphasizes national interests and facilitates the firm's efforts to satisfy local or cultural differences.

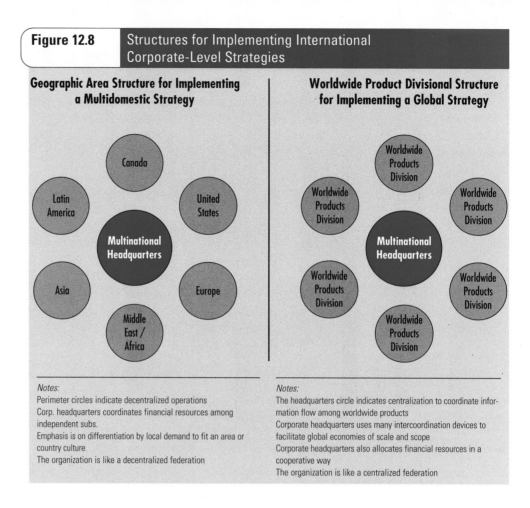

Figure 12.8 Structures for Implementing International Corporate-Level Strategies

Geographic Area Structure for Implementing a Multidomestic Strategy

Canada
Latin America
United States
Multinational Headquarters
Asia
Europe
Middle East / Africa

Notes:
Perimeter circles indicate decentralized operations
Corp. headquarters coordinates financial resources among independent subs.
Emphasis is on differentiation by local demand to fit an area or country culture
The organization is like a decentralized federation

Worldwide Product Divisional Structure for Implementing a Global Strategy

Worldwide Products Division
Worldwide Products Division
Worldwide Products Division
Multinational Headquarters
Worldwide Products Division
Worldwide Products Division
Worldwide Products Division

Notes:
The headquarters circle indicates centralization to coordinate information flow among worldwide products
Corporate headquarters uses many intercoordination devices to facilitate global economies of scale and scope
Corporate headquarters also allocates financial resources in a cooperative way
The organization is like a centralized federation

The multidomestic strategy/worldwide geographic area structure match evolved as a natural outgrowth of the multicultural European marketplace. Friends and family members of the main business who were sent as expatriates into foreign countries to develop the independent country subsidiary often implemented this type of structure for the main business. The relationship to corporate headquarters by divisions took place through informal communication among "family members."[98]

To implement its multidomestic strategy, InBev—the parent company of Labatt—which, by acquiring local brands, has become one of the world's largest brewers, uses the worldwide geographic area structure with regional and country division headquarters throughout the world.[99] Decentralization at its regional and country headquarters allows for strong marketing that adapts the acquired brands to the local cultures and for some improved cost structures, especially in avoiding significant transportation costs across geographic regions. Similarly, the strategy/structure fit at SABMiller has contributed significantly to the success of the firm throughout the world.[100]

A key disadvantage of the multidomestic strategy/worldwide geographic area structure match is the inability to create strong global efficiency. With an increasing emphasis on lower-cost products in international markets, the need to pursue worldwide economies of scale has also increased. These changes have fostered the use of the global strategy and its structural match, the worldwide product divisional structure.

Using the Worldwide Product Divisional Structure to Implement the Global Strategy

With the corporation's home office dictating competitive strategy, the *global strategy* is one through which the firm offers standardized products across country markets. The firm's success depends on its ability to develop and take advantage of economies of scope and economies of scale on a global level. Decisions to outsource some primary or support activities to the world's best providers are particularly helpful when the firm tries to develop economies of scale.[101]

The worldwide product divisional structure supports use of the global strategy. In the **worldwide product divisional structure,** decision-making authority is centralized in the worldwide division headquarters to coordinate and integrate decisions and actions among divisional business units (see the right side of Figure 12.8). As opposed to the common retail practice of customizing products to meet local markets' needs, the Swedish home products retailer IKEA has employed a global strategy approach when selling its products worldwide.

IKEA has successfully employed a standardized go-to-market strategy; however, this same strategy that led to cost savings in Europe and North America was criticized as being insensitive of cultural differences in some significant markets, namely China and Japan. To its dismay, IKEA was received by Chinese consumers as a high-price, premium brand, and so consumers were not prepared to pay such a premium for the lack of service that comes from the "do it yourself" factor of IKEA's value proposition.[102]

Integrating mechanisms are important in the effective use of the worldwide product divisional structure. Examples of these mechanisms include direct contact between managers, liaison roles between departments, temporary task forces, and permanent teams. One researcher describes the use of these mechanisms in the worldwide structure: "There is extensive and formal use of task forces and operating committees to supplement communication and coordination of worldwide operations."[103] The evolution of a shared vision of the firm's strategy and how structure supports its implementation is one of the important outcomes resulting from these mechanisms' effective use. The disadvantages of the global strategy/worldwide structure combination are the difficulty involved with coordinating decisions and actions across country borders and the inability to quickly respond to local needs and preferences.

In response to some problems brought on by standardization, franchising is an increasingly common practice that IKEA employs when moving into new, higher-risk markets. IKEA's franchisees are given standardized products but have the room to customize their selling prices and promotions to fit the local market demands. In order for IKEA to maintain a standard level of service and quality across different markets, it frequently audits its franchisees and provides extensive training and operational support from headquarters.[104]

In stable markets that carry similar characteristics to that of the Scandinavian market IKEA enters using fully owned subsidiaries, which are responsible for training, logistics, marketing, and specifics to the location. As a result, IKEA's brand remains standardized, and corporate maintains operational control.[105]

Using the Combination Structure to Implement the Transnational Strategy

The *transnational strategy* calls for the firm to combine the multidomestic strategy's local responsiveness with the global strategy's efficiency. Thus, firms using this strategy are trying to gain the advantages of both local responsiveness and global efficiency. The combination structure is used to implement the transnational strategy. The **combination structure** is a structure drawing characteristics and mechanisms from both the worldwide geographic area structure and the worldwide product divisional structure. The transnational strategy is often implemented through two possible combination structures: a global matrix structure or a hybrid global design.[106]

The global matrix design brings together both local market and product expertise into teams that develop and respond to the global marketplace. The *global matrix design* (the

In the **worldwide product divisional structure,** decision-making authority is centralized in the worldwide division headquarters to coordinate and integrate decisions and actions among divisional business units.

The **combination structure** is a structure drawing characteristics and mechanisms from both the worldwide geographic area structure and the worldwide product divisional structure.

basic matrix structure was defined earlier) promotes flexibility in designing products and responding to customer needs. However, it has severe limitations in that it places employees in a position of being accountable to more than one manager. At any given time, an employee may be a member of several functional or product group teams. Relationships that evolve from multiple memberships can make it difficult for employees to be simultaneously loyal to all of them. Although the matrix places authority in the hands of managers who are most able to use it, it creates problems in regard to corporate reporting relationships that are so complex and vague that it is difficult and time-consuming to receive approval for major decisions. The hybrid structure is illustrated in Figure 12.9. In this design, some divisions are oriented toward products while others are oriented toward market areas. Thus, in some divisions where the geographic area is more important, the division managers are area-oriented. In other divisions where worldwide product coordination and efficiencies are more important, the division manager is more product-oriented.

The fits between the multidomestic strategy and the worldwide geographic area structure, and between the global strategy and the worldwide product divisional structure are apparent. However, when a firm wants to implement the multidomestic and the global strategies simultaneously through a combination structure, the appropriate integrating mechanisms for the two structures are less obvious. The structure used to implement the transnational strategy must be simultaneously centralized and decentralized; integrated and nonintegrated; formalized and nonformalized. These seemingly opposite characteristics must be managed by an overall structure that is capable of encouraging all employees to understand the effects of cultural diversity on a firm's operations. This is illustrated in the Strategic Focus on Unilever's teams approach.

The teams approach exemplified in the Strategic Focus on Unilever highlights the need for a strong educational component to change an organization's entire culture. If the cultural change is effective, the combination structure should allow the firm to learn how to gain competitive benefits in local economies by adapting its core competencies, which often have been developed and nurtured in less culturally diverse competitive environments. As firms globalize and move toward the transnational strategy, the idea of a corporate headquarters has become increasingly important in fostering leadership and a shared vision to create a stronger company identity.[107]

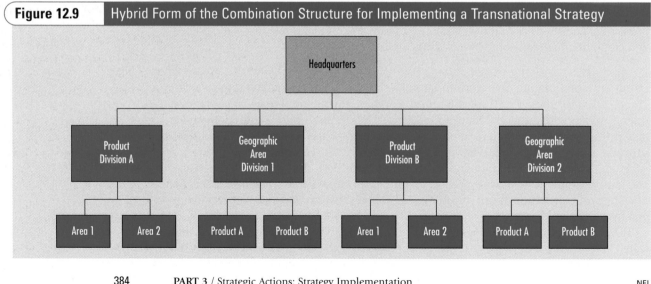

Figure 12.9   Hybrid Form of the Combination Structure for Implementing a Transnational Strategy

Unilever: Reorganized for Transnational Strategy and Combination Structure

Unilever is a large consumer products firm headquartered historically in two locations, the Netherlands and the United Kingdom. Unilever has adopted a structure similar to the reorganization adopted by Procter & Gamble (P&G), with global managers overseeing consumer marketing and product development and regional bosses controlling areas such as sales, media buying, and trade marketing.

This organizational structure has moved Unilever away from the location-specific dominance that is associated with a multidomestic strategy and worldwide area structure. In the restructuring, "Unilever sought to reduce the influence of country heads by forming global teams for some products." As such, it is clear that Unilever is using the combination structure to implement a transnational strategy.

Unilever's organization system differs from P&G's in a significant respect: "profit-and-loss responsibility lies with regional presidents rather than with global category organizations that control marketing, product mixes and strategy." Although brand managers and directors in global brand categories sign off on overall strategic plans for each business unit, regional organizations have the power to set marketing budgets and to buy actual media applications (i.e., TV, radio, Internet, or newspaper advertisements). This power was previously in the hands of local country managers. One veteran P&G executive commented on that restructuring by noting: "You are essentially moving decision rights around, and that is very difficult since new kings are crowned and others dethroned." With this system, "country managers can't tinker with [the product's] packaging, formulation or advertising," and with fewer layers of management Unilever hopes to facilitate faster decision making and faster execution.

One example of how the restructuring worked in the regions is the home and personal care business in Asia. Country heads for Asian countries had relocated to Singapore to form a team to manage investments in innovation and marketing across the region. Instead of reporting to marketing directors in each country, they sought to build a regional team to manage brands across the region, and thus only sales would remain an exclusively local function.

Although this realignment could speed up decision making, improve cost management, and provide stronger brand consistency in the region, this ran the risk of decreased insights from local-consumer-oriented marketers. "It's not exactly clear how a strategy devised in Singapore for the Thai market will work in the Indian context." The bottom line is that there is more global and regional brand-management centralization than under the previous strategy. Thus, Unilever is moving from a multidomestic strategy developed in continental Europe to a transnational strategy as it moves globally. To a degree it mirrors the strategy that competitors such as P&G and L'Oréal have implemented in the past but with more regional control versus product control.

SOURCES: 2005, Can Unilever create a masterpiece? *Strategic Direction*, May, 11–14; 2005, Unilever's restructure "Makes us more like P&G," *Marketing Week*, February 24, 8; D. Ball, 2005, Too many cooks: Despite revamp, unwieldy Unilever falls behind rivals, *Wall Street Journal*, January 3, A1; D. Ball, 2005, Unilever weighs adding CEO post to alter structure, *Wall Street Journal*, February 7, B5; D. Baishya, 2005, Will realignment aid Unilever marketing strategies?, *Media*, January 4, A20; G. Jones & P. Miskell, 2005, European integration and corporate restructuring: The strategy of Unilever c.1957–c.1990, *Economic History Review*, 58(1): 113–139; J. Neff, 2005, Unilever gets snarled in its own untangling, *Advertising Age*, May 2, 63–64; J. Neff, 2005, Unilever reorganization shifts P&L responsibility, *Advertising Age*, February 28, 13; 2007, Unilever Company Structure, http://www.unilever.com/ourcompany/aboutunilever/companystructure/default.asp,retrieved December 29.

Matches between Cooperative Strategies and Network Structures

As discussed in Chapter 10, a network strategy exists when partners form several alliances in order to improve the performance of the alliance network itself through cooperative endeavours.[108] The greater levels of environmental complexity and uncertainty that companies face in today's competitive environment are causing increasing numbers of firms to use cooperative strategies such as strategic alliances and joint ventures.[109]

The breadth and scope of firms' operations in the global economy create many opportunities for firms to cooperate.[110] In fact, a firm can develop cooperative relationships with many of its stakeholders, including customers, suppliers, and competitors.[111] When a firm becomes involved with combinations of cooperative relationships it is part of a strategic network, or what others call an alliance constellation.[112]

A *strategic network* is a group of firms that has been formed to create value by participating in multiple cooperative arrangements, such as alliances and joint ventures. An effective strategic network facilitates the discovery of opportunities beyond those identified by individual network participants.[113] A strategic network can be a source of competitive advantage for its members when its operations create value that is difficult for competitors to duplicate and that network members can't create by themselves.[114] Strategic networks are used to implement business-level, corporate-level, and international cooperative strategies.

Commonly, a strategic network is a loose federation of partners who participate in the network's operations on a flexible basis. At the core or centre of the strategic network, the *strategic centre firm* is the one around which the network's cooperative relationships revolve (see Figure 12.10).

Because of its central position, the strategic centre firm is the foundation for the strategic network's structure. Concerned with various aspects of organizational structure, such as formal reporting relationships and procedures, the strategic centre firm manages what are often complex, cooperative interactions among network partners. In order to

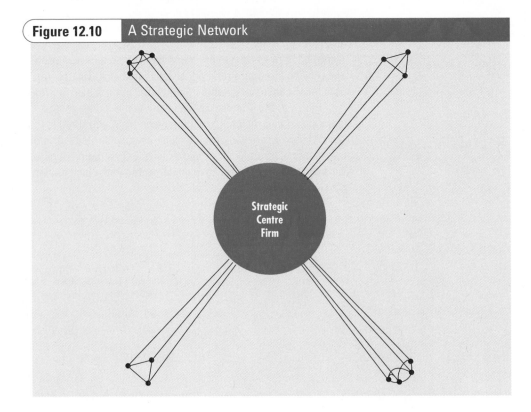

Figure 12.10 A Strategic Network

perform the primary tasks discussed next, the strategic centre must make sure that incentives for participation in the network are aligned so that network firms continue to have a reason to remain connected.[115] The strategic centre firm is engaged in four primary tasks as it manages the strategic network and controls its operations:[116]

Strategic Outsourcing

The strategic centre firm outsources and partners with more firms than do other network members. At the same time, the strategic centre firm requires network partners to be more than contractors. Members are expected to find opportunities for the network to create value through its cooperative work.

Competencies

To increase network effectiveness, the strategic centre firm seeks ways to support each member's efforts to develop core competencies that can benefit the network.

Technology

The strategic centre firm is responsible for managing the development and sharing of technology-based ideas among network members. The structural requirement that members submit formal reports detailing the technology-oriented outcomes of their efforts to the strategic centre firm facilitates this activity.[117]

Race to Learn

The strategic centre firm emphasizes that the principal dimensions of competition are between value chains and between networks of value chains. Because of this, the strategic network is only as strong as its weakest value-chain link. With its centralized decision-making authority and responsibility, the strategic centre firm guides participants in efforts to form network-specific competitive advantages. The need for each participant to have capabilities that can be the foundation for the network's competitive advantages encourages friendly rivalry among participants seeking to develop the skills needed to quickly form new capabilities that create value for the network.[118]

Interestingly, strategic networks are being used more frequently, partly because of the ability of a strategic centre firm to execute a strategy that links other firms more cheaply. Improved information systems and communication capabilities (i.e., the Internet) make this possible.[119]

Implementing Business-Level Cooperative Strategies

As noted in Chapter 10, there are two types of business-level complementary alliances: vertical and horizontal. Firms with competencies in different stages of the value chain form a vertical alliance to cooperatively integrate their different, but complementary, skills. Firms that agree to combine their competencies to create value in the same stage of the value chain form a horizontal alliance. Vertical complementary strategic alliances are formed more frequently than horizontal alliances, though, and the Toyota Motor Company is a good example of such an arrangement. Acting as the strategic centre firm, Toyota has fashioned its lean production system around a network of supplier firms.[120]

A strategic network of vertical relationships, such as the network in Japan between Toyota and its suppliers, often involves a number of implementation issues.[121] First, the strategic centre firm encourages subcontractors to modernize their facilities and provides them with technical and financial assistance to do so, if necessary. Second, the strategic centre firm reduces its transaction costs by promoting longer-term contracts with subcontractors, so that supplier-partners increase their long-term productivity. This approach is diametrically opposed to that of continually negotiating short-term contracts based on unit pricing. Third, the strategic centre firm enables engineers in upstream companies (suppliers) to have better communication with those companies with whom it has contracts for services. As a result, suppliers and the strategic centre firm become more interdependent and less independent.[122]

The lean production system pioneered by Toyota and others has been diffused throughout the global auto industry.[123] However, no auto company has learned how to duplicate the manufacturing effectiveness and efficiency Toyota derives from the cooperative arrangements in its strategic network.[124] A key factor accounting for Toyota's manufacturing-based competitive advantage is the cost other firms would incur to imitate the structural form used to support Toyota's application. In part, then, the structure of Toyota's strategic network that it created as the strategic centre firm facilitates cooperative actions among network participants that competitors cannot fully understand or duplicate.

In vertical complementary strategic alliances, such as the one between Toyota and its suppliers, the strategic centre firm is obvious, as is the structure that firm establishes. However, this is not always the case with horizontal complementary strategic alliances where firms try to create value in the same part of the value chain, as with airline alliances that are commonly formed to create value in the marketing and sales primary activity segment of the value chain (refer to Table 4.7).[125] Because air carriers commonly participate in multiple horizontal complementary alliances, such as the Star Alliance between Air Canada, Lufthansa, United Airlines, Thai Airways International, Singapore Airlines, SAS, and others, it is difficult to determine the strategic centre firm. Moreover, participation in several alliances can cause firms to question partners' true loyalties and intentions. Also, if rivals band together in too many collaborative activities, one or more governments may suspect the possibility of illegal collusive activities. For these reasons, horizontal complementary alliances are used less frequently than their vertical counterpart.

Implementing Corporate-Level Cooperative Strategies

Corporate-level cooperative strategies (such as franchising) are used to facilitate product and market diversification. As a cooperative strategy, franchising allows the firm to use its competencies to extend or diversify its product or market reach, but without completing a merger or an acquisition.[126] Research suggests that knowledge embedded in corporate-level cooperative strategies facilitates synergy.[127] For example, the world's largest fast-food chain, McDonald's, has restaurants in 120 countries and territories around the world, serving nearly 54 million customers a day.[128] The McDonald's franchising system is a strategic network. McDonald's headquarters office serves as the strategic centre firm for the network's franchisees. The headquarters office uses strategic controls and financial controls to verify that the franchisees' operations create the greatest value for the entire network. One strategic control issue is the location of franchisee units. McDonald's believes that its greatest expansion opportunities are outside of North America. For instance, in 2005 McDonald's expected "to open at least 100 units a year in China through 2008."[129] As a result, as the strategic centre firm, McDonald's is devoting its capital expenditures (over 70 percent in the last three years) primarily to develop units in foreign markets. Financial controls are framed around requirements an interested party must satisfy to become a McDonald's franchisee as well as performance standards that are to be met when operating a unit.[130]

Implementing International Cooperative Strategies

Strategic networks formed to implement international cooperative strategies result in firms competing in several countries.[131] Differences among countries' regulatory environments increase the challenge of managing international networks and verifying that, at a minimum, the network's operations comply with all legal requirements.[132]

Distributed strategic networks are the organizational structure used to manage international cooperative strategies. As shown in Figure 12.11, several regional strategic centre firms are included in the distributed network to manage partner firms' multiple cooperative arrangements. Strategic centres for Ericsson (a supplier of telecommunications exchange equipment) and Electrolux (a producer of white goods, such as washing machines) are located in countries throughout the world, instead of only in Sweden where the firms are headquartered. Ericsson, for example, is active in more than 140 countries and employs more than 90,000 people. Using the SBU structure, Ericsson has five strategic business units and has formed cooperative agreements with companies throughout the world in each unit. As a founding member of an Ethernet alliance (Intel and Cisco are also members), Ericsson acts as the strategic centre firm for this cooperative arrangement, which seeks to solve the wireline access bottleneck by promoting open industry standards.[133]

Organizational Structure and Controls: An Additional Perspective

As noted in Chapter 5, no business-level strategy is inherently superior to the others. In this chapter, we note that the same is true for organizational structures. The objective when dealing with strategy and structure is to design a way for the firm's work to be completed, as called for by a strategy's focus and details. Peter Drucker's words address this matter: "There is no one right organization anymore. Rather, the task . . . is to select the organization for the particular task and mission at hand."[134] In our context, Drucker

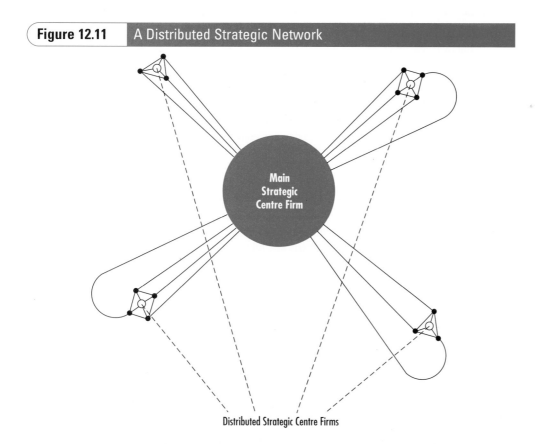

Figure 12.11   A Distributed Strategic Network

Main Strategic Centre Firm

Distributed Strategic Centre Firms

is suggesting that the firm must select a structure that is right for the particular strategy that has been chosen to pursue the firm's strategic intent and strategic mission.

The increasingly competitive global economy finds firms continuously modifying the use of their strategies to improve performance. An important **theme of this chapter** is that once a strategy has been modified, the firm should also change how its work is to be done through changing its structure, control, and reward systems. Thus, 21st-century companies, especially global competitors, are in a stream of strategy and structure changes. In all cases, the outcome sought is to develop an effective match between what the firm intends to do (as indicated by strategy) and how it intends to do it (as indicated by structure, controls, and reward systems). Firms do well to remember that there is no inherently superior strategy or structure, and there is no inherently superior strategy-structure match.

> An important **theme of this chapter** is that once a strategy has been modified, the firm should also change how its work is to be done through changing its structure, control, and reward systems.

Summary

- Organizational structure specifies the firm's formal reporting relationships, procedures, and controls, and its authority and decision-making processes. Influencing managerial work, structure essentially details the work to be done and how that work is to be accomplished. Organizational controls guide the use of strategy, indicate how to compare actual and expected results, and suggest actions to take to improve performance when it falls below expectations. When properly matched with the strategy for which they were intended, structure and controls can be a competitive advantage.

- Strategic controls (largely subjective criteria) and financial controls (largely objective criteria) are the two types of organizational controls used to implement a firm's chosen strategy. Both types of controls are critical, although their degree of emphasis varies based on individual matches between strategy and structure.

- Strategy and structure influence each other, although overall, strategy should have a stronger influence on structure. Research indicates that firms tend to change structure when declining performance forces them to do so. Effective managers anticipate the need for structural change, quickly modifying structure to better accommodate the firm's strategy implementation needs when evidence calls for that action.

- The functional structure is used to implement business-level strategies. The cost leadership strategy requires a centralized functional structure—one in which manufacturing efficiency and process engineering are emphasized. The differentiation strategy's functional structure decentralizes implementation-related decisions, especially those concerned with marketing, to those involved with individual organizational functions. Focus strategies, often used in small firms, require a simple structure until such time that the firm diversifies in terms of products and/or markets.

- Unique combinations of different forms of the multidivisional structure are matched with different corporate-level diversification strategies to properly implement these strategies. The cooperative M-form, used to implement the related-constrained corporate-level strategy, has a centralized corporate office and extensive integrating mechanisms. Divisional incentives are linked to overall corporate performance. The related-linked SBU M-form structure establishes separate profit centres within the diversified firm. Each profit centre may have divisions offering similar products, but the centres are unrelated to each other. The competitive M-form structure, used to implement the unrelated diversification strategy, is highly decentralized, lacks integrating mechanisms, and utilizes objective financial criteria to evaluate each unit's performance.

- The multidomestic strategy, implemented through the worldwide geographic area structure, emphasizes decentralization and locates all functional activities in the host country or geographic area. The worldwide product divisional structure is used to implement the global strategy. This structure is centralized in order to coordinate and integrate different functions' activities so as to gain global economies of scope and economies of scale. Decision-making authority is centralized in the firm's worldwide division headquarters.

- The transnational strategy—a strategy through which the firm seeks the local responsiveness of the multidomestic strategy and the global efficiency of the global strategy—is implemented through the combination structure. Because it must be simultaneously centralized and decentralized, integrated and nonintegrated, and formalized and nonformalized, the combination structure is difficult to organize and manage successfully. However, two structural designs are suggested: the matrix and the hybrid structure with both geographic and product-oriented divisions.

- Increasingly important to competitive success, cooperative strategies are implemented through organizational structures framed around strategic networks. Strategic centre firms play a critical role in managing strategic networks.

1. What is organizational structure and what are organizational controls? What are the differences between strategic controls and financial controls?

2. What does it mean to say that strategy and structure have a reciprocal relationship?

3. What are the characteristics of the functional structures that are used to implement the cost leadership, differentiation, integrated cost leadership/differentiation, and focused business-level strategies?

4. What are the differences among the three versions of the multidivisional (M-form) organizational structures that are used to implement the related-constrained, related-linked, and unrelated corporate-level diversification strategies?

5. What organizational structures are used to implement the multidomestic, global, and transnational international strategies?

6. What is a strategic network? What is a strategic centre firm?

1. In the opening case of this chapter we noted the inability of Sony's divisions to work together to develop a product that they had the resources and capabilities to produce. Is it possible that there is a natural limit to corporate power in that there may be a natural limit to people's ability to organize very large organizations? Or did Sony simply not understand the need to integrate the disparate technologies involved in its new product? Can an organization grow too large? In May 2008, Encana announced that it was splitting into two different firms to create more shareholder wealth. The organization had grown large to be able to resist being taken over by large firms headquartered outside of Canada. Which is being more socially responsible (and to whom)— being large to ensure the ability to resist takeover by foreign firms, or splitting into two smaller, better-run firms with a higher risk of being taken over?

2. Do you think that a properly arranged network has the potential to allow firms the power to collude and set prices? In other words, is there the potential for *socially irresponsible* behaviour when potential competitors get together?

3. If it is possible for managers to create very large organizations (if they are properly structured), should governments put limits on the size of corporations in order to limit corporate power? Why, or why not? Is it being socially responsible to allow governments to have more power so that they can impose more limitations on organizations through taxation, regulations, and stricter laws?

Organizational Structure and Controls

As an executive board member for a successful 50-partner firm that provides accounting services to corporate clients, you are interested in expanding to offer management consulting services to these clients. Another possibility for your firm is offering both types of services to smaller clients.

Part One. You are concerned about how your organizational structure may need to change to support these services. Based on the material in the chapter, use the chart to rank each type of organizational structure against the activities—information processing, coordination, and control—that you anticipate will need to be strengthened.

Part Two. You are also very concerned that there may be a potential conflict of interest if your firm provides both accounting and management consulting services to the same client. In small groups, discuss whether it is possible for a firm to use organizational structure and controls to achieve its strategic objectives and also to prevent conflicts of interest among its divisions.

	Information processing	Coordination	Control
Simple structure			
Functional structure			
Multidivisional structure			

Structural Issues of Related and Unrelated Diversification

Power Corporation of Canada maintains interests in a number of businesses in a number of industries. Go to www.powercorporation.com and click on their organization chart. Using the materials in this chapter to inform your analysis:

1. Does the way in which Power Corp. has arranged its businesses make sense?

2. Why do you think the company is organized in this manner?

3. How might you alter the organization chart to make the groupings of companies more synergistic?

Notes

1. M. S. Gary, 2005, Implementation strategy and performance outcomes in related diversification, *Strategic Management Journal*, 26: 643–664; J. Hauser, 2003, Organizational lessons for nonprofits, *The McKinsey Quarterly*, Special Edition: 60–69.

2. H. Barth, 2003, Fit among competitive strategy, administrative mechanisms, and performance: A comparative study of small firms in mature and new industries, *Journal of Small Business Management*, 41(2), 133–147; R. E. Miles & C. C. Snow, 1978, *Organizational Strategy, Structure and Process*, New York: McGraw-Hill.

3. N. Nohria, W. Joyce, & B. Roberson, 2003, What really works, *Harvard Business Review*, 81(7): 42–52.

4. T. Amburgey & T. Dacin, 1994, As the left foot follows the right? The dynamics of strategic and structural change, *Academy of Management Journal*, 37: 1427–1452.

5. B. Keats & H. O'Neill, 2001, Organizational structure: Looking through a strategy lens, in M. A. Hitt, R. E. Freeman, & J. S. Harrison (eds.), *Handbook of Strategic Management*, Oxford, UK: Blackwell Publishers, 520–542.

6. R. E. Hoskisson, C. W. L. Hill, & H. Kim, 1993, The multidivisional structure: Organizational fossil or source of value? *Journal of Management*, 19: 269–298.

7. E. M. Olson, S. F. Slater, G. Tomas, & M. Hult, 2005, The performance implications of fit among business strategy, marketing organization structure, and strategic behavior, *Journal of Marketing*, 69(3): 49–65.

8. T. Burns & G. M. Stalker, 1961, *The Management of Innovation*, London: Tavistok; P. R. Lawrence & J. W. Lorsch, 1967, *Organization and Environment*, Homewood, IL: Richard D. Irwin; J. Woodward, 1965, *Industrial Organization: Theory and Practice*, London: Oxford University Press.

9. H. Kim, R. E. Hoskisson, L. Tihanyi, & J. Hong, 2004, Evolution and restructuring of diversified business groups in emerging markets: The lessons from chaebols in Korea, *Asia Pacific Journal of Management*, 21: 25–48; M. Bower, 2003, Organization: Helping people pull together, *The McKinsey Quarterly*, Number 2, www.premium.mckinseyquarterly.com.

10. Keats & O'Neill, Organizational structure, 520–542; J. R. Galbraith, 1995, *Designing Organizations*, San Francisco: Jossey-Bass, 6.

11. Keats & O'Neill, Organizational structure, 533; Galbraith, *Designing Organizations*, 6.

12. H. J. Leavitt, 2003, Why hierarchies thrive, *Harvard Business Review*, 81(3): 96–102.

13. R. L. Priem, L. G. Love, & M. A. Shaffer, 2002, Executives' perceptions of uncertainty sources: A numerical taxonomy and underlying dimensions, *Journal of Management*, 28: 725–746.

14. S. K. Ethiraj & D. Levinthal, 2004, Bounded rationality and the search for organizational architecture: An evolutionary perspective on the design of organizations and their evolvability, *Administrative Science Quarterly*, 49: 404–437; J. D. Day, 2003, The value in organization, *The McKinsey Quarterly*, Number 2: 4–5; V. P. Rindova & S. Kotha, 2001, Continuous "morphing": Competing through dynamic capabilities, form, and function, *Academy of Management Journal*, 44: 1263–1280.

15. Barth, Fit among competitive strategy, administrative mechanisms, and performance; J. G. Covin, D. P. Slevin, & M. B. Heeley, 2001, Strategic decision making in an intuitive vs. technocratic mode: Structural and environmental consideration, *Journal of Business Research*, 52: 51–67.

16. E. M. Olson, S. F. Slater, & G. T. M. Hult, 2005, The importance of structure and process to strategy implementation, *Business Horizons*, 48(1): 47–54; H. Barkema, J. A. C. Baum, & E. A. Mannix, 2002, Management challenges in a new time, *Academy of Management Journal*, 45: 916–930.

17. L. Donaldson, 2001, *The contingency theory of organizations*, Thousand Oaks, CA: Sage; Jenster & Hussey, *Company Analysis*, 169; L. Donaldson, 1997, A positivist alternative to the structure-action approach, *Organization Studies*, 18: 77–92.

18. M. A. Schilling & H. K. Steensma, 2001, The use of modular organizational forms: An industry-level analysis, *Academy of Management Journal*, 44: 1149–1168.

19. C. B. Dobni & G. Luffman, 2003, Determining the scope and impact of market orientation profiles on strategy implementation and performance, *Strategic Management Journal*, 24: 577–585; D. C. Hambrick & J. W. Fredrickson, 2001, Are you sure you have a strategy? *Academy of Management Executive*, 15(4): 48–59.

20. T. J. Andersen, 2004, Integrating decentralized strategy making and strategic planning processes in dynamic environments, *Journal of Management Studies*, 41: 1271–1299.

21. J. Rivkin & N. Siggelkow, 2003, Balancing search and stability: Interdependencies among elements of organizational design, *Management Science*, 49: 290–321; G. A. Bigley & K. H. Roberts, 2001, The incident command system: High-reliability organizing for complex and volatile task environments, *Academy of Management Journal*, 44: 1281–1299.

22. K. D. Miller & A. T. Arikan, 2004, Technology search investments: Evolutionary, option reasoning, and option pricing approaches, *Strategic Management Journal*, 25: 473–485; J. Child & R. M. McGrath, 2001, Organizations unfettered: Organizational form in an information-intensive economy, *Academy of Management Journal*, 44: 1135–1148.

23. S. K. Ethiraj & D. Levinthal, 2004, Modularity and innovation in complex systems, *Management Science*, 50: 159–173; T. W. Malnight, 2001, Emerging structural patterns within multinational corporations: Toward process-based structures, *Academy of Management Journal*, 44: 1187–1210; A. Sharma, 1999, Central dilemmas of managing innovation in firms, *California Management Review*, 41(3): 146–164; H. A. Simon, 1991, Bounded rationality and organizational learning, *Organization Science*, 2: 125–134.

24. S. K. Maheshwari & D. Ahlstrom, 2004, Turning around a state owned enterprise: The case of Scooters India Limited, *Asia Pacific Journal of Management*, 21(1–2): 75–101; B. W. Keats & M. A. Hitt, 1988, A causal model of linkages among environmental dimensions, macroorganizational characteristics, and performance, *Academy of Management Journal*, 31: 570–598.

25. A. Chandler, 1962, *Strategy and Structure,* Cambridge, MA: MIT Press.
26. R. E. Hoskisson, R. A. Johnson, L. Tihanyi, & R. E. White, 2005, Diversified business groups and corporate refocusing in emerging economies, *Journal of Management,* 31: 941–965; J. D. Day, E. Lawson, & K. Leslie, 2003, When reorganization works, *The McKinsey Quarterly,* Number 2, 20–29.
27. M. Robb, P. Todd, & D. Turnbull, 2003, Untangling underperformance, *The McKinsey Quarterly,* Number 2, 52–59; Keats & O'Neill, Organizational structure, 535.
28. C. H. Noble, 1999, The eclectic roots of strategy implementation research, *Journal of Business Research,* 45: 119–134.
29. P. K. Mills & G. R. Ungson, 2003, Reassessing the limits of structural empowerment: Organizational constitution and trust as controls, *Academy of Management Review,* 28: 143–153.
30. R. Reed, W. J. Donoher, & S. F. Barnes, 2004, Predicting misleading disclosures: The effects of control, pressure, and compensation, *Journal of Managerial Issues,* 16: 322–336.
31. C. Sundaramurthy & M. Lewis, 2003, Control and collaboration: Paradoxes of governance, *Academy of Management Review,* 28: 397–415.
32. Y. Li, L. Li, Y. Liu, & L. Wang, 2005, Linking management control system with product development and process decisions to cope with environment complexity, *International Journal of Production Research,* 43: 2577–2591; D. F. Kuratko, R. D. Ireland, & J. S. Hornsby, 2001, Improving firm performance through entrepreneurial actions: Acordia's corporate entrepreneurship strategy, *Academy of Management Executive,* 15(4): 60–71.
33. S. D. Julian & E. Scifres, 2002, An interpretive perspective on the role of strategic control in triggering strategic change, *Journal of Business Strategies,* 19: 141–159.
34. R. E. Hoskisson, M. A. Hitt, & R. D. Ireland, 1994, The effects of acquisitions and restructuring strategies (strategic refocusing) on innovation, in G. von Krogh, A. Sinatra, & H. Singh (eds.), *Managing Corporate Acquisition,* London: MacMillan, 144–169.
35. M. A. Hitt, R. E. Hoskisson, R. A. Johnson, & D. D. Moesel, 1996, The market for corporate control and firm innovation, *Academy of Management Journal,* 39: 1084–1119.
36. 2005, Shaking up Intel's insides, *BusinessWeek,* January 31.
37. Ibid.
38. R. E. Hoskisson & M. A. Hitt, 1988, Strategic control and relative R&D investment in multiproduct firms, *Strategic Management Journal,* 9: 605–621.
39. D. J. Collis, 1996, Corporate strategy in multibusiness firms, *Long Range Planning,* 29: 416–418.
40. M. L. Songini, 2003, Oracle tools designed to help monitor financial controls, *Computerworld,* 37(22): 49.
41. J. B. Barney, 2002, *Gaining and Sustaining Competitive Advantage,* 2nd ed., Upper Saddle River, NJ: Prentice Hall.
42. X. Yin & E. J. Zajac, 2004, The strategy/governance structure fit relationship: Theory and evidence in franchising arrangements, *Strategic Management Journal,* 25: 365–383.
43. Keats & O'Neill, Organizational structure, 531.
44. Chandler, *Strategy and Structure.*
45. Keats & O'Neill, Organizational structure, 524.
46. M. E. Sosa, S. D. Eppinger, & C. M. Rowles, 2004, The misalignment of product architecture and organizational structure in complex product development, *Management Science,* 50: 1674–1689.
47. S. Karim & W. Mitchell, 2004, Innovating through acquisition and internal development: A quarter-century of boundary evolution at Johnson & Johnson, *Long Range Planning,* 37: 525–547; C. Williams & W. Mitchell, 2004, Focusing firm evolution: The impact of information infrastructure on market entry by U.S. telecommunications companies, 1984–1998, *Management Science,* 50: 1561–1575.
48. C. Levicki, 1999, *The Interactive Strategy Workout,* 2nd ed., London: Prentice Hall.
49. J. J. Chrisman, A. Bauerschmidt, & C. W. Hofer, 1998, The determinants of new venture performance: An extended model, *Entrepreneurship Theory &*

Practice, 23(3): 5–29; H. M. O'Neill, R. W. Pouder, & A. K. Buchholtz, 1998, Patterns in the diffusion of strategies across organizations: Insights from the innovation diffusion literature, *Academy of Management Review,* 23: 98–114.
50. 2005, Welcome to CasketFurniture Store, CasketFurniture.com Web page, www.casketfurniture.com, August 25.
51. Galbraith, *Designing Organizations,* 25.
52. Keats & O'Neill, Organizational structure, 539.
53. Lawrence & Lorsch, *Organization and Environment.*
54. O. E. Williamson, *Markets and Hierarchies: Analysis and Anti-trust Implications,* New York: The Free Press.
55. Chandler, *Strategy and Structure.*
56. J. Greco, 1999, Alfred P. Sloan Jr. (1875–1966): The original organizational man, *Journal of Business Strategy,* 20(5): 30–31.
57. Hoskisson, Hill, & Kim, The multidivisional structure, 269–298.
58. H. Zhou, 2005, Market structure and organizational form, *Southern Economic Journal,* 71: 705–719; H. Itoh, 2003, Corporate restructuring in Japan Part I: Can M-form organization manage diverse businesses? *Japanese Economic Review,* 54: 49–73; W. G. Rowe & P. M. Wright, 1997, Related and unrelated diversification and their effect on human resource management controls, *Strategic Management Journal,* 18: 329–338.
59. C. E. Helfat & K. M. Eisenhardt, 2004, Inter-temporal economies of scope, organizational modularity, and the dynamics of diversification, *Strategic Management Journal,* 25: 1217–1232; A. D. Chandler, 1994, The functions of the HQ unit in the multibusiness firm, in R. P. Rumelt, D. E. Schendel, & D. J. Teece (eds.), *Fundamental Issues in Strategy,* Cambridge, MA: Harvard Business School Press, 327.
60. O. E. Williamson, 1985, *The Economic Institutions of Capitalism: Firms, Markets, and Relational Contracting,* New York: Macmillan.
61. Keats & O'Neill, Organizational structure, 532.
62. M. F. Wolff, 1999, In the organization of the future, competitive advantage will be inspired, *Research Technology Management,* 42(4): 2–4.
63. R. H. Hall, 1996, *Organizations: Structures, Processes, and Outcomes,* 6th ed., Englewood Cliffs, NJ: Prentice Hall, 13; S. Baiman, D. F. Larcker, & M. V. Rajan, 1995, Organizational design for business units, *Journal of Accounting Research,* 33: 205–229.
64. L. G. Love, R. L. Priem, & G. T. Lumpkin, 2002, Explicitly articulated strategy and firm performance under alternative levels of centralization, *Journal of Management,* 28: 611–627.
65. Hall, *Organizations,* 64–75.
66. Barney, *Gaining and Sustaining Competitive Advantage,* 257.
67. Olson, Slater, Tomas, & Hult, The performance implications of fit among business strategy, marketing organization structure, and strategic behavior.
68. 2005, Wal-Mart stores "pricing philosophy," www.walmart.com, August 26.
69. Olson, Slater, Tomas, & Hult, The performance implications of fit among business strategy, marketing organization structure, and strategic behavior.
70. T. Koplyay, 2002, Research In Motion, Hi-Tech Strategy Formulation, *Corporate Culture,* December 17, http://cata.ca/files/PDF/Resource_Centres/hightech/ reports/studies/quebec-RIM.pdf.
71. Ibid.
72. http://www.gmcanada.com/inm/gmcanada/english/about/MissionGreen/Daily/Sep27.html.
73. http://www.fivewinds.com/uploadedfiles_shared/MECGreenBuilding040127.pdf.
74. Chandler, *Strategy and Structure.*
75. Gary, Implementation strategy and performance outcomes in related diversification.
76. R. Rumelt, 1974, *Strategy, Structure and Economic Performance,* Boston: Harvard University Press.
77. Wikipedia, Magna International, http://en.wikipedia.org/wiki/Magna_International#Products_and_services.
78. http://www.magna.com/magna/en/about/structure/default.aspx.
79. Ibid.

80. C. C. Markides & P. J. Williamson, 1996, Corporate diversification and organizational structure: A resource-based view, *Academy of Management Journal*, 39: 340–367; C. W. L. Hill, M. A. Hitt, & R. E. Hoskisson, 1992, Cooperative versus competitive structures in related and unrelated diversified firms, *Organization Science*, 3: 501–521.

81. P. F. Drucker, 2002, They're not employees, they're people, *Harvard Business Review*, 80(2): 70–77; J. Robins & M. E. Wiersema, 1995, A resource-based approach to the multibusiness firm: Empirical analysis of portfolio interrelationships and corporate financial performance, *Strategic Management Journal*, 16: 277–299.

82. J. R. Baum & S. Wally, 2003, Strategic decision speed and firm performance, *Strategic Management Journal*, 24: 1107–1129.

83. C. C. Markides, 1997, To diversify or not to diversify, *Harvard Business Review*, 75(6): 93–99.

84. J. G. March, 1994, *A Primer on Decision Making: How Decisions Happen*, New York: The Free Press, 117–118.

85. M. Goold & A. Campbell, 2003, Structured networks: Towards the well designed matrix, *Long Range Planning*, 36(5): 427–439.

86. Wikipedia, The Goodyear Tire and Rubber Company, http://en.wikipedia.org/wiki/Goodyear_Tire_and_Rubber_Company#Corporate_Structure_and_Leadership.

87. P. A. Argenti, R. A. Howell, & K. A. Beck, 2005, The strategic communication imperative, *MIT Sloan Management Review*, 46(3): 84–89.

88. Hoskisson, Hill, & Kim, The multidivisional structure; R. E. Hoskisson & M. A. Hitt, 1990, Antecedents and performance outcomes of diversification: A review and critique of theoretical perspectives, *Journal of Management*, 16: 461–509.

89. Hill, Hitt, & Hoskisson, Cooperative versus competitive structures, 512.

90. J. Birkinshaw, 2001, Strategies for managing internal competition, *California Management Review*, 44(1): 21–38.

91. 2005, Textron profile, www.textron.com, August 27.

92. M. Maremont, 2004, Leadership (a special report); More can be more: Is the conglomerate a dinosaur from a bygone era? The answer is no—with a caveat, *Wall Street Journal*, October 24, R4; T. R. Eisenmann & J. L. Bower, 2000, The entrepreneurial M-form: Strategic integration in global media firms, *Organization Science*, 11: 348–355.

93. S. E. Christophe & H. Lee, 2005, What matters about internationalization: A market-based assessment, *Journal of Business Research*, 58: 636–643; Y. Luo, 2002, Product diversification in international joint ventures: Performance implications in an emerging market, *Strategic Management Journal*, 23: 1–20.

94. T. M. Begley & D. P. Boyd, 2003, The need for a corporate global mind-set, *MIT Sloan Management Review*, 44(2): 25–32; Tallman, Global strategic management, 467.

95. T. Kostova & K. Roth, 2003, Social capital in multinational corporations and a micro-macro model of its formation, *Academy of Management Review*, 28: 297–317.

96. Malnight, Emerging structural patterns, 1188.

97. J. Wolf & W. G. Egelhoff, 2002, A reexamination and extension of international strategy-structure theory, *Strategic Management Journal*, 23: 181–189.

98. C. A. Bartlett & S. Ghoshal, 1989, *Managing across Borders: The Transnational Solution*, Boston: Harvard Business School Press.

99. 2008, InBev Web site, http://www.inbev.com/, retrieved March 3.

100. G. Makay, 2005, Challenging conventional wisdom in the global beer business, www.sabmiller.com, August 29.

101. S. T. Cavusgil, S. Yeniyurt, & J. D. Townsend, 2004, The framework of a global company: A conceptualization and preliminary validation, *Industrial Marketing Management*, 33: 711–716.

102. 2007, IKEA Strategy Dilemma, http://www.customerthink.com/article/IKEA_china_branded_experience, July 2.

103. Malnight, Emerging structural patterns, 1197.

104. 1996, IKEA of Sweden, http://www.geocities.com/TimesSquare/1848/ikea.html, January 12.

105. Ibid.

106. Goold & Campbell, Structured networks: Towards the well designed matrix.

107. R. J. Kramer, 1999, Organizing for global competitiveness: The corporate headquarters design, *Chief Executive Digest*, 3(2): 23–28.

108. Y. L. Doz & G. Hamel, 1998, *Alliance Advantage: The Art of Creating Value through Partnering*, Boston: Harvard Business School Press, 222.

109. K. Moller, A. Rajala, & S. Svahn, 2005, Strategic business nets—Their type and management, *Journal of Business Research*, 58: 1274–1284; S. X. Li & T. J. Rowley, 2002, Inertia and evaluation mechanisms in interorganizational partner selection: Syndicate formation among U.S. investment banks, *Academy of Management Journal*, 45: 1104–1119; A. C. Inkpen, 2001, Strategic alliances, in M. A. Hitt, R. E. Freeman, & J. S. Harrison (eds.), *Handbook of Strategic Management*, Oxford, UK: Blackwell Publishers, 409–432.

110. T. H. Reus & W. J. Ritchie III, 2004, Interpartner, parent, and environmental factors influencing the operation of international joint ventures: 15 years of research, *Management International Review*, 44: 369–395; Luo, Product diversification in international joint ventures, 2.

111. Goold & Campbell, Structured networks: Towards the well designed matrix; M. Sawhney, E. Prandelli, & G. Verona, 2003, The power of innomediation, *MIT Sloan Management Review*, 44(2): 77–82; R. Gulati, N. Nohria, & A. Zaheer, 2000, Strategic networks, *Strategic Management Journal*, 21 (Special Issue): 203–215; B. Gomes-Casseres, 1994, Group versus group: How alliance networks compete, *Harvard Business Review*, 72(4): 62–74.

112. B. Comes-Casseres, 2003, Competitive advantage in alliance constellations, *Strategic Organization*, 1: 327–335; T. K. Das & B.-S. Teng, 2002, Alliance constellations: A social exchange perspective, *Academy of Management Review*, 27: 445–456.

113. S. Tallman, M. Jenkins, N. Henry, & S. Pinch, 2004, Knowledge, clusters, and competitive advantage, *Academy of Management Review*, 29: 258–271; C. Lee, K. Lee, & J. M. Pennings, 2001, Internal capabilities, external networks, and performance: A study on technology-based ventures, *Strategic Management Journal*, 22 (Special Issue): 615–640.

114. A. Zaheer & G. G. Bell, 2005, Benefiting from network position: Firm capabilities, structural holes, and performance, *Strategic Management Journal*, 26: 809–825; M. B. Sarkar, R. Echambadi, & J. S. Harrison, 2001, Alliance entrepreneurship and firm market performance, *Strategic Management Journal*, 22 (Special Issue): 701–711.

115. V. G. Narayanan & A. Raman, 2004, Aligning incentives in supply chains, *Harvard Business Review*, 82(11): 94–102.

116. S. Harrison, 1998, *Japanese Technology and Innovation Management*, Northampton, MA: Edward Elgar.

117. T. Keil, 2004, Building external corporate venturing capability, *Journal of Management Studies*, 41: 799–825.

118. P. Dussauge, B. Garrette, & W. Mitchell, 2004, Learning from competing partners: Outcomes and duration of scale and link alliances in Europe, North America and Asia, *Strategic Management Journal*, 21: 99–126; G. Lorenzoni & C. Baden-Fuller, 1995, Creating a strategic centre to manage a web of partners, *California Management Review*, 37(3): 146–163.

119. N. C. Carr, 2005, In praise of walls, *MIT Sloan Management Review*, 45(3): 10–13.

120. J. H. Dyer & K. Nobeoka, 2000, Creating and managing a high-performance knowledge-sharing network: The Toyota case, *Strategic Management Journal*, 21 (Special Issue): 345–367; J. H. Dyer, 1997, Effective interfirm collaboration: How firms minimize transaction costs and maximize transaction value, *Strategic Management Journal*, 18: 535–556.

121. M. Kotabe, X. Martin, & H. Domoto, 2003, Gaining from vertical partnerships: Knowledge transfer, relationship duration and supplier performance improvement in the U.S. and Japanese automotive industries, *Strategic Management Journal*, 24: 293–316.

122. T. Nishiguchi, 1994, *Strategic Industrial Sourcing: The Japanese Advantage*, New York: Oxford University Press.

123. P. Dussauge, B. Garrette, & W. Mitchell, 2004, Asymmetric performance: The market share impact of scale and link alliances in the global auto industry, *Strategic Management Journal*, 25: 701–711.

124. C. Dawson & K. N. Anhalt, 2005, A "China price" for Toyota, *BusinessWeek,* February 21, 50–51; W. M. Fruin, 1992, *The Japanese Enterprise System,* New York: Oxford University Press.
125. A. Andal-Ancion & G. Yip, 2005, Smarter ways to do business with the competition, *European Business Forum,* April 1, 32–36.
126. P. J. Brews & C. L. Tucci, 2004, Exploring the structural effects of internet-working, *Strategic Management Journal,* 25: 429–451.
127. B. B. Nielsen, 2005, The role of knowledge embeddedness in the creation of synergies in strategic alliances, *Journal of Business Research,* 58: 1194–1204.
128. Wikipedia, 2007, McDonalds, Corporate Overview, December 19.
129. 2005, McDonald's plans for the future, *Restaurant and Institutions,* June 1, 19.
130. 2005, McDonald's USA franchising, www.mcdonalds.com, August 31.
131. P. H. Andersen & P. R. Christensen, 2005, Bridges over troubled water: Suppliers as connective nodes in global supply networks, *Journal of Business*

Research, 58: 1261–1273; C. Jones, W. S. Hesterly, & S. P. Borgatti, 1997, A general theory of network governance: Exchange conditions and social mechanisms, *Academy of Management Review,* 22: 911–945.
132. A. Goerzen, 2005, Managing alliance networks: Emerging practices of multi-national corporations, *Academy of Management Executive,* 19(2): 94–107; J. M. Mezias, 2002, Identifying liabilities of foreignness and strategies to minimize their effects: The case of labor lawsuit judgments in the United States, *Strategic Management Journal,* 23: 229–244.
133. R. E. Miles, C. C. Snow, J. A. Mathews, G. Miles, & J. J. Coleman, Jr., 1997, Organizing in the knowledge age: Anticipating the cellular form, *Academy of Management Executive,* 11(4): 7–20; Ericsson, 2002, Ericsson NewsCenter, Ericsson Web site, http://www.ericsson.com, February 10.
134. M. F. Wolff, 1999, In the organization of the future, competitive advantage will be inspired, *Research Technology Management,* 42(4): 2–4.

Chapter Thirteen

Strategic Leadership

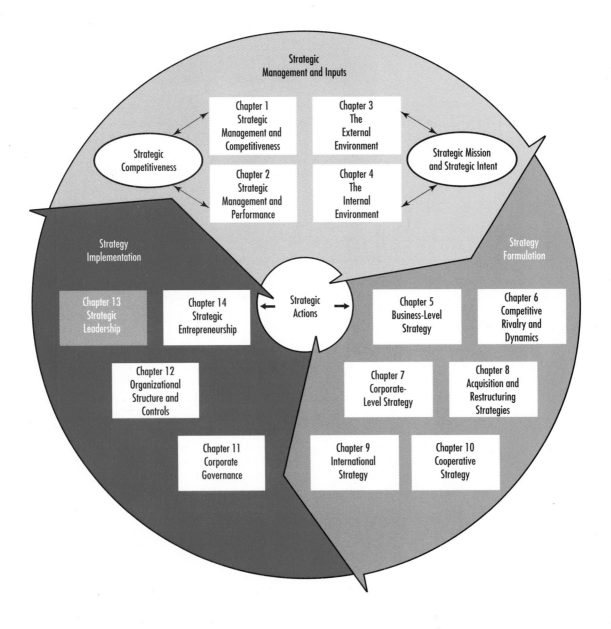

Knowledge Objectives

Studying this chapter should provide you with the strategic management knowledge needed to:

1. Define strategic leadership and describe the importance of top-level managers as a resource.

2. Differentiate among the concepts of strategic, visionary, and managerial leadership.

3. Define top management teams and explain their effects on firm performance.

4. Describe the managerial succession process using internal and external managerial labour markets.

5. Discuss the value of strategic leadership in determining the firm's strategic direction.

6. Describe the importance of strategic leaders in managing the firm's resources, with emphasis on exploiting and maintaining core competencies, human capital, and social capital.

7. Define organizational culture and explain what must be done to sustain an effective culture.

8. Explain what strategic leaders can do to establish and emphasize ethical practices.

9. Discuss the importance and use of organizational controls.

The Change of Reins at Hewlett-Packard

In 2005, after almost six years as CEO of Hewlett-Packard, Carly Fiorina was fired by the firm's board of directors. They were unhappy with the stock price, which closely paralleled the firm's operating performance. After firing Fiorina, the board of directors at HP hired Mark Hurd as CEO and president. Originally pigeonholed as an "operations executive," Hurd was respected by most employees for the "slash and burn reputation" he acquired from his previous reign as CEO at NCR Corporation. However, Hurd proved to be a better leader at HP and "a better strategist than many expected." Just one year after he was appointed CEO, HP boasted annual revenue figures of US$91.7 billion, exceeding revenues for IBM and making HP the world's largest technology vendor in terms of revenue. In 2007, HP's revenue surpassed the US$100 billion mark, making HP the first IT company to ever do so.

www.hp.com

At the time Fiorina lost her job, she was one of a very small group of women CEOs at Fortune 500 companies. Women make up 51 percent of the management, professional, and related jobs in these companies but hold only 2 percent of the CEO positions, 15.6 percent of the corporate officer positions, and are 14.6 percent of the members on boards of directors. Three women who were in the CEO position as of December 2007 were Brenda Barnes (chairman and CEO of Sara Lee), Meg Whitman (president and CEO of eBay), and Indra Nooyi (chairman and CEO of PepsiCo).

Fiorina was well known and perhaps the most powerful woman executive in the world when she was fired—so why did this smart, powerful woman lose her job? One reason relates to a season of discontent with top executives in many North American firms: a large number of top executives lost their jobs in 2005 because investors and boards of directors wanted stronger firm performance. Other reasons why Fiorina lost her job were because of her presence and some of the decisions that she made.

Perhaps the biggest decision Fiorina made during her tenure was to acquire a rival company, Compaq. She encountered significant resistance to this decision from within and outside the company. Her decision to acquire Compaq was based on the charge given to her by the board of directors when she was hired; they asked her to change the company and enhance its competitiveness. She felt that integrating Compaq would give HP market power in the personal computer market and would also enrich HP's ability to compete with IBM in information services. Because it was a high-profile acquisition and because many such mergers are not successful, her decision was risky. She had to fight members of the board, major investors, and some managers in her own company. She won the battle but staked her future on the performance of the combined company.

In late 2004 HP badly missed its sales and profit targets, and Fiorina fired three top sales executives. But she also did not heed the warnings of analysts and her own board to shore up HP's operations. Some believe that she did not have the right talent in this area. Because of HP's poor operating performance, the firm's stock price lagged badly and investors were quite concerned.

Some believe that Fiorina was unlikely to succeed because she was an outsider. She had a significantly different approach than her predecessors. She was the spokesperson for the company. She appeared in commercials for the company and held high-profile pep rallies for employees. Because of these actions, many current and former HP executives and managers never accepted her leadership. They viewed her more in a promotional role than as a strategic leader. In short, Fiorina had a vision but was unable to muster the support needed to achieve the vision.

The acquisition of Compaq turned out to be a great strategic move for HP in terms of growing sales and capturing market share. However, it was Hurd, and not Fiorina, who was able to get the two companies to work in concert. In addition, Hurd's intense focus on cutting costs and eliminating inefficiencies has resulted in profits increasing faster than revenues. It goes without saying, then, that HP's board is pleased with Hurd's ability to lead HP. What will be interesting is to see whether the switch from Fiorina's visionary style to Hurd's apparent managerial style will be successful over the next decade.

SOURCES: D. K. Berman & A. Latour, 2005, Too big: Learning from mistakes, *Wall Street Journal*, www.wsj.com, February 10; B. Elgin, 2005, The inside story of Carly's ouster, *BusinessWeek*, www.businessweek.com, February 10; J. Markoff, 2005, Fiorina's confrontational tenure at Hewlett comes to a close, *New York Times*, www.nytimes.com, February 10; C. de Aenlle, 2005, See you, Carly, goodbye, Harry, hello, investors, *New York Times*, www.nytimes.com, March 13; J. Markoff, 2005, A break with style not with strategy, *New York Times*, www.nytimes.com, March 30; P. Burrows & P. Elgin, The un-Carly unveils his plan, 2005, *BusinessWeek*, www.businessweek.com, June 16; 2007, Hurd takes Hewlett-Packard from "dinosaur" to tech-industry dynamo, Knight Ridder Tribune Business News, April 15; 2007, Hewlett-Packard, Wikipedia, http://en.wikipedia.org/wiki/Hewlett-Packard; 2006, Hewlett-Packard's Taskmaster, *InformationWeek*, September 18; G. Blair, 2007, Women taking charge, *Jungle*, December, 25–27.

As the Opening Case illustrates, all CEOs encounter significant risk, but they also can make a major difference in how a firm performs. If a strategic leader can create a strategic vision for the firm using forward thinking, she may be able to energize the firm's human capital and achieve positive outcomes. However, the challenge of strategic leadership is significant. Carly Fiorina seems to have exercised visionary leadership at Hewlett-Packard and ignored the advice of more down-to-earth managerial leaders. She was hired with much publicity and she had the media spotlight on her during much of her tenure with HP. The controversial acquisition of Compaq and the attempts to change the company appeared to be unsuccessful as the firm suffered weakening performance-and Fiorina paid the ultimate corporate price: she lost her job.

As this chapter makes clear, it is through effective strategic leadership that firms are able to successfully use the strategic management process. As strategic leaders, top-level managers must guide the firm in ways that result in the formation of a vision and mission (as explained in Chapter 1). This guidance may lead to goals that stretch everyone in the organization to improve performance.[1] Moreover, strategic leaders must facilitate the development of appropriate strategic actions and determine how to implement them. These actions on the part of strategic leaders culminate in strategic competitiveness and above-average returns,[2] as shown in Figure 13.1.

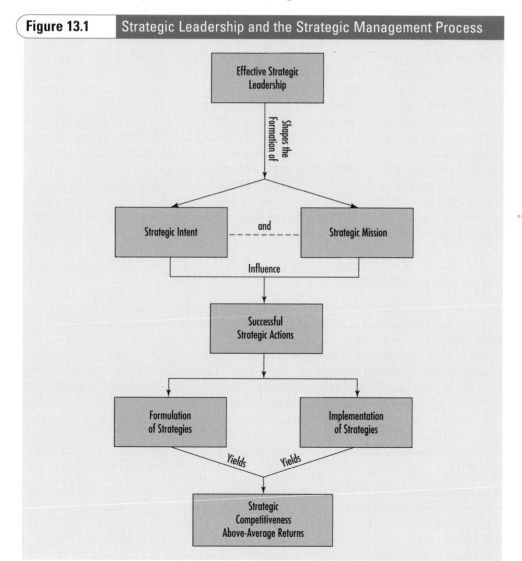

Figure 13.1   Strategic Leadership and the Strategic Management Process

Chapter 13 / Strategic Leadership

As noted in the Opening Case, it is difficult to be a successful strategic leader. The Opening Case suggests that the job of CEO is challenging and stressful, but more importantly it implies that the responsibility of the CEO has changed over the years. Largely due to increased governance requirements, as outlined in Chapter 11, there is a higher correlation today between CEO tenure and corporate performance than there was in the past. If a firm is performing poorly today, research suggests that the CEO's job becomes quite vulnerable, as was the case with Carly Fiorina.

Booz Allen Hamilton, one of the oldest management consulting firms in the world,[3] conducted a study entitled, "CEO Succession 2006: The Era of the Inclusive Leader," and found that between the years 1995 to 2006 annual CEO turnover increased by 59 percent.[4] During that same time frame, "performance-related turnover increased by 318 [percent]."[5]

This study revealed that over nearly a decade there has been a "fundamental shift in the way corporate boards address CEO selection and oversight."[6] Booz Allen suggests that boards today are "less tolerant of poor performance."[7] This explains the change from 1996, when one out of eight CEOs that left office were forced out, compared to 2006, when one in three CEOs left because they were forced to do so.[8]

Additionally, boards of directors over the years have shown an increased tendency to go outside the firm for new CEOs, or to select "dark horses"[9] from within the firm. (A dark-horse candidate is one who is nominated unexpectedly, without previously having been discussed or considered as a likely choice.) Members of boards seem to be searching for an executive who is unafraid to make changes in the firm's traditional practices. Still, many new CEOs do fail (as we learn later in this chapter).[10]

This chapter begins with a definition of strategic leadership, its importance as a potential source of competitive advantage, and the styles that are most effective. Next, we examine top management teams and their effects on innovation, strategic change, and firm performance. Following this discussion is an analysis of the internal and external managerial labour markets from which strategic leaders are selected. Closing the chapter are descriptions of the five key components of effective strategic leadership: determining a strategic direction, effectively managing the firm's resource portfolio (which includes exploiting and maintaining core competencies along with developing human capital and social capital), sustaining an effective organizational culture, emphasizing ethical practices, and establishing balanced organizational control systems.

Strategic Leadership

The word *strategy* originated with the Greeks. Originally, *strategos* alluded to a role such as a general in command of an army. Subsequently, it referred to the psychological and behavioural skills with which the general occupied the role, and it came to mean the "art of the general." By 450 B.C. it had come to mean managerial skills such as administration, leadership, oration, and power. And by 330 B.C. it meant the ability to employ forces to defeat opposing forces and to develop a unified system of global governance.[11]

Strategic leadership is defined as the ability to influence those with whom you work in your organization to *voluntarily* make decisions on a day-to-day basis that enhance the long-term viability of the organization, while at the same time maintaining the short-term financial stability of the organization.[12] This definition of strategic leadership presumes:

- an ability to influence those with whom one works—subordinates, peers, and superiors.
- that the leader understands the emergent strategy process, which, according to Henry Mintzberg,[13] is more important than the intended strategic process.
- a shared vision of what the organization is to be, so that the day-to-day decision making, or the emergent strategy process, is consistent with this vision.

Strategic leadership is defined as the ability to influence those with whom you work in your organization to *voluntarily* make decisions on a day-to-day basis that enhance the long-term viability of the organization, while at the same time maintaining the short-term financial stability of the organization.

- agreement among the senior managers and board members on the opportunities that can be taken advantage of and the threats that can be neutralized, given the resources and capabilities of the organization.[14]
- visionary leadership that entails many characteristics, such as a willingness to take risks.
- managerial leadership that entails many characteristics, such as an intended rational way of looking at the world.
- that visionary leadership and managerial leadership can exist together.
- that strategic leadership synergistically combines visionary leadership and managerial leadership.
- leaders' beliefs in their ability to change their organizations in such a way that the environment in which the organization operates will also change versus believing that the actions they take are constrained by the environment and organization in which they work.

In the next two sections, the concepts of managerial and visionary leadership are discussed. A major portion of this discussion is based on the classic *Harvard Business Review* (HBR) article by Abraham Zaleznik.[15]

A Comparison of Managerial, Visionary, and Strategic Leadership

In the 21st century, many managers who work in nations around the world will be challenged to change their frames of reference to cope with the rapid and complex changes occurring in the global economy. A **managerial frame of reference** is the set of assumptions, premises, and accepted wisdom that bounds—or *frames*—a manager's understanding of the firm, the industry or industries in which it competes, and the core competencies it uses in the pursuit of strategic competitiveness. A frame of reference is the foundation on which a manager's mind-set is built (see Chapter 4).

A **managerial frame of reference** is the set of assumptions, premises, and accepted wisdom that bounds—or *frames*—a manager's understanding of the firm, the industry or industries in which it competes, and the core competencies it uses in the pursuit of strategic competitiveness.

A firm's ability to achieve strategic competitiveness and earn above-average returns is compromised when leaders fail to respond appropriately and quickly to the mindset—related changes an increasingly complex and global competitive environment demands. Research suggests that a firm's "long-term competitiveness depends on managers' willingness to challenge continually their managerial frames," and that global competition is more than product versus product or company versus company—it is also a case of "mind-set versus mind-set, managerial frame versus managerial frame."[16] Competing on the basis of mind-set requires that strategic leaders learn how to deal with diverse and cognitively complex competitive situations. One of the most challenging mind-set changes is overcoming one's own success when change is required. Managers who are able, early and frequently in their career, to successfully complete challenging assignments that are linked to achieving strategic competitiveness appear to improve their ability to make appropriate changes to their mind-set.[17]

Managerial Leadership

Organizations implicitly and explicitly train their people to be managerial leaders. For example, in governments, managerial leaders are required to address public accountability for every penny spent, to provide unrelated diversification as an organization, and to work within the political context. These factors lead to the imposition of a financial control system that enhances the use of managerial leadership and curtails the use of strategic and visionary leadership. Managerial leaders adopt impersonal, passive attitudes toward goals, leading to goals that arise from necessity rather than from desires or dreams. These goals are based on the organization's history and are deeply embedded in the history and culture of the organization as it currently stands.[18] Managerial leaders view work as an enabling process that involves some combination of ideas and people interacting to establish strategies and make decisions. In this process, they negotiate and bargain and/or use rewards, punishments, or other forms of coercion.[19]

In their relations with others, managerial leaders relate to people according to their role in the decision-making process. Although managerial leaders may seek out involvement with others, they will maintain a low level of emotional involvement in these relationships. They may lack empathy; managerial leaders need order, not the potential chaos inherent in human relations.[20] Managerial leaders see themselves as conservators and regulators of the existing order of affairs with which they personally identify. Strengthening and perpetuating the existing institution enhances these managers' self-worth. For example, if people feel that they are members of an institution and contributing to that institution's well-being, then they will consider that a mission in life has been fulfilled and will feel rewarded for having measured up to an ideal. This reward transcends material gains and answers the more fundamental desire for personal integrity that is achieved by identifying with existing institutions.[21] However, when managerial leaders have devoted their career to perpetuating and strengthening an institution that then gets ripped apart and put back together again, as happens in restructuring, these leaders feel as if they are being torn apart, too.

Managerial leaders influence only the actions and decisions of those with whom they work.[22] They are involved in situations and contexts characteristic of day-to-day activities,[23] and they are concerned with, and more comfortable in, functional areas of responsibilities.[24] They possess more expertise about their functional areas than visionary leaders.[25] In some instances, managerial leaders make decisions that are not subject to value-based constraints,[26] which does not mean that these leaders are not moral, ethical people on a personal level; as managers, values might not be included in their decision making because of certain pressures, such as being financially controlled. These leaders engage in, and support, short-term, least-cost-behaviour activities, to enhance financial performance figures in the short term.[27] They focus on managing the exchange and combination of explicit knowledge and ensuring compliance to standard operating procedures.[28] They use a linear thought process. Finally, managerial leaders believe in determinism—that is, they believe that their organization's internal and external environments determine what they do.[29]

To summarize, **managerial leaders** want stability and order, and they strive to preserve the existing order. They are more comfortable handling day-to-day activities, and are short-term-oriented. They guide without a strategic vision constrained by values and by using explicit knowledge. We need to emphasize that this is not a bad way to be—it is more a recognition of some of the defining characteristics of managerial leadership. Organizations need managerial leadership; however, it is possible that too many organizations are led by managerial leaders. In the longer term, managerial leadership causes organizational performance to decline.

Visionary Leadership

Visionary leadership is touted as the cure for many of the ills that affect organizations in today's fast-changing environment. Unfortunately, visionary leaders are not readily embraced by organizations, and without the support of managerial leaders they may not be appropriate for most organizations. Being visionary and having an organizational tendency to use visionary leaders is risky. Ultimately, visionary leadership requires power to influence people's thoughts and actions. This means putting power in the hands of one person, which entails risk on several dimensions. First, there is the risk of equating power with the ability to achieve immediate results; second, there is the risk of losing self-control in the desire for power; and third, the presence of visionary leaders may

Managerial leaders want stability and order, and they want to preserve the existing order. They are more comfortable handling day-to-day activities, and are short-term-oriented. They guide without a strategic vision constrained by values and by using explicit knowledge.

undermine the development of managers who become anxious in the relative disorder that visionary leaders tend to generate.

Because they are relatively more proactive, visionary leaders have attitudes toward goals that are different from those of managerial leaders. Visionary leaders shape ideas, as opposed to reacting to them. They exert influence in a way that determines the direction an organization will take, by altering moods, evoking images and expectations, and establishing specific desires and objectives. Their influence changes the way people think about what is desirable, possible, and necessary.[30] Visionary leaders strive to develop choices and fresh approaches to long-standing problems. They create excitement in work. Visionary leaders work from high-risk positions; in fact, they seek out risky ventures, especially when the rewards are high.[31]

Visionary leaders are concerned with ideas and relate to people in intuitive and empathetic ways, focusing on what events and decisions mean to people. With visionaries in charge, human relations are more turbulent, intense, and, sometimes, even disorganized. This atmosphere may intensify individual motivation and produce unanticipated, positive outcomes.[32] With respect to their sense of self, visionary leaders feel separate from their environment, and, sometimes, from other people. The key point is that they work in—but do not belong to—organizations. Their sense of identity does not depend on their work, roles, or memberships, but on their created sense of identity, which may result from major events in their lives.[33]

Visionary leaders influence the opinions and attitudes of others within their organizations.[34] They are concerned with ensuring the future of an organization through the development and management of people.[35] Visionaries immerse themselves in complexity, ambiguity, and information overload. Their task is multifunctional, and because they have a much more complex integrative task,[36] they come to know less than their functional area experts about each of the functional areas for which they are responsible.[37]

Visionaries are more likely to make decisions that are based on values,[38] and they are more willing to invest in innovation, human capital, and creating and maintaining an effective culture to ensure long-term viability.[39] Visionary leaders focus on tacit knowledge and develop strategies as communal forms of tacit knowledge that promote the enactment of a vision.[40] They utilize nonlinear thinking, and they believe in strategic choice—that is, they believe that their choices make a difference in what their organizations do, and these differences affect their organizations' environments.[41]

In summary, visionary leadership is future-oriented and concerned with risk taking, and visionary leaders are not dependent on their organizations for their sense of identity. Under these leaders, organizational control is maintained through socialization and the sharing of, and compliance to, a commonly held set of norms, values, and shared beliefs. Organizations need visionary leadership to ensure their long-term viability; however, organizations that are led by visionaries without the constraining influence of managerial leaders are probably more in danger of failing in the short term than those led by managers. One solution is a combination of managers and visionaries to lead organizations, with visionaries having more influence than managers.[42] This was the solution used by The Body Shop, with Anita Roddick as the visionary leader and Gordon Roddick (her husband) as the managerial leader. A better solution is to have an individual who can exercise both visionary and managerial leadership. Herein is the problem; Zaleznik argues that leaders and managers are different and that no one person can exercise both types of leadership simultaneously.[43] His perspective suggests that visionary leaders and managerial leaders are at opposite ends of a continuum and that trying to be both causes the individual to end up in the centre and unable to exercise either style of leadership.

This is not an unreasonable perspective when we consider the following: managerial leaders want stability and order, and they strive to preserve the existing order; **visionary leaders** want creativity, innovation, and chaos, and they strive to change the existing order. For an organization in a transition phase, being driven by a visionary is very hard

Visionary leaders want creativity, innovation, and chaos, and they strive to change the existing order.

on those who are managerial leaders. The organization they have worked so hard to build, and that is part of their identity, is being ripped apart and put together as something else. Under visionary leaders, this climate of transition will be more the norm than the stability and order experienced under managerial leadership. In fact, the environment being created by today's technological and global forces is one of change and complexity. John Kotter, one of the foremost experts on organizational leadership, suggests that organizations need leaders to cope with change and managers to cope with complexity.[44]

Having said this, it is necessary to reiterate and emphasize that both visionary and managerial leadership are vital for long-term viability and short-term financial stability. As we said earlier, visionary leadership without managerial leadership may be more detrimental to organizational performance in the short term.[45] Having visionary and managerial leadership can be accomplished by having the two different organizational mind-sets co-exist—but with the visionary approach being more influential than the managerial approach. However, an organization will be more viable in the long term, and better able to maintain its financial stability in the short term, if strategic leadership is prevalent. To conceptualize strategic leadership, it is necessary to think of visionary leadership and managerial leadership as existing on separate continuums that are perpendicular to each other. This conceptualization of strategic leadership provides a synergistic combination of visionary and managerial leadership that was not possible under previous thinking.

Strategic Leadership

Earlier, *strategic leadership* was defined as the ability to influence those with whom you work in your organization to *voluntarily* make decisions on a day-to-day basis that enhance the long-term viability of the organization, while at the same time maintaining the organization's short-term financial stability. Strategic leaders are different from managerial and visionary leaders. They are a synergistic combination of managerial and visionary leadership. This means that a strategic leader creates more wealth than a combination of two individuals, one of whom is a visionary leader and one of whom is a managerial leader.[46] Strategic leaders emphasize ethical behaviour.[47] Strategic leaders are probably very rare in most organizations.[48] They oversee operating (day-to-day) and strategic (long-term) responsibilities.[49] They formulate and implement strategies for immediate impact and the preservation of long-term goals to enhance organizational growth, survival, and long-term viability. Strategic leaders have strong, positive expectations of the performance they expect from their superiors, peers, subordinates—and from themselves. They use strategic controls and financial controls—with the emphasis on strategic controls.[50] They utilize and interchange tacit and explicit knowledge on both the individual and organizational levels.[51] And they use both linear and nonlinear thinking patterns. Finally, they believe in strategic choice—that is, they believe that their choices make a difference in what their organizations do and that their choices will affect their organizations' environments,[52] while at the same time they understand that managerial leaders are deterministic.

In summary, **strategic leaders** manage the paradox created by the use of managerial and visionary leadership models. They use metaphors, analogies, and models to allow the juxtaposition of apparently contradictory concepts by defining boundaries of mutual co-existence. They guide the organizational knowledge creation process by encouraging contradictory combinative capabilities—that is, the organization's ability to combine individual, group, and organizational tacit and explicit knowledge to generate organizational and technological innovations.[53] Organizations need to let a critical mass of their managers develop the skills and abilities required to exercise strategic leadership.[54] This means that managerial leaders need to bear with and actively support the strategic

Strategic leaders manage the paradox created by the managerial and visionary leadership models. They use metaphors, analogies, and models to allow the juxtaposition of apparently contradictory concepts by defining boundaries of mutual co-existence. They guide the organizational knowledge creation process by encouraging contradictory combinative capabilities.

leaders, who create chaos, destroy order, take risks, and maybe destroy a part of the organization that is near and dear to them. This does not mean throwing out managerial leadership—it means including visionary and managerial leadership to enhance long-term viability and short-term financial stability. In fact, strategic leaders need to understand what managerial and visionary leaders bring to the organization and utilize the skills, knowledge, and abilities of both.

Multifunctional in nature, strategic leadership involves managing through others, managing an entire enterprise (rather than a functional subunit), and coping with change that seems to be increasing exponentially in today's new competitive landscape. Because of the complexity and global nature of this new landscape, strategic leaders must learn how to influence human behaviour effectively in an uncertain environment. By word and/or personal example and through their ability to dream pragmatically, strategic leaders meaningfully influence the behaviours, thoughts, and feelings of those with whom they work.[55] The ability to manage human capital may be the most critical of the strategic leader's skills.[56] In the opinion of one well-known leadership observer, the key to competitive advantage ". . . will be the capacity of top leadership to create the social architecture capable of generating intellectual capital. . . . By intellectual capital, I mean know-how, expertise, brainpower, innovation (and) ideas."[57] Strategic leaders also establish the context through which stakeholders (e.g., employees, customers, and suppliers) are able to perform at peak efficiency.[58]

Strategic leaders are willing to make candid, courageous, yet pragmatic, decisions—decisions that may be difficult, yet necessary, in light of internal and external conditions facing the firm.[59] Strategic leaders solicit corrective feedback from their peers, superiors, and employees about the value of their difficult decisions. Often, this feedback is sought through face-to-face communications. The unwillingness to accept feedback may be a key reason why other talented executives fail, highlighting the need for strategic leaders to consistently solicit feedback from those affected by their decisions.[60]

The primary responsibility for strategic leadership rests at the top—in particular with the CEO, but other commonly recognized strategic leaders include members of the board of directors, the top management team, and division general managers. Regardless of title and organizational function, strategic leaders have substantial decision-making responsibilities that cannot be delegated.[61]

Strategic leadership is an extremely complex but critical form of leadership. Strategies cannot be formulated and implemented to achieve above-average returns without strategic leadership. Because it is a requirement of strategic success, and because organizations may be poorly led and over-managed, firms competing in the new competitive landscape are challenged to develop strategic leaders.[62] Wayne Calloway, PepsiCo's former CEO, has suggested that " . . . most of the companies that are in life-or-death battles got into that kind of trouble because they didn't pay enough attention to developing their leaders."[63]

Constraints on Strategic Leadership

Unfortunately, many organizations may constrain the exercise of strategic leadership. Some of these constraints are examined using government as an example, because some of the principles that affect large businesses also affect governments. Governments are sometimes thought of as a monopoly with the power to impose its will on the people. However, governments compete with other organizations for human resources and with other governments for tax dollars and for new businesses to set up in their constituency (country, province, or state). Unfortunately, they also grow large and unrelatedly diversified. This high level of diversification *plus* the debt loads of many national, provincial, and state governments *plus* public accountability for every cent spent *plus* the political context of an election every four years forces governments to use financial controls only and to push the use of strategic controls aside. This forces leaders with the potential to be strategic leaders to do one of three things: (1) to be managerial leaders, (2) to leave the organization, or (3) to fight within the system that uses the strategic energy they should be expending on leading and managing their part of the organization.[64]

Is strategic leadership possible in this type of organization? The answer is "probably not," except under two very hard to impose conditions: autonomy and protection.[65] Giving a subunit some autonomy could enhance the exercise of strategic leadership in the subunit if the autonomy is coupled with protection from those to whom the strategic leaders report. In this way, the subunit can exercise strategic controls as well as financial controls. Unfortunately, as the subunit becomes more successful and achieves visibility (because it is taking risks and "bruising" the bureaucracy), it is much more difficult to maintain this autonomy and to be protected from the managerial leadership of the organization—especially when that leadership controls financially and bureaucratically because the organization is unrelatedly diversified, has a massive debt load, operates in a political context, and must be publicly accountable for every dollar it spends. Doug House, a professor of sociology from Memorial University of Newfoundland who was seconded to the Provincial Government of Newfoundland and Labrador, considers it difficult to exercise strategic leadership in government:

> The organization of the Newfoundland and Labrador public service is very bureaucratic and hierarchical. There is a place for everyone and everyone should know his or her place. Communications go up the hierarchy from officer to manager to director to assistant deputy minister to deputy minister, and possibly to the minister, and down the hierarchy in a reverse chain. Much gets lost or reinterpreted along the way, and it is often a slow process. Not surprisingly, the public and the business community who deal with government as "clients," often complain about "red tape" and "bureaucracy."
>
> Such a system is not well suited to dealing with change. To the extent that change has to occur—and able senior officials recognize that it does—they prefer that it takes place at a modest pace under their control and direction. They are naturally sceptical about and resistant to premiers, ministers, and other agencies that want to initiate a lot of change on a number of fronts within a short period of time.
>
> This system also tends to select out or mould certain personality types for career success. The premium is on reliability, steadfastness, and loyalty to the service rather than on creativity, innovation, and critical thinking. People who do not fit the mould either stagnate, leave, or are forced out of the service. Creative individuals are usually damned with faint praise in epithets such as "He's a smart guy but he can't manage people" or "She's got some good ideas but she's a bit of a loose cannon."[66]

Managers as an Organizational Resource

As we have suggested, top-level managers are an important resource for firms seeking to formulate and implement strategies effectively. The strategic decisions made by top-level managers influence how the firm is designed and whether goals will be achieved. Thus, a critical element of organizational success is having a top-management team with superior managerial skills.[67]

A poll of Canadian CEOs suggested that an increasingly important part of the CEO's skill set is to build respect for their firm among the general public. Two-thirds (67 percent) of CEOs engaged in this activity. The reason why a firm's reputation is becoming more important is that 90 percent of the CEOs surveyed believe that firms that are more respected by the public enjoy a premium in their share price.[68]

Managers often use their discretion (or latitude for action) when making strategic decisions, including those concerned with the effective implementation of strategies.[69] Managerial discretion differs significantly across industries. The primary factors that determine the amount of decision-making discretion a manager (especially a top-level manager) has include (1) external environmental sources (e.g., the industry structure, the rate of market growth in the firm's primary industry, and the degree to which products can be differentiated), (2) characteristics of the organization (e.g., its size, age, resources, and culture), and (3) characteristics of the manager (e.g., commitment to the firm and its strategic outcomes, tolerance for ambiguity, skills in working with different people, and aspiration levels) (see Figure 13.2).

Because strategic leaders' decisions are intended to help the firm gain a competitive advantage, how managers exercise discretion when determining appropriate strategic actions is critical to the firm's success.[70] Top executives must be action-oriented; thus, the decisions that they make should spur the company to action. In addition to determining new strategic initiatives, top-level managers also develop the appropriate organizational

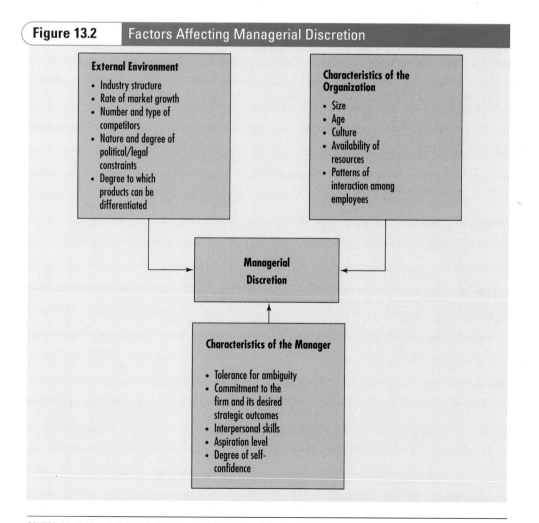

Figure 13.2   Factors Affecting Managerial Discretion

External Environment

- Industry structure
- Rate of market growth
- Number and type of competitors
- Nature and degree of political/legal constraints
- Degree to which products can be differentiated

Characteristics of the Organization

- Size
- Age
- Culture
- Availability of resources
- Patterns of interaction among employees

Managerial Discretion

Characteristics of the Manager

- Tolerance for ambiguity
- Commitment to the firm and its desired strategic outcomes
- Interpersonal skills
- Aspiration level
- Degree of self-confidence

SOURCE: Adapted from S. Finkelstein & D.C. Hambrick, 1996, *Strategic Leadership: Top Executives and Their Effects on Organizations*, St. Paul, MN: West Publishing Company.

structure and reward systems of a firm. (In Chapter 12, we described how organizational structure and reward systems affect strategic actions taken to implement different types of strategies.) Furthermore, top-level managers have a major effect on a firm's culture. Evidence suggests that managers' values are critical in shaping a firm's cultural values.[71] As this discussion shows, top-level managers have an important effect on organizational activities and performance.[72] The significance of this effect should not be underestimated.

Strategic Leadership and Style

Strategic leadership involves managing through others, managing an entire enterprise rather than a functional subunit, and coping with change that continues to increase in the 21st-century competitive landscape. Because of this landscape's complexity and global nature strategic leaders must learn how to effectively influence human behaviour, often in uncertain environments. By word or by personal example, and through their ability to envision the future, strategic leaders meaningfully influence the behaviours, thoughts, and feelings of those with whom they work.[73]

Sam Pollock, the legendary general manager (GM) of the Montreal Canadiens in the National Hockey League (NHL), was known for his "uncanny knack for recognizing [talent]" and his ability to find and shape the skills of his players. As a result, Pollock made a profound impact on the success of his team. This is largely apparent in his 14 years as the general manager of the Montreal Canadiens, in that his team won the Stanley Cup nine times.[74] He is the only GM in NHL history to have won the Cup in more than 50 percent of the years he served in the GM role. Two other GMs won seven Stanley Cups but took 30 years and 35 years, respectively, to do so. NHL commissioner Gary Bettman explained that Pollock could "see genius in others—players, coaches, future executives—before anyone else did, and his influence around the hockey world was unmatched."[75] Pollock's leadership was said to be "contagious," and he inspired many throughout his time with the NHL.[76] Pollock served in various subordinate roles with the Canadiens for 16 years before serving as the Canadiens' GM.

In a 2007 study of the "50 Best Employers in Canada," EllisDon—the international construction firm operated out of London, Ontario—won the distinction of being rated the No. 1 employer.[77] One long-time employee gave his account of EllisDon by saying, "I've never come across a large group of diverse people who are all committed to the same thing, and who all have relatively the same outlook on their profession and how they treat people. And senior management believe it themselves."[78] CEO Geoff Smith "steered EllisDon back to health through several crises and a recession in the early and mid-1990s that hit the construction industry particularly hard."[79] Today, more than 50 percent of the company is owned by EllisDon employees, and Smith has gained a lot of trust and credibility among them. Due to several factors, 94 percent of EllisDon employees said that "they'd highly recommend the firm to their friends."[80]

As indicated in the EllisDon story, the primary responsibility for strategic leadership rests at the top, in particular with the CEO. Other commonly recognized strategic leaders include members of the board of directors, the top management team, and divisional general managers. Regardless of their title and organizational function, strategic leaders have substantial decision-making responsibilities that cannot be delegated.[81] Strategic leadership is an extremely complex, but critical, form of leadership. Strategies cannot be formulated and implemented to achieve above-average returns without strategic leaders.

The styles used to provide leadership often affect the productivity of those being led. The most effective leadership style used by strategic leaders is visionary leadership. Visionary leadership entails motivating followers to do more than expected (a characteristic ascribed to Sam Pollock), to continuously enrich their capabilities, and to place the interests of the organization above their own. Visionary leaders develop and communicate a vision for the organization and formulate a strategy to achieve the vision.

They make followers aware of the need to achieve valued organizational outcomes. And they encourage followers to continuously strive for higher levels of achievement.

Marked as 2007's "CEO of the Year" by *The Globe and Mail*, Canadian National Railway's (CN) CEO, Hunter Harrison, has been labelled a "sermonizer" because he spends so much time "guiding CN employees . . . through so-called Hunter Camps—three-day sessions devoted to the gospel of efficiency."[82] Harrison explains that, "If you can develop five or six disciples out of those 25 people that really start to believe in it, that start to think this company is really doing the right thing for the right reasons, that becomes powerful. Because chances are, they go back to the workplace and maybe they convert two or three more, and before it's over with, you have a real renaissance."[83]

Harrison's ability to "turn the company into the continent's best-managed railway" and contribute to nearly doubling profits was so appreciated by CN's board of directors that he was asked to extend his contract as CEO for another year into 2009. The board's chairman said this about Hunter: "[He] has been a tremendous leader, transforming CN into one of the continent's leading railroads."[84]

The Role of Top-Level Managers

Top-level managers play a critical role in firms as they are charged with formulating and implementing strategies effectively.[85] The strategic decisions made by top-level managers influence how the firm is designed and whether or not goals will be achieved. Thus, a critical element of organizational success is having a top management team with superior managerial skills.[86]

In addition to determining new strategic initiatives, top-level managers develop the appropriate organizational structure and reward systems of a firm. In Chapter 12, we described how the organizational structure and reward systems affect strategic actions taken to implement different strategies. Top executives also have a major effect on a firm's culture. Evidence suggests that managers' values are critical in shaping a firm's cultural values.[87] Accordingly, top-level managers have an important effect on organizational activities and performance.[88] Because of the challenges top executives face, they often are more effective when they operate as top management teams.

Top Management Teams

In most firms, the complexity of challenges and the need for substantial amounts of information and knowledge require strategic leadership by a team of executives. Use of a team to make strategic decisions also helps to avoid another potential problem when these decisions are made by the CEO alone: managerial hubris or pride. Research has shown that CEOs are more likely to make poor strategic decisions when they begin to believe glowing press accounts and to feel that they are unlikely to make errors.[89] Some felt that part of Carly Fiorina's problem was that she seemed to be the primary spokesperson for HP, and her refusal to focus more on the operational details of the business may have been partly the result of her celebrity status. Top executives need to have self-confidence but must guard against allowing it to become arrogance and a false belief in their own invincibility.[90] To guard against CEO overconfidence and poor strategic decisions firms often use the top management team to consider strategic opportunities and problems and to make strategic decisions.

The **top management team** comprises the key managers who are responsible for selecting and implementing the firm's strategies. Typically, the top management team includes the officers of the corporation, defined by the title of vice-president and above or by service as a member of the board of directors.[91] The quality of the strategic decisions made by a top management team affects the firm's ability to innovate and engage in effective strategic change.[92]

The **top management team** is composed of the key managers who are responsible for selecting and implementing the firm's strategies.

Top Management Team, Firm Performance, and Strategic Change

The job of top-level executives is complex and requires a broad knowledge of the firm's operations, as well as the three key parts of the firm's external environment—the general, industry, and competitor environments, as discussed in Chapter 3. Therefore, firms try to form a top management team that has the appropriate knowledge and expertise to operate the internal organization, yet that also can deal with all the firm's stakeholders as well as its competitors.[93] This normally requires a heterogeneous top management team. A **heterogeneous top management team** is composed of individuals with different functional backgrounds, experience, and education. The more heterogeneous a top management team is, with varied expertise and knowledge, the more capacity it has to formulate an effective strategy.

Members of a heterogeneous top management team benefit from discussing the different perspectives advanced by team members. In many cases, these discussions increase the quality of the top management team's decisions, especially when a synthesis emerges from the diverse perspectives that is generally superior to any one individual perspective.[94] The net benefit of such actions by heterogeneous teams has been positive in terms of market share and above-average returns. Research shows that more heterogeneity among top management team members promotes debate, which often leads to better strategic decisions. In turn, better strategic decisions produce higher firm performance.[95]

It is also important that the top management team members function cohesively. In general, the more heterogeneous and larger the top management team is, the more difficult it is for the team to effectively implement strategies.[96] Comprehensive and long-term strategic plans can be inhibited by communication difficulties among top executives who have different backgrounds and different cognitive skills.[97] Alternatively, communication among diverse top management team members can be facilitated through electronic communications, sometimes reducing the barriers before face-to-face meetings.[98] However, a group of top executives with diverse backgrounds may inhibit the process of decision making if it is not effectively managed. In these cases, top management teams may fail to comprehensively examine threats and opportunities, leading to a sub-optimal strategic decision. Thus, the CEO must attempt to achieve behavioural integration among the team members.[99]

Having members with substantive expertise in the firm's core functions and businesses is also important to the effectiveness of a top management team. In a high-technology industry, it may be critical for a firm's top management team members to have R&D expertise, particularly when growth strategies are being implemented.[100] Yet their eventual effect on strategic decisions depends not only on their expertise and the way the team is managed but also on the context in which they make the decisions (the governance structure, incentive compensation, etc.).[101]

The characteristics of top management teams are related to innovation and strategic change.[102] For example, more heterogeneous top management teams are associated positively with innovation and strategic change. The heterogeneity may force the team or some of the members to "think outside of the box" and thus be more creative in making decisions. Therefore, firms that need to change their strategies are more likely to do so if they have top management teams with diverse backgrounds and expertise. When a new CEO is hired from outside the industry, the probability of strategic change is greater than if the new CEO is from inside the firm or inside the industry.[103] While hiring a new CEO from outside the industry adds diversity to the team, the top management team must be managed effectively to use the diversity in a positive way. Thus, to create strategic change, the CEO should exercise visionary leadership.[104] A top management team with various areas of expertise is more likely to identify environmental changes (opportunities and threats) or changes within the firm that require a different strategic direction.

A **heterogeneous top management team** is composed of individuals with different functional backgrounds, experience, and education.

CEO Power Relative to the Board and the Top Management Team

As noted in Chapter 11, the board of directors is an important governance mechanism for monitoring a firm's strategic direction and for representing stakeholders' interests, especially those of shareholders. In fact, higher performance normally is achieved when the board of directors is more directly involved in shaping a firm's strategic direction.[105]

Boards of directors, however, may find it difficult to direct the strategic actions of powerful CEOs and top management teams.[106] It is not uncommon for a powerful CEO to appoint to the board a number of sympathetic outside members or to have inside board members who are also on the top management team and report to the CEO.[107] In either case, the CEO may have significant control over the board's actions. Thus the amount of discretion a CEO has in making strategic decisions is related to the board of directors and how it chooses to oversee the CEO's actions and the top management team. In the poor performance of Hewlett-Packard, as explained in the Opening Case, the board of directors shares part of the blame. While some members on the board opposed Fiorina's decision to acquire Compaq, the majority supported her. Interestingly, recent research shows that social ties between the CEO and board members may actually increase board members' involvement in strategic decisions. Thus, strong relationships between the CEO and the board of directors may have positive or negative outcomes.[108]

CEOs and top management team members can achieve power in other ways. A CEO who also holds the position of chairman of the board usually has more power than the CEO who does not.[109] Although this practice of CEO duality (when the CEO and the chairperson of the board are the same) has become more common today, it has come under heavy criticism. Duality has been blamed for poor performance and slow response to change in a number of firms.[110]

The problems with poor top management decisions and lack of board oversight are evident in the recent problems at General Motors (GM) and Ford. Some have suggested that both firms seem stuck in neutral while customers buy automobiles from other manufacturers. In fact, following continuing losses of market share, GM had plans to cut at least 25,000 jobs in North America during 2008.[111] Rather than focus on a long-term vision to make the firm's products competitive again, top management has continually emphasized the need to cut costs.[112]

As discussed in Chapter 3, Toyota is taking advantage of GM's and Ford's lack of vision; Toyota's vision is to become the largest and most important auto manufacturer in the world.[113] To further complicate matters for the two companies, it was reported early in 2007 that Standard & Poor's credit rating for GM and Ford's debt was downgraded to "junk status."[114] This makes it very difficult for the firms to recover from their slump.

Although it varies across industries, CEO duality occurs most commonly in the largest firms. Increased shareholder activism, however, has brought CEO duality under scrutiny and attack in both North American and European firms. Historically, an independent board leadership structure in which the same person did not hold the positions of CEO and chair was believed to enhance a board's ability to monitor top-level managers' decisions and actions, particularly in terms of the firm's financial performance.[115] And, as reported in Chapter 11, many believe these two positions should be separate in most companies today to make the board more independent from the CEO. Stewardship theory, on the other hand, suggests that CEO duality facilitates effective decisions and actions. In these instances, the increased effectiveness gained through CEO duality accrues from the individual who wants to perform effectively and desires to be the best possible steward of the firm's assets. Because of this person's positive orientation and actions, extra governance and the coordination costs resulting from an independent board leadership structure would be unnecessary.[116]

Top management team members and CEOs who have long tenure—on the team and in the organization—have a greater influence on board decisions. And CEOs with greater influence may take actions in their own best interests, the outcomes of which increase their compensation from the company.[117] Long tenure is known to restrict the breadth of an executive's knowledge base. With the limited perspectives associated with a restricted knowledge base, long-tenured top executives typically develop fewer alternatives to evaluate in making strategic decisions.[118] However, long-tenured managers also may be able to exercise more effective strategic control, thereby obviating the need for board members' involvement because effective strategic control generally produces higher performance.[119]

To strengthen the firm, boards of directors should develop an effective relationship with the firm's top management team. The relative degrees of power held by the board and top management team members should be examined in light of an individual firm's situation. For example, the abundance of resources in a firm's external environment and the volatility of that environment may affect the ideal balance of power between boards and top management teams. Moreover, a volatile and uncertain environment may create a situation where a powerful CEO is needed to move quickly, but a diverse top management team may create less cohesion among team members and prevent or stall necessary strategic actions. Through the development of effective working relationships, boards, CEOs, and other top management team members are able to serve the best interests of the firm's stakeholders.[120]

Managerial Succession

The choice of top executives—especially CEOs—is a critical board of directors decision with important implications for a firm's performance.[121] Many companies use leadership screening systems to identify individuals with managerial and strategic leadership potential. The most effective of these systems assess people within the firm and gain valuable information about the capabilities of other companies' managers, particularly their strategic leaders.[122] Based on the results of these assessments, training and development programs are provided for current managers in an attempt to pre-select and shape the skills of people who may become tomorrow's leaders.

Organizations select managers and strategic leaders from two types of managerial labour markets—internal and external.[123] An **internal managerial labour market** consists of a firm's opportunities for managerial positions and the qualified employees within that firm. An **external managerial labour market** is the collection of managerial career opportunities and the qualified people who are external to the organization in which the opportunities exist. Several benefits are thought to accrue to a firm when the internal labour market is used to select an insider as the new CEO. Because of their experience with the firm and the industry environment in which it competes, insiders are familiar with company products, markets, technologies, and operating procedures. Also, internal hiring produces lower turnover among existing personnel, many of whom possess valuable firm-specific knowledge. When the firm is performing well, internal succession is favoured to sustain high performance. It is assumed that hiring from inside keeps the important knowledge necessary to sustain the performance. The well-known management consultant and author Jim Collins found that high-performing firms almost always appoint an insider to be the new CEO. Collins argues that bringing in a well-known outsider, to whom he refers as a "white knight," is a recipe for mediocrity.[124]

It is not unusual for employees to strongly prefer that the internal managerial labour market be used to select top management team members and the CEO, as was the case with Jeffrey Immelt described in the Strategic Focus. In the past, companies have also had a preference for insiders to fill top-level management positions because of a desire for continuity and a continuing commitment to the firm's current vision, mission, and chosen strategies.[125] However, because of a changing competitive landscape and varying

An **internal managerial labour market** consists of a firm's opportunities for managerial positions and the qualified employees within that firm.

An **external managerial labour market** is the collection of managerial career opportunities and the qualified people who are external to the organization in which the opportunities exist.

Managing the CEO Succession Process

Global turnover of CEOs has hit record highs in recent years, and with a wave of retirements approaching CEO succession should be on the forefront of many company agendas. However, according to a study by the National Association of Corporate Directors, nearly 50 percent of companies with revenues exceeding $500 million lack a meaningful CEO succession plan.

As stated in an article by the *Harvard Business Review*, "The [North American] CEO succession process is broken." According to a study conducted by PricewaterhouseCoopers, 65 percent of CEOs intend to leave their company within 10 years, while 42 percent plan to leave within five years. To compound this, 50 percent of CEOs who were surveyed had not done any "real succession planning" and 61 percent of them lacked a potential candidate who could succeed them. The result of this is that "too often new CEOs are plucked from the well-worn Rolodexes of a remarkably small number of recruiters." And oftentimes, as the *Harvard Review* suggests, this results in appointing a CEO who does not fit well with the company.

In contrast, given General Electric's (GE) phenomenal success and its highly effective management development program, insider Jeffrey Immelt was chosen ahead of time to succeed Jack Welch. The former CEO took succession planning seriously and made it his prerogative to prepare Immelt for the role. Welch introduced Immelt to the job early by involving him in meetings with security analysts and having him "lead several key internal meetings." Research suggests that this was the "most successful succession in recent years." By giving Immelt a head start, "Welch made the transition smoother," and in turn reduced anxiety that stakeholders could have been feeling about his departure. It should also be noted that Welch's actions helped stabilize GE's stock price during this transition.

Equally as important as determining who will succeed the CEO is the timing of the succession, which many experts agree is also critical for success. For instance, "if the CEO leaves before a decision is made, there can be a scramble to find a successor, and the succession process is short circuited, often with mixed results." Typically, investors do not respond well to this and their resulting dissatisfaction will negatively impact the share price.

As researchers at the Richard Ivey School of Business concluded in their leader succession research using the National Hockey League, the performance of NHL teams is closely related to the "particular pattern of succession" of both coaches and general managers. Their study on general manager succession in the NHL revealed that "teams that changed coaches or general-managers during the previous season performed significantly better than teams that did not . . . [And] . . . teams that changed coaches or general-managers during the current season performed significantly worse than teams that did not."

One can conclude, then, that CEOs must be very strategic in both determining a successor and choosing the appropriate timing for their transition.

SOURCE: 2005, C. Ram, Ending the CEO succession crisis, *Harvard Business Review*, February 1; 2007, Succession planning, Ray & Berndtson Global Leaders in Executive Search, www.rayberndtson.ca, May 9; 2006, CEO succession plan essential for reassuring shareholders, *PRWeek*, http://www.prweekus.com/CEO-succession-plan-essential-for-reassuring-shareholders/article/54162/February 13; 2003, Leadership succession: What can we learn from National Hockey League?, W. G. Rowe & D. Rankin, *Ivey Business Journal*, http://www.iveybusinessjournal.com/view_article. asp?intArticle_ID=397, January/February, retrieved March 4, 2008.

levels of performance, an increasing number of boards of directors have been turning to outsiders to succeed CEOs.[126] A firm often has valid reasons to select an outsider as its new CEO: Long tenure with a firm seems to reduce the number of innovative ideas top executives are able to develop to cope with conditions facing their firm. Given the importance of innovation for a firm's success in today's competitive landscape (see Chapter 14), an inability to innovate or to create conditions that stimulate innovation throughout a firm is a liability for a strategic leader. Figure 13.3 on page 414 shows how the composition of the

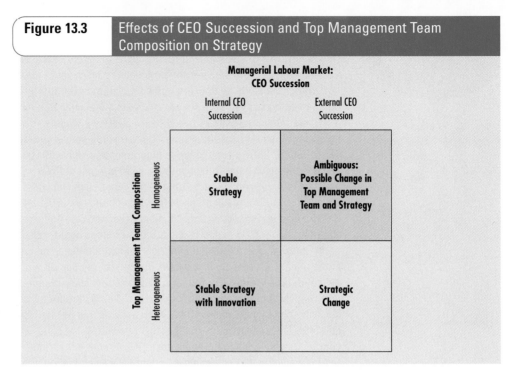

Figure 13.3 Effects of CEO Succession and Top Management Team Composition on Strategy

Managerial Labour Market:
CEO Succession

Internal CEO Succession   External CEO Succession

Top Management Team Composition

Homogeneous

| Stable Strategy | Ambiguous: Possible Change in Top Management Team and Strategy |

Heterogeneous

| Stable Strategy with Innovation | Strategic Change |

top management team and the CEO succession (managerial labour market) interact to affect strategy. For example, when the top management team is homogeneous (its members have similar functional experiences and educational backgrounds) and a new CEO is selected from inside the firm, the firm's current strategy is unlikely to change.

Alternatively, when a new CEO is selected from outside the firm and the top management team is heterogeneous, there is a high probability that strategy will change. When the new CEO is from inside the firm and a heterogeneous top management team is in place, the strategy may not change, but innovation is likely to continue. An external CEO succession with a homogeneous team creates a more ambiguous situation. The selection of Sir Howard Stringer as CEO of Sony suggested changes in the firm's future. He is not only an outsider but also a foreigner; a British businessman taking over a Japanese company. His selection as Sony's new CEO was perhaps a result of increased globalization and may be a harbinger of future appointments like it.[127]

To have an adequate number of top managers firms must take advantage of a highly qualified labour pool, including one source of managers as strategic leaders that has been overlooked in prior years: women. Firms have begun to utilize women's potential managerial talents with substantial success. A few firms have gained value by using the significant talents of women leaders. But many more have not done so, which represents an opportunity cost to them. Alternatively, women are being recognized for their leadership skill and are being selected for prominent strategic leadership positions, such as those held by Anne Mulcahy, CEO of Xerox, and Meg Whitman, CEO of eBay.

More women are also being appointed to the boards of directors for organizations in both the private and public sectors. These additional appointments suggest that women's ability to represent stakeholders' and especially shareholders' best interests in for-profit companies at the level of the board of directors is being more broadly recognized. However, in addition to appointments to the board of directors, firms competing in the complex and demanding global economy may be well served by adding more female executives to their top management teams. It is important for firms to create diversity in leadership positions.

Key Strategic Leadership Actions

Several identifiable actions characterize strategic leadership that positively contributes to the effective use of the firm's strategies.[128] We present the most important of these actions in Figure 13.4. Many of the actions interact with each other. For example, managing the firm's resources effectively includes developing human capital and contributes to establishing a strategic direction, fostering an effective culture, exploiting core competencies, using effective organizational control systems, and establishing ethical practices.

Determining Strategic Direction

Determining the strategic direction involves specifying the image and character the firm seeks to develop over time.[129] The strategic direction is framed within the context of the conditions (such as opportunities and threats) strategic leaders expect their firm to face in five, ten, or more years.

The ideal long-term strategic direction has two parts: a core ideology and an envisioned future. While the core ideology motivates employees through the company's heritage, the envisioned future encourages employees to stretch beyond their expectations of accomplishment and requires significant change and progress in order to be realized.[130] The envisioned future serves as a guide to many aspects of a firm's strategy implementation process, including motivation, leadership, employee empowerment, and organizational design.

Most changes in strategic direction are difficult to design and implement, and Jeffrey Immelt has faced such a challenge at General Electric. The company performed exceptionally well under Jack Welch's leadership, and even though there is need for a change due to a shifting competitive landscape stakeholders accustomed to Jack Welch and high performance may not readily accept Immelt's changes, especially in strategy. Immelt has been trying to effect critical changes in GE's culture, strategy, and governance and

Determining the strategic direction involves specifying the image and character the firm seeks to develop over time.

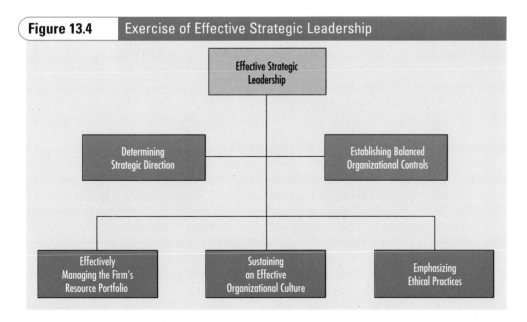

Figure 13.4   Exercise of Effective Strategic Leadership

simultaneously gain stakeholders' commitment to them. He is shifting GE managers' mind-set to innovation, which he believes is critical to GE's future competitiveness. He is linking managerial bonuses to the development and introduction of new ideas, customer satisfaction, and sales growth, as opposed to bottom-line results as used in the past. He is investing significant resources (billions of dollars) into a fund called "Imagination Breakthrough," for projects that extend the boundary of GE. Immelt reviews up to 12 proposals a month and determines whether he will allocate resources to a new project depending on whether it can generate up to US$100 million a year for the company.[131]

It generally takes a CEO with visionary capabilities to foster stakeholders' commitment to a new vision and strategic direction. Furthermore, it is important not to lose sight of the organization's strengths when making changes required by a new strategic direction. Immelt is finding that he must use the strengths of GE to ensure continued positive performance. The challenge is to pursue the firm's short-term need to adjust to a new vision and strategic direction while maintaining GE's long-term survival by managing a strong portfolio. So far, Immelt's innovation strategy has been successful; since its inception, Immelt has signed off on more than 120 ideas, and the program generates nearly US$3 billion in revenue per year.[132]

Effectively Managing the Firm's Resource Portfolio

Probably the most important task for strategic leaders is effectively managing the firm's portfolio of resources. Firms have multiple resources that can be categorized into one of the following: financial capital, human capital, social capital, and organizational capital (including organizational culture).[133] The importance of these resources is shown in the Strategic Focus. The importance of managing financial capital is well accepted, although managers use different approaches.[134] Many small business owners, as discussed in the Strategic Focus, use personal forms of credit to obtain access to needed financing. More to the point, the Strategic Focus argues the need for firms to use their full complement of human capital, especially making full use of the capabilities of women employees. Finally, the Strategic Focus shows the value of intangible resources such as brand and information/knowledge of customers. Wal-Mart has a large amount of valuable data on its customers that allows it and its suppliers to better serve them. For Wal-Mart to be able to extract the value from its data the company must manage its resources effectively.

Strategic leaders manage the firm's portfolio of resources by organizing them into capabilities, structuring the firm to use the capabilities, and developing and implementing a strategy to leverage those resources to achieve a competitive advantage.[135] In particular, strategic leaders must exploit and maintain the firm's core competencies and develop and retain the firm's human and social capital.

Exploiting and Maintaining Core Competencies

Examined in Chapters 1 and 4, *core competencies* are capabilities that serve as a source of competitive advantage for a firm over its rivals. Typically, core competencies relate to an organization's functional skills, such as manufacturing, finance, marketing, and research and development. As shown by the descriptions that follow, firms develop and exploit core competencies in many different functional areas. Strategic leaders must verify that the firm's competencies are emphasized when implementing strategies. Capabilities are developed over time as firms learn from their actions and enhance their knowledge about specific actions needed. For example, some firms have excellent capabilities to deal with customers developed over time with increasing knowledge of their customers and their

How Do Managers Acquire, Protect, and Use Resources Wisely?

Resources are the lifeblood of any company. Firms must have them to operate and they must protect them because of their value to competitors. Finally, resources must be used effectively in order to create value for customers and gain an advantage over competitors. A critical resource for all organizations is financial capital, but it is especially important for smaller companies. Entrepreneurs and large firms alike often experience problems in maintaining adequate cash flow to continue operations.

While financial capital is highly important to business, other resources are equally or perhaps even more important. One incredibly vital resource for most firms is human capital. Because of its importance, a firm must make certain that it accesses and uses human capabilities to the greatest extent possible. Some firms have not made full use of their human capital resources, especially women. In the early 1970s, women received fewer than 10 percent of all graduate degrees in law, medicine, dentistry, and veterinary medicine. A Statistics Canada study showed that in Canada in 2007 women comprised the majority in full-time undergraduate studies, and at the graduate level enrolment of women was equal to that of men. Therefore, women are capable, educated, and available. Firms must fully utilize their human capital and break the glass ceilings that stall women's opportunities for higher-level positions.

Not all resources are as easy to identify as financial capital and human capital. For example, a valuable resource held by Wal-Mart is information about customers and their purchases. Wal-Mart amasses data on the types of products consumers buy, their buying habits, when they are most likely to buy, and so forth. In fact, Wal-Mart stores 583 terabytes of data and shares part of these data with suppliers. For example, Kraft can access a private extranet provided by Wal-Mart to obtain real-time information on how its products are selling. However, Wal-Mart is careful about sharing its information with others. The information can be highly valuable to the company. For example, when Hurricane Frances, a major Atlantic hurricane in 2004, was predicted to hit Florida, Wal-Mart was able to analyze its data on sales prior to previous hurricanes to identify the expected sales of flashlights and many other products in order to have adequate amounts on hand for customers. Such predictive knowledge translates into profits for the firm.

SOURCES: W. M. Cox & R. Alm, 2005, Scientists are made, not born, *New York Times*, www.nytimes.com, February 28; G. Bounds, 2004, The great money hunt, *Wall Street Journal*, www.wsj.com, November 29; C. L. Hays, 2004, Wal-Mart's hoard of data staggering, *Houston Chronicle*, November 14, D4; 2006, Data, data, everywhere, *InformationWeek*, http://www.informationweek.com/story/showArticle.jhtml?articleID= 175801775, January 9; 2007, The Daily, 2007 education indicators, Statistics Canada, December 12.

needs.[136] Firms with capabilities in R&D that develop into core competencies are rewarded by the market because of the critical nature of innovation in many industries.[137]

Firms must continuously develop and, when appropriate, change their core competencies to stay ahead of competitors. If they have a competency that provides an advantage but do not change it, competitors will eventually imitate that competency and reduce or eliminate the firm's competitive advantage. Additionally, firms must guard against the competency becoming a liability or core rigidity thereby preventing change. Some firms are reluctant to change competencies because they helped them gain competitive advantages. However, competencies can become outdated and result in the loss of competitive advantages if not changed. If this occurs, competitors will eventually develop a more valuable competency, eliminating the firm's competitive advantage and taking away its market share.[138] Most core competencies require high-quality human capital.

Developing Human Capital and Social Capital

Human capital refers to the knowledge and skills of a firm's entire workforce. From the perspective of human capital, employees are viewed as a capital resource that requires investment.[139] Furthermore, "as the dynamics of competition accelerate, people are perhaps the only truly sustainable source of competitive advantage."[140] So, then, human capital's increasing importance suggests a significant role for the firm's human resource management activities.[141] As a support activity (see Chapter 4), human resource management practices facilitate people's efforts to successfully select and especially to use the firm's strategies.[142]

Human capital is important in all types of organizations, large and small, new and established. For example, a major factor in the decision by venture capitalists to invest in an entrepreneurial venture is the quality of the human capital involved. In fact, it may be of equal or more importance to the quality of the entrepreneurial opportunity.[143] J. W. Marriott, Jr., CEO of Marriott International, argued strongly that the primary reason for the long-term success of the company has been the belief that its human capital is the firm's most important asset. Thus, the company built and maintained a homelike and friendly environment that supports the growth and development of its employees, called "associates in Marriott." He also suggested that the firm invests significant effort in hiring caring and dependable people who are ethical and trustworthy. The firm then trains and rewards them for high-quality performance.[144]

Effective training and development programs increase the probability that a manager will be a successful strategic leader. These programs have grown progressively important to the success of firms as knowledge has become more integral to gaining and sustaining a competitive advantage.[145]

Additionally, such programs build knowledge and skills, inspire a common set of core values, and offer a systematic view of the organization, thus promoting the firm's vision and organizational cohesion. The programs also contribute to the development of core competencies.[146] Furthermore, they help strategic leaders improve skills that are critical to completing other tasks associated with effective strategic leadership, such as determining the firm's strategic direction, exploiting and maintaining the firm's core competencies, and developing an organizational culture that supports ethical practices. Thus, building human capital is vital to the effective execution of strategic leadership.[147]

Strategic leaders must acquire the skills necessary to help develop human capital in their areas of responsibility. When human capital investments are successful, the result is a workforce capable of learning continuously. Continuous learning and leveraging the firm's expanding knowledge base are linked with strategic success.[148]

Learning also can preclude making errors. Strategic leaders tend to learn more from their failures than their successes because they sometimes make the wrong attributions for the successes.[149] For example, the effectiveness of certain approaches and knowledge can be context specific.[150] Some "best practices," for example, may not work well in all situations. We know that using teams to make decisions can be effective, but there are times when it is better for leaders to make decisions alone, especially when the decisions must be made and implemented quickly (i.e., in crisis situations).[151] It is important to learn from both successes and failures.

Learning and building knowledge are important for creating innovation in firms.[152] Innovation leads to competitive advantage.[153] Overall, firms that create and maintain greater knowledge usually achieve and maintain competitive advantages. However, as noted with core competencies, strategic leaders must guard against allowing high levels of knowledge in one area to lead to myopia and overlooking knowledge development opportunities in other important areas of the business.[154]

Usually during serious and prolonged economic downturns, like in 2001–2002, many firms will lay off key people. Such layoffs can result in a significant loss of the knowledge possessed by a firm's human capital. Research has shown that moderate-sized layoffs may improve firm performance, but large layoffs produce stronger performance downturns in firms because of the loss of human capital.[155] Although it is also not uncommon for restructuring firms to reduce their expenditures on, or investments in, training and development programs, restructuring may actually be an important time to increase investments in these programs. Restructuring firms have less slack and cannot absorb as many errors; moreover, the employees who remain after layoffs may find themselves in positions without all of the skills or knowledge they need to perform the required tasks effectively.[156] Improvements in information technology can facilitate better use of human resources when a downsizing event occurs.[157]

Viewing employees as a resource to be maximized rather than a cost to be minimized facilitates the successful implementation of a firm's strategies, as does the strategic leader's ability to approach layoffs in a manner that employees believe is fair and equitable.[158] A critical issue for employees is the fairness in the layoffs and in treatment in their jobs.[159]

Social capital involves relationships inside and outside the firm that help the firm accomplish tasks and create value for customers and shareholders.[160] Social capital is a critical asset for a firm. Inside the firm, employees and units must cooperate to get the work done. In multinational organizations, units often must cooperate across country boundaries on activities such as R&D to produce outcomes needed by the firm (i.e., new products).[161]

Social capital involves relationships inside and outside the firm that help the firm accomplish tasks and create value for customers and shareholders.

External social capital has become critical to firm success in the last several years. Few, if any, firms have all the resources they need to compete in global (or domestic) markets. Thus, they establish alliances with other firms that have complementary resources in order to gain access to them. These relationships must be effectively managed to ensure that the partner trusts the firm and is willing to share the desired resources.[162] In fact, the success of many types of firms may partially depend on social capital. Large multinational firms often must establish alliances in order to enter new foreign markets. Likewise, entrepreneurial firms often must establish alliances to gain access to resources, venture capital, or other types of resources (i.e., special expertise that the entrepreneurial firm cannot afford to maintain in-house.)[163] Retaining quality human capital and maintaining strong internal social capital can be affected strongly by the firm's culture.

Sustaining an Effective Organizational Culture

In Chapter 1, we defined **organizational culture** as a complex set of ideologies, symbols, and core values that is shared throughout the firm and influences the way business is conducted. Evidence suggests that a firm can develop core competencies in terms of both the capabilities it possesses and the way the capabilities are leveraged by strategies to produce desired outcomes. In other words, because the organizational culture influences how the firm conducts its business and helps regulate and control employees' behaviour, it can be a source of competitive advantage.[164] Thus, shaping the context within which the firm formulates and implements its strategies—that is, shaping the organizational culture—is a central task of strategic leaders.[165]

An **organizational culture** consists of a complex set of ideologies, symbols, and core values that is shared throughout the firm and influences the way business is conducted.

The founders of Calgary's low-cost airline, WestJet, have been quite successful in building a strong corporate culture. In fact, WestJet is consistently named Number 1 by *Canadian Business* magazine and Waterstone Human Capital Ltd. in the Canadian Corporate Culture Study entitled "Canada's 10 Most Admired Corporate Cultures." The top attributes of WestJet's culture that contribute to its fame are its "entrepreneurial spirit," "delivering what they promise," and its "winning attitude."[166]

In the 2006 Canadian Corporate Culture Study 185 executives were interviewed about the importance of corporate culture; 99.9 percent claimed there is "a direct correlation between corporate culture and financial performance."[167]

Entrepreneurial Mind-Set

An organizational culture often encourages (or discourages) the pursuit of entrepreneurial opportunities, especially in large firms.[168] Entrepreneurial opportunities are an important source of growth and innovation.[169] Therefore, a key role of strategic leaders is to encourage and promote innovation by pursuing entrepreneurial opportunities.[170] One way in which this activity might be promoted is to invest in opportunities as real options—that is, invest in an opportunity to provide the potential for exercising the option to take advantage of the opportunity at some point in the future.[171] For example, a firm might buy a piece of land to have the option to build on it at some time in the future should the company need more space and should that location increase in value to the firm. Firms might enter strategic alliances for similar reasons. For example, they might do so to have the option of acquiring the partner later or of building a stronger relationship with it (e.g., developing a joint new venture).[172]

In Chapter 14, we describe how large firms use strategic entrepreneurship to pursue entrepreneurial opportunities and to gain first-mover advantages. Medium and small-sized firms also rely on strategic entrepreneurship when trying to develop innovations as the foundation for profitable growth. In firms of all sizes, strategic entrepreneurship is more likely to be successful when employees have an entrepreneurial mind-set.[173] Five dimensions characterize a firm's entrepreneurial mind-set: autonomy, innovativeness, risk taking, proactiveness, and competitive aggressiveness.[174] In combination, these dimensions influence the actions a firm takes to be innovative and launch new ventures.

The first of an entrepreneurial orientation's five dimensions, *autonomy*, allows employees to take actions that are free of organizational constraints and permits individuals and groups to be self-directed. The second dimension, *innovativeness*, "reflects a firm's tendency to engage in and support new ideas, novelty, experimentation, and creative processes that may result in new products, services, or technological processes."[175] Cultures with a tendency toward innovativeness encourage employees to think beyond existing knowledge, technologies, and parameters in efforts to find creative ways to add value. *Risk taking* reflects a willingness by employees and their firm to accept risks when pursuing entrepreneurial opportunities. These risks can include assuming significant levels of debt and allocating large amounts of other resources (e.g., people) to projects that may not be completed. The fourth dimension of an entrepreneurial orientation, *proactiveness*, describes a firm's ability to be a market leader rather than a follower. Proactive organizational cultures constantly use processes to anticipate future market needs and to satisfy them before competitors learn how to do so. Finally, *competitive aggressiveness* is a firm's propensity to take actions that allow it to consistently and substantially outperform its rivals.[176]

Changing the Organizational Culture and Restructuring

Changing a firm's organizational culture is more difficult than maintaining it, but effective strategic leaders recognize when change is needed. Incremental changes to the firm's culture typically are used to implement strategies.[177] More significant and sometimes even radical changes to organizational culture are used to support the selection of strategies that differ from those the firm has implemented historically. Regardless of the reasons for change, shaping and reinforcing a new culture require effective communication and problem solving, along with the selection of the right people (those who have the values desired for the organization), effective performance appraisals (establishing goals and measuring individual performance toward goals that fit in with the new core values), and appropriate reward systems (rewarding the desired behaviours that reflect the new core values).[178]

Evidence suggests that cultural changes succeed only when the firm's CEO, other key top management team members, and middle-level managers actively support them.[179] To effect change, middle-level managers in particular need to be highly disciplined to energize the culture and foster alignment with the strategic vision.[180]

Emphasizing Ethical Practices

The effectiveness of processes used to implement the firm's strategies increases when they are based on ethical practices. Ethical companies encourage and enable people at all organizational levels to act ethically when doing what is necessary to implement the firm's strategies. In turn, ethical practices and the judgment on which they are based create "social capital" in the organization in that "goodwill available to individuals and groups" in the organization increases.[181] Alternatively, when unethical practices evolve in an organization, they may become acceptable to many managers and employees throughout the organization. One study found that in these circumstances managers were particularly likely to engage in unethical practices if they had not been able to meet their goals. In other words, they engaged in such practices to help them meet their goals.[182]

To properly influence employees' judgment and behaviour, ethical practices must shape the firm's decision-making process and be an integral part of its culture. In fact, research has found that a value-based culture is the most effective means of ensuring that employees comply with the firm's ethical requirements.[183] As discussed in Chapter 11, in the absence of ethical requirements, managers may act opportunistically, making decisions that are in their own best interests but not in the firm's best interests. In other words, managers acting opportunistically take advantage of their positions, making decisions that benefit themselves to the detriment of the firm's owners (shareholders).[184] But managers are most likely to integrate ethical values into their decisions when the company has explicit ethics codes, the code is integrated into the business through extensive ethics training, and shareholders expect ethical behaviour.[185] They are less likely to make value-based decisions when there is increased financial pressure because of dwindling revenues.

On March 29, 2007, Canada's Minister of Public Safety, Stockwell Day, affirmed the investigation into the misuse of RCMP pension and insurance funds; what some sources say amounted to several million dollars of misplaced funds.[186] Back in 1995, when the scandals were estimated to have begun, Canada was facing "deep budget cuts and wage freezes," and some suggest that this pressure could have led the RCMP's human resources branch to "improperly divert some of the money from the members' insurance fund to shore up other budgets."[187] Moreover, some officers have claimed that, "when they tried to report the wrongdoing, they were either stonewalled or punished by top officials in the force."[188] This behaviour could be considered unethical and seems to have resulted from the financial "squeeze" senior RCMP officers found themselves subjected to by the federal government of Canada.

Firms should employ ethical strategic leaders—leaders who include ethical practices as part of their strategic direction for the firm, who desire to do the right thing, and for whom honesty, trust, and integrity are important.[189] Strategic leaders who consistently display these qualities inspire employees as they work with others to develop and support an organizational culture in which ethical practices are the expected behavioural norms.[190]

Additional actions strategic leaders can take to develop an ethical organizational culture include (1) establishing and communicating specific goals to describe the firm's ethical standards (e.g., developing and disseminating a code of conduct); (2) continuously revising and updating the code of conduct, based on inputs from people throughout the firm and from other stakeholders (e.g., customers and suppliers); (3) disseminating the code of conduct to all stakeholders to inform them of the firm's ethical standards and practices; (4) developing and implementing methods and procedures to use in achieving the firm's ethical standards (e.g., using internal auditing practices that are consistent with the standards); (5) creating and using explicit reward systems that recognize acts of courage (e.g., rewarding those who use proper channels and procedures to report observed wrong-doings); and (6) creating a work environment in which all people are treated with dignity.[191] The effectiveness of these actions increases when they are taken simultaneously and thereby are mutually supportive. When managers and employees do not engage in such actions—perhaps because an ethical culture has not been created—problems are likely to occur. As we discuss next, formal organizational controls can help prevent further problems and reinforce better ethical practices.

Establishing Balanced Organizational Controls

Organizational controls are basic to a capitalistic system and have long been viewed as an important part of strategy implementation processes.[192] Controls are necessary to help ensure that firms achieve their desired outcomes.[193] Defined as the "formal, information-based . . . procedures used by managers to maintain or alter patterns in organizational activities," controls help strategic leaders build credibility, demonstrate the value of strategies to the firm's stakeholders, and promote and support strategic change.[194] Most critically, controls provide the parameters within which strategies are to be implemented, as well as corrective actions to be taken when implementation-related adjustments are required. In this chapter, we focus on two organizational controls—strategic and financial—that were introduced in Chapter 12 (refer to Table 12.1). Our discussion of organizational controls here emphasizes strategic and financial controls because strategic leaders, especially those at the top of the organization, are responsible for their development and effective use.

Evidence suggests that, although critical to the firm's success, organizational controls are imperfect. *Control failures* have a negative effect on the firm's reputation and divert managerial attention from actions that are necessary to effectively use the strategic management process.

As explained in Chapter 12, financial control focuses on short-term financial outcomes. In contrast, strategic control focuses on the *content* of strategic actions, rather than their *outcomes*. Some strategic actions can be correct but still result in poor financial outcomes because of external conditions, such as a recession in the economy, unexpected domestic or foreign government actions, or natural disasters.[195] Therefore, an emphasis on financial control often produces more short-term and risk-averse managerial decisions, because financial outcomes may be caused by events beyond managers' direct control. Alternatively, strategic control encourages lower-level managers to make decisions that incorporate moderate and acceptable levels of risk because outcomes are shared between the business-level executives making strategic proposals and the corporate-level executives evaluating them.

The Balanced Scorecard

The **Balanced Scorecard** is a framework that firms can use to verify that they have established both strategic and financial controls to assess their performance.

As mentioned in Chapter 2, the **Balanced Scorecard** is a framework that firms can use to verify that they have established both strategic and financial controls to assess their performance.[196] This technique is most appropriate for use when dealing with business-level strategies, but can also apply to corporate-level strategies.

The underlying premise of the Balanced Scorecard is that firms jeopardize their future performance possibilities when financial controls are emphasized at the expense of strategic controls,[197] in that financial controls provide feedback about outcomes achieved from past actions but do not communicate the drivers of the firm's future performance.[198] Thus, an overemphasis on financial controls could promote managerial behaviour that has a net effect of sacrificing the firm's long-term value-creating potential for short-term performance gains.[199] An appropriate balance of strategic controls and financial controls, rather than an overemphasis on either, allows firms to effectively monitor their performance.

Four perspectives are integrated to form the Balanced Scorecard framework: *financial* (concerned with growth, profitability, and risk from the shareholders' perspective), *customer* (concerned with the amount of value customers perceive was created by the firm's products), *internal business processes* (with a focus on the priorities for various business processes that create customer and shareholder satisfaction), and *learning and growth* (concerned with the firm's effort to create a climate that supports change, innovation, and growth). Thus, using the Balanced Scorecard framework allows the firm to understand how it looks to shareholders (financial perspective), how customers view it (customer perspective), the processes it must emphasize to successfully use its competitive advantage (internal perspective), and what it can do to improve its performance in order to grow (learning and growth perspective).[200] Generally speaking, strategic controls tend to be emphasized when the firm assesses its performance relative to the learning and growth perspective, while financial controls are emphasized when assessing performance in terms of the financial perspective.

Firms use different criteria to measure their standing relative to the scorecard's four perspectives. Sample criteria are shown in Figure 13.5. The firm should select the number of criteria that will allow it to have both a strategic understanding and a financial understanding of its performance without becoming immersed in too many

Figure 13.5 Strategic and Financial Controls in a Balanced Scorecard Framework

Perspectives	Criteria
Financial	• Cash flow • Return on equity • Return on assets
Customer	• Assessment of ability to anticipate customers' needs • Effectiveness of customer service practices • Percentage of repeat business • Quality of communications with customers
Internal Business Processes	• Asset utilization improvements • Improvements in employee morale • Changes in turnover rates
Learning and Growth	• Improvements in innovation ability • Number of new products compared to competitors' • Increases in employees' skills

details.[201] For example, we know from research that a firm's innovation, quality of its goods and services, growth of its sales, and its profitability are all interrelated.[202]

Strategic leaders play an important role in determining a proper balance between strategic controls and financial controls for their firm. This is true in single-business firms as well as in diversified firms. A proper balance between controls is important, in that "wealth creation for organizations where strategic leadership is exercised is possible because these leaders make appropriate investments for future viability [through strategic control], while maintaining an appropriate level of financial stability in the present [through financial control]."[203] In fact, most corporate restructuring is designed to refocus the firm on its core businesses, thereby allowing top executives to re-establish strategic control of their separate business units.[204] Thus, as emphasized in Chapter 12, both strategic controls and financial controls support effective use of the firm's corporate-level strategy.

Successful use of strategic control by top executives frequently is integrated with appropriate autonomy for the various subunits so that they can gain a competitive advantage in their respective markets.[205] Strategic control can be used to promote the sharing of both tangible and intangible resources among interdependent businesses within a firm's portfolio. In addition, the autonomy provided allows the flexibility necessary to take advantage of specific marketplace opportunities. As a result, strategic leadership promotes the simultaneous use of strategic control and autonomy.[206]

Balancing strategic and financial controls in diversified firms can be difficult. Failure to maintain an effective balance between strategic controls and financial controls in these firms often contributes to a decision to restructure the company. For example, Jean-Pierre Garnier, CEO of GlaxoSmithKline, a British-based pharmaceutical, biological, and healthcare company,[207] worked to reinvent the company by streamlining its costs (financial controls) and simultaneously enhancing its development of innovative and valuable new drugs (strategic controls). The firm required a sufficient balance between these controls in order to survive in the strongly competitive pharmaceuticals industry.[208]

Summary

- Effective strategic leadership is a prerequisite to successfully using the strategic management process. Strategic leadership is the ability to influence those with whom you work in your organization to *voluntarily* make decisions on a day-to-day basis that enhance the long-term viability of the organization, while at the same time maintaining the short-term financial stability of the organization.

- Top-level managers are an important resource for firms to develop and exploit competitive advantages. In addition, when they and their work are valuable, rare, imperfectly imitable, and organized to be exploited, strategic leaders can themselves be a source of competitive advantage.

- The top management team comprises key managers who play a critical role in selecting and implementing the firm's strategies. Generally, they are officers of the corporation or members of the board of directors.

- There is a relationship among the top management team's characteristics, a firm's strategies, and its performance. For example, a top management team that has significant marketing and R&D knowledge positively contributes to the firm's use of growth strategies. Overall, most top management teams are more effective when they have diverse skills.

- When the board of directors is involved in shaping a firm's strategic direction, that firm generally improves its performance. However, the board may be less involved in decisions about strategy formulation and implementation when CEOs have more power. CEOs increase their power when they appoint people to the board and when they simultaneously serve as the CEO and board chair.

- In managerial succession, strategic leaders are selected from either the internal or the external managerial labour market. Because of their effect on performance, the selection of strategic leaders has implications for a firm's effectiveness. There are valid reasons to use either the internal or the external market when choosing the firm's strategic leaders. In most instances, the internal market is used to select the firm's CEO, but the number of outsiders chosen is increasing. Outsiders often are selected to initiate change.

- Effective strategic leadership has five major components: determining the firm's strategic direction, effectively managing the firm's resource portfolio (including exploiting and maintaining core competencies and managing human capital and social capital), sustaining an effective organizational culture, emphasizing ethical practices, and establishing balanced organizational controls.

- Strategic leaders must develop the firm's strategic direction. The strategic direction specifies the image and character the firm wants to develop over time. To form the strategic direction, strategic leaders evaluate the conditions (e.g., opportunities and threats in the external environment) they expect their firm to face over the next five to ten or more years.

- Strategic leaders must ensure that their firm exploits its core competencies, which are used to produce and deliver products that create value for customers, through the implementation of strategies. In related diversified and large firms in particular, core competencies are exploited by sharing them across units and products.

- A critical element of strategic leadership and the effective implementation of strategy is the ability to manage the firm's resource portfolio. This includes integrating resources to create capabilities and leveraging those capabilities through strategies to build competitive advantages. Human capital and social capital are perhaps the most important resources.

- As a part of managing the firm's resources, strategic leaders must develop a firm's human capital. Effective strategic

leaders and firms view human capital as a resource to be maximized, rather than as a cost to be minimized. Resulting from this perspective is the development and use of programs intended to train current and future strategic leaders to build the skills needed to nurture the rest of the firm's human capital.

- Effective strategic leaders also build and maintain internal and external social capital. Internal social capital promotes cooperation and coordination within and across units in the firm. External social capital provides access to resources that the firm needs to compete effectively.

- Shaping the firm's culture is a central task of effective strategic leadership. An appropriate organizational culture encourages the development of an entrepreneurial orientation among employees and an ability to change the culture as necessary.

- In ethical organizations, employees are encouraged to exercise ethical judgment and to behave ethically at all times. Improved ethical practices foster social capital. Setting specific goals to describe the firm's ethical standards, using a code of conduct, rewarding ethical behaviours, and creating a work environment in which all people are treated with dignity are examples of actions that facilitate and support ethical behaviour within the firm.

- Developing and using balanced organizational controls is the final component of effective strategic leadership. The Balanced Scorecard is a tool used by the firm and its strategic leaders to develop an appropriate balance between its strategic and financial controls. An effective balance between strategic and financial controls allows for the flexible use of core competencies, but within the parameters indicated by the firm's financial position.

Review Questions

1. What is strategic leadership? How are top executives considered important resources for a firm?

2. What is a top management team, and how does it affect a firm's performance and its abilities to innovate and make appropriate strategic changes?

3. How do the internal and external managerial labour markets affect the managerial succession process?

4. How does strategic leadership affect the determination of the firm's strategic direction?

5. How do strategic leaders effectively manage their firm's resource portfolio such that its core competencies are exploited, and the human capital and social capital are leveraged to achieve a competitive advantage?

6. What is organizational culture? What must strategic leaders do to develop and sustain an effective organizational culture?

7. What are organizational controls? Why are strategic controls and financial controls important parts of the strategic management process?

1. As a strategic leader, what could you do to establish and emphasize ethical practices in your firm?

2. How important is creating an ethical corporate culture in creating an ethical organization? How would you create an ethical culture and ensure that your organization is being socially responsible?

3. Should executives be held accountable and legally liable if their organization pursues unethical actions that an organi-

zation with an ethical culture would have steered clear of? Why or why not?

4. How is behaving ethically as an organization different from being socially responsible? Is it possible to be an ethical organization but not a socially responsible organization or vice versa?

Experiential Exercises

Key Strategic Leadership Actions

As discussed in this chapter, several actions characterize effective strategic leadership. In this exercise, you will use these actions to evaluate three top-level managers who are widely known and who have served as CEO and/or chairman of their respective firm for a long period. The length of time these individuals have served their firms allows you to find a wealth of information about their actions as strategic leaders as well as the results of those actions. You can consult each firm's Web site as well as search engines to find the information and materials you will need to complete this exercise.

In the chart below, provide an example of each strategic leadership action for each of the three individuals. (*Note:* You are

not being asked to provide an example of the "exploiting and maintaining core competencies" action. The reason for this is that this action is internal to the firm, meaning that it would be difficult for you to find an example of this action to include in the chart.) Each example you provide in terms of the five strategic actions included in the chart should be an important indicator of the action it represents. Be ready to defend your choices when you present them to the class. Be prudent in your selection of examples of each leader's actions, as there are writers who will have a biased opinion (either positive or negative in nature) of the top-level manager about whom they are offering comments. To the degree possible, it is best to find at least two writers or analysts who comment identically about a strategic leader's action before you include that action in the chart.

	Determining strategic direction	Establishing balanced organizational controls	Effectively managing the firm's resource portfolio	Sustaining an effective organizational culture	Emphasizing ethical practices
Clive Beddoe WestJet					
Robert Milton Air Canada					
Howard Schultz Starbucks					

Notes

1. R. D. Ireland, M. A. Hitt, S. M. Camp, & D. L. Sexton, 2001, Integrating entrepreneurship and strategic management actions to create firm wealth, *Academy of Management Executive*, 15(1): 49–63; K. R. Thompson, W. A. Hochwarter, & N. J. Mathys, 1997, Stretch targets: What makes them effective? *Academy of Management Executive*, 11(3): 48–59.

2. A. Cannella Jr., A. Pettigrew, & D. Hambrick, 2001, Upper echelons: Donald Hambrick on executives and strategy, *Academy of Management Executive*, 15(3): 36–52; R. D. Ireland & M. A. Hitt, 1999, Achieving and maintaining strategic competitiveness in the 21st century: The role of strategic leadership, *Academy of Management Executive*, 12(1): 43–57.

3. Wikipedia, 2007, Booz Allen Hamilton, December 30, http://en.wikipedia.org/wiki/Booz_Allen_Hamilton.

4. 2007, CEO turnover remains high at world's largest companies, Booz Allen study finds, boozallen.com, http://www.boozallen.com/publications/article/36608085, May 22.

5. Ibid.

6. Ibid.

7. Ibid.

8. Ibid.

9. Wikipedia, Dark Horse, http://en.wikipedia.org/wiki/Dark_horse.

10. A. Barrionuevo, 2005, As directors feel their oats, chiefs are put out to pasture, *New York Times Online*, www.nytimes.com, March 15; L. Greiner, T. Cummings, & A. Bhambri, 2002, When new CEOs succeed and fail: 4-D theory of strategic transformation, *Organizational Dynamics*, 32: 1–16.

11. R. Evered, 1980, So what is Strategy? working paper, Monterey, CA: Naval Postgraduate School; J. B. Quinn, 1980, *Strategies for Change: Logical Incrementalism*, Homewood, IL: Richard D. Irwin; H. Mintzberg & J. B. Quinn, 1996, *The Strategy Process: Concepts, Contexts, Cases*, 3rd ed., Upper Saddle River, New Jersey: Prentice Hall.

12. W. G. Rowe, 2001, Creating wealth in organizations: The role of strategic leadership, *Academy of Management Executive*, 15(2), 81–94.

13. H. Mintzberg, 1987, Five Ps for Strategy, *California Management Review*, fall, in H. Mintzberg & J. B. Quinn, 1996, *The Strategy Process: Concepts, Contexts, Cases*, 3rd ed., Upper Saddle River, NJ: Prentice Hall, 10–17; H. Mintzberg, 1987, Crafting strategy, *Harvard Business Review*, July–August, in H. Mintzberg & J. B. Quinn, 1996, *The Strategy Process: Concepts, Contexts, Cases*, 3rd ed., Upper Saddle River, NJ: Prentice Hall, 101–9.

14. J. Barney, 1997, *Gaining and Sustaining Competitive Advantage*, New York: Addison-Wesley Publishing Company, 65–133.

15. A. Zaleznik, 1977, Managers and leaders: Are they different? *Harvard Business Review*, May–June, 67–78.

16. G. Hamel & C. K. Prahalad, 1993, Strategy as stretch and leverage, *Harvard Business Review*, 71(2), 75–84.

17. S. Sherman, 1995, How tomorrow's best leaders are learning their stuff, *Fortune*, November, 27, 99; R. Calori, G. Johnson, & P. Sarnin, 1994, CEOs' cognitive maps and the scope of the organization, *Strategic Management Journal*, 15: 437–57.

18. Zaleznik, Managers and leaders: Are they different? 70–71.

19. Ibid., 71–72.

20. Ibid., 72–74.

21. Ibid., 74–75.

22. L. T. Hosmer, 1982, The importance of strategic leadership, *Journal of Business Strategy*, 3(2), fall, 47–57.

23. D. Schendel, 1989, Introduction to the special issue on "strategic leadership," *Strategic Management Journal*, special issue, 10, 1–3.

24. D. Hambrick, 1989, Guest editor's introduction: Putting top managers back in the strategy picture, *Strategic Management Journal*, special issue, 10, 5–15.

25. Ibid., 5–15.

26. Hosmer, 1982, The importance of strategic leadership; R. Evans, 1997, Hollow the leader, *Report on Business*, November, 56–63; L. Sooklal, 1989, The leader as a broker of dreams, *Human Relations*, 44(8), 833–56; A. Zaleznik, 1990, The leadership gap, *Academy of Management Executive*, 4(1), 7–22.

27. C. W. L. Hill & R. E. Hoskisson, 1987, Strategy and structure in the multiproduct firm, *Academy of Management Review*, 12(2), 1987, 331–41; R. E. Hoskisson & M. A. Hitt, 1994, *Downscoping: How to Tame the Diversified Firm*, New York: Oxford University Press; A. Zaleznik, The leadership gap, 7–22.

28. G. Hedlund, 1994, A model of knowledge management and the N-Form corporation, *Strategic Management Journal*, 15 (special issue), summer, 73–90; B. Kogut & U. Zander, 1992, Knowledge of the firm, combinative abilities, and the replication of technology, *Organization Science*, 3, 383–97.

29. R. Trigg, 1996, *Ideas of Human Nature: An Historical Introduction*, Cambridge, MA: Blackwell Publishers; J. Child, 1972, Organizational structure, environment and performance: The role of strategic choice, *Sociology*, 6, 1–22.

30. Zaleznik, Managers and leaders: Are they different? 70–71.

31. Ibid., 71–72.

32. Ibid., 72–74.

33. Zaleznik, Managers and leaders: Are they different? 74–75; A. Zaleznik, 1990, The leadership gap, *Academy of Management Executive*, 4(1), 7–22.

34. Hosmer, 1982, The importance of strategic leadership, 47–57.

35. Schendel, 1989, Introduction to the Special Issue on "Strategic Leadership," 1–3.

36. Hambrick, 1989; Guest editor's introduction: Putting top managers back into the strategy picture, 5–15; H. Mintzberg, 1973, *The Nature of Managerial Work*, chapters 15–17, New York: Harper and Row.

37. Hambrick, 1989, Guest editor's introduction: Putting top managers back into the strategy picture, 5–15.

38. Evans, 1997, Hollow the leader, 56–63; Hosmer, 1982, The importance of strategic leadership, 47–57; Sooklal, 1991, The leader as a broker of dreams, 833–56; Zaleznik, 1990, The leadership gap, 7–22.

39. Hoskisson and Hitt, 1994, *Downscoping: How to Tame the Diversified Firm*.

40. M. Polanyi, 1966, *The Tacit Dimension*, Garden City, NY: Anchor; R. Reed and R. J. deFillippi, 1990, Causal ambiguity, barriers to imitation, and sustainable competitive advantage, *Academy of Management Review*, 15, 88–102; R. Nelson and S. Winter, 1982, *An Evolutionary Theory of Economic Change*, Cambridge, Mass: Belknap Press; H. Itami, 1987, *Mobilizing Invisible Assets*, Cambridge, MA: Harvard University Press; J. Kotter and J. Heskett, 1992, *Corporate Culture and Performance*, New York: The Free Press; W. G. Ouchi and M. Maguire, 1975, Organizational control: Two functions, *Administrative Sciences Quarterly*, 20, 559–569; E. H. Schein, 1993, On dialogue, culture, and organizational learning, *Organizational Dynamics*, 22(2), 40–51.

41. R. Trigg, 1996, *Ideas of Human Nature: An Historical Introduction*; Child, 1972, Organizational structure, environment and performance: The role of strategic choice, 1–22; H. Mintzberg, B. Ahlstrand and J. Lampel, 1998, *Strategy Safari*, chapter 5, New York: The Free Press.

42. J. P. Kotter, 1990, What leaders really do, *Harvard Business Review*, May–June, reprinted *Harvard Business Review on Leadership*, Boston: Harvard Business School Press, 37–60.

43. Zaleznik, 1977, Managers and leaders: Are they different?, 74–75; Zaleznik, 1990, The leadership gap, 7–22.

44. Kotter, 1990, What leaders really do.

45. Ibid.

46. W. G. Rowe, 2001, Creating wealth in organizations: The role of strategic leadership, 81–94.

47. Ireland and Hitt, 1999, Achieving and maintaining strategic competitiveness in the 21st century, 43–57.

48. J. Conger, 1991, Inspiring others: The language of leadership, *The Academy of Management Executive*, 5(1), 31–45; M. Nathan, 1996, What is organizational vision? Ask chief executives, *The Academy of Management Executive*, 10(1), 82–83.

49. Hambrick, 1989, Guest editor's introduction: Putting top managers back in the strategy picture, 5–15; Schendel, 1989, Introduction to the Special Issue on "Strategic Leadership," 1–3.

50. Hoskisson and Hitt, 1994, *Downscoping: How to Tame the Diversified Firm*.

51. I. Nonaka, 1994, A dynamic theory of organizational knowledge creation, *Organization Science*, 5(1), 14–37; I. Nonaka and H. Takeuchi, 1995, *The Knowledge Creating Company*, New York: Oxford University Press.

52. Trigg, 1996, *Ideas of Human Nature: An Historical Introduction*; Child, 1972, Organizational structure, environment and performance: The role of strategic choice, 1–22.

53. I. Nonaka and H. Takeuchi, 1995, *The Knowledge Creating Company*; Kogut & Zander, 1992, Knowledge of the firm, combinative abilities, and the replication of technology, 383–97; S. Sherman & W. Glenn Rowe, 1996, Leadership and strategic value: A resource-based typology, Proceedings of the Texas Conference on Organizations, March 1.

54. H. Mintzberg, 1975, The manager's job: Folklore and fact, *Harvard Business Review*, July-August, reprinted in *Harvard Business Review on Leadership*, Boston: Harvard Business School Press, 1998, 1–36.

55. H. Gardner, 1995, *Leading Minds: An Anatomy of Leadership*, New York: Basic Books; S. Sherman, 1995, How tomorrow's best leaders are learning their stuff, *Fortune*, November 27, 90–102.

56. J. B. Quinn, P. Anderson, and S. Finklestein, 1996, Managing professional intellect: Making the most of the best, *Harvard Business Review*, 74(2): 71–80.

57. M. Loeb, 1994, Where leaders come from, *Fortune,* September 19, 241–242.

58. M. F. R. Kets de Vries, 1995, *Life and Death in the Executive Fast Lane,* San Francisco: Jossey-Bass.

59. Loeb, Where leaders come from, 241; N. Nohria and J. D. Berkley, 1994, Whatever happened to the take-charge manager? *Harvard Business Review,* 72(1): 128–37.

60. M. Hammer and S. A. Stanton, 1997, The power of reflection, *Fortune,* November 24, 291–296.

61. S. Finkelstein and D. C. Hambrick, 1996, *Strategic Leadership: Top Executives and Their Effects on Organizations,* St. Paul, Minn.: West Publishing Company, 2.

62. J. A. Byrne and J. Reingold, 1997, Wanted: A few good CEOs, *BusinessWeek,* August 11, 64–70; Kotter, 1990, What leaders really do?

63. Sherman, How tomorrow's best, 102.

64. Rowe, 2001, Creating wealth in organizations: The role of strategic leadership, 81–94.

65. Ibid, 81–94.

66. J. D. House, 1999, *Against the Tide: Battling for Economic Renewal in Newfoundland and Labrador,* Toronto: University of Toronto Press.

67. R. Castanias & C. Helfat, 2001, The managerial rents model: Theory and empirical analysis, *Journal of Management,* 27: 661–678; H. P. Gunz & R. M. Jalland, 1996, Managerial careers and business strategy, *Academy of Management Review,* 21: 718–756; M. Beer & R. Eisenstat, 2000, The silent killers of strategy implementation and learning, *Sloan Management Review,* 41(4): 29–40; C. M. Christensen, 1997, Making strategy: Learning by doing, *Harvard Business Review,* 75(6): 141–156; M. A. Hitt, B. W. Keats, H. E. Harback, and R. D. Nixon, 1994, Rightsizing: Building and maintaining strategic leadership and long-term competitiveness, *Organizational Dynamics,* 23: 18–32.

68. 2004, For second year running, Paul Tellier named most respected CEO by peers, *Ipsos News Center,* January 20, www.ipsos-na.com/news/, retrieved May 10.

69. M. Wright, R. E. Hoskisson, L. W. Busenitz, & J. Dial, 2000, Entrepreneurial growth through privatization: The upside of management buyouts, *Academy of Management Review,* 25: 591–601; M. J. Waller, G. P. Huber, & W. H. Glick, 1995, Functional background as a determinant of executives' selective perception, *Academy of Management Journal,* 38: 943–974; N. Rajagopalan, A. M. Rasheed, & D. K. Datta, 1993, Strategic decision processes: Critical review and future directions, *Journal of Management,* 19: 349–384.

70. W. G. Rowe, 2001, Creating wealth in organizations: The role of strategic leadership, 81–94; Finkelstein & Hambrick, *Strategic Leadership,* 26–34; D. C. Hambrick & E. Abrahamson, 1995, Assessing managerial discretion across industries: A multimethod approach, *Academy of Management Journal,* 38: 1427–1441; D. C. Hambrick & S. Finkelstein, 1987, Managerial discretion: A bridge between polar views of organizational outcomes, in B. Staw & L. L. Cummings (eds.), *Research in Organizational Behavior,* Greenwich, CT: JAI Press, 369–406.

71. R. C. Mayer, J. H. Davis, & F. D. Schoorman, 1995, An integrative model of organizational trust, *Academy of Management Review,* 20: 709–734.

72. N. Rajagopalan and D. K. Datta, 1996, CEO characteristics: Does industry matter? *Academy of Management Journal,* 39: 197–215.

73. S. Green, F. Hassan, J. Immelt, M. Marks, & D. Meiland, 2003, In search of global leaders, *Harvard Business Review,* 81(8): 38–45; T. J. Peters, 2001, Leadership: Sad facts and silver linings, *Harvard Business Review,* 79(11): 121–128.

74. 2007, Passing of Pollock hits Canadians Hard, Yahoo! Sports, August 16.

75. Ibid.

76. Passing of Pollock hits Canadians Hard, Yahoo! Sports.

77. 2007, 50 Best Employers in Canada, *The Globe and Mail,* December 20.

78. Ibid.

79. Ibid.

80. Ibid.

81. S. Finkelstein & D. C. Hambrick, 1996, *Strategic Leadership: Top Executives and Their Effects on Organizations,* St. Paul, MN: West Publishing Company, 2.

82. 2007, CEO of the Year, *The Globe and Mail,* November 29.

83. Ibid.

84. 2007, CN Media, news release, http://www.cn.ca/about/media/news_releases/2006/4th_quarter/en_News20061130.shtml; Wikipedia, E. Hunter Harrison, http://en.wikipedia.org/wiki/Hunter_Harrison, December 31.

85. R. Castanias & C. Helfat, 2001, The managerial rents model: Theory and empirical analysis, *Journal of Management,* 27: 661–678; H. P. Gunz & R. M. Jalland, 1996, Managerial careers and business strategy, *Academy of Management Review,* 21: 718–756.

86. M. Beer & R. Eisenstat, 2000, The silent killers of strategy implementation and learning, *Sloan Management Review,* 41(4): 29–40; C. M. Christensen, 1997, Making strategy: Learning by doing, *Harvard Business Review,* 75(6): 141–156.

87. J. A. Petrick & J. F. Quinn, 2001, The challenge of leadership accountability for integrity capacity as a strategic asset, *Journal of Business Ethics,* 34: 331–343; R. C. Mayer, J. H. Davis, & F. D. Schoorman, 1995, An integrative model of organizational trust, *Academy of Management Review,* 20: 709–734.

88. S. Gove, D. Sirmon, & M. A. Hitt, 2003, Relative resource advantages: The effect of resources and resource management on organizational performance, Paper presented at the Strategic Management Society Conference, Baltimore; J. J. Sosik, 2001, Self-other agreement on charismatic leadership: Relationships with work attitudes and managerial performance, *Group & Organization Management,* 26: 484–511.

89. M. L. A. Hayward, V. P. Rindova, & T. G. Pollock, 2004, Believing one's own press: The causes and consequences of CEO celebrity, *Strategic Management Journal,* 25: 637–653.

90. N. J. Hiller & D. C. Hambrick, 2005, Conceptualizing executive hubris: The role of (hyper-) core self-evaluations in strategic decision making, *Strategic Management Journal,* 26: 297–319.

91. I. Goll, R. Sambharya, & L. Tucci, 2001, Top management team composition, corporate ideology, and firm performance, *Management International Review,* 41(2): 109–129.

92. J. Bunderson, 2003, Team member functional background and involvement in management teams: Direct effects and the moderating role of power and centralization, *Academy of Management Journal,* 46: 458–474; L. Markoczy, 2001, Consensus formation during strategic change, *Strategic Management Journal,* 22: 1013–1031.

93. Post, Preston, & Sachs, Managing the extended enterprise; C. Pegels, Y. Song, & B. Yang, 2000, Management heterogeneity, competitive interaction groups, and firm performance, *Strategic Management Journal,* 21: 911–923.

94. Markoczy, Consensus formation during strategic change; D. Knight, C. L. Pearce, K. G. Smith, J. D. Olian, H. P. Sims, K. A. Smith, & P. Flood, 1999, Top management team diversity, group process, and strategic consensus, *Strategic Management Journal,* 20: 446–465.

95. J. J. Distefano & M. L. Maznevski, 2000, Creating value with diverse teams in global management, *Organizational Dynamics,* 29(1): 45–63; T. Simons, L. H. Pelled, & K. A. Smith, 1999, Making use of difference, diversity, debate, and decision comprehensiveness in top management teams, *Academy of Management Journal,* 42: 662–673.

96. Finkelstein & Hambrick, *Strategic Leadership,* 148.

97. S. Barsade, A. Ward, J. Turner, & J. Sonnenfeld, 2000, To your heart's content: A model of affective diversity in top management teams, *Administrative Science Quarterly,* 45: 802–836; C. C. Miller, L. M. Burke, & W. H. Glick, 1998, Cognitive diversity among upper-echelon executives: Implications for strategic decision processes, *Strategic Management Journal,* 19: 39–58.

98. B. J. Avolio & S. S. Kahai, 2002, Adding the "e" to e-leadership: How it may impact your leadership, *Organizational Dynamics,* 31: 325–338.

99. Z. Simsek, J. F. Veiga, M. L. Lubatkin, & R. H. Dino, 2005, Modeling the multilevel determinants of top management team behavioral integration, *Academy of Management Journal,* 48: 69–84.

100. U. Daellenbach, A. McCarthy, & T. Schoenecker, 1999, Commitment to innovation: The impact of top management team characteristics, *R&D Management,* 29(3): 199–208; D. K. Datta & J. P. Guthrie, 1994, Executive succession: Organizational antecedents of CEO characteristics, *Strategic Management Journal,* 15: 569–577.

101. M. Jensen & E. J. Zajac, 2004, Corporate elites and corporate strategy: How demographic preferences and structural position shape the scope of the firm, *Strategic Management Journal,* 25: 507–524.

102. W. B. Werther, 2003, Strategic change and leader-follower alignment, *Organizational Dynamics,* 32: 32–45; S. Wally & M. Becerra, 2001, Top management team characteristics and strategic changes in international diversification: The case of U.S. multinationals in the European community, *Group & Organization Management,* 26: 165–188.

103. Y. Zhang & N. Rajagopalan, 2003, Explaining the new CEO origin: Firm versus industry antecedents, *Academy of Management Journal,* 46: 327–338.

104. T. Dvir, D. Eden, B. J. Avolio, & B. Shamir, 2002, Impact of transformational leadership on follower development and performance: A field experiment, *Academy of Management Journal,* 45: 735–744.

105. L. Tihanyi, R. A. Johnson, R. E. Hoskisson, & M. A. Hitt, 2003, Institutional ownership and international diversification: The effects of boards of directors and technological opportunity, *Academy of Management Journal,* 46: 195–211.

106. B. R. Golden & E. J. Zajac, 2001, When will boards influence strategy? Inclination times power equals strategic change, *Strategic Management Journal,* 22: 1087–1111.

107. M. Carpenter & J. Westphal, 2001, Strategic context of external network ties: Examining the impact of director appointments on board involvement in strategic decision making, *Academy of Management Journal,* 44: 639–660.

108. J. D. Westphal, 1999, Collaboration in the boardroom: Behavioral and performance consequences of CEO-board social ties, *Academy of Management Journal,* 42: 7–24.

109. J. Roberts & P. Stiles, 1999, The relationship between chairmen and chief executives: Competitive or complementary roles? *Long Range Planning,* 32(1): 36–48.

110. J. Coles, N. Sen, & V. McWilliams, 2001, An examination of the relationship of governance mechanisms to performance, *Journal of Management,* 27: 23–50; J. Coles & W. Hesterly, 2000, Independence of the chairman and board composition: Firm choices and shareholder value, *Journal of Management,* 26: 195–214.

111. 2007, General Motors to cut at least 25,000 U.S. jobs by 2008: CEO, CBC News, June 7.

112. B. Simon, 2005, GM shuts plants and cuts 25,000 jobs, Financial Times Online, www.ft.com, June 7; D. Hakim, 2005, GM and Ford stuck in neutral as buyers look beyond Detroit, New York Times Online, www.nytimes.com, April 15.

113. Y. Kageyama, 2005, Toyota sets it sights on being no. 1 in the world, *Houston Chronicle,* March 18, D4.

114. 2007, General Motors to cut at least 25,000 U.S. jobs by 2008: CEO, CBC News, June 7.

115. C. M. Daily & D. R. Dalton, 1995, CEO and director turnover in failing firms: An illusion of change? *Strategic Management Journal,* 16: 393–400.

116. R. Albanese, M. T. Dacin, & I. C. Harris, 1997, Agents as stewards, *Academy of Management Review,* 22: 609–611; J. H. Davis, F. D. Schoorman, & L. Donaldson, 1997, Toward a stewardship theory of management, *Academy of Management Review,* 22: 20–47.

117. J. G. Combs & M. S. Skill, 2003, Managerialist and human capital explanations for key executive pay premiums: A contingency perspective, *Academy of Management Journal,* 46: 63–73.

118. N. Rajagopalan & D. Datta, 1996, CEO characteristics: Does industry matter? *Academy of Management Journal,* 39: 197–215.

119. R. A. Johnson, R. E. Hoskisson, & M. A. Hitt, 1993, Board involvement in restructuring: The effect of board versus managerial controls and characteristics, *Strategic Management Journal,* 14 (Special Issue): 33–50.

120. M. Schneider, 2002, A stakeholder model of organizational leadership, *Organization Science,* 13: 209–220.

121. M. Sorcher & J. Brant, 2002, Are you picking the right leaders? *Harvard Business Review,* 80(2): 78–85; D. A. Waldman, G. G. Ramirez, R. J. House, & P. Puranam, 2001, Does leadership matter? CEO leadership attributes and profitability under conditions of perceived environmental uncertainty, *Academy of Management Journal,* 44: 134–143.

122. W. Shen & A. A. Cannella, 2002, Revisiting the performance consequences of CEO succession: The impacts of successor type, postsuccession senior executive turnover, and departing CEO tenure, *Academy of Management Journal,* 45: 717–734.

123. R. E. Hoskisson, D. Yiu, & H. Kim, 2000, Capital and labor market congruence and corporate governance: Effects on corporate innovation and global competitiveness, in S. S. Cohen & G. Boyd (eds.), *Corporate Governance and Globalization,* Northampton, MA: Edward Elgar, 129–154.

124. M. Hurlbert, 2005, Lo! A white knight! So why isn't the market cheering? New York Times Online, www.nytimes.com, March 27.

125. W. Shen & A. A. Cannella, 2003, Will succession planning increase shareholder wealth? Evidence from investor reactions to relay CEO successions, *Strategic Management Journal,* 24: 191–198.

126. Greiner, Cummings, & Bhambri, When new CEOs succeed and fail.

127. K. Belson & T. Zaun, 2005, Land of the rising gaijin chief executive, New York Times Online, www.nytimes.com, March 27.

128. B. Dyck, M. Mauws, F. Starke, & G. Mischke, 2002, Passing the baton: The importance of sequence, timing, technique and communication in executive succession, *Journal of Business Venturing,* 17: 143–162.

129. M. A. Hitt, B. W. Keats, & E. Yucel, 2003, Strategic leadership in global business organizations, in W. H. Mobley & P. W. Dorfman (eds.), *Advances in Global Leadership,* Oxford, UK: Elsevier Science, Ltd., 9–35.

130. I. M. Levin, 2000, Vision revisited, *Journal of Applied Behavioral Science,* 36: 91–107; J. C. Collins & J. I. Porras, 1996, Building your company's vision, *Harvard Business Review,* 74(5): 65–77.

131. 2007 Profit Innovation Awards, Oracle.com, http://www.oracle.com/oramag/profit/07-feb/p17cfos.html, February.

132. Ibid.

133. J. Barney & A. M. Arikan, 2001, The resource-based view: Origins and implications, in M. A. Hitt, R. E. Freeman, & J. S. Harrison (eds.), *Handbook of Strategic Management,* Oxford, UK: Blackwell Publishers, 124–188.

134. E. T. Prince, 2005, The fiscal behavior of CEOs, *Managerial Economics,* 46(3): 23–26.

135. D. G. Sirmon, M. A. Hitt, & R. D. Ireland, 2006, Managing firm resources in dynamic markets to create value: Looking inside the black box, *Academy of Management Review,* in press.

136. S. K. Ethiraj, P. Kale, M. S. Krishnan, & J. V. Singh, 2005, Where do capabilities come from and how do they matter? A study in the software services industry, *Strategic Management Journal,* 26: 25–45.

137. S. Dutta, O. Narasimhan, & S. Rajiv, 2005, Conceptualizing and measuring capabilities: Methodology and empirical application, *Strategic Management Journal,* 26: 277–285.

138. Barney & Arikan, The resource-based view.

139. N. W. Hatch & J. H. Dyer, 2004, Human capital and learning as a source of sustainable competitive advantage, *Strategic Management Journal,* 25: 1155–1178; C. A. Lengnick-Hall & J. A. Wolff, 1999, Similarities and contradictions in the core logic of three strategy research streams, *Strategic Management Journal,* 20: 1109–1132.

140. M. A. Hitt, L. Bierman, K. Shimizu, & R. Kochhar, 2001, Direct and moderating effects of human capital on strategy and performance in professional service firms: A resource-based perspective, *Academy of Management Journal,* 44: 13–28.

141. S. E. Jackson, M. A. Hitt, & A. S. DeNisi (eds.), 2003, *Managing Knowledge for Sustained Competitive Advantage: Designing Strategies for Effective Human Resource Management,* Oxford, UK: Elsevier Science, Ltd.

142. A. McWilliams, D. D. Van Fleet, & P. M. Wright, 2001, Strategic management of human resources for global competitive advantage, *Journal of Business Strategies,* 18(1): 1–24; J. Pfeffer, 1994, *Competitive Advantage through People,* Cambridge, MA: Harvard Business School Press, 4.

143. W. Watson, W. H. Stewart, & A. Barnir, 2003, The effects of human capital, organizational demography, and interpersonal processes on venture partner perceptions of firm profit and growth, *Journal of Business Venturing,* 18: 145–164.

144. H. B. Gregersen & J. S. Black, 2002, J. W. Marriott Jr. on growing the legacy, *Academy of Management Executive,* 16(2): 33–39.

145. R. A. Noe, J. A. Colquitt, M. J. Simmering, & S. A. Alvarez, 2003, Knowledge management: Developing intellectual and social capital, in S. E. Jackson, M. A. Hitt, & A. S. DeNisi (eds.), 2003, *Managing Knowledge for Sustained Competitive Advantage: Designing Strategies for Effective Human Resource Management,* Oxford, UK: Elsevier Science, Ltd., 209–242.

146. G. P. Hollenbeck & M. W. McCall Jr., 2003, Competence, not competencies: Making a global executive development work, in W. H. Mobley & P. W. Dorfman (eds.), *Advances in Global Leadership,* Oxford, UK: Elsevier Science, Ltd., 101–119; J. Sandberg, 2000, Understanding human competence at work: An interpretative approach, *Academy of Management Journal,* 43: 9–25

147. Hitt, Keats, & Yucel, Strategic leadership in global business organizations; J. J. Distefano & M. L. Maznevski, 2003, Developing global managers integrating theory, behavior, data and performance, in W. H. Mobley & P. W. Dorfman (eds.), *Advances in Global Leadership,* Oxford, UK: Elsevier Science, Ltd., 341–371.

148. J. S. Bunderson & K. M. Sutcliffe, 2003, Management team learning orientation and business unit performance, *Journal of Applied Psychology,* 88: 552–560; C. R. James, 2003, Designing learning organizations, *Organizational Dynamics,* 32(1): 46–61.

149. J. D. Bragger, D. A. Hantula, D. Bragger, J. Kirnan, & E. Kutcher, 2003, When success breeds failure: History, Hysteresis, and delayed exit decisions, *Journal of Applied Psychology,* 88: 6–14.

150. M. R. Haas & M. T. Hansen, 2005, When using knowledge can hurt performance: The value of organizational capabilities in a management consulting company, *Strategic Management Journal,* 26: 1–24; G. Ahuja & R. Katila, 2004, Where do resources come from? The role of idiosyncratic situations, *Strategic Management Journal,* 25: 887–907.

151. Hitt, Miller, & Colella, *Organizational Behavior.*

152. J. W. Spencer, 2003, Firms' knowledge-sharing strategies in the global innovation system: Empirical evidence from the flat-panel display industry, *Strategic Management Journal*, 24: 217–233; M. Harvey & M. M. Novicevic, 2002, The hyper-competitive global marketplace: The importance of intuition and creativity in expatriate managers, *Journal of World Business*, 37: 127–138.

153. S. Rodan & C. Galunic, 2004, More than network structure: How knowledge heterogeneity influences managerial performance and innovativeness, *Strategic Management Journal*, 25: 541–562; S. K. McEvily & B. Charavarthy, 2002, The persistence of knowledge-based advantage: An empirical test for product performance and technological knowledge, *Strategic Management Journal*, 23: 285–305.

154. K. D. Miller, 2002, Knowledge inventories and managerial myopia, *Strategic Management Journal*, 23: 689–706.

155. R. D. Nixon, M. A. Hitt, H. Lee, & E. Jeong, 2004, Market reactions to corporate announcements of downsizing actions and implementation strategies, *Strategic Management Journal*, 25: 1121–1129.

156. J. Di Frances, 2002, 10 reasons why you shouldn't downsize, *Journal of Property Management*, 67(1): 72–73.

157. A. Pinsonneault & K. Kraemer, 2002, The role of information technology in organizational downsizing: A tale of two American cities, *Organization Science*, 13: 191–208.

158. Nixon, Hitt, Lee, & Jeong, Market reactions to corporate announcements of downsizing actions.

159. T. Simons & Q. Roberson, 2003, Why managers should care about fairness: The effects of aggregate justice perceptions on organizational outcomes, *Journal of Applied Psychology*, 88: 432–443; M. L. Ambrose & R. Cropanzano, 2003, A longitudinal analysis of organizational fairness: An examination of reactions to tenure and promotion decisions, *Journal of Applied Psychology*, 88: 266–275.

160. P. S. Adler & S.-W. Kwon, 2002, Social capital: Prospects for a new concept, *Academy of Management Review*, 27: 17–40.

161. A. Mendez, 2003, The coordination of globalized R&D activities through project teams organization: An exploratory empirical study, *Journal of World Business*, 38: 96–109.

162. R. D. Ireland, M. A. Hitt, & D. Vaidyanath, 2002, Managing strategic alliances to achieve a competitive advantage, *Journal of Management*, 28: 413–446.

163. J. Florin, M. Lubatkin, & W. Schulze, 2003, *Academy of Management Journal*, 46: 374–384; P. Davidsson & B. Honig, 2003, The role of social and human capital among nascent entrepreneurs, *Journal of Business Venturing*, 18: 301–331.

164. A. K. Gupta & V. Govindarajan, 2000, Knowledge management's social dimension: Lessons from Nucor Steel, *Sloan Management Review*, 42(1): 71–80; C. M. Fiol, 1991, Managing culture as a competitive resource: An identity-based view of sustainable competitive advantage, *Journal of Management*, 17: 191–211; J. B. Barney, 1986, Organizational culture: Can it be a source of sustained competitive advantage? *Academy of Management Review*, 11: 656–665.

165. V. Govindarajan & A. K. Gupta, 2001, Building an effective global business team, *Sloan Management Review*, 42(4): 63–71; S. Ghoshal & C. A. Bartlett, 1994, Linking organizational context and managerial action: The dimensions of quality of management, *Strategic Management Journal*, 15: 91–112.

166. 2005, Culture shock: A survey of Canadian executives reveals that corporate culture is in need of improvement, Canadian Business Online, http://www.canadianbusiness.com/managing/employees/article.jsp?content=20060106_160426_5512, October.

167. 2006, WestJet: Canada's Most Admired Corporate Culture of 2006, Canada NewsWire, October 10.

168. D. F. Kuratko, R. D. Ireland, & J. S. Hornsby, 2001, Improving firm performance through entrepreneurial actions: Acordia's corporate entrepreneurship strategy, *Academy of Management Executive*, 15(4): 60–71.

169. A. Ardichvili, R. Cardoza, & S. Ray, 2003, A theory of entrepreneurial opportunity identification and development, *Journal of Business Venturing*, 18: 105–123; T. E. Brown, P. Davidsson, & J. Wiklund, 2001, An operationalization of Stevenson's conceptualization of entrepreneurship as opportunity-based firm behavior, *Strategic Management Journal*, 22: 953–968.

170. D. S. Elenkov, W. Judge, & P. Wright, 2005, Strategic leadership and executive innovation influence: An international multi-cluster comparative study, *Strategic Management Journal*, 26: 665–682.

171. R. G. McGrath, W. J. Ferrier, & A. L. Mendelow, 2004, Real options as engines of choice and heterogeneity, *Academy of Management Review*, 29: 86–101.

172. R. S. Vassolo, J. Anand, & T. B. Folta, 2004, Non-additivity in portfolios of exploration activities: A real options analysis of equity alliances in biotechnology, *Strategic Management Journal*, 25: 1045–1061.

173. R. D. Ireland, M. A. Hitt, & D. Sirmon, 2003, A model of strategic entrepreneurship: The construct and its dimensions, *Journal of Management*, 29: 963–989.

174. G. T. Lumpkin & G. G. Dess, 1996, Clarifying the entrepreneurial orientation construct and linking it to performance, *Academy of Management Review*, 21: 135–172; R. G. McGrath & I. MacMillan, 2000, *Entrepreneurial mindset*, Boston: Harvard Business School Press.

175. Lumpkin & Dess, Clarifying the entrepreneurial orientation construct, 142.

176. Ibid., 137.

177. R. R. Sims, 2000, Changing an organization's culture under new leadership, *Journal of Business Ethics*, 25: 65–78.

178. R. A. Burgelman & Y. L. Doz, 2001, The power of strategic integration, *Sloan Management Review*, 42(3): 28–38.

179. J. S. Hornsby, D. F. Kuratko, & S. A. Zahra, 2002, Middle managers' perception of the internal environment for corporate entrepreneurship: Assessing a measurement scale, *Journal of Business Venturing*, 17: 253–273.

180. B. Axelrod, H. Handfield-Jones, & E. Michaels, 2002, A new game plan for C players, *Harvard Business Review*, 80(1): 80–88.

181. Adler & Kwon, Social capital.

182. M. E. Scheitzer, L. Ordonez, & M. Hoegl, 2004, Goal Setting as a motivator of unethical behavior, *Academy of Management Journal*, 47: 422–432.

183. L. K. Trevino, G. R. Weaver, D. G. Toffler, & B. Ley, 1999, Managing ethics and legal compliance: What works and what hurts, *California Management Review*, 41(2): 131–151.

184. C. W. L. Hill, 1990, Cooperation, opportunism, and the invisible hand: Implications for transaction cost theory, *Academy of Management Review*, 15: 500–513.

185. J. M. Stevens, H. K. Steensma, D. A. Harrison, & P. L. Cochran, 2005, Symbolic or substantive document? Influence of ethics codes on financial executives' decisions, *Strategic Management Journal*, 26: 181–195.

186. 2007, New allegations coming in RCMP scandal: CTV.com, http://www.ctv.ca/servlet/ArticleNews/story/CTVNews/20070422/george_rcmp_070422/20070422?hub=QPeriod, April 22.

187. Ibid.

188. Zaccardelli denies coverup in RCMP pension fund scandal, CBC News, April 17, 2007.

189. C. J. Robertson & W. F. Crittenden, 2003, Mapping moral philosophies: Strategic implications for multinational firms, *Strategic Management Journal*, 24: 385–392; E. Soule, 2002, Managerial moral strategies—In search of a few good principles, *Academy of Management Review*, 27: 114–124.

190. L. M. Leinicke, J. A. Ostrosky, & W. M. Rexroad, 2000, Quality financial reporting: Back to the basics, *CPA Journal*, August, 69–71.

191. P. E. Murphy, 1995, Corporate ethics statements: Current status and future prospects, *Journal of Business Ethics*, 14: 727–740.

192. G. Redding, 2002, The capitalistic business system of China and its rationale, *Asia Pacific Journal of Management*, 19: 221–249.

193. J. H. Gittell, 2000, Paradox of coordination and control, *California Management Review*, 42(3): 101–117.

194. M. D. Shields, F. J. Deng, & Y. Kato, 2000, The design and effects of control systems: Tests of direct- and indirect-effects models, *Accounting, Organizations and Society*, 25: 185–202.

195. K. J. Laverty, 1996, Economic "short-termism": The debate, the unresolved issues, and the implications for management practice and research, *Academy of Management Review*, 21: 825–860.

196. R. S. Kaplan & D. P. Norton, 2001, The strategy-focused organization, *Strategy & Leadership*, 29(3): 41–42; R. S. Kaplan & D. P. Norton, 2000, *The Strategy-Focused Organization: How Balanced Scorecard Companies Thrive in the New Business Environment*, Boston: Harvard Business School Press.

197. B. E. Becker, M. A. Huselid, & D. Ulrich, 2001, *The HR Scorecard: Linking People, Strategy, and Performance*, Boston: Harvard Business School Press, 21.

198. Kaplan & Norton, The strategy-focused organization.

199. R. S. Kaplan & D. P. Norton, 2001, Transforming the balanced scorecard from performance measurement to strategic management: Part I, *Accounting Horizons*, 15(1): 87–104.

200. R. S. Kaplan & D. P. Norton, 1992, The balanced scorecard-Measures that drive performance, *Harvard Business Review*, 70(1): 71–79.

201. M. A. Mische, 2001, *Strategic Renewal: Becoming a High-Performance Organization*, Upper Saddle River, NJ: Prentice-Hall, 181.

202. H.-J. Cho & V. Pucik, 2005, Relationship between innovativeness, quality, growth, profitability and market value, *Strategic Management Journal*, 26: 555–575.

203. Rowe, Creating wealth in organizations: The role of strategic leadership.

204. R. E. Hoskisson, R. A. Johnson, D. Yiu, & W. P. Wan, 2001, Restructuring strategies of diversified business groups: Differences associated with country institutional environments, in M. A. Hitt, R. E. Freeman, & J. S. Harrison (eds.), *Handbook of Strategic Management*, Oxford, UK: Blackwell Publishers, 433–463; R. A. Johnson, 1996, Antecedents and outcomes of corporate refocusing, *Journal of Management*, 22: 437–481; R. E. Hoskisson & M. A. Hitt, 1994, *Downscoping: How to Tame the Diversified Firm*, New York: Oxford University Press.

205. J. Birkinshaw & N. Hood, 2001, Unleash innovation in foreign subsidiaries, *Harvard Business Review*, 79(3): 131–137.

206. Ireland & Hitt, Achieving and maintaining strategic competitiveness.

207. Wikipedia, 2007, GlaxoSmithKline, http://en.wikipedia.org/wiki/GlaxoSmithKline, December 31.

208. R. C. Morais, 2003, Mind the gap, *Forbes,* www.forbes.com, July 21.

Chapter Fourteen

Strategic Entrepreneurship

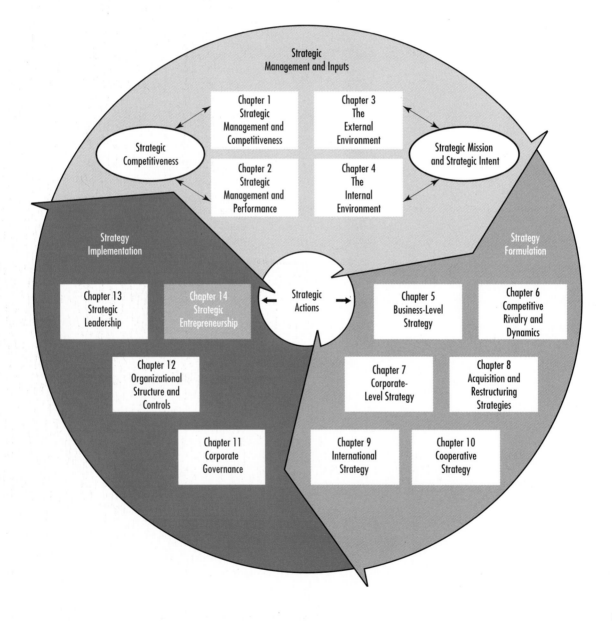

Knowledge Objectives

Studying this chapter should provide you with the strategic management knowledge needed to:

1. Define strategic entrepreneurship and corporate entrepreneurship.

2. Define entrepreneurship and entrepreneurial opportunities and explain their importance.

3. Define invention, innovation, and imitation and describe the relationship among them.

4. Describe entrepreneurs and the entrepreneurial mind-set.

5. Explain international entrepreneurship and its importance.

6. Describe how firms internally develop innovations.

7. Explain how firms use cooperative strategies to innovate.

8. Describe how firms use acquisitions as a means of innovation.

9. Explain how strategic entrepreneurship helps firms create value.

Robbery? Recovery. Absolutely!

In 1992, freelance writer Fraser Cain had his $2,200 notebook computer stolen in Vancouver. He and associate Christian Cotichini formed Absolute Software. Two years and $15,000 later, they had created what can best be thought of as a computer virus called CompuTrace. Once installed, CompuTrace periodically takes control of a laptop's modem and silently contacts the company with the computer's serial number and other relevant facts about its Internet connection and location. Any thief who has taken possession of the computer has no idea CompuTrace is installed, and once installed—like any well-made virus—it is incredibly difficult to get rid of: CompuTrace can survive system crashes or hard drive reformatting. If the computer is stolen, the company will be able to track its location.

www.absolute.com

http://lojack.com

www.lojackforlaptops.com

While the Vancouver firm did well enough to survive, people did not pave a path to Cain and Cotichini's door. So in 1995 the company brought on John Livingston to serve as chairman and CEO. Under Livingston, the firm grew by evolving a broader range of business solutions that encompassed physical, data, and network security and IT asset management. After completing a traditional venture capital round of financing in 1998 the company went public, completing a $22-million IPO in 2000.

Over the next five years, the company continued to grow slowly, and to continuously develop new product features. For example, if your computer goes missing, Absolute's software now lets you delete data from the missing machine. Getting the technical aspects of the product to work together was only part of the battle. The company not only must coordinate its developers, but also must set up systems whereby it organizes the efforts of the 800 police departments with which it works, and, more importantly, ensure the company's efforts are consistent with those of LoJack Corporation of Westwood, Massachusetts, its alliance partner since 2005.

Another innovative company, LoJack had become the premier provider of wireless tracking and recovery systems for mobile assets: cars, trucks, commercial vehicles, construction equipment, and motorcycles. Since LoJack began in the 1980s it has helped recover more than 200,000 stolen vehicles worth over $4 billion—a success rate of more than 90 percent. LoJack's systems are based on radio frequency technology that is highly effective even when the vehicle is hidden. Because of the effectiveness of its system, LoJack had created a brand name that was well known, recognized, and trusted. By re-branding CompuTrace as "LoJack for laptops," Absolute was able to tap into LoJack's reputation for guaranteed recovery.

The name recognition allowed Absolute to gain an award-winning reputation by 2006. The company's data protection product was the recipient of the Emerging Technology Award at the 9th annual International West Coast Security Forum. In 2006 alone, the company was software runner-up for the Wall Street Journal Technology Innovation Awards, a finalist for the Canadian Information Productivity Awards, and a finalist in the 14th Annual Canadian Information Productivity Awards.

Besides being innovative, the product also works—even when the company has to track the computer halfway around the world. For example, one Absolute-equipped computer was stolen from a hospital in Minnesota. The following day, the computer reappeared online in a nearby town before being shut down again. Before the end of the week, the machine had been reformatted with a new operating system and was accessing the Internet in Vietnam. Within days, the thief was back in the U.S., where local police were able to tap into a larger, international theft ring. In early 2008 Absolute's software helped recover its 5,000th computer, but getting to that point was not an easy process.

All these things have allowed Absolute to garner agreements with most major computer makers—including Dell, Fujitsu, Gateway, HP, Toshiba, and others. These companies embed Absolute's software in the BIOS firmware of their computers, and then buyers have the option of activating a subscription for security services. Given that only 7 percent of buyers activate a subscription, the potential market is significant. The adoption rate is comparable to anti-virus, anti-spam software of 10 years ago. According to securities analyst Ranjit Narayanan, Absolute's product may move from a "nice-to-have thing" to a "must-have" in the next few years. It seems well on its way; the company's subscriber base grew from 1.6 million in 2006 to 2.1 million in 2007—a 31-percent annual increase.

SOURCES: 2008, Absolute Web site, http://www.absolute.com, retrieved January 29; 2008, Absolute Software recovers 5,000th stolen computer, Canada News Wire, http://www.newswire.ca/en/releases/archive/January2008/15/c8913.html; G. Shaw, 2007, Absolute Software has a fabulous year, *Vancouver Sun*, November 7, D3; 2005, Absolute Software and LoJack Corporation announce branding partnership to introduce "LoJack for Laptops," Canada News Wire, June 27, 1; D. Smith, 1994, Innovators hope to sell software anti-theft device to big guys, *Vancouver Sun*, July 29.

In Chapter 1, we indicated that *organizational culture* refers to the complex set of ideologies, symbols, and core values that are shared throughout the firm and that influence how the firm conducts business. Thus, culture is the social energy that drives—or fails to drive—the organization. Given Absolute Software's orientation toward continuous technical advancement, we can expect that the company's culture would also be oriented toward, and supportive of, continuous product and organizational innovations. Increasingly, a firm's ability to engage in both types of innovation is linked to performance improvements.[1] You will see from reading this chapter that Absolute's ability to innovate in both ways shows that the firm successfully practises strategic entrepreneurship. While product innovation's importance has long been recognized, the equally critical importance of organizational innovations is a more recent recognition.[2]

Strategic entrepreneurship is taking entrepreneurial actions using a strategic perspective. When engaging in strategic entrepreneurship, the firm simultaneously focuses on finding opportunities in its external environment that it can try to exploit through innovations. Identifying opportunities to exploit through innovations is the *entrepreneurship* part of strategic entrepreneurship, while determining the best way to manage the firm's innovation efforts is the *strategic* part. Thus, strategic entrepreneurship finds firms integrating their actions to find opportunities and to successfully innovate as a primary means of pursuing them.[3] In the 21st-century competitive landscape, firm survival and success increasingly is a function of a firm's ability to continuously find new opportunities and quickly produce innovations to pursue them.[4]

> **Strategic entrepreneurship** is taking entrepreneurial actions using a strategic perspective.

To examine strategic entrepreneurship, we consider several topics in this chapter. First, we examine entrepreneurship and innovation in a strategic context. Definitions of entrepreneurship, entrepreneurial opportunities, and entrepreneurs as those who engage in entrepreneurship to pursue entrepreneurial opportunities are included as parts of this analysis. We then describe international entrepreneurship, a phenomenon reflecting the increased use of entrepreneurship in economies throughout the world. After this discussion, the chapter shifts to descriptions of the three ways firms innovate. Internally, firms innovate through either autonomous or induced strategic behaviour. We then describe actions firms take to implement the innovations resulting from those two types of strategic behaviour.

In addition to innovating through internal activities, firms can develop innovations by using cooperative strategies, such as strategic alliances, and by acquiring other companies to gain access to their innovations and innovative capabilities. Most large, complex firms use all three methods to innovate. The method the firm chooses to innovate can be affected by the firm's governance mechanisms. Research evidence suggests, for example, that inside board directors with equity positions favour internal innovation, while outside directors with equity positions prefer acquiring innovation.[5] The chapter closes with summary comments about how firms use strategic entrepreneurship to create value and earn above-average returns.

As you will see from studying this chapter, innovation and entrepreneurship are vital for young and old and for large and small firms, for service companies as well as manufacturing firms, and for high-technology ventures.[6] In the global competitive landscape, the long-term success of new ventures and established firms is a function of the ability to meld entrepreneurship with strategic management.[7]

Before moving to the next section, we should mention that our focus in this chapter is on innovation and entrepreneurship within established organizations. This phenomenon is called **corporate entrepreneurship,** which is the use or application of entrepreneurship within an established firm.[8] An important part of the entrepreneurship discipline, corporate entrepreneurship increasingly is thought to be linked to survival and success of established corporations.[9] Indeed, established firms use entrepreneurship to strengthen their performance and to enhance growth opportunities.[10] Of course, innovation and entrepreneurship play a critical role in the degree of success achieved by start-up entrepreneurial ventures as well.

> **Corporate entrepreneurship** is the use or application of entrepreneurship within an established firm.

Our focus in this chapter is on corporate entrepreneurship. However, the materials we will describe are equally important in entrepreneurial ventures (sometimes called "start-ups"). Moreover, we will make specific reference to entrepreneurial ventures in a few parts of the chapter as we discuss the importance of strategic entrepreneurship for firms competing in the 21st-century competitive landscape.

Entrepreneurship and Entrepreneurial Opportunities

Entrepreneurship is the process by which individuals or groups identify and pursue entrepreneurial opportunities without being immediately constrained by the resources they currently control.[11] **Entrepreneurial opportunities** are conditions in which new goods or services can satisfy a need in the market. These opportunities exist because of competitive imperfections in markets and among the factors of production used to produce them[12] and when information about these imperfections is distributed asymmetrically (that is, not equally) among individuals.[13] Firms should be receptive to pursuing entrepreneurial opportunities whenever and wherever they may surface. These opportunities come in a host of forms (e.g., the chance to sell an existing product in a new market or the chance to develop and sell a new product).[14] Some new products are so radically different that they it may be considered a new industry. Cirque du Soleil's redefinition of the circus, Honda's reconfiguration of the motorcycle market, or Nintendo's simplified gaming interface with the Wii are all examples of this type of change.[15] INSEAD professors W. Chan Kim and Renée Mauborgne call such moves Blue Ocean Strategies. Kim and Mauborgne's view is "that tomorrow's leading companies will succeed *not* by battling competitors, but by creating 'blue oceans' of uncontested market space ripe for growth. Such strategic moves—termed 'value innovation'—create powerful leaps in value for both the firm and its buyers, rendering rivals obsolete and unleashing new demand."[16]

As these two definitions suggest, the essence of entrepreneurship is to identify and exploit entrepreneurial opportunities—that is, opportunities others do not see or for which they do not recognize the commercial potential.[17] As a process, entrepreneurship results in the "creative destruction" of existing products (goods or services) or methods of producing them and replacing them with new products and production methods.[18] Thus, firms engaging in entrepreneurship place high value on individual innovations as well as the ability to continuously innovate across time.[19]

We study entrepreneurship at the level of the individual firm. However, evidence suggests that entrepreneurship is the economic engine driving many nations' economies in the global competitive landscape.[20] Thus, entrepreneurship, and the innovation it spawns, is important for companies competing in the global economy and for countries seeking to stimulate economic climates with the potential to enhance the living standard of their citizens.[21]

Entrepreneurship is the process by which individuals or groups identify and pursue entrepreneurial opportunities without being immediately constrained by the resources they currently control.

Entrepreneurial opportunities are conditions in which new goods or services can satisfy a need in the market.

Innovation

Peter Drucker argued that "innovation is the specific function of entrepreneurship, whether in an existing business, a public service institution, or a new venture started by a lone individual."[22] Moreover, Drucker suggested that innovation is "the means by which the entrepreneur either creates new wealth-producing resources or endows existing resources with enhanced potential for creating wealth."[23] Thus, entrepreneurship and the innovation resulting from it are important for large and small firms, as well as for start-up ventures, as they compete in the 21st-century competitive landscape.[24] In fact, some argue that firms failing to innovate will stagnate.[25] The realities of competition in the 21st-century competitive landscape suggest that, "No company can maintain a long-term leadership position in a category unless it is in a continuous process of developing innovative new products desired by customers."[26] This means that innovation should be an intrinsic part of virtually all of a firm's activities.[27]

Innovation is a key outcome firms seek through entrepreneurship and is often the source of competitive success, especially in turbulent, highly competitive environments.[28] For example, research results show that firms competing in global industries that invest more in innovation also achieve the highest returns.[29] In fact, investors often react positively to the introduction of a new product, thereby increasing the price of a firm's stock. Innovation, then, is an essential feature of high-performance firms.[30] Furthermore, "innovation may be required to maintain or achieve competitive parity, much less a competitive advantage in many global markets."[31] The most innovative firms understand that financial slack should be available at all times to support the pursuit of entrepreneurial opportunities.[32]

In his classic work, Schumpeter argued that firms engage in three types of innovative activity.[33] **Invention** is the act of creating or developing a new product or process. **Innovation** is the process of creating a commercial product from an invention. Innovation begins after an invention is chosen for development.[34] Thus, an invention brings something new into being, while an innovation brings something new into use. Accordingly, technical criteria are used to determine the success of an invention, whereas commercial criteria are used to determine the success of an innovation.[35] Finally, **imitation** is the adoption of an innovation by similar firms. Imitation usually leads to product or process standardization, and products based on imitation often are offered at lower prices, but without as many features. Entrepreneurship is critical to innovative activity in that it acts as the linchpin between invention and innovation.[36]

In North America, innovation is the most critical of the three types of innovative activity. Many companies are able to create ideas that lead to inventions, but commercializing those inventions through innovation has, at times, proved difficult. This difficulty is suggested by the fact that approximately 80 percent of R&D occurs in large firms, but these same firms produce fewer than 50 percent of the patents.[37] Patents are a strategic asset and the ability to regularly produce them can be an important source of competitive advantage, especially for firms competing in knowledge-intensive industries[38] (e.g., pharmaceuticals).

Invention is the act of creating or developing a new product or process.

Innovation is the process of creating a commercial product from an invention.

Imitation is the adoption of an innovation by similar firms.

Entrepreneurs

Entrepreneurs are individuals, acting independently or as part of an organization, who see an entrepreneurial opportunity and then take risks to develop an innovation to pursue it. Often, entrepreneurs are the individuals who receive credit for making things happen![39] Entrepreneurs are found throughout an organization—from top-level managers to those working to produce a firm's goods or services. For example, entrepreneurs are found throughout W. L. Gore—the makers of GORE-TEX. Part of the job of all Gore associates is to use roughly 10 percent of their time to develop innovations. Entrepreneurs tend to demonstrate several characteristics, including those of being optimistic,[40] highly motivated, willing to take responsibility for their projects, and courageous.[41] In addition, entrepreneurs tend to be passionate and emotional about the value and importance of their innovation-based ideas.[42]

Evidence suggests that successful entrepreneurs have an entrepreneurial mind-set. The person with an **entrepreneurial mind-set** values uncertainty in the marketplace and seeks to continuously identify opportunities with the potential to lead to important innovations.[43] Because they have the potential to lead to continuous innovations, individuals' entrepreneurial mind-sets can be a source of competitive advantage for a firm.[44] Howard Schultz, founder of Starbucks, believes that his firm has a number of individuals with an entrepreneurial mind-set. Making music a meaningful part of the experience for Starbucks customers is an example of an evolving product offering resulting from an entrepreneurial

Entrepreneurs are individuals, acting independently or as part of an organization, who see an entrepreneurial opportunity and then take risks to develop an innovation to pursue it.

The person with an **entrepreneurial mind-set** values uncertainty in the marketplace and seeks to continuously identify opportunities with the potential to lead to important innovations.

mind-set. In Schultz's words, "The music world is changing, and Starbucks and Starbucks Hear Music will continue to be an innovator in the industry. It takes passion, commitment, and even a bit of experimentation to maintain that position."[45] Of course, changes in the music industry create the uncertainties that lead to entrepreneurial opportunities that can be pursued by relying on an entrepreneurial mind-set.

As our discussions have suggested, "innovation is an application of knowledge to produce new knowledge."[46] As such, entrepreneurial mind-sets are fostered and supported when knowledge is readily available throughout a firm. Indeed, research has shown that units within firms are more innovative when they have access to new knowledge.[47] Transferring knowledge, however, can be difficult, often because the receiving party must have adequate absorptive capacity (or the ability) to learn the knowledge.[48] This requires that the new knowledge be linked to the existing knowledge. Thus, managers need to develop the capabilities of their human capital to build on their current knowledge base while incrementally expanding that knowledge[49] to facilitate the development of entrepreneurial mind-sets.

For example, look at the entrepreneurial mind-set at Vancouver's Lululemon Athletica. Founder and chairman Chip Wilson says that, "We're always asking ourselves, 'What problem can we solve for athletes?'" To get the answers, Lululemon solicits feedback from frequently held focus groups, selected yoga instructors, and athletes who receive free yoga wear in return for reporting on its performance. Senior managers spend one day a week in a retail store staying in touch with what clothing is moving and what is not. The first-hand knowledge Lululemon gathers helps the company stay on the leading edge of innovation. As a result, it has scored a number of industry firsts: flat seams that eliminate chafing, and using microfabrics that are intended to wick away moisture. Thus, Lululemon employees—from the top down—use their entrepreneurial mind-set to identify opportunities and then integrate knowledge available throughout the firm to develop an innovation to exploit the identified opportunity.[50]

International Entrepreneurship

International entrepreneurship is a process in which firms creatively discover and exploit opportunities that are outside their domestic markets in order to develop a competitive advantage.

International entrepreneurship is a process in which firms creatively discover and exploit opportunities that are outside their domestic markets in order to develop a competitive advantage.[51] As the practices suggested by this definition shown, entrepreneurship is a global phenomenon.[52]

A key reason why entrepreneurship has become a global phenomenon is that in general internationalization leads to improved firm performance.[53] Nonetheless, decision makers should recognize that the decision to internationalize exposes their firms to various risks, including those of unstable foreign currencies, problems with market efficiencies, insufficient infrastructures to support businesses, and limitations on market size.[54] Thus, the decision to engage in international entrepreneurship should be a product of careful analysis.[55]

Because of its positive benefits, entrepreneurship is at the top of public policy agendas in many of the world's countries, including Finland, Germany, Ireland, and Israel. Some argue that placing entrepreneurship on these agendas may be appropriate in that regulation hindering innovation and entrepreneurship is the root cause of Europe's productivity problems.[56] In Ireland, for example, the government is "particularly focused on encouraging new innovative enterprises that have growth potential and are export oriented."[57] Some believe that entrepreneurship is flourishing in New Zealand, a trend having a positive effect on the productivity of the nation's economy.[58]

While entrepreneurship is a global phenomenon, the rate of entrepreneurship differs across countries. A study of 42 countries found that the percentage of adults involved in entrepreneurial activity ranged from a high of about 40 percent in Peru to a low of approximately 3 percent in Belgium. Canada had a rate of 7.1 percent (the median is 7.35).

Importantly, this study also found a strong positive relationship between the rate of entrepreneurial activity and economic development in a country.[59]

Culture is one of the reasons for the differences in rates of entrepreneurship among different countries. For example, the tension between individualism and collectivism is important in that entrepreneurship declines as collectivism is emphasized. Simultaneously, however, research results suggest that exceptionally high levels of individualism might be dysfunctional for entrepreneurship. Viewed collectively, these results appear to call for a balance between individual initiative and a spirit of cooperation and group ownership of innovation. For firms to be entrepreneurial, they must provide appropriate autonomy and incentives for individual initiative to surface, but also promote cooperation and group ownership of an innovation if it is to be implemented successfully. Thus, international entrepreneurship often requires teams of people with unique skills and resources, especially in cultures where collectivism is a valued historical norm.[60]

The level of investment outside of the home country made by young ventures is also an important dimension of international entrepreneurship. In fact, with increasing globalization, a greater number of new ventures have been "born global."[61] Research has shown that new ventures that enter international markets increase their learning of new technological knowledge and thereby enhance their performance.[62] Because of the positive outcomes associated with its use, the amount of international entrepreneurship has been increasing in recent years.[63]

The probability of entering international markets increases when the firm has top executives with international experience.[64] Furthermore, the firm has a higher likelihood of successfully competing in international markets when its top executives have international experience.[65] Because of the learning and economies of scale and scope afforded by operating in international markets, both young and established internationally diversified firms often are stronger competitors in their domestic market as well. Additionally, as research has shown, internationally diversified firms are generally more innovative.[66]

Next, we discuss the three ways firms innovate.

Internal Innovation

In established organizations, most innovation comes from efforts in research and development (R&D). This is the case with the innovations through which Toyota Motor Company produced the Prius, a gas–electric hybrid.[67] As explained in the Strategic Focus, this is also the case at Smart Technologies. While reading about Smart, observe how the firm relies on its R&D activities to continuously improve the quality of the products it makes as well as to continuously provide customers with innovative product features.

Effective R&D often leads to firms filing for patents to protect their innovative work. Increasingly, successful R&D results from integrating the skills available in the global workforce. Firms seeking internal innovations through their R&D must understand that, "Talent and ideas are flourishing everywhere—from Bangalore to Shanghai to Kiev—and no company, regardless of geography, can hesitate to go wherever those ideas are."[68] Thus, in the years to come, the ability to have a competitive advantage based on innovation may accrue to firms able to meld the talent of human capital from countries around the world. Absolute Software and Smart Technologies appear to be two companies with an ability to do this.

Increasingly, it seems possible that in the 21st-century competitive landscape R&D may be the most critical factor in gaining and sustaining a competitive advantage in some industries, such as pharmaceuticals. Larger, established firms, certainly those competing globally, often try to use their R&D labs to create competency-destroying new technologies and products.[69] Being able to innovate in this manner can create a competitive advantage for a firm in many industries.[70] Although critical to long-term

As Smart as Can Be: Canada's Most Innovative Firm?

Your company puts the latest in technology into its products, but your competitors are not far behind. In addition, your competitors have introduced new styling into their product and it makes yours look dated. You need to make a change quickly. Yet, how can you show the engineers in India how you want to restyle the cover on the product, have the component manufacturer in Italy still make it economically, view how the assembler in China will ensure it fits with the finished product correctly, and guarantee the creative consultants in Montreal are happy with the change? You need to hash out everything quickly. A good old-fashioned meeting is what you need!

At this point, Bridgit steps in. No, Bridgit doesn't find cheap flights and get everyone together in one place. Bridgit is a communications software product created by Calgary-based Smart Technologies. What Bridgit does is allow Windows and Mac users to start or join a conference over the Internet from their desktops. Bridgit creates a conference and then invites participants via an e-mail message that contains a link to the online meeting. Users choose their preferred language interface from 13 languages, and the software has built-in voice over Internet protocol (VoIP) to allow high-quality voice calls over computer networks as well as multi-point webcam support and Smart Board interactive whiteboard support.

The Smart Board interactive whiteboard is Smart Technologies' premier product. A Smart Board is a touch-sensitive screen that can be used to control and manipulate computer applications, with handwriting and voice recognition software that can convert such input into text. With Bridgit, participants using a Smart Board can write over shared information, and these notes will be shown in real time on all sites in the conference. Television anchors touch Smart screens to show election results, new weather patterns, or football plays. Smart Boards are used in NASA control centres and government situation centres. The North Atlantic Treaty Organization, the U.S. Central Intelligence Agency, and the U.S. National Security Agency all use the product. Children in remote Mexican classrooms can get interactive teaching information complete with sound and video using Smart Boards. Other clients include former U.S. President Bill Clinton, and former U.S. Secretary of State Madeleine Albright. The boards sell for $1,000 to $3,500 each, depending on size. Supporting projector technology drives the price higher.

Smart Technologies was founded in 1987 as a home-based business by Nancy Knowlton, the current chief executive, and her spouse, current executive chairman David Martin. Smart pioneered its industry and is still the largest provider of the technology worldwide—and sales are growing 40 to 50 percent each year. This is why the company's new plant in Kanata, Ontario is designed for growth. The 400-plus-employee plant churns out 1,600 interactive whiteboards daily and is designed to triple that capacity.

The company's growth is fuelled by research and development. In fact, Smart Technologies was selected as the Most Innovative Company of the Year for 2006. Executive chairman Martin notes that "Researching and redesigning products never ends." This is why Smart Technologies created a research chair at the University of Calgary. Professors Saul Greenberg and Sheelagh Carpendale were jointly named to serve as Technologies Industry Research chairs at the university's Human Computer Interaction Lab. The lab has about 30 graduate students and a third professor working on developing technology based on the way people behave and interact with each other. "There's no menus or keyboards—everything is operated by touch and voice commands," explains Carpendale. Currently, the lab has a working prototype of a table that is essentially one of Smart's interactive whiteboards on four legs with innovative software that allows employees to gather and work online simultaneously. Instead of physical charts and reports, everyone can see and manipulate information by touching the tabletop screen. Professor Greenberg notes, "The technology allows us to talk and communicate in the way we would in everyday life and see what each other is doing." When the lab hits upon an innovation that Smart believes may be marketable, the company steps in and further develops the product.

The massive new three-wing headquarters the company is building in the University Research Park will allow for closer interaction between the school and the firm. When complete, the 19,200-square-metre structure will include underground parking, a day care, and health club and dining facilities. The $60-million building's design has incorporated top environmental standards for improved natural light, fresh air circulation, and energy efficiency. Why go to such lengths? Smart needs to attract not only heads of state and corporations, but also top research personnel to continue with its product development.

SOURCES: 2008, Smart Technologies Web site, http://www2.smarttech.com/st/en-US/About+Us/, retrieved February 2; Stevie Awards for Women Web site, http://www.stevieawards.com/pubs/women/awards/282_1943_13636.cfm, retrieved February 2; B. Hill, 2007, Smart move in Kanata: Firm is bullish on making a profit building display screens in Canada, *Ottawa Citizen*, October 1, E1; S. Myers, 2007, Smart creates research chair, *Calgary Herald*, March 9, D3; G. Scotton, Smart wins $30M Mexican contract, *Calgary Herald*, January 19, C3; C. Howes, 2000, Even Bubba schemes on Smart Board: Calgary firm's clients include Bill Clinton, NASA and NATO, *National Post*, November 24, C6.

corporate success, the outcomes of R&D investments are uncertain and often not achieved in the short term,[71] meaning that patience is required as firms evaluate the outcomes of their R&D efforts.

Incremental and Radical Innovation

Firms produce two types of internal innovations when using their R&D activities: incremental and radical. Most innovations are *incremental*—that is, they build on existing knowledge bases and provide small improvements in the current product lines. Incremental innovations are evolutionary and linear in nature.[72] "The markets for incremental innovations are well-defined, product characteristics are well understood, profit margins tend to be lower, production technologies are efficient, and competition is primarily on the basis of price."[73] Adding a different kind of whitening agent to a soap detergent is an example of an incremental innovation, as are improvements in televisions over the last few decades (moving from black-and-white to colour, improving existing audio capabilities, etc.). Companies launch far more incremental innovations than radical innovations.[74]

In contrast to incremental innovations, *radical innovations* usually provide significant technological breakthroughs and create new knowledge.[75] Recall from the Strategic Focus that Smart Technologies seeks to develop primarily radical rather than incremental innovations through its R&D activities. Radical innovations, which are revolutionary and non-linear in nature, typically use new technologies to serve newly created markets. The development of the personal computer (PC) is an example of a radical innovation. Reinventing the computer by developing a "radically new computer-brain chip" is an example of what could be a radical innovation. If researchers are successful in their efforts, superchips (with the capability to process a trillion calculations per second) will be developed.[76] Obviously, such a radical innovation would seem to have the capacity to revolutionize the tasks computers could perform.

Because they establish new functionalities for users, radical innovations have strong potential to lead to significant growth in revenue and profits.[77] Developing new processes is a critical part of producing radical innovations. Both types of innovation can create value, meaning that firms should determine when it is appropriate to emphasize either incremental or radical innovation.[78] However, radical innovations have the potential to contribute more significantly to a firm's efforts to earn above-average returns.

Radical innovations are rare because of the difficulty and risk involved in developing them.[79] The value of the technology and the market opportunities are highly uncertain.[80] Because radical innovation creates new knowledge and uses only some or little of a firm's current product or technological knowledge, creativity is required. However, creativity does not create something from nothing. Rather, creativity discovers,

Chapter 14 / Strategic Entrepreneurship

combines, or synthesizes current knowledge, often from diverse areas.[81] This knowledge is then used to develop new products that can be used in an entrepreneurial manner to move into new markets, capture new customers, and gain access to new resources.[82] Such innovations are often developed in separate business units that start internal ventures.[83]

Internally developed incremental and radical internal innovations result from deliberate efforts. These deliberate efforts are called *internal corporate venturing*, which is the set of activities firms use to develop internal inventions and especially innovations.[84] As shown in Figure 14.1, autonomous and induced strategic behaviour are the two types of internal corporate venturing. Each venturing type facilitates incremental and radical innovations. However, a larger number of radical innovations spring from autonomous strategic behaviour, while the greatest percentage of incremental innovations come from induced strategic behaviour.

Autonomous Strategic Behaviour

Autonomous strategic behaviour is a bottom-up process in which product champions pursue new ideas, often through a political process, by means of which they develop and coordinate the commercialization of a new good or service until it achieves success in the marketplace. A *product champion* is an organizational member with an entrepreneurial vision of a new good or service who seeks to create support for its commercialization. Product champions play critical roles in moving innovations forward.[85] Indeed, in many corporations, "Champions are widely acknowledged as pivotal to innovation speed and success."[86] The primary reason for this is that "no business idea takes root purely on its own merits; it has to be sold."[87] Commonly, product champions use their social capital to develop informal networks within the firm. As progress is made, these networks become more formal as a means of pushing an innovation to the point of successful commercialization.[88] Internal innovations springing from autonomous strategic behaviour tend to diverge from the firm's current strategy, taking it into new markets and perhaps new ways of creating value for customers and other stakeholders.

Autonomous strategic behaviour is based on a firm's wellsprings of knowledge and resources that are the sources of the firm's innovation. Thus, a firm's technological capabilities and competencies are the basis for new products and processes.[89] GE depends on

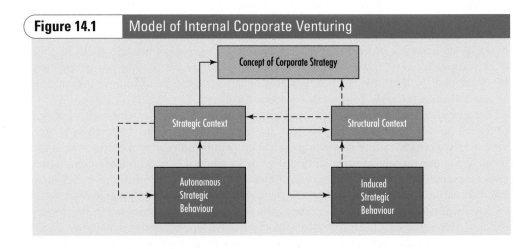

| Figure 14.1 | Model of Internal Corporate Venturing |

SOURCE: Adapted from R.A. Burgelman, 1983, A Model of the Interactions of Strategic Behavior, Corporate Context, and the Concept of Strategy, *Academy of Management Review*, 8:65. Permission by CCC.

autonomous strategic behaviour on a regular basis to produce innovations.[90] Essentially, "the search for marketable services can start in any of GE's myriad businesses. [For example], an operating unit seeks out appropriate technology to better do what it already does. Having mastered the technology, it then incorporates it into a service it can sell to others."[91]

Changing the concept of corporate-level strategy through autonomous strategic behaviour results when a product is championed within strategic and structural contexts (see Figure 14.1). The strategic context is the process used to arrive at strategic decisions (often requiring political processes to gain acceptance). The best firms keep changing their strategic context and strategies because of the continuous changes in the current competitive landscape. Thus, some believe that the most competitively successful firms reinvent their industry or develop a completely new one across time as they compete with current and future rivals.[92]

To be effective, an autonomous process for developing new products requires that new knowledge be continuously diffused throughout the firm. In particular, the diffusion of tacit knowledge is important for development of more effective new products.[93] Interestingly, some of the processes important for the promotion of autonomous new product development behaviour vary by the environment and country in which a firm operates. For example, the Japanese culture is high on uncertainty avoidance. As such, research has found that Japanese firms are more likely to engage in autonomous behaviours under conditions of low uncertainty.[94]

Induced Strategic Behaviour

The second of the two forms of internal corporate venturing, *induced strategic behaviour*, is a top-down process whereby the firm's current strategy and structure foster innovations that are closely associated with that strategy and structure. In this form of venturing, the strategy in place is filtered through a matching structural hierarchy. In essence, induced strategic behaviour results in internal innovations that are highly consistent with the firm's current strategy.

Norwegian furniture manufacturer Stokke recently introduced a high-end baby stroller (at the time of its introduction, the base price was $749). This stroller is based on the company's design of its most famous product, a high chair called the KinderZeat. Using the KinderZeat's design concept (which was to develop a seat that can "grow" with babies), the firm relied on its existing strategy and structure to develop its high-end stroller. When contemplating the product, the firm's managers knew that they wanted a different "design approach to create a vehicle that would both bring baby closer to mom and dad and be flexible enough to navigate the modern landscape (everything from Starbucks tables to escalators)."[95] Thus, by using the differentiation strategy and a particular form of the functional structure (see Chapter 12), Stokke's strategy and structure have created a very successful product through an internal innovation.

Implementing Internal Innovations

An entrepreneurial mind-set is required to be innovative and to develop successful internal corporate ventures. Valuing environmental and market uncertainty are key parts of an entrepreneurial mind-set. Individuals and firms with these elements of an entrepreneurial mind-set demonstrate their willingness to take risks to commercialize innovations. While they must continuously attempt to identify opportunities, they must also select and pursue the best opportunities and do so with discipline. Thus, employing an entrepreneurial mind-set entails not only developing new products and markets but also placing an emphasis on execution. This means that those with an entrepreneurial mind-set "engage the energies of everyone in their domain," both inside and outside the organization.[96]

Having processes and structures in place through which a firm can successfully implement the outcomes of internal corporate ventures and commercialize the innovations is critical. Indeed, the successful introduction of innovations into the marketplace reflects implementation effectiveness.[97] In the context of internal corporate ventures, processes are the "patterns of interaction, coordination, communication, and decision making employees use" to convert the innovations resulting from either autonomous or induced strategic behaviours into successful market entries.[98] As we describe in Chapter 12, organizational structures are the sets of formal relationships supporting organizational processes.

Effective integration of the various functions involved in innovation processes—from engineering to manufacturing and, ultimately, market distribution—is required to implement the incremental and radical innovations resulting from internal corporate ventures.[99] Increasingly, product development teams are being used to integrate the activities associated with different organizational functions. Such integration involves coordinating and applying the knowledge and skills of different functional areas in order to maximize innovation.[100] Effective product development teams also create value when they "pull the plug" on a project.[101] Although ending a project is difficult, sometimes because of emotional commitments to innovation-based projects, effective teams recognize when conditions change in ways that preclude the innovation's ability to create value as originally anticipated.

Cross-Functional Product Development Teams

Cross-functional teams facilitate efforts to integrate activities associated with different organizational functions, such as design, manufacturing, and marketing.[102] In addition, new product development processes can be completed more quickly and the products more easily commercialized when cross-functional teams work effectively.[103] Using cross-functional teams, product development stages are grouped into parallel or overlapping processes to allow the firm to tailor its product development efforts to its unique core competencies and to the needs of the market.

Horizontal organizational structures support the use of cross-functional teams in their efforts to integrate innovation-based activities across organizational functions.[104] Therefore, instead of being built around vertical hierarchical functions or departments, the organization is built around core horizontal processes that are used to produce and manage innovations. Some of the core horizontal processes that are critical to innovation efforts are formal; they may be defined and documented as procedures and practices. More commonly, however, these processes are informal: "They are routines or ways of working that evolve over time."[105] Often invisible, informal processes are critical to successful innovations and are supported properly through horizontal organizational structures more so than through vertical organizational structures.

Two primary barriers that may prevent the successful use of cross-functional teams as a means of integrating organizational functions are independent frames of reference of team members and organizational politics.[106]

Team members working within a distinct specialization (e.g., a particular organizational function) may have an independent frame of reference typically based on common backgrounds and experiences. They are likely to use the same decision criteria to evaluate issues such as product development efforts as they do within their functional units. Research suggests that functional departments vary along four dimensions: time orientation, interpersonal orientation, goal orientation, and formality of structure.[107] Thus, individuals from different functional departments having different orientations on these dimensions can be expected to perceive product development activities in different ways. For example, a design engineer may consider the characteristics that make a product functional and workable to be the most important of the product's characteristics. Alternatively, a person from the marketing function may hold characteristics that satisfy customer needs most important. These different orientations can create barriers to effective communication across functions.[108]

Organizational politics is the second potential barrier to effective integration in cross-functional teams. In some organizations, considerable political activity may centre on allocating resources to different functions. Interunit conflict may result from aggressive competition for resources among those representing different organizational functions. This dysfunctional conflict between functions creates a barrier to their integration.[109] Methods must be found to achieve cross-functional integration without excessive political conflict and without changing the basic structural characteristics necessary for task specialization and efficiency.

Facilitating Integration and Innovation

Shared values and strategic leadership are important for achieving cross-functional integration and implementing innovation.[110] Highly effective shared values are framed around the firm's vision and mission, and become the glue that promotes integration between functional units. Thus, the firm's culture promotes unity and internal innovation.[111]

Strategic leadership is also highly important for achieving cross-functional integration and promoting innovation. Leaders set the goals and allocate resources. The goals include integrated development and commercialization of new goods and services. Effective strategic leaders also ensure a high-quality communication system to facilitate cross-functional integration. A critical benefit of effective communication is the sharing of knowledge among team members.[112] Effective communication thus helps create synergy and gains team members' commitment to an innovation throughout the organization. Shared values and leadership practices shape the communication systems that are formed to support the development and commercialization of new products.[113]

Creating Value from Internal Innovation

The model in Figure 14.2 shows how firms can create value from the internal corporate venturing processes they use to develop and commercialize new goods and services. An entrepreneurial mind-set is necessary so that managers and employees will consistently try to identify entrepreneurial opportunities the firm can pursue by developing new goods and services and new markets. Cross-functional teams are important for promoting integrated new product design ideas and commitment to their subsequent

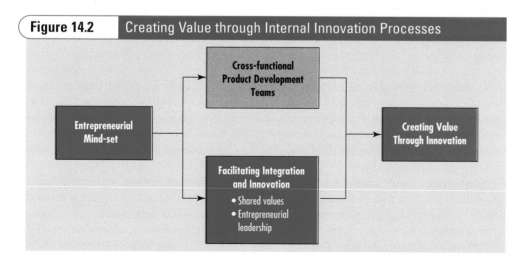

Figure 14.2 Creating Value through Internal Innovation Processes

implementation. Effective strategic leadership and shared values promote integration and vision for innovation and commitment to it. The end result for the firm is the creation of value for the customers and shareholders by developing and commercializing new products.[114]

In the next two sections, we discuss the other ways firms innovate—by using cooperative strategies and by acquiring companies.

Innovation through Cooperative Strategies

Virtually all firms lack the breadth and depth of resources (e.g., human capital and social capital) in their R&D activities needed to internally develop a sufficient number of innovations. Even in light of its success and widely respected ability to consistently produce incremental and primarily radical innovations, Smart Technologies still felt the need to enter into a cooperative arrangement with the University of Calgary to develop new innovations.[115] In other instances, firms use cooperative strategies to align what they believe are complementary assets, sometimes with the potential to lead to future innovations, as explained in the Strategic Focus.

The rapidly changing technologies of the 21st-century competitive landscape, globalization, and the need to innovate at world-class levels are primary influences on firms' decisions to innovate by cooperating with other companies. Evidence shows that the skills and knowledge contributed by firms forming a cooperative strategy to innovate tend to be technology-based, a fact suggesting how technologies and their applications continue to influence the choices firms make while competing in the 21st-century competitive landscape.[116] Indeed, some believe that because of these conditions, firms are becoming increasingly dependent on cooperative strategies as a path to successful competition in the global economy.[117]

Both entrepreneurial ventures and established firms use cooperative strategies (e.g., strategic alliances and joint ventures) to innovate. An entrepreneurial venture, for example, may seek investment capital as well as established firms' distribution capabilities to successfully introduce one of its innovative products to the market.[118] Alternatively, more established companies may need new technological knowledge and can gain access to it by forming a cooperative strategy with entrepreneurial ventures.[119] To increase its financial returns, Sony Corp. is forming alliances with smaller firms to develop innovative technologies.[120] Alliances between large pharmaceutical firms and biotechnology companies increasingly have been formed to integrate the knowledge and resources of both to develop new products and bring them to market.[121]

Because of the importance of strategic alliances, particularly in the development of new technology and in commercializing innovations, firms are beginning to build networks of alliances that represent a form of social capital to them.[122] This social capital in the form of relationships with other firms helps them to obtain the knowledge and other resources necessary to develop innovations.[123] Knowledge from these alliances helps firms develop new capabilities.[124] Some firms now even allow other companies to participate in their internal new product development processes. It is not uncommon, for example, for firms to have supplier representatives on their cross-functional innovation teams because of the importance of the suppliers' input to ensure quality materials for any new product developed.[125]

However, alliances formed for the purpose of innovation are not without risks. In addition to conflict that is natural when firms try to work together to reach a mutual goal,[126] cooperative strategy participants also take a risk that a partner will appropriate a firm's technology or knowledge and use it to enhance its own competitive abilities.[127] To prevent or at least minimize this risk, firms, particularly new ventures, need to select

Working with Others to Bring Innovations to Market

In this chapter we have discussed how companies work together to get their products to market. For example, Absolute Software worked with LoJack to market its computer recovery product, and Smart Technologies worked with the University of Calgary to develop new ways to use the Smart Board. However, we do not want to end the book with the notion that all innovations are high-tech computerized devices. Some devices that are simpler lower-tech versions of state-of-the-art tools can also be innovative.

Let us start with a device so incredibly simple that people who see it cannot figure out why no one invented it before. The Hangman is an invention that turns your rectangular guitar case into a guitar stand. The Hangman looks like a model of the Stealth Bomber with a crescent cutout missing from the tail section. When The Hangman is placed at the top of an upright, open, hard-sided guitar case, it allows the case to be used as a guitar stand by simply placing the instrument into the crescent hole and hanging the guitar by its neck. Cole Smith, of Kamsack, Saskatchewan, worked with others to develop the product and with a Canadian plastics maker to come up with a simple, virtually indestructible device. Smith claims, "Sales are starting to climb. We have an estimated market of 20 million rectangular cases out there in North America that can be retro-fitted with The Hangman."

Who's afraid of a rubber knife? No one—and that's the problem. It's pretty hard to get police officers or any one involved in edged-weapons training to take the exercise seriously when someone is wielding a rubber knife. For obvious reasons, a real knife cannot be used. So, Winnipeg police officer Jeff Quail and high-school business teacher Rory Bochinski pooled $100,000 of their own money to create the Shocknife. They outsourced the production, and since 2006 have been selling their $900 product to the RCMP, half a dozen Canadian police departments, border guards, and U.S. air marshals. In their first year alone, the FBI bought 110 of the knives (15 percent of their production). The *Shocknife* is exactly what it sounds like—an imitation knife that can deliver a shock of up to 7,500 volts. It's simple and non-lethal, but painful enough to put the right amount of fear into anyone facing it.

In 2000, 27-year-old Ken Rempel of Rosenort, Manitoba, was working with potato farmers in the land-reforming and irrigation business. At that time, most of the earthmovers they were using came with an attached drive engine. They were therefore expensive to operate given the size of the jobs with which he was involved. He knew the equipment could be more efficient, and many of the folks he knew already possessed a drive engine—more commonly known as a farm tractor. So Rempel built a prototype. Within three years, his Lo-Pel Manufacturing was selling $4.2 million worth of earthmovers across North America and as far away as Australia. Rempel worked with five local workshops to develop a line of earthmovers and land levellers sold under the name KTec. Though not quite as simple as The Hangman or the Shocknife, KTec products are far simpler, and thus more dependable, than an earthmover you might buy from Caterpillar or Komatsu. In 2006, Rempel was named the Business Development Bank of Canada's best young entrepreneur for Manitoba.

While all of the above-mentioned products and companies enlisted help to develop their product, some companies simply build on the well-known work of other firms. This brings us to our last company. Titan Metal Werks of Wheeling, Illinois, is obviously not a Canadian company. What drew our attention to them is that they have placed a quintessentially Canadian product on one of America's most iconic landmarks. Atlantic City's boardwalk is a wood structure that is more than 6.6 kilometres long and 18 metres wide. It is essentially a short pier behind the beach that follows the shoreline instead of jutting out into the ocean. If you look down at what's holding it together, you will see a most Canadian thing—millions of Robertson-head screws!

As the story goes, one day in the early 1900s a young Canadian salesman, P. L. Robertson, was setting up his sales stall when the slot-headed screwdriver he was using slipped and gashed his hand. He vowed to make something better, and in 1908 he created a square recess impression in the head of a screw and began producing these screws in Milton, Ontario—where the company is still headquartered. Today, 85 percent of screws sold in Canada have Robertson's square recess impression. The CBC ranked the Robertson screw as one of Canada's ten greatest inventions—ahead of the BlackBerry, the game of basketball, and the zipper!

Since the last of Robertson's patents ran out in 1964, anyone can make a screw with a square recess impression, and this is where our American friends re-enter the picture. Knowing a good thing when they see one, Titan Metal Werks adopted the square recess because, according to them, "the drive recess ensures better engagement with the drill bit and less slippage." Or, as Mr. Robertson and most Canadians would tell it, it works better! Yet the real reason why these very Canadian-looking screws—which Titan sells under the name SplitStop—ended up in the Boardwalk are two additional inventions. The screws feature a unique slot on the tip for self-drilling, and special ridges where the threads end so they will not split wood even when placed three millimetres from the edge of a plank. The Robertson screw is a great simple invention, and great as it is, with help, even it has been improved. Fortunately, people only see the top of Titan's SplitStop screw, and only 10 percent of the screws sold in the U.S. are of a Robertson type. So you can probably still convince your American friends that those are Canadian screws holding together their Boardwalk.

SOURCES: 2008, CBC Inventions Web site, http://www.cbc.ca/inventions/inventions.html; 2008, Robertson Screw Web site, http://www.robertsonscrew.com/index.html; 2008, Suite 101 Web site, http://homerenorepair.suite101.com/article.cfm/types_of_screwdrivers; 2008, SplitStop Screw Web site, http://www.splitstop.com/products/index.asp and http://www. splitstop.com/about.asp; 2008, KTec Earthmovers Web site, http://www.ktecearthmovers.com/; 2008, Vision Pop Web site, http://visionpop.com/; all Web sites retrieved February 2; 2006, Simple idea becomes a guitar's best friend, *Saskbusiness*, 27(3): S8; J. Waytiuk, 2007, Cuts like a knife?, *Financial Post Business*, May, 16; R. Gage, 2006, Efficiency Spurs Invention, *Manitoba Business*, 28(2): 6–8.

their partners carefully. The ideal partnership is one in which the firms have complementary skills as well as compatible strategic goals.[128] However, because companies are operating in a network of firms and thus may be participating in multiple alliances simultaneously, they encounter challenges in managing the alliances.[129] Research has shown that firms can become involved in too many alliances, which can harm rather than facilitate their innovation capabilities.[130] Thus, effectively managing a cooperative strategy to produce innovation is critical. The Strategic Focus shows how effectively managing a cooperative strategy can help organizations.

Innovation through Acquisitions

Firms sometimes acquire companies to gain access to their innovations and to their innovative capabilities. One reason why companies do this is that the capital market values growth; acquisitions provide a means to rapidly extend one or more product lines and increase the firm's revenues. Acquisitions pursued for this reason should, nonetheless, have a strategic rationale. Pharmaceutical company Novartis AG, for example, is acquiring other companies to make progress toward its growth goal of becoming one of the world's pharmaceutical giants. However, the transactions being completed are part of what Novartis envisions as a set of "strategic acquisitions to create the world leader in the generic drug industry."[131] Pfizer also uses acquisitions to innovate. In fact, Pfizer recently announced that it intends to intensify its ". . . efforts to acquire new products and technologies to further strengthen (its) new product pipeline."[132]

Similar to internal corporate venturing and strategic alliances, acquisitions are not a risk-free approach to innovating. A key risk of acquisitions is that a firm may substitute an ability to buy innovations for an ability to produce innovations internally. In support of this contention, research shows that firms engaging in acquisitions introduce fewer new products into the market.[133] This substitution may take place because firms lose strategic control and focus instead on financial control of their original and especially of their acquired business units.

We note in Chapter 8 that companies can also learn new capabilities from firms they acquire. In the case of this chapter's topic, this would mean that firms may gain capabilities to produce innovation from an acquired company. Additionally, firms that emphasize innovation and carefully select companies for acquisition that also emphasize innovation are likely to remain innovative.[134]

This chapter closes with an assessment of how strategic entrepreneurship, as we have discussed it, helps firms create value for stakeholders through its operations.

Creating Value through Strategic Entrepreneurship

Newer entrepreneurial firms often are more effective than larger established firms when it comes to identifying entrepreneurial opportunities.[135] As a consequence, it seems that entrepreneurial ventures produce more radical innovations than do their larger, more established counterparts. Entrepreneurial ventures' strategic flexibility and willingness to take risks may account for their ability to spot opportunities and then develop radical innovations to pursue them.

On the other side of the coin, larger and well-established firms often have more resources and capabilities to exploit identified opportunities.[136] Younger entrepreneurial firms generally excel with the opportunity-seeking part of strategic entrepreneurship, while more established firms generally excel with the advantage-seeking part. However, to compete effectively in the 21st-century competitive landscape, firms not only must identify and exploit opportunities but also must do so while achieving and sustaining a competitive advantage.[137] Thus, on a relative basis, newer entrepreneurial firms must learn how to gain a competitive advantage, and older, more established firms must relearn how to identify entrepreneurial opportunities. Another way of saying this is that, in general, entrepreneurial ventures need to improve their advantage-seeking behaviours while larger firms need to improve their opportunity-seeking skills.

In some large organizations, action is being taken to deal with these matters. For example, an increasing number of widely known, large firms, including AstraZeneca, Nortel Networks, Blockbuster Inc., RBC Financial Group, and Wendy's International, have created new, top-level managerial positions generally labelled something like "vice president of emerging opportunities." The essential responsibility for people holding these positions is to find entrepreneurial opportunities for their firms. If innovations are to be developed to pursue one or more identified opportunities, this person also leads the analysis to determine whether the innovations should be internally developed, pursued through a cooperative venture, or acquired. The objective is for these activities to help firms successfully develop both incremental and radical innovations.

To be entrepreneurial, firms must develop an entrepreneurial mind-set among their managers and employees. Managers must emphasize the management of their resources, particularly human capital and social capital.[138] The importance of knowledge to identify and exploit opportunities as well as to gain and sustain a competitive advantage suggests that firms must have strong human capital.[139] Social capital is critical for access to complementary resources from partners in order to compete effectively in domestic and international markets.[140]

Many entrepreneurial opportunities continue to surface in international markets, a reality that is contributing to firms' willingness to engage in international entrepreneurship. By entering global markets that are new to them, firms can learn new technologies and management practices and diffuse this knowledge throughout the entire enterprise. Furthermore, the knowledge firms gain can contribute to their innovations. Research has shown that firms operating in international markets tend to be more innovative.[141] Entrepreneurial ventures and large firms now regularly enter international markets. Both types of firms must also be innovative to compete effectively. Thus, by developing resources (human and social capital), taking advantage of opportunities in domestic and international markets, and using the resources and knowledge gained in these markets to be innovative, firms achieve competitive advantages.[142] In so doing, they create value for their customers and shareholders.

Firms practising strategic entrepreneurship contribute to a country's economic development. In fact, some countries such as Ireland have made dramatic economic progress by changing the institutional rules for businesses operating in the country. This could be construed as a form of institutional entrepreneurship. Likewise, firms that seek to establish their technology as a standard, also representing institutional entrepreneurship, are engaging in strategic entrepreneurship because creating a standard produces a competitive advantage for the firm.[143]

Research shows that because of its economic importance and individual motives, entrepreneurial activity is increasing around the globe. Furthermore, more women are becoming entrepreneurs because of the economic opportunity entrepreneurship provides and the individual independence it affords.[144] In North America, for example, women are the nation's fastest-growing group of entrepreneurs.[145] In future years, entrepreneurial activity may increase the wealth of less-affluent countries and continue to contribute to the economic development of the more-affluent countries. Regardless, the entrepreneurial ventures and large, established firms that choose to practise strategic entrepreneurship are likely to be the winners in the 21st century.[146]

After identifying opportunities, entrepreneurs must act to develop capabilities that will become the basis of their firm's core competencies and competitive advantages. The process of identifying opportunities is entrepreneurial, but this activity alone is not sufficient to create maximum shareholder value or even to survive over time.[147] As we learned in Chapter 4, to successfully exploit opportunities a firm must develop capabilities that are valuable, rare, difficult to imitate, and organized to be exploited. When capabilities satisfy these four criteria, the firm has one or more competitive advantages to exploit the identified opportunities (as described in Chapter 4). Without a competitive advantage, the firm's success will be only temporary (as explained in Chapter 1). An innovation may be valuable and rare early in its life, if a market perspective is used in its development. However, competitive actions must be taken to introduce the new product to the market and protect its position in the market against competitors to gain a competitive advantage. These actions combined represent strategic entrepreneurship.

- Strategic entrepreneurship is taking entrepreneurial actions using a strategic perspective. Firms engaging in strategic entrepreneurship find themselves simultaneously engaging in opportunity-seeking and advantage-seeking behaviours. The purpose of doing this is to continuously find new opportunities and quickly develop innovations to take advantage of them.

- Entrepreneurship is a process used by individuals and groups to identify entrepreneurial opportunities without being immediately constrained by the resources they control. Corporate entrepreneurship, the focus of this chapter, is the application of entrepreneurship (including the identification of entrepreneurial opportunities) within ongoing, established organizations. Entrepreneurial opportunities are conditions in which new goods or services can satisfy a need in the market. Increasingly, entrepreneurship is positively contributing to individual firms' performances and is stimulating growth in entire economies.

- Firms engage in three types of innovative activity: (1) invention, which is the act of creating a new good or process, (2) innovation, or the process of creating a commercial product from an invention, and (3) imitation, which is the adoption of an innovation by similar firms. Invention brings something new into being while innovation brings something new into use.

- Entrepreneurs see or envision entrepreneurial opportunities and then take actions to develop innovations to pursue them. The most successful entrepreneurs (whether they are establishing their own venture or are working in an ongoing organization) have an entrepreneurial mind-set, which is an orientation that values the possibilities suggested by marketplace uncertainties.

- International entrepreneurship, or the process of identifying and exploiting entrepreneurial opportunities outside the firm's domestic markets, is becoming important to firms around the globe. Some evidence suggests that firms capable of effectively engaging in international entrepreneurship outperform those competing only in their domestic markets.

- Three basic approaches are used to produce innovation: (1) internal innovation, which takes place by forming internal corporate ventures, (2) cooperative strategies such as strategic alliances, and (3) acquisitions. Autonomous strategic behaviour and induced strategic behaviour are the two forms of internal corporate venturing. Autonomous strategic behaviour is a bottom-up process through which a product champion facilitates the commercialization of an innovative good or service. Induced strategic behaviour is a top-down process in which a firm's current strategy and structure facilitate product or process innovations that are associated with them. Thus, induced strategic behaviour is driven by the organization's current corporate strategy and structure while autonomous strategic behaviour can result in a change to the firm's current strategy and structure arrangements.

- Firms create two types of innovation—incremental and radical—through internal innovation that takes place in the form of autonomous strategic behaviour or induced strategic behaviour. Overall, firms produce more incremental innovations, although radical innovations have a higher probability of significantly increasing sales revenue and profits. Increasingly, cross-functional integration is vital to a firm's efforts to develop and implement internal corporate venturing activities and to commercialize the resulting innovation. Additionally, integration and innovation can be facilitated by developing shared values and effectively using strategic leadership.

- To gain access to the kind of specialized knowledge that often is required to innovate in the complex global economy, firms may form a cooperative relationship such as a strategic alliance with other companies, some which may be competitors.

- Acquisitions are another means firms use to innovate. Innovation can be acquired through direct acquisition, or firms can learn new capabilities from an acquisition, thereby enriching their internal innovation abilities.

- The practice of strategic entrepreneurship by all types of firms, large and small, new and more established, creates value for all stakeholders, especially for shareholders and customers. Strategic entrepreneurship also contributes to the economic development of entire nations.

Review Questions

1. What is strategic entrepreneurship? What is corporate entrepreneurship?

2. What is entrepreneurship and what are entrepreneurial opportunities? Why are these important for firms competing in the 21st-century competitive landscape?

3. What are invention, innovation, and imitation? How are these concepts related?

4. What is an entrepreneur and what is an entrepreneurial mind-set?

5. What is international entrepreneurship? Why is it important?

6. How do firms develop innovations internally?

7. How do firms use cooperative strategies to innovate and to have access to innovative abilities?

8. How does a firm acquire other companies to increase the number of innovations it produces and improve its capability to produce innovations?

9. How does strategic entrepreneurship help firms to create value as they compete in the 21st-century competitive landscape?

Social Responsibility Review

1. Reginald Fessenden was born in East Bolton, Quebec in 1866. At the age of 34 he would do something no human had ever done before—he talked on radio. His transmission across 1.6 kilometres was the world's first radio voice transmission. At the age of 40, he would again perform another radio first: the first radio entertainment transmission. Fessenden played "O Holy Night" on the violin to ships off the coast of New England. Fessenden eventually would claim 500 patents to his name, but his financial success was limited and involved numerous legal battles with business partners. Fessenden was even dismissed from the company he helped found. His is not an uncommon story in this regard—at one point, Apple Computer fired founder Steve Jobs. Why do you think business people and innovators often get involved in bitter feuds? Given what the chapter has discussed, how can we keep this creative resource in the organization?

2. Tim Collings of Stratford, Ontario became concerned about the impact of television violence on children, so he developed a decoding device that uses infrared signals to follow an interactive menu that parents can program to block out certain levels of violent programming. Broadcasters agreed to code their programming to indicate the level of violence, and the V-chip was born. It has been a standard feature on all televisions since 2000. The V, by the way, stands for Viewer. There are, however, objections to the V-chip.

The V-chip has been criticized for being an infringement on basic human rights as it allows government interference in what viewers watch on television. According to this argument, because the government regulates the rating system, it is also regulating parents' decision-making processes on their children's viewing habits. Do you see this as a valid criticism? Why, or why not?

3. Despite the amount of funding spent on educating parents on use of the V-chip noted above, there are still an insufficient number of users. Only 15 percent of parents who have access to the chip use it—in part because it is somewhat difficult to use, but more likely because it is unknown. Almost 40 percent of parents who have access to the V-chip were unaware of its existence. As a technical feature it has great potential, but as a practical matter it is underutilized. If reducing exposure to violence is a good thing, why have we as business people not found a way to get people to use a product feature they are buying? What would be a way to get people to use it more? Should government, in the public's interest, be doing more to get the chip used? If so, then what should it be doing?

Experiential Exercises

Entrepreneurship Goes Better with Koch

One of the most entrepreneurially successful large companies is Koch (pronounced "coke") Industries. Do not try to find the price of a share of this firm's stock, though—Koch is a private company. In fact, in 2006 *Forbes* magazine named Koch the world's largest privately held company, as measured by sales volume. Koch achieved this status in 2005 after it acquired paper producer Georgia Pacific. One of the reasons why the

firm remains private is that those leading the company strongly believe it is far easier to be entrepreneurial when not facing pressures from Wall Street analysts and investors. Interestingly, during the negotiations for his firm to be acquired, Georgia Pacific CEO Pete Correll specifically noted that "not having to be on the defensive" with respect to Wall Street when acquisition or restructuring activities take place was an important factor in his firm's decision to be acquired by Koch.

Koch's success comes from acquiring businesses with growth potential, even if those businesses compete in industries that are often perceived as old-line, mature-product, and commodity-like, such as paper products. At Georgia Pacific, CEO Correll tried to shift to an entrepreneurial model with more value-added products and by eliminating products that were poor performers. As part of Koch Industries, this transition within the former parts of Georgia Pacific is expected to accelerate. A reason for this is that entrepreneurship has been integrated throughout Koch's operations. Koch's market-based management philosophy includes "principled entrepreneurship." Activities associated with principled entrepreneurship are suggested by the following statement: "Our values also include a discovery mentality, which is reflected in our employees' initiative and desire to learn. The result is 'principled entrepreneurship'—doing well by doing good."

To further consider how entrepreneurship is embedded throughout Koch Industries, visit the firm's Web site. First, study Koch's guiding principles as presented at www.kochind.com/about/ guiding_principles.asp. Second, study Koch's ideas regarding business development as presented at www.kochind.com/industry/bus_development.asp. Look also at Koch's philosophy and principles, the firm's "living values," the Koch vision and mission statements, and the firm's "keys to success." Continue to browse the site and perform Google searches for more insights on the Koch orientation toward corporate entrepreneurship.

In discussions involving the entire class, address the following questions:

- What actions and orientations does Koch Industries take to establish an entrepreneurial culture?

- Is it likely that Koch will be more successful in corporate entrepreneurship because it is a private company? Why or why not?

- What role does Koch Genesis Company play in Koch's large entrepreneurship focus? Why is it separated from the established firm?

Entrepreneurial Culture

One of your responsibilities as a strategic leader in an entrepreneurial firm is to build shared values that will support entrepreneurial behaviour. Choose one of the two following options and describe the steps you would follow to build an entrepreneurial culture.

Option A. Take the perspective of a manager in a large corporation who has just been given the responsibility to lead a newly acquired business unit that has an innovative product. As the manager, prepare a report for the top management team that describes the actions you will take to lead the newly acquired business unit. Using materials from this chapter provide a brief rationale for the actions you intend to take.

Option B. Take the perspective of an entrepreneur who has personally developed an invention and is establishing a new venture to produce and market it. Prepare a report for investors about how you, the entrepreneur, plan to build an entrepreneurial culture so that the investors will be willing to provide financial resources to support the venture you want to launch to convert your invention into a commercially viable innovation. Explain how your efforts to build an entrepreneurial culture will lead to strategic competitiveness and above-average returns.

Notes

1. D. S. Elenkov & I. M. Manev, 2005, Top management leadership and influence on innovation: The role of sociocultural context, *Journal of Management,* 31: 381–402.

2. S. D. Dobrev & W. P. Barnett, 2005, Organizational roles and transition to entrepreneurship, *Academy of Management Journal,* 48: 433–449; V. Govindarajan & C. Trimble, 2005, Building breakthrough businesses within established organizations, *Harvard Business Review,* 83(5): 58–68.

3. M. A. Hitt, R. D. Ireland, S. M. Camp, & D. L. Sexton, 2002, Strategic entrepreneurship: Integrating entrepreneurial and strategic management perspectives, in M. A. Hitt, R. D. Ireland, S. M. Camp, & D. L. Sexton (eds.), *Strategic Entrepreneurship: Creating a New Mindset,* Oxford, UK: Blackwell Publishers, 1–16; M. A. Hitt, R. D. Ireland, S. M. Camp, & D. L. Sexton, 2001, Strategic entrepreneurship: Entrepreneurial strategies for wealth creation, *Strategic Management Journal,* 22 (Special Issue): 479–491; R. D. Ireland, M. A. Hitt, S. M. Camp, & D. L. Sexton, 2001, Integrating entrepreneurship and strategic management actions to create firm wealth, *Academy of Management Executive,* 15(1): 49–63.

4. D. A. Shepherd & D. R. DeTienne, 2005, Prior knowledge, potential financial reward, and opportunity identification, *Entrepreneurship Theory and Practice,* 29(1): 91–112; W. J. Baumol, 2004, Entrepreneurial cultures and countercultures, *Academy of Learning & Education,* 3(3): 316–326.

5. R. E. Hoskisson, M. A. Hitt, R. A. Johnson, & W. Grossman, 2002, Conflicting voices: The effects of institutional ownership heterogeneity and internal governance on corporate innovation strategies, *Academy of Management Journal,* 45: 697–716.

6. K. G. Smith, C. J. Collins, & K. D. Clark, 2005, Existing knowledge, knowledge creation capability, and the rate of new product introduction in high-technology firms, *Academy of Management Journal,* 48: 346–357.

7. R. D. Ireland, M. A. Hitt, & D. G. Sirmon, 2003, A model of strategic entrepreneurship: The construct and its dimensions, *Journal of Management,* 29: 963–989.

8. B. R. Barringer & R. D. Ireland, 2006, *Entrepreneurship: Successfully Launching New Ventures,* Upper Saddle River, NJ: Pearson Prentice Hall, 5; G. G. Dess, R. D. Ireland, S. A. Zahra, S. W. Floyd, J. J. Janney, & P. J. Lane, 2003, Emerging issues in corporate entrepreneurship, *Journal of Management,* 29: 351–378.

9. H. A. Schildt, M. V. J. Maula, & T. Keil, 2005, Explorative and exploitative learning from external corporate ventures, *Entrepreneurship Theory and Practice,* 29: 493–515.

10. G. T. Lumpkin & B. B. Lichtenstein, 2005, The role of organizational learning in the opportunity-recognition process, *Entrepreneurship Theory and Practice,* 29: 451–472.

11. Barringer & Ireland, *Entrepreneurship;* H. H. Stevenson & J. C. Jarillo, 1990, A paradigm for entrepreneurship: Entrepreneurial management, *Strategic Management Journal,* 16 (Special Issue): 17–27.

12. S. A. Alvarez & J. B. Barney, 2005, Organizing rent generation and appropriation: Toward a theory of the entrepreneurial firm, *Journal of Business Venturing,* 19: 621–635.

13. M. Minniti, 2005, Entrepreneurial alertness and asymmetric information in a spin-glass model, *Journal of Business Venturing,* 19: 637–658.

14. W. Kuemmerle, 2005, The entrepreneur's path to global expansion, *MIT Sloan Management Review,* 46(2): 42–49.

15. Wikipedia, 2008, Blue Ocean Strategy,http://en.wikipedia.org/wiki/Blue_ Ocean_Strategy, retrieved May 5; C. W. Kim & R. Mauborgne, 2005, *Blue Ocean Strategy,* Cambridge, MA: Harvard University Press.

16. W. C. Kim & R. Mauborgne, 2008, Make the competition irrelevant, http://www.blueoceanstrategy.com/downloads/BlueOceanStrategySummary.pdf, retrieved May 5.

17. S. Shane & S. Venkataraman, 2000, The promise of entrepreneurship as a field of research, *Academy of Management Review,* 25: 217–226.

18. J. Schumpeter, 1934, *The Theory of Economic Development,* Cambridge, MA: Harvard University Press.

19. R. Katila, 2002, New product search over time: Past ideas in their prime? *Academy of Management Journal,* 45: 995–1010; B. R. Barringer & A. C. Bluedorn, 1999, The relationship between corporate entrepreneurship and strategic management, *Strategic Management Journal,* 20: 421–444.

20. R. G. Holcombe, 2003, The origins of entrepreneurial opportunities, *Review of Austrian Economics,* 16: 25–54; C. M. Daily, P. P. McDougall, J. G. Covin, & D. R. Dalton, 2002, Governance and strategic leadership in entrepreneurial firms, *Journal of Management,* 28: 387–412.

21. R. D. Ireland, J. W. Webb, & J. E. Coombs, 2005, Theory and methodology in entrepreneurship research, in D. J. Ketchen Jr. & D. D. Bergh (eds.), *Research Methodology in Strategy and Management* (Volume 2), San Diego: Elsevier Publishers, 111–141; S. D. Sarasvathy, 2005, The questions we ask and the questions we care about: Reformulating some problems in entrepreneurship research, *Journal of Business Venturing,* 19: 707–717.

22. P. F. Drucker, 1998, The discipline of innovation, *Harvard Business Review,* 76(6): 149–157.

23. Ibid.

24. J. D. Wolpert, 2002, Breaking out of the innovation box, *Harvard Business Review,* 80(8): 77–83.

25. K. Karnik, 2005, Innovation's importance: Powering economic growth, *National Association of Software and Service Companies,* www.nasscom .org, January 24.

26. 2005, Innovation challenge, *Extraordinary Dairy,* www.extraordinarydairy .com, January 24.

27. M. Subramaniam & M. A. Youndt, 2005, The influence of intellectual capital on the types of innovative capabilities, *Academy of Management Journal,* 48: 450–463.

28. J. E. Perry-Smith & C. E. Shalley, 2003, The social side of creativity: A static and dynamic social network perspective, *Academy of Management Review,* 28: 89–106.

29. R. Price, 1996, Technology and strategic advantage, *California Management Review,* 38(3): 38–56; L. G. Franko, 1989, Global corporate competition: Who's winning, who's losing and the R&D factor as one reason why, *Strategic Management Journal,* 10: 449–474.

30. J. W. Spencer, 2003, Firms' knowledge-sharing strategies in the global innovation system: Empirical evidence from the flat panel display industry, *Strategic Management Journal,* 24: 217–233; K. M. Kelm, V. K. Narayanan, & G. E. Pinches, 1995, Shareholder value creation during R&D innovation and commercialization stages, *Academy of Management Journal,* 38: 770–786.

31. M. A. Hitt, R. D. Nixon, R. E. Hoskisson, & R. Kochhar, 1999, Corporate entrepreneurship and cross-functional fertilization: Activation, process and disintegration of a new product design team, *Entrepreneurship: Theory and Practice,* 23(3): 145–167.

32. J. P. O'Brien, 2003, The capital structure implications of pursuing a strategy of innovation, *Strategic Management Journal,* 24: 415–431.

33. Schumpeter, *The Theory of Economic Development.*

34. R. Katila & S. Shane, 2005, When does lack of resources make new firms innovative? *Academy of Management Journal,* 48: 814–829.

35. P. Sharma & J. L. Chrisman, 1999, Toward a reconciliation of the definitional issues in the field of corporate entrepreneurship, *Entrepreneurship: Theory and Practice,* 23(3): 11–27; R. A. Burgelman & L. R. Sayles, 1986, *Inside Corporate Innovation: Strategy, Structure, and Managerial Skills,* New York: Free Press.

36. D. K. Dutta & M. M. Crossan, 2005, The nature of entrepreneurial opportunities: Understanding the process using the 4I organizational learning framework, *Entrepreneurship Theory and Practice* 29: 425–449.

37. R. E. Hoskisson & L. W. Busenitz, 2002, Market uncertainty and learning distance in corporate entrepreneurship entry mode choice, in M. A. Hitt, R. D. Ireland, S. M. Camp, & D. L. Sexton (eds.), *Strategic Entrepreneurship: Creating a New Mindset,* Oxford, UK: Blackwell Publishers, 151–172.

38. D. Somaya, 2003, Strategic determinants of decisions not to settle patent litigation, *Strategic Management Journal,* 24: 17–38.

39. S. D. Sarasvathy, 2004, Making it happen: Beyond theories of the firm to theories of firm design, *Entrepreneurship Theory and Practice,* 28: 519–531.

40. 2004, Rules to live by, and break, Knowledge@Wharton, http://knowledge .wharton.upenn.edu, June 17.

41. D. Duffy, 2004, Corporate entrepreneurship: Entrepreneurial skills for personal and corporate success, *Center for Excellence,* www.centerforexcellence.net, June 14.

42. M. S. Cardon, C. Zietsma, P. Saparito, B. P. Matheren, & C. Davis, 2005, A tale of passion: New insights into entrepreneurship from a parenthood metaphor, *Journal of Business Venturing,* 19: 23–45.

43. R. G. McGrath & I. MacMillan, 2000, *The Entrepreneurial Mindset,* Boston, MA: Harvard Business School Press.

44. R. D. Ireland, M. A. Hitt, & J. W. Webb, 2005, Entrepreneurial alliances and networks, in O. Shenkar and J. J. Reuer (eds.), *Handbook of Strategic Alliances,* Thousand Oaks, CA: Sage Publications, 333–352; T. M. Begley & D. P. Boyd, 2003, The need for a corporate global mind-set, *MIT Sloan Management Review,* 44(2): 25–32.

45. H. D. Schultz, 2005, Starbucks' founder on innovation in the music biz, *BusinessWeek,* July 4, 16–17.

46. H.-J. Cho & V. Pucik, 2005, Relationship between innovativeness, quality, growth, profitability, and market value, *Strategic Management Journal,* 26: 555–575.

47. W. Tsai, 2001, Knowledge transfer in intraorganizational networks: Effects of network position and absorptive capacity on business unit innovation and performance, *Academy of Management Journal,* 44: 996–1004.

48. S. A. Zahra & G. George, 2002, Absorptive capacity: A review, reconceptualization, and extension, *Academy of Management Review,* 27: 185–203.

49. M. A. Hitt, L. Bierman, K. Shimizu, & R. Kochhar, 2001, Direct and moderating effects of human capital on strategy and performance in professional service firms, *Academy of Management Journal,* 44: 13–28.

50. K. Aaserud, C. Cornell, J. McElgunn, K. Shiffman, R Wright, 2007, The golden rules of growth, *Profit,* 26(2), 66–75.

51. Zahra & George, Absorptive capacity: 261.

52. T. M. Begley, W.-L. Tan, & H. Schoch, 2005, Politico-economic factors associated with interest in starting a business: A multi-country study, *Entrepreneurship Theory and Practice,* 29: 35–52; J. W. Lu & P. W. Beamish, 2001, The internationalization and performance of SMEs, *Strategic Management Journal,* 22 (Special Issue): 565–585.

53. L. Tihanyi, R. A. Johnson, R. E. Hoskisson, & M. A. Hitt, 2003, Institutional ownership differences and international diversification: The effects of boards of directors and technological opportunity, *Academy of Management Journal,* 46: 195–211.

54. R. D. Ireland & J. W. Webb, 2006, International entrepreneurship in emerging economies: A resource-based perspective, in S. Alvarez, A. Carrera, L. Mesquita, & R. Vassolo (eds.), *Entrepreneurship and Innovation in Emerging Economies,* Oxford, UK: Blackwell Publishers: in press; A. E. Ellstrand, L. Tihanyi, & J. L. Johnson, 2002, Board structure and international political risk, *Academy of Management Journal,* 45: 769–777.

55. S. Andersson, 2004, Internationalization in different industrial contexts, *Journal of Business Venturing,* 19: 851–875.

56. D. Farrell, H. Fassbender, T. Kneip, S. Kriesel, & E. Labaye, 2003, Reviving French and German productivity, *The McKinsey Quarterly,* Number One, 40–53.

57. 2004, *GEM 2004 Irish Report,* www.gemconsortium.org/download, July 13.

58. J. McMillan, 2005, Creative destruction thrives, *New Zealand Herald,* January 13, C2.

59. N. Bosma & R. Harding, 2007, *Global Entrepreneurship: GEM 2006 Summary Results,* Boston, Global entrepreneurship Monitor, http://www.gemconsortium .org/download/1201834176939/GEM_2006_Global_Results_Summary_V2.pdf, retrieved January 31, 2008.

60. M. H. Morris, 1998, *Entrepreneurial Intensity: Sustainable Advantages for Individuals, Organizations, and Societies,* Westport, CT: Quorum Books, 85–86.

61. N. Nummeia, S. Saarenketo, & K. Puumalainen, 2005, Rapidly with a rifle or more slowly with a shotgun? Stretching the company boundaries of internationalizing ICT firms, *Journal of International Entrepreneurship,* 2: 275–288; S. A. Zahra & G. George, 2002, International entrepreneurship: The state of the field and future research agenda, in M. A. Hitt, R. D. Ireland, S. M. Camp, & D. L. Sexton (eds.), *Strategic Entrepreneurship: Creating a New Mindset,* Oxford, UK: Blackwell Publishers, 255–288.

62. S. A. Zahra, R. D. Ireland, & M. A. Hitt, 2000, International expansion by new venture firms: International diversity, mode of market entry, technological learning and performance, *Academy of Management Journal,* 43: 925–950.

63. P. P. McDougall & B. M. Oviatt, 2000, International entrepreneurship: The intersection of two paths, *Academy of Management Journal,* 43: 902–908.

64. A. Yan, G. Zhu, & D. T. Hall, 2002, International assignments for career building: A model of agency relationships and psychological contracts, *Academy of Management Review,* 27: 373–391.

65. H. Barkema & O. Chvyrkov, 2002, What sort of top management team is needed at the helm of internationally diversified firms? in M. A. Hitt, R. D. Ireland, S. M. Camp, & D. L. Sexton (eds.), *Strategic Entrepreneurship: Creating a New Mindset,* Oxford, UK: Blackwell Publishers, 290–305.

66. T. S. Frost, 2001, The geographic sources of foreign subsidiaries' innovations, *Strategic Management Journal,* 22: 101–122.

67. C. Dawson, 2005, Proud papa of the Prius, *BusinessWeek,* July 20, 20.

68. R. Underwood, 2005, Walking the talk? *Fast Company,* March, 25–26.

69. J. Battelle, 2005, Turning the page, *Business 2.0,* July, 98–100.

70. J. Santos, Y. Doz, & P. Williamson, 2004, Is your innovation process global? *MIT Sloan Management Review,* 45(4): 31–37; C. D. Charitou & C. C. Markides, 2003, Responses to disruptive strategic innovation, *MIT Sloan Management Review,* 44(2): 55–63.

71. J. A. Fraser, 2004, A return to basics at Kellogg, *MIT Sloan Management Review,* 45(4): 27–30; P. M. Lee & H. M. O'Neill, 2003, Ownership structures and R&D investments of U.S. and Japanese firms: Agency and stewardship perspectives, *Academy of Management Journal,* 46: 212–225.

72. S. Kola-Nystrom, 2003, Theory of conceptualizing the challenge of corporate renewal, Lappeenranta University of Technology, Working Paper.

73. 2005, Radical and incremental innovation styles, *Strategies 2 innovate,* www.strategies2innovate.com, July 12.

74. W. C. Kim & R. Mauborgne, 2005, Navigating toward blue oceans, *Optimize,* February: 44–52.

75. G. Ahuja & M. Lampert, 2001, Entrepreneurship in the large corporation: A longitudinal study of how established firms create breakthrough inventions, *Strategic Management Journal,* 22 (Special Issue): 521–543.

76. O. Port, 2005, Mighty morphing power processors, *BusinessWeek,* June 6, 60–61.

77. 2005, Getting an edge on innovation, *BusinessWeek,* March 21, 124.

78. J. E. Ashton, F. X. Cook Jr., & P. Schmitz, 2003, Uncovering hidden value in a midsize manufacturing company, *Harvard Business Review,* 81(6): 111–119; L. Fleming & O. Sorenson, 2003, Navigating the technology landscape of innovation, *MIT Sloan Management Review,* 44(2): 15–23.

79. J. Goldenberg, R. Horowitz, A. Levav, & D. Mazursky, 2003, Finding your innovation sweet spot, *Harvard Business Review,* 81(3): 120–129.

80. G. C. O'Connor, R. Hendricks, & M. P. Rice, 2002, Assessing transition readiness for radical innovation, *Research Technology Management,* 45(6): 50–56.

81. R. I. Sutton, 2002, Weird ideas that spark innovation, *MIT Sloan Management Review,* 43(2): 83–87.

82. K. G. Smith & D. Di Gregorio, 2002, Bisociation, discovery, and the role of entrepreneurial action, in M. A. Hitt, R. D. Ireland, S. M. Camp, & D. L. Sexton (eds.), *Strategic Entrepreneurship: Creating a New Mindset,* Oxford, UK: Blackwell Publishers, 129–150.

83. J. G. Covin, R. D. Ireland, & D. F. Kuratko, 2005, Exploration through internal corporate ventures, Indiana University, Working Paper; Hoskisson & Busenitz, Market uncertainty and learning distance.

84. R. A. Burgelman, 1995, *Strategic Management of Technology and Innovation,* Boston: Irwin.

85. S. K. Markham, 2002, Moving technologies from lab to market, *Research Technology Management,* 45(6): 31–42.

86. J. M. Howell, 2005, The right stuff: Identifying and developing effective champions of innovation, *Academy of Management Executive,* 19(2): 108–119.

87. T. H. Davenport, L. Prusak, & H. J. Wilson, 2003, Who's bringing you hot ideas and how are you responding? *Harvard Business Review,* 81(2): 58–64.

88. M. D. Hutt & T. W. Seph, 2004, *Business Marketing Management* (8th ed.), Cincinnati, OH: Thomson South-Western.

89. M. A. Hitt, R. D. Ireland, & H. Lee, 2000, Technological learning, knowledge management, firm growth and performance, *Journal of Engineering and Technology Management,* 17: 231–246; D. Leonard-Barton, 1995, *Wellsprings of Knowledge: Building and Sustaining the Sources of Innovation,* Cambridge, MA: Harvard Business School Press.

90. A. Taylor III, 2005, Billion-dollar bets, *Fortune,* June 27, 139–154.

91. S. S. Rao, 2000, General Electric, software vendor, *Forbes,* January 24, 144–146.

92. H. W. Chesbrough, 2002, Making sense of corporate venture capital, *Harvard Business Review,* 80(3): 90–99.

93. M. Subramaniam & N. Venkatraman, 2001, Determinants of transnational new product development capability: Testing the influence of transferring and deploying tacit overseas knowledge, *Strategic Management Journal,* 22: 359–378.

94. M. Song & M. M. Montoya-Weiss, 2001, The effect of perceived technological uncertainty on Japanese new product development, *Academy of Management Journal,* 44: 61–80.

95. R. Underwood, 2005, Hot wheels, *Fast Company,* May, 64–65.

96. McGrath & MacMillan, *Entrepreneurial Mindset.*

97. 2002, Building scientific networks for effective innovation, *MIT Sloan Management Review,* 43(3): 14.

98. C. M. Christensen & M. Overdorf, 2000, Meeting the challenge of disruptive change, *Harvard Business Review,* 78(2): 66–77.

99. L. Yu, 2002, Marketers and engineers: Why can't we just get along? *MIT Sloan Management Review,* 43(1): 13.

100. P. S. Adler, 1995, Interdepartmental interdependence and coordination: The case of the design/manufacturing interface, *Organization Science,* 6: 147–167.

101. I. Royer, 2003, Why bad projects are so hard to kill, *Harvard Business Review,* 81(2): 48–56.

102. P. Evans & B. Wolf, 2005, Collaboration rules, *Harvard Business Review,* 83(7): 96–104.

103. B. Fischer & A. Boynton, 2005, Virtuoso teams, *Harvard Business Review,* 83(7): 116–123.

104. Hitt, Nixon, Hoskisson, & Kochhar, Corporate entrepreneurship.

105. Christensen & Overdorf, Meeting the challenge of disruptive change.

106. Hitt, Nixon, Hoskisson, & Kochhar, Corporate entrepreneurship.
107. A. C. Amason, 1996, Distinguishing the effects of functional and dysfunctional conflict on strategic decision making: Resolving a paradox for top management teams, *Academy of Management Journal*, 39: 123–148; P. R. Lawrence & J. W. Lorsch, 1969, *Organization and Environment*, Homewood, IL: Richard D. Irwin.
108. D. Dougherty, L. Borrelli, K. Muncir, & A. O'Sullivan, 2000, Systems of organizational sensemaking for sustained product innovation, *Journal of Engineering and Technology Management*, 17: 321–355; D. Dougherty, 1992, Interpretive barriers to successful product innovation in large firms, *Organization Science*, 3: 179–202.
109. Hitt, Nixon, Hoskisson, & Kochhar, Corporate entrepreneurship.
110. E. C. Wenger & W. M. Snyder, 2000, Communities of practice: The organizational frontier, *Harvard Business Review*, 78(1): 139–144.
111. Gary Hamel, 2000, *Leading the Revolution*, Boston: Harvard Business School Press.
112. McGrath & MacMillan, *Entrepreneurial Mindset*.
113. Q. M. Roberson & J. A. Colquitt, 2005, Shared and configural justice: A social network model of justice in teams, *Academy of Management Review*, 30: 595–607.
114. S. W. Fowler, A. W. King, S. J. Marsh, & B. Victor, 2000, Beyond products: New strategic imperatives for developing competencies in dynamic environments, *Journal of Engineering and Technology Management*, 17: 357–377.
115. S. Myers, 2007, Smart creates research chair, *Calgary Herald*, March 9, D3.
116. F. T. Rothaermel & D. L. Deeds, 2004, Exploration and exploitation alliances in biotechnology: A system of new product development, *Strategic Management Journal*, 25: 201–221; R. Gulati & M. C. Higgins, 2003, Which ties matter when? The contingent effects of interorganizational partnerships on IPO success, *Strategic Management Journal*, 24: 127–144.
117. J. Hagel III & J. S. Brown, 2005, Productive friction, *Harvard Business Review*, 83(2): 82–91.
118. A. C. Cooper, 2002, Networks, alliances and entrepreneurship, in M. A. Hitt, R. D. Ireland, S. M. Camp, & D. L. Sexton (eds.), *Strategic Entrepreneurship: Creating a New Mindset*, Oxford, UK: Blackwell Publishers, 204–222.
119. S. A. Alvarez & J. B. Barney, 2001, How entrepreneurial firms can benefit from alliances with large partners, *Academy of Management Executive*, 15(1): 139–148; F. T. Rothaermel, 2001, Incumbent's advantage through exploiting complementary assets via interfirm cooperation, *Strategic Management Journal*, 22 (Special Issue): 687–699.
120. B. Brenner, C. Edwards, R. Grover, T. Lowry, & E. Thornton, 2005, Sony's sudden samurai, *BusinessWeek*, March 21, 28–32.
121. Alvarez & Barney, How entrepreneurial firms can benefit from alliances with large partners; F. T. Rothaermel, 2001, Incumbent's advantage through exploiting complementary assets via interfirm cooperation, *Strategic Management Journal*, 22 (Special Issue): 687–699.
122. D. Kline, 2003, Sharing the corporate crown jewels, *MIT Sloan Management Review*, 44(3): 89–93.
123. H. Yli-Renko, E. Autio, & H. J. Sapienza, 2001, Social capital, knowledge acquisition and knowledge exploitation in young technology-based firms, *Strategic Management Journal*, 22 (Special Issue): 587–613.
124. C. Lee, K. Lee, & J. M. Pennings, 2001, Internal capabilities, external networks and performance: A study of technology-based ventures, *Strategic Management Journal*, 22 (Special Issue): 615–640.
125. A. Takeishi, 2001, Bridging inter- and intra-firm boundaries: Management of supplier involvement in automobile product development, *Strategic Management Journal*, 22: 403–433.
126. J. Weiss & J. Hughes, 2005, Want collaboration? Accept—and actively manage—conflict, *Harvard Business Review*, 83(3): 92–101.
127. R. D. Ireland, M. A. Hitt, & D. Vaidyanath, 2002, Strategic alliances as a pathway to competitive success, *Journal of Management*, 28: 413–446.
128. M. A. Hitt, M. T. Dacin, E. Levitas, J.-L. Arregle, & A. Borza, 2000, Partner selection in emerging and developed market contexts: Resource-based and organizational learning perspectives, *Academy of Management Journal*, 43: 449–467.
129. J. J. Reuer, M. Zollo, & H. Singh, 2002, Post-formation dynamics in strategic alliances, *Strategic Management Journal*, 23: 135–151.
130. F. Rothaermel & D. Deeds, 2002, More good things are not always necessarily better: An empirical study of strategic alliances, experience effects, and new product development in high-technology start-ups, in M. A. Hitt, R. Amit, C. Lucier, & R. Nixon (eds.), *Creating Value: Winners in the New Business Environment*, Oxford, UK: Blackwell Publishers, 85–103.
131. 2005, Novartis announces completion of Hexal AG acquisition, Novartis Web page, www.novartis.com, June 6.
132. 2005, Pfizer sees sustained long-term growth, Pfizer Web page, www.pfizer.com, April 5.
133. M. A. Hitt, R. E. Hoskisson, R. A. Johnson, & D. D. Moesel, 1996, The market for corporate control and firm innovation, *Academy of Management Journal*, 39: 1084–1119.
134. M. A. Hitt, J. S. Harrison, & R. D. Ireland, 2001, *Mergers and Acquisitions: A Guide to Creating Value for Stakeholders*, New York: Oxford University Press.
135. Ireland, Hitt, & Sirmon, A model of strategic entrepreneurship.
136. Ibid.
137. Hitt, Ireland, Camp, & Sexton, Strategic entrepreneurship.
138. D. G. Sirmon, M. A. Hitt, & R. D. Ireland, 2007, Managing firm resources in dynamic environment to create value: Looking inside the black box, *Academy of Management Review*, in press.
139. Hitt, Bierman, Shimizu, & Kochhar, Direct and moderating effects of human capital.
140. M. A. Hitt, H. Lee, & E. Yucel, 2002, The importance of social capital to the management of multinational enterprises: Relational networks among Asian and Western firms, *Asia Pacific Journal of Management*, 19: 353–372.
141. M. A. Hitt, R. E. Hoskisson, & H. Kim, 1997, International diversification: Effects on innovation and firm performance in product diversified firms, *Academy of Management Journal*, 40: 767–798.
142. M. A. Hitt & R. D. Ireland, 2002, The essence of strategic leadership: Managing human and social capital, *Journal of Leadership and Organization Studies*, 9(1): 3–14.
143. R. Garud, S. Jain, & A. Kumaraswamy, 2002, Institutional entrepreneurship in the sponsorship of common technological standards: The case of Sun Microsystems and JAVA, *Academy of Management Journal*, 45: 196–214.
144. Reynolds, Camp, Bygrave, Autio, & Hay, *Global Entrepreneurship Monitor*.
145. J. D. Jardins, 2005, I am woman (I think), *Fast Company*, May, 25–26.
146. Hitt, Ireland, Camp, & Sexton, Strategic entrepreneurship.
147. C. W. L. Hill & F. T. Rothaermel, 2003, The performance of incumbent firms in the face of radical technological innovation, *Academy of Management Review*, 28: 257–274.

Name Index

A

Aaserud, K., 454
Abbott, A., 291
Abboud, A. L., 254
Abell, D. F., 127
Abrahamson, E., 194, 428
Abratt, R., 326
Adler, P. S., 430, 455
Adner, R., 37
Aeppel, T., 289
Afuah, A., 95, 96, 194
Agami, A. M., 253
Agarwal, R., 195
Aggarwal, R. K., 222
Agle, B. R., 38
Aguilera, R. V., 356, 358
Ahlstrand, B., 427
Ahlstrom, D., 95, 129, 292,
    323, 360, 392
Ahuja, G., 37, 127, 128, 254,
    429, 455
Aiello, R. J., 255
Ajinkya, B., 358
Albanese, R., 429
Albright, Madeleine, 440
Alcacer, J., 289
Alchian, A., 61
Alden, D. L., 127
Alexander, G. J., 62
Allen, L., 291
Almeida, J. G., 127
Almeida, P., 292, 325
Almond, P., 291
Alptert, B., 36
Alred, B. B., 290
Altman, E. I., 62
Altman, Edward, 46
Alvarez, S. A., 128, 429, 454,
    455, 456
Amason, A. C., 456
Ambos, B., 289
Ambrose, M. L., 430
Ambrosini, V., 129
Amburgey, T., 392
Ames, C., 129
Amihud, Y., 224, 357
Amit, R., 127, 129, 456
An, J. M., 289
Anand, J., 253, 255, 323,
    325, 359, 430
Andal-Ancion, A., 95,
    126, 395
Anders, G., 253

Andersen, P. H., 395
Andersen, T. J., 392
Anderson, P., 128, 254, 427
Anderson, R. C., 224,
    357, 358
Andersson, S., 289, 455
Andersson, U., 294
Andrews, T. G., 294
Aneiro, M., 162
Angwin, J., 96
Anhalt, K. N., 395
Anthanassiou, N., 357
Antoine, A., 293, 323
Aoyama, Y., 290
Ardichvilli, A., 430
Argenti, P. A., 38, 394
Argote, L., 128
Argyres, N., 95
Arikan, A. M., 429
Arikan, A. T., 392
Arino, A., 293
Armstrong, J. C., 195
Armstrong, L., 195
Armstrong, Lance, 314
Armstrong, R. W., 164
Arndt, M., 323, 358
Arnott, R., 360
Arora, A., 127, 292
Arregle, J.-L., 292, 325, 456
Artz, K., 326
Artz, K. W., 96, 127
Asakawa, K., 37, 289
Ashton, J. E., 455
Asper, Izzy, 241
Atamer, T., 95
Au, K. Y., 94
Audia, P. G., 127
Aukutsionek, S., 360
Aulakh, P. S., 292
Auster, E. R., 252
Autio, E., 94, 127, 456
Avolio, B. J., 428
Axelrod, B., 430
Azamhuzjaev, M., 62

B

Babakus, E., 292, 323
Baden-Fuller, C., 325, 394
Baek, H. Y., 294
Baek, J.-S, 360
Baglole, J., 95
Bagnall, J., 38
Bailey, J. V., 62

Baiman, S., 393
Bakan, J., 333, 356
Baker, H. K., 357
Baker, Richard, 158
Baljko, J., 163
Balsillie, James, 347, 348
Bamford, J., 292
Banerji, K., 291
Banhonacker, W. R., 95
Bannert, V., 254
Barber, B. N., 255
Barkema, H., 95, 253,
    392, 455
Barker, R. G., 291
Barner-Rasmussen, W., 294
Barnes, Brenda, 398
Barnes, J. G., 61
Barnes, S. F., 393
Barnett, W. P., 453
Barney, J. B., 36, 37, 61, 62,
    127, 129, 162, 163, 255,
    322, 324, 393, 427, 429,
    430, 454, 456
Barney, Jay, 9, 43, 66, 309
Barnir, A., 429
Baron, Carol, 133
Barr, P. S., 294
Barrett, A., 162
Barringer, B. R., 453, 454
Barrionuevo, A., 427
Barsade, S., 428
Barth, H., 392
Bartlett, C. A., 95, 291, 292,
    394, 430
Bartram, A., 293
Barwise, P., 37
Bass, K. E., 288
Bates, K. A., 128, 222
Bates, T., 36
Bates, T. W., 224, 357
Batra, R., 127
Battelle, J., 455
Bauerschmidt, A., 393
Baum, I. R., 38
Baum, J. A. C., 392
Baum, J. R., 394
Baumol, W. J., 453
Baur, A., 162
Baysinger, B. D., 358
Bayus, B. L., 127, 325
Beal, B. D., 94, 290
Beamish, P. W., 95, 222,
    254, 290, 291, 292, 293,
    294, 324

Beatty, Perrin, 77
Beauchesne, E., 325
Bebchuk, L. A., 359
Becerra, M., 428
Beck, K. A., 38, 394
Becker, B. E., 430
Beddoe, C., 163
Beer, M., 428
Begley, T. M., 127, 288,
    394, 454
Belderbos, R., 36, 194, 293
Bell, G. G., 325
Belson, K., 429
Bendor-Samuel, P., 129
Benedict, J., 127
Bengtsson, L., 326
Benner, M. J., 129
Bentson, G., 62
Bergen, M., 36, 126, 222
Bergh, D. D., 36, 162, 222,
    223, 253, 255, 256,
    359, 454
Berkley, J. D., 428
Berle, A., 358
Berman, D. K., 222, 252, 253
Berman, S. L., 128, 323
Bernardo, A. E., 223, 324
Berner, R., 163
Berryman, K., 357
Berthon, P., 128
Best, A., 255
Bethel, J. E., 255
Bettis, J. C., 359
Bettis, R. A., 36
Bettman, Gary, 408
Bhambri, A., 427, 429
Bhojraj, S., 358
Biemans, W. G., 326
Bierly, P., 323
Bierman, L., 126, 129, 254,
    429, 454
Bigley, G. A., 294, 392
Biller, S., 163
Birkinshaw, J., 290, 394
Birkinshaw, J., 431
Bish, E. K., 163
Biziak, J. M., 359
Bizjak, J. M., 224, 357
Bjorkman, I., 294
Black, Conrad, 30, 44, 241,
    331–332, 345, 353
Black, J. S., 429
Black, S. S., 323
Blankson, C., 289

Company Index

Subject Index

Note: Page numbers followed by *f* or *t* indicate figures and tables, respectively.

M

Management
  acquisitions decisions, 241–242
  boards of directors and, 341–344
  compensation, 331–333, 345–348
  cooperative strategies, 318–319
  defence tactics, 218, 350–351, 351*t*
  discretion of, 407, 407*f*
  diversification decisions, 217–218, 337–339
  ethics, 421
  managers as resource, 406–409
  multinational firms, 282, 285–286
  opportunism, 337, 421
  ownership concentration, 340–341
  ownership separated from, 335–340
  role of top-level, 409
  selection of, 412
  succession, 412–415, 414*f*
  top teams, 409–412, 414*f*
  women in, 414–415
  See also Chief executive officers (CEOs); Strategic leadership
Management buyouts, 248
Managerial competencies, 104
Managerial discretion over accounting measures, 49
Managerial frame of reference, 401
Managerial leadership, 401–402
Managerial opportunism, 337, 421
Market-based performance measures, 51–54
Market commonality, 171–174
Market dependence, 184–185
Market for corporate control, 349–351
Market microstructure, 82
Market power, 209–211, 231–233
Market segmentation, 138–139, 138*t*
Market size, 264
Markets of one, 83
Market Value Added (MVA), 54–56
Matrix organization, 377, 377*f*

Mergers, 230. *See also* Acquisitions
M-form structure. *See* Multidivisional (M-form) structure
Mission, 24–25
Monitoring, 72, 318
Motivation, competitors', 174–175
Multidivisional (M-form) structure, 365, 371–372
  corporate-level strategies, 380, 381*t*
    related-constrained diversification, 375–378
    related-linked diversification, 378–379
    unrelated diversification, 379–380
  types
    competitive, 379–380
    cooperative, 375–378
    strategic business unit, 378–379
  variations, 375*f*
Multidomestic strategy, 269, 381–382
Multimarket competition, 169, 172
Multipoint competition, 209–210
Mutual forbearance, 308

N

National advantage, 266*f*, 267–268
National Innovation Initiative (U.S.), 99
National Research Council, 137
Needs, customer, 139–140
Network cooperative strategy, 315–316
Network structure, 386–387
New entrants
  acquisitions, 233, 235
  barriers, 83–85, 147–148, 233, 235
  cost leadership strategy, 147–148
  differentiation strategy, 151
  industry analysis, 82–85
Newfoundland and Labrador, 406
New wholly owned subsidiaries, 278–279
New Zealand, 438
Nonequity strategic alliances, 300

Nonsubstitutable capabilities, 116
Normal performance, 43–44
North American Free Trade Agreement (NAFTA), 272
North Atlantic Treaty Organization, 440
Norway, 274
NutraSweet, 86

O

Offshore outsourcing, 280
Oil reserves, 6
Operational relatedness, 205, 206*f*, 207–208, 211–212
Opportunism, managerial, 337, 421
Opportunistic behaviours, corporate, 316
Opportunities, 71
Opportunity maximization, 318–319
Organizational change, 19–20, 384, 420–421
Organizational controls, 366–367, 368*t*, 389–390, 422–424
Organizational culture, 28, 384, 419–422
Organizational design, 112
Organizational politics, 445
Organizational structure, 363–390
  business-level strategies, 372–374, 387–388
  controls, 366–367, 368*t*, 389–390, 422–424
  cooperative strategies, 386–389
  corporate-level strategies, 375–381, 388
  defined, 365
  flexibility, 366
  functional, 371–374
  growth patterns, 369–370, 370*f*
  ineffective, 363–364
  inertia, 366
  international strategies, 381–385, 382*f*, 388–389
  multidivisional, 371–372, 375–381
  network, 386–387
  overview, 365–366
  simple, 370–371
  stability, 366
  strategy in relation to, 368–370
  types, 369–387
  worldwide, 381–385
Organization of American States (OAS), 272
Organizations
  best interests of, 333

conflict within, 107
  defined, 43
  knowledge in, 111, 112
  size of, 179–180, 217–218, 242
  slack in, 178
  stakeholders in, 27
Organized to be exploited, 116–117
Outsiders, on boards of directors, 342, 343
Outsourcing
  defined, 121
  globalization and, 79
  offshore, 280
  overview, 121, 123
  as strategic alliance, 299, 302
  strategic network and, 387
Ownership
  concentration of, 340–341
  institutional, 340–341
  management separated from, 335–340

P

Palm Pilot, 17
Patents, 186, 437
Pattern, strategy as, 10
Percentage of sales, 34
Performance
  conceptual definition of, 43–44
  diversification and, 215, 215*f*, 219*f*
  levels of, 43–44
  value and, 45*t*
  See also Performance measures
Performance measures
  accounting measures, 47, 48–49*t*, 49–50
  Balanced Scorecard, 56, 57*t*
  Economic Value Added (EVA), 55–56
  firm survival, 45–47
  market-based measures, 51–54
  Market Value Added (MVA), 54–56
  multiple stakeholder approach, 50
  present value, 51
  reputation, 59
  return, 34
  social responsibility, 57
  triple bottom line, 41–42, 58
Perpetual innovation, 15
Perspective, strategy as, 10
Peru, 438
Pet industry, 99–100
Plan, strategy as, 9–10